Woolf Studies Annual

Volume 31, 2025

Pace University Press • New York

Pace University Press
41 Park Row, 15th Floor, Rm. 1510
New York, NY 10038

Printed in the United States of America

ISSN: 1080-9317
ISBN: 978-1-965246-01-6

Member

Council of Editors of Learned Journals

∞ Paper used in this publication meets the minimum requirements of American National Standard for Information Sciences–Permanence of Paper for Printed Library Materials, ANSI Z39.48–1984

(continued on next page)

Editorial Advisory Board (continued)

Many thanks to readers for Volume 31 (in addition to the Editorial Board): Candis Bond (Augusta U), Catherine Brown (Northeastern U London), Laura Cernat (KU Leuven), Barbara Green (U of Notre Dame), Kate Haffey (U of Mary Washington), Clara Jones (King's College London), Caroline Marie (U Paris 8), Natasha Periyan (U of London), Davi Pinho (UERJ), Amy C. Smith (Vicki Tromanhauser (SUNY New Paltz), Lauryl Tucker (U of the South).

Woolf Studies Annual is indexed in *Humanities International Complete, ABELL,* and the *MLA Bibliography.*

Contents

*W*oolf *S*tudies *A*nnual

Volume 31, 2025

vii Abbreviations

ix Editor's Note

ARTICLES

Ramathi Bandaranayake **1** Shellshocked "Idiots": Septimus Smith, *Mrs. Dalloway*, and Dostoevsky's *The Idiot*

Han Au Chua **21** The Letters between Virginia Woolf and Ling Shuhua

Anne E. Fernald **47** Two Pacifists: Vera Brittain and Virginia Woolf

Cristina Testa **77** Virginia Woolf's *Choephori Notebook*: An Annotated Transcription

GUIDE

125 Guide to Library Special Collections

INDEX OF WOOLF STUDIES ANNUAL VOLUMES 21–30 (2015–2024)

Benjamin D. Hagen **147** Introduction

Skylar Kovacs and Benjamin D. Hagen **148** Part One: Names and Places

Oliver Case and Benjamin D. Hagen **182** Part Two: Source References

Jenny Ann Cubin and Benjamin D. Hagen — **235** Part Three: Topics

Skylar Kovacs and Benjamin D. Hagen — **255** Part Four: Woolf References

Benjamin D. Hagen — **265** Part Five: Bibliography of Articles, Reviews, and Other Materials in Volumes 21–30 (2015–2024)

REVIEWS

Elizabeth Berkowitz — **277** *The Artist Helen Coombe: The Tragedy of Roger Fry's Wife*, Martin Ferguson Smith

283 *In and out of Bloomsbury: Biographical Essays on Twentieth-Century Writers and Artists*, Martin Ferguson Smith

Debra Rae Cohen — **286** *Edible Arrangements: Modernism's Queer Forms*, Elizabeth Blake

Mark Hussey — **288** *Bring No Clothes: Bloomsbury and the Philosophy of Fashion*, Charlie Porter

291 *Virginia Woolf and Capitalism*, Clara Jones (editor)

Shawna Ross — **296** *Cybernetic Aesthetics: Modernist Networks of Information and Data*, Heather A. Love

301 Notes on Contributors

303 Submission Guidelines

Abbreviations

AHH	*A Haunted House*
AROO	*A Room of One's Own*
BP	*Books and Portraits*
BTA	*Between the Acts*
CDB	*The Captain's Death Bed and Other Essays*
CE	*Collected Essays (4 vols.)*
CR1	*The Common Reader*
CR2	*The Common Reader, Second Series*
CSF	*The Complete Shorter Fiction*
D	*The Diary of Virginia Woolf (5 vols.)*
DM	*The Death of the Moth and Other Essays*
E	*The Essays of Virginia Woolf (6 vols.)*
F	*Flush*
FR	*Freshwater*
GR	*Granite & Rainbow: Essays*
JR	*Jacob's Room*
L	*The Letters of Virginia Woolf (6 vols.)*
M	*The Moment and Other Essays*
MEL	*Melymbrosia*
MOB	*Moments of Being*
MT	*Monday or Tuesday*
MD	*Mrs. Dalloway*
ND	*Night and Day*
O	*Orlando*
PA	*A Passionate Apprentice*
RF	*Roger Fry: A Biography*
TG	*Three Guineas*
TTL	*To the Lighthouse*
TW	*The Waves*
TY	*The Years*
VO	*The Voyage Out*

Editor's Note

I had originally hoped, during the centenary of *Mrs. Dalloway* (2025), to feature several new pieces in *Woolf Studies Annual* on this foundational modernist novel. As it turns out, such work will probably span across this and the next few volumes, as did pieces marking the centenary of *Jacob's Room* (1922) [see vols. 28–30]. The first article of a cross-volume *Mrs. Dalloway* cluster—by Ramathi Bandaranayake—appears here in volume 31. As Cristina Testa notes in her acknowledgments, her contribution to this volume also relates significantly to the composition of Woolf's 1925 novel.

Though *WSA* 2025 does not feature the cluster I envisioned, it has serendipitously become a comparativist volume, with content that explores critical resonances between Woolf and Fyodor Dostoevsky (Bandaranayake) as well as the resonances and relationships (personal and textual) between Woolf and Ling Shuhua (Chau), Vera Brittain (Fernald), and Aeschylus (Testa). Moreover, volume 31 presents new material from the archives, including a transcription of Virginia Stephen's "*Choephori* Notebook," scans of which are freely available on the new digital archive *WoolfNotes.com*.

In addition to these articles and new book reviews, *WSA* 31 concludes the Index Project, started in *WSA* 28 and continued in *WSA* 29 and 30. This time, readers will find an index of articles published in *WSA* 21–30 (2015–2024), bringing the index fully up to the "Present Day." I repeat a hope I shared in the last few Editor's Notes: that this project will be a help to those navigating the thirty years of scholarship that has found a home in this journal. I will also repeat that I remain stunned, even after four years working on this index, by the brilliance and breadth of the journal's scholarship, which remains relevant to new pathways that contemporary Woolf studies, modernist studies, and literary studies continues to forge. I hope readers of *WSA* will agree.

Lastly, volume 31 sees the transfer of Amanda Golden (the former book review editor) and Vara Neverow (the former associate editor) to the Editorial Board. On behalf of Mark Hussey and myself, I would like to thank them for the years of intellectual and editorial labor they put into this publication. I'm grateful that they will continue to support the journal as new members of the board. The board itself has also been updated and will see additional updates in the coming year. I would like to conclude by thanking those members cycling off the board for their unwavering support of *WSA* and for their time and wisdom over the years: Pamela L. Caughie, Beth Rigel Daugherty, Michael Lackey, Gill Lowe, Celia Marshik, Patricia Moran, Steven Putzel, Bonnie Kime Scott, Diana L. Swanson, and Janine Utell. This volume is dedicated to Morris Beja, who died on 6 February 2025. He was a longtime member of the WSA board and a foundational figure in Woolf studies. He will be missed.

– B.H.

Shellshocked "Idiots": Septimus Smith, *Mrs. Dalloway*, and Dostoevsky's *The Idiot*

Ramathi Bandaranayake

Abstract: In 1915, living in Richmond in the aftermath of a suicide attempt, Virginia Woolf recorded in her diary that she had been reading Dostoevsky's *The Idiot* (1868–69). She was impressed by the "wonders" Dostoevsky conjured, "with very subtle brains, & fearful sufferings." Later, while composing *Mrs. Dalloway* (1925) in 1923, she wrote in her diary, "One must write from deep feeling, said Dostoevsky." Both *The Idiot* and *Mrs. Dalloway* feature central characters who are ill: the saintly, epileptic Prince Myshkin and the shellshocked World War I veteran Septimus Smith, respectively. The illnesses of both characters grant them unique viewpoints on and make them misfits and irritants to society. Materialistic, ego-driven Petersburg cannot tolerate the compassionate, selfless Myshkin while the shellshocked Septimus is an unwelcome specter in a London that would rather forget the war. The protagonists' alienated statuses become occasions for Woolf and Dostoevsky to "criticise the social system," one of Woolf's explicit intentions for *Mrs. Dalloway*. While there is a body of scholarship on Woolf's relationship to Russian literature, little criticism has focused on *The Idiot*'s influence, and there has been no extensive discussion of the links between Myshkin and Septimus. I argue that comparing Myshkin and Septimus enables us to understand an important influence on Woolf's deployment of illness not just as a personal disruptor but also as the very means of social critique.

> *The main idea of the novel is to portray a positively beautiful person ... it's a measureless task. The beautiful is an ideal, and the ideal—both ours and that of civilized Europe—is far from having been achieved.* (Dostoevsky, *Letters III* 17)

> *But now what do I feel about my writing?—this book, that is, The Hours, if thats its name? One must write from deep feeling, said Dostoevsky. ... I want to give life & death, sanity & insanity; I want to criticise the social system, & to show it at work, at its most intense.* (*D*2 248)

Introduction

In 1915, living in Richmond in the aftermath of a suicide attempt, Virginia Woolf recorded in her diary that she had been reading Fyodor Dostoevsky's *The Idiot* (1868–69).[1] She writes of the novel, "I cant bear the style of it very often; at the same time, he seems to me to have the same kind of vitality in him that

[1] This essay relies on Constance Garnett's 1913 translation of *The Idiot,* as this is the version in the Woolfs' library (King and Miletic-Vejzovic).

Scott had … D. creates wonders, with very subtle brains, & fearful sufferings" (*D*1 23). Woolf recognized the artistic potential of deep mental distress, its ability to engender "vitality" even as it causes severe pain. Woolf's attraction to the fictional depiction of mental suffering, however, did not necessarily extend to "idiots" in the real world. Just nine days before her entry on *The Idiot*, she describes an encounter of her own with "a long line of imbeciles" thus:

> On the towpath we met & had to pass a long line of imbeciles. The first was a very tall young man, just queer enough to look twice at, but no more; the second shuffled, & looked aside; & then one realized that every one in that long line was a miserable ineffective shuffling *idiotic* creature, with no forehead, or no chin, & an imbecile grin, or a wild suspicious stare. It was perfectly horrible. They should certainly be killed. (*D*1 13, emphasis added)

The diary entry is uncharitable and disparaging, a marked contrast to the "wonders" Woolf enthused over in Dostoevsky's representation. While this split reaction appears jarring at first, it reflects the paradoxical fascination and revulsion that the figure of the "idiot" inspired in Woolf, even as she dealt with her own mental illness.[2]

That an "idiot's" mind could be a source of moral revelation even as such a person is shunned by society was very much in Dostoevsky's thoughts as he composed *The Idiot* between 1867 and 1869.[3] In the novel, the saintly, epileptic Prince Myshkin arrives in St. Petersburg after receiving treatment at a Swiss sanitarium. He finds himself in a world "locked in the grip of conflicting egoisms, a world in which the desire for wealth and social advantage, for sexual satisfaction, for power over others, dominates and sweeps away all other humane feelings" (Frank 580). In particular, he becomes embroiled in the machinations of his relative Lizaveta Prokofyevna Epanchin and her husband to marry off their daughters as well as Parfyon Roghozin's obsessive pursuit of the beautiful Nastasya Filippovna. Myshkin, however, refuses to participate in these sexual intrigues. He refrains from single-mindedly pursuing a socially and economically advantageous bride, preferring universal compassionate love to exclusive romantic love. His behavior frustrates the "conflicting egoisms" of Petersburg high society, who denounce him as "an idiot."[4]

[2] While Woolf's mental illness and the condition of the "imbeciles" are not the same, a degree of personal identification is likely embedded in this otherizing horror. As Janet Lyon points out in her discussion of the diary entry, "This kind of shock, for someone like Woolf, must surely extend to her own tenuous mental sovereignty" (559). Both conditions involve loss of control over the mind.

[3] For a composition history of *The Idiot*, see Frank 555–91.

[4] Some examples: the character Varya observes, "The prince has hooked [the Epanchins' youngest daughter Aglaia], in the first place, because he wasn't fishing for her; and secondly, because he is looked upon by every one as an idiot" (471–72). Myshkin's refusal to "fish" for a bride makes him appear like an "idiot" (and ironically makes Aglaia fall in love with him, according to Varya). When Myshkin receives an angry note from Aglaia telling him not to visit, Lizaveta Prokofyevna scoffs; "she didn't consider that it wouldn't do to write

His "idiocy" is directly associated with his epilepsy.[5] As Brian Johnson notes, despite the characters' difficulties in fathoming who Myshkin is, that Myshkin is an "idiot" is "the one point upon which there is universal agreement… in the eyes of everyone in the novel" (377). While others hurl the epithet "idiot," at him, however, Myshkin's epilepsy is important to his characterization as "a positively beautiful person." In the notebooks Dostoevsky kept while composing *The Idiot,* he recorded as a "chief point" that his "idiot" "*is in very frail health*" (143). Dostoevsky himself suffered from epilepsy, writing to his friend Apollon Maikov in 1867 that "[t]he attacks had begun to repeat themselves every week, and clearly sensing and *recognizing* that nervous and *cerebral* disorder was unbearable. My reason really was coming unhinged—that's the truth. I sensed that, and the derangement of my nerves sometimes led to moments of frenzy" (*Letters II* 252). Drawing on his own experiences, Dostoevsky provided an account of the illness largely consistent with the medical understanding of epilepsy at the time (Rice 44). Myshkin's epileptic fits serve as gateways to perceiving goodness, beauty, and seemingly divine revelation, granting him insights unavailable to the healthy.[6]

Ten years after reading *The Idiot,* Woolf published *Mrs. Dalloway* (1925). Dostoevsky was very much in mind during the novel's composition, especially the need to "write from deep feeling" (*D*2 248). As Dostoevsky drew on his epilepsy to create Myshkin, Woolf channeled her illness into the shellshocked Septimus Smith, whom the novel associates with lunacy (*MD* 107). According to Julia Briggs, creating Septimus was "an act of exorcism, in which she summoned up her own experiences in order to write them out of her system and into his, and ultimately into the imagination of her readers" (146). Septimus is an unwelcome reminder of the War in a city that wants to pretend that "[t]he War was over … thank Heaven—over" (*MD* 3). The returning soldier disturbs this complacency, as "[t]hose who receive him at home encounter through him an otherness within the home that had, it seems, been there all along but could only come to light by way of the displacements war has effected" (Bonikowski 133). Septimus's shell shock gives the lie to masculine ideals of heroism in the face of death and the triumphalism of the military victory, which are integral parts of the British national-imperial image expounded by the ruling classes (including the Dalloways and their circle).

---

like that to an idiot, because he'd take it literally, as he has done" (323). In a cynical society, Myshkin's innocent sincerity is often interpreted as idiocy.

[5] For example, as Myshkin muses, "Everyone looks on me as an idiot, too, for some reason. I was so ill at one time that I really was almost like an idiot. But can I be an idiot now, when I am able to see for myself that people look upon me as an idiot?" (72).

[6] It is worth noting that Dostoevsky also used epilepsy to portray vice. As Anupama Iyer observes, "Dostoevsky uses epilepsy as a metaphor for both goodness and guilelessness in Myshkin and for evil in Smerdyakov [the villain in *The Brothers Karamazov*], where it provides an alibi for a criminal act. Smerdyakov, who suffers from epileptic seizures for most of his life, murders his father Fyodor Pavlovich Karamazov while simulating status epilepticus" (313).

There are strong parallels between the epileptic Myshkin and the shellshocked Septimus in that their illnesses set them apart from and grant them a unique viewpoint on their respective sociopolitical worlds. Their alienated statuses allow Dostoevsky and Woolf to use them, as Woolf famously puts it, to "criticise the social system" (*D*2 248). Martin Halliwell notes that both Woolf and Dostoevsky, among others, "explored bodily, cerebral and neurological illnesses as disabling and often life-threatening afflictions that paradoxically enable the artist to look beyond the veneer of bourgeois values to identify social unrest beneath" (116). Woolf was keenly attuned to the revelatory power of illness, writing in "On Being Ill" (1926) that "There is … a childish outspokenness in illness; things are said, truths blurted out, which the cautious respectability of health conceals" (11). The sick are "outlaws," their "rashness" capable of revealing profound truths (22).[7] She shared this awareness with Dostoevsky.

Myshkin and Septimus straddle many of the meanings contained in the term "idiot." The word "idiot" (in English and Russian) derives from the Greek *ἰδιώτης*, meaning "private person," "ignorant, ill-informed person" (idiot).[8] Their illness sometimes seems to grant them access to higher truths, but given that these truths remain incommunicable to the healthy, they remain "private." Hence, Myshkin and Septimus appear "ignorant" and "ill-informed" to an exasperated public. Dostoevsky observed this "enigm[a]" in his notes—"Who is [the idiot]? A terrible scoundrel or a mysterious ideal?" (124). Disability studies scholars have observed that it is difficult to specifically define "idiot," which has meant different things at different historical moments and has been used interchangeably with related terms such as "imbecile" or "feeble-minded" (McDonagh et al. 1, 13).[9] Nonetheless, as Anne Digby points out, "Implicit in the language describing these individuals was, and is, the notion of the Other" (3). Regardless of the specific definition, therefore, the designation "idiot" always marks out an "other" who does not think and behave as wider society expects them to, curtailing the thoughts and actions of those called "idiots." As Patrick McDonagh argues elsewhere, "the study of idiocy is the study of a particular form of exile, through which some humans are removed in order

[7] As Sarah Pett points out, in "On Being Ill," for Woolf "'rashness' signifies both a sense of detachment, even liberation, from social norms and an unmediated, profoundly phenomenological engagement with the world and its inhabitants" (33). Illness, therefore, enables a fresh look at the world, uninhibited by societal structures, priming the sick to be vehicles of social critique.

[8] For a further discussion of the etymology of the word "idiot" in relation to Dostoevsky's title *The Idiot,* see Murav 88–90.

[9] Illustrating the problem of historical "slipperiness" in the conception of "idiocy," McDonagh et al. ask, "what does the term 'intellectual disability' or, for that matter, 'learning disability' refer to? And what, glancing further back in time, of idiocy? Or folly?" (1). Moreover, as C. F. Goodey contends, changing historical and social contexts also play a role in who gets classified as intellectually disabled: "there are always people around who seem unable to grasp certain complex everyday activities. What changes, though, is the content of those activities and their centrality to the life which the rest of us in any one era expect to lead" (1).

to enable the remainder to believe in their own unalloyed intelligence. 'Idiocy' is thus a term to designate *other* people, or other groups of people" (2). The label "idiot," therefore, isolates potentially disturbing "others" for the comfort of the rest of society, who can remain complacent in their "unalloyed intelligence" and ignore uncomfortable truths. Rebecah Pulsifer argues in her study of *Between the Acts* (1941) that "[t]he idiot allows [Woolf] to imagine a being who experiences sensations and may translate those sensations into forms of self-signification, yet whose mind remains completely inaccessible to others" (102). Pulsifer also notes that apart from *Between the Acts,* Woolf seldom wrote about idiocy in her fiction or nonfiction (101). While the word "idiot" is never used in *Mrs. Dalloway* (although words such as "lunatic" are), it was not uncommon at the time to refer to shellshocked soldiers as "idiots."[10] Harriet Murav points out that in nineteenth century Russia, "medical and legal handbooks defined 'idiotism' as a defect present from birth or as the result of another disease, such as epilepsy" (90). The term "idiot," therefore, is associated with both disability and illness and has been used to describe victims of epilepsy and shell shock, encompassing both Myshkin and Septimus's afflictions.[11]

Woolf's fascination with Russian literature and Dostoevsky more particularly is well recorded. Like many of her contemporaries, she was swept up in what Helen Muchnic called Britain's "Dostoevsky cult," when Constance Garnett's Dostoevsky translations were published between 1912 and 1921 (62). British critics were drawn to Dostoevsky's treatment of madness, describing "the atmosphere of the lunatic asylum" and "the extraordinary handling of psychological abnormality" in his works (qtd. in Protopopova 71). Woolf even took Russian language lessons while writing *Mrs. Dalloway.* Her notebook contains several exercises and notes on Russian grammar, writing, and pronunciation (dated February 1921), situated between the "First Sketch of Mrs. Dalloway," and the manuscript version of *Mrs. Dalloway* (9 November 1922) [Reinhold 10–11]. She also collaborated with S. S. Koteliansky on several Russian-to-English translations for the Hogarth Press, including formerly unpublished segments from Dostoevsky's *The Possessed* (1922).[12] In her essay "The Russian Point of View" (1925), published the same year as *Mrs. Dalloway,* she enthused over "the stuff of the soul" in Dostoevsky's novels, the "seething whirlpools, gyrating sandstorms, waterspouts which hiss and boil and suck us in" (*CR1* 182). Echoing her 1915 comments on *The Idiot,* she is deeply drawn

[10] See, for example, "howling idiots" (qtd in Meinhart 169); another example: "they were just laying, gibbering idiots. I've seen a soldier laying on a stretcher, gibbering like an idiot just from the shell shock" (qtd. in "Voices").

[11] Additionally, given how poorly shell shock was understood, various conditions thought to be connected to war-induced psychological afflictions tended to be clumped under the "unstable diagnosis" of "shell-shock," including epilepsy (Loughran 52). This tendency indicates that epilepsy and shell shock were sometimes conceived of similarly during the First World War, although they are not equivalent.

[12] For more on the Woolfs' collaborations with Koteliansky, see Diment 122–41.

to the tortured agitation in Dostoevsky's works, finding a new, expansive way of exploring seemingly unfathomed aspects of the human psyche. "But what keyword could be applied to Raskolnikov, Mishkin, Stavrogin, or Alyosha?" she contends in "Mr. Bennett and Mrs. Brown" (1923) before continuing, "We go down into them as we descend into some enormous cavern. Lights swing about; we hear the boom of the sea; it is all dark, terrible and uncharted" (*E*3 386) Similarly, Septimus's shell shock takes him into "uncharted" territory, to places that complacent London society cannot go.

Scholarly attention has been paid to the influence of Dostoevsky (and of Russian literature generally) on Woolf, but little criticism has focused on *The Idiot*'s influence.[13] There has been no extensive discussion of the links between Myshkin and Septimus.[14] Comparing Septimus to Myshkin enables us to understand an important influence on Woolf's deployment of illness not just as a personal but also a *social* disruptor. I contend that while Myshkin and Septimus do not revolutionize the "social system," they nonetheless succeed in changing the outlook of individual characters, thereby planting the seeds of potential change.[15] Just as Myshkin's compassion is a rebuke to the avaricious sexual scheming of Petersburg, Septimus's

[13] This lack of critical attention initially seems warranted, given that Woolf left a limited paper trail of her engagement with this novel versus Dostoevsky's other works. Her reading notes on *The Possessed* survive (Rubenstein 165–73). She reviewed translations of shorter Dostoevsky works such as *The Eternal Husband* ("More Dostoevsky" [1917]) and *The Gambler* ("A Minor Dostoevsky" [1917]) (*E*2 83–7, 165–67). Her commentary on *The Idiot,* however, is confined to a few cursory mentions in diaries and essays. In addition to her diary entry on reading *The Idiot* and the reference to Myshkin in "Mr. Bennett and Mrs. Brown," Woolf comments on "the plethoric state of mind" evoked by *The Idiot* and *Jude the Obscure* in a 1916 essay on Charlotte Brontë (*E*2 28). Critical linkages between *The Idiot* and Woolf tend to focus on *Night and Day* (1919), where Katharine Hilbery quotes a line from the novel (Briggs 23–24; Rubenstein 35–37). Connections between *The Idiot* and *Mrs. Dalloway* are sparse, although Emily Dalgarno notes that both Peter Walsh and Myshkin fall asleep in parks (93–94). Roberta Rubenstein also points to the novels' common theme of suicide, since the terminally ill Ippolit in *The Idiot* makes a failed suicide attempt (44). She also links Ippolit's comment that "it's life that matters" to Clarissa Dalloway's posthumous encounter with Septimus (37). (On the other hand, there has been deeper analysis of the influence of Tolstoy's *Anna Karenina* on *Mrs. Dalloway*. See Dalgarno 73–76 and Knapp, *Anna Karenina* 206–23.)

[14] Septimus has been compared to other Dostoevsky characters, such as *Crime and Punishment*'s Raskolnikov (Richter 90), but not Myshkin.

[15] It would, of course, be misleading to argue that Myshkin was Woolf's *primary* influence for Septimus. In addition to her own struggles with mental illness, she had plenty of inspiration in her immediate environment, including her soldier brother-in-law Phillip Woolf (Levenback 74). Elaine Showalter has made the case for Siegfried Sassoon's influence (192–94). In 1922, the War Office Committee of Enquiry into "Shell-Shock" submitted its report to Parliament. The report's dismissal of shell shock as the result of cowardice and mental weakness is echoed in Dr. Holmes and Dr. Bradshaw's evaluations of Septimus (Zwerdling 29–31). There are also important differences between Myshkin and Septimus, such as social class (Myshkin is of the nobility, Septimus is not), and their specific medical conditions (epilepsy in peacetime as opposed to shell shock attributable to wartime experiences).

presence is a reproof of an imperial Britain that discards people who fought and suffered on its behalf. The social system in both novels mistreats the vulnerable and different and, particularly in the case of *Mrs. Dalloway*, takes advantage of them for the system's own ends.

This comparison also sheds light on a relatively understudied part of Woolf's rich relationship to Russian literature, specifically in the composition of *Mrs. Dalloway*. As Rubenstein observes, "For [Woolf and Dostoevsky], writing was a means of subduing inner chaos as well as harnessing their most visionary moments" (28). Peter Kaye contends that for Woolf, Dostoevsky "may have played the role of a Septimus Smith ... like Smith, Dostoevsky challenged all certainties and proprieties, but he also brushed aside all the order and art of civilization" (85). Woolf may have identified in Dostoevsky a kindred spirit willing to "write from deep feeling," (*D*2 248) drawing on "subtle brains" and "fearful sufferings" (*D*1 23) to throw out a "challeng[e]" to "all the order and art of civilization" (Kaye 85). With this in mind, let us turn to the texts.

Splitting Time

Both Myshkin and Septimus experience an altered sense of time due to their illnesses, indicating that they have access to modes of thought and perception that others do not. Just before an epileptic fit, Myshkin experiences an "unendurable" second of "gleams and flashes," which gives rise to "the acme of harmony and beauty, and gives a feeling, unknown and undivined till then, of completeness, of proportion, of reconciliation, and of ecstatic devotional merging in the highest synthesis of life" (224–25). Time seems to dilate, where an entire lifetime is experienced in a second—"Yes, for this moment one might give one's whole life!" (225). Similarly, Septimus experiences time dilation, where "The word 'time' split its husk; poured its riches over him; and from his lips fell like shells, like shavings from a plane ... hard, white, imperishable words, and flew to attach themselves to their places in an ode to Time; an immortal ode to Time" (75). As Myshkin experiences harmony and beauty, Septimus observes that "Beauty was everywhere" (74); like Myshkin's sense "of completeness, of proportion, of reconciliation, and of ecstatic devotional merging in the highest synthesis of life," Septimus partakes "of this relief, of this joy, of this astonishing revelation" (75). The anaphoric repetition and the listing in both texts suggests a compounding intensity of experience and mental clarity. The altered sense of time creates a gateway to perception beyond the ordinary.

Myshkin and Septimus's experiences of altered time have strong religious overtones, indicating that their illnesses serve as pathways to near-divine revelations inaccessible to the rest of society. Myshkin's sensations are directly connected to religious passion—"ecstatic devotional merging" (225). He also experiences a sense of ultimate truth and the removal of uncertainty—"he could not doubt, and could not admit the possibility of doubt" (225). Moreover, he explains to Rogozhin, "at that moment I seem somehow to understand the extraordinary saying that *there shall be no more time*" (225), echoing Revelation on the end of time.[16] Indeed, Dostoevsky has Christ explicitly in mind when creating Myshkin's character. In his notebooks, Dostoevsky describes Myshkin as "Prince Christ" (198), and in a letter about *The Idiot* to his niece, Sofia Ivanova, Dostoevsky writes, "There's only one positively beautiful person in the world—Christ" (*Letters III* 17). Likewise, Septimus feels he is receiving divine revelation. He seems to hear his dead friend Evans singing in response to his "ode to Time," and then hallucinates a vision: "A man in grey was actually walking towards them. It was Evans! But no mud was on him; no wounds; he was not changed" (75). Evans, Christlike, has been resurrected. Time moves backward, reversing death and life. Indeed, Septimus responds to the vision as though it is a divine revelation, and he feels he must spread word of Evans's resurrection:

> I must tell the whole world, Septimus cried … raising his hand like some colossal figure who has lamented the fate of man for ages in the desert alone with his hands pressed to his forehead, furrows of despair on his cheeks, and now sees light on the desert's edge which broadens and strikes the iron-black figure. (75)

Woolf references the temptation of Christ in the desert by Satan, shifting the parallel from Evans/Christ to Septimus/Christ. There is a clear link between illness and divinity. As Harriet Murav points out, epilepsy had in ancient times been thought of as a "sacred disease" (75), and in Myshkin we find "the coincidence of the holy and the pathological" (73). The same "coincidence" takes place in Septimus, where his shell shock, like Myshkin's epilepsy, gives him insight into higher truths that the healthy cannot access. Jane de Gay argues that "[the] identification between Septimus and Christ is reinforced by his compulsion to take the sins of society upon himself," where Septimus kills and experiences death on behalf of his society (203). That this society now ignores Septimus is an indictment of the "social system" Woolf intends to criticize.[17]

That Myshkin and Septimus's gnostic insights are intrinsically tied to illness means that both pay a personal and social penalty for their revelations. For Myshkin, as Sarah Young notes, "the prelude to his fit demonstrates his access to a higher reality and the possibility of true clarity, with regard to the nature of both the self and existence" (105). However, Myshkin gloomily reflects that "Stupefaction, spiritual

[16] "And sware by him that liveth for ever and ever, who created heaven, and the things that therein are, and the earth, and the things that therein are, and the sea, and the things which are therein, that there should be time no longer" (*The Bible: Authorized King James Version*, Rev. 10.6).

[17] In her later essay "Phases of Fiction" (1929), Woolf would express annoyance with Dostoevsky's religiosity: "The novels of Dostoievski are pervaded with mysticism; he speaks not as a writer but as a sage … But in a novel the voice of the teacher, however exalted, is not enough" (278). Interestingly, she nonetheless shares a strong exegetical sensibility with Dostoevsky in these above passages.

darkness, idiocy stood before him conspicuously as the consequence of these 'higher moments'" (225). Likewise, Septimus's shell shock is the gateway to higher truths, but the sense of impending triumph in Septimus's/Christ's tussle with the Devil is immediately undercut by the rest of the sentence: "with legions of men prostrate behind him he, the giant mourner, receives for one moment on his face the whole" (75). Septimus may be a prophet carrying a revelation, but he is leading dead men; a "giant mourner" and a prophet not of life but of death. Moreover, since Myshkin and Septimus's revelations are the result of illness, they cannot communicate them to the (ostensibly healthy) public. As Robin Feuer Miller argues, "*The Idiot* itself treats problems of communication … [W]ords can never fully express a thought" (2). Karen DeMeester makes a similar contention about Septimus, that "[his] death is the result of his inability to communicate his experiences to others and thereby give those experiences meaning and purpose" (649). As sick people in a supposedly healthy society, as Christlike figures in apparently godless worlds, both characters are shunned.[18] And, like Christ, both pay for their revelations, as we shall see next.

"Original" Men

Due to the aforementioned communication gap, Myshkin and Septimus's behavior appear peculiar in the public realm, as both characters refuse their socially prescribed roles. In *The Idiot*, Myshkin refuses the role of a suitor looking for a bride. According to the narrator, Russian society believes that the most practical profession is an army general, where one rises through predictable ranks and attains social standing and financial security (326). Those who are "original" upset things: "The only person among us who can fail to reach the general's rank is the original man—in other words, the man who won't be quiet" (326). Myskhin will not "be quiet" not because he is attention seeking but because his nonconformity is disturbing. He looks after the fallen woman Marie in Switzerland not out of romantic attraction but because he pities her loneliness, to the mocking disbelief of the Epanchin family: "No, don't laugh … It was not a question of love. If only you knew what an unhappy

[18] Dal's Russian Dictionary defines "idiot" as a "weak-minded" person but also includes "*iurodivyi*" (holy fool) (Murav 90). In Eastern Orthodoxy, holy fools "feign madness in order to provide the public with spiritual guidance yet shun praise for their saintliness and attract abuse in imitation of the suffering Christ" (Kobets 15). In the original Russian version of *The Idiot,* Rogozhin compares Myshkin to a "*iurodivyi*" (14). (For more on Myshkin as *iurodivyi* see Miller 65–66.) Garnett's translation uses "regular blessed innocent" (11), a similar term, although it does not exactly capture the same concept. Patrick McDonagh argues that nineteenth century British novelists such as Charles Dickens, George Eliot, and Sir Walter Scott deployed the figure of the "holy innocent and trickster fool" to advance "social and moral critiques" in *Little Dorritt* (1857), *Brother Jacob* (1860), and *Waverly, or 'Tis Sixty Years Since* (1814), respectively (153). The concept of "the innocent Christian idiot" did exist historically in Britian (McDonagh 18), although there are cultural differences compared to the Russian holy fool. Society certainly scorns both Myshkin and Septimus even though they convey important moral truths, but since the Garnett translation does not specifically use the word "holy fool," I have not further explored the potential parallel here.

being she was, you would be very sorry for her, as I was" (65). He writes a letter to the Epanchins' daughter Aglaia out of brotherly love ("Are you happy? That was all I wanted to say to you") rather than romantic desire, signing the note, "Your brother" (187). Tellingly, Aglaia puts the letter between the pages of a volume of *Don Quixote* (187), implying that Myshkin's disinterested compassion is quixotic, or chivalrously impractical and idealistic, in a society fraught with sexual intrigue.[19] Even his one seemingly overt romantic gesture—attempting to marry Nastasya Filippovna—is performed out of pity and not sexual attraction to the disbelief and irritation of everyone else. As Radomsky, the "raisonneur" (Knapp, "Introduction" 37) of the novel, exclaims, "What will compassion lead you to next? … How can you, loving a girl [i.e., Aglaia], humiliate her like this before her rival [i.e., Nastasya Filippovna], jilt her for the sake of another woman, in the very presence of that other, after you had yourself made her an honorable offer [of marriage]?" (585). Myshkin never directly proposes to Aglaia, but everyone assumes he is courting her. In frustration at Myshkin, "Aglaia suddenly whispered to herself wrathfully: 'Idiot!'" (348), tying his unusual behavior back to his epilepsy. Even the more charitable Radomsky concedes, "You're too clever to be called [an idiot]. But you're so strange that you're not like other people—you must admit that yourself" (583). Myshkin's illness, therefore, gives rise to "original" behavior that conflicts with social norms.

Septimus too exhibits originality by refusing his proper social place, confinement in a home as a shell shock victim, by committing suicide: "He did not want to die. Life was good. The sun hot. Only human beings—what did *they* want?" (162). Throughout the novel, Septimus is regarded as an oddity by others. The physical manifestations of his illness inspire wariness. Woolf writes that Septimus had "hazel eyes which had that look of apprehension in them which makes complete strangers apprehensive too" (14). Maisie Johnson, asking Rezia and Septimus for directions, thinks, "this couple on the chairs gave her quite a turn … the man looking queer; so that should she be very old she would still remember and make it jangle again among her memories … the man—he seemed awfully odd" (26). Seeing a distraught Rezia and Septimus talking to himself in the park, Peter Walsh muses, "To be having an awful scene—the poor girl looked absolutely desperate—in the middle of the morning" (76). To observers, Septimus is "queer," "odd," the creator of "awful scene[s]," the kind of man who will not "be quiet" (as Dostoevsky's narrator puts it), and therefore should be put away. But contemplating his suicide, Clarissa Dalloway muses: "Death was defiance. Death was an attempt to communicate; people feeling the impossibility of reaching the center which, mystically, evaded them; closeness drew apart; rapture faded, one was alone. There was an embrace in death" (201). Clarissa understands that Septimus's "defiance" is an attempt to "communicate" in action what cannot be

[19] Dostoevsky did have the character Don Quixote in mind while developing *The Idiot* but opined that "he is only beautiful because he's ridiculous at the same time" (*Letters III* 17).

said in words. She even thinks of Septimus as a poet or a thinker (201), occupations associated with creating original works and ideas. Both Myshkin and Septimus's refusals turn a critical lens back onto society. Petersburg society's intolerance of Myshkin's compassion exposes that society's materialism and selfishness, while Septimus's suicide discloses how society discards the men that fought on its behalf after they return from war damaged and in need.

Moreover, if a sense of originality is socially undesirable ("odd," "queer" [*MD* 26]) and linked to illness, then there is a societal interest in curing the illness as a means to correct the troublesome behavior that it inspires. Both Myshkin and (more so) Septimus have ambivalent relationships with doctors. In *The Idiot*, Myshkin describes his treatment:

> Frequent attacks of his illness had made him almost an idiot … Pavlishtchev [Myshkin's benefactor] had met in Berlin Professor Schneider, a Swiss, who was a specialist in such diseases and had an institution in Switzerland in the canton of Valais, where he had patients suffering even from idiocy and insanity, and treated them on his own method with cold water and gymnastics, training them also, and superintending their mental development generally. … Schneider … had not completely cured him, [but] he had greatly improved his condition. (24–25)

While Myshkin remains personally loyal to Schneider, the narrator is skeptical and sarcastic; it is unclear what "cold water and gymnastics" could do for epilepsy. The conditions Schneider treats ("idiocy," "insanity"), and the treatments ("training," "superintending their mental development generally") are vague. Moreover, the events of the novel drive Myshkin insane and send him back to the asylum, which leaves ambiguous the extent to which Myshkin's "idiocy" is due to his illness or to the callous society that amplifies his insanity.

Woolf is also skeptical of the medical treatment handed out to Septimus, far more critical of Septimus's dismissive doctors Dr. Holmes and Sir William Bradshaw than *The Idiot*'s narrator is of Schneider. Woolf famously despised her own doctors and channeled her frustrations into *Mrs. Dalloway*. Writing about Septimus's suicide in a letter to Gwen Raverat, she states, "It was a subject that I have kept cooling in my mind until I felt I could touch it without bursting into flame all over. You can't think what a raging furnace it is still to me—madness and doctors and being forced" (*L3* 180). Like Schneider's "cold water and gymnastics," Holmes and Bradshaw's diagnoses and treatments are suspect. Holmes refers to Septimus's condition as "Talking nonsense to frighten your wife" (101). Sir William's advice to Septimus is to "Try to think as little about [himself] as possible" (106). Septimus tries to tell Sir William, "I have … committed a crime" (104) but cannot articulate the crime, presumably survivor's guilt over Evans's death. His private thoughts cannot be expressed, leading to misunderstanding in the public world. In fact, Bradshaw's obsession with his public role causes him to neglect Septimus's private needs. Evelyn Chan contextualizes the depiction of Bradshaw within the professionalization of medicine in early twentieth-century Britain, noting that while Sir William gives his patients only fifteen-minute appointments, he spends a great deal of time on public works such as legal and institutional reform (35). Citing the party conversation between Bradshaw and Richard Dalloway about Septimus's suicide, where Bradshaw argues that an upcoming Bill must account for "the deferred effects of shell shock," Chan observes that "this macroscopic and public view of healing, indicating a mass and impersonal approach to medicine, could come at the expense of the individual patient like Septimus" (35). Septimus's private struggles have public significance (he is one among many shellshocked veterans), but the public does not understand his message. If illness breeds non-conformity, medicine—the cure—attempts to maintain the social order by banishing the "idiot." At the end of *The Idiot,* Myshkin, driven insane, is confined again to a Swiss sanitarium. Septimus escapes confinement but only at the cost of his life. But the two characters are even more troubling because they disturb not only their immediate societies, but the national self-images of Russia and England as a whole.

Empire and the "idiot"

Dostoevsky and Woolf use Myshkin and Septimus to criticize various forms of imperialism. For Septimus, the War causes disillusionment with the national and imperial ideal. At first, "Septimus was one of the first to volunteer. He went to France to save an England which consisted almost entirely of Shakespeare's plays and Miss Isabel Pole in a green dress .... There in the trenches ... he developed manliness; he was promoted; he drew the attention, indeed the affection of his officer, Evans" (93). The pre-traumatized Septimus is culturally literate, competent, and masculine, but these very qualities precipitate his breakdown. Upon Evans's death, Septimus, "far from showing any emotion or recognizing that here was the end of a friendship, congratulated himself upon feeling very little and very reasonably" (93). Like the army general, the practical ideal in *The Idiot,* Septimus's success in the army is contingent on sublimating his "original" character to social and military norms. Sir William attempts to fix Septimus by shoehorning him back into the national ideal Septimus lost at the front—"Worshipping proportion, Sir William not only prospered himself but made England prosper, secluded her lunatics, forbade childbirth, penalized despair, made it impossible for the unfit to propagate their views until they, too, shared his sense of proportion" (107). Figures like Septimus threaten the nation-building project through the "propagat[ion]" of undesirable traits, necessitating their "seclu[sion]" in the social Darwinian philosophy of Sir William.

Sir William's philosophy is not only national, however, but also imperial, as Woolf suggests that the forces that forcibly export and enforce Englishness abroad destroy Septimus at home. In addition to proportion, Sir William prizes "Conversion," found "in the heat and sands of India, the mud and swamp of Africa, the purlieus of London" (108). Conversion "feasts on the wills of the weakly, loving to impress, to impose, adoring her own features stamped on the face of the populace" (108). While Septimus is not identical to British imperial subjects in Africa or India, he too is a misfit from "the purlieus of London" that must undergo "conversion," to have English "features" "stamped" on his face. As Alex Zwerdling points out, "The passage clearly connects the 'case' of Septimus Smith with British imperialism and social repression and reveals the iron hand in the velvet glove. It is entirely appropriate that this psychiatrist-policeman and the Prime Minister should be invited to the same party" (129). All the social critique Woolf has channeled through Septimus comes to a head at Clarissa's party. As Kathy Philips argues, "The society gathered at Clarissa's party … claims to spread light to colonies but instead uses Lady Bruton's brute force to increase darkness. It distributes wealth disproportionally while hypocritically worshipping Proportion. It hates the slightest divergence from a narrow norm, converting offenders by ostracism or violence, both at home and in the overseas Empire" (26). Empire is an extension of the homogenizing drive that Woolf sees in the coercive social system, which seeks to control misfits at home and abroad.

The Idiot too deploys Myshkin to protest what Dostoevsky saw as cultural imperialism imported from Western Europe that undermines Russian culture, although there are some key differences between *The Idiot* and *Mrs. Dalloway.* Sarah Hudspith notes that

> Dostoevsky was concerned about the Europeanization of the educated classes and believed that a foreign culture was being forcibly imposed upon the true Russian tradition. Therefore it is to Myshkin's credit that he seems a stranger in his own country: he stands out in an environment populated by Westernized aristocrats … It is feasible that his mental condition protected him from this fate [becoming Westernized], an interesting possibility that suggests that his idiocy may be viewed as a positive attribute (151).

While abroad in Europe, Dostoevsky, in an 1867 letter to Apollon Maikov, railed against "all these trashy little liberals and progressives [… who] find their greatest pleasure and satisfaction in criticizing Russia" (*Letters II* 257–58). In Part IV of *The Idiot,* Myshkin launches into a nationalistic, anti-Catholic tirade, exclaiming, "Our Christ whom we have kept and they have never known must shine forth and vanquish the West. Not letting ourselves be slavishly caught by the wiles of the Jesuits, but carrying our Russian civilization to them, we ought to stand before them and not let it be said among us … that their preaching is skillful" (547). Moreover, this tirade occurs just before the onset of an epileptic fit, indicating that Myshkin's illness brings him closer to true Russian patriotism. At the end of the novel, Lizaveta Prokofyevna declares, "I've had a good Russian cry over this poor fellow [the now insane Myshkin]," thereby further connecting Myshkin's illness to Russian national identity (620).

Insofar as Dostoevsky is criticizing a form of Western linguistic and cultural imperialism, *The Idiot* may be aligned with the anti-imperialism of *Mrs. Dalloway.*

However, Myshkin's protest against Western cultural imperialism also goes together with an advocacy of Russian imperialism and Russian Orthodox exceptionalism. In fact, Myshkin's statements about "carrying our Russian civilization to them" has echoes of Sir William's goddess of Conversion bringing civilization to the uncivilized. Like Sir William, Myshkin believes that this national exceptionalism is inherently good and should be exported abroad—"Show him the whole of humanity, rising again, and renewed by Russian thought alone, perhaps by the Russian God and Christ, and you will see into what a mighty and truthful, what a wise and gentle giant he will grow" (549). While it seems strange at first to hear this forceful imperialism from the compassionate Myshkin, as Olga Maiorova notes, Dostoevsky's brand of militant religious imperialism was imbued with a paradoxical belief in brotherly love:

> He saw the Russian people, charged with "preserving the truth of Christ … which has been obscured in all other … nations," as the main agent for establishing harmony on earth. … Russia was destined, he preached, to conquer the world in order to transform it into a community of universal brotherhood—a concept Josef Bohatec called "an imperialism of love." (91)

There exists, therefore, an important difference between *Mrs. Dalloway* and *The Idiot,* as the strain of militarism in Myshkin's tirade contrasts with the anti-militarism Woolf channels through Septimus. Septimus is an outcast in the imperial capital of London because his experiences give the lie to the national-imperial project, but Myshkin is an outcast in the imperial capital of Petersburg because Petersburg society has forgotten its true national-imperial identity.

While both Woolf and Dostoevsky harness the outsider status of the "idiot" for the purposes of political critique, then, this figure's otherness can be deployed in a variety of, even in contradictory, ways. Especially in Dostoevsky's case, the "idiot" is paradoxically a figure of imperialism and anti-imperialism at the same time. This disparity perhaps illustrates some of the limitations of Woolf's engagement with Dostoevsky. In "The Russian Point of View" (1925), she contrasts the "teapot," socially stratified culture of England that seeps into English literature with what she sees as the universal egalitarian "samovar" culture of Russia. "It is all the same to [Dostoevsky] whether you are noble or simple, a tramp or a great lady … The soul is not restrained by barriers," she argues (*CR1* 184). While there is some truth in this claim, nineteenth-century Russia was itself deeply socially stratified. And Woolf's observation of Dostoevsky's egalitarianism jars against the xenophobic nationalism evident in some of Myshkin's thought. For all her political and social astuteness, Woolf does not appear to have left any evidence that she ever interrogated Dostoevsky's imperial ideology.[20] Therefore, while the "idiot" can be

[20] Rebecca Beasley elaborates on the complex political relationship of Russian literature to British modernism. Of particular note, she points out the deployment of Russian literature as propaganda during World War I, observing that "[Russian literature] was central to efforts to construct a more favorable perception of Britain's new ally, tsarist Russia, but this entailed

used to protest certain forms of marginalization (a concept that Woolf shares with Dostoevsky), the use of the figure is not inherently precluded from advancing other forms of majoritarian exceptionalism.

The "Idiot's" Point of View

Both Myshkin and Septimus's deviations from the social roles expected of them is reflected in their roles in the novels' narrative structures. In her essay "Dostoevsky in Cranford" (1919), Woolf writes that "the fervor of [Dostoevsky's] genius goads him across the boundary. … He is incapable, even when his story is hampered by the digression, of passing by anything so important and loveable as a man or a woman without stopping to consider their case and explain it. Thus at one moment it occurs to him that there must be a reason why an unfortunate clerk could not afford to pay for a bottle of wine" (*E*3 114). Myshkin is a master of digressions, too absorbed in trying to be kind to everyone that he muddles the socially sanctioned marriage narrative. Septimus's story is itself an extended digression. When we first meet him, he is one face in a crowd, but he ends up as the co-protagonist of a novel with the singular title *Mrs. Dalloway.* Echoing her own analysis of Dostoevsky, Woolf's narrator refuses to "pass" Septimus "by" "without stopping to consider [his] case and explain[ing] it." Just like the clerk who could not pay for the wine, there is no reason that Septimus's story should be considered less important than those of the social and political power brokers who converge at the Dalloways' party.

Do the digressions, however, pay off? At first, one might argue that the two novels end in failure for their respective protagonists: the insane Myshkin is back in the Swiss sanitarium and Septimus is dead. We have already observed that "the idiot" struggles to express private thoughts to the wider public. At the end of *The Idiot,* the narrator tells us that "many of the other persons of our story go on living as before and have changed but little" (617). Nonetheless, the boy Kolya, who is impressed by Myshkin's behavior earlier in the novel, "was greatly affected by what had happened" (617), and although his mother "is uneasy at his being too thoughtful for his years; he may become an active and useful man" (617–18). Kolya recognizes Radomsky's potential for compassion and communicates Myshkin's fate to him. Radomsky takes it upon himself to get the insane Myshkin back to Switzerland and continues to visit and care for him. As per the narrator, Radomsky "has a heart, which is evident from the fact that Kolya writes to him, and that he even sometimes answers him" (618). Myshkin's illness also puts Radomsky into correspondence, and an emerging friendship, with another of *The Idiot*'s supporting

a rearrangement of the interpretations of Russian literature with which British readers were familiar, since this had been achieved … through a careful ideological separation of the Russian people from the Russian State by liberal and revolutionary critics" (242). The use of Russian literature as propaganda was a topic of fierce dispute among British modernists (Beasley 253). I could not find evidence that Woolf herself engaged publicly in these debates.

characters, Vera Lebedyev, who "was so distressed [by Myshkin's breakdown] that she fell positively ill" (618). While Myshkin's own story ends in tragedy, he inspires kindness in Kolya, Radomsky, and Vera, who form a Dostoevskian "accidental family … bound together by love rather than blood and genes" (Knapp, "Myshkin" 204). Some hope is here.

Likewise, through his self-annihilation, Septimus inspires a moral awakening in Clarissa Dalloway. She realizes that "A thing there was that mattered; a thing, wreathed about with chatter, defaced, obscured in her own life, let drop every day in corruption, lies, chatter. This he [Septimus] had preserved" (201). Septimus's "revelation" communicates itself to Clarissa, who juxtaposes the "thing there was that mattered" with the "corruption, lies, chatter" of the social system she is a part of, one that has "obscured … her own life." Septimus's death may not have generated mass awareness of the problems of the social system; most of Clarissa's guests remain blissfully ignorant, as Sir William's complacent conversation with Richard Dalloway shows. But his death touches one person at least, in the private recesses of her own mind, as Clarissa comes to understand that there may be more to her own life than the "corruption, lies, chatter" of the society around her. Neither Myshkin nor Septimus publicly revolutionizes the social system, but their lives, lived out of the privacy of their "idiotic" minds, give rise to private acts of decency and empathy.

Conclusion

Let us return to Woolf's wish to "write from deep feeling" (*D*2 248), the lesson she takes from Dostoevsky. I have contended that for both Dostoevsky and Woolf, an "idiot's" mind can afford moral revelation and social critique even as they are shunned by wider society as an "other." There are limits to this comparison. Given Myshkin's imperialist attitudes, we cannot quite have "a good Russian cry" over Septimus (like Lizaveta Prokofyevna). However, these "odd," "queer" (*MD* 26) figures serve as foils to social ills, whether materialism and selfishness in *The Idiot* or the discarding of young veterans in *Mrs. Dalloway.* In both novels, the "idiot's" own story ends in tragedy, but his "exile" (McDonough 2) challenges the social system not through grand public gestures but by influencing individual minds one by one, planting the first seeds of potential future change. From a place of "deep feeling," embodying the "very subtle brains, & fearful sufferings" that Woolf identified in *The Idiot*, Septimus gets to have his say (*D*2 248; *D*1 23).

Works Cited

Beasley, Rebecca. *Russomania: Russian Culture and the Creation of British Modernism, 1881–1922*. Oxford UP, 2020.
The Bible. Authorized King James Version, Oxford UP, 2008.

Bonikowski, Wyatt. *Shell Shock and the Modernist Imagination: The Death Drive in Post-World War I British Fiction.* Routledge, 2016.

Briggs, Julia. *Virginia Woolf: An Inner Life.* Harcourt, 2005.

Chan, Evelyn Tsz Yan. *Virginia Woolf and the Professions.* Cambridge UP, 2014.

Dalgarno, Emily. *Virginia Woolf and the Migrations of Language.* Cambridge UP, 2012.

De Gay, Jane. *Virginia Woolf and Christian Culture.* Edinburgh UP, 2018.

DeMeester, Karen. "Trauma and Recovery in Virginia Woolf's *Mrs. Dalloway.*" *Modern Fiction Studies,* vol. 44, no. 3, 1998, pp. 649–73.

Digby, Anne. "Contexts and Perspectives." *From Idiocy to Mental Deficiency: Historical Perspectives on People with Learning Disabilities,* edited by David Wright and Anne Digby, Routledge, 1996, pp. 1–21.

Diment, Galya. *A Russian Jew of Bloomsbury: The Life and Times of Samuel Koteliansky.* McGill-Queen's UP, 2011.

Dostoevsky, Fyodor. *Fyodor Dostoevsky Complete Letters: Volume II 1860–1867.* Edited and translated by David A. Lowe, Ardis, 1989.

———. *Fyodor Dostoevsky Complete Letters: Volume III 1868–1871.* Edited and translated by David A. Lowe, Ardis, 1990.

———. *Idiot.* In *Polnoe sobranie sochinenii v tridtsati tomakh,* vol. 8. Nauka, 1973.

———. *The Idiot.* Translated by Constance Garnett, William Heineman, 1913.

———. *The Notebooks for The Idiot.* Edited by Edward Wasiolek, translated by Katherine Stresky, U of Chicago P, 1967.

Frank, Joseph. *Dostoevsky: A Writer in His Time.* Princeton UP, 2010.

Goodey, C. F. *A History of Intelligence and 'Intellectual Disability': The Shaping of Psychology in Early Modern Europe.* Routledge, 2016.

Halliwell, Martin. *Images of Idiocy: The Idiot Figure in Modern Fiction and Film.* Routledge, 2016.

Hudspith, Sarah. *Dostoevsky and the Idea of Russianness: A New Perspective on Unity and Brotherhood.* Routledge, 2004.

idiot, noun & adjective. *Oxford English Dictionary*, Oxford UP, June 2024, https://doi.org/10.1093/OED/6390117550.

Iyer, Anupama. "Epilepsy in Dostoyevsky's Life and Fiction—Psychiatry in Literature." *The British Journal of Psychiatry,* vol. 216, no. 6, 2020, p. 313.

Johnson, Brian R. "Diagnosing Prince Myshkin." *The Slavic and East European Journal*, vol. 56, no. 3, 2012, pp. 377–93.

Kaye, Peter. *Dostoevsky and English Modernism, 1900–1930.* Cambridge UP, 1999.

King, Julia, and Laila Miletic-Vejzovic, editors and compilers. *The Library of Leonard and Virginia Woolf.* Washington State UP, 2003. Accessed 30 June 2023, http://ntserver1.wsulibs.wsu.edu/masc/onlinebooks/woolflibrary/woolflibraryonline.htm

Knapp, Liza. *Anna Karenina and Others: Tolstoy's Labyrinth of Plots.* U of Wisconsin P, 2016.

———. "Introduction to *The Idiot*: Part 2: The Novel." *Dostoevsky's The Idiot: A Critical Companion,* edited by Liza Knapp, Northwestern UP, 1998, pp. 27–50.

———. "Myshkin Through a Murky Glass, Guessingly." *Dostoevsky's The Idiot: A Critical Companion,* edited by Liza Knapp, Northwestern UP, 1998, pp. 191–215.

Kobets, Svitlana. "Lice in the Iron Cap: Holy Foolishness in Perspective." *Holy Foolishness in Russia: New Perspectives,* edited by Priscilla Hunt and Svitlana Kobets, Slavica, 2011, pp. 15–40.

Levenback, Karen L. "Virginia Woolf and the Returning Soldiers: The Great War and the Reality of Survival in *Mrs. Dalloway* and *The Years*." *Woolf Studies Annual,* vol. 2, 1996, pp. 71–88.

Loughran, Tracey. *Shell-Shock and Medical Culture in First World War Britain.* Cambridge UP, 2017.

Lyon, Janet. "On the Asylum Road with Woolf and Mew." *Modernism/modernity,* vol. 18, no. 3, 2011, pp. 551–74.

Maiorova, Olga. "Empire." *Dostoevsky in Context,* edited by Deborah A. Martinsen and Olga Maiorova, Cambridge UP, 2015, pp. 86–97.

McDonagh, Patrick. *Idiocy: A Cultural History.* Liverpool UP, 2008.

McDonagh, Patrick, et al. "Introduction: The Emergent Critical History of Intellectual Disability." *Intellectual Disability: A Conceptual History, 1200–1900*, edited by Patrick McDonagh, C. F. Goodey, and Tim Stainton, Manchester UP, 2018.

Meinhart, Michelle. "'Unearthly Music', 'Howling Idiots', and 'Orgies of Amusement': The Soundscapes of Shell Shock at Edinburgh's Craiglockhart War Hospital, 1917–18." *Nineteenth-Century Music Review*, vol. 20, no. 1, 2023, pp. 53–84.

Miller, Robin Feuer. *Dostoevsky and* The Idiot*: Author, Narrator, and Reader.* Harvard UP, 1981.

Muchnic, Helen. *Dostoevsky's English Reputation (1881–1936).* Smith College Studies in Modern Languages, Volume XX, no. 3 and 4, 1939.

Murav, Harriet. *Holy Foolishness: Dostoevsky's Novels and the Poetics of Cultural Critique.* Stanford UP, 1992.

Pett, Sarah. "Rash Reading: Rethinking Virginia Woolf's *On Being Ill*." *Literature and Medicine,* vol. 37, no. 1, 2019, pp. 26–66.

Phillips, Kathy J. *Virginia Woolf Against Empire.* U of Tennessee P, 1994.

Protopopova, Daria. *Virginia Woolf's Portraits of Russian Writers: Creating the Literary Other.* Cambridge Scholars, 2019.

Pulsifer, Rebecah. "'Contemplating the Idiot' in Virginia Woolf's *Between the Acts*." *Journal of Modern Literature,* vol. 42, no. 2, 2019, pp. 94–112.

Reinhold, Natalya. "Virginia Woolf's Russian Voyage Out." *Woolf Studies Annual,* vol. 9, 2003, pp. 1–27.

Rice, James. *Dostoevsky and the Healing Art: An Essay in Literary and Medical History.* Ardis, 1985.

Richter, Harvena. *Virginia Woolf: The Inward Voyage*. Princeton UP, 1970.

Rubenstein, Roberta. *Virginia Woolf and the Russian Point of View.* Palgrave Macmillan, 2009.

Showalter, Elaine. *The Female Malady: Women, Madness, and English Culture, 1820–1980.* Penguin, 1985.

"Voices of the First World War: Shell Shock." *Imperial War Museum,* n.d., www.iwm.org.uk/history/voices-of-the-first-world-war-shell-shock. Accessed 9 Jan. 2025.

Woolf, Virginia. *The Common Reader.* Harcourt, Brace & World, 1925.

———. *The Diary of Virginia Woolf: 1915–1919,* edited by Anne Oliver Bell, introduction by Quentin Bell, Harcourt Brace Jovanovich, 1977. Vol. 1 of *The Diary of Virginia Woolf.*

———. *The Diary of Virginia Woolf: 1920–1924,* edited by Anne Oliver Bell, assisted by Andrew McNeillie, Harcourt Brace Jovanovich, 1978. Vol. 2 of *The Diary of Virginia Woolf.*

———. *The Essays of Virginia Woolf: 1912–1918,* edited by Andrew McNeillie, Harcourt Brace Jovanovich, 1987. Vol. 2 of *The Essays of Virginia Woolf.*

———. The *Essays of Virginia Woolf: 1919–1924,* edited by Andrew McNeillie, Harcourt Brace Jovanovich, 1988. Vol. 3 of *The Essays of Virginia Woolf.*

———. *The Letters of Virginia Woolf: 1923–1928,* edited by Nigel Nicolson and Joanne Trautmann, Harcourt Brace Jovanovich, 1977. Vol. 3 of *The Letters of Virginia Woolf.*

———. *Mrs. Dalloway.* Harcourt Brace & Company, 1925.

———. *On Being Ill.* Paris Press, 2002.

———. "Phases of Fiction: In Three Parts: Part Two." *The Bookman; a Review of Books and Life (1895–1933)*, vol. 69, no. 3, 1929, pp. 269–79.

Young, Sarah J. *Dostoevsky's* The Idiot *and the Ethical Foundations of Narrative: Reading, Narrating, Scripting.* Anthem, 2004.

Zwerdling, Alex. *Virginia Woolf and the Real World.* U of California P, 1986.

The Letters between Virginia Woolf and Ling Shuhua

Han Au Chua

Introduction

From 1935 to 1937, Virginia Woolf's nephew Julian Bell taught English literature at Wuhan University and met the Chinese painter and writer Ling Shuhua (凌叔华) (1900–1990) in China.[1] Ling was married to Chen Yuan [陈源]), dean of Wuhan's Faculty of Letters, and had a brief intimate affair with Bell, who often referred to Ling in his letters to Vanessa Bell and Woolf.[2] Bell and Ling's relationship was short-lived because of its scandalous nature and Bell's relocation to Spain. In 1937, during the Spanish Civil War, Bell worked for the British Medical Aid Unit and died when a bomb destroyed the ambulance that he was driving. Bell's death was devastating for his family and for Ling, who was also grappling with the horrors of the Second Sino-Japanese War in China. On 3 March 1938, Ling started a correspondence with Woolf. Between 1938 and 1939, Ling and Woolf discussed grief, gender, imperialism, race, nationality, sexuality, and Ling's developing autobiography, which would be published by the Hogarth Press as *Ancient Melodies* (1953). There are a total of seventeen extant letters constituting the Ling-Woolf correspondence: Ling sent Woolf eleven letters and Woolf returned six.[3]

The unevenness of the correspondence has been overlooked in discussions of the Ling-Woolf correspondence. Scholars tend to emphasize Woolf's mentorship, arguing that she influenced Ling by giving her regular advice on *Ancient Melodies*.[4] This consensus on Woolf's cross-cultural mentorship participates in the ongoing global/planetary/transnational expansions in modernist studies.[5] But the critical account of Woolf's mentorship is symptomatic of a methodological tendency in global modernist studies and world literature in general to read an individual's

[1] Some biographical records state that Ling was born in 1904. I have noted 1900 as her birth year to honour Ling's intention of changing her original year of birth from 1904 to 1900 (Welland 4).

[2] Bell and Ling's affair inspired the contemporary Chinese writer Hong Ying (虹影) to write the controversial biofiction *K: The Art of Love* (2002). The work is generally regarded as being far from factual and Hong was charged with defamation in China in December 2002. But I have discussed how such assessments may be unfair to Hong and her work. See Chua, "Rethinking the biofiction."

[3] This number updates my reference to sixteen letters in my recent article in the previous volume of WSA "We Misunderstood Them: The Correspondence between Virginia Woolf and Ling Shuhua" (2024).

[4] In chronological order, see Ng; Shih; Laurence; Welland; Cheng; Berman; Zhang and Wang; Lei; and Meng.

[5] See discussions of these critical orientations (listed chronologically) in Mao and Walkowitz; Friedman; Moody and Ross; and Callison et al.

engagement with the culture, figures, and politics of a different geography as examples of genuine commitment.[6]

Regarding the full Ling-Woolf correspondence, I see two related areas of potential interest for scholars. The first is methodological. Many extant studies of the correspondence arise from selective and consequently overdetermined readings of the letters. Access to the full correspondence will thus facilitate more thorough evaluations of the Ling-Woolf exchange. The second area of interest is theoretical and political. As mentioned, scholars often take Woolf's letters to Ling as proof of Woolf's influence on the writing of *Ancient Melodies*. I have engaged with the issue of Woolf's mentorship elsewhere, and I would like to respond to critics who read Woolf's letters to Ling as testament to Woolf's Eurocentrism.[7] After all, Woolf's racism, her Ethnocentrism, and the concomitant ethics of studying works embroiled in racial/colonial politics are increasingly popular topics of discussion in literary studies. The Virginia Woolf Podcast, made in association with Literature Cambridge, released the episode "Making Sense of the Dreadnaught {*sic*} Hoax with Danell Jones" (2024), in which Karina Jakubowicz (the host) and Danell Jones revisit the 1910 blackfacing prank involving Woolf. Anne E. Fernald notes that "Woolf's occasional participation in discourses of race are notable, but seldom innovative, and often racist" (3). When I spoke about the Ling-Woolf correspondence at a conference in 2022, two scholars asked me whether Woolf was disengaged from her correspondence with Ling because she was racist toward the Chinese. I responded to these questions by saying that there is insufficient evidence to suggest these conclusions. As I will show later, the letters that Woolf sent Ling do not reflect Eurocentrism or racism. We must be careful in our analysis of Woolf's interactions with Ling because our conclusions have implications on the ways in which we remember, read, and teach Woolf's legacies. It is crucial to avoid transferring our impressions of Woolf across different contexts. In the case of the Ling-Woolf exchange, the fact that analyses of Woolf's Eurocentrism have not been supported by the full set of letters should encourage us to reconsider this contention.

Shu-mei Shih argues that Woolf's "subtle Eurocentric attitude" "urged Ling to write a work … in English" (216). But Shih fails to consider the rest of Woolf's letters and, quite alarmingly, all of Ling's letters written to Woolf. Shih's estimate of Woolf's Eurocentrism has been selectively supported by three of Woolf's letters in the sixth volume of Woolf's collected letters. We only have to read two letters—one by Woolf that Shih has excluded from her analysis and another by Ling—to recognise the implausibility of Shih's claim. In a letter sent to Ling, Woolf acknowledges that Ling has begun writing her autobiography: "And the only thing of any interest I had to say was to ask you to write your autobiography […] Now your other letter (March 24th) has just come, in which you tell me that you have begun to write this. I am so glad" (9 April 1938; *L*6 222). In another letter by Ling, she apprises Woolf

[6] See Chua, "We Misunderstood Them: The Correspondence between Virginia Woolf and Ling Shuhua."

[7] See Chua, "We Misunderstood Them."

of her own intention to write an autobiography for English speakers: "[i]f I could write this book in a very natural way—from it people could see some truths of life and art or sex which Westerners never have a chance even to think about them, that would be something worth doing" (25 May 1938).

Patricia Laurence holds that Woolf's disregard for Ling's Chinese culture is problematic, stating that "Virginia Woolf, like many who are foreign to the culture of China, understood some things about it, misunderstood others, and may have been culturally ignorant or insensitive" (249). Laurence then supports her assertion by writing, "Woolf, responded, not understanding the title of respect in China, 'Please call me Virginia. I do not like being Mrs. Woolf'" (272). Laurence's stance may have been influenced by the matrix in which she was writing her book, which saw a scholarly expansion on Woolf's xenophobia and racism.[8] Yet Woolf's letters to Ling cannot be simplified in this way. By stating that Woolf was culturally ignorant because she wishes to be called by her first name "Virginia," Laurence does not seem to be familiar with Woolf's habit of letter writing. When Vita Sackville-West addresses Woolf as "Mrs Woolf" during the early stages of their friendship, Woolf prefaces her reply to Sackville-West, "But I wish you could be induced to call me Virginia" (Sackville-West 37–8); in response to David Garnett's letter, Woolf begins comparably: "Dear Bunny, / I hope you dont mind, but as I always hear of you as Bunny and you of me as Virginia, I think we might venture—" (*L2* 167); to W. J. H. Sprott, Woolf writes, "Dear Sebastian, / (I hope you don't mind, and will call me Virginia)" (*L3* 55); in a letter to Daphne Sanger, she starts her letter, "Dear Daphne—I wish you would call me Virginia, or I shall have to call you Miss Sanger—" (*L3* 184). There is a clear pattern here: Woolf wishes simply to be called "Virginia" as opposed to "Mrs Woolf." Straightforwardly, the formal register of "Mrs Woolf" resists intimacy between Woolf and her friends. What appears to be the issue with Woolf's earnest appeal to Ling—"Please call me Virginia"—is not an issue of culture, but salutation.

The Ling-Woolf letters first gained public attention at the 1991 Sotheby's auction in London, where they were in a dossier of unpublished materials related to the Bloomsbury Group. Sold to Steve Crook, then head archivist of the New York Public Library, the letters have since been kept at the Berg collection for private study and research. Yet few scholars have examined these letters and those who refer to the correspondence have misquoted the letters. In Ling's letter dated 24 July 1938, Ling writes, "If my book could give English readers some pictures of real Chinese lives …." But Laurence misquotes Ling by writing, "If my book could give English readers some *picture* of real Chinese lives …" (274, my emphasis). Additionally, the phrase following "Chinese lives" in Ling's original letter is "some impression about Chinese who …" but Laurence writes, "some *experience* about Chinese who …" (274, my emphasis). Similarly, in Harcourt Brace Jovanovich's

[8] See, for instance, (listed chronologically) Rosenfeld; Rodríguez; Linett; Schröder; Seshagiri; Gruber; and Trubowitz.

1980 edition of Woolf's letters, her letters to Ling contain words, paragraphing, and punctuation marks that deviate from the original letters. The 1980 edition also does not include word cancellations and spelling mistakes that would be especially useful for scholars working in codicology, the digital humanities, and genetic criticism today.

At the top left-hand corner of each transcribed letter, there is one of the following designations in bold: autograph letter signed (ALS); typed letter signed (TLS); or typed letter unsigned (TLU). Some of the letters were airmailed and this has been indicated in the transcription as 'Airmailed letter' in bold. At the top right-hand corner, there is the date of the letter also in bold. Non-standard spelling, punctuation marks, word spacing, and paragraph breaks in the letters have been retained. Editorial symbols accompanying the transcription of each letter are explained below:

Word written by author's hand: *italics*
Word inserted by author by hand: ^
Word cancelled by author: ~~strikethrough~~

Acknowledgments

I received a great deal of advice and support from many people when I began this project in 2019. My first thanks go to Tania Roy, whose wisdom helped to sharpen my views on Ling and Woolf when I was working on these two writers during my undergraduate studies. I am also thankful to Dirk Van Hulle for his comments on an early version of this project, and to my supervisor at Oxford, Rebecca Beasley, who supported my research grant applications, enabling me to develop my findings on Woolf and Ling in archives at the New York Public Library, the University of Cambridge, and The Keep.

I would also like to express my appreciation to Sarah Baxter and her team at The Society of Authors representing the Estate of Virginia Woolf for their permission to publish new transcriptions of Woolf's letters. I am also deeply grateful to Ling's family, Colin Chinnery and Hsiaoying Chinnery, for entrusting me with the transcription of Ling's letters and for their permission to include quotations from them in my WSA 30 article and publish them in this volume. My thanks are also to Carolyn Vega and Emma Davidson from the New York Public Library for helping me with the manuscripts of Ling and Woolf.

I am interminably thankful to Benjamin Hagen and Mark Hussey for publishing "We Misunderstood Them: The Correspondence between Virginia Woolf and Ling Shuhua" in the 30th volume of *Woolf Studies Annual* (2024). This transcription is a companion piece to that article.

Works Cited

Berman, Jessica. *Modernist Commitments Ethics, Politics, and Transnational Modernism*. Columbia UP, 2011.

Callison, Jamie et al., editors. *The Bloomsbury Handbook of Modernist Archives*. Bloombury Academic, 2024.

Cheng, Eileen. "Virtue in Silence: Voice and Femininity in Ling Shuhua's Boudoir Fiction." *NAN NÜ*, vol. 9, no. 2, 2007, pp. 330–70. doi:10.1163/138768007X244370.

Chua, Han Au. "Rethinking the biofiction." *Prose Studies*, vol. 43, no. 3, 2022, pp. 213–31. doi:10.1080/01440357.2024.2410429

———. "We Misunderstood Them: The Correspondence between Virginia Woolf and Ling Shuhua." *Woolf Studies Annual*, vol. 30, no. 2, 2024, pp. 31–52.

Friedman, Susan Stanford. *Planetary Modernisms: Provocations on Modernity across Time*. Columbia UP, 2016.

Gruber, Ruth. *Virginia Woolf: The Will to Create as a Woman*. Basic Books, 2005.

Jakubowicz, Karina. "Making Sense of the Dreadnaught Hoax with Danell Jones." *The Virginia Woolf Podcast*, season 4, episode 4, 1 August 2024, open.spotify.com.

Laurence, Patricia. *Lily Briscoe's Chinese Eyes: Bloomsbury, Modernism, and China*. Columbia UP, 2003.

Lei, Jun. "Capitalizing China: Writing Autography into World Literature." *Modern Chinese Literature and Culture*, vol. 30, no. 1, 2018, pp. 87–109.

Linett, Maren. "The Jew in the Bath: Imperiled Imagination in Woolf's *The Years*." *Modern Fiction Studies*, vol. 48 no. 2, 2002, pp. 341–61. doi:10.1353/mfs.2002.0031

Ling, Shuhua. *Ancient Melodies*. Hogarth Press, 1953.

———. Letter to Virginia Woolf. 25 May 1938. Henry W. and Albert A. Berg Collection of English and American Literature. New York Public Library. Manuscript.

———. Letter to Virginia Woolf. 24 July 1938. Henry W. and Albert A. Berg Collection of English and American Literature. New York Public Library. Manuscript.

———. Letter to Virginia Woolf. 16 November 1938. Henry W. and Albert A. Berg Collection of English and American Literature. New York Public Library. Typescript.

———. Letter to Virginia Woolf. 12 December 1938. Henry W. and Albert A. Berg Collection of English and American Literature. New York Public Library. Typescript.

———. Letter to Virginia Woolf. 31 December 1938. Henry W. and Albert A. Berg Collection of English and American Literature. New York Public Library. Typescript.

———. Letter to Virginia Woolf. 11 January 1939. Henry W. and Albert A. Berg Collection of English and American Literature. New York Public Library. Typescript.

———. Letter to Virginia Woolf. 20 January 1939. Henry W. and Albert A. Berg Collection of English and American Literature. New York Public Library. Typescript.

———. Letter to Virginia Woolf. 28 February 1939. Henry W. and Albert A. Berg Collection of English and American Literature. New York Public Library. Typescript.

———. Letter to Virginia Woolf. 16 March 1939. Henry W. and Albert A. Berg Collection of English and American Literature. New York Public Library. Manuscript.

———. Letter to Virginia Woolf. n.d., 1938. Henry W. and Albert A. Berg Collection of English and American Literature. New York Public Library. Manuscript.

———. Letter to Virginia Woolf. n.d., 1939. Henry W. and Albert A. Berg Collection of English and American Literature. New York Public Library. Manuscript.

Mao, Douglas and Rebecca L. Walkowitz. "The New Modernist Studies." *PMLA*, vol. 123, no. 3, 2008, pp. 737–48.

Meng, Deyan. "Ling Shuhua and Virginia Woolf: Female Communion, Resistance, and Individuality." *Virginia Woolf, Europe, and Peace: Vol. 1 Transnational Circulations*, edited by Ariane Mildenberg and Patricia Novillo-Corvalán, Liverpool UP, 2020, pp. 203–18.

Moody, Alys and Stephen J. Ross, editors. *Global Modernists on Modernism: An Anthology*. Bloomsbury Academic, 2020.

Ng, Janet. "Writing in her father's world: The feminine autobiographical strategies of Ling Shuhua." *Prose Studies*, vol. 16, no. 3, 1993, pp. 235–50.

Rodríguez, Laura María Lojo. "Contradiction and Ambivalence: Virginia Woolf and the Aesthetic Experience in 'The Duchess and the Jeweller.'" *Journal of English Studies*, 2002, vol. 3, pp. 115–29.

Rosenfeld, Natania. *Outsiders Together: Virginia and Leonard Woolf*. Princeton UP, 2000.

Seshagiri, Urmila. "Orienting Virginia Woolf: Race, Aesthetics, and Politics in To the Lighthouse." *Modern Fiction Studies*, vol. 50 no. 1, 2004, p. 58–84.

Schröder, Leena Kore. "Tales of Abjection and Miscegenation: Virginia Woolf's and Leonard Woolf's 'Jewish' Stories." *Twentieth Century Literature*, vol. 49, no. 3, Duke UP, 2003, pp. 298–327.

Trubowitz, Lara. "Concealing Leonard's Nose: Virginia Woolf, Modernist Antisemitism, and 'The Duchess and the Jeweller.'" *Twentieth Century Literature*, 2008, vol. 54, no. 3, pp. 273–306.

Sackville-West, Vita, and Virginia Woolf. *The Letters of Vita Sackville-West to Virginia Woolf*. Edited by Louise Desalvo and Mitchell Leaska, Cleis P, 1984.

Shih, Shu-mei. *The Lure of the Modern: Writing Modernism in Semicolonial China, 1917–1937*. U of California P, 2001.

Welland, Sasha Su-Ling. *A Thousand Miles of Dreams: The Journeys of Two Chinese Sisters*. Rowman & Littlefield, 2006.

Woolf, Virginia. Letter to Ling Shuhua. 5 April 1938. Henry W. and Albert A. Berg Collection of English and American Literature. New York Public Library. Manuscript.

———. Letter to Ling Shuhua. 9 April 1938. Henry W. and Albert A. Berg Collection of English and American Literature. New York Public Library. Manuscript.

———. Letter to Ling Shuhua. 27 July 1938. Henry W. and Albert A. Berg Collection of English and American Literature. New York Public Library. Typescript.

———. Letter to Ling Shuhua. 15 October 1938. Henry W. and Albert A. Berg Collection of English and American Literature. New York Public Library. Typescript.

———. Letter to Ling Shuhua. 17 April 1939. Henry W. and Albert A. Berg Collection of English and American Literature. New York Public Library. Typescript.

———. Letter to Ling Shuhua. 16 July 1939. Henry W. and Albert A. Berg Collection of English and American Literature. New York Public Library. Typescript.

———. *The Letters of Virginia Woolf: 1912–1922*, edited by Nigel Nicolson and Joanne Trautmann, Harcourt Brace Jovanovich, 1976. Vol. 2 of *The Letters of Virginia Woolf*.

———. *The Letters of Virginia Woolf: 1923–1928*, edited by Nigel Nicolson and Joanne Trautmann, Harcourt Brace Jovanovich, 1977. Vol. 3 of *The Letters of Virginia Woolf*.

———. *The Letters of Virginia Woolf: 1936–1941*, edited by Nigel Nicolson and Joanne Trautmann, Harcourt Brace Jovanovich, 1980. Vol. 6 of *The Letters of Virginia Woolf*.

Zhang, Yuanling and Wang Yunxia. 章元羚；汪云霞. "从此岸到彼岸———论凌叔华《古韵》的跨文化书写, 华文文学 ["From This Side to That Side—Discussing the Transcultural Styles in Ling Shuhua's *Ancient Melodies*." *Huawen Wenxue*, no. 3, 2017, pp. 113–18.]

ALS

5th April 1938

Dear Sue Ling

I hope you have had the letter I wrote in answer to your first letter. I wrote only a few days after I had yours. Now Vanessa has just sent on your letter of March 3rd. I wish I could help you. I know that you have much more reason to be unhappy than we have even; & therefore how foolish any advice must be. But my only advice — & I have tried to take it myself — is to work. So let us think how you could fix your mind upon something worth doing in itself. I have not read any of your writing, but Julian often wrote ^to me about it, & meant to show me some of it. He said too that you had lived a most interesting life; indeed, we had discussed — I think in letters — the chance that you would try to write an account of your life in English. That is what I would suggest now. Your English is quite good enough to give the impression you ~~have~~ wish to make; & I could change anything difficult to understand. Will you make a beginning, & put down exactly anything you remember? As no one in England knows you, the book could be more free than usual. Then I would see if it could not be printed. But please think of this: not merely as a distraction, but as a work that would be of great value to other people too. I find autobiographies much better than novels. You ask what books I would advise you to read: I think the English in the 18th Century wrote in the best way for a foreigner to learn from. Do you like letters? There are Cowpers, Walpoles; very clear and easy; Scotts novels; (~~Redgauntlet~~Rob Roy); Jane Austen: then Mrs Gaskells Life of Charlotte Brontë: then among modern writers, George Moore's novels — they are simply written too. I could send you English books, but I do not know if you have them already. But from your letters I see that you write very well; you need not copy others, only find new words by reading quickly. I say nothing about politics. You know from what I said before how ^strongly the English are on your side but cannot do anything to help. We hear about China from friends here. But perhaps now there will be a change. The worst may be over. At any rate please remember that I am always glad if you will write & tell me anything about yourself: ^or politics & it would be a great pleasure to me to read some of your writing, & criticise it: so think of writing your life, & if you only write a few pages at a time, I could read them & we could discuss it. I wish I could do more. We send our best sympathy.

Yours
Virginia Woolf

ALS

April 9th 1938

Dear Sue Ling,

I got your letter written on March 3rd a few days ago, and answered it at once. But stupidly I forgot to send it by air mail — so I write this to tell you that I have written. And the only thing of any interest I had to say was to ask you to write your autobiography, & to say I will gladly read it & give it any correction it needs. Now your other letter (March 24th) ~~other letter~~ has just come, in which you tell me that you have begun to write this. I am so glad. Julian always told me that you had lived a most interesting life: & you say he also wanted to write it down — simply, as it comes, not bothering about grammar at all. I also ~~said~~ asked if you would like me to send you any old English books — 18th century ones perhaps — so that you could learn words. But you will find this in my letter. Let me know if I can do anything to help you in your work. I am certain work is the only way in which one can love at the moment. I will send this now. I hope you will get it soon.

We send our sympathy & shall always wish for news both of you & of your war, & politics.

Yrs
Virginia Woolf

ALS
Airmailed letter

May 25, 1938

Dear Virginia Woolf,

I feel more familiar with your pen name, if this is not polite, please excuse me. Your letter dated April 5th reached me two days ago. It is beyond words to tell my deep gratitude to-ward your good letter. The only thing I want to say is if some day I could write something which could be good value to ^other people is all from your kind encouragement. I'm by nature a careful person but very have to do things ^in a rush when I feel it ~~and~~ I like it. Lately I have been thinking very often on the things which was happening in my life ^& which would be worth writing. Since Julian and I became intimate friends, I had almost got an habit to ~~tell~~ make him ~~about~~ understand China in telling him stories which I know really happened to some people and they were interesting. I think Julian had a good taste of life and art from an Eastern point of view, he sometimes reminded me of my father who died 5 years ago while he was 70 by age. I'm thinking to choose all the stories I had told Julian and write them down could be something anyway to the Western people. perhaps some ~~young~~ people with ~~new~~ his thoughts or those who sympathise with all things human. If I could write this book in a very natural way — from it people could see some truths of life and art or sex which Westerners would never have a chance to ^even to think ~~of~~ about them, that would be something worth doing. Do you think so? ~~From~~ I'm writing this sort of

stories, it would do me good ~~which I~~ because that will make me recall all the happy hours with Julian when he was here. I have written ~~a~~ some parts of my early childhood — about my father when he was the last mayor of the capital city (Peking) and how we celebrating a new comedian ~~had~~ entered our home. Another part is I went to see an execution with a servant who was a soldier before. Another part is [~~illegible~~] tell a festival day, what unhappy life mother lived, and ~~aroundt~~ but among all concubines, mother was ^a very kind friend to them. And how I had to understand the word "fate" from my mother's sad [~~illegible~~] life. I'm going to try to describe my father he was a very charming man indeed, I hope I could give a real picture of him. He by all means, a type of a Chinese gentleman, who never missed a chance of enjoying life, and he was lucky he got all. These should be from the eye of a child, it is not very easy to ~~make~~ express it naturally and good well. Thank you very much for suggesting some English books for me to read. I had only read J. Austen, all of hers. The rest you suggest are Cooper, Walpoles, [illegible] Scott's Rob Roy, Mr Gaskell's Life of Charlotte Brontë, I have never read them. If it will not be too much trouble to you, will you please send them to me in two parcels (big parcels always delay for months) to the following address: Ling Su Hua of Mr Yih-Chuan Koo General manager of ~~Canton~~ The Provincial Bank of Canton
Canton ~~City~~, China
Please remember to tell me how much I shall pay for these books when you write me. And please register these parcels in the post, because we always lose things in post recently. I have been persuaded to go to Szechuan to avoid the disaster of frequent bombing, I shall go there with my child for some time, ~~and I know~~ Because I can't do much work here, I like to go away for a relief. Please write to my house P.O. box 59. They will forward it to me.

As soon as I can sit down in a quiet corner, I will copy some parts I have written in a clearer way and send ^them to you, to see whether or not ^worth to continue writing them. I often feel, if my English could write as well as my Chinese, that would be a real book which perhaps last for sometime. But I'm afraid I'm too proud of myself by all means, and expecting too much.

Since we had knocked down 21 Japanese airplanes 3 weeks ago, there has ^not been seen any enemy plane in the sky. Some people need to be [~~illegible~~] beatten in this world. How I hope Westerners will learn a lesson from our war ^with Japan to stop power by power, don't hesitate and ^try to compromise. Please write to ^tell me about your opinion about my suggestion from my book, ~~when~~ after you get my letter. I'm always anxious to hear from you.

Yours,
Sue Ling

ALS

1938 undated

Dear Virginia,

I'm afraid a person with a most miserable mind can't express her thought as half good as ordinary. I don't think my English is half as good as my Chinese, so my writing must be a bore for you to read. But I know you'll excuse me when you feel impatient to read it. Last night, a girl of our university jumped down from the third stored house windows. She was killed cruelly. Her simple reason for to commit suicide is that she could not hear from her family after Hankow occupied^by the enemy. I began to feel ~~a~~ surprice of ~~myself~~my exicestence because I have more reason to commit suicide than this girl, beside the general desaster, I have my person deep sorrow which I will never get out of my mind. The worst of all, I have to face all this helpless condition every day. Japanese airplanes had come to visit West China 3 times a week recently, I feel quite the same as a month ago. Death does not make any difference to my thought now.

Please write a few line to tell me how do you think about my writing. I will be most grateful if only I know you have read it.

With love and respect,
Sue Ling

Please call me Sue when you write again. I feel it's not becoming being a Mrs. C. to write this letter to you.

ALS
Airmailed letter

July 24, 1938

My dear Virginia Woolf,

I and my family members came to Szechuan(West China) with a group of university staffs a month already. We are living in a room situated in South of Szechuan which we think we are safe from bombing by our enemy but we might be killed by several kind of special deseases which outsiders of this place can not resist. It's alright for us at present because I always think being a Chinese, one has to look for hardships, preparing the worst of life, then by and by one may ^learn to amuse oneself with misery. An European person perhaps would not understand what I mean by amuse oneself with misery, but here we are seeing everyday in the street or ^when look into oneself daily life. I have been very busy and unwell about some time, to look for a house or look after relatives all bore me to death, because I can't do my work as I want to. During these last few days I made up my mind to continue to write my book, I finished a chapter yesterday. I will copy it in a more neat way and will send to you. I hope ~~they~~it will not give you too much trouble in reading. If my book could give English readers some pictures of real Chinese lives, some impression about Chinese who are as ordinary as any English people, some truth of life and sex which your people never have a chance to see but [illegible] even seen by a child in the East, I shall be contended. I'm not those who only want satisfy readers curiosity and neglect whether ^or not its true to themselves. ~~or not~~[illegible]. I dislike a book like "Great Earth" by P. Buck though it has been a great success, I don't admire it. It seems to me she create every character all by herself and make a good story to satisfy her readers. To write an autobiography perhaps can be avoid these mistakes, at least I will try to leave out things I don't know well. My chief difficulty in my book is that ^there are too many people ^appearing in my mind when I think of my past days. It's hard to manage and to select them. I hope you will be good enough to tell me what would you do if you were writing such a books. Please do let me know if the part I will send to you is no good or ~~even~~need to be rewrite. I'm very anxious to know my faults and more anxious to write a good book. When you tell me I'm ^not hopeless in writing, will you allow me to call you my teacher or my tutor when I ^next write to you? A teacher to a real Chinese's mind (I mean who have not been changed by Western influence) is equally highly respect and ^feeling intimate as well as parents as brothers. I'm not certain what is this word mean to English people. Julian had suggested I can write my autobiography in two books, my first one is life to the time before I attended college. (before ^my fifteen) I think that perhaps easier for me but it's rather a pity to tell all things in a Chinese book out of time and tide. All new movement had meant very little to me before I entered college, but it is true of most Chinese. That people live in the country, if you ask them what is the name or our national flag like, they can't answer you.

Recently I read again your "The Years" and Mr. Proust Swann's Way. I've admired both of you so much, you bring in all people so naturally without letting your readers to see your intention. And I learn words in reading The Years. I begin to notice all good literature are alike. I tried to translate the words you use, especially about [illegible], I could put them into very good (I mean correct) Chinese words easily. Julian often said to me that my English is not enough to tell a thing very well, yet he often found ^out that many words I used give good suggestion for the thing, and made him understand well. I think perhaps this had been helpt by my knowledge of learning Chinese words. I hope it will help me to learn ^good English. What do you think about this? Please write to me to my old letter box in Hankow. No. 59. P.O. Hankow. I'm always anxious to hear from you.

With love and respect,
Sue

P.S. we believe within 3 months, Japan would be here to occupy Hankow.

TLS

27th July 1938

Dear Madame Sue Ling,

I have just seen Christopher Isherwood, who gave me the lovely little box with the two little gifts from you. I need not say that I am much touched that you should have got them for me, and I shall keep them on my table — not as a moemory of you, for I have never seen you, but all the same I think of you often. Thank you so much. I heard from him how much they had enjoyed seeing you. But he was only here for a moment, and I did not have time to get much information from him. I hope however that you are going on with your work. I am sending you two little books ~~ofxx~~ one is the life of Charlotte Brontë, the other Lambs Essays. I think Lamb wrote very good English prose — but do not bother *to* read it a an exercise; only for pleasure — The life of Charlotte Bronte will perhaps give you a feeling for the lives of women writers in England in the 19th century — their difficulties, and how she overcame them. And it is a very interesting life *in other ways*. But I will send other books from time to time, on condition that you do not think you must thank me for them. And certainly you must never think of paying for them. hey are so cheap in England. I can buy them for a few pence. Tell me the names of any you think you would like.

We are just going down to Sussex, and I hope to have more time there. London is so crowded. There is a quiet time here politically for the moment. That is to say we are waiting for what Hitler may do next. People are getting tired of talking about war; but all the same we do nothing but buy arms. The air is full of aeroplanes at the moment.

I hope some day you will write again and tell me how you are getting on with your work. And please remember how glad I shall be to give you any help I can in reading it and correcting any mistakes. But write exactly as you think — that is the only way.

With my love, good bye. Please call me Virginia. I do not like being Mrs Woolf.

Virginia Woolf

TLS
Monks House, Rodmell, Lewes Sussex
15th Oct. 1938

I am typing this, so as to save your eyes, for my writing is so hard to read. At last I have read the chapter you sent me — I put it off, for one reason and another. Now I write to say that I like it very much. I think it has a great charm. It is also of course difficult for an English person, at first, there is some incoherence, and one does not understand the different wives; who they are; which is speaking. But this becomes clear after a time; and then I feel a charm in the very unlikeness. I find the similes strange and poetical. How far it can be read by the public as it stands, I do not know. That I could only say if you would go on sending me more chapters. Then I should get the whole impression. This is only a fragment. Please go on; write freely: do not mind how directly you translate the Chinese into the English. In fact

I would advise you to come as close to the Chinese both in style and in meaning as you can. Give as many natural details of the life, of the house, of the furniture as you like. And always do it as you were writing for the Chinese. Then if it were to some extent made easy grammatically by someone English I think it might be possible to keep the Chinese flvour and make it both understandable yet strange for the English.

One of the reasons why I did not read it or write before was that we have been so uneasy in England; we were almost sure of war. Everything was ready, even the gas masks served out, and orders given to house children from London. This atmosphere made it difficult to fix ones mind on books. Now for the time at least that strain is over.

Please forgive me then for having been so long in writing. Next time you send me more chapters — soon I hope — I will write back more quickly.

We are just going back to London. The houses there are still protected many of them with sand bags. But in China I know things are far worse. I find the only relief is to work. And I hope you will go on, writing, for it might be a very interesting book.

Did you get a letter I wrote in August, and a parcel of books? Tell me, for if they came safe I will send more. It is easy to get books cheaply in London. Please never think of paying for them. It is a great pleasure to me to send them. Tell me what you like. It is difficult to know. I am keeping the manuscript you sent. I can read your writing quite easily. so dont bother to type.

Yours with love,
Virginia Woolf
52 Tavistock Square
London WC 1

TLS

November 16th 1938
Kaitung, West China

Dear Virginia,

I realise recently that time passes quickly too when on is miserable for I still remember all deaster happened to me some monthes ago as clear as if it were yesterday. Since I arrived Szechun[1], I wrote you two or three letters, one was sending with a part of my autobiography I wonder all these things had been lukily reached you. I ~~too~~, am ~~afri~~ *afraid* when they were arriving, you were having your most busy time to ward the possibility of a next great war, ~~and this~~ Hiteler would never beleive that his darn policy even brings distress to a poor little woman in the far East in the very begining. But I'm glad it is not like so serious as a month ago. I hope you ha~~ve~~d kindly read my manuscri*pt* and perhaps would write to tell me. But I hope you had not sent this letter to Hankow, for you know it has ^been occupied by Japenese about some time. During these last weeks as all bad news brought out

[1] Ling misspells Szechuan as Szechun in the subsequent typed letters.

at once; we lost Canton unexpectfully and Hankow had to withdraw our trops, and the West being in a helpless condition, and our money had been reduced its value that made life harder for Chinese, I almost lost my head. As I understood that It is useless to go to the front to fight for we can not find our anemy, we only see the machines. I could not sleep in the night, if I fell to sleep I would dream the most unpleasant thing I ~~was dread~~ [x] had in my thought. I saw my house in the ruin and broken funitures, out side of the house the ^laying corpse, the unburried corpses smelling badly. I think perhaps you would like to know a bit of extrem miserable kind feeling, so I wrote this to tell you, I hope you would not think I like to write long letter. As I could not make myself work well, so I made up my mind to learn something which need not use my mind, I chose typewriting. I 'm glad I got a teacher finally. Typ~~w~~riting is useful to me as I want to write ~~myself~~. I feel sorry that I had sent that manuscript to you I'm afraid it is difficult to read.

Please write to tell me frankly when you have read this part which I send with this letter. I hope it will not take much of your time. my life seems ~~tome~~ to me quite long, it begins in time of something like your dark age, it suddenly turns out to the very up to date time. The developement of my mind likes the life, though only thirty years, it happens to ~~learn~~ see many unusal thing. I think it would be something if one puts down in paper. Although sometime I can't help to fear ^at time like this, there is no one care about to read something personal, for there is many ~~great~~ important things in the world one ~~want~~ to ~~know~~ read. But what shall I do, since I can't write those stuff. One must be honest to one's work. I decide to continue my book. Do you think it right?

Your leeter dated July 27th reached ^me tow months ago, I was grateful to know that you're going to send me books. I hope you had not sent out them, because all places have been in a upset condition. I dont trust the post office in Hankow would forward my letters too. Please use the following address: Ling Su Hua, Mrs Chen, Mrs B. Bassett, American Baptist Mission, Kiating, Szechun Province, West China.

TLS

Dec. 12, 1938. Kaiting, Szechun,
West china.

Dear Virginia,

Herewith I am sending you the first part of my autobiography I hope it will reach you safely and you will let me know what do you think of it. Some months ago I had sent two ^parts of my autobiography to you, but I do not dare to think what have become of them. I fear that two months ago you would not have time to read my writing, there had been many important things before you. But now perhaps you have read them, will you kindly to tell me what do you think of them? If they were not hopeless to be a ~~real~~ book, I mean to become a book which you think not <u>too</u> bad, please tell me to continue it. My work is the only single sparker which gives me fire and strength to linger upon life. Being faced this great disater of a whole nation, one feel personal sorrow is not something worth to mention, yet it is *the* ~~thing~~ very thing one has to taste everyday and night. Just a few weeks ago, a college girl of the Wu Han University had commited suicid by jamping down from a three storied house at night. Her death gives me a surprise because I know I have been much unhappy than what she has had, but she had courage to put an end to it. She dies because Hankow was occupied by Japanese and she could not hear from her family. The war in China seems last longer and longer than any one could think about it only half year ago, one can not help feeling it might be God's will that He intends to put an end on the yellow race. Some times I feel that the best result would be for those yellow-faced human beings to find out a new way of ^to live ~~life~~ and a ^real *new* world through all struggles. In my heart, I often feel I love Japenese ordinary people not less than I do to Chinese. But why do we have to fight?

The place where I live now is situated in south Szechun province. Two years ago Julian had been visited here. He told us he had seen the remote part of China. ~~in a~~ ^He was proud of his trip ~~way~~. But now this tiny town has filled up with thousands of outsiders. Recently we have had the honnor of ^maybe being bombed, because the enemy planes had visited in the air several times. The people here who live a life of a sixteen century and with thoughts of sixteen century, know to fear of morden airoplanes. Little children who never have the pleasure of ride ion a train or a motor car, but they can tell you the difference between the enemy's plan e or Chinese. Isen't this world ridiculus? I begin to realize the world will turn out faster than one's ~~mind~~thoughts. The old Chinese saying says " When one is aged, (we mean old), one will become a ghost" The word ghost means a kind of immotal being who has lived long years, who has seen all strange things so knows all sort of queer things. I feel if we could live through this great period, one day we would become a ghost in the human world. One ^of those days I thought perhaps it ~~might~~would be something to put down all these experiences which a lucky nation may find it amusing if I write them in English. Will you care to read these sort of writing?

Please write me a few lines when you have read my writing and *please do* send your letter by air mail. An ordinary mail takes three months to this place. I hope you will use this following address which the post ^man will take to me easily.

Ling Su Hua, ————> *(This is my pen name in Chinese)*
c/o Miss B. Bassett,
Kaiting, Szechun Province,
China.

I am sorry I have change my address often, but I need not tell you how much I have been touched by your sympathy and kind letter.

Love
Sue (Su Hua)

TLS

December 31, 1938.

Dear Virginia,

To-day is the last day of the year, I still have not got your letter from which I shall *expect to* hear what you think about my writing of an autobiography." No flowers, no wine the festival day passes" I thought of this famous line, I could not keep back my tears during this day.

Just a few moment ago, I was wondering about in the street I had thought of you and envyed your work. The people here live a life of five hundred years ago. There are small temples where they worship gods and ghosts, when they come to ask bliss or to beg to cure their illness they worship both mighty powers. They believe they will get what they want. Beside the roads there are fortune tellers who now and then are telling soldiers about their future fate in the battle feilds where they are going to meet the morden armement. The soldiers of course know as well as the fortune tellers that they never in their lives have the honor of seeing a tank nor a machine gun, how could they know the~~y~~ chance of hitting. But in fact the soldiers listen to the fortune tellers very siriously and the speakers say honestly. I felt dislike of this scene at first, but now I feel I symperthise with the soldiers. I even want to weep ^or to laugh with them. For you see, if this only left tiny comfort to them were also robbed, it would be too cruel. Since we know that there is nothing left in their hope, and their lives now and then are too sad to tell. When I came back to think of myself, especially about my work, I felt I am [illegible] the same fate as these soldiers. I know there is very little chance for me to write a good book in English for the ~~s~~tool I use to do my work is something which I can not handle well. It is true in cooking too, if one uses a forgin pin or stove to cook a Chinese dish, it won't come out the same one as the original. It often loses some good taste. In writing, I don't know how far it counts. When I read a good translation, I feel a releif at once though I do not dare to think every book can be well translated. Dear Virginia, I want you to tell me what shall I do since I am in a state of nurves tension. Oh, yet, how I hope you would be as kind as before to tell me to try it, don't dispair.

Now I send you another part of my book, I hope it will reach you safely. I almost decide to go to the temple to beg the ghosts or gods to protect my letter and to make you read it early if only I know it would do me some good.

This part I send now is very bad ^writing, I hope someday you will tell me which parts can be kept which should be left out.

The weather changed suddenly here. It has been very cold recently. My hands feel frozen when I type this. People tell us that there has never been so cold almost fifty years. It seems a refugee's fate: disaster ~~never falls~~ comes alone.

When Julian was here in China, he often told me that my life is a poem. I said because of the sadness and the character of my strong personality make him think so. He smiled. I need not to tell you more of my life. I only hope with this unfavour*able* parts of my nature, it may help me in my writing. Among many women, I think I am ~~more less~~ a fighter.

Please use the following address when you write to me: Ling Su Hua c/o Miss B. Bassett, Baptist Mission, Kaiting, Szechun, China.

Love from Su Hua

TLS

Kaiting, Szechun
Jan 11, 1939

Dear Virginia,

Yesterday (Jan. 10), I got Vanesa's letter, she tells me that my manuscripe has reached you safely and you had written me a long letter about it. She said you sent out this letter long ago, perhaps in August. What shall I do, this letter must have been lost *obviously* in the same fate with Canton and Hankow. As I now count the date and the days which took the letter to Hankow and Canton just about the time of the capture~~d~~ by the Japanese. How I regret now that I had given you those address of both captured towns! It is impossible to inquire you or to do anything to look for it ^now though it means so valuable and precious to me. And the books you sent to me were lost too, how bad my fate it, I can't help to complaint to ~~a~~ this unseen and misterious power. But how silly one is when one knows it is useless! Dear Virginia, I don't know wheter I ask you too much or not if I ask you to write me another long letter to tell me what you think about my writing on my autobiography. Please excuse me if you are too busy at present and perhaps feel I should not ask too much. I think you will understand at once how important this lost letter is meant to me when you read this letter. This week, ~~I~~ inspite of all hopeless condition of this dreary and chill weather I did write my book continuely. I am going to post it tomorrow. This part I have done better than the previous one I think. In which I tell how clearly in my childhood I had found the meaning of the word fate. This ~~part of~~ story has been written in Chinese which I did not use my real name and which had von sympathy and good critiscium by a few literary critics. I hope you would not feel ^too different. The part I sent to you ten days ago is bad. I think there will be many things I must leave out when I finish the whole book. At present, I just keep writing on. Do you think so?

The chapter written about a new concubine of my fathers' enter*ing* our family' had been appeared in Chinese as a short story. When I use it in my autobiography it still with something left like a story As I recall it now, it is too ~~perfect~~ clear a recall of daily life. Though sometimes I can remember a especial day as clearly as this chapter. I wonder you will tell me what mistakes I have made beside what I said. Recently, I have read some books of ~~biography or~~ autobiography in English. Such as Mark Twain's Lincoln Steffens, H. G. Wells' (I happened to read them because I only found these in the library, as I don't have got any things to read) they seem to me none of them I like much, I often thought they were things written by sucessful men. Sometimes they could not help to give people some impression how they have come up to such a luky possition. Perhaps this opion of mine is come merely because of my jealousy. I don't know. But to tell the truth I dont admire them. Will you be good to tell me the names of some good books when you write? I know there are many good books I don't know the name yet. There are some books of the Wu Han university have been moved here, some of them I can get in the library. For years I have read blindly, it is a vast, I suppose.

Our war with Japan seems to turn out a hopeless case for both countries. Every one wants peace, but no body dares to tell it. It is said Japan is going to send out a large number of airoplanes to bomb the rest part of uncaptured earth as she thinks now it is the only thing she could do to Chinese. But ~~we~~ Chinese know that bombs are very expensive nowadays, how [illegible] we do not mind of this threat. The most ugly and pitiful scenes are those conscriped soldiers in Szechun I *see* every day. There are tow real stories I heard a few days ago which make me sick when I think of this war which we suppose to call it a 'holy one' There are ~~men~~ groups of conscriped men coming into this town from the near by countries, they are treating like prisoners, when they are out in the street, they are bound with strings on their aims. When they sleep, the door is l~~a~~ocked. A few days ago, two men of them were killed by earing too hot porrige. They eat in a limited time, they are too hungry as they don't have enough food as they *want* to, so these two men eat in a fast speed, their porrige is too hot, it burned their throat and hi~~n~~t their stomach. They died. When the conscriped soldiers were examined by the office here, a man suddenly cried bitterly, saying that he is willing to return the money to the man he buys him, till this day he begins to understand that he would be sent to the place where he may get to be killed, and he can't see his family any more. He implored to return the money ~~who~~ to whom he received. He thought that would be a fair thing. Almost amony these conscriped men, none of them know what this war mean to them and of course a morden war they never dreamed aout. When one sees all these scens, one feel sinful to tell them any truth. Since one ~~does~~[can] not ~~have~~[do] any ~~power~~[thing] to help them. this is a life I see every day. After all I doubt it is lu^[c]ky my fate has been to~~ld~~ me ~~that~~ when I compare with them.

Please write to my new address as following when you write,

For—

Ling Su Hua, (Mrs Chen)

c/o Miss B. Bassett,

American Baptist Mission, Kaiting, Szechun Province, West China, read them, please send them the following address, they will forword to send them to me by special mail as in care of Miss Bassett's,

Miss B. E. Bassett, (for Mrs. Y. Chen)

American Express Co., 4, Des Voeu Rd. Central, Hongkong, China.

(Kaiting Szechun) Please write this [^underneearth], they will understand where send it at once.

I need not to tell you again how I feel when you are so kind to me. Some day ^perhaps I may show that I have not been ruined myself since I know you. Meantime please accept my love,

Su Hua.

TLS
Airmailed letter

Jan 20, 1939
China

Dear Virginia,

I wrote to you a week ago telling you that I am going to send you another part of my book the next day, but I failed to do so because I caught cold then. Now I am glad to tell you I have done it and send it to you with this letter.

This part seems to be better than the last one. I plan to write each chapter every week, after some months, it would be something. I think by now I just keep on writing on the thing I want to put down, ~~then~~, when it become a book, I will look (I mean read) it carefully and do some cancel work. Do you think this attitude would help me? Will you give me some suggestions ~~when~~ about ~~one~~ writing a long book? I wrote hundreds of short stories before but never had tried a long one. I fear when I write short chapters of a book, they still like short stories: they don't connet well. But I dont like to write an autobiography like a novel. I often feel funny when I read those story-like autobiographys. But it would be certainly difficult if one wants to tell oneself but without telling clearly as a story.
' My eyes ^is high, my hand is low' a Chinese expression of a writer, in this attitude I often feel discouraged when I write. But after all, I think one must set one' eyes higher than one's hand could do, by and by, one will find out some way to meet his eye's stander. Do you agree?

The address I gave you before is useless. Both Canton and Hankow are captured by Japenese. We can not write to those places. How I regret that I gave you those addresses! Your letter for me must gave been lost. There is no way to inquire about. How grateful I shall be if some day you will kindly write me another letter to my new address. This new address is trustful. The post office only can read this much English, and I know they never have lost a letter to this missionary. So I use it. The person who takes care of my letter is very good and careful. though I only know her a few mouths.

We had a good air raid in Chung king afew days ago, about 200 ordinary people were killed. Chungking is only three hours trip by airoplane from this place, so we expect some day when Japenese like to pay us avisit, they may allowed. Just a few days ago, we had air raid, all people made haste to do every thing they thought could avoid danger, but all in vain, because the enemy's plane had not come. The next day we found out ^it was that the enemy's airoplans had been visiting a near by place before yesterday, the office from that city meant to tell us at once, but by some mistakes, they sent the news next day. People here had not complain on their carelessness, out of my expectation, they rather appreciate what they had done, because we shan't fear as much as before if there will be an air raid again. Do you think this funny?

When you write to me please use this address:
Ling Su Hua, / Miss B. Bassett, American Baptist Mission,
Kaiting, Szechun Province, China.

Love from
Su Hua

TLS

28 Feb 1939

Dear Virginia,

I like to tell you once more that your letter written in October has been at last reached me.[2] I was very grateful to know you have read my manuscripe and you said you like it. Since I wrote to tell you in my last letter, I need not to say much here.

I am going to send you another chapter, I hope it will reach you safely and you will read it early, that seems all I can hope. My manuscripes have never *been* shown to any one here, except when I want to know an English ^word which I have not in my mind, I show a part of my manuscripe to an American friend she is an old miss, working in the missionary. I am timid to show people my work, for writing an English book, it would be something harder than in Chinese. I quite agree to what you suggest to my writing *of* this book, I always have this idea in my mind to keep the Chinese flavour as much as I can. For I often notice in the art work, a Chi*n*ese better keep a Chi*n*ese idea while he works, if he admires something he knows little *if* ~~but~~ he wants to adopt it simply because its being smart nee, he always fails. Perhaps this belief would help me a little as I have never been abroad nor read ~~in~~ forign language thouroghly. The three little poems I translate in this chapter. I have worked hard, every word I had thought carely. But the translation is a word for word one, *p*lease tell me in your next letter how far you could read them, I have in my mind I shall try to translate more in other chapter as I ~~told of~~write on *my* early education on poetry. Most translater had tried to translate the popular poems, if I ^will work in the different way, it might be interesting to some one.

I had been leading a vigorous life mixed with joy and sorrow, despair and hope before I marry. It may be plain to some Chinese, but it could not be common to forigners. If I could write in a way I have planned, it would be at least a book which is defferent from the ordinary. There is ^a proverb in ^a old Chinese book that a mice drinks at the river, he only can ~~make~~drink water filling his stomach, that is all. For a

[2] Ling is referring to Woolf's letter dated 15 October 1938.

little writer like me, all I wish is to write a book only defferent from the rest. I have no more ambition. will you laugh at me for this, or you will pity me?

Our war, we all see will last longer and longer than any one had told a year ago. It is good to have some thing to work with since one can do nothing to save the misery nor to stop the desaster. Oh, I don't know how to say my thanks.

Love
Su Hua

Please use my previous address as following
Ling Su Hua, c/o Miss B. Bassett.
American Baptist Mission, Kaiting, Szechun Province, China

TLS

[undated 1939]

March I,

Recently I felt more and ^more thirsty for reading good English books, I felt I can read faster than before. But here are few books in the university library, some of them were lent out to the professers. How I wish I could get those books you had sent me!

Reading is the only amusement and pleasure in my daily life. Only reading can occupy my mind and releive me from thinking ^& feeling *of* all sort of misery and greif. I am delifgted to know that you will send me some more books, but the communication is bad in China, and it seems to become worse and worse later on. I just heard from a friend that the post office in Hongkong does receive parcels sending to Szechun Province. Because it is difficult to send over since the Southern Sea irland has been captured by Japan. This news is bad enough, not only for the munition which our government ^has bought from abroad, can not take over to these near by war district, but it is also ^bad for my plan which I asked you to send the books to Hongkong inorder to be deliver*ed* to me early. I don't know wheter you have sent them out or not yet, please tell me. Some books had been at last arrived here from England in the university, it takes almost about three months, but safely reached here. May I ask you to send some ^more books which you think I can read? Please send them to the same address I gave you in the other page. I know you do not mind me pay back the money, so I don't bother ^myself to take any "adventure" to send the money at present, but I hope some day I could do something to show my thought of you.

I just heard a reliable news about what Japan's new plan in the Yang Tze regime which will effect British markect in ^future in those places. They now try to take hold and reorganize the steamer company of every town, Japanese ^now occupy two third of the share in each company. When the war stops, they naturally mannage all markects. If they do not allow the steamer shippin to what regime with English or other country's good, one has to listen to them. I don't know how far your government mind about her markect in the far east, at mean time, it seems could do nothing with Japan.

We have had no air raid during a long time. I **even** sometimes feeling miss something. If one day, human beings were beleive to drink human blood for some good reason, I can beleive one would feel missing if a certain day without a living person killed. Do you think so? What a mad world we live.

Su Hua

P.S. Please send your letter by air raid, because the ordinary mail takes for months and months to reach here.

ALS

16 March '39

Dear Virginia,

I hope you will think this chapter has done better than some I have sent you. I've not heard from you ^since the letter you wrote in last October. I hope you were not too busy when this reaches your place. Please write to tell me if your opinion of my book. Now it seems I have tried half of my book. My address is as before: care of Miss ^B. Bassett American Baptist Mission, Kaitung, Szechun, China.

With love & respect,
Ling Su Hua

TLS

Monks House Rodmell Lewes Sussex
17th April 1939

Dear Sue,

I am so glad to hear you have at last got my letter safely. I will always send them by air mail in future. I have heard several times from you, and I am keeping your chapters as they come. But I hope you keep copies, so that there may be no risk through the post. It is difficult to know what to advise you to do, except that I am sure you ought to go on writing.

The difficulty is as you say about the English. I feel that the whole feeling of the book would be very much spoilt if some English person were to put what you write into formal English prose, yet of course as it stands it is difficult for English readers to get at your full meaning. I suppose you could not dictate to an educated English person? Perhaps in that way the sense and the feeling could be combined. But it would depend entirely upon finding someone who could be quick ~~to~~ enough to understand and able to express. I must of course leave this to you, as I do not know what opportunities you have. Meanwhile, I think it is best to get toegether as many chapters as possible; and then to read them all through together. One cannot get a true impression if one reads in little bits. But I have seen enough to be interested and charmed. Publication would of course depend upon many things so that it is useless to think of it — things we cannot control. But please go on, and let us hope that it will ^come more hopeful for books later. At the moment, we are finding it very difficult to continue our publishing for nobody will read anything except politics; and we have had to make plans for taking our press away from London, and of course have to face the prospect, should there be war, of shutting up our publishing house altogether. It is very difficult to go on working under such uncertainty. But I myself feel it is the only possible relief from the perpetual strain. It has become worse here, since Italy has also began to steal land. We do not know if the American president's appeal will be heard. If not, then nothing can prevent war. We are spending Easter in the country; but all the time aeroplanes are crossing the house and every we hear of some unfortunate refugee who asks for help. I am reading Chaucer and trying to write about our freind Roger Fry. Also Vanessa and her children come over and we play bowls, and try to go on with our painting and gardening as if we were sure of living another ten years. When I go to London I will see if I can find some books to send you. Only I find it so difficult to guess what you would like. Never mind; books are very cheap; and you can always throw them away.

I have not seen Christopher Isherwood as I had hoped but he and Mr Auden like so many people have gone to America. They dont like it, I hear; but at any rate there is more feeling of security there; and they can work better so they say. But I had wanted to hear more about you. It seems millions of miles away — your life, from this. It is full spring here; and our garden has blue, pink, white flowers—and all the hills are deep green; but very small; and our little river is about as big as a large snake; Julian used to wade across it; and sail a tiny boat. On the other hand, people crowd together. We are hardly ever alone even for a day. Would you like this change of proportion? I often envy you, for being in a large wild place with a very old civilisation. I get hints of it in what you write. Do you ever send Vanessa your paintings? Please write whatever you like; and whatever happens please go on with your autobiography; for even though I cannot help yet with it, it will be a great thing to do it thoroughly. I am giving you the advice I try to take myself — that is to work without caring what becomes of it, for the sake of doing something impersonal.

I will send this by air, and let me know if it comes safely. If so, I will go on if you dont mind these very scrappy letters; written in a garden house, after my morning working at my book.

Yours
Virginia Woolf

TLU

52 Tavistock Square London W.C. 1
16th July 39

Dear Sue,

I am ~~farid~~[afraid] that I have been very bad about answering your letters. It is partly that I am a very bad letter writer — after writing all the morning about Roger Fry. I hate the type writer. And then we went to France for a holiday, driving about Brittany; and directly after that my mother in law had an accident; was ill and died. And now we have to turn out of this house, which is carmmed with books and papers and type and furniture and go to another. 37 Mecklenburgh Square will be our address in September. So I hope you will write there.

Also it is difficult to think of any news worth sending. One only caps stories of war — and you have enough of your own. Here they say it must come next month. That is what Harold Nicolson who is in Parliamnt told me two nights ago. By this time one is so numb that it seems impossible to feel anything, save that dull vague gloom. We are getting used, I suppose. But it will be different when it comes. Like you, I find work the best thing; and have more than I can do. it is dull work — sorting letters, trying to find quotations; trying to fit them together. Roger Fry left such masses of papers; and they are full of interest; but full too of detail. I keep wanting Julian to help me. I am keeping all your chapters together.

As told you, I shant read them till the book is done. And please go on with it, as it might be of such great interest. I am also sorry that I have never sent more books — I began to feel for one thing that books would never reach you. but I will get some cheap ones this week; chancing that you may like them. There again, I dont know what to send. Whether new or old, poetry or fiction or biography. But tell me some time what it is that you would like. Thank you very much for the red and black poster, which I liked. And you say you are sending something else to Vanessa. I am just going to dine with her. That is a great pleasure. And I wish you lived near and could come in.

These little meetings are the best things we have at present. We talk about pictured not about war. I am so sorry for all you are having to suffer—but what is the ise of saying that, all these miles away? Any time you want to write please do. The letter will be sent on. Next week we go to Sussex, Monks house Rodmell Lewes that is the address. Will one be able to work? Will one have to fill the house with refugees? There are aeroplanes always round us; and air raid shelters — but I still believe we shall have peace. And there I will stop. With my love and believe in my sympathy, futile as it seems.

Yours

Two Pacifists: Vera Brittain and Virginia Woolf

Anne E. Fernald

Abstract: Two previously unpublished letters from Virginia Woolf to Vera Brittain and a little-known memorial essay by Brittain published in 1941 in her subscription-only series, *Letters to Peace Lovers*, form the occasion for this reconsideration of Woolf's connection to Brittain. Appendices reprint these documents. Brittain cherished her several contacts with Woolf and framed her memorial essay on the moments when their lives touched. More surprisingly, and despite Woolf's many aesthetic differences from Brittain, she learned much from Brittain, and cited her column (without naming her) in an early draft of "Professions for Women," a citation that persists in a footnote in *Three Guineas*. Tracing Brittain's acquaintance with Woolf as she outlined it: hearing talk about her from the suffragist pacifist Helena Maria Swanwick, joining her in support of Radclyffe Hall, citing her experiences at Somerville in a speech, and finally, soliciting her support on behalf of the Austrian antifascist Paula Wallisch, these documents reveal a surprising feminist connection. This connection, while minor, illuminates the unappreciated web of feminist activism and surprising connections across cultural barriers. Finally, both women's continued pacifism during World War II subjected them to ridicule and reputational damage which Brittain documents and empathizes within her essay. In Woolf's relationship to Holtby and Brittain, we see the truth of Woolf's insistence that "masterpieces are not single and solitary births": theirs is an example of the powerful proximity and mutual dependence of great writers on good ones.

While Vera Brittain's extensive archive (over 36m of materials) at McMaster University in Hamilton, Ontario, has unusually detailed finding aids, Woolf's letters to Brittain were not listed at the time of my visit in September 2023. While the folder itself was carefully filed, accurately labeled, and known to several of the archivists, without a place on the finding aids, it could only be found by serendipity. I was surprised, looking for a letter to Brittain from Leonard, to come upon an adjacent folder containing six document sheets pertaining to Virginia: three letters from Woolf to Brittain, one of which, from January 2, 1940, is included in volume five of the letters, a fourth letter from Woolf written at Brittain's request on behalf of a political prisoner, and two pages of notes toward a memorial essay by Brittain. All told, there are three previously unpublished letters from Woolf in the McMaster University archive [see Appendix B].

This is a story of archival discovery. Mindful of Melanie Micir's caution that "everything scholars 'discover' in an institutional archive has already been processed and catalogued by professional archivists and librarians," discoveries are still possible (13). The OED's first definition of "discovery" has three components: "The action of finding out or becoming aware of something for the first time; the action of being the first to find (a place); the action of bringing to light something (as a substance, scientific phenomenon, etc.) which was previously unknown" ("discovery"). The first attestation is to Richard Hakluyt's *Voyages and Discoveries* (1527). Hakluyt's collection of sea-faring narratives was foundational to the creation of the British Empire (and among Woolf's favorite childhood books). So, there is good reason that the second of these three meanings of discovery—the discovery of a new place, with its attendant connotations of imperial acquisition—is so prominent. However, rather than reject the entire concept of discovery as imperialist, we can reimagine discovery in its other senses of becoming aware for the first time, of sharing something previously unknown. Even the lexicographers note that Hakluyt's usage may more properly belong with obsolete meaning 1.b., "exploration, reconnaissance." Thus, in the spirit of legal or scientific discovery and with the intent of feminist collaboration, this paper shares a discovery. These previously unpublished letters, alongside Brittain's notes for a memorial essay on Woolf reshape not only our understanding of Woolf and Brittain's relation to each other, but our understanding of a network of feminist pacifist women in the interwar period. These women were not close collaborators; the ties between them were weak. Instead, their network functioned to bring women from different circles together under the banner of pacifism. As such, it operated as Mark Granovetter describes the strength of weak ties in his pioneering article on network theory: "whatever is to be diffused can reach a larger number of people, and traverse greater social distance … when passed through weak ties rather than strong" (1366). Understanding the importance and ongoing reverberations of these weak ties helps us understand the history of feminist pacifism and, more generally, how social movements grow and how writers contribute to them.

The online finding aid at McMaster University's archive has since been updated, describing a folder of "6 document sheets. Include[ing] commentary by Brittain regarding Woolf's death."[1] Brittain's notes, in her usual black fountain pen, have a brief penciled list at the bottom:

Meetings w. V.W. A) H.M. Swanwick
B) Radclyffe Hall meeting
C) London Soc. of Women's Service. Senior partner.
D) three letters to me.
W.H. [Winifred Holtby] + V.W.
Now V.W. Gone while E.S. [Ethel Smyth] left. Obituaries feeble
We will never know whether she protested
War + the artist. [Brittain, Commentary; see Fig. 1; for full transcription see Appendix A]

[1] See Vera Brittain fonds, finding aid, section J: Incoming Correspondence, which now lists: "Woolf, Virginia 3 H.L.S. 1934 - 1941. 6 document sheets. Includes commentary by Brittain regarding Woolf's death, and a copy of Woolf's letter to Austrian Chancellor Dollfuss requesting clemency for Paula Wallisch, an Austrian resistance fighter and wife of Koloman Wallisch." The William Ready Division of Archives and Research Collections, Mills Library, McMaster University, Hamilton, OT.

It is a poignant list, made more so when we recognize that only two of the four meetings were directly with Woolf, and even those were large gatherings, not intimate conversations.[2] It was simple enough to establish that three of these four letters did not appear in the *Letters of Virginia Woolf*, but the purpose of the closely written two pages of notes was a little trickier to determine. Eventually, I figured out that these pages were the holograph draft of Brittain's April 24, 1941 "Letter to Peace Lovers."

The April 24, 1941 "Letter" is a memorial essay dedicated to Virginia Woolf. This little-known work is uncollected in anthologies of obituaries and early assessments of Woolf's life and work. It is one of many twice-monthly letters that Brittain wrote from 1939 through the end of the war, for an average of between one and two-thousand subscribers (Mellown 3). The publication was subscription-only because Brittain was censored by the British Government for her criticism of English war policy. A staunch pacifist and a prominent member of the Peace Pledge Union, she questioned the conduct of saturation bombing of Germany and advocated for an end to war at a time when all government efforts were focused on uniting for victory. Her travel, lecturing, publishing, and correspondence were all restricted. During the war, she was twice denied travel visas, even though, for several years, her children were in the United States (Wisor 143). So, in April 1941, at a time when the progress of the war seemed particularly bleak, Brittain dedicated issue 55 of her "Letters" entirely to Woolf's death. In it, she reviewed Woolf's role in her life and career and the broader significance of her suicide to all pacifists: "To me her loss is more grievous and significant than the process of a military campaign …, since it typifies in its stark unalleviated tragedy what war does to the finest flowering of a civilisation" (Brittain, *Testament of a Peace* 67). And, in dedicating her letter to Woolf, she laments what she found missing in other tributes:

> The 'appreciations' written of Virginia Woolf by friends and critics on the Sunday following the announcement of her disappearance struck me as extraordinarily inept..... It seemed to me that these friends had been hurried over their threnodies, as though the manner of Virginia Woolf's death at this time was an embarrassment best tidied out of the way. (*Peace* 69)

Although Brittain avoids the word suicide, she faces the fact of it with more forthrightness than many. Suicide was nothing new to her. Brittain knew loss and, with her 1933 World War I memoir *Testament of Youth*, she became one of the period's most painstaking chroniclers of personal loss and what it means to survive after the death of intimates. Having lost her father to suicide in 1935, Brittain was personally acquainted with the taboos surrounding suicide. She was alert to the shame and self-censorship that often overcomes the bereft and found fault with

[2] Ethel Smyth recalls both Woolf and Brittain as guests at her 75th birthday concert at the Royal Albert Hall and "the improvised 'Mad Tea Party' at an adjacent Lyons" (Smyth 355), but Woolf does not mention this event and Brittain's account of it does not mention Woolf (*Friendship* 356).

remarks that she found "hurried" and "embarrassed." Woolf mattered to Brittain, even more than we have recognized. Moreover, as we shall see, Brittain mattered to Woolf.

Both Woolf (1882–1941) and Brittain (1893–1970) were pacifists. While Woolf was a pacifist during both World Wars, Brittain became a pacifist only after her war service. As a VAD nurse during World War I, she came to her pacifism after the loss of her fiancé, two of his friends, her brother, and while nursing German soldiers. After the publication of her 1933 war memoir *Testament of Youth*, Brittain joined Dick Sheppard's Peace Pledge Union and remained a vocal pacifist for the rest of her life. The ways in which Brittain and Woolf paid for their beliefs during World War II, and how they spoke of each other to their mutual friend Ethel Smyth, offers us new insight into the intersection of British feminism and pacifism in the first half of the twentieth century.

There is a strong tradition in Woolf scholarship of analyzing her pacifism, and many scholars have outlined the intellectual genealogy of how Woolf linked her feminism to her anti-imperial, anti-war thinking. Scholars have also linked Woolf to Brittain, most notably Marion Shaw, Rebecca Wisor, Margot Kotler, and Jacqueline Eglin.[3] Each of them notes the surprising nature of juxtaposing the highbrow, modernist writer with the middlebrow realist. Woolf was eleven years Brittain's senior, but the difference between her birth in 1882 and Brittain's in 1893 became a vast gulf with the advent of World War I. That gulf only seemed to widen in the twenties, when Woolf was at the peak of her experimentation and success as a high modernist while the younger Brittain was trying to find her footing as a reviewer and novelist, lecturing widely, publishing often, and working in a community of more popular feminist writers through the Six Point Group and their journal *Time and Tide*. However, in the 1930s, Brittain and Woolf's subject matter and approach to feminist pacifism began to converge.

Wisor focuses on ways their thinking grew toward each other in the thirties, especially their shared "insistence that the causes of women's rights and the struggle against war were intimately connected" (139). Kotler builds on these ideas, emphasizing both writers' embrace of the idea of counterpublics in the 1930s. As Winifred Holtby's biographer, Shaw considers Holtby and Brittain together and traces a powerful case for understanding generational influence in reverse: for all that Holtby and Brittain admired Woolf, Shaw shows how interested Woolf was in the younger women and documents several important ways in which their ideas and experiences shaped Woolf's writing.

Uncited by any of these literary sources is Jacqueline Eglin's 1999 historical study, "Women Pacifists in Interwar Britain." There, Eglin offers an account of the women involved in the overwhelmingly male movement. Following Martin Ceadel's categories, Eglin names three main strands of pacifism, "socialist anti-

[3] In addition to these scholars, Charles Andrews discusses Woolf and Brittain in both *Writing Against War* and "Christian Pacifism and Modern Witness"; Karen Levenback also briefly discusses Brittain and Woolf in her book.

militarists, pacif*ic*ists, and pacifists" (Eglin 149). In Eglin's piece, as in the work of historians of pacifism more broadly, pacifists are distinguished by the intensity of their commitment to peace, the point at which they will assent to violence. This commitment was animated and profoundly challenged in the 1930s by the League of Nations, the Spanish Civil War, and, most of all, the rise of Hitler and the Nazi Party.[4] The socialist anti-militarists, whose most prominent women adherents included Sylvia Pankhurst, Ellen Wilkinson, and Ethel Mannion, found the rise of fascism called for a military response. The pacif*ic*ists, a clumsy term for strong-but-not-absolutist pacifists, included Mary Hamilton, Storm Jameson, and Mary Sheepshanks in their number. They took a bit longer to change their minds and accept the necessity of military response, but each did so in the mid-1930s. Only the third group, the pacifists, insisted on an antiwar stance even after World War II was underway. Eglin's exemplars for that group are Helena Swanwick, Virginia Woolf, and Vera Brittain. Although she discusses each woman in turn, she makes no note of their connections to each other. She does note, however, the special intensity of Brittain's turn to pacifism: "It was not until 1936, when many others felt that they could no longer subscribe to pacifism that she [Brittain] committed herself irrevocably to it" (Eglin 156).

This paper builds on and is distinct from prior work on Brittain and Woolf in its archival and biographical approach. Even those who discuss Brittain's *Letters to Peace Lovers* do not engage in extensive discussion of her memorial essay to Woolf. Charles Andrews is one of the only scholars to discuss it, emphasizing Brittain's understanding of Woolf's suicide as a protest, which he sees as inaccurate (Andrews, *Writing* 192). While he is right that Brittain's reading is at best eccentric and perhaps incorrect, her linkage of Woolf's death to war reveals the intensity of Brittain's sense of the war's cost: whatever Woolf's reasons for committing suicide, it was easy for Brittain to imagine the War's role in precipitating that choice. In attempting to understand the suicide, Brittain cautions that "The minds of those who deliberately seek death are seldom open to analysis," yet she speculates that "Her end was perhaps a kind of protest" against a world that had become "tough" (*Peace* 69). If, as Andrews writes, Brittain's sense of the reason is mistaken, her interpretation participates in the period's interest in the causes of suicide and suggests how strong the war presented itself as a plausible reason for despair to a fellow pacifist.[5] Reading these private letters and Brittain's memorial essays from *Letters to Peace Lovers* reveals not only their relationship to each other, but an entire network of pacifist women. Moreover, as Eglin's research suggests, they were at the forefront of the most radical branch of the movement.

These two previously unpublished letters from Woolf to Brittain enhance the story, not only of Woolf's relation to the next generation of women writers, but of the costs of being a pacifist woman during World War II. Theirs was not

[4] See Lukowitz 119 ff. for a discussion of how the movement responded to historical events leading up to World War II.

[5] For a discussion of suicidology in the period, see Laird.

an intimate connection: they never even properly met. Moreover, in a time of highly segregated cultural registers, they wrote in different styles. The younger Brittain remained a social realist writer, in the mode of George Eliot and Olive Schreiner, the writers she revered most. While their politics converged in the 1930s, Brittain moved away from recognizably Woolfian themes and ideas in the years that followed. In the 1940s and after, her career and reputation damaged by her consistent and strengthening commitment to peace work, she turned increasingly to Christianity, writing a biography of John Bunyan, entitled *Valiant Pilgrim*, in 1950. Nevertheless, in the 1930s, their tenacious commitment to pacifism during WWII and the scorn, rejection, and vitriol they faced for retaining that stance reveal unexpected similarities that are underscored by Woolf's unpublished remarks.

In her notes, Brittain lists four "meetings with V.W." although she is not using "meeting" in the usual sense. The meeting with Helena Swanwick (1864–1939) was an afternoon in Swanwick's house in Kew Gardens. There, Brittain sat "listening to her reminiscences of Sir Leslie Stephen's family." On that day, Brittain recalls, Swanwick "spoke particularly of his beautiful daughter Virginia and of an early period of mental illness through which her devoted husband had nursed her and of which she had always dreaded a return" (67–68). Woolf was not there, but Swanwick's intimate stories of Woolf and the Stephen family made Brittain feel Woolf's presence.

Second, in 1928, Brittain and Woolf both attended a meeting to strategize the defense of Radclyffe Hall. Several years later, she heard Woolf speak at a London Society of Women's Service Event with Ethel Smyth. Although Brittain was an audience member that day, she had the heady experience of hearing Woolf quote her from the platform. Finally, there is the material token of their connection: the three letters she received from Woolf.

Feminist Pacifism: Woolf, Brittain, and Swanwick

In 1920, Margaret, Lady Rhondda founded *Time and Tide,* a feminist and (originally) leftist political review, designed to support The Six Point Group, a feminist collective dedicated to six points of political reform: securing legislation against child assault and for child protection, for the protection of single and widowed mothers, and for equal pay for teachers and civil servants.[6] *Time and Tide* was originally edited by Helen Archdale, but Rhondda took over as editor in 1926 and remained in that role until death in 1958. Brittain and her close friend and writing companion Winifred Holtby had been sent the very first issue of the magazine while still undergraduates at Somerville College in 1920. Rhondda's guess was right: they were not merely likely subscribers; they quickly became frequent contributors (Berry and Bostridge 175).

Swanwick, though thirty years Brittain's senior, was, like Brittain, a regular contributor to *Time and Tide*. Born in 1864, she was the only daughter of the Sickert

[6] Reproduced from McMaster University, https://www.timeandtidemagazine.org/history.

family, family friends of the Stephens, and the younger sister of the artist, Walter Sickert. She remembers watching Leslie Stephen playing on the beach with his children, "his naked babies running about the beach or being towed into the sea between his legs" (Swanwick 107). Woolf wonders at not remembering this herself in "A Sketch of the Past": "Why remember the hum of bees in the garden going down to the beach, and forget completely being thrown naked by father into the sea? (Mrs. Swanwick says she saw that happen)" (*MOB* 70).[7] Swanwick attended Girton College, Cambridge, beginning her studies there in 1882. Her first book was on gardening, but her political interests expanded over the years. In the early 20th century, she became active in the non-violent, moderate wing of the suffrage movement, editing the suffragist paper *Common Cause* from 1909–1914. Breaking with the suffragists over their support for World War I, Swanwick chaired the Women's International League for Peace from 1915–1922. Swanwick was a fierce critic of the Treaty of Versailles and the League of Nations. Her husband's death in 1931 increased her isolation. Few supported her stance: which was isolationist and non-interventionist, but not an absolute pacifism, and which characterized Hitler's foreign policy as equivalent to other imperial actions.[8] She committed suicide in November 1939, shortly after the outbreak of World War II (Harris). Her death is but one of the many costs of radical pacifism.

In her 1935 memoir, Swanwick records first meeting Holtby and Brittain at a League of Nations Conference in Geneva in 1926 (468).[9] Brittain spent an afternoon with Swanwick in England, likely before 1928 and summarized that afternoon in her memorial letter on Woolf:

> My personal contacts with Virginia Woolf were few but memorable. I recall sitting, perhaps fifteen years ago, among tall spring irises in Mrs H. M. Swanwick's devotedly cultivated little garden at Kew, and listening to her reminiscences of Sir Leslie Stephen's family. She spoke particularly of his beautiful daughter Virginia and of an early period of mental illness through which her devoted husband had nursed her and of which she had always dreaded a return. (*Peace* 67–68)

This description is written in the tone of a social note from the women's pages of a local newspaper. She describes Swanwick's "devotedly cultivated little garden at Kew." While likely accurate (Swanwick was a passionate gardener), starting with the garden obscures both Swanwick's stature as a feminist suffragist and Brittain's relationship to her. It also serves as a reminder of a difference between Woolf and Brittain's tone. The presence of this detail in Brittain's memorial essay on Woolf—not only the garden, but the afternoon itself, hints at Woolf's importance to Brittain and Brittain's unguarded pride in having been admitted to intellectual London. For

[7] Swanwick's visit to St. Ives may have been before Woolf's birth.
[8] In 1938, the Peace Pledge "Union published a pamphlet by Clive Bell in which he stated that 'I see no reason why Germany should not have colonies too'" (Lukowitz 121).
[9] For more on Brittain's involvement with the League of Nations, see Mellown 2.

a provincial girl from Buxton, this alone represented an achievement. And yet her ongoing delight in being included ensured that some members of that intellectual class, Woolf among them, would often sneer her to others.

From the late 1920s onward, Swanwick, Holtby, and Brittain would have had many opportunities to meet and be aware of each other's work through their close association with *Time and Tide*. Swanwick's university education, her work as a feminist peace advocate, her journalism, and her willingness to take unconventional and unpopular public stands make her a natural mentor for Brittain. However, in 1933, Brittain was "taken aback" when Swanwick "suggested, after reading *Testament of Youth*, that she and Vera 'shouldn't have had a word to say to each other' had they met during the war" (Berry and Bostridge 123). Having come to her pacifism after the War, Brittain was understandably sensitive about the value of her war work. She remained insistently proud of her service, even as her opinion of the conflict changed. She responded by suggesting that, had peace activists such as Swanwick made their case to her in 1917, all might have been different. There is little evidence to support that claim. Nevertheless, the incident offers a glimpse into Brittain's sensitivity and Swanwick's uncompromising nature. Both Woolf and Swanwick could be ungenerous to newcomers. Brittain, though a snob in her own way, was more welcoming. She retained her humility about her provincial origins and knew that, for a movement to grow, it would need to welcome newcomers, however belated.

Brittain's experiences with Swanwick—the embarrassing combination of being thrilled to be included and then, on a later occasion, being insulted as a latecomer to pacifism—indicates that her insecurities were well-founded. Brittain writes about "a more cynical post-war generation" throughout *Testament* (210), but she herself does not become cynical: numb, traumatized, disillusioned, but not cynical. This consistency means that her look back on the war rarely has the bite of irony. Instead, it offers something different that is also of value in resisting war. She remembers how hard she and the other VAD nurses worked, seeing the hard labor not with resentment but as having "a sacred glamour which redeemed it equally from tedium and disgust" (*Testament of Youth* 210). Her awareness of the power of that desire to be inspired remains an asset and a distinctive feature in her pacifism. Unlike other pacifists, Brittain, having come from a conventional patriotic background, understands the appeal of the fight. She writes: "It is, I think, this glamour, this magic, this incomparable keying up of the spirit in a time of mortal conflict, which constitute the pacifists' real problem—a problem still incompletely imagined, and still quite unsolved" (292).

Sapphic Solidarity

Brittain's first actual meeting with Woolf was at a gathering to discuss defending Radclyffe Hall and her 1928 lesbian novel *The Well of Loneliness* against charges of obscenity. 1928 was the banner year for lesbian visibility and for the prosecution of lesbianism (which was still a crime in England). It saw the publication of Woolf's *Orlando* and the censorship trial of *The Well*, an episode which has been well-documented elsewhere (see e.g., Doan and Prosser). Brittain and Woolf were among the forty or so supporters who gathered in support of Hall, although none were called to testify. (Desmond MacCarthy took the stand but was not permitted to answer.) Woolf's support—full-throated for Hall's rights to have her book published and distributed but cool on its literary merits—mattered because in 1928 Woolf was at the crest of her career and was publicly closely associated with her friend and lover Vita Sackville-West. She had also just published *Orlando*, a queer mock-biography of Sackville-West that evaded the censors. By contrast, Brittain's support for Hall came at a much more vulnerable moment: before the publication of *Testament of Youth* (1933), which brought her the literary success she had long sought.

In 1928, Brittain had a lot of reasons not to publicly support Hall, and yet she did. Her review for *Time and Tide* calls the book "a plea, passionate, yet admirably restrained and never offensive, for the extension of social toleration, compassion and recognition to the biologically abnormal woman" (rptd. Doan and Prosser 59). To our ears, this seems tepid, but it was enough, and published in a sufficiently prominent place, to earn Brittain notice as a potential witness for the defense.

As Micir notes, Brittain seems to want to support Hall for feminist reasons while distancing herself from Hall's sexuality. Brittain had strong reasons for this. Her intimacy with Holtby often gave rise to speculation that she was a lesbian, a label that her homophobic husband was eager to avoid, and one which Brittain frequently denied. The women lived together for several years after university, traveled together across Europe, and, after Brittain's marriage, Holtby rejoined the family household, living with the Brittain-Catlin clan and helping with the children during Catlin's long absences. Brittain was a staunch and outspoken advocate for what she called the "semi-detached marriage" (what we would now call a commuter marriage) and persisted in publicly extolling its virtues despite frequent snide remarks and unkind comments about her choice to retain her "maiden" name after marriage (Brittain, *Testament of Experience* 45).

No single word can describe Brittain's most intimate relationships. She loved Roland Leighton (her fiancé who was killed in World War I), married and had children with George Catlin (who had many extramarital affairs), had an affair in the late 1930s with the American publisher George Brett, and yet she was happiest when living, working, and traveling with Holtby. There is no evidence of a sexual affair between them, but their intimacy was the most important relationship of her life.

Biographers and critics have taken "sides" on how to label the relationship between Brittain and Holtby, but Shaw and Catherine Clay's approach of allowing it to be complex and taking the time to characterize it richly seems the most valuable. Clay acknowledges the pressure that an intense bond between two feminists in 1928 faced: "Their [Holtby and Brittain's] shared professional investments converge with intense desires for intimacy in a friendship which (in light of new 'scientific' discourses around lesbianism) may be placed under censorious scrutiny. I argue that in Brittain's stated professional need of Holtby she also articulates a desire that calls forth Holtby's (more passionate) response" (4). Moreover, Clay continues, some biographical accounts have been anxious to de-sexualize or erase the "readable traces of desire" in their relationship (27). Ultimately, Clay follows Shaw in rejecting the reductive nature of deciding whether they were lesbians:

> These 'rivalrous' positions on the Brittain-Holtby friendship which attempt either to prove or disprove 'lesbianism' are ultimately reductive, and the more recent work of Marion Shaw has done much to reveal the greater complexity of this friendship … [H]er observation that the friendship was 'intense, hungry, and anxious in ways that Brittain herself did not want, or could not bring herself, to acknowledge' allows for an erotic intensity in Brittain's feelings for Holtby which the biographies of Brittain deny. (38)

As Micir writes in her extended discussion of "Chloe liked Olivia," we would do well to remember Woolf's deliberate ambiguity: did she like her *like that*? Or were they "just" work colleagues? (2). There can be no single answer, after all, as Lily Briscoe thinks, "Love had a thousand shapes" (*TTL* 192), and no one label suffices to capture the ties of a heart. In Brittain, particularly in *Testament of Youth*, there is a restraint and propriety, a buttoned-up quality, and a love of romance over sex that makes it narratively convenient to shape the story of her love for Roland, Catlin, and Holtby as she does, despite evidence that pulls the story in slightly different directions. Woolf inflects her passage on how "Chloe liked Olivia" in *A Room of One's Own* with an allusion to Sir Chartres Biron, the jurist who presided over Radclyffe Hall's trial. The narrator demands to be assured that no men—and certainly not Biron—are present before she discussed the small revolutionary difference made by this friendship between women. Brittain and Holtby lived the revolutionary female intimacy that Woolf imagined.

When Brittain attended the meeting and agreed to make herself available to testify on Hall's behalf, she may have been supporting a fellow War noncombatant participant against the lesbian panic that arose around women's service (Marshik 146–47); standing up for the rights of artists to free expression; seeking to burnish her status as a public intellectual; making a statement on behalf of freedom of sexual expression; defying her homophobic husband. Brittain's 1928 review for *Time and Tide*, with its muted language of "tolerance," hardly stands on the barricades, and yet she placed herself in clear public opposition to the censors. Her curiosity about the book's confusion "between what is 'male' or 'female' and what is merely human in our complex makeup" (Doan and Prosser 60) testifies to her liberal intellect and her courage. Whatever her reasons, Brittain's public support for Hall remained steadfast. Indeed, in 1968, she published *Radclyffe Hall: A Case of Obscenity?* helping usher in what Laura Doan and Jay Prosser call "the second wave of *The Well*'s critical reception" (14).

A Society

Brittain's second encounter with Woolf was at the January 21, 1931 meeting of the London and National Society for Women's Service. Both Woolf and Ethel Smyth spoke that night and Brittain was in the audience. There, Woolf gave the speech that became "Professions for Women" and the germ of *Three Guineas* and *The Years*, and Brittain heard Woolf quote from her regular column from *The Nation*, "A Woman's Notebook," in her speech. Brittain wrote up the evening for the January 31 issue:

> I went on to a delicious entertainment provided for a large audience by Dame Ethel Smyth and Mrs. Virginia Woolf. This hilariously serious party was organized, incidentally, by the Junior Council … Dame Ethel, whose superb humour gives the lie to the common belief that all women are heavy and conscientious speakers, told us that … she accepted her D.B.E. with alacrity … I was interested … to hear both Dame Ethel and Mrs. Woolf attribute their success largely to the possession of a private income … Women, Mrs. Woolf maintained, had succeeded better in literature than the other arts because paper was cheap and pens made no noise. I am delighted to record, from the internal evidence of a quotation in her speech, that Mrs. Woolf is a reader of this Notebook. (qtd. *E5* 636).

Woolf, too, recorded the event: "Two hundred people; well dressed, keen, & often beautiful young women. Ethel in her blue kimono & wig. I by her side. Her speech rollicking & direct; mine too compressed & allusive. Never mind. Four people wish the speeches printed" (*D4* 7). Three nights earlier, she marked the conception of *Three Guineas*: "I have this moment, while having my bath, conceived an entire new book—a sequel to a Room of One's Own—about the sexual life of women: to be called Professions for Women perhaps—Lord how exciting! This sprang out of my paper to be read on Wednesday to Pippa's society" (*D4* 6). Brittain returns to this evening in her 1941 memorial essay, recollecting Woolf's "rare public appearance … on an after-dinner platform … The contrast between the two celebrated women was striking indeed. Dame Ethel, the senior by a quarter of a century, kept the audience convulsed by a pungent and witty speech which she evidently enjoyed delivering …. By comparison Virginia Woolf appeared the more gentle and diffident. In a low voice, audible only through the microphone, she gave a scholarly address which she accompanied with shy but elegant gestures of her thin pale hands" (Brittain, *Peace* 68).

Woolf's "Speech to the London and National Society for Women's Service" was preserved in typescript and was reprinted in Mitchell A. Leaska's edition of *The Pargiters* as well as in an appendix to volume five of *The Essays*. This early version of what became "Professions for Women" continues a central argument from *A Room of One's Own*: a comparison of the endowments of men's and women's colleges.[10]

[10] For a discussion of this speech's place in Woolf's evolving understanding of women's

In the speech, Woolf's main example of the gender-based economic gap comes from two articles in the January 17, 1931 issue of *The Nation*: John Maynard Keynes's glowing review of an expensively bound and illustrated gift book on Clare College and Vera Brittain's reminiscence of her mice-infested undergraduate apartment. Keynes begins by mentioning that "this book cost it is rumoured six thousand pounds to produce" and "ends with an eloquent description" of the luxury object, "[c]lothed," Keynes writes, "in the finest dress of paper and black buckram." Keynes is dazzled by the luxury. Woolf answers his wonder with contempt and sketches an alternative review: "Had the Editor of the Nation sent it to me, I should have been compelled by that different sense of values to write in a very different vein. O you old humbugs. I should have begun" (*E*5 641). Her outrage at the waste of money in self-advertisement, especially considering how the money might have been better spent on woefully under-funded women's education. To illustrate how poor women's colleges are by comparison, she quotes Brittain.

In her January 17th column, Brittain had written, "When I lived out during my last year at Somerville, my one room was a cold, gloomy, ground-floor bedroom, which faced due north and was overrun with mice" (*Nation* 509; qtd. *E*5 648). Brittain continues, "To provide these things, they require, above all, money. Virginia Woolf's little masterpiece, 'A Room of One's Own,' is the classic expression of the need' (*Nation* 509; qtd. *E*5 648). Just four days later, in her January 21st speech, Woolf said, "would it not be better to spend your six thousand pounds not upon a book…but upon a girl…who tried to do her work, as you will read if you turn the very next page in the Nation in one cold gloomy ground-floor bedroom which faces due north and is overrun with mice" (*E*5 641), quoting Brittain word for word. "(Somerville it seems is very hard up.)," Woolf writes in parentheses, adding: "If the members of Clare college handed over the six thousand pounds that they have spent upon a book to Girton some of the difficulties … would be removed" (*Pargiters* xxxv; *E*5 641). As Leaska notes, these details, including the reference to Brittain's column, survive in a footnote to *Three Guineas*:

> The book "it is rumoured cost six thousand pounds to produce." Rumour has it also that a band of students returning at dawn from some festivity about that time saw a cloud in the sky; why as they gazed assumed the shape of a woman; who, being supplicated for a sign, let fall in a shower of radiant hail the one word "Rats." This was interpreted to signify what from another page of The Nation would seem to be the truth; that the students of one of the women's colleges suffered greatly from "cold gloomy ground floor bedrooms overrun with mice." … There is nothing mythical … about the fact recorded in the same number of *The Nation* that "Somerville received with pathetic gratitude the £7,000 which went to it last year from the Jubilee gift and a private bequest." (*TG* 151)

---

place in the professions, see Chan.

Twice, then, Woolf quotes Brittain's description of her "cold, gloomy, ground-floor bedroom, which faced due north and was overrun with mice." This reciprocity and collaboration, painstakingly documented by Leaska and Clarke in the notes and discussed briefly by Karen Levenback in *Virginia Woolf and the Great War* (114ff.), has not been fully appreciated, even by the scholars most sympathetic to finding a connection between Brittain and Woolf.

Woolf's and Brittain's arguments build on each other. Brittain was among the first women to take a degree at Oxford (rather than matriculate as a non-degree student) shortly after World War I; Woolf's visits to Oxford and Cambridge help her build the arguments about women's education in *A Room of One's Own*; Brittain recognized her experience in the descriptions there; her subsequent details about the mice reactivated Woolf's imagination. Working together through print, Brittain played a key role in affirming Woolf's point about the economic impact of a failure to invest in women's education.

"Professions for Women" was central to Woolf's thinking and the ideas she developed in it continued to occupy her for years as she developed what would become *The Years* and *Three Guineas*. Shaw has explored several important ways that Holtby (and, to a lesser extent, Brittain) may have influenced Woolf, even speculating that Holtby may be a source for Kitty Malone in *The Years*, an unusually tall, brainy woman with a Yorkshire mother: "More important was the field of reference that women like Holtby and Brittain created for Woolf as representatives of a linked feminism and pacifism and the radical philosophical and social implications this linkage raised" (Shaw 43–44). For Shaw, Woolf's turn to politics in *The Years* and *Three Guineas* has its roots in her engagement "with the complex tissue of men's, and woman's, relation with their environment … That she was able to make so complex and radical an analysis in fiction and essay bears its own relation to the work of 'down on the ground' women activists and writers like Holtby and Brittain" (50). Stephen Barkway's publication of a dozen unpublished letters from Holtby to Woolf show a genuine intimacy and friendship developing between the women, cut short only by Holtby's illness and untimely death.

In March of 1931, Woolf learned of Winifred Holtby's proposed book about her. They met several times while Holtby was writing, and then several more times after the book's publication: a sign of Woolf's respect for Holtby and her work. On one occasion, Woolf seems to have invited her over to discuss some of the ideas she was developing from her 1931 speech into *Three Guineas*: "it was my fault if we wandered into Yorkshire and professions and so on. I have it at the back of my mind that I will re-write a paper on professions that I read a year or two ago; and thus tend to pick peoples brains" (Woolf, "Letters" 23). To Shaw and Barkway's documentation of Holtby's contribution to Woolf's thinking, we can now add this fuller view of Brittain's contribution.

Three Letters

The collected *Letters of Virginia Woolf* only include one letter to Brittain, a January 1940 thank you note for sending *Testament of Friendship*, Brittain's memoir of her friendship with Winifred Holtby, who died in 1935:

> Dear Vera Brittain,
>
> It was very good of you to send me your book. I waited to thank you until I had read it. And now that I have read it I feel that, thanks to you, I know her much better than I did before. I was puzzled by something about her when we met—I think I only saw her two or three times—perhaps you'll understand. I think I see now what it was. (*L*6 378)

For a writer as specific and imaginative as Woolf, this is a strikingly ambiguous compliment: she seems to be going out of her way to say little. But she takes the gift of a 500-page book seriously and conveys to Brittain that it revealed "something" about Holtby that she had not understood before. The next letter is to Ethel Smyth, a friend of both women, and it undoes much of the complimentary tone we might extract from the letter to Brittain. Woolf writes: "But tho' I wrote Vera a polite letter, I didn't somehow enjoy or wholly like her Life: too petty and that horrid little reviewer's gossip; she had a good deal more to her than V.B. saw .... [I]t was a scrambling gasping affection book: and W. H. deserved a better" (*L*6 379). A second letter to Smyth clarifies that the "she" who had "a good deal more to her" was Holtby while continuing the insults to both: "I think I meant that W. H. [Winifred Holtby] was a barrel organ writer. Vera [Brittain] is a scrambling and enthusing chatterbox, but of course very competent .... And oh Lord how I loathe that scribbling business: 35 novels to be reviewed for Harpers Bazaar in one morning in a bungalow. So I'm not unprejudiced, but will try to be" (*L*6 380–81). These letters to Smyth, who was also friends with Brittain and Holtby, remind us of how dramatically Woolf's tone changes depending on the recipient. The letters also show the complexity of Woolf's relationship to the middlebrow and her continual inability to appreciate what it meant for Holtby and Brittain, women without family money, to make their livings as professional writers. Still, Woolf has a point: *Testament of Friendship* is unwieldy. Shaped by Brittain's anxiety to secure a posthumous reputation for her friend, it is full of anxious over-praise, even imagining how all future generations will make pilgrimages to Holtby's Yorkshire home.

The two McMaster letters pre-date this one and, combined with Brittain's poignant "three letters to me" in her private notes, demand a reconsideration of their relationship. Woolf's attention, however fleeting, mattered to and impressed Brittain. She was marked by those moments when she crossed paths with Woolf. And, during 1941, separated from her children by the Atlantic, with her letters to them censored and delayed, she responded to Woolf's suicide as a significant casualty of war. And she should know. The First World War had taken her fiancé, his two friends, and her brother, whose death may have been a suicide. In 1935, she lost her father to suicide. Without judgment or personal pleading, Brittain marks Woolf's death and connects it to the ways that war intrudes on civilian life, making ordinary pleasures—and the more extraordinary and miraculous gifts of art—impossible. The deaths of her brother and father especially prepared her to see the extended ramifications of war, far beyond what shows up on any official reckoning of casualties. In this, she and Woolf shared a vision of the extensive costs of war. And Woolf, whose letters shift and change according to the recipient, was more sympathetic to Brittain than her gossip about her to Smyth and others indicates.

The first letter is very brief—a cover note from Woolf enclosing a letter of appeal for clemency to the Austrian chancellor on behalf of Frau Wallisch. Paula Wallisch (1893–1986) was an Austrian politician and resistance fighter. Her husband, Koloman Wallisch, was a socialist labor leader. In 1934, he took up arms in the Austrian Civil War, fleeing to the mountains to wage guerrilla warfare against the fascists, but he was arrested, tried, and executed. Naomi Mitchison witnessed the trial, publishing her account in England shortly afterward as *Vienna Diary* (Gollancz 1934). Wallisch, too, was imprisoned and later released. She visited refugee camps, took on an assumed name, and worked for the Austrian resistance during the War. She was a member of the Austrian National Council from 1945–56. While it would be impossible to gauge the effect of this campaign on Wallisch's release, released she was and able to carry on her work for decades.

In this letter, Woolf was engaged in the type of intellectual political labor of international feminism that she describes with such skepticism in *Three Guineas*. Here, an acquaintance asks her to write a letter for a cause, and she does so. This was the work of Holtby and Brittain's lives: journalism, travel, conferences, and advocacy. But what makes this more than just a covering document is the added remark, "May I take this opportunity of saying how much your book, A Testament of Youth, interests me?" (Woolf, Three unpublished). As an acknowledgment of a book that she had read the year before, Woolf's remark is noncommittal, but when added to what she wrote elsewhere about *Testament of Youth*, it suggests how moved Woolf was by Brittain's memoir. As Shaw notes, Woolf read the memoir at a particularly gloomy time, not only internationally, but within her own home. There was no way, in 1933, for Woolf to understand *Testament of Youth* outside the context of a coming war. The book came out at a moment when Leonard had lost faith in the League of Nations and saw war as inevitable: "No wonder that Virginia Woolf's hand shook in 1933, reading Brittain's 'hard, anguished' account of the slaughter of the previous war" (Shaw 41–42). Brittain, too, had lost faith in the League of Nations at this time, a loss which alienated her from the Labour Party and began the political isolation she was to suffer until the end of WWII (Mellown 2).

Testament of Youth more than interested Woolf. Markedly different from the aversion she expresses about the later and less well-written *Testament of Friendship,* the remarks in her diary describe a very strong reaction:

> I am reading with extreme greed a book by Vera Britain, called The Testament of Youth. Not that I much like her. A stringy metallic mind, with I suppose, the sort of taste I should dislike in real life. But her story, told in detail, without reserve, of the war, & how she lost lover & brother, & dabbled her hands in entrails, & was forever seeing the dead, & eating scraps, & sitting five on one WC, runs rapidly, vividly across my eyes.
>
> A very good book of its sort. The new sort, the hard anguished sort, that the young write; that I could never write. Nor has anyone written that kind of book before. Why now? What urgency is there on them to stand bare in public? She feels that these facts must be made known, in order to help--what? herself partly I suppose. And she has the social conscience. I have still to read how she married the infinitely dreary Catlin & found beauty & triumph in poor, gaping Holtby. But I give her credit for having lit up a long passage to me at least. I read & read & read & neglect Turgenev & Miss C. Burnett. But why does my hand shake? Why cant I write clearly? (*D*4 177)

This is a rollercoaster of a diary entry, beginning and ending with strong feelings which she seems to try to bring into check in the middle. Woolf loved to be captured by her reading, whether a classic or a gossipy biography, and for her to be "reading with extreme greed" is a compliment. But as she begins listing the suffering Brittain endured in her war service, she turns admiration toward parody, listing how "she lost lover & brother, & dabbled her hands in entrails, & was forever seeing the dead, & eating scraps, & sitting five on one WC."

This list, moving from tragic to ridiculous, permits her to classify it as merely a "very good book of its sort … the hard anguished sort … that I could never write." "Dabbled her hands in entrails" is a particularly good Woolfian remark, transforming Brittain's earnest account of the hard work of nursing into a tasteless display. Still, Woolf admits that no one has "written that kind of book before." Lest we think this a simple compliment, however, she proceeds to wonder what the value of such a book might be: what does it help to share so much suffering? What good can come of so much sharing? Brittain's final chapters, on "the infinitely dreary Catlin" and "poor, gaping Holtby" would seem to cap her rejection, but she continues, not only "giving her credit," but marking an intense physical reaction to the story: "But why does my hand shake? Why cant I write clearly?" Woolf's intense response to Brittain shows her taste at odds with her emotions: everything tells her that this is not her "kind of book," but the story has gripped her, overtaking her day. She knows how she should feel, she perceives the differences in their styles and generations, but she keeps interrupting herself to say how she feels. The book moves her deeply. She also recognizes its newness, its revolutionary candor: it is "told in detail, without reserve." It is book of a kind that no one has written before, something that she simultaneous admires and feels a little embarrassed about. For a writer who recognized the value and difficulty of "telling the truth about my own experiences as a body" and doubted "that any woman has solved it yet," Woolf sees that Brittain has come close to doing something she could not (*E*6 483).

Woolf's second letter to Brittain is much more personal: a letter of condolence on Winifred Holtby's death:

> Dear Miss Brittain,
>
> Although I have [sic] met you, I hope you will let me say how unhappy I am at the news of Winifred Holtby's death.
>
> I knew her very little, but she gave me the impression of a most generous + delightful nature. I am very proud of the book she wrote about me I know you will understand if I say that the fact that she wrote about me, so generously, made me shy of seeing her. How I wish now that I had seen her more, + known her better! She had said she would come see us this summer, but I suppose, though I didn't know it, that she was too ill.
>
> I am talking selfishly of my own feelings, because it is impossible to say anything about what her death must mean to you.
>
> Please believe me how much we both feel for you.
>
> Yours sincerely
> Virginia Woolf
> Of course, do not think of answering.
>
> My husband has been telling me how greatly he admired her.

The postscript—the sense of Leonard coming into the room, asking what she is writing, and adding his comment—gives this letter an uncanny immediacy. It is a true sympathy letter, written feelingly with Brittain in mind. Woolf did not know Brittain; they had barely met, but she knew Holtby's importance to her well enough to take the time to write a letter of condolence. Woolf's letters to Holtby bear out that Holtby had been as much Leonard's friend as hers: on one occasion, arranging a meeting, Woolf urges Holtby to keep her meeting with Leonard despite her inability to join them (Woolf, "Letters" 20–21). (And, following convention, Leonard leaves the work of mourning to his wife.) For all of Woolf's jokes to Smyth about "gaping Holtby" and even her diary's arch allusion to "dabbling in entrails," Woolf took the time to write to a distant acquaintance. It is a moving condolence letter that recognizes the loss of a friend as monumental. The sympathy Woolf extended Brittain on this occasion seems to have redounded back to Woolf at her death: Brittain is as generous to her in her absence as Woolf had once been to Brittain in her grief.

The third (and published) letter from Woolf to Brittain is also about Winifred Holtby, making her the subject of two of Woolf's three letters to Brittain. In this case, the 1940 letter is Woolf's thanks to Brittain for sending her book on Holtby, *Testament of Friendship*. Brittain expresses gratitude for this and the first letter in her memorial essay, grateful that she had liked both her books.

Pacifism

In *Three Guineas*, Woolf describes the informal, passive "lessons" that women pick up under patriarchy, including "derision." She writes: "You must refuse all methods of advertising merit, and hold that ridicule, obscurity and censure are preferable, for psychological reasons, to fame and praise. Directly badges, orders, or degrees are offered you, fling them back in the giver's face" (*TG* 80). Throughout this period, her diary recounts the pain and frustration of this stance. However clearly Woolf felt about the importance of rejecting honors, she found this time difficult and lonely.

Woolf's stance connects to Brittain's own doctrine of humiliation. Their ideas are distinct, but cousins to each other. Brittain's humiliation differs from Woolf's derision, primarily in the Christian overtones of sacrifice in Brittain's thinking. More important is the way that both women found it necessary to articulate a philosophy of being disliked, even despised, for their beliefs. Different as they were, both suffered under the pain of losing readers because of their anti-war writing and in both of their works we see them wrestling with the pain of being outsiders. Brittain propounded humiliation as an important element of her pacificism. Her book *Humiliation with Honor* (1943), structured as a series of letters to her son, explains the importance of accepting humiliation as a step toward spiritual resurrection (Mellown 4). As Mellown notes, Brittain was painfully aware of the ways her combative disposition and her feminism both challenged the value of humiliation. Only after the war, she argues, was Brittain able to reconcile her pacifism and feminism, by stressing the fundamental differences between men and woman (Mellown 5).

Woolf's 1936 essay "Why Art To-Day Follows Politics" and Brittain's memorial essay both articulate a theme that is at the heart of their anti-war writing: no one escapes the trauma of war. Woolf writes that "Art is the first luxury to be discarded in times of stress; the artist is the first of the workers to suffer. But intellectually also he depends upon society. Society is not only his paymaster but his patron. If the patron becomes too busy or too distracted to exercise his critical faculty the artist will work in a vacuum and his art will suffer and perhaps perish from lack of understanding" (*E6* 76). Brittain speculates of Woolf that "Her end was perhaps a kind of protest, the most terrible and effective that she could make, against the real hell which international conflict creates for the artist" (*Testament of a Peace* 69). Elsewhere in both pieces, they are at pains not to do special pleading for themselves, but to imagine the struggles of all who are affected by war: Woolf speculates that war may be most difficult for visual artists; Brittain speculates that it may be most difficult for serious writers like Woolf. For Brittain, especially, there is a lament and a weariness in her admission that her career has been dedicated to something other than art alone.

Both Brittain and Woolf understand that a death by suicide can contain a message: in *Mrs. Dalloway*, Woolf imagines it as an offering; Brittain wonders if Woolf's death is a protest. Brittain's survival, beyond Swanwick and Woolf, is undeniably brave. In her memorial essay, she reflects on the strangeness of Ethel Smyth's continual survival, left to mourn her much younger friend. The grace she affords Woolf is lovely, considering all of Brittain's own losses and griefs. Brittain implicitly understands what Rosi Braidotti posits in her recent discussion of Woolf's suicide in light of her pacifism: "you can suppress your own life, in its specific and radically immanent form, and still affirm the potency (*potentia*) of life" (145).

One might wish that Woolf was always as generous to Brittain as she was to the fictional Mary Carmichael: "Considering that Mary Carmichael was no genius, but an unknown girl writing her first novel in a bed-sitting room, without enough of those desirable things, time, money, and idleness, she did not do so badly, I thought" (*AROO* 94). Perhaps, in borrowing Brittain's description of her room in college, she was. When we look at even at these glancing relationships, we uncover a network of women advocating for and learning from other women. In Brittain's work, in her loyalty to Holtby and her women friends, we have a living example of what happens "if Chloe likes Olivia and Mary Carmichael knows how to express it": we have begun to "light a torch in that vast chamber where nobody has yet been," a world of women, supporting each other (*AROO* 84).

Acknowledgments

Texts by Vera Brittain are © The Literary Executors of the Vera Brittain Will Trust (1970) and are reproduced with permission. Texts by Virginia Woolf are reproduced with permission from The Society of Authors as the Literary Executors of Virginia Woolf. The images in the appendices are reproduced with permission from The William Ready Division of Archives and Research Collections, McMaster University Library.

Works Cited

Andrews, Charles. "Christian Pacifism and Literary Witness: The Political Theology of Vera Brittain's *Born 1925*." *Religion & Literature*, vol. 51, no. 2, 2019, pp. 69–90.

———. *Writing against War: Literature, Activism, and the British Peace Movement.* Northwestern UP, 2017.

Barkway, Stephen. "Virginia Woolf, Winifred Holtby and Her Virginia Woolf." *Virginia Woolf Bulletin*, no. 32, September 2009, pp. 5–10.

Beeston, Alix, and Stephan Solomon. "Pathways to the Feminist Incomplete: An Introduction, a Theory, a Manifesto." *Incomplete: The Feminist Possibilities of the Unfinished Film*, U of California P, 2023, pp. 1–36.

Berry, Paul, and Mark Bostridge. *Vera Brittain: A Life*. Northeastern UP, 2002.

Braidotti, Rosi. "Virginia Woolf, Immanence and Ontological Pacifism." *Comparative Critical Studies*, vol. 19, no. 2, 2022, pp. 131–48. https://doi.org/10.3366/ccs.2022.0439.

Brittain, Vera. Commentary regarding Woolf's death. Vera Brittain fonds, section J: Incoming Correspondence, "Woolf, Virginia 3 H.L.S. 1934 - 1941. 6 document sheets. Includes commentary by Brittain regarding Woolf's death, and a copy of Woolf's letter to Austrian Chancellor Dollfuss requesting clemency for Paula Wallisch, an Austrian resistance fighter and wife of Koloman Wallisch." The William Ready Division of Archives and Research Collections, Mills Library, McMaster University, Hamilton, OT.

———. *Testament of a Peace Lover: Letters from Vera Brittain*. Edited by Winifred Eden-Green and Alan Eden-Green, Virago, 1988.

———. *Testament of Experience*. 1957. Seaview Books, 1981.

———. *Testament of Friendship: The Story of Winifred Holtby*. Edited by Mark Bostridge, Virago, 2012.

———. *Testament Of Youth*. Penguin, 1995.

Ceadel, Martin. "A Legitimate Peace Movement: The Case of Interwar Britain, 1918–1945." *Challenge to Mars: Essays on Pacifism from 1918 to 1945*, edited by Peter Brock and Thomas Paul Socknat, U of Toronto P, 1999, pp. 134–48.

———. *Thinking about Peace and War*. Oxford UP, 1987.

Chan, Evelyn T. "Professions, Freedom, and Form: Reassessing Woolf's *The Years* and *Three Guineas*." *The Review of English Studies*, vol. 61, no. 251, 2010, pp. 591–613.

Clay, Catherine. *British Women Writers, 1914–1945: Professional Work and Friendship*. Ashgate, 2006.

DiCenzo, Maria. "'Our Freedom and Its Results': Measuring Progress in the Aftermath of Suffrage." *Women's History Review*, vol. 23, no. 3, 2014, pp. 421–40. https://doi.org/10.1080/09612025.2013.820598.

discovery, n. *Oxford English Dictionary*. Accessed June 3, 2024. www.oed.com/dictionary/discovery_n.

Doan, Laura L. *Fashioning Sapphism: The Origins of a Modern English Lesbian Culture*. Columbia UP, 2001.

Doan, Laura, and Jay Prosser, editors. *Palatable Poison: Critical Perspectives on The Well of Loneliness*. Columbia UP, 2001.

Eglin, Josephine. "Women Pacifists in Interwar Brittain." *Challenge to Mars: Essays on Pacifism from 1918 to 1945*, edited by Peter Brock and Thomas Paul Socknat, U of Toronto P, 1999, pp. 149–68.

Ewins, Kristin. "'Revolutionizing a Mode of Life': Leftist Middlebrow Fiction by Women in the 1930s." *ELH*, vol. 82, no. 1, 2015, pp. 251–79.

Gorham, Deborah. *Vera Brittain: A Feminist Life*. Blackwell, 1996.

Granovetter, Mark S. "The Strength of Weak Ties." *American Journal of Sociology*, vol. 78, no. 6, 1973, pp. 1360–80.

Harris, Jose. "Swanwick [Née Sickert], Helena Maria Lucy (1864–1939), Suffragist." *Oxford Dictionary of National Biography*. Accessed December 22, 2023. https://doi.org/10.1093/ref:odnb/38040.

Kotler, Margot. "The Impersonal Is Political: Virginia Woolf, Vera Brittain, and Feminist Counterpublics." *Virginia Woolf Miscellany*, no. 97, 2021, pp. 26–30.

Laird, Holly A. "Between the (Disciplinary) Acts: Modernist Suicidology." *Modernism/modernity*, vol. 18, no. 3, 2011, pp. 525–50.

Levenback, Karen L. *Virginia Woolf and the Great War*. Syracuse UP, 1999.

Lukowitz, David C. "British Pacifists and Appeasement: The Peace Pledge Union." *Journal of Contemporary History*, vol. 9, no. 1, 1974, pp. 115–27. https://doi.org/10.1177/002200947400900107.

Marshik, Celia. "History's 'Abrupt Revenges': Censoring War's Perversions in The Well of Loneliness and Sleeveless Errand." *Journal of Modern Literature*, vol. 26, no. 2, 2003, pp. 145–59.

McCleery, Alistair. "Banned Books and Publishers' Ploys: The Well of Loneliness as Exemplar." *Journal of Modern Literature*, vol. 43, no. 1, 2019, pp. 34–52.

Medd, Jodie. *Lesbian Scandal and the Culture of Modernism*. Cambridge UP, 2012.

Mellown, Muriel. "One Woman's Way to Peace: The Development of Vera Brittain's Pacifism." *Frontiers: A Journal of Women Studies*, vol. 8, no. 2, 1985, pp. 1–6. https://doi.org/10.2307/3346044.

Micir, Melanie. *The Passion Projects: Modernist Women, Intimate Archives, Unfinished Lives*. Princeton UP, 2019.

Rosenblum, Lauren M. "Beyond Recovery: Towards a New Feminist Methodology of the Archive." *Modernism/Modernity Print Plus*, November 12, 2020. https://modernismmodernity.org/forums/posts/rosenblum-beyond-recovery.

Shaw, Marion. "'Alien Experiences': Virginia Woolf, Winifred Holtby and Vera Brittain in the Thirties." *Rewriting the Thirties: Modernism and After*, edited by Keith Williams and Steven Matthews, Longman, 1997, pp. 37–52.

Simpson, Kathryn, "Friends and Lovers," *The Oxford Handbook of Virginia Woolf*, edited by Anne E. Fernald, Oxford UP, 2021, pp. 27–43.

Smyth, Ethel. *The Memoirs of Ethel Smyth*. Edited by Ronald Crichton, Viking, 1987. archive.org/details/memoirsofethelsm00smyt.

Swanwick, Helena Maria. *I Have Been Young*. Victor Gollancz, 1935.

Wisor, Rebecca. "Virginia Woolf & Vera Brittain: Pacifism and the Gendered Politics of Public Intellectualism." *Studies in the Humanities*, vol. 35, no. 2, 2008, pp. 137–53.

Woolf, Virginia, Three unpublished letters. Vera Brittain fonds, section J: Incoming Correspondence, "Woolf, Virginia 3 H.L.S. 1934 - 1941. 6 document sheets. Includes commentary by Brittain regarding Woolf's death, and a copy of Woolf's letter to Austrian Chancellor Dollfuss requesting clemency for Paula Wallisch, an Austrian resistance fighter and wife of Koloman Wallisch." The William Ready Division of Archives and Research Collections, Mills Library, McMaster University, Hamilton, OT.

———. *The Diary of Virginia Woolf: 1931–1935*. Edited by Anne Olivier Bell, assisted by Andrew McNeillie, Harcourt Brace, 1982. Vol. 4 of *The Diary of Virginia Woolf*.

———. *The Letters of Virginia Woolf: 1932–1935*. Edited by Nigel Nicolson and Joanne Trautmann, Harcourt, 1982. Vol. 5 of *The Letters of Virginia Woolf*.

———. "Letters to Winifred Holtby." Edited by Stephen Barkway. *Virginia Woolf Bulletin*, no. 32, September 2009, pp. 11–24.

———. *Moments of Being: A Collection of Autobiographical Writing*. 2nd ed. Edited with introduction by Jeanne Schulkind, Harcourt, 1985.

———. *The Pargiters, the Novel-Essay Portion of The Years*. Edited by Mitchell A. Leaska. 1st ed. New York: New York Public Library : distributed by Readex Books, 1977.

———. *A Room of One's Own*. San Diego: Mariner Books, 1989.

———. "Speech to the London and National Society for Women's Service." *The Essays of Virginia Woolf: 1929–1932*, edited by Stuart N. Clarke, Houghton Mifflin Harcourt, 2009, pp. 635–48. Vol. 5 of *The Essays of Virginia Woolf*.

———. *Three Guineas*. Harcourt, 1966.

———. *To the Lighthouse*. Harcourt, 1981.

———. "Why Art To-Day Follows Politics." *The Essays of Virginia Woolf: 1933–1941*, edited by Stuart N. Clarke, Hogarth, 2011, pp. 75–79. Vol. 6 of *The Essays of Virginia Woolf*.

Appendix A: Holograph Notes for Woolf Memorial Letter

During World War II, Brittain wrote nearly two hundred twice-monthly Letters to Peace Lovers *as a subscription offering for members of the Peace Pledge Union. These letters were closely printed on both sides of single sheet of paper and reached one- to two-thousand subscribers. They combined news and personal reflection, offering solidarity to pacifists who seldom found their interests or ideas represented in the national news or mainstream journalism. Most letters began with an epigraph. Letter #55, dated April 24, 1941, memorialized Virginia Woolf on the occasion of her death and is reprinted in* Testament of a Peace Lover: Letters from Vera Brittain. *Edited by Winifred Eden-Green and Alan Eden-Green. London: Virago, 1988. This appendix transcribes her holograph notes.*

Quote Elinor Wylie.

Virginia Woolf.

1) I wanted to write to W.H. [Winifred Holtby], but she has moved too far away from this warring world for any illusions to be left of her reassuring presence.

2) I suppose she felt that this war, for too long, had put an end to anything she cared about; that she had no contribution to make to the type of society which is has created. Her end was a kind of protest—the most terrible, the most effective that she could make - against the real hell that war brings to the artist.

3) Of all those whom war penalises, the musicians, the painters, & the writers suffer most. (See 6) They need ~~an orderly world~~ a world on the up grade [?] in which to create [illegible superscript] - a world such as the Greeks had in the time of Pericles, the Italians during the Renaissance, Shakespeare + ~~Milton +~~ Spencer [sic] during the Elizabethan Age, the great Victorians (and also Goethe during the Victorian Age. Their world is always so full, so deeply interesting, they don't need war to give them aims or provide them with occupation. You can't escape from this type of war—not even by retiring to California like Aldous Huxley + James Hilton. It seeks you out + runs you down. \ quote J. J./ The only method of adaptation is to acquire what the Quakers call "a concern" for the problems that war creates for mankind, + for exploring routes out of them - an essentially political pursuit. And that, ^in a certain sense endows being a minor artist ^instead of a major artist. So [sic] of us have adapted ourselves in that way, sacrificing the integrity of our art to the overwhelming bludgeonings of circumstance ~~maintenance~~. \Perhaps/ V.W. preferred to die.

She was not ~~open~~ young enough to adapt herself, and too fragile. Anyhow she would not, I think, have wanted to—any more than James Joyce, the protesting invalid exile was able to do. She preferred to say - in her own words at the end of

"The Waves" — "Against you I will fling myself, unvanquished and unyielding, O Death." Written ten years ago, they might stand for her epitaph.

4) Last Sunday I felt that the "appreciations" written over her, even V. S-W.'S poem were inept and inadequate as though ~~the~~ her protest were too overwhelming, too breathtaking for those who are attempting to square their own ideal of civilisation with impossible barbarisms—~~It~~ The protest could not be ignored, so it had to be hurriedly tidied out of the way.

5) CF W.'s comment on "Jacob's Room" (T of F. p. 357)

6) The artist's world is always so full, so deeply interesting; they don't need war to give them arms or provide them w occupation. It is in fact the most grievous kind of interruption of everything they do & are ~~to one~~. So, as her last & final ~~official~~ argument against the breakdown of civilisation, V.W. choose chose death. Was that it?

meetings w V. W. —
a) H.M. Swanwick
b) Radclyffe Hall meeting
c) London Soc. Of Women's Service. Senior partner
d) three letters to me

W.H. + V. W.
Now V.W. gone while E. S. [Ethel Smyth] left. Obituaries feeble.
We shall never know whether she protested.
War + the artist.

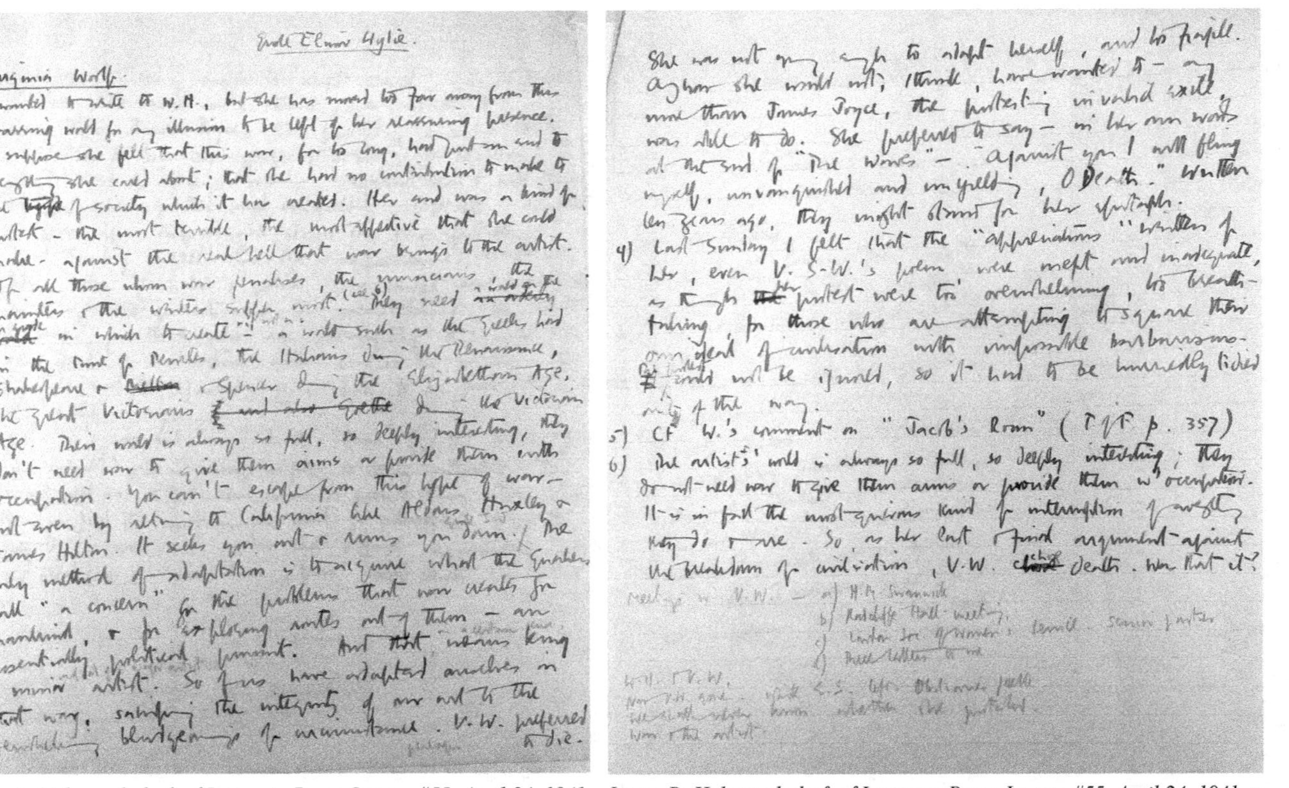

Image A: Holograph draft of Letters to Peace Lovers, #55, April 24, 1941, p. 1 of 2. Texts by Vera Brittain are © The Literary Executors of the Vera Brittain Will Trust (1970) and are reproduced with permission. Courtesy The William Ready Division of Archives and Research Collections, McMaster University Library.

Image B: Holograph draft of Letters to Peace Lovers, #55, April 24, 1941, p. 2 of 2. Texts by Vera Brittain are © The Literary Executors of the Vera Brittain Will Trust (1970) and are reproduced with permission. Courtesy The William Ready Division of Archives and Research Collections, McMaster University Library.

Appendix B: Two Unpublished Letters to Vera Brittain from Virginia Woolf

Vera Brittain fonds, box 203, McMaster University Archives

[Tavistock Square stationery]
~~14~~ 15 June [n.d.; likely 1933]

Dear Miss Brittain,
I am of course glad to sign the letter, which I enclose with hopes that it may succeed. May I take this opportunity of saying how much your book, A Testament of Youth, interests me?

Yours sincerely
Virginia Woolf

****

Typed. N.d.

Your Excellency, Considerable anxiety is being expressed in this country with regard to Frau Wallisch who was recently sentenced to a year's hard labour for having distributed food to the Schutsbundlers during the disturbances in Bruck.

We understand that the condition of her health is so grave that her sentence has been postponed and that she is at present in a sanatorium receiving medical attention.

In view of the fact that her husband has already been executed for his part in the disturbances and that Frau Wallisch's action was such as would naturally be prompted by her position as his wife, we are approaching you in the hope that you may see your way to remit her sentence and allow her to recover her health without the prospect of prison in front of her.

We have the honour to remain,
Yours faithfully,
Virginia Woolf

His Excellency Chancellor Dollfuss

*****

52 Tavistock Square
WC 1 Oct 4th [1935]

Dear Miss Brittain,

Although I have met you, I hope you will let me say how unhappy I am at the news of Winifred Holtby's death.

I knew her very little, but she gave me the impression of a most generous + delightful nature. I am very proud of the book she wrote about me. I know you will understand if I say that the fact that she wrote about me, so generously, made me shy of seeing her. How I wish now that I had seen her more, + known her better! She had said she would come see us this summer, but I suppose, though I didn't know it, that she was too ill.

I am talking selfishly of my own feelings, because it is impossible to say anything about what her death must mean to you.

Please believe me how much we both feel for you.

Yours sincerely

Virginia Woolf

Of course, do not think of answering.

My husband has been telling me how greatly he admired her.

52,
Tavistock Square,
W.C.1.
Telephone : Museum 2621.

15th June

Dear Miss Brittain,

I am of course glad to sign the letter, which I return, with hopes that it may succeed.

May I take this opportunity of saying how much your book, a Testament of Youth, interested me?

Yours sincerely
Virginia Woolf

Image C: Holograph letter from Virginia Woolf to Vera Brittain, 15 June [n.d.; likely 1933]. Courtesy The Society of Authors, the Literary Representative of the Estate of Virginia Woolf, and The William Ready Division of Archives and Research Collections, McMaster University Library.

Your Excellency,

Considerable anxiety is being expressed in this country with regard to Frau Wallisch who was recently sentenced to a year's hard labour for having distributed food to the Schutzbundlers during the disturbances in Bruck.

We understand that the condition of her health is so grave that her sentence has been postponed and that she is at present in a sanatorium receiving medical attention.

In view of the fact that her husband has already been executed for his part in the disturbances and that Frau Wallisch's action was such as would naturally be prompted by her position as his wife, we are approaching you in the hope that you may see your way to remit her sentence and allow her to recover her health without the prospect of prison in front of her.

We have the honour to remain,

Yours faithfully,
Virginia Woolf

His Excellency
Chancellor Dollfuss.

Virginia

Image D: Typescript letter from Virginia Woolf to Chancellor Dollfus on behalf of Frau Wallisch [n.d.; likely 1933]. Courtesy The Society of Authors, the Literary Representative of the Estate of Virginia Woolf, and The William Ready Division of Archives and Research Collections, McMaster University Library.

52 Tavistock Square
W.C.1 Oct 4th [ ]

Dear Miss Brittain,

Although I have met you, I hope you will let me say how unhappy I am at the news of Winifred Holtby's death.

I knew her very little, but she gave me the impression of a most generous & delightful nature. I am very proud of the book she wrote about me. I know you will understand if I say that the fact that she wrote about me, so generously, made me shy of seeing her. How I wish now that I had seen her more, & known her better!

Image E: Holograph letter from Virginia Woolf to Vera Brittain, 4 October [n.d.; 1934], p. 1 of 2. Courtesy The Society of Authors, the Literary Representative of the Estate of Virginia Woolf, and The William Ready Division of Archives and Research Collections, McMaster University Library.

She had said she would come & see us this summer, but I suppose, though I didn't know it, that she was too ill.

I am talking selfishly of my own feelings, because it is impossible to say anything about what her death must mean to you.

Please believe how much we both feel for you.

Yours sincerely
Virginia Woolf.

Of course, do not think of answering. My husband has been telling me how greatly he admired her.

Image F: Holograph letter from Virginia Woolf to Vera Brittain, 4 October [n.d.; 1934], p. 2 of 2. Courtesy The Society of Authors, the Literary Representative of the Estate of Virginia Woolf, and The William Ready Division of Archives and Research Collections, McMaster University Library.

Virginia Woolf's *Choephori Notebook*: An Annotated Transcription

Cristina Testa

Introduction

Woolf never said that she had a favorite tragedian among the Greeks, but her reading notebooks make evident that Aeschylus and Sophocles are both in the running. The latter's work attracted her for its political themes (consider the recurrence of the *Antigone* in Woolf's fiction and notebooks) while she was fascinated by the former's human characters and by a power of language capable of expressing emotions and conveying crises of epochal passage.

Woolf filled various papers with notes on books that she read and studied across her life. While notes dedicated to Sophoclean production outnumber pages on other works of Greek antiquity, her single most extensive commentary is dedicated to the *Choephori* (or, *The Libation Bearers*), the second tragedy of Aeschylus's *Oresteia* trilogy, in which the death of Mycenae's king Agamemnon is avenged by his children Orestes and Electra.

The *Choephori Notebook*, as I will refer to it here and which Brenda Silver numbers RN27, corresponds to the manuscript, "*Choephori of Aeschylus. Edited by A. W. Verrall.* Holograph Reading Notes, Dated January 1907," kept in the Berg Collection of the New York Public Library (Silver 146–47). Years after her study of the *Choephori*, probably between 1922 and 1923, Woolf also composed a bilingual edition of the first *Oresteia* tragedy *Agamemnon*, whose main event is the murder of the titular protagonist by his wife Clytemnestra. This edition appears in another notebook (unnumbered by Silver), also catalogued in the Berg Collection as "Holograph English translation Aeschylus's *Agamemnon*, and her marginal MS notes" (Silver 125). In an important breakthrough in the study of these manuscripts, a full reproduction of both notebooks is now available on the website *WoolfNotes*,[1] an inestimable online resource that allows free and immediate consultation of many archived writings. In her analysis of these manuscripts, noting the early tragedian's influence on Woolf's literary production, Emily Dalgarno suggests that "Woolf's passion for Aeschylus, in whose work her own is most deeply grounded, was instilled in her … by Janet Case," the teacher with whom she first studied the *Oresteia* trilogy in Greek but also the friend who put her on a path toward feminist thought and activism (42).

Woolf seems to have come to the *Choephori* in 1907 with a different purpose than her later translation of *Agamemnon*, for in Aeschylus's second tragedy, Woolf

[1] On *WoolfNotes.com*, the *Agamemnon Notebook* is numbered WN100 and is included in the "Additions Index," while *Choephori* appears on the back of *Mrs. Dalloway*'s notes as document RN28 in "Silver Index."

may have found ways to face loss and look for atonement, needs she may still have been feeling strongly after the death of her father Leslie Stephen, which preceded her mental breakdown in 1904. (More practically, since the *Choephori* is generally considered less linguistically complex than *Agamemnon*, the second tragedy is also a more suitable starting point for a new student of ancient Greek).

The *Choephori Notebook* consists of sixteen holograph pages bound in a brown leather cover with a decorated paper interior. The notes on Aeschylus's work, dated January 1907, are written on the recto in black ink and are found in the same volume as notes on the composition of *Mrs. Dalloway* (1925), mainly preliminary ideas on the novel's narrative development and structure.[2] The dates Woolf affixes to the thirteen holograph pages relating to the novel (beginning November 9th, 1922 and running to August 2nd, 1923) suggests contemporaneousness with her translation of *Agamemnon*. (This coincidence might be not casual.) Though appearing in the same notebook as her study of the *Choephori*, Woolf's notes toward *Mrs. Dalloway* begin at the *end* of the notebook. When she began working on her novel, Woolf flipped the notebook upside down and worked backward from the last page as if it were the first page of a fresh notebook. Five blank sheets separate the 1907 and the 1922–23 notes.

It is not difficult to sense continuity between *Mrs. Dalloway* and Woolf's studies of Aeschylus. Jean Mills contextualizes this connection in light of historical events:

> It seems to me Aeschylus' problem in *The Libation Bearers* is the same problem Woolf poses in *Mrs. Dalloway.* What do we as a society do now with all of these dead bodies? It is as if the texts of both 'The Libation Bearers Notebook' and *Mrs. Dalloway* perform a kind of ritual, regardless of intention, with the manuscript asking the translation, how do I perform this task? How do I write this novel? And how does the content of that novel unfold, tap out the rhythm, bang the drum, pour out the libations over the sacrifice? And who, after all, is being sacrificed and why? (101)

If the legacy of war (the First World War; the Trojan War) and the need for sacrifice (Septimus Smith's suicide; Electra's offering for a dead father) are recurring themes in *Mrs. Dalloway* and the *Choephori*, then it follows that Woolf's later work on the novel may have recalled her 1907 study and inspired a new study of *Agamemnon*. Perhaps she wanted to resume her work on Aeschylus and thus returned to the first tragedy of the *Oresteia* trilogy.

[2] These notes are catalogued as "*[Mrs. Dalloway] Holograph notes*. Bound 1922 Nov. 9–1923 Aug. 2. 13 p." and are preceded by three pages containing notes on the Russian alphabet and language. There seems to be no connection between the notes on Russian and the notes on *Mrs. Dalloway*.

The *Choephori Notebook* is not as ambitious as her later study of *Agamemnon*,[3] but the two notebooks reward comparison because they present similarities in compositional method. Both, indeed, are openly based on volumes edited and translated by Arthur Verrall, a Cambridge professor. These editions are suitable for academic work but also for individual study because they include book-length introductions, appendices, the original Greek text with voluminous scholarly footnotes that offer explanations, interpretations, and translations that often differ from the English translation that appears separately.[4] Mills notes that Verrall's version of Aeschylus's *Agamemnon* (1889) and *Choephori* (1893) circulated among scholars who were, spiritually or directly, Woolf's mentors:

> This is the same text used by Jane Harrison as an undergraduate at Newnham College, the same edition from which she taught her direct method as an instructor there, and the same edition Janet Case used to teach Woolf her lessons. It is the same edition, years later in 1922, that Woolf uses again when she revisits her Greek study and devises her 'Agamemnon Notebook' (49).

The choice of Verrall as preferred text is thus a fixed point in Woolf's study of Aeschylus. While Verrall's presence is more evident in the *Agamemnon* notebook (his translation is almost entirely transcribed), his importance for Woolf's notes on the *Choephori* is perhaps more radical for both linguistic and ideological reasons.

Woolf's Greek

When copying or annotating an expression in Greek, as Rowena Fowler notes, "Woolf rarely used accents or breathings ... and never marked scansion" not caring much about syllabic subdivision and phonetics (Fowler 220). Except in formal writing, as in the case of the quotations in "On Not Knowing Greek" (1925) and in *The Years* (1937) where the meter and accents are indicated correctly, Woolf read and wrote Greek more like a cultured amateur than an academic, as can be clearly seen in this 1907 reading notebook as well as in later notebooks.[5]

[3] Referring to *Agamemnon*, Woolf writes in her diary, "I should be at Aeschylus, for I am making a complete edition, text, translation, & notes of my own—mostly copied from Verrall; but carefully gone into by me" (*D*2 215).

[4] In the *Choephori Notebook*, Woolf signals attributions to Verrall's commentary and translation with the initial "V" and to his introduction with "V. intro"; she also credits her gloss on line 216 of the tragedy to "verallian subtlety" (CN6; see Verrall 31).

[5] Woolf generally omits accents and spirits in the "Greek Notebook" (RN34) and in the notes on the *Bacchae* (RN19). She employs some but not all accents and spirits in the extracts from the *Odyssey* (RN25). In the *Agamemnon Notebook* (WN100), the Greek text is "glued" onto its pages and therefore already has all the diacritical marks printed. Even so, Woolf makes changes to the punctuation and sometimes also to the words themselves, rewriting them in

Woolf's somewhat simplified Greek, analogous to what in *Aurora Leigh* (1856) Elizabeth Barrett Browning calls "Lady's Greek,"[6] may be the result of what she often represented as a private education, which did not provide formally rigorous or continuous instruction on certain aspects of grammar and, above all, was external to the restricted, male-centered, and inward-looking university elite. And yet, Woolf's instruction in Greek was more consistent and better structured than she ever admits.[7] Indeed, she participated in classes at the King's College Ladies' Department from 1897 to 1901 with Sir George Warr and Clara Pater and at home from 1902 to 1907 with Janet Case, a classicist and activist who became an intimate friend.[8] Although Woolf always lamented her aversion to grammar—and while accenting is difficult for those first learning ancient Greek—I agree with Theodore Koulouris that "it is not conceivable" that the scholars who taught her "did not know how to correctly or adequately stress their Greek" (65). It seems more likely to me that Woolf deliberately omits accents due either to a lack of interest in that feature of the language (rather than a lack of skill) or, as Koulouris suggests,[9] due to a specific political commitment that she intends to carry forward, engaging in what we might call a democratic exercise. From this point of view, unaccented Greek becomes an instrument to oppose an elitism that aimed to reserve classical studies as a prerogative of the leading class (of educated men). In this sense, "feminine Greek" is code shared by non-professionals who rebel against the canons of education, forming a sort of counter-society to the "Oxbridge" inner circle, from which they are excluded. Recalling Case's classes in an obituary, Woolf remarks that, due to her own amateur condition and her desire to remain

---

the margin, where the accents are ignored.

[6] *Lady's Greek* is easily recognizable by the young man who discovers the protagonist's notebook for being written "without the accents" (II.76–77). The general opinion of the time sees in Aurora's study an undue appropriation of an instrument, ancient Greek, which should be protected from women, in order to keep it from being reduced to a vulgarized, unofficial, and even occult version of the language, something that "had witchcraft in 't" and whose reading "calls up dangerous spirits" (II, 78–79).

[7] See Snaith and Jones; Daugherty.

[8] Woolf writes about her relationship with her tutor not only in letters and diary entries but also in two works expressly dedicated to her. Case's lessons and method are the object of the 1903 sub-section of the early journal *A Passionate Apprentice* called "Miss Case" and in a commemorative article for the *Times*, written on the occasion of her death in 1937. Case is remembered as the "noble Athena, breaking down the tradition that only men acted in the Greek play" (*PA* 181–84; *E*6 111).

[9] Koulouris reasons, "The perceived defiance of grammar and appropriate accentuation does not so much point towards inability as it does towards a will to redirect the study of Greek from the academic cloister to the drawing room, from the scholar's library to the High Street tea-rooms, from the pomp and circumstance of the academic ceremony to the democracy of the social gathering, and from the conformity and intellectual idleness of the Victorian gentleman-scholar to the activism of the committee for the emancipation of the Victorian and Edwardian woman; in other words, from the masculine socio-cultural and educational domain to the traditionally designated space of female *struggle*, as well as to the larger socio-political aspiration of femininity at large" (65).

an amateur, "somehow the masterpieces of Greek drama were stormed, without grammar, without accents," adopting a direct and captivating approach that made them "supremely desirable" (*E*6 111). Thus, in Woolf's conception, the conscious avoidance of accents must not be considered a result of poor training in translation, which is ultimately unattainable even for experts,[10] but rather a way to make the ancient language and literature more accessible, especially for women who were usually denied higher education.[11] As Prins states, "Woolf here turns the Victorian denigration of 'Lady's Greek, without the accents' into a revelation of Greek as a language of and for desire … beyond a (merely) scholarly reading" (170).

Woolf's Greek notebooks afford her personal language exercise and pleasure, and for this reason she chooses subjects according to her own taste and their utility for her literary work. Though the 1907 manuscript begins, "Orestes:," suggesting the beginning of a full transcription or translation, the *Choephori Notebook* presents neither the whole Greek text nor the full English translation by Verrall (CN1). Rather, Woolf studies specific words and expressions, always indicating the line of reference in Verrall's edition, giving the literal meaning, and often adding explanatory notes. She usually provides the original phrase first and then the translation and her attention is particularly attracted by Aeschylus's figurative language.[12]

At the top of the fourth page of the *Choephori Notebook*, Woolf quotes Verrall's commentary, "In the obscurity of the language lies its dramatic merit" (CN4; Verral 18n108). This quotation may express, Mills suggests, Woolf's general thoughts on Aeschylus's work (even if this reading pulls the passage out of its original context) [Mills 102]. In "On Not Knowing Greek," indeed, Woolf echoes Verrall's comment and suggests that the ancient language itself is the darkest and at the same time most fascinating part of Hellenic culture; talking specifically about Aeschylus's enigmatic and metaphorical expressions, moreover, she observes that "to understand him it is not so necessary to understand Greek as to understand poetry … There is an ambiguity which is the mark of the highest poetry; we cannot know exactly what it means" (*E*4 44). Verrall's compelling phrase forecasts Woolf's belief, stated in the 1925 essay, that "meaning is just on the far side of language"

[10] Woolf famously expresses this idea in her 1925 essay "On Not Knowing Greek": "For it is vain and foolish to talk of knowing Greek ... between this foreign people and ourselves there is not only difference of race and tongue but a tremendous breach of tradition. All the more strange, then, is it that we should wish to know Greek, try to know Greek, feel for ever drawn back to Greek, and be for ever making up some notion of the meaning of Greek" (*E*4 38).

[11] Whom she taught in evening classes at Morley College for Working Men and Women from 1905 to 1907. See Daugherty.

[12] Woolf will cultivate this aspect even more specifically in the *Agamemnon Notebook*, where she puts emphasis on the image of the fire beacons that signal the return of the king and represent Clytemnestra's inner state, and an even more precise reflection is dedicated to the red tapestry spread on the protagonist's way. The latter announces the bloodshed expecting Agamemnon in the palace and by extension symbolizes the familiar massacre that will close its circle in the next tragedy in the death of Clytemnestra.

(*E4* 45). By studying the *Choephori Notebook* and Woolf's careful engagement with Verrall's commentary, we gain insight into Woolf's views of language and languages—especially ancient ones.

Woolf and Verrall

The above-mentioned comment by Verrall on the obscurity of Aeschylus's language may have attracted Woolf's curiosity because it represents both an indication and a challenge. Indeed, after providing her own translation, she looks for the hidden meaning of the passage, to which the scholar seems to allude.

Line 108 of the *Choephori* (bolded below in the English version) reads "φθέγγου χέουσα σεμνά τοῖσιν εὔφροσιν" (Verrall 18) and is part of an early conversation between Electra and female slaves attending the grave of her murdered father Agamemnon. Here is Verrall's translation:

> *Electra.* Women, who serve our house, who give it order, since ye are here to attend in this rite upon me, share ye my counsels respecting the bewilderment of our case. When I pour these offerings of sorrow, how can I speak, how can I pray, in terms of kindness to my father? … Keep not your counsel in your heart for fear of ... those whom I name not. For our fate is fixed for us all, for the free not less than for him whom destiny governs by an instrumental hand.
>
> O speak, if thou canst grasp aught beyond this present world!
>
> *Slave.* In reverence for thy father's tomb, as it were an altar, I will speak, as thou commandest, the very thought of my heart.
>
> *El.* Speak, as thou dost reverence my father's grave.
>
> ***Sla.* Utter, when thou pourest, such words as religion permits to those who love.**
>
> *El.* And to which of those bound to me may I give this name?
>
> *Sla.* Name first thyself, then... all that loathe Aegisthus. (Verrall 214)

In her notebook, Woolf translates lines 108–09 straightforwardly: "[Slave] When you pour out, speak what is sacred to those who love. [Electra] Whom of our friends can I address as people who love?" (CN3).[13] The repetition found in

[13] In this Introduction, I quote Woolf's manuscript without her lineation, incorporating possible modifications that Woolf made in the holograph and writing in full the words she abbreviates. I keep the exact form of Woolf's script in the transcription below. See my Note to the transcription. Whenever the antecedent of a pronoun is unclear, I specify the person or object in brackets.

Woolf's phrases "those who love" and "people who love" is not present in the original Greek—or in Verrall's translation—but still draws out attention to a phrase in Verrall's commentary on line 108. (This is the same footnote from which Woolf draws the quotation, "In the obscurity of the language lies its dramatic merit"). In his commentary, Verrall emphasizes the phrase *those who love* with italics and develops over 200 words of explication that contest other reckonings with the phrase in classical scholarship (see CN3n47 below). At stake here is a sense of the inner purpose of those who offer prayers and libation: the heart of the tragedy, in short, and what Woolf investigates through her careful engagement with Verrall's scholarship.

The early exchange between Electra and the female slaves may have triggered Woolf's critical interest, for she follows up her translation with some brief commentary: "A. parodies, it seems, from the matter in hand" (CN3). Woolf seems to mean that Electra's final question is rhetorical since the implicit answer would be "nobody." Woolf's follows her commentary with the quotation from Verrall noted above (i.e., "In the obscurity …") before concluding, "Electra is urging [the slaves] on to commit themselves in speech by feigning ignorance," thus making a guess at Electra's intentions (CN4). Here, Woolf again echoes Verrall's commentary, this time of line 109: "She [Electra] wishes them to name themselves" (Verrall 18). However, as the slaves' answer proves, they will not help Electra: she must rely on herself alone, and later on Orestes.

In her attempts to translate Aesychlus's lines, Woolf benefits from Verrall's commentary, drawing out, through her rearrangements and English idiom, the literal meaning of expressions that Verrall indicates in his commentary but often does not include in his final translation (which follows the Greek text in his volume). As I show in my transcription and transcription notes, Woolf prefers clear and concise renditions that nonetheless capture key points of Verrall's commentary. For example, she translates νερτέροις μειλίγμασιν (line 15), "after propitiation," specifying in simple terms that ceremonies like the bearing of libations to Agamemnon's grave are made both "after the death" and "to propitiate one of the dead" (CN1; see CN1n10).

Also, when Electra invokes the Earth at a crucial point of the tragedy (lines 127–28), bearing libations to her father's grave and praying that gods avenge his death at her mother's hand, Woolf translates the process of the natural cycle, "producest everything and nourishing it conceives it again" (CN4). Here she deviates from Verrall's compound and outdated expression, "summon Earth herself, who bringeth all things to birth, reareth them, and receiveth again into her womb" (Verrall 214; see C4n61). Woolf gives emphasis to the maternal acceptation of the term "κῦμα," which means "concept, embryo" (CN4). Woolf follows this allusion to rebirth with a comment about the possibility of resurrection that deviates from Verrall's notes. Here, she develops an interpretation that, as far as it concerns religious doctrine, departs from Verrall's comparison of Electra's prayer with the

Christian doctrine of resurrection (see CN4n63).[14] Woolf turns to a more ancient and pagan canon: namely, philosophy. She mentions Lucretius, probably alluding to the "atomic theory" expressed in *De Rerum Natura* and, more specifically, to the concept according to which nothing in nature dies but, rather, turns back into what is called "first bodies," that is, original components and materials. Electra hopes that Agamemnon's blood will come to her aid not only in spirit but concretely, forecasting the imminent appearance of her brother Orestes less than a hundred lines later.

When she studies single words or expressions, Woolf usually makes a summary of Verrall's notes to highlight the core sense of his explanation. Instead of a proper translation, she paraphrases the Greek text in a synthetic way that conveys both the literal meaning and the acceptation suggested by the scholar. The first example of this process occurs in line 5, where κλύειν and ἀκοῦσαι are translated, respectively, "listen with your ear" and "hear with your mind," which allude to the fact that a spirit (Agamemnon's in this case) is in some way affected by the prayers and sacrifices of the living, namely Orestes's (CN1; see CN1n7).

Very emblematic of Woolf's critical synthesis is also line 85 in the manuscript, when Electra asks her attendants to give her counsel about the present situation, which Aesychylus describes as an atmospheric disaster or "τυφώς." (From Verrall's notes: "This energetic figure cannot be rendered in English, because the terrible phaenomenon of the 'whirlwind' or 'dust-storm' is to us practically unknown" [14; see CN3n37]). In his final translation, Verrall strips the line of any reference to a specific natural disaster, instead rendering the reference to the present moment as "the bewilderment of our case" (213). Woolf recovers the figurative meaning of Electra's line, noting that "the bewilderment of a dust-storm reflects Electra's [state of mind]: bewilderment as well as shock" (CN3).

Another case worth noting is line 161, where Woolf avoids the literal translation of weapons referenced by the chorus: that is "the Scythian weapon" and "the weapon firm to its hilt" (215). To clarify Aeschylus's intention to indicate two distinct objects, Woolf prefers to employ concrete nouns: "bow" and "sword," drawing on Verrall's synopsis (Verrall 24–25; CN5; see CN5n82 below).

Also, in the recognition scene, during which Orestes proves his identity to Electra by showing her a lock of his hair, Woolf retranslates Electra's reply and develops commentary on the passage. Her rendition of line 233, "Yet I know that our closest are our enemies" (CN7), changes the order of the words, making them more linear than Verrall's translation, "Ah yes, I know how sharp against us both are our kin" (Verrall 217; see CN7n112). Woolf makes here different semantic interpretations: φιλτάτους becomes, more generally, people who are nearby, not only those with a parental relation, which Verrall's "kin" implies. Woolf also translates πικρούς as "enemies" rather than the more literal adjective "sharp." Of

[14] Verrall references Paul's statement in 1 Corinthians 15:36, which reads "You fool! What you sow does not come to life unless it dies" in the standard English translation.

this passage, Woolf notes that Electra is "so anxious to believe" that her brother is back "that she opposes each hope with a doubt," discovering a state of mind that is concealed behind Electra's wise and cautious words: namely, an obscured fear that Orestes's return is a ruse (CN7).

There are other cases in the notebook in which Woolf simply gives the semantic meaning of single words and reports in a synthetic or simplified way Verrall's commentary on the whole passage. (I quote the wider context of Verrall's commentary in the notes to the transcription below).

Of particular interest is the analysis of lines referring to proper aspects of ancient religious ritual. From the very beginning, it seems that special attention in the manuscript is dedicated to prayers and ceremonial behaviors. The *Choephori Notebook* opens by explaining three valences of Hermes's cult, which invokes him as "God of the dead; God of ancestry" and "God of victory" (CN1). Woolf goes on to record the significance of Orestes's early offering of two locks of hair (line 5): "one to the river God 'for nurture', for this was the God of his country; and the other to the dead" (CN1). Both offerings derive from ancient and local religion and are aimed to be propitiatory for central events of the tragedy (see CN1n1). Later, in another reference to ancient religion, Woolf reflects on the chorus's reference in lines 37–41 to the dream that inspired Clytemnestra's demand that Electra journey to her father's grave to appease and calm his ghost:

> For there came a spirit true, lifting the hair, who prophesied to the house in dreams of sleep; angry his breath; and in the dead hour of dark his cry from the inmost room rang out with terror, breaking upon our women's chambers. And they who read this dream spake bold as from a god to whom they must answer, and said that it was the wrathful complaint of a soul below, angry against the slayer (Verrall 212–13).

This passage is immediately preceded by a note on the word φοιβος (line 32). Drawing on Verrall's remarks (Verrall 5), Woolf identifies this word with divine "inspiration, which is here an allusion to Clytaemnestra" and her dream, which the chorus later explains to Orestes (CN2; see CN2n16). According to Verrall's commentary, which Woolf records, Aeschylus words "signify that the interpreters were inspired by the Gods; they do not say what the interpretation was. This is to show that the facts" seen by the queen in her dream "are a divine and true symbol; but that the interpretation" given by the experts "is wrong" (CN2; see CN2n17). In short, Clytemnestra will eventually be killed by an immediate family member, but this person will be her son Orestes, not Agamemnon's ghost (as she feared).

In other parts of the notebook, Woolf reports Verrall's translation justifications, thus showing her reliance on his linguistic and philological expertise. Indeed, to mark her agreements with his renditions, she often records key steps of the scholar's reasoning. For example, with regard to line 104, Woolf's manuscript signals a disambiguation that Verrall draws out in his commentary. Woolf summarizes the scholar's interpretation of a moment in which Electra, speaking to the chorus of slaves, "expresses doubt" about "whether they [the slaves] can rise higher than the present time—& [she] thus stimulates their self-respect" (CN3). Woolf then reports another possible translation ("if you have any better suggestion to make") that Verrall explicitly discards in his commentary ("Speak, if you have any suggestion better than mine") [CN3; Verrall 17]. In keeping with Verrall's commentary, Woolf further motivates this choice, adding that the discarded translation "would throw doubt on their [the slaves'] power to give her advice which is precisely what [Electra] does not want to do. [Otherwise, this] would be … pointless remark" (CN3). This example further evinces Woolf's trust in Verrall's interpretation, which once more she finds convincing, and her fascination with Aeschylus's language, never plain or unequivocal but full of hidden meaning.

Woolf's most careful and detailed study corresponds to lines 320–25 of the tragedy. Woolf notes that the passage is "very difficult" and then she analyzes two sentences of the passage separately. Here is Verrall's translation of the passage:

> *Or*. . . . Darkness and light are parted and opposite: and in like manner is barred the office of love, the dirge which in time past has glorified the sires of our house.
>
> *Cho*. Child, the spirit of one that is dead is not conquered by all the fierceness of the devouring fire. He does make known his desires, but not so soon. As the parting soul can receive a lament, so the delaying soul can be brought to light. And the dirge for a father, for a parent, is a rightful, natural seeker, embracing with wide range both the worlds. (Verrall 219)

The first sentence, uttered by Orestes, wonders how prayers and sacrifices could possibly alleviate the suffering of his father Agamemnon's soul. Woolf summarizes the "[s]ense" of the passage, writing, "Darkness is severed from light, and all the loves between the two are alike barred and that lamentation which has done honour to the chief of our house of old" (CN9). The second sentence Woolf studies comes from the chorus' reply, which is introduced as "further subtleties, dependent some of them upon the tradition" (CN9). Verrall explains in his commentary that this "tradition" implies the division of the world of the dead from the one of the living and the possibility to bring back a spirit through the sincere moaning of a son (see CN9n147). Woolf does not report all the information Verrall covers in his notes but provides instead a translation of her own based on the literal meaning of the words: "As the dying man is wailed so the man's delaying is longest to light, and the true dirge for sake of the father and parent, his fathering the whole world" (CN9). Finally, she summarizes the main themes here as follows: "a dying man, one whose body is still there, is lamented; and so also may the delaying soul of one whose body has long been lost, be brought to light. And there is no cry much potent to reach such a soul than the cry of a child" (CN9). Again, the concept that Woolf emphasizes is not casual. It refers to the power of sincere mourning and the need to honor the dead. These themes, strictly linked to one another, are not only central in the tragedy of the *Choephori*, but also, as I stated from the beginning, in the writer's personal and artistic reflection at that time.

Another example of Woolf's engagement with and elaboration of Verrall concerns line 583 and its context. Here, Woolf notes that, as the chorus begins a new scene, "preparations for the slaughter go on," referring to the machinations of Orestes and Electra's vengeance (CN11). This note is a stronger assertion than the commentary found in Verrall's notes. While Verrall identifies the function of the chorus's ode as a scene-shifting device (Verrall 84; see CN11n182), Woolf emphasizes a sense of continuity and simultaneity: as the ode carries on, Orestes and Electra carry forward their plan to avenge their father. Of the chorus, Woolf reports, in her own rendition, a very striking phrase that hints to Clytemnestra's impetus: "The passion of beast and man is topped by the passion of a woman who shrives against wedlock" (CN11). Such words are in my view a sign of an admiration for the queen's strong character, in plain contrast with the "timid & lukewarm, like a fireless heath" temper of Aegisthus (line 628), Clytemnestra's lover and cousin of the king who helps in projecting vengeance but eventually does not carry out an active part in it (CN11).

Woolf's positive portrayal of Clytemnestra contrasts with the common interpretation that depicts her as an absolute evil. Here, Woolf only implies more explicit defenses of the queen in later studies of Aeschylus and in Woolf's more mature works.[15] In "Character in Fiction," an essay contemporaneous to the later *Agamemnon Notebook*, discussing the variable attitudes toward characters and human relationships, Woolf states: "Read the *Agamemnon*, and see whether, in process of time, your sympathies are not almost entirely with Clytemnestra" (*E*3 422). Reading the tragedy, Woolf must have wondered about the reasons for the extreme act of a woman who comes to betray her husband by plotting and ultimately accomplishing his murder. Clytemnestra is, in fact, not only a wife who remained away from a soldier and her king for the long interval of the Trojan War, but also a mother who suffered the loss of her beloved daughter Iphigenia, sacrificed by Agamemnon at the beginning of the war to propitiate the voyage of the ships on their expedition. By reversing the most widely shared point of view at the time, Woolf presents the queen as the offended party and a forerunner of a rebellion against patriarchal systems. As Mills notes, in Woolf's eyes Clytemnestra behaves "as she must, for the good of the family, the community, and civilization, itself, as

[15] A critical-literary line of the defense of Clytemnestra, in the wake of which Woolf evidently places herself, can be traced in Janet Case's article "Women in the Plays of Aeschylus" (1914), in which the queen's freedom of thought and strength of speech are praised and valued (not obscured by her sins). According to Case's interpretation, the most ancient tragedian would actually be the most innovative. Mills reports that, according to Case, Aeschylus is not only the one able to bridge the (only apparent) gap between the women he represents in his plays and those who really lived in Athens in the fifth century, but it is to him "to whom we must look for an alternative perspective on feminism in her own time" (50).

she has known it" (Mills 87). What is not accepted, by the character or by Woolf, is that a woman and mother has to be deprived of her offspring; moreover, the reasons given for this deprivation are considered unjustifiable.

In *A Room of One's Own* (1929), Woolf pays attention to the collective bonds that unite women, also talking about the female literary figures who have marked the collective imagination of Western culture. Referring to Trevelyan's opinion, according to which women of Shakespearean plays "do not seem wanting in personality and character," in order to underline the great strength of these characters, she declares: "Not being a historian, one might go even further and say that women have burnt like beacons in all the works of all the poets from the beginning of time" (*AROO* 64). It is certainly no coincidence that she uses again the similarity of fire signals, reminiscent of those of the palace of Mycenae, and, indeed, the first name that opens her list of examples is "Clytemnestra."

In some cases, Woolf feels confident enough in her notes to express an opinion on a phrase's meaning. However, in doing so, it is evident that she is still anchored by the version of the text she studies. Most of the time, she writes not what she thinks about the meaning of a sentence, but, rather, whether she agrees with Verrall's interpretation, making conjectures that follow the path he traces or that at least start from the points he makes. The most evident example of such a procedure is when Woolf, commenting on the question of whether the lock of hair is Orestes's, summarizes Verrall's assumption that "the natural inference, if you determine that the hair is Orestes' is that he is dead, and it is sent as remembrance" (CN5). But Woolf also notes that "Electra hopes that it is her brother's hair" and asks herself, "Why she [Electra] … hopes, if it might be so ominous?" (CN6). The hypothesis she makes is that the "emphatic 'ειναι'" in line 192 "shows that she is determined to regard it [the lock] hopefully" (CN6).

Another case in which Woolf develops a line of reasoning is in her notes on line 317 (which she misidentifies as 316). In this scene, Orestes is planning his vengeance and invokes Agamemnon's assistance by saying, in Verrall's translation: "*Or.* O father strange and terrible, what can I say, what do, to waft my signal from so far thither, **where thou art anchored fast**?" (Verrall 219). For the line at issue, bolded in English above, Woolf accepts Verrall's interpretation but with an explicit disagreement about the best reason to translate εὐναί as "anchors" instead of "beds." Indeed, while Verrall thinks, as Woolf reports, that a "waft with a favouring breeze would be ineffective to wake a sleeper" in bed but "would reach one" who is simply "anchored," Woolf remarks, "But is it not the point of Orestes' exclamation that he doubts that anything can waken him?" (CN8–9). The protagonist, she reflects, is (ideally) trying to speak to the spirit of his father Agamemnon, who is dead and so eternally sleeping, and posing the recurrent question whether the souls of ancestors can perceive and benefit from the prayers of their descendants. Woolf declares, nevertheless, that the presence of the word ἔχουσιν, which means "they hold, detain," seems to her "a better argument for anchor than the other" argument given by Verrall (CN9; see CN9n142–45).

Throughout her notebook, Woolf marks doubts or inquiries, after translation or comment, with self-posed questions that help her interpret the text. For instance, she asks if the pronoun ὑμας (you) in line 151 "refer[s] to [the] Chorus" (CN4), whom Electra invites to sing (see CN4n73). And when in line 224 Orestes wonders why his sister catches the traces of him in the lock of hair and in his footsteps but does not recognize him in person (see CN6n107–08), Woolf writes: "Might not this be an oblique way of hinting that the poet himself is a little amazed at her acuteness?" (CN6). Later, Woolf also comments on Clytemnestra's request for an axe (line 890) by putting quotation marks around the phrase "this evil has now reached such a point" (CN11), which is similar in sense to Verrall's translation (see CN11n191), and adding that "one can only kill or be killed" (CN11). Woolf thinks on this "evil" by asking, "Does she [Clytemnestra] mean the whole tragedy of the house, in which case she is a passive instrument; or her own private act, in which she is active and responsible?" (CN11–12). In a later question, Woolf imagines possible stagings and asks whether what she defines as "a cryptic chorus" in lines 934–70 is sung "while the murder [of Clytemnestra] is being done off or on the stage" (CN12). What finally emerges from these few moments of self-reflection is that Woolf is particularly interested in investigating human instincts and especially women's. In particular, it is evident that here she starts her careful judgment of Clytemnestra's presumed guilt and the (in)justice of the treatment she suffers.

Woolf's original interventions, not numerous but interesting, for the most part converge on the description and appreciation of Aeschylus's literary style. She defines a "packed description of Electra's weeping" (CN5–6) that the playwright makes in line 184, when the protagonist confesses her inability to avoid crying over Orestes's tress. Here, the focus is on the word δίψιοι, with reference to which Woolf translates the whole line, "thirsty for the omen drops which are restrained" (CN6). Woolf thus captures but condenses a sense of Verrall's explanation given in his commentary (see CN6n 91–93).

Another example of Woolf's originality concerns the word δυσχειμέρους (line 270), which Aesychlus uses to describe Orestes's inner state. Here, Woolf does not put the English meaning of "wintry" (see CN7n120–21) yet "observe[s] that almost all Aeschylus' epithets profit by a literal translation" (CN7), which is in this case would be something like "bearing winter hardly" (my translation). Shortly after, Orestes is described in line 274 as "scowling upon compensations which would beggar" his mother and her lover usurper (CN7n122). Following Verrall's interpretation (CN8n124), Woolf remarks that he "demands life and not money" and supplies the following explanation, which summarizes the scholar's comment on this passage: "If you take it to mean that he scowls on losses of property due him you belittle his action and the whole story" (CN8). Indeed, Orestes's vengeance must be much greater because he was forced to leave not only his house but also his family, hiding in exile after Agamemnon's murder. "The beauty" of this passage, Woolf claims, "lies in the majestic arrangement" of the words (CN8). In her next note on lines 277–81, she praises the "astonishing closeness of description and metaphor," where the corruption of the flesh is described as a spinning web (CN8; see CN8n126).

Other annotations express in short sentences the hidden intentions that Woolf thinks some passages convey, trying to articulate Aeschylus's dramatic strategies. In some cases, she reports ideas found in Verrall's critical apparatus, summarizing and re-arranging them. This procedure is observable in a pair of comments that start with the letter "A." (for Aeschylus). In the first, Woolf notes that the playwright "expresses the poignancy of the suggestion by contradicting it," by describing as a laughter a cry in line 30 (CN1–2; see CN2n13). In the second example, he "supposes foreknowledge of the story on the part of his audience" so that the meaning of the queen's prophecy-dream would be clear (CN2; see CN2n20). Elsewhere, Woolf's comments on Aeschylus's subtext are original and apparently not derived from the interpretation of another scholar. For example, in introducing the prayer to Hermes to summon the spirits of the dead from line 125, she notes that Electra "has waked her audience to a fit state to receive it," meaning that the character wants to impress people in Thebes by evoking their ancestors (CN4).

Finally, in the final pages of the manuscript, Woolf translates Orestes's long monologue in lines 971–1004 without note or explanation. (This is a procedure which she also adopts in some pages of her study of *Agamemnon.*) Verrall appreciates Orestes's monologue and writes in his note: "The rapid fall of this speech, as the speaker's mind gives way, from the dignity of the commencement to the confusion and ruin of the close, has always appeared to me, as doubtless to many, one of the finest things in literature" (139). This comment must have piqued Woolf's curiosity to study the passage more scrupulously and to challenge herself with its translation. However, this might not be the only or the main reason she chose it as a conclusion to her study.

Indeed, I believe that at least two other factors inspire Woolf to focus on Orestes's monologue at the close of her notebook: the problem of lifeless bodies, associated with Orestes's uneasiness, and the treatment of Clytemnestra, which is unfair in Woolf's eyes. The horror of the death, though it is the result of a sacrifice that is considered necessary, is the striking image that preludes the later notes leading to *Mrs. Dalloway*. Clytemnestra's death, in particular, cannot be justified, though her son attempts to demonstrate his rightness with reference to Apollo's law. Indeed, in 1907 Woolf does not and never seems to study the *Eumenides*, the third play of the trilogy, in which Orestes is freed from the fury of avenging spirits. Instead, she goes back to *Agamemnon* in the early 1920s, in which the queen plays the decisive role in killing her husband. Woolf herself defends Clytemnestra's action, understanding her reasons as a betrayed wife and mother. In "On Not Knowing Greek," she explicitly claims that "Clytemnestra is no unmitigated villainess" (*E*4 41). Quoting line 770 of Sophocles's *Electra*, "'δεινὸν τὸ τίκτειν ἐστίν' . . . 'there is a strange power in motherhood,'" Woolf advocates on the queen's behalf, concluding that "[i]t is no murderess, violent and unredeemed, whom Orestes kills within the house, and [whom] Electra bids him utterly destroy" (*E*4 41). Woolf insists on Clytemnestra's motivation as a mother; however noble their intentions, her persecutors (her children) are ruthless killers. By building the discourse on a series of negations, Woolf highlights the extreme humanity of the queen, whose character is made up of lights and shadows and in the end is the very center of both the *Choephori* and *Agamemnon* notebooks.

Note to the Transcription

The following is an annotated transcription of Virginia Woolf's *Choephori Notebook*. I keep the pagination and lineation of the original text throughout and place emphasis where Woolf does (underlining specific words). I place in chevrons < __ > writing that Woolf cancelled or modified, adding in note an explanation or hypothesis of what she meant to write (whenever it is needed and if it is possible to guess).

I always use the en-dash "–" and not a hyphen "-" for consistency and because it is not possible to establish a distinction between the two in the holograph. I do differentiate the equal sign (=) from the colon (:), generally used by the author to introduce translations or linguistic explanation (equal sign) and summary or comment (colon). I keep the distinction between single and double quotation marks, which Woolf uses without specific criterion.

I supply in brackets missing parts of the manuscript's abbreviations, as well as apostrophes in possessive nouns and dots after line numbers. I insert a quotation mark in brackets after a word ([?]) whenever I am unable to decipher Woolf's handwriting. Everything that appears in brackets ([__]) is my intervention, unless otherwise noted (as in line 320). Everything that appears in parentheses (__) is attributable to Woolf.

In notes, I specify the tragedy's line numbers in Verrall's edition of the *Cheophori* and indicate when Woolf miscounts lines. In notes, I also rewrite in their canonical form all Greek words or expressions that Woolf "simplifies" (without accents or spirits), and I give the English literal meaning of the quotations in original language whenever it is omitted.

Finally, I also report in full the passages from Verrall's critical apparatus where Woolf took information to make evident her research, summary, and re-elaboration.

Key of symbols used in transcription

For further clarity I provide a list of symbols used in the transcription:

< > contain cancelled or modified text by Woolf
[ ] contain my interventions
[?] stands for uncertain deciphering

Acknowledgments

I first discovered this manuscript while I was researching the *Agamemnon Notebook* for my PhD. Looking for unedited writings about Greek literature and culture in her personal studies, I found out that not only one, but two texts on Aeschylus's trilogy were held in the New York Public Library, and the second was the *Choephori Notebook*. At first, I read and analyzed it for the purpose of my thesis, comparing it with other notebooks, but then I decided that it deserved "a room of its own" in the wide field of Woolf's relationship with the classics. What finally got me to make the choice to transcribe the notebook was the centennial of *Mrs. Dalloway*, which I consider tightly related to the manuscript.

This project found its way thanks to the following people, to whom I would like to express gratitude for their help and support. First, my work owes its birth to Julie Carlsen and Emma Davidson from the Berg Collection of the New York Public Library. They provided me high-definition scans of all the pages of the manuscript when I could not travel to U.S. due to the Covid pandemic and helped me also with the in-person study of the manuscript when I finally visited the archive, being also very patient and kind during the whole follow-up process. I would also like to thank Theodore Koulouris from the University of Sussex, always ready to help whenever I had doubts with some transcription but also of great support and encouragement. He suggested that I consider publishing this work and get in contact with Michelle Barrett, who is also very enthusiastic at the idea and collaborated to make Woolf's notebooks freely available on WoolfNotes.com. Also, I am very grateful to the Society of Authors for granting me permission, as the representative of the Literary Estate of Virginia Woolf, to publish my transcription of the manuscript. Finally, I would like to thank Benjamin D. Hagen and the journal's editorial board for accommodating this important resource in *Woolf Studies Annual*.

Works Cited

"Additions Index." Barrett and Silver.

Barrett, Michèle and Brenda Silver. *WoolfNotes*. King's London College, woolfnotes.com.

Browning, Elizabeth Barrett. *Aurora Leigh*. London: Chapman and Hall, 1857.

Dalgarno, Emily. *Virginia Woolf and the Visible World*. Cambridge UP, 2007.

Daugherty, Beth Rigel. *Virginia Woolf's Apprenticeship: Becoming an Essayist*. Edinburgh UP, 2022.

Fowler, Rowena. "Moments and Metamorphoses: Virginia Woolf's Greece." *Comparative Literature*, vol. 60, no. 3, 1999, pp. 217–42.

Koulouris, Theodore. *Hellenism and Loss in the Work of Virginia Woolf*. Ashgate, 2011.

———. "Virginia Woolf's 'Greek Notebook' (VS Greek and Latin Studies): An

Annotated Transcription." *Woolf Studies Annual*, vol. 25, 2019, pp. 1–72.

Mills, Jean. *Virginia Woolf, Jane Ellen Harrison, and the Spirit of Modernist Classicism*. Ohio State UP, 2014.

Prins, Yopie. "OTOTOTOI: Virginia Woolf and 'The Naked Cry' of Cassandra." *'Agamemnon' in Performance 458 BC to AD 2004*, edited by Fiona Macintosh et al., Oxford UP, 2005, pp. 163–85.

Silver, Brenda R. *Virginia Woolf's Reading Notebooks*. Princeton UP, 1983.

"Silver Index." Barrett and Silver.

Snaith, Anna and Kenyon-Jones, Christine. "Tilting at Universities: Virginia Woolf at King's College London." *Woolf Studies Annual*, vol. 16, 2010, pp. 1–44.

Verrall, Arthur Woollgar. *The 'Choephori' of Aeschylus*. Macmillan & Company, 1893.

Woolf, Virginia. "Character in Fiction." *The Essays of Virginia Woolf: 1919–1924*. Edited by Andrew McNeillie, Hogarth, 1988, pp. 420–38. Vol. 3 of *The Essays of Virginia Woolf*.

———. *Choephori of Aeschylus. Edited by A. W. Verrall.* Holograph reading notes. 1907 Jan., 16 p (Berg RN28). The Henry W. and Albert A. Berg Collection of English and American Literature," The New York Public Library, Astor, Lenox and Tilden Foundations. New York, NYPL:

———. *The Diary of Virginia Woolf: 1920–1924*. Edited by Anne Olivier Bell, Hogarth, 1978. Vol. 2 of *The Diary of Virginia Woolf*.

———. "Miss Case." *A Passionate Apprentice: The Early Journals, 1897–1909*. Edited by Mitchell A. Leaska, Hogarth, 1990, pp. 181–84.

———. "Miss Janet Case: Classical Scholar and Teacher." *The Essays of Virginia Woolf: 1933–1941 and Additional Essays: 1906–1924*, edited by Stuart N. Clarke, Hogarth, 2011, pp. 111–14. Vol. 6 of *The Essays of Virginia Woolf*.

———. "On Not Knowing Greek." *The Essays of Virginia Woolf: 1925–1928*, edited by Andrew McNeillie, Hogarth, 1994, pp. 38–51. Vol. 4 of *The Essays of Virginia Woolf*.

———. *A Room of One's Own*. Hogarth, 1929.

CN0 [Title Page]

Choephori
of Aeschylus.
Edited by
A. W. Verrall.
–
Jan.[uary] 1907

CN1

1.

Orestes:
1. Hermes is invoked in three aspects – as
God of the dead; God of ancestry –
specially interested in the house of
Atreus – God of victory. because he
was God of good fortune.[1]
3. ἡκω[2] = present perfect: I am come
κατερχομαι[3] = continuous present: am here[4]
5. κλυειν[5] = listen with your ear.
ακουσαι[6] = hear with your mind.[7]

[1] Woolf notes here each of the three aspects of Hermes's divinity that appear in Verrall's translation, the first line, uttered by Orestes, reads: "O Hermes, god of the underworld, god of my fathers, god before whom are done feats of strength" (Verrall 212). In his earlier note to the Greek text, Verrall elaborates on these aspects, "Hermes is invoked in three aspects, each bearing upon the prayer of Orestes for his aid, (1) as χθόνιος or ψυχοπομπός, as a *god of the lower world* and specially conductor of the dead; (2) as πατρώιος, *god of ancestry*, not only as being (with Zeus, Apollo, and others) one of the gods with whom the worship of ancestors was connected but also as specially interested in the house of Atreus; and (3) as *president* or *overseer of victory*, an allusion to his functions as the god of *good fortune* and *success* in general, particularly in contests of strength and of craft" (Verrall 1).
[2] ἥκω. Here, Woolf records the spirit but omits the accent.
[3] κατέρχομαι.
[4] Woolf expresses here two aspects of these verbs: grammatical and lexical; Verrall translates these verbs, "I have entered" and "standing" (212). Elaboration found in Verrall's commentary: "Note that these are different tenses, and each appropriate: ἥκω is *present perfect*, the mere arrival is complete: κατέρχομαι a *continuous* present; the κάθοδος or *return* from exile is in progress only, and will be complete when Orestes is restored to his rights" (1).
[5] κλύειν.
[6] ἀκοῦσαι.
[7] Woolf paraphrases the original meaning through a poetic English rendition, drawing a figurative distinction between ear (external sense organ) and mind (internal understanding). Verrall's commentary explains: "κλύειν, ακούσαι. The idea is repeated for pathos and emphasis, but with an increase of meaning, ακούσαι signifying not merely *hear*, but *hearken*, *i.e. respond*, *comply*" (2). Verrall translates this latter verb, "to hear and respond" (212). See my Introduction.

Gives two locks of hair – one to
the river God 'for nurture', for
this was the God of his
country; and the other to the
dead.[8]
15. νερτεροις μειλιγμασιν[9] = after
propitiation – so called
either because it was after the
death – or because it was
to propitiate one of the dead[.][10]
30. 'αγελαστος'[11] = epithet applied
to the <noise> miserable plight
of the woman, which led her to
tear her clothes; the noise of the
rending having suggested laughter,[12] A[eschylus]:

[8] In Verrall's translation, Orestes offers "a lock to Inachus for nurture and this second lock for mourning" (212). Woolf summarizes the conceptual elaboration of this offering that Verrall develops in his notes. For Verrall, Orestes "performs two religious duties, which he had been compelled to neglect, the offering of hair to *the dead* and to *the river-god* of Argos. The latter was done upon attaining manhood. … The association of the customs here is interesting, and it is unfortunate that we have not the whole passage. Probably they were based upon the same notion, the wish to bring the person of the giver into permanent connexion with a source of help and strength, that is, in the one case with the deceased ancestor, in the other with the god of his country, supposed to be especially embodied in the life-giving river. … The offering to Inachus has been made already; that to Agamemnon Orestes now makes, by laying the lock upon the tomb.— θρεπτήριον, an offering *for nurture*, πενθητήριον, *for mourning*" (2).
[9] νερτέροις μειλίγμασιν.
[10] Woolf summarizes here Verrall's notes to the Greek text: "14—15. 'Shall I suppose this libation-bearing to be an after-propitiation of my father?' [...] νερτέροις, which is strictly comparative, combines the signification of (1) *later* and (2) *lower*. The first conjecture of Orestes is that the funeral ceremony is for a *recent* death (*v.* 13). As compared with offerings made at or immediately after a funeral, offerings made to a person long deceased, like Agamemnon, might be called νέρτερα for two reasons, either (1) because in themselves *later*, *subsequent*, […] or certainly (2), by transference of epithet, because made to one absolutely departed and belonging to the νέρτεροι, which, in the primitive view, a person whose body was yet among the living could hardly be said to do. It is reasonable to suppose that the epithet was or had been technically used for such offerings" (Verrall 3).
[11] ἀγελάστος, literally "grave, gloomy," masculine. Here and later in her notebook, Woolf indicates the nominative singular (base form that is found in most dictionaries) of the words even if they appear in the text in another case or number. In this example the dative plural ἀγελάστοις is found in Aeschylus's line.
[12] Verrall translates this word as "laughter-mocking woe" (212). See also following note.

CN2

expresses the poignancy of the suggestion
by contradicting it.[13]
(32).[14] φοιβος:[15] the inspiration, which is
here an allusion to Clytaemnestra.[16]
The lines about the dream (37-41)
signify that the interpreters
were inspired by the Gods; they
do not say what the interpretation

[13] Woolf summarizes here Verrall's notes on this line: "ἀγελάστοις. This epithet, at first sight feeble, is to be explained by the fondness of Greek poets, and of Aeschylus especially, for description *by contrast*. A figure is suggested, and the inapplicable parts of it are excluded by contrary epithets. … So here the words λακίς and ἔφλαδον (cf. παφλάζω) suggested to the ear of Aeschylus the sound of *laughter* rather than of *lamentation*; and he makes a fresh point by correcting this suggestion with the contrary epithet ἀγελάστος" (Verrall 4).

[14] On this page, the line numbers are circled. The parentheses here represent these circles.

[15] φοῖβος.

[16] Woolf accepts Verrall's interpretation of the Greek text and focuses on his reference to Queen Clytemnestra. Verrall translates lines 32–36: "For there came a *spirit true*, lifting the hair, who prophesied to the house in dreams of sleep; angry his breath; and in the dead hour of dark his cry from the inmost room rang out with terror, breaking upon our women's chambers" (212–13, emphasis added).

Verrall explicates the obscure sense of these allusions in his commentary: "… φοῖβος, ὀνειρόμαντις, μυχόθεν … [refer] directly to the inner women's chamber of the house, but figuratively to the oracular *adytum*, such as the sanctuary and subterranean grotto at Delphi, commonly called μυχός … It appears not improbable, since the purpose of these details is to connect the dream with the impending vengeance of *Delphi* … that there was an analogy between the circumstances of the dream and those of the divine command. It has been noticed in the Introduction that, in the story of Aeschylus, Orestes did not, so far as appears, consult Apollo on a project of revenge, or conceive such a project independently at all. The special injunction came originally from the god, and may well have been given, through the prophetess, in some such way as this parallel would suggest.

"... φοῖβος. I think, though it is of little importance, that, as this word … signifies *an inspiring power*, making prophetic the person (here Clytaemnestra) into whom it enters. Whatever may be the etymology of the name φοῖβος, or the true origin of its application to Apollo, it was in fact associated, as usage proves, with *inspiring possession*, and practically had this meaning. Such a use was probably far older than the identification of the φοῖβος at Delphi with Apollo, the invader and appropriator of that sanctuary … [T]he inspiring power was exercised *through a dream* and *in a private house*, in these respects otherwise than as that of the great φοῖβος commonly was. … The 'terror' and 'cry' are literally those of Clytaemnestra, who is figuratively identified with the φοῖβος" (Verrall 5).

was.[17] This <sh>[18] is to show that
the facts (of the snake born of C.[lytaemnestra] which
stung her) are a divine and true
symbol; but that the interpret<ers>ation
<interpret it> is wrong<ly>.[19] A[eschylus]:
supposes foreknowledge of the story
on the part of his audience.[20]

[17] Verrall translates these chorus lines: "And they who read this dream spake bold as from a god to whom they must answer, and said that it was the wrathful complaint of a soul below, angry against the slayer" (212–13). The explanation he gives in his notes to the Greek text are essential for understanding Woolf's notes and are worth quoting here in full: "38. θεόθεν ἔλακον ὑπέγγυοι: 'uttered from the gods to whom they are responsible.' ... The reason for insisting thus on the guarantee of the interpreters is that the interpretation is *misleading*, false as well as true, and that this whole character of it, the falsehood as well as the truth, is no human error or deception, but calculated for the divine purpose. …

"39—41. It is important to observe, with regard to the dream, that this 'interpretation' is a true and scientific piece of mantic art, but nevertheless essentially and fatally *wrong*. Clytaemnestra dreamed that she gave birth to a snake which, when put to her breast, wounded her. Now a snake was the regular symbol of things subterranean, and especially of the *grave*; it pointed therefore to danger from the dead (οἵ γᾶς νέρθεν). The interpreters, fixing upon this, took the birth of the snake to be *metaphorical*, and supposed it to signify merely that the danger threatened Clytaemnestra as the person who had *produced* or *caused* the death (τοῖς κτανοῦσι). They accordingly advised her to appease the spirit of Agamemnon. They did not think of danger from Orestes, supposed to be far away and helpless, and therefore did not see that the birth was meant *literally*; still less did they foresee that Orestes, though alive, was to execute his vengeance by pretending to be *dead*, and in this way, as well as by representing his dead father, corresponded to the symbol of the snake. Least of all did they observe that, as the casual expressions of the chorus have just indicated, the minor circumstances of the warning pointed to danger *from Delphi*. In fact the dream was κάρτα μάντις, far more significant than they supposed. This is just one of those providential schemes in which Aeschylus and his instructors delighted. If the advisers of Clytaemnestra had been suffered to read the warning fully, Orestes must have been detected and lost. But though miraculously exact, it was framed and intended to mislead; and the only effect of it is, that Electra is sent by Clytaemnestra herself to Agamemnon's grave, and there quietly and without suspicion *meets Orestes*, a thing which, but for this divine assistance, must have been hard to effect. And since the warning conveyed by the imperfect interpretation is itself inspired and true in fact, as far as it goes, the triumph of 'Phoebus the true" is (according to Delphic doctrine) absolutely immaculate and complete" (6).

[18] Here Woolf probably intended to write "shows."

[19] Woolf here modifies the phrase "the interpreters interpret it wrongly" to "the interpretation is wrong." This a comment summarizes the sense of Aesychlus's lines.

[20] Woolf records information drawn from Verrall's notes on Aeschylus's narrative strategy: "With regard to the dream, as elsewhere, we remark that Aeschylus assumes the story, in all its parts and bearings, to be known, as no doubt it was, to the audience, and makes his performers speak as they probably would in the supposed circumstances, not as they have to do in the ordinary conditions of the drama. To talk of an interpretation without mentioning what was interpreted is perfectly natural: indeed the prevailing stiffness of stage-dialogue is due to the fact that such natural phaenomena of speech can rarely be imitated. But unless the audience knew all beforehand, the arrangement adopted would be practically unintelligible"

(60). It is simplest to take this
as referring to the three stages
light, twilight and darkness.
Comparing them with the [three][21]
punishments soon, late & never.[22]
(69)[.][23] παναρκετας[24] may be[25] <n>[26]
nom[inative]: with ατη,[27] as it
precedes <no>[28] νοσου.[29]

(Verrall 6–7).

[21] Woolf writes the numeral "3 here. I adopt "three" for a stylistic reason, since all over the manuscript the author uses ciphers for line numbers and letters for explanations (as the "three" of the previous line proves). My intervention is only meant to maintain consistency in the transcript.

[22] In this line, the chorus reflects on the apparent impunity of Clytemnestra. Woolf records the meaning of a metaphor that Verrall elaborates in his notes: "60–63. 'Coming swiftly upon some in the day, though sometimes the punishment bides in the twilight and grows, and sometimes darkness takes the offender ere aught is done'. This reservation suggests itself naturally in the present case, when justice has already been long delayed, and the criminals are still in apparent strength and prosperity ... It is simplest to take the stages of *day*, *twilight*, *darkness* as typical merely of three possibilities in punishment, *soon*, *late*, and (in this life) *never*. ... At any rate this is part of the meaning. Others ... refer them rather, or also, to three varieties of crime, *manifest*, *concealed for a time*, *concealed to the end.* The vague words certainly admit this; but we should observe on the contrary that, in the case in view, the murder of Agamemnon, concealment is out of the question, nor is 'concealment' plainly mentioned anywhere in the passage" (9).

[23] Actually line 68.

[24] παναρκέτας. Literally "all-sufficing."

[25] Here the chorus predicts misfortunes that will results from bad behavior. In his notes, Verrall explains: "*a plague runs penetrating through the sinner, and breeds in every part disease* [...] παναρκέτας νόσου βρύειν: 'inexhaustible in producing disease', *i.e.* 'which will go on spreading till it overcomes'. παναρκέτας, a unique word, but unexceptionable, may be either nom. ... If we follow the common opinion in supposing the subject of βρύειν to be τὸν αἴτιον ('so that he is full of disease'), then παναρκέτας must be genitive ... But there is much to be said for referring the adj. to ἄτη, an alternative which has not been sufficiently considered. For (1) in the phrase 'all-sufficing (inexhaustible) to teem (produce) disease', the connexion of the infinitive is close and natural, whereas, if it depends on διαφέρει τὸν αἴτιον, the connexion is loose, remote, and not easily apprehended: (2) the hearer must naturally in the first instance refer παναρκέτας to the preceding ἄτη, and will not change his opinion, when νόσου follows" (10).

[26] Here Woolf probably started to write "nominative," but then she decided to put it in the following line, giving the explanation immediately afterward. Note that, in a departure from Verrall, although she leaves "may be" to frame the sentence as a hypothesis, she does not record the two possibilities analyzed by the scholar. However, she records the possibility that he considers more believable, indicating that she is persuaded by his reasoning.

[27] ἄτη. Literally "reckless guilt" or "sin," feminine. In the text it is found the nominative singular ἄτη, which Woolf reports as it is also the base form (see CN1n11).

[28] Here Woolf probably started to transliterate νόσου but then decided to leave it in Greek.

[29] νόσος. Literally "disease," feminine. In the text it is found the genitive singular νόσου but

(83)[.][30] παχνουμινη[31] frozen rigid –
applied to the attitude of Electra
because <El[ectra]> it is like that of Niobe.[32]

CN3

85.[33] τυφω[34]= gen.[itive] fr.[om] τυφως[35] –
governs τωνδε.[36]
the bewilderment of a dust-storm[37]
reflects E[lectra']s: bewilderment as well
as shock.[38]
91.[39] εστ'[40] emphatic – the law is –
a continuous present.[41]

Woolf reports the base form as in the other examples showed before.

[30] Actually line 82.

[31] παχνουμένη.

[32] Here a servant is mourning on behalf of his mistress. Woolf records the comparison and the still image that Verrall analyzes in his notes: "*80—82. Yet I weep, veiling my tears (so wild is the destiny of my lords), for one whom sorrow hidden is freezing into ice* [...] παχνουμένη, Electra, whom, during these last words, they timidly approach. Since the entrance she has been sitting at the tomb, motionless, and probably with her face covered, pondering and forming the resolve which she presently discloses. The fondness of Aeschylus for such a situation in the opening of a play is noticed in the *Frogs*; where his Niobe is cited as a famous example of it. The expression παχνουμένη looks like an actual reminiscence of Niobe 'frozen to stone' [in Ovid's *Metamorphoses*], and probably suggested to Sophocles the explicit comparison between Niobe and Electra which occurs in his corresponding scene in *Electra*" (13).

[33] Actually 86.

[34] τυφῶ. Literally "of a typhoon." For this word and the following explanation see note 37.

[35] τυφώς. Nominative form.

[36] τῶνδε. Demonstrative pronoun, "of this."

[37] Electra is speaking to the chorus. See Verrall's commentary: "85—86. *Give me your counsel upon our bewildering situation.* τῶνδε (*the present matter*) depends, as gen. of equivalent, on τυφῶ: the situation is metaphorically a τυφώς. This energetic figure cannot be rendered in English, because the terrible phaenomenon of the 'whirlwind' or 'dust-storm' is to us practically unknown. It is powerfully described by Sophocles [in the *Antigone*]. By the sudden attack of its stifling cloud men were sometimes even deprived of their senses; and popular language borrowed from it a synonym for *idiotic* … The command of Clytaemnestra, that offerings shall be made on her behalf at the grave of her victim, is compared to a τυφώς, not only as an astounding surprise, but also because it has placed Electra in a position of bewildering difficulty … The author of the MS. reading took τύφω for an intransitive verb, connected with τῦφος *smoke*, and meaning 'I am perplexed'" (14).

[38] Woolf's re-elaboration of Verrall's assessment of Aeschylus's meaning. See previous note and my Introduction.

[39] Actually line 93.

[40] ἔστ(ι). Third person singular of verb "to be" in indicative present.

[41] In Verrall's translation, Electra prays in a way that "stands in the costume of men" (213). Woolf records a grammatical remark found in his notes on Aesychlus's use of the verb: "ἔστι:

97. καθαρμαθ'[42] = the thing cleansed
away – thus, the pollution.[43]
104. [Electra] expresses doubt whether they [the slaves]
can rise higher than the present
time – & thus stimulates their
self-respect[44] – not 'if you have
any better suggestion to make'
The effect in such a case would
throw doubt on their power to
give her advice wh.[ich] is precisely
what she does not want to do.
The present would be a correct
but pointless remark.[45]
110:[46] When you pour out, speak
what is sacred to those who
love.
Whom of our friends can I address
as people who love?[47]

---

not 'is' but 'has been and is' … The word marks the custom as immemorial and 'standing' ... The general assumption is certainly right, that ἐστί (not emphatic) is here inappropriate ... As I think the emphasis intentional, I make no change" (15).

[42] καθάρμαθ(α).

[43] Verrall renders the whole line as follows: "Or without word or rite, in such fashion as my father was put away, shall I pour this out for earth to drink [?]" (213). Electra refers to the libations that Clytemnestra asked her to put on Agamemnon's grave. In his notes, Verrall also adds: "'Am I to offer them without a word and thus repeat the insult of his death [and funeral], flinging them out like so much pollution?' Electra so words the proposal as to assign a reason for rejecting it" (16). Woolf records the sense of something thrown away or wasted.

[44] As I claim in the Introduction, Woolf gives here the sense of Electra's line, addressed to the slaves, following Verrall's notes: "104. *Speak, if thou canst grasp anything beyond this present!* Seeing that they still hesitate, she tries a solemn and personal appeal to one of the oldest, pointing, as she speaks, to Agamemnon's grave … The fear of Electra is, that, demoralized by subjection, the slaves may *not* have faith enough to rise above their habitual acquiescence in the will of Clytaemnestra. It has been seen, that they have but a weak trust in the justice of this world, and no outlook beyond. As it is essential to the plot that they should play a very dangerous and heroic part, this awakening of their conscience is a fit commencement. The form λέγοις ἄν implies here not merely a softening of the command, but also a doubt whether it will be effectual" (17).

[45] In his notes, Verrall writes: "The common interpretation 'Speak, if you have any suggestion better than mine' leads naturally to the conjecture ἔχεις, since, by expressing doubt of the slaves' capacity to advise her, Electra would only make her appeal weaker. It is also in itself pointless and inappropriate, as is seen by those who, assuming ἔχεις, propose to omit the whole verse" (17). Woolf agrees with Verrall discarding of this translation, as I note in my Introduction.

[46] Actually 108.

[47] New translation of an exchange between a slave and Electra, presenting differences from Verrall's translation. See Introduction and Verrall's commentary: "108. 'Speak, when thou

A.[eschylus] parodies, it seems, from
the matter in hand.[48]

CN4

'In the obscurity of the language lies
its dramatic merit.'[49]
Electra is urging them on to
commit themselves in speech by
feigning ignorance.[50]
125. E[lectra']s. prayer[51] – now that she
has waked her audience to a fit
state to receive it.[52]
125. "δαιμονας"[53] her ancestors.[54]
'επισκοπους'[55] which look towards[56]

---

pourest, as religion bids *those who love*', literally 'utter what is religious for those who love (to utter)', *i.e.* the only proper and permitted prayer, that the dead will vouchsafe his presence and blessing *to those who love him* … What she [the slave] means, but as yet dares only hint, is that to which Electra has directly led, that the impious offering of Clytaemnestra should be converted into a pious offering on behalf of Electra herself ...

"109. *To whom among our friends am I to apply your 'τοῖς εὔφροσιν'?* She [Electra] wishes them to name themselves" (Verrall 18). Regarding issues in notes 47–50 below, see also my Introduction.

[48] Woolf comments on the ironic meaning of the question.

[49] Woolf quotes this sentence directly from Verrall's note to line 108, which reads: "The objections to this verse proceed on the assumption that we are to find in it, plainly expressed, the ἐπεύχου which Electra reads into it. Hence, since φθέγγου σεμνά cannot mean 'invoke blessings', many read κεδνά. But why not then εὔχου κεδνά, since φθέγγεσθαι. is not 'to invoke'? In the obscurity of the language lies its dramatic merit.—The [Scholia] would undoubtedly disprove the reading σεμνά, and φθέγγου … if we knew (1) that the writer is trustworthy, and also (2) that he is translating word for word. As we know nothing of him but this note, we conclude in the alternative, that if he was a good scholar, he is giving only the implied sense, which he gives rightly, and if he is translating, his εὖξαι ἀγαθὰ is no more than an ignorant guess" (18).

[50] Woolf's own summary of the sense of these lines.

[51] Woolf refers to the invocation to Hermes at the beginning of Electra's speech, which Verrall translates, "O Messenger, mightiest to pass between those above and below, O Hermes of the Deep, be messenger for me, and summon the spirits under earth to hear my prayers, my prayers that seek the regard of paternal eyes; summon Earth herself, who bringeth all things to birth, reareth them, and receiveth again into her womb" (214).

[52] Woolf's own comment on Aeschylus's strategies. See my Introduction.

[53] δαίμονας.

[54] See Verrall's notes: "125. τοὺς δαίμονας: the spirits of her ancestors … [Electra] imagines that the rite brings the ancestral ghosts themselves to the tomb (as Darius comes visibly in the *Persae*), that she, or rather her personified 'prayer', is now face to face with them, though they are not seen, and that they will be affected by the look of their daughter's eyes" (19–20).

[55] ἐπισκόπους.

[56] Literal translation given by Verrall in his note: "ομμάτων ἐπισκόπους, literally, 'which look towards eyes', that they may be looked upon in return" (20).

taken with ευχας[57] – not with
δαιμονας[58] because of the order.[59]
127.[60] "& you earth, I pray, who
producest everything &
nourishing it conceives it again"[61]
κυμα[62] = concept, embryo. She
may therefore bring back the
dead. This argument is used
by Lucretius.[63]
132. πεπραγμενοι[64] bargained away[65]
μετα[66] = by way of change instead.[67]

[57] εὐχάς.
[58] δαίμονας.
[59] See Verrall: "In the conjectural texts … ἐπισκόπους is mostly referred to δαίμονας: but the order indicates that it belongs to εὐχάς … Thus here the description πατρώων ομμάτων επισκόπους is by δε marked as a correction or extension of the preceding εὐχάς, 'prayers, which are not common prayers, but more, when they thus meet my ancestors face to face'" (20).
[60] Actually 127–28.
[61] Woolf's translation differs from Verrall's: "summon Earth herself, who bringeth all things to birth, reareth them, and receiveth again into her womb" (214). The last word that Woolf adopts seems to derive from Verrall's note on the Greek text: "128. αὖθις … λαμβάνει: *doth again conceive them*. κῦμα (*concept*) is correlative to τίκτεται, and τῶνδε is gen. of equivalent; literally 'receives them again, as a concept'" (20). See my Introduction.
[62] κῦμα. In line 128.
[63] Woolf's departs from Verrall's notes, referring to *The Rerum Natura* instead of the New Testament (Verrall's comparative text). See my Introduction and Verrall's notes: "This, as τὰ πάντα shows, is not to be limited to plants, which drop their seed, though that is the fact which suggests the idea and the application. *All things*, men among them, are born of the earth, and received again into her womb. The prayer implied is that, as she restores the plants, so she will now permit the return of the dead. In fact the thought is precisely that which St. Paul (1 Cor. 15. 36) adopts with an immense extension of meaning" (20).
[64] πεπραγμένοι.
[65] Woolf records the core word of Electra's speech, which resumes her and her brother's situation. The whole sentence covers lines 132–37, which in Verrall's translation reads: "For now *are we vagabonds* as it were, b*argained away* by our mother (to purchase for a husband Aegisthus, partner with her in thy death), I into slavery, and Orestes into banishment from his wealth, while they proudly revel instead in that which thy labour won" (214, emphasis added). Verrall specifies in *Appendix I* that "in πεπραγμένοι, πράσσειν means 'to deal with by way of a πρᾶξις' or 'bargain', especially a dishonest bargain" (166).
[66] μέτα. In line 137.
[67] Woolf here takes information from Verrall's commentary in *Appendix I*: "Lastly, for μέτα … It is used in the primitive manner, as an independent adverb, meaning 'by way of change', *i.e. instead*. … The adverb signifies that Aegisthus the exile has *changed places* with Orestes the heir (see [*Agamemnon*]), and thus repeats the general conception of this passage" (167).

143.[68] ἡμιν[69]= in reference to us.[70]
151.[71] 'ὑμας[72]' – refer[s] to [the] Chorus?[73]

CN5

153.[74] ερυμα[75] – barrier against good & ill
= Grave mound.[76]
155. αγος[77] – an obscure word – combining
sense of reverence & horror – applied to
the grave.[78]
156.[79] εξ αμαυρας φρενος[80] –
applied to Agamemnon – his

[68] Line 142.

[69] ἡμῖν. Personal pronoun, first person plural.

[70] See Verrall's notes: "142. ἡμῖν…τοῖς ἐναντίοις datives 'of the person concerned', *in reference to us*, as in *v*. 146" (21).

[71] Line 150.

[72] ὑμᾶς. Literally "you" or "your."

[73] Woolf's questions the antecedent of the pronoun, asking to whom Electra is speaking (that is, the chorus). The whole sentence is rendered as follows by Verrall's translation: "To *you* it belongs by custom to crown the prayer with lamentation, swelling with *your* voices the hymn of the dead" (215, emphasis added). See also Introduction.

[74] Actually 154.

[75] ἔρυμα.

[76] See Verrall's commentary: "ἔρυμα. *This barrier of* (against) *good and ill*; the grave-mound, which, by its resemblance to a rampart, suggests and figures the separation between this world and the other" (23). This expression and the following lines are part of the chorus speech, which Verrall translates: "*Cho.* Let the tear fall with a plash, and be lost in the deep where our lord is lost, fall on this mound (which bars both ill things and good, this horror, from which men turn, against which they pray) as the offerings have been poured thereon. Hark to me, hark, O Majesty, O Master; let thy dim soul hear. Woe, woe, woe! O for some mighty man of arms to deliver the house, a warrior whose hands should shake at the foe the Scythian weapon back-bent in the using, and wield in closer fight the weapon firm to its hilt!" (215).

[77] ἄγος.

[78] Woolf summarizes Verrall's extensive note on line 155: "*This awful thing, from which we turn, against which we pray*, literally 'averting, prayed against'.— ἄγος. This word is extremely obscure to us, partly from its rarity, partly because the sphere of thought to which it belongs is remote from ours, partly because it is liable to confusion with ἄγος (conn. with ἅγιος). [...] What seems certain is that it meant (1) *pollution* and (2) *expiatory offering*, ideas which we conceive as contradictory. I believe that the account in L. and Sc. is correct, and that primarily it meant simply *a religious thing* or *emotion*; it described the object of that ancient (and savage) feeling, which combines *reverence* and *horror* in a manner to us hardly intelligible, in spite of the abundant explanations of anthropologists. In this sense the grave is here called an ἀπότροπον ἄγος, because it is a thing which men keep away from their lives and thoughts. To touch a grave was of course a religious *pollution*, and this is part of the idea, but a part only" (24).

[79] Actually lines 157.

[80] ἐξ ἀμαυρᾶς φρενός. See following note.

remote mind. Questioned.[81]
161. The Scythian (bow) & the
close fighting sword.[82]
164. Beginning of recognition
Scene.[83]
168.[84] τοδ[']85 = refers to the question
whether it were man[']s or woman[']s
hair. E.[lectra] has no doubt.[86]

[81] Woolf reports Verrall's interpretation. Verrall specifies in his commentary that "ἐξ ἀμαυρᾶς φρενός. ἀμαυρός is either literally 'dark, obscure', or metaphorically 'week'. The scholia hesitate between referring the φρήν (1) to the speakers themselves, and (2) to Agamemnon ... *Prima facie* it seems that the φρήν must be that of ὁ κλύων (*Let thy dark soul hear*), the consciousness of the dead being ἀμαυρός, because it belongs to the dim world" (24).
[82] Woolf adapts a translation based on the following note from Verrall: "161–163. 'Shaking at (the foe) the bow and wielding the sword'.— Σκυθικά: the epithet, like the grandiose Ἄρης and the double equipment, mark the deliverer as utterly remote and visionary, in contrast to the plain reality of the deliverer close at hand, whose presence they are just about to discover.— βέλη *weapons* generally ... The Scythian bow was shaped somewhat like a Σ ... and παλίντονα signifies that the pull of it was in the reverse direction from the setting on of its limbs.— σχέδια αὐτόκωπα: *close-fighting, hilt and all* ... because the swordsman's weapon remains entire in his grasp, whereas the arrow parts from the bow and wounds at a distance. The contrasted types are together put for 'every weapon'.— βέλη in *v.* 162 is perhaps to be omitted as an explanation; but Greek writers had not at all the modern dislike of mere repetition, and the omission makes some obscurity" (24–25). See my Introduction.
[83] Verrall labels this scene (lines 164–233), "The *Anagnorisis* or *Recognition*" (25). Verrall dedicates an extensive part of his critical Introduction to a comparison of this scene with a correspondent one in Euripides's and Sophocles's *Electra*. He underlines the following aspect: "The story of Aeschylus differs from those of the two other dramatists in nothing more essentially than in this, that between the brother and sister there is no intermediary whatever. No one in Argos knows him, nor he any one in Argos. He brings with him no *paedagogus*, as in Sophocles, and therefore must put himself in communication with some one in the house of Clytaemnestra, before his design can proceed. Nor, as in Euripides, is there any *paeadagogus* to recognize him. To Electra he is an absolute stranger. Now in this situation it is a question of high romantic interest, how the orphan pair are to be brought together, and how Electra is to be assured that her brother is actually before her. And that she shall be so assured, in some rational and effective manner, is required by her character, and by the important part which in Aeschylus, in Aeschylus only, she takes in the execution of the plan" (xliii). This commentary explains why the question of the lock (if it is Orestes's or not) in the following lines is so important.
[84] Actually line 169.
[85] τόδ(ε). Literally "this," demonstrative.
[86] Woolf summarizes here Verrall's commentary: "Electra, who has inspected the lock closely, has already marked its peculiar quality, and thinks that the slave's recognition will confirm her own. But the interlocutor, scared half out of her senses, and naturally less quick to such an observation than one of the family, does *not* notice the quality, until Electra, after several attempts at suggestion, points it out expressly, *v.* 175.— τόδε refers strictly to the question last raised, whether the hair is possibly a woman's. Given the assumption (that it is the hair of a Pelopid) made in her own mind, there exists no woman, but Electra, whose hair it could be" (25).

171. νιν: it. (the lock)[87]
173. ὁμοπτερος[88] (V. intro).[89]
180. The natural inference, if you
determine that the hair is O[reste]s['].
is that he is dead, & it is
sent as remembrance.[90]
184. packed description of E[lectra']s.

[87] Woolf accepts Verrall's notes, which explain that "'νιν must be the lock [as in *v.* 188], not Agamemnon, as Linwood and Conington take it; for (1) there is no example of κείρασθαι τινα 'to cut hair off in mourning for a person': (2) there is no mention of Agamemnon for νιν to refer to: (3) κείρασθαι κόμην is the regular construction both in Homer (*Od.* 4. 198, 24. 96) and Tragedy (Eur. *Tro.* 1183, *Phoen.* 326)'. Sidgwick.— Con.'s objection is that 'Electra could never mean to say *There is no one but myself who would cut off this lock.*' This however, reading 'might' for 'would', is what she does mean; but it becomes intelligible only when the basis of the scene is correctly conceived" (26).
[88] ὁμόπτερος. See the following note.
[89] In his critical Introduction, Verrall references this line and explains: "In discussing the resemblance of hair, Electra [in the homonymous play by Euripides] uses, for *like*, the fanciful expression ὁμόπτερος, *of like feather*. The slave, whom she is criticizing, has not used the word or any like it. As involving a needless and merely decorative metaphor, it is alien from the Euripidean style, and jars perceptibly with the tone of the dialogue. The very alert and positive critic might perhaps have convinced himself, that Euripides could not have used this word without a purpose ... However the *Choephori* is before us: and we find, not only that the alien ὁμόπτερος is borrowed from Aeschylus, in whose style it is natural, not only that a verse of Euripides, in itself unnoticeable, is in fact an echo from Aeschylus, but that the three objects which the slave suggests as likely, if Orestes should return, to convince his sister of his identity, that is to say, his hair, his foot-prints, and a piece of her work which he may be supposed to possess, are the very three from which, and from which alone, she actually appears to infer his identity in the *Choephori*. Manifestly therefore the contempt expressed by the Euripidean Electra implies a judgment, on the part of her creator, that the proofs in the *Choephori* are inadequate, and that to a ridiculous and offensive degree. We have to consider, as critics of Aeschylus, whether this judgment is well founded, and what defence, if any, can be made for him" (xxxviii).
[90] This explanation is given in full by Verrall in note: "The argument, which, as is natural in one reasoning with herself, is hinted rather than expressed, would, if set out fully, run thus: 'No ordinary Argive could have this hair; for it is the hair of a Pelopid. There *is* indeed something about it like that of my mother; but it is certainly not hers either. I dare not assent positively to the conclusion that it is that of Orestes, partly because it may very well be that of Aegisthus, partly because, if it is that of Orestes, there is reason to fear that he is dead. I may flatter myself with the *hope* that it is his, and that he lives: but I know only that it belongs to him or Aegisthus. To which, only the hair itself could say'. Given the story, as known beforehand to the audience, the reasoning is perfectly clear; and the form of expression is admirably true to nature. But without the story it would be unintelligible" (28).

CN6

weeping.[91] ‘διψιοι’.[92] thirsty for the
omen drops which are restrained.[93]
190.[94] E[lectra] hopes that it is her
brother’s hair.[95]
‘ειναι’[96] – emphatic.[97] Why she, she
hope[s], if it might be so ominous?
The emphatic ‘ειναι’ perhaps
shows that <she> <he> she is determined to
regard it hopefully.[98]
204. foll[owing]: recognition tokens. V. intro.[99]

[91]Woolf here refers to the whole line, which Verrall translates: “Out of my eyes drop, thirsty-like, driblets of a strong flood forcing the dyke, as I behold this tress” (216). See Introduction.
[92] δίψιοι. See following note.
[93] Woolf here adopts the meaning that Verrall leads up to in the following note: “δίψιοι is somewhat obscure … The σταγόνες are the drops which, oozing through the barrier, mark that it is yielding and about to give way. In what sense can this first water be said to ‘fall, thirsty’? Only, I think, because it is the precursor which invites the flood to follow. Aeschylus, by one of his personifying glances regards the situation from the point of view, so to speak, of the drops, which call for, or ‘thirst for’, the mass of water from which they are parted. As applied to the tears, the comparison marks both the difficulty of weeping in a great agony and the volume of the passion which seeks escape” (27–28). See Introduction.
[94] Actually lines 191–93, which Verrall translates, “How I myself can say right out ‘Yes, this is indeed the cherished pride of him I love best in the world, Orestes’....... Nay, but I am flattered by the hope...” (216; ellipses original).
[95] See CN5n83.
[96] εἶναι. In line 192. It is the verb “to be.”
[97] See Verrall’s commentary: “192. εἶναι: ‘that it really *is*’. The position of the word would perhaps not import a stress, but it is probably intended” (28).
[98] Woolf here gives her own comment and suggestion on the above-discussed word and follows the path traced by Verrall. See my Introduction.
[99] Woolf again references Verrall’s critical introduction: “First then, is it of importance to the effect of the *Choephori*, as a story, whether the proofs are adequate or not? That is a question which can be answered only by considering what the particular story is, and what part the alleged proofs play in it. It would be absurd to lay down, as a general rule of criticism, either that the evidence by which an imaginary personage is convinced must always be adequate, or that it never need be. In this as in other things the imagination, within wide limits, gives the law to itself; and the measure of proof requirable is proportioned not to the necessities of real life, but simply to that expectation which the author chooses to raise. How little the question depends on the facts of real experience may be easily seen by putting cases. Suppose for example that in the *Choephori* Orestes, from his striking resemblance to his father, had been recognized, immediately on his appearance, by two or three old slave-women among the chorus. Or suppose again, that he had simply claimed to be recognized by his sister, and she, after a moment’s hesitation, had declared that her memory confirmed his claim. Judged by reality, these two methods of recognition would be at opposite poles of likelihood. The first, which is in substance identical with the way of Euripides, would have been perfectly natural; the second, by a careful collection of passages from the trilogy, might have been shown to be practically impossible. But for the purpose of a story, for the demands of the imagination,

210.[100] She[101] prays that the gods may
fulfil her prayers in future, as
they have – she may announce
to them – <they have> fulfilled them
now.[102]
216. 'εκπαγλουμενος'[103] surprised that
you don[']t welcome O.[restes] himself[104]–
a verallian subtlety.[105]
224.[106] O.[restes] points out her inconsistency.
When she sees him she doesn't
know him; yet she <suspec[ts]> recognised
his hair & his footsteps.[107] Might
not this be an oblique way
of hinting that the poet himself
is a little amazed at her
acuteness?[108]

---

either way would be equally good and sufficient; and assuredly neither of them would have provoked the criticism of Euripides, or of any one deserving an answer" (xl–xli).

[100] Actually line 211.

[101] Electra.

[102] Here Orestes speaks to his sister. Verrall translates his exhortation, "Say unto the gods that thy prayers have brought accomplishment, and pray for such success hereafter" (216). Woolf summarizes what Verrall further explains in his commentary to the Greek text: "211. τοῖς θεοῖς…ἐπαγγέλλουσα: *announcing to the gods the fulfilment of thy prayers* … Electra may ask the gods to fulfil her prayers in future, *as* they have fulfilled them now. The form of expression belongs to a polytheism which did not, at least steadily and permanently, conceive the gods as omniscient. We should rather say '*thanking* God for the fulfilment'" (30).

[103] ἐκπαγλούμενος. Literally, "wondering, being surprised." See following note.

[104] See Verrall's commentary: "216. *I know that thou wast invoking Orestes, and much I am amazed at thee, i.e.* 'that thou dost not welcome Orestes himself'" (31). Verrall expresses the implicit object of the surprise, and Woolf accepts his guess.

[105] Should be read as "Verrall's subtlety." "Verallian" is Woolf's coinage, misspelled with one only "r." Woolf explicitly references the point Verrall makes when explaining this line (see previous note).

[106] Actually lines 225–27.

[107] Woolf summarizes Verrall's explanation: "225–227. 'Orestes is pointing out Electra's inconsistency in doubting ocular demonstration after having just accepted much more equivocal evidence … The order of the verses 226 and 227 (which some transpose) is in fact the only natural order, when what is meant is not 'you were excited by the two indications together' but 'you were excited by the lock, and again by the foot-marks'" (32).

[108] Woolf's personal reflection on Aeschylus's intentions. See Introduction.

CN7

7.
229.[109] ["] whose head has the proportions
of thine"[110] a point for the info:[111]
233. [']Yet I know that our closest
are our enemies –'[112] so anxious to
believe that she opposes each
hope with a doubt.[113]
234.[114] The chorus without such anxious
subt[l]ety burst out into acclamation.[115]
265. γλωσσης χαριν:[116] for the
pleasure of talking – not for
the profit of talking – wh.[ich] w[oul]d.
imply that the tyrants
had friends.[117]

[109] Actually line 228.
[110] Here Orestes gives Electra physical evidence of his identity (and return)—as Woolf remarks hereafter. Woolf copies the literal translation of this passage in Verrall's note: "228. *The lock is from the head of thine own brother, formed as thine own* … The order of the sentence is arranged so as to emphasize these words, which contain the clinching proof of Orestes' identity [...] συμμέτρου τῷ σῷ κάρᾳ: 'whose *head* has the proportions of thine' … The alterations, transpositions, and mistranslations of this passage all proceed from the tacit assumption that συμμέτρου τῷ σῷ κάρᾳ has *not* the only meaning which the words will bear. … But the labour has not been wasted; for it helps to show that the text is sound" (32).
[111] Woolf's comment to emphasize the importance of the information for the purposes of the identification of Orestes, which is here the main point.
[112] Woolf's own rendition. Verrall's translation reads, "I know how sharp against us both are our kin" (217). For a comparison of the translations see also Introduction.
[113] Here Woolf comments on the speaker's state of mind, as I point out in the Introduction, following Verrall's notes (which attribute the question to Electra). Verrall writes, "I take this verse to be said by Electra, to herself rather than to Orestes, as she controls with difficulty the outbreak of her joy. After this, all remain silent and overcome for some moments, and the by-standers, as seems natural, are the first to speak collectedly.—M marks no change of speaker at *v.* 233, leaving this verse to Orestes; but it is then perhaps necessary to change οἶδα to οἶσθα. Since Orestes cannot suppose Electra to require information respecting the position of the family, οἶδα in his mouth seems pointless, unless we suppose some rather artificial ellipse, such as 'Be calm (and I shall not misunderstand your feelings) for' etc." (33).
[114] Woolf refers to the whole passage uttered (according to Verrall) by the chorus, so lines 234–36.
[115] See Verrall notes for more on the chorus's outburst: "234. μέλημα 'object of attention', or 'observance'. The word expresses anxious respect and is appropriate to the speakers … So also δώμασιν *to the house* is a proper term to include the slaves; and it is natural that they, rather than the brother and sister, should fix at once upon material interests and the hard facts of the situation" (33).
[116] γλώσσης χάριν. See following note.
[117] Here Woolf copies Verrall's literal translation given by Verrall in note and summarizes his interpretation of the scholius, which he reports in Greek: "265. γλώσσης χάριν: '*for the pleasure of talking*', μὴ δυνάμενος ἐχεμυθεῖν [lit. "unable to lie"] schol[ia]. This is put in,

270. ἐπορθριαζω[118] = to utter a
morning cry: a significant
word. O.[restes] heard Apollo
in the morning wh.[ich] was the
true hour. & many times.[119]
δυσχειμερους[120] observe
that almost all A.[eschylus'] epithets
profit by a literal translation.[121]
274. [']scowling upon compensations
wh.[ich] w[oul]d. beggar them.'[122]

CN8

8.
<B[123]> He demands life & not money.
If you take it to mean that
he scowls on <the> losses of
property due him you belittle

---

because the whole play forbids us to suppose that the tyrants had now any active partizans among the people of the country. Nevertheless if the arrival of Orestes were known, some careless and gossiping person might let it out" (36).

[118] ἐπορθριάζω. This verb occurs in *Agamemnon*, and Verrall draws on it as evidence for his explanation of ἐξορθριάζων (see following note). This word is found in *Choephori* in the contracted form of the participle κἀξορθριάζων (standing for καί ἐξορθιάζων).

[119] Here Woolf copies the literal translation and summarizes the following explanation given by Verrall in note: "I believe ἐξορθριάζων to be right and highly significant. The word ὀρθριάζω occurs at *Ag.* 29 Ἀγαμέμνονος γυναικὶ σημαίνω … εὐνῆς ἐπαντείλασαν … ὀλολυγμὸν εὐφημοῦντα τῇδε λαμπάδι ἐπορθιάζειν, where it has been wrongly changed to ὀρθιάζειν. It signifies 'to utter as a morning-cry', at the time of awaking and arising, a specially ominous and significant hour. Now we have already seen that the command of Apollo to Orestes was probably not given in the common way, in answer to consultation, but by a dream or dreams, sent either to him or to the Pythia, or perhaps to both. This is what is meant by ἐξορθριάζων πολλὰ. The stress of the injunction was shown by its being given repeatedly (πολλὰ) and always at *the hour of truth*, the time of waking. The word was probably technical in this *mantic* sense. Whether ὀρθιάζειν would be an appropriate word, it is, in the rarity of the examples, not easy to say; but it does not appear at all events to be specially appropriate" (36–37).

[120] δυσχειμέρους. Still at v. 270. Meaning "wintry, stormy." See following note.

[121] Contrary to most of the other cases, Woolf does not copy the English periphrasis that Verrall gives in note. She prefers instead to comment on the best rendition of Aeschylus's word, even if not recording the literal translation to which she alludes. In his note, Verrall writes, "δυσχειμέρους … θερμὸν: 'plagues to make the warm heart cold as winter' with horror" (37). See also Introduction. Orestes uses this phrase to express his feelings.

[122] Woolf copies the literal translation that Verrall gives in note. Verrall also supplies an interpretation of the line's general meaning—"274: *refusing the payment of all their wealth*"—and a full explanation of all the terms that form the line "ἀποχρημάτοισι ζημίαις ταυρούμενον" (37). See CN8n124.

[123] Woolf may have initially intended to write "beggar" or "because" here.

his action & the whole story.[124]
The beauty lies in the majestic arrangement.[125]
277-81. astonishing closeness of description & metaphor.[126]
289. πλαστιγγι[127] – commonly taken

[124] The subject here is Orestes. Verrall claims in his note that "ἀποχρημάτοισι" must be intended as "'wealth-depriving' in the full and literal sense" and provides the following explanation: "As ἀπόπολις, ἀποφύλιος etc. mean 'city-less, tribe-less', totally deprived of city or tribe, so a person beggared would be ἀποχρήματος 'wealth-less'; here the epithet is transferred, with active sense, to the fine which beggars.—In a certain stage of society the rule 'a life for a life' might well be preached as an improving doctrine, when compared with the callous savagery of universal 'were-gild'; and this passage suggests that it was at one time zealously supported by the civilizing authority of Delphi.—The current interpretation 'exasperated by my losses' is, I venture to think, certainly wrong. No authority is cited for ταυροῦσθαι in this sense; and it seems strangely below the office of a god to stimulate unscrupulous cupidity. If Orestes had killed his mother *because she had robbed him*, he would surely have been a villain by the consent of all ages.—It is possible to interpret ἀποχρημάτοισι by 'paid from' *i.e.* in 'money': but I prefer the explanation given above" (37–38). Woolf gives the core sense of this interpretation by remarking that wanting for material goods can not be considered a reason good enough for the atrocious crime Orestes is going to commit. He does not mean to take from Clytemnestra and Aegisthus only the royal palace and all its riches, but also their life, as they took that of Agamemnon. See also CN8n125.

[125] One of Woolf's comments on Aeschylus's style (see Introduction). The passage she refers to reads in Verrall's translation: "I did not make quest for my father against the guilty, who bade me slay them, even as they slew, answering with a scowl the offer of all their wealth" (218).

[126] In his long speech (lines 268–95), Orestes explains that his pursuit of vengeance is demanded by Apollo and that he faces consequences if he does not answer this demand. Woolf's comment here addresses the language that expresses these consequences, figured as the corruption of the body. Verrall notes that "the penalties which attend the avenger of blood, if he neglects his duty … are the same as those inflicted upon the murderer; bodily corruption, by the corrupted fruits of the earth, haunting and pursuing fiends, and banishment from social intercourse for life" (38). Verrall continues in his next note: "277–281. *For the (gift), with which earth appeases men's cares, doth, as he declared for their instruction, breed in them certain threading corruptions, things which climb over the flesh, with cruel cancerous jaws eating away its natural state; and by this corruption a whiteness breaks forth upon the temples.* … ἐννῆν: lit. *spin in them* like a thread … the metaphor of *spinning* … seems admirably to express the peculiarity of cancerous diseases, which reach out in filaments from the tainted centres and cover the surface as with a web. The following expressions … develop the idea, hinting a comparison of the self-producing plague not only to the web, but also to a sort of loathsome, devouring *arachne*" (38). In his Appendix, Verrall further explains the theory of the "fruits of the earth" and the philological problems of this passage: "Here there is not a letter to mend, and in v. 278 scarcely a letter: νῶν in the Ms. represents the infinitive, whatever that should be, of the verb *to spin*" (169). Woolf's comment is a sort of continuation of Verrall's discourse, with which she evidently agrees, that underlines the most convincing points for her and focuses the attention on Aeschylus's stylistic choices, namely the metaphor of the web. See also Introduction.

[127] πλάστιγγι. See following notes.

for 'whip'[128] from πλησσω.[129]
V[errall]:[130] takes it for a small metal
plate, such as used in scales.[131]
295. ταριχευθεντα[132] – mummied.[133]
μορω[134] = be corpse.[135]
316.[136] does ευνη[137] = bed or anchor?[138]
V[errall]: <su>[139] believes anchor, because
ουριζω:[140] waft with a favouring
breeze would be ineffective
to wake a sleeper. And it

[128] Here Woolf refers to a possible meaning assumed by previous scholars ("whip" or, more precisely, "scourge") that differs from Verrall's interpretation, which she reports immediately hereafter.

[129] πλήσσω. Literally "to hit / beat / wound." This etymology is not found in Verrall. Woolf must have done her own research elsewhere on this term (maybe consulting a dictionary or another edition). Verrall translates Orestes's description of the persecution of the Furies, to which each murderer is condemned, as "phantoms which the victim, though his eye-brows twitch in the dark, can clearly see … and frenzy and causeless fear of the nights vex him and harrow; and they make him be chased from his town, with *metal scare* in his tortured body" (218, emphasis added).

[130] Here and a few lines later on the same page Woolf indicates that she reports Verrall's interpretation by explicitly writing the scholar's initial. See Introduction, note 5.

[131] Woolf here records details from Verrall's commentary: "289. πλάστιγγι. As to the meaning of this word we have no evidence but that of the context. Elsewhere it means a *balance*, or some part of one, the *scale* or sometimes the *tongue*. The context, taken in connexion with known practices about lepers, madmen, and other such outcasts, suggests that here it is some metal object, which was attached in a painful way … to the victim, so that he could not easily remove it, and was so made as to give a sound, warning people of his approach. Small metal plates, suspended so as to clash, would have the effect and correspond to the name" (41).

[132] ταριχευθέντα. See following note.

[133] Woolf draws this word from Verrall's note: "295. κακῶς ταριχευθέντα: lit. 'vilely mummied', a metaphor for the wasting of the body and hardening of the skin by the disease" (41).

[134] μόρῳ. See line 295 and following note.

[135] In his note, Verrall writes, "παμφθάρτῳ μόρῳ: lit. 'with utterly corrupted corpse' … On μόρος *funus*, for which we have no complete equivalent … [I]t means (1) *death*, (2) *corpse*, (3) *funeral*" (41–42).

[136] Actually 317.

[137] εὐνή. Singular of εὐναί, which occurs in the text.

[138] This word raises some doubts, as both Verrall and Woolf note. The whole line, in which Orestes asks how his prayers and invocations could reach Agamemnon, reads in Verrall's translation, "O father strange and terrible, what can I say, what do to waft my signal from so far thither, where thou art anchored fast?" (219).

[139] Woolf may be about to copy Verrall's comment on this passage, starting with "surely" (44). See CN8n141.

[140] οὐρίζω. The verb, meaning "carry with a fair wind, waft on the way," from which οὐρίσας in the text derives. See Verrall: "316. τύχοιμ' ἂν κτλ.: *can I succeed in wafting it* (the word or act which expresses my feelings) *from this distance to the (shore) where* etc" (44).

w[oul]d. reach one anchored.[141] But
is it not the point of O[reste]s[’].
exclamation that he doubts

CN9

9.

that anything can waken him?[142]
εχουσιν[143] = holds, detains[144] seems to me
a better argument for anchor
than the other.[145]
320 &:[146] a very difficult passage.[147]
Sense[148]: [‘]Darkness is severed
from light, & all the loves between
the two are alike barred
[and?][149] that lamentation wh.[ich]
has done honour to the
chief of our house of old’[150]

[141] Verrall justifies his rendering, which Woolf draws on here, thus: “ἔνθα … εὐναί: *where thou art anchored fast*. Surely εὐναί here means *anchors*, and not, as commonly thought, *bed*. The comparison of the interval between the living and the dead to a ‘great water’ is familiar to all poetry, ancient poetry in particular. … The dead is said to be ‘anchored fast,’ to signify the impossibility or difficulty of return. If εὐναί be rendered *bed*, οὐρίσας is pointless and incongruous, since a sleeper is not to be reached by means of a breeze” (44).

[142] Here Woolf continues the reasoning traced by Verrall but for the first time questions his interpretation, as I point out in my Introduction.

[143] ἔχουσιν. See line 317.

[144] Literal translation, given by Verrall in note: “ἔχουσιν: *hold, detain*” (44). Woolf uses (incorrectly) the third person singular instead of plural.

[145] This comment, like the previous one, is related not to the primary text, but to Verrall’s translational choice and, particularly, the reasons with which he justifies his decision. Woolf disagrees with his justification.

[146] Actually lines 318–20.

[147] Woolf’s comment, in line with Verrall’s opinion: “The obscurity of the passage has arisen partly because this antithesis has been missed, and partly from the difficulty that we have in realizing the primitive notions, about death and the dead, which are here implied. Orestes is thinking of his father’s neglected funeral, when he ought to have been honoured, like his predecessors, with the customary lament. *Then* (such is the conception) the dead father, being present and not yet wholly departed, could have heard and been consoled by his son’s voice; *now* he is gone far away, perhaps altogether beyond reach” (45). See my Introduction.

[148] Woolf identifies what follows as an explanation or interpretation rather than a translation.

[149] Woolf’s brackets, word, and question mark. Woolf’s insertion separates the two concepts of darkness and light. See following note.

[150] Verrall renders these lines, which continue the previous discourse, as follows in his translation: “Darkness and light are parted and opposite: and in like manner is barred the office of love, the dirge which in time past has glorified the sires of our house” (219). Verrall also notes that Ἀτρείδαις refers to “the family in general, not Agamemnon and Menelaus, the sons of one individual Atreus” (45).

325.[151] further subtleties, dependent
some of them upon the tradition.[152]
As the dying man is wailed
so <the> the man's delaying is longest to
light, & the true dirge for sake of the father
& parent, his fathering the whole
world.[153]
The sense may be: a dying man,
one whose body is still there, is
lamented; & so also may the
delaying soul of one whose body
has long been lost, be brought
to light. And there is no
cry much potent to reach such a

[151] Actually line 326.

[152] Woolf takes the following information on the religious meaning, which is helpful to interpret correctly, from Verrall's commentary: "a dirge (γόος) takes effect on the dead not only (according to the thought of Orestes) to console him at his funeral, but also to bring him back long after his death. ὁ θνῄσκων. Observe the tense, and contrast τοῦ θανόντος: the difference is, in every sense of the word, vital, and contains the point of the whole passage. According to this primitive doctrine 'death' is not regarded as complete before the destruction of the body; the severed corpse and soul, at a γόος or *lykewake*, make up a θνῄσκων not a θανών ... The dead is a 'delayer' or 'hinderer' because (to put the matter quite simply and prosaically) he keeps waiting those who desire to communicate with him. The expression is (to us) obscure, but no doubt was explained by conventional and religious use. The doctrine is this. The soul is not destroyed with the body, but goes out of it. In the case of one just 'dead' (in the modern sense), whose body is with us, the soul, scarcely parted, is not far off, and we reach it, with some difficulty, by the *lament* or *dirge* ... The soul of a man long since burnt on the pyre has of course gone far away into the world of darkness, and we cannot expect that it will respond to us *quickly*. But it exists, and it will respond to us in some way, if we call with perseverance; and (adds the speaker) the most mighty of calls is the voice of a child lamenting a parent, which will range the universe till it finds him. ... τε couples the whole clause to the preceding, and signifies that the relation of Orestes to the soul he seeks is an assurance added to the general doctrine above laid down.—The first words of the sentence have the emphasis, represented in the translation by 'more especially'. — καὶ τεκόντων: 'and a parent *in particular*' ... The addition is important, since in this scene and context, πατέρων *fathers* might naturally have its wider sense ... ἔνδικος (*right and true*) is part of the predicate and in effect adverbial. It combines here both its senses, and implies not only that the lament is in this case a 'right seeker', *i.e.* a seeker who will go right, but also that the child has a just and natural claim to communicate with the parent" (46–47).

[153] Verrall's translation reads, "As the parting soul can receive a lament, so the delaying soul can be brought to light. And the dirge for a father, for parent, is a rightful, natural seeker, embracing with wide range both the worlds" (233). Woolf makes here her own translation on the basis on Verrall's note, which reads: "326–327: literally 'And as he that is dying is lamented, so he that is delaying is brought to light' ... 328–330. 'And more especially in the case of a father and parent is the lamentation of him a true seeker, whose wide (pursuit) embraces the universe'" (46).

soul than the cry of a child.[154]

CN10

10.
330.[155] <en[156]> εν μερει[157] = in their turn[158]
373. δυνασαι γαρ[159] = for that thou canst do.[160]
415.[161] a mended phrase [?].[162]
420.[163] 'from their mother'[164] their suffering are bitter as her that caused them.[165]
449.[166] βασει[167] = foundation, solidity.[168]
515. The dead can[']t take such pleasure in gifts as the living

[154] Here also Woolf paraphrases the text to offer a more succinct and clearer explanation.
[155] Line 331.
[156] Here Woolf probably starts to transliterate ἐν μέρει but then decides to leave it in Greek.
[157] ἐν μέρει. See following note.
[158] Literal translation. In this line Electra says that she and Orestes alternate in their mourning of Agamemnon. Verrall explains, "ἐν μέρει of voices in succession taking up one burden [...] The expression was probably technical, and fits here naturally, at the beginning of the first responsion or antistrophe" (47).
[159] δύνασαι γάρ. Meaning in the following note.
[160] Woolf draws on Verrall's note: "φωνεῖς· δύνασαι γάρ … 'thou givest words to these wishes, for that thou canst do', with the implication, 'but thou canst do no more'" (53). The chorus considers Electra's plan to avenge her father almost impractical.
[161] Line 416.
[162] Woolf remarks the uncertain meaning of this line, uttered by the chorus, which Verrall thus translates: "boldness turns sorrow away in answer to the happy sign (?)" (221). The scholar explains in note (60-61) that the whole passage is "hopelessly corrupted" and also the scholius "presume the corrupt text and give no assistance".
[163] Line 421.
[164] Literal translation of ἐκ ματρός.
[165] According to Verrall, whom Woolf paraphrases in part here, Electra means that Orestes's and her cruelty is a result of what Clytemnestra did to them (rather a fact of nature or family/species resemblance). See Verrall's note: "420–421: *for their spirit, like that of a cruel wolf, is implacable by derivation from the mother of them.* ματρός: metaphorical, the cruelty of Clytaemnestra. There is of course an allusion to the physical relationship of the persons, but it is an allusion only; and the interpretation '*we* (Orestes and Electra) are naturally cruel *as our mother*' misses the point" (61).
[166] Actually 450.
[167] βάσει. See following note.
[168] See Verrall: "ἡσύχῳ φρονῶν βάσει: 'by thinking ἡσύχως καὶ βεβαίως lit. *on* or *with steady foundation* … βάσις here signifies not *step, movement* but *ground*" (66). In this scene Orestes has just been told in every detail how his father Agamemnon was killed and dishonored by Clytemnestra. Electra then encourages him to fix the things he heard in his mind and the chorus adds, in Verrall's final translation: "but aid them first to pierce thy sense by calm, **steady** thought" (221, bold added).

tho'[169] of lovers as the whole
play shows, they can be
<pleased by> pleasantly
affected.[170]
530.[171] <o>[172] ωστε[173] = so far as that.[174]
545.[175] As she dreamed she nursed a snake
she is fated to a violent death.[176]
555.[177] ερκειους[178] = outer wall of
the castle.[179] The reference
is to be as much like

[169] Transcription uncertain, but I interpret this word as an abbreviation of "though."

[170] In this line Orestes wonders about the significance of Clytemnestra's late offerings on the grave of her murdered husband. In Verrall's translation he defines the libation as "a wretched boon, sent to her victim dead, unconscious" (223). Woolf summarizes the general sense of that Verrall offers earlier in note: "strictly speaking this language is inconsistent … But what is really meant, that no gifts can affect the dead with a pleasure *equivalent* to the life taken away, is perfectly consistent with the foregoing doctrine: and οὐ φρονοῦντι is but an exaggeration of rhetoric" (72).

[171] Line 531.

[172] Here Woolf probably started to transliterate ὥστε but then decided to leave it in Greek.

[173] ὥστε. In the Greek text, this word is found in the contracted form: ὥστ'. See following note.

[174] The chorus tells Orestes that Clytemnestra breastfed the snake to which she gave birth in her dream but escaped "hurt from the venom" (Verrall 223). Woolf's note draws from Verrall's note, which explains the chorus's description of the dream: "531. 'The teat was unhurt by the poison only because with the milk the snake sucked out the clotted blood'. **ὥστε: literally 'so far as that':** the snake bit, and injected its poison, which produced the natural effect of clotting the blood; but as the blood injected was drawn out by the sucking, there was no other effect: *to this extent* the teat escaped hurt" (74–75, bold added).

[175] Line 546.

[176] Orestes refers to Clytemnestra's dream. Woolf summarizes the following explanation given by Verrall: "546. 'The meaning plainly is that "to dream of giving suck to a monster means violent death"; the snake is to reach her breast'. ὡς ἔθρεψεν: 'in accordance with the fact that she suckled', lit. 'as' or 'since she suckled'" (76). The scholar's later translation of this passage reads, "nursing so strange a prodigy, she is fated to a violent death," concluding, "and I, turned serpent, am her slayer, according as this dream declares" (224). See also Introduction.

[177] Line 559.

[178] ἑρκείους. See following note.

[179] The castle wall is the place where Orestes plans to carry out his vengeance. In lines 552–82, he presents the plan, which in Verrall's translation reads as follows: "The instruction is but simple. My sister here must go home, with charge to cover the plan contrived by me … In the guise of a traveller, with full and complete equipment, I shall come to the *outer gate*—and Pylades here (such is his name) along with me … And if once I pass the threshold of the *outer gate*, and find that man … swift death from my steel shall arrest his whence with a full stop" (224, emphasis added). In his notes, Verrall also explains that "the ἕρκειοι πύλαι here and hereafter signify and distinguish the outer gate of the castle, the 'gate of the wall', as opposed to the entrances of the various buildings within the precinct, two of which are represented in the subsequent scene" (78).

the original crime[180] as
possible.
Pylades – a propitious name for

CN11

11.

one having business with gates,
& thus quoted here for the first
time.[181]
583. Chorus, while the preparations
for the slaughter go on.[182]
The passion of beast & man is
topped by the passion of a woman
who shrives against wedlock.[183]

[180] Clytemnestra's murder of Agamemnon.

[181] Referring to Pylades (see last line of CN10), Verrall's offers the following commentary in note: "560. Πυλάδῃ This name of course conveys nothing to Electra and the rest, who neither in this scene nor elsewhere show any knowledge of Orestes' history. The reason why Orestes mentions the name of his apparently unimportant subordinate is curiously characteristic of Greek feeling, and especially of Aeschylus. So far as I am aware, it has not been observed, and there has been much debate in consequence over the verse. The words ἐφ' ἑρκείους πύλας suggest that the appellation of his friend, implying familiarity with *gates*, is apt and 'of good omen' for a plot, in which the first step will be to win admission at a closed and guarded portal: and for this reason only he cites it, indicating the point by the juxtaposition of πύλας Πυλάδῃ, and by the tone. From what precedes we may fairly infer that this application of the name had even received the very highest 'mantic' sanction … Orestes here puts forward Pylades as the sole companion of his enterprise: and on this ground the text and the plot have been subjected to injurious alteration. But there is nothing said here about the number of Orestes' company, which for his declared purpose must be large. He notices Pylades partly because he is there, but mainly in order to cite, for the encouragement of the others, the significance attributed by Apollo to his title" (58–59).

[182] In my Introduction, I point out that Woolf's comment underlines the juxtaposition between the chorus and the murder. See Verrall's note: "583. The ode, which follows, covers a large interval of time, from the morning to the evening of the day, which is the natural hour for the plan. It is plain that the preparations alluded to in the preceding verses could not be hastily made; and the poet has in fact given as much time as he conveniently could. The ode itself is carefully adapted to its function as a mere symbolic interlude, being in theme and treatment wholly non-dramatic. Whether the scenery was in any way changed, we cannot positively say; but a very simple change would be sufficient to suggest what in any case, I think, we must suppose, that the tomb was at some distance from the palace and not in sight of it. … Nothing would be easier than to screen, during the first scene, the simple wooden erections, which in Aeschylus' day probably stood for the 'palace', and to remove the screen (and perhaps the 'tomb') at this point. I should myself suppose that something of this sort was done. If, in order to do it, it was necessary that the Chorus should withdraw by the *parodos* (with Electra), that also would be far from disadvantageous to the effect intended" (84).

[183] Woolf paraphrases here a small part of a longer chorus, which Verrall summarizes in note: "583–648. 'Many are the terrible marvels of brute nature (583–591), but more marvellous is the daring of man and the passion of woman (592–596): and this passion, when it is seen

626.[184] 'harmony fuel hearth
without a fire'[185] O.[restes] has paid Ae.[gisthus]'
the compliment of fighting him
with as great treachery as
Ae.[gisthus]' has used:[186] Ae.[gisthus]' temper is
timid & lukewarm, like a fireless
heath.[187]
890.[188] Here Clytennestra [sic] comes
out,[189] asks for a manslaying
axe[190]: "this evil has now
reached such a point"[191] one
can only kill or be killed.

---

in rebellion against the bond of wedlock, surpasses all the terrors both of brute nature and human (597–600). Woman's recklessness we see in Althaea sacrificing her son, in Scylla sacrificing her father (601–620). And if these legends are not perfect parallels—for it is another crime, the murder of a husband, which Orestes is about to avenge—legend and language tell us that treason to wedlock is the crime of all crimes, most abhorred, most surely punished, containing all horrors in itself (621–636). Such a punishment is now to be seen. Justice and Fate forge the sword ; and Vengeance leads to the work (637–648)" (84). Woolf paraphrases only the core of lines 597–600, which Verrall further explains, "There is a triple ascending scale, the terrors of nature, the passions of mankind, and a special case surpassing all, *female passion in revolt against wedlock*" (86).

[184] Line 627.

[185] The translation given in note by Verrall is "*that hearth without fire*," which the scholar further explains: "ἀθέρμαντον ἑστίαν δόμων. I take this phrase to be purely metaphorical. So taken, it is obscure indeed, but not, I think, by any means unintelligible. Unless we resort to emendation, which has not proved efficient, we plainly must identify the *fireless* or *warmthless hearth* with the *spiritless temper*. Since warmth is a natural and known figure for *courage*, spirit, the simile was ready to hand; and it expresses the intended contempt" (90). The expression is a metaphor of Aegisthus' weak character. See Introduction.

[186] See Verrall's explanation in note: "The plot of Orestes is (it is true) in itself fit rather for Aegisthus, but in this Orestes pays a proper compliment to the genius of his opponent. To meet a man at his own game, with his own weapons, is (in an ordinary case) to show respect for the art which he practises: the application of the term to the case of meeting a traitor with treachery is of course bitterly ironical" (90).

[187] Woolf's paraphrase of the explanation given by Verrall. See CN11n185.

[188] Line 888.

[189] Verrall writes in note that "Clytaemnestra comes out from her door" (126).

[190] See Verrall's note: "ἀνδροκμῆτα πέλεκυν. The epithet seems to describe a kind of axe, a *battle-axe* in fact, as distinct from other like instruments. A needless epithet, such as *murdering*, would be weak and out of place" (126). After engaging with other scholars and sources, Verrall continues, "But other references point rather, though not perhaps conclusively, to a sword; and as no allusion is here required, the passage itself affords no evidence. It is however likely enough that this πέλεκυν helped to establish the axe as the weapon of Clytaemnestra, and led, even if unintentionally, to the later versions of the murder" (126).

[191] Woolf's paraphrases Verrall's final translation: "Give me a battle-axe, some one, and quick! Let us know whether we are victors or vanquished. For to this point this woeful way hath brought me" (230). See my Introduction.

Does she mean the whole
tragedy of the house, in which
case she is a passive
instrument; or her own

CN12

12.
<act> private act, in which
she is active & responsible?.[192]
There is a cryptic chorus[193]

[192] Woolf considers here her own interpretation of the text. See Introduction.
[193] Woolf refers to the chorus at lines 934–70. Verrall's commentary tracks the ambiguity of this difficult passage due to its incomplete and questionable tradition: "934–970. The text is in a curious condition. The first half is in the usual state, that is to say, almost entirely correct … In the second half on the contrary there is scarcely a sentence which, without considerable change, can be scanned or interpreted. The phenomenon suggests some local accident, such as the blotting of a page. But whatever the cause, it has made restoration impossible. The general sense is visible … The loss is deplorable, for the ode (what is left of it) is superb.
934–940. 'Even as upon Troy Justice, long-delayed, fell all the heavier at last, so now at last she has come from Delphi to the house of Agamemnon, in the shape of Orestes and his friend, and has taken a vengeance complete'. …
936–938. *So now hath Vengeance come into the house of Agamemnon, twofold to prey, two-fold to fight, crying 'To the uttermost!'.* διπλοῦς λέων, διπλοῦς Ἄρης. The vengeance was 'double' in every aspect, two victims to avenge (Agamemnon and Cassandra), two agents (Orestes and Pylades), and two criminals (Aegisthus and Clytaemnestra). The reason for insisting here upon this essential doubleness (note again δυοῖν in *v.* 943) is to remind us that Clytaemnestra, whose death we have just commiserated, could not have been lawfully spared …
939–940: *the exile fitly urged by warning from Pytho's oracle divine*, *i.e.* Orestes stimulated by Pylades … This reference points again to the leading thought, the necessity of not sparing Clytaemnestra. …
945–951. 'Again, because the crime was planned with guile, so was her vengeance; and when it came to fighting, she hit, doing justice in all to her most happy name— Δίκη, whose wrath is fatal to those she hates'. The subject, continued from the preceding strophe, is still throughout the personified Δίκη; and the point is still to justify Orestes, by dwelling on the exactness of the retribution. …
952–955. Nothing is certain here, except that there is a reference to Apollo as author of the vengeance. …
956–957 have again neither metre nor sense. Even the general meaning is disputable, and restoration apparently hopeless.
958. If it were certain that this verse formed a complete sentence, either ἄξια δ' (Hermann) or θέμις δ' [Heimsoeth] might be accepted. But in the wreck of the whole we cannot even be sure that there was a full stop at κακοῖς.
959–960 are more promising and (with μέγα for μέγαν Stanley) possibly right, 'Light has appeared, and I am delivered from the strong curb which held the house' …
963–966. 'But soon the house shall be thoroughly purged.' This must be the general sense; but the details are wholly uncertain. …
967–969. 'The luck shall be turned, the house have new possessors'. This again is in ruins. … In a general way it is manifest, if only from the future tenses of the verbs, that the conclusion

while the murder<s> <are> is[194] being
done off or on? the stage.[195]
Then Orestes comes on
bearing an olive bough. &
speaks over the bodies of
Ae.[gisthus] & Cly.[taemnestra][196]
971. Look now upon the twofold
tyranny of the land murderers
of my father, wasters of my
house.
Majestic they were once,
seated <on here> on the throne<,> here,
& fond, & now, as it suits
them, their fortunes follow
them,[197] & the oath of their

---

refers not to the fall of the tyrants but to *the sequel*, the abolition of the tyranny and restoration of the old order" (134–38).

[194] Woolf changes plural into singular because Aegisthus is already dead. She refers to Clytaemnestra's death.

[195] Woolf's conjecture. See Introduction.

[196] Here Woolf introduces Orestes's monologue in lines 971–1004, which she retranslates at conclusion of the notebook, though the monologue does not coincide with the end of the tragedy. See Verrall's comment on the tragedies final section: "971–1074. *Finale*. Orestes is about to throw himself upon the protection of Apollo at Delphi, as the god himself commanded. Bearing, in sign of this purpose, the wool-wreathed olive-bough of the suppliant, he comes to pronounce over the bodies of Clytaemnestra and Aegisthus a justification of his act, producing to his fellow-citizens in support the actual 'entangled robe' which was used in the murder of his father. He speaks at first with a certain fierce solemnity, but soon becomes violent and confused: and when after a pause he resumes, it is manifest, and he himself presently declares, that he has not the control of his mind. It is the approach of the Erinnyes. With a last protest he prepares to depart, when suddenly he perceives the avenging fiends. The by-standers (for the forms are visible to him alone) vainly endeavour to persuade him that it is a delusion; he rushes away, and the play concludes with a god-speed and a few words of retrospect and doubtful anticipation. —With regard to the scenic arrangements it seems to be clear, as generally supposed, that the bodies of the tyrants are brought before the audience; but it is not so clear that this was done by the *eccyclema* [a machine used to display an interior scene, as dead bodies after a murder, in the classic theatre]. The scene takes place, not in the interior of the house, but outside before the public, as is shown by the character of Orestes' speeches … There would therefore be no need for the mechanism; and we should suppose rather that the bodies are brought out" (139).

[197] See Verrall's note: "973–975. *Majestic they were and loving they were, when yet they sat upon their thrones; and still, it may be judged, their condition abides with them, and their oath stands true to the pledge*. That the condition of the dead in the other world continued and corresponded in some sort to that of the living man was a general Greek belief. Orestes applies this to the two corpses laid side by side, half in irony, as if to signify that their guilty splendour and pleasure is all at an end, but also with some half-voluntary recognition of the pathos inherent in their union and the σεμνότης inseparable from death. To render the fine and delicate language we require a word (which I cannot find) exactly covering the Greek

pledge is unbroken, for they die tonight & their faith
<in> holds <good> past.[198]

CN13

13.
See once more,[199] you that hear <my>
the vow, the plot, the prison
of my poor sire the coupling
grasp of his hands and feet.
Stretch it out among you,[200]
clustered close in a circle,
th<is>e <men[']s covering> men[']s thing that covered up [?] him,[201] so
that the father – & not my
father – but the Sun who
sees all, <these deeds> this,[202] & the

σεμνός: death, and the dead, as such, are not exactly *majestic*, which best fits the first part of the sentence, but they are in themselves σεμνά, *solemn* or *impressive*, as darkness is, and the open sky, and all things which make man little. It is essential here to realize that the scene (to repeat it once more) takes place long after the murders, and that the bodies do not lie as they fell. They are solemnly laid out, and Orestes, who comes to make over them a solemn oration in his own defence, strikes in his opening the proper note, though he is unable to maintain it— πάθη πάρεστι: *their conditions (fortunes) are with them* or *belong to them*, *i.e.* the continuation of their story is like what went before, πάθος is here neutral in sense (*fact*, *experience*, *incident*)" (139).

[198] See Verrall's commentary: "ὅρκος: the oath personified, 'those who swore' … 977. καὶ ξυνθανεῖσθαι stands in apposition to ὅρκος, *their oath 'to be joined even unto death'; this also hath been truly kept*. Literally *that they would even* (or *also*) *die together*: καὶ signifies 'to be joined in death *as well as in all else*', in their enterprise, their lives, etc. The point which Orestes makes is that the addition καὶ ξυνθανεῖσθαι has been no idle form, but has been fulfilled for the conspirators more exactly than they hoped or intended" (139).

[199] See Verrall's note: "978. αὖτε, *again*, as at the time of the murder" (140).

[200] See Verrall's note: "981. ἐκτείνατ' αὐτοί: *spread it with your own hands*. Orestes, or more probably an attendant by his direction, delivers the robe to some of the ἐπήκοοι, the natural action of one who is courting publicity" (141).

[201] This sentence is quite hard to read in the manuscript. I believe Woolf wrote, "this," then cancelled "is" and added "e" to transform the word into "the." Then she wrote and cancelled what seems to read as "men's covering" in favor of "men's thing that covered," I think she meant to use the same word, but the cancelled version is not perfectly readable. Finally, there is a word I cannot confidently transcribe; I interpret it as "up" mainly for the sense of "covered up" (meaning "hid"), and what looks like "him." The result would be "the men's thing that covered up him." It should correspond line 982—"στέγαστρον ἀνδρὸς δείξαθ'"—which Verrall renders, "show this net for a man" (233).

[202] See Verrall's note: "983. πάντα...τάδε: not 'all these events ', but 'all things *here*', 'all things in this world' … It is a solemn way of saying that 'this thing is not done in a corner'" (141). Of the reference to the sun, Verrall continues, "The question raised, whether there is any allusion here to the future appearance of Apollo (not Helios) as an actual witness at the trial before the Areopagus in the *Eumenides*, is to be answered by a distinction. Orestes is not thinking of the Delphian god, or of an actual trial. His appeal to Helios is merely figurative.

impious work of my mother
<he> that he may[203]
may he be with me as a
witness in all truth how
justly I achieved this doom.
My mother's doom I mean (for I
speak not of the fate that
befell Aegisthus: he has the
justice that the law <by>
pays a seducer.[204]) but she
planned shame for her husband,
<the wei[205]> through whom she
bore the weight of children

CN14

14.
beneath her girdle, a dear
weight once, <I kn> but now
a bitter sorrow, I know;
Ah! How think you?.
Had she been born eel or viper
the touch of her would have
rotted one without the bite,
such was her boldness, < or the>
& the hasten of her <will> soul.[206]

… But on the other hand the poet must have been conscious that he meant to bring on Apollo, a god associated with light, as an actual witness, and he does by this figure … point our minds to it, if we already know the whole work" (141).

[203] Variation of the following sentence.

[204] Woolf draws on Verrall's note to this line: "988. 'He has received, as from the law, the penalty of the seducer' ... The slaying of Aegisthus might be regarded rather as the act of the law than of the hand that did it" (142).

[205] Perhaps Woolf meant to write "weight" here but then decided to postpone this word.

[206] Orestes here expresses all the hatred he feels for his mother. The words he uses convey the totally negative portrayal that is commonly made of Clytemnestra. Anyway, such brutality gives also proof of his own wild temperament, as Verrall also notes in his long comment: 988–994. *But as for one who etc...., what think you of her? I say that, were she eel or viper, she 'would rot another with her touch, without a bite, if boldness and native will could do it.* … In these 'almost grotesque words' (Sidgwick) the violent nature of Orestes, which has been already exhibited before the murder, and is felt, under the curb as it were, in the opening part of this speech, suddenly breaks from control, the sight of the robe, now outspread, being more than he can bear. His language marks the utmost degree of fury, which could be called sane. Just here, with thrilling power and truth, the poet places the invasion of the mysterious madness. After a brief pause Orestes resumes; and feeling that he has spoken of his mother otherwise than as he intended, he tries to refer to her in a milder tone, 'the mildest that he may find', a phrase exhibiting in itself the struggle within. But … he hesitates, his eye falls again

What words could I use, if
all were mine?[207]
Is it a snare for a wild beast –
a sheet such as you wrap
round the feet of a dead
man?[208] – a net then?
One might call it a toil –
something that snares the feet –
a cloak[209] – such as a highway
robber is wont to use, one
who saves his head by the
cheering & fleecing of travellers.[210]

---

upon the ensnaring robe … and he loses himself altogether, talks of the instrument, when he would be thinking of the murderess, tries to return, but only plunges again, with a wild and wandering imagination, into the same topic, then, with a last effort, remembers just so much as that the thing he wanted to speak of was a wicked woman, flings at this theme a desperate platitude, utterly wide of the true mark, ...and comes to a helpless stop … Note also that the effort of Orestes to speak of his dead mother not without tenderness is the last turn which makes the tension unbearable … The soul of Clytaemnestra was so deadly that, had it dwelt in a viper, it would have been the *nature* of that viper to sting by mere contact" (142–43).

[207] The verb προσείπω means literally "to call, to name" and therefore requires an object, which here is νιν. See Verrall's note: "995. νιν: *her* or *it*. Orestes means *her*, but the possible ambiguity is essential to the sequel, and the passage therefore cannot be really translated into English" (143). Both Woolf and Verrall use an expedient, namely they slightly change the verb into "words to use" to maintain the uncertainty present in the passage.

[208] See Verrall's notes on this line: "996. νεκροῦ ποδένδυτον δροίτης κατασκήνωμα: *a bath-curtain fit to wrap the feet of a corpse*, the invention of a clouded and labouring mind, entangled in the notions of *bathing* and *death* … If the interpretation covers δροίτης (and not only κατασκήνωμα), it asserts that δροίτης had the secondary sense of *bier* (or *coffin*) … This would aid the confusion of figures; but it may be based only on a hasty view of this very passage, which does not prove it. … [W]e want more information on the Greek customs both of bathing and burying, and also a fuller account of the murder than Aeschylus anywhere gives." (143).

[209] See Verrall's notes on this line: "997. δίκτυον μὲν οὖν … πέπλους. These words, in the frightful simplicity with which they exhibit the symptoms of mental agony, are comparable only to certain passages of *King Lear*. The disease of speech is more than perplexity, it is a kind of aphasia; and the worst of the horror is the semi-consciousness of the victim. He knows that it is *not* of the robe at all that he wants to speak, that *snare* and *wrapping* and *curtains* are all wrong and irrelevant: *No, it is not that, it is a...net...or rather a...trap as you might say, or again ...*: but it will not do; nothing but *net*, *trap*, *snare* can he say. The 'entangling robe' has fettered his senses and his intellect; he gives himself up to it; and his language at once becomes perfectly fluent and perfectly insane" (143–44).

[210] See Verrall's note on these lines for more on "travellers": "999–1002. 'What profits might be made on the highway by a robber who should set himself up (in a hostelry) with such a thing as this, and give 'the murderer's bath 'to any travellers (ξένοι) who turned in!' Aeschylus has not forgotten that even the extravagance of the mind is obedient, in its own fashion, to memory and association. It is the welcome of Clytaemnestra to the pretended 'travellers' of yesterday, with its gruesome hints of 'bath' and 'bed' and 'honest eyes', which

<Glad is his heart> His heart
laughed merrily when he has

CN15

caught his full bag in such a
fix trap.[211] Ah may
such a woman never be
fellow lodger in the house
with me! Might I
die by the gods will first –
& childless.[212]

---

is reflected in this nightmare of the imagination.
999. τοιοῦτον ἂν Turnebus.—φηλήτης Scaliger … This shows that the spelling φιλήτης is very ancient, and explains the origin of it, but φηλήτης appears to be the true form. It signifies *cozener, cheat,* but was or had been used, as the text suggests, specially for a robber who carried on his 'trade' under the pretence of entertaining travellers, a species found in all disorderly times and countries. Φηλῆται are favourites of fiction, and some strange devices have been attributed to them, but not, by any sane person, the bath of Clytaemnestra" (144).

[211] See Verrall's note to the original text: "1001. *With this deceit might he take off many a life, and his heart often glow with* … The metaphor θερμαίνεσθαι *to be warmed* is not uncommon, in Greek as in English, for exultation, hope, and other such feelings. … The wandering speaker, after another pause of distress, succeeds in recovering his intended theme. But his situation is such, that he cannot say even a few vague words without some fresh shock to his feelings; and at the terrible ὀλοίμην πρόσθεν … ἄπαις he stops dead, gazing, as we see from the words of the chorus and his next speech, in a sort of stupor at his mother's corpse" (144–45).

[212] Compare this passage with Verrall's translation at the end of his edition: *"Orestes.* Behold this pair, who were tyrants of the land, who slew the sire and usurped the house. Majestic they were in the past, when they sat on their thrones, and loving they were: and still, it may be judged, their condition abides with them, and their oath stands true to the pledge, that they would share, as in all, so in death; this, like the rest, hath been truly kept. "Behold now once more, ye that take cognizance of our sad story, this crafty thing, wherewith my unhappy father was bound, a fetter for his arms and a lock for his feet. Spread it out with your own hands; approach and stand about it, and show this net for a man, that our father—not mine, but our father, who surveyeth all things here, the Sun—may see my mother's unclean work, and so perchance may appear one day as my witness in trial, that I had my just cause in pursuing this death,—my mother's. As for Aegisthus' death I reckon it not; he hath, as from the law, the seducer's penalty. But she, who contrived against her husband so vile a thing as this, against him whose children she conceived and carried beneath her girdle, a burden some time dear but now no dearer than ye see—What thinkest thou of her? I say that, were she eel or viper, her touch would turn a man rotten without any bite, if hardness and native will could do it. "What words shall I use of such, to take the very gentlest? A trap were it for beast ? … Or bath-curtain, fit to wrap the feet of a corpse? Nay, rather a seine … no, a snare, you might say...and a foot-entangling … garment—This were the kind of thing for a man to get, who cozened travellers, and practised for his living to beguile and then to rob them with such a cunning weapon might he take off many a life, and his heart often glow with. … Ah, such an one as she may I never have in my dwelling for house-fellow! God strike me dead sooner—having no child!" (233, ellipses original).

Guide to Library Special Collections

This list reflects updates or changes received by the end of January 2025. Suggestions for additions to this list are always welcome.

Name of Collection: The Beinecke Rare Book and Manuscript Library

Contact: Nancy Kuhl, Curator of American Literature

Address: Yale University Library
P.O. Box 208240
New Haven, CT 06520-8240

URL: http://beinecke.library.yale.edu/

Access Requirements: Registration required at first visit.

Holdings Relevant To Woolf: General Collection includes autograph manuscript of "Notes on Oliver Goldsmith." Comments on Edward Gibbon, William Beckford Collection. Letters from Virginia Woolf in the Bryher Papers, the Louise Morgan and Otto Theis Papers, the Rebecca West Papers, the James Lees-Milne Papers, and the Mary Smyth Hunter correspondence. Related material: 41 letters from Vita Sackville-West to Violet Trefusis; files relating to Robert Manson Myers's From Beowulf to Virginia Woolf in the Edmond Pauker Papers.

Yale Collection of American Literature includes typewritten manuscripts of "The Art of Walter Sickert," "Augustine Birrell," "Aurora Leigh," "How Should One Read a Book?" "Letter to a Young Poet," "The Novels of Turgenev," "Street Haunting." Dial/Scofield Thayer Papers: manuscripts of "The Lives of the Obscure," "Miss Ormerod," and "Mrs. Dalloway in Bond Street." Letters from Virginia Woolf in the William Rose Benet Papers, the Benet Family Correspondence, Henry Seidel Canby Papers, the Seward Collins Papers, the Dial/Scofield Thayer Papers, and the Yale Review archive. Material relating to translations of Woolf in the Thornton Wilder papers. Related material: Clive Bell, "Virginia Woolf" (Dial/Scofield Thayer Papers); 43 letters from Leonard Woolf to Helen McAfee

(Yale Review); 11 letters from Leonard Woolf to Gertrude Stein.

Name of Collection: The Henry W. and Albert A. Berg Collection of English and American Literature

Contact: Carolyn Vega, Curator

Address: The New York Public Library
Stephen A. Schwarzman Building
476 Fifth Avenue, Room 320
New York, NY 10018

Telephone: 212-930-0815
Email: carolynvega@nypl.org; berg@nypl.org
URL: https://www.nypl.org/locations/divisions/berg-collection-english-and-american-literature

Hours: Tue–Sat, 11am–5:45pm
Closed Sun., Mon. and legal holidays

Access Requirements: A New York Public Library card and current government-issued photo identification are required to complete registration. Please go to specialcollections.nypl.org to book an appointment, or contact the division with any questions you may have.

Restrictions: Virginia Woolf's bound manuscripts, because of their fragile condition, are made available on microfilm or through digital surrogates.

Holdings Relevant To Woolf: The Virginia Woolf collection of papers (Berg Coll MSS Woolf) includes the manuscripts and/or typescripts of all of Woolf's novels except Orlando, including: Between the Acts, Flush, Jacob's Room, Mrs. Dalloway (notes and fragments), Night and Day, To the Lighthouse, The Voyage Out, The Waves, The Years; 12 notebooks of articles, essays, fiction and reviews, 1924–1940; 36 volumes of diaries; 26 volumes of reading notes; and correspondence with Vanessa Bell, Violet Dickinson, Shuhua Ling, Ethel Smyth, Vita Sackville-West and others.

Since 2019, the Berg Collection has acquired

the William Beekman Collection of Virginia Woolf and Her Circle, which comprises extensive correspondence, remarkable examples of scarce printed books, and unique material such as photographs, original artwork by Vanessa Bell, and ephemera, including Woolf's 1923 passport; the the Hills-Duckworth papers, which consist primarily of personal and family correspondence and photographs; Vanessa Bell's original dust jacket design for Mrs. Dalloway; and individual letters from Virginia Woolf to Ellery Sedgwick, Susan Lushington, and Roger L. Scaife. The Berg also holds related collections of Vita Sackville-West, Leslie Stephen, and others.

Finding aid for the Virginia Woolf collection of papers: http://archives.nypl.org/brg/19159

Finding aid for the William Beekman Collection of Virginia Woolf and Her Circle: http://archives.nypl.org/brg/25777

List of all finding aids in the Berg Collection: http://archives.nypl.org/brg

Name of Collection: The British Library, Modern Archives and Manuscripts

Contact: Manuscripts and Maps Reference Team

Address: 96 Euston Road
London NW1 2DB
England

Telephone: 0207-412-7513
Fax: 0207-412-7745
Email: mss@bl.uk

Hours: The British Library, Manuscripts Reading Room: Mon, 10am–5pm; Tues–Sat, 9:30am–5pm

Access Requirements: British Library Reader Pass (to register for a free Reader Pass a state-issued photo ID, printed with your photo, name and address (driving licence or national ID card) is required or two separate documents, one showing your name and one showing your home address – see www.bl.uk/help/how-to-get-a-reader-pass).

Restrictions: Most manuscript and archive items can be seen by anyone with a valid British Library Reader Pass, but access restrictions may apply for some items of significant historical or literary importance. See individual catalogue entries for details. Photography of selected items available upon receipt of written authorization for photo duplication from the copyright holder.

Holdings Relevant To Woolf: Diaries 1930–1931 (microfilm); *Mrs. Dalloway* and other writings (1923–1925) three volumes (Add MS 51044–51046); letter from Leonard Woolf to H. G. Wells (1941) (Add MS 52553); two letters from Virginia Woolf and three letters from Leonard Woolf to John Lehmann (1941) (Add MS 56234); letters from Virginia Woolf (1923–1927) and one written on behalf of Leonard Woolf to S. S. Koteliansky (1946) (Add MS 48974); notebook of Virginia Stephen (1906–1909) (Add MS 61837); Stephen family papers (Add MS 88954); travel and literary notebook of Virginia Woolf (Add MS 61837); A sketch of the past, revised (1940) (Add MS 61973); letters from Virginia Woolf in the correspondence files of Lytton and James Strachey (Add MS 60655-60734); letter from Virginia Woolf to Mildred Massingberd (Add MS 61891); letter from Virginia Woolf to Harriet Shaw Weaver (1917) (Add MS 57353); (in the same volume as the letter on behalf of Leonard); letter from Virginia Woolf to Frances Cornford (1929) (Add MS 58422); copy of Frances Cornford's *Spring Morning* annotated and decorated by Virginia Woolf (1915) (Add MS 89477/1/1); letter from Virginia Woolf to Ernest Rhys (1930) (Egerton MS 3248); correspondence of Virginia Woolf in the Society of Authors archive (1934–1937) (Add MS 63206–63463); letter and postcard from Virginia Woolf to Bernard Shaw (1940) (Add MS 50522); three letters (suicide notes) from Virginia Woolf (1941) (Add MS 57947). "Hyde Park Gate News" (1891–1892, 1895) (Add. MSS 70725, 70726). Letters of Virginia and Leonard Woolf to Lady Aberconway, (1927–1941) (Add MS 70775).

List related to a fund for Desmond MacCarthy, annotated by Virginia Woolf, (1927) (Add MS 70776). Letters from Virginia Woolf to Macmillan Co. (1903, 1908) (Add MS 54786–56035). Letters from Virginia Woolf to P. Strachey, (1935–1937) (Add MS 81956). Letter to Marie Stopes from Adeline Virginia Woolf, (1941) (Add MS 58495). Collection of RPs ("reserved photocopies"–copies of manuscripts exported, some subject to restrictions).

Name of Collection: Harry Ransom Center

Contact: Head of Reference Services

Address: Harry Ransom Center
The University of Texas at Austin
P.O. Box 13246
Austin, TX 78711

Email: reference@hrc.utexas.edu
URL: www.hrc.utexas.edu

Hours: Exhibitions: Monday, closed,
Tue–Fr, 10am–5pm
Sat–Sun, 12pm–5pm
Reading and Viewing Room:
Mon–Sat, 9am–5pm
Sun, closed

Access Requirements: Completed online research application; current photo identification.

Holdings Relevant To Woolf: The manuscript collection includes the typed manuscript with autograph revisions of Kew Gardens, and the typed manuscript and autograph revisions of "Thoughts on Peace in an Air Raid." The Center holds 571 of Woolf's letters, including correspondence to Elizabeth Bowen, Lady Ottoline Morrell, Mary Hutchinson, William Plomer, Hugh Walpole and others. Further mss. relating to Virginia Woolf include letters to her from T. S. Eliot and reviews of her work. A substantial collection of the first British and American editions of Woolf's published works, as well as 130 volumes from Leonard and Virginia Woolf's library and a collection of books published by the Hogarth Press, is also housed.

An art collection holds a landscape painting of Virginia's garden and a series of Cockney cartoons in a sketch book, signed "V.W." The center also has extensive holdings of materials related to Leonard Woolf, Ottoline Morrell, Mary Hutchinson, Lytton Strachey, Dora Carrington, E. M. Forster, Clive Bell, Roger Fry, Vanessa Bell, Bertrand Russell, Elizabeth Bowen, William Plomer, Stephen Spender and Hugh Walpole.

Name of Collection: Houghton Library (Monk's House Photograph Albums)

Contact: Houghton Public Services

Address: Harvard Yard
Cambridge, MA 02138
United States

Telephone: 617-495-2440
Email: houghton_library@harvard.edu
URL: https://library.harvard.edu/libraries/houghton

Hours: Mon-Fri, 10am–5pm

Access Requirements: https://library.harvard.edu/how-to/access-materials-houghton-library

Holdings Relevant To Woolf: Houghton Library holds Virginia Woolf's Monk's House Photographs, a collection consisting of six albums (MS Thr 557, MS Thr 559–MS Thr 563) and a photographic series (MS Thr 564) composed of an additional album, loose photographs, cabinet cards, and negatives. The photographs are primarily snapshots of Virginia Woolf, her friends, and her family and were also likely taken by Woolf and members of her social circle. Subjects include Woolf herself, Leonard Woolf, Clive Bell, Quentin Bell, Vanessa Bell, Dora de Houghton Carrington, Margaret Llewelyn Davies, T. S. Eliot, Roger Fry, E. M. Forster, Angelica Garnett, Duncan Grant, John Maynard Keynes, Lydia Lopokova, Ralph Partridge, Vita Sackville-West and Lytton

Strachey. The collection also includes photographs of Virginia and Leonard Woolf's homes and snapshots from their travels, including images documenting Leonard Woolf's civil service in Sri Lanka.

Frederick R. Koch gifted the Monk's House Photographs to Houghton's Harvard Theatre Collection in 1983 and all of the materials are available digitally. Finding aids, which include links to the digital material, are available here:

The first album (MH-1): https://id.lib.harvard.edu/ead/hou02067/catalog

The second album (MH-2): https://id.lib.harvard.edu/ead/hou02069/catalog

The third album (MH-3): https://id.lib.harvard.edu/ead/hou02070/catalog

The fourth album (MH-4): https://id.lib.harvard.edu/ead/hou02071/catalog

The fifth album (MH-5): https://id.lib.harvard.edu/ead/hou02072/catalog

The sixth album (MH-6): https://id.lib.harvard.edu/ead/hou02073/catalog

Related photographic series (MS Thr 564): https://id.lib.harvard.edu/ead/hou02507/catalog

Houghton also holds several other archives with relevant correspondence. Of particular note are 9 letters and 1 postcard from Virginia Woolf to T.S. Eliot (MS Am 1432), 7 letters to Theodora Bosanquet (MS Eng 1213.3), 22 letters and 3 postcards to Victoria Ocampo (MS Span 117), and 7 letters to Sir William Rothenstein (MS Eng 1148). A small number of letters sent by or to Woolf can be found in the personal papers of Henry Goddard Leach (MS Eng 854), Logan Pearsall Smith (2005M-4), James Russell Lowell (MS AM 1659), and Charles Eliot Norton (MS Am 1088).

In addition, publishing records related to Woolf's "Nurse Lugton's Golden Thimble" can be found in The Little, Brown and Company collection (MS AM 3171).

Name of Collection: King's College Archive Centre

Contact: Patricia McGuire, Archivist King's College

Address: Archive Center
King's College
Cambridge CB2 1ST

Telephone: 01223 331444
Email: archivist@kings.cam.ac.uk
URL: https://www.kings.cam.ac.uk/archive-centre

Hours: Mon–Thu, 9:30am–12:30pm and 1:30pm–5:15pm. *Closed during public holidays and the College's annual periods of closure.*

Access Requirements: Proof of ID, letter of introduction, appointment in advance.

Holdings Relevant To Woolf: Woolf MSS and letters: Minute book, written up by Clive Bell, of the meetings of a play-reading society, with cast lists and comments on performances by CB. Dec. 1907–Jan. 1909, Oct. 1914– Feb. 1915. Players included variously Clive and Vanessa Bell, Roger and Margery Fry, Duncan Grant, Walter Lamb, Molly MacCarthy, Adrian and Virginia Stephen, Saxon Sydney-Turner. Freshwater, A Comedy—photocopy of editorial typescript prepared from the MSS at Sussex University and Monk's House; photocopy of covering letter from the publisher to "Robert Silvers," Jan. 29, 1976. Papers relating to the Virginia Woolf Centenary Conference held at Fitzwilliam College, Cambridge, Sept. 20–22, 1982. TS with corrections of "Nurse Lugton's Curtain." Typed transcript of R. Fry's memoir of his schooldays. Correspondence with Clive Bell, Julian Bell, Vanessa Bell, Richard Braithwaite, Rupert Brooke, Mrs. Brooke, Katharine Cox, Julian Fry, Roger Fry, John Davy Hayward, J.

M. Keynes, Lydia Keynes, Rosamond Lehmann, Charles Mauron, Raymond Mortimer, Frances and Ralph Partridge, G. H. W. Rylands, J. T. Sheppard, W. J. H. Sprott, Thoby Stephen, Madge Vaughan.

Woolf-related archival collections held: Charleston Papers; Rupert Brooke Papers; E. M. Forster Papers; Roger Fry Papers; J. M. Keynes Papers; Frances Partridge Papers; George Humphrey Wolferstan ('Dadie') Rylands Papers; J. T. Sheppard Papers; W. J. H. Sprott Papers. Various works of art by Vanessa Bell, Duncan Grant, and Roger Fry, held in various locations around King's College. Access via Second Bursar's secretary.

Name of Collection: The Lilly Library

Contact: Joel Silver, Director and Curator of Early Books and Manuscripts
Erika Dowell, Executive Associate Director and Curator of Modern Manuscripts
Rebecca Baumann, Curator of Modern Books

Patrons wishing to use collections would be best served by contacting our Teaching and Research Department email account at liblilly@iu.edu to check on availability and access.

Holdings Relevant To Woolf: Corrected page proofs for the British edition of Mrs. Dalloway; letters to Woolf from Desmond and Mary (Molly) MacCarthy; 77 letters (published in Letters) from Woolf to correspondents including Donald Clifford Brace, Robert Gathorne-Hardy, Barbara (Strachey) Halpern, Richard Arthur Warren Hughes, Desmond MacCarthy and Molly MacCarthy; "Preliminary Scheme for the formation of a Partnership between Mr Leonard Sidney Woolf and Mr John Lehmann to take over The Hogarth Press" (includes contract signed by Lehmann, Leonard Woolf, and Virginia Woolf and receipt for Lehmann's payment to Virginia Woolf to purchase Virginia Woolf's share in the Hogarth Press); photographs of Virginia Woolf, Leonard Woolf, Lytton Strachey, Strachey family, Roger Fry, and Vanessa Bell (Hannah Whitall Smith mss.); (Richard) Kennedy mss. (four hand-colored lithographs of Virginia Woolf: artist's proofs for RK's portfolio, VIRGINIA WOOLF: "AS I KNEW HER"; Sackville-West, V. mss. (10,529 items: includes the correspondence of Vita Sackville-West, and Harold Nicolson); MacCarthy mss. (ca. 10,000 items: papers of Desmond and Molly MacCarthy); correspondence between LW and Mary Gaither regarding publication of A Checklist of the Hogarth Press (1976, repr. 1986); Todd Avery, Close and Affectionate Friends: Desmond and Molly MacCarthy and the Bloomsbury Group (The Lilly Library/Indiana University Libraries, 1999); Notable books (The [sic] Voyage out (1915) – 1st ed. (PR6045.O7 V6 1915); Two stories (1917) – 1st ed., written and published by Virginia and L.S. Woolf, copy 1 signed by both. (PR6045.O7 T9); Kew Gardens (1919) – 1st ed., signed by Woolf (PR6045.O7 K4); Kew Gardens (1927) – 3rd English ed., signed by Woolf and illustrator (PR6045.O7 K44 1927)

Name of Collection: Jane Marcus Collection

Note: This collection is closed and will be moving to the CUNY Graduate Center later in 2025.

Name of Collection: Monks House Papers/Leonard Woolf Papers/ Charleston Papers/Nicolson Papers

Contact: University of Sussex, Special Collections

Address: The Keep
Woollards Way
Brighton & Hove
BN1 9PB

Telephone: 01273 482349
Email: library.specialcoll@sussex.ac.uk
URL: http://www.thekeep.info

Access Requirements: Seats in the reading room can be booked in advance. Identification is required to complete registration on your first visit to The Keep. Registration and material requests can be made through our website.

Restrictions: Access to some of the papers is by surrogate. Digital photography is allowed for private research, charges apply.

Holdings Relevant To Woolf: The University of Sussex holds two large archives relating to Leonard and Virginia Woolf: The Monks House Papers, primarily correspondence and MSS of Virginia Woolf, including the three scrapbooks relating to Three Guineas, and Virginia Woolf's engagement diaries from 1930 to her death in 1941; and The Leonard Woolf Papers, primarily correspondence and other papers of Leonard Woolf. (Monks House Papers are available on microfilm in many research libraries.) The Charleston Papers consist in the main of letters written to or by Clive and Vanessa Bell and Duncan Grant which had accumulated in their home; the library houses Quentin Bell's photocopied set; letters from Roger Fry, Maynard Keynes, Lytton Strachey, Virginia Woolf, Vita Sackville-West, E. M. Forster, T. S. Eliot, Frances Partridge and others. The Maria Jackson letters comprise some 900 letters from Maria Jackson to Julia and Leslie Stephen. The Nicolson Papers complement these three Sussex archives relating to the Bloomsbury Group and consist of Nigel Nicolson's correspondence relating to his editorial work as principal editor of the six-volume Letters of Virginia Woolf, published between 1975 and 1980.

The Bell Papers. A. O. Bell's correspondence relating to her editorial work on Virginia Woolf's diaries, a parallel collection to the Nicolson Papers. Collection level description may be accessed at www.archiveshub.ac.uk.

Name of Collection: The Morgan Library & Museum

Contact: Reading Room

Address: 225 Madison Avenue
New York, NY 10016

Telephone: 212-590-0315
Email: readingroom@themorgan.org
URL: www.themorgan.org

Access Requirements: Admission to the Reading Room is by application and by appointment. See www.themorgan. org/ research/reading.asp for application form.

Holdings Relevant To Woolf: Virginia Woolf. Autograph manuscript notebook, 1931 Sept. 24. 1 item (52 p.); 265 x 208 mm. Contains drafts of "A Letter to a Young Poet," a brief letter to the press entitled "The Villa Jones" [ff. 3–5] and a monologue by a working-class woman [ff. 44–46]. MA 3333. Purchased on the Fellows Fund with the special assistance of Anne S. Dayton, Enid A. Haupt, Mrs. James H. Ripley, Mr. and Mrs. August H. Schilling, and John S. Thacher,1979.

Virginia Woolf. Autograph letters signed (2) and typed letter signed, dated London [etc.], to E. McKnight Kauffer, 1931 Apr. 4 and 23, and undated. 3 items (4 p.). Concerning a drawing of her and a bibliography of her works. MA 1679. Purchased from Marion Dorn Kauffer in 1955.

Vanessa Bell. 84 autograph letters, 3 typed letters, 7 postcards, and 3 telegrams. Most, but not all, are written by Vanessa Bell to John Maynard Keynes. Concerning Duncan Grant, Roger Fry, Clive Bell, the Bell children, Leonard and Virginia Woolf, Lytton Strachey, John Maynard and Lydia Lopokova Keynes, David Garnett, Ottoline Morrell, and others. MA 3448. Items in this collection are described in 97 individual records (MA 3448.1-97). Purchased on the Fellows Fund, special gift of the Gramercy Park Foundation (Mrs. Michael Tucker), 1980.

Vanessa Bell. 2 letters (7 June and 8 July 1908) to J. Pierpont Morgan regarding the sale of Adrian Stephen's collection of Thackeray drawings and manuscripts (ARC 3247–48). Bill of sale dated 6 Feb 1909 (ARC 1310).

Letter from Virginia Woolf, London to R. W. Chapman, 1930 November 13. 1 item (1 p.). Concerning revisions to the criticism section of a bibliography of Jane Austen. Accompanied by carbon copy of a letter from Chapman to Woolf dated 1930 November 11. MA 8893. Purchased on the Drue Heinz Fund, 2017.

Twenty-four letters from Leslie Stephen to W.E. Henley, 1876–1881. MA 1617.411-MA 1617.434. Purchased as the gift of Edwin J. Beinecke, 1955.

Five letters from John Ruskin to Julia Marshall and Julia Stephen, 1877–1879 and undated. MA 14342.1-5. Bequest of Gordon N. Ray, 1987

Recent Acquisitions: Eleven letters and postcards from Virginia Woolf to Clive Bell, 1908–1931, one letter from Virginia Woolf to Eric Duthie, 1927 October 2, one postcard from Virginia Woolf to A.W. Brickett, 1937 February 17, and one photograph of Virginia Woolf at Monk's House, between 1919 and 1941. MA 22718-22731. Gift from the estate of Nancy N. Brooker, 2018.

Name of Collection: 1. Katherine Mansfield Papers
2. Arts Club of Chicago Papers

Contact: Alison Hinderliter, Lloyd Lewis Curator of Modern Manuscripts and Archives

Address: The Newberry Library, 60 West Walton Street, Chicago, IL, 60610

Telephone: (312) 255-3694 (Hinderliter)
Email: hinderlitera@newberry.org

Hours: Tue–Sat, 10am–4pm

Access Requirements: The Newberry's reading rooms are open to researchers who are at least 14 years old or first years in high school. Before using the collections, all researchers must apply for and receive a reader's card. Issued in the Welcome Center on the first floor, cards require a valid photo ID, proof of current home address, and a research interest that is supported by the Newberry's collections.

Holdings Relevant To Woolf: The papers of the Arts Club of Chicago—since 1916, a private club and preeminent exhibitor of international art—contain material related to Bloomsbury artists and how they were received in Chicago. The papers of Katherine Mansfield contain manuscript copies of some of Mansfield's most important work, and outgoing correspondence—the bulk to artist Dorothy Brett and Lady Ottoline Morrell. The Fanny Butch Papers includes a subject file and photograph file on Virginia Woolf.

Name of Collection: University of Reading Special Collections

Contact: Special Collections Service
Address: Special Collections Service
University of Reading
6 Redlands Road
Reading RG1 5EX

Telephone: 0118-378-8660
Email: specialcollections@reading.ac.uk
URL: https://collections.reading.ac.uk/special-collections/

Access Requirements: Prior appointment suggested to consult material. Permission required to consult or copy material in the Hogarth Press, Jonathan Cape, and Chatto & Windus collections from Penguin Random

House: Penguin Random House Archive and Library
1 Cole Street
Crown Park
Rushden
Northants. NN10 6RZ
archive@penguinrandomhouse.co.uk

Holdings Relevant To Woolf: The Hogarth Press (MS 2750): Editorial and production correspondence relating to publications of the Press, including Virginia Woolf and Leonard Woolf's own titles. These files feature letters from Leonard Woolf and the employees of The Hogarth Press, including various managers (such as John Lehman) and secretarial staff, 1922–1955 (MS 2750/1-627). Of note, there is one letter dictated by Leonard Woolf but written by Virginia Woolf (MS 2750/255/64); Ledgers and albums, 1920–1994

(MS 2750/A) including order books e.g., lists of booksellers, book clubs and how many books they have ordered for a particular title, and newspaper cuttings e.g., press clippings of advertisements for Hogarth Press books including Virginia Woolf publications; Outgoing letter books, 1947–1951; 1965–1967 (MS 2750/B). Correspondence files regarding translation rights of Virginia Woolf's publications, 1924–1983 (MS 2750/C); Photographs of Leonard Woolf, Virginia Woolf, and other Bloomsbury figures, 1860s–1980s (MS 2750/D).

Chatto & Windus (CW): small number of letters 1915–1925; 1929–1931.Various letters and notes by Leonard Woolf; outgoing letters to Leonard Woolf: 22 November 1927 (CW A/119); outgoing letters to Virginia Woolf: 29 January 1936 (CW A/172), 22 December 1931 (CW A/135), 31 December 1931 (CW A/135), 15 December 1920 (CW A/100), 20 December 1920 (CW A/100).
George Bell & Sons (MS 1640): 5 letters from Leonard Woolf 1930–1966.

Routledge (RKP): Reader's report by Leonard Woolf on George Padmore's "Britannia rules the blacks" (1935); "How Britain rules Africa." 1 letter from Leonard Woolf (June 1941) from Miscellaneous publishing correspondence 1941–1942 Wi-Wy RKP 174/15. Draft introduction by Leonard Woolf to Letters on India by Mulk Raj (1942) and 1 letter to Leonard Woolf from Mulk Raj Anand 1942-1943 RKP 178/3. Correspondence concerning the publication of The War for Peace by Leonard Woolf, 1939–1940 RKP 160/5. 1 letter from Virginia Woolf declining an invitation from Routledge to write a biography of Margaret Bondfield, 25 May 1940 RKP 160/5.

Megroz (MS 1979/68): 2 letters from Leonard Woolf, 1926.

Allen & Unwin (MS 3282): Allen & Unwin (AU): correspondence with Leonard Woolf c.1914-1918 (concerning his book "International Government"), 1923-1924; 1939-1940; 1943;

1946 (concerning progress with Woolf's collected edition of the works of Freud); 1950-1951; 1953; 1965 (concerning ill-founded rumours about the Hogarth Press); 1967 (concerning a reprint of Empire and Commerce in Africa).

Jonathan Cape (JC): All correspondence from file JC A43. Correspondence between Jonathan Cape and Virginia Woolf and Cape and A. C. Gissing concerning Virginia Woolf's introduction to George Gissing's Ionian Sea to which A. C. Gissing objects. 1 postcard (1935), 1 letter (1933), 2 letters (1932) from Virginia Woolf. 1 letter (1932) from Virginia Woolf declining to write an introduction to Jane Austen's Northanger Abbey. 4 letters (1931) from Virginia Woolf declining to write an introduction to one of Miss Thackeray's books.

Letters from Vanessa Bell: 1 letter from Bell CW 152/2; 1 letter from Bell CW 171/10; 2 letters from Bell CW 578/1; 1 letter from Bell CW 59/9; 1 letter from Bell (1936) CW 61/10. Artwork by Vanessa Bell for various Virginia Woolf titles.

Artwork by Angelica Garnett, Philippa Bramson and others for various books in the Chatto & Windus archive.

Name of Collection: Smith College Special Collections

Contact: Smith College Special Collections

Address: Smith College Special Collections
Neilson Library, 3rd floor
83 Green Street
Northampton, MA 01063

Telephone: 413-585-2970
Email: specialcollections@smith.edu
URL: https://libraries.smith.edu/special-collections

Hours: Mon–Fri, 10am–4:45pm

Access Requirements: Open to all—no appointment necessary but appreciated: https://libraries.smith.edu/specialcollections/about/visit

Holdings Relevant To Woolf: Virginia Woolf papers: https://findingaids.smith.edu/repositories/3/resources/405
Frances Hooper papers on Virginia Woolf : https://findingaids.smith.edu/repositories/3/resources/430
Elizabeth P. Richardson papers: https://findingaids.smith.edu/repositories/3/resources/407
Leslie Stephen photograph album: https://findingaids.smith.edu/repositories/3/resources/428
Additional published work by Virginia Woolf and other members of the Bloomsbury Group can be searched via https://libraries.smith.edu/ (click on "More search options" under Discover Advanced and limit by location to "Smith College Special Collections"), among other collections related to Virginia Woolf and her circle.

The Virginia Woolf papers and Francis Hooper papers on Virginia Woolf include many Hogarth Press first editions, limited editions of Woolf's works, and translations. The collection includes page proofs of Orlando, To the Lighthouse, and The Common Reader, corrected by Woolf for the first American editions, a proof copy of The Waves that Woolf inscribed to Hugh Walpole, and the proof copies of The Years and of Flush. The Collection also has one of the deluxe editions of Orlando that was printed on green paper. Other items include twenty-two pages of reading notes from 1926, three pages of notes on D. H. Lawrence's Sons and Lovers, thirty-three pages of notes for Roger Fry, a six-page ms. "As to criticism," a five-page ms. of "The Searchlight," and a fourteen-page ms. of "The Patron and The Crocus." The Hooper Collection also owns 140 letters between Woolf and Lytton Strachey as well as other correspondence, including a 13 February [1921] letter to Katherine Mansfield and ten letters to Mela and Robert Spira

The Richardson papers is a working collection of books and materials used by Richardson in preparing her Bloomsbury Iconography. It includes ninety-eight original exhibition catalogs dating back to 1929, clippings and photocopies of such items as reviews of early Woolf works, and

Bloomsbury material from British Vogue of the 1920s. The Collection also has three preliminary pencil drawings by Vanessa Bell for Flush.

Smith College Special Collections also owns Woolf's 1916 Italian ms. notebook and her corrected typescripts of "Reviewing" and "The Searchlight." In addition, there is a 1923 photograph of Woolf at Garsington. Original cover designs for Hogarth Press publications include The Common Reader, On Being Ill, and Duncan Grant. The collection also includes Woolf's 26 February 1939 letter to Vita Sackville-West, a 1923 Hogarth Press edition of T. S. Eliot's The Waste Land, a 1919 Hogarth Press edition of Paris by Hope Mirrlees and first editions of Vita Sackville-West and Katherine Mansfield publications. Additional Bloomsbury items include Original Woodcuts (Omega Workshops, 1918), Vanessa Bell's original woodcut for the cover of Monday or Tuesday (1921), and exhibition catalogs for Manet and the Post-Impressionists (Grafton Galleries, 1911), Friday Club Members (Mansard Gallery, 1921) Paintings and Drawings by Vanessa Bell (Independent Gallery, 1922). Additional photographs include the Mary L. S. Bennett (née Fisher) Family Photographs and Leslie Stephen's photograph album.

Name of Collection: Woolf/Hogarth Press/Bloomsbury

Contact: Roma Kail (Interim Chief Librarian)

Address: Victoria University Library
71 Queens Park, Crescent E.
Toronto M5S 1K7
Ontario, Canada

Email: victoria.library@utoronto.ca
URL: https://library.vicu.utoronto.ca/collections/special_collections/bloomsbury_group/

Hours: Mon–Fri, 9:30 am–4:30 pm

Access Requirements: Prior notification; identification.

Restrictions: Limited reproduction.

Holdings Relevant To Woolf: This collection, the most comprehensive of its kind with over 6,000 items, contains all the work of Virginia and Leonard Woolf in various editions, issues, variants and translations; all the books hand-printed by Leonard and Virginia Woolf at the Hogarth Press, including many variant issues and bindings, association copies and page proofs; a nearly comprehensive collection of Hogarth Press machine printed books to 1946 (the year Leonard Woolf and the Press joined Chatto & Windus) including presentation copies, signed limited editions, page proofs, variants as well as substantial amounts of ephemera, such as the Catalogue of Publications to 1939 with annotations by Leonard Woolf. The collection is also very strong in Bloomsbury Art and Artists, especially the decorative arts, including important examples of Omega Workshops publications and exhibition catalogues. Materials include the catalogue of the second post-impressionist exhibition, 1912; catalogues relating to Vanessa Bell and Duncan Grant exhibitions; bronze medal of Virginia Woolf by Marta Firlet; oil on canvas portrait of Amaryllis Garnett by Vanessa Bell (c.1958); Portrait sketch of Leonard Woolf by Vanessa Bell; portrait of Leonard Woolf by Duncan Grant; portrait of Julia Duckworth by Henry Holiday (1839–1927); Duncan Grant and Vanessa Bell designed Clarice Cliff dinner plates; original Vanessa Bell and Duncan Grant sketches and designs for dust jackets, novels, and other special projects; Duncan Grant charcoal portrait of Virginia Woolf (1968); Quentin Bell set of five pottery plates based on the novels of Virginia Woolf (ca. 1979); Quentin Bell pottery figurine in aid of Charleston (ca. 1980); a selection of other pottery by Quentin Bell; bronze busts of Lytton Strachey, Duncan Grant and Virginia Woolf by Stephen Tomlin (1901–1937); as well as the Marcel Gimond bust of Vanessa Bell and the Tomlin bust of Henrietta Bingham. Book hand bound by Virginia Woolf. Wooden plaque from the Hogarth Press at 24 Tavistock. Examples of programmes, posters, and handbills relating to productions of plays, movies, and dance productions with content relating to Bloomsbury group members. Original correspondence and mss.

material includes that by Vanessa Bell; Leonard Woolf; Ritchie family re: Anne Thackeray Ritchie/ Stephen family; Duncan Grant; Quentin Bell; S. P. Rosenbaum mss. Letters from E. M. Forster, Bertrand Russell, James Strachey, Raymond Mortimer, David Garnett, Nigel Nicolson and others in the Bloomsbury Circle; as well as biographers, scholars and bibliographers such as Joanne Trautmann, Carolyn Heilbrun, J. Howard Woolmer, Leon Edel, Leila Luedeking, P. N. Furbank, Noel Annan and others. Large Ephemera Collection includes items revealing Virginia Woolf's effect on popular culture.

Name of Collection: Library of Leonard and Virginia Woolf (Washington S U)

Contact: Trevor James Bond
Head, Manuscripts, Archives, and Special Collections

Address: Washington State University Libraries
Pullman, WA 99164-5610

Email: tjbond@wsu.edu
URL: www.wsulibs.wsu.edu/holland/masc/masc.htm

Hours: Mon–Fri, 8:30am–4:30pm

Access Requirements: Letter stating nature of research preferred; student or other identification.

Restrictions: Materials must be used in the MASC area under supervision. Photocopying or photographing is permitted only when it will not harm the materials and is permitted by copyright.

Holdings Relevant To Woolf: WSU has the Woolfs' basic working library including many works which belonged to Woolf's father, Sir Leslie Stephen, and other family members. Over 800 titles came from their Sussex home, Monks House, including some works bought at auction soon after Leonard Woolf died in 1969. Later additions include: 1,875 titles from his house in Victoria Square, London; 400 titles from his nephew Cecil Woolf; and over 60 titles from Quentin and Anne Olivier Bell. WSU has been actively collecting: all works in all editions by Virginia Woolf; all titles by Leonard Woolf; dust jackets; works published by the Woolfs at the Hogarth Press through 1946; books by their friends and associates, especially those by Bloomsbury authors and about Bloomsbury artists; relevant correspondence and original works of art. Original artwork by Vanessa Bell; scattered letters by Vanessa Bell, E. M. Forster, Roger Fry, Leslie Stephen, Lytton Strachey, and Leonard Woolf. Original artwork by Richard Kennedy for illustrations in his book A Boy at the Hogarth Press; scattered letters by Roger Fry, Leslie Stephen, Ethel Smyth, and Leonard Woolf. Virginia Woolf's initialed copy of Cornishiana; Leonard Woolf's annotated copy of An Anatomy of Poetry by A. Williams-Ellis; Leslie Stephen's copy of Lapsus Calami and Other Verses, inscribed by James Kenneth Stephen. Several letters from Virginia Woolf, including two written in 1939 to Ronald Heffer, and a letter to Edward McKnight Kauffer. New in the Hogarth Press Collection are a copy of E. M. Forster's Anonymity, an Enquiry, bound in cream paper boards, and what Woolmer calls the third label state of Forster's The Story of the Siren. The Library of Leonard and Virginia Woolf is once again shelved separately so that scholars visiting Pullman may see the collection apart from the other rare book collections

Recent Acquisitions: Correspondence to Clive and Vanessa Bell (approximately 30 items), with most items addressed to Clive. Correspondents include Stephen Tallant, Eric MacLagan, John Pollock, H. J. Norton, Lyn Irvine (including one letter mentioning Mrs. Raven Hill), Sir George Grahame, Karen Costelloe, John Alford, Ivor Churchill, the Earl of Sandwich, George Lansbury, Clifford Sharp, F. H. S. Shepherd, Gilbert Seldes, Lord Evan Tredegar, C. E. Stuart, Max Eastman, E. Hilton Young, Col. Heward Bell.

Name of Collection: Yale Center for British Art

Contact: Study Room, Yale Center for British Art

Address:	1080 Chapel Street P.O. Box 208280 New Haven, CT 06520-8280
Telephone:	(203) 432-2840
Fax:	(203) 432-7314
Email:	ycba.studyroom@yale.edu
URL:	https://collections.britishart.yale.edu/
Hours:	Tue–Fri, 10am-12pm and 1pm-4pm
Access Requirements:	Study Room access is by appointment, patrons are required to register with Yale Special Collections. Can provide images upon request but cannot grant permissions.
Holdings Relevant To Woolf:	Rare Books & Mss Department: 94 letters from Vanessa Bell and Duncan Grant to Sir Kenneth Clark; 6 letters from Lytton Strachey (to Clive Bell, Siegfried Sassoon, et al.). Prints & Drawings Department: 7 drawings by Vanessa Bell; 6 drawings by Duncan Grant; 16 drawings by Wyndham Lewis; 1 drawing by Frederick Etchells; 2 photographs by Julia Margaret Cameron. Paintings Department: 3 paintings by Vanessa Bell, 7 paintings by Duncan Grant (including 2 portraits of Vanessa Bell); 4 paintings by Roger Fry.

Index of *Woolf Studies Annual* volumes 21–30 (2015–2024)

Compiled by Oliver Case, Jenny Ann Cubin, Benjamin D. Hagen, and Skylar Kovacs

Introduction to the *Woolf Studies Annual* Index Project: Part Four

Like the first three installments of the *Woolf Studies Annual* index project (2022, 2023, 2024), this fourth and final installment is divided into four primary sections: Names and Places, Sources, Topics, and Woolf References. A fifth section offers a bibliography of the articles, reviews, archival materials, and more included in volumes 21–30 (2015–24) of the journal. The Index Team continues to hope that this organization is self-explanatory and that the organizing logic of our four-year collaboration will become clearer as readers and researchers flip and look through the following pages.

For convenience, I repeat here a few clarifications:

- We have indexed articles and not book reviews or published archival materials.
- The "Names" in the index's first section are names of historical (not fictional) persons. We decided it would not be worthwhile to track references to "Woolf, Virginia" (a *passim* might suffice). We made the same decision about other ubiquitous place names like "England" and "London."
- Part Two (Sources) is subdivided into three subsections: A) Works by Literary Figures and Artists; B) Scholarship and Miscellaneous Texts; and C) Woolf and Woolf-Adjacent Scholarship.
- Part Three (Topics) no doubt misses a great deal, but we have included "See also" subheadings that should help readers build connections of their own across articles. The indexers have tried to retain categories from the first two installments so as to maintain consistency across and communication between *WSA* 28, 29, 30, and 31.
- Part Four (Woolf References) inventories citations and references to Woolf's fiction and nonfiction, and it also lists which diary entries (by date) and which letters (by letter no., date, and addressee) authors cite/reference as well.
- Section Five (Bibliography) provides a full list of content included in *WSA* 21–30 (2015–2024).

Two last things: first, the completion of this index no doubt contains, as past installments did, errors and oversights. Though the WSA *Index Project* is complete, we welcome corrections and amendments, which will be useful should we pursue a revision of the index in the future. (See the "Submission Policy" page for the contact information of the *WSA* editor.) Second, I want to thank Oliver Case, Jenny Ann Cubin, and Skylar Kovacs for returning to work on Part Four of this project.

—Benjamin D. Hagen
University of South Dakota

Part 1: Names and Places
Compiled by Benjamin D. Hagen and Skylar Kovacs

10 Downing Street Wisor 21.17, 21, 24
22 Hyde Park Gate de Gay 30.100; Sullam 30.117
Abbott, Wilbur Cortez Gillespie 25.102
Abe, Juri Czarnecki 21.58
Abel, Elizabeth Rutherford 24.135
Abercrombie, Patrick Jones 22.82–84
Abrahams, William Gallego Larrarte 30.115
Abrams, M.H. Shin 23.124
Abramson, Ben Gilman 29.30n11
Abyssinia (now Ethiopia) Graeber 24.166; Rutherford 24.153; Wisor 21.22n36
Ackerley, Joe Davison 29.144
Ackerman, Robert McVicker 28.72n8
Acland, Henry W. Schwartz 29.89
Adair, Robin Gillespie 25.99n4
Adam Gallery Chua 30.31
Adams, David McVicker 28.81n20, 87
Adams, Henry C. Golden 23.89n15
Adams, Rachel Chua 30.34
Addison, Joseph Gilman 29.34
Adkins, Peter Jenkins (Amber) 27.14n18; Ryan 30.69
Adlington, William Rutherford 24.155
Aegean Sea Bunting 30.13
Aeschylus Golden 23.85n8, 87n13, 89n15; Jenkins (Gwyn) 27.27, 31, 41; Koulouris 25.5, 50n159, 69n240, 70; White 24.108
Africa Gillespie 25.102; Graeber 24.170n4, 180n14; Novillo-Corvalán 23.42, 52, 54, 56; Schwartz 29.94
Agathon Dalgarno 22.8; Koulouris 25.50–54, 57
Agree, James Berkowitz 29.129n8
Ahmed, Sara Caputi 29.5n2; Favre 30.64; Kotler 24.37–38, 40, 44–47, 50, 52; Livingstone 26.98; van Straten 30.88
Aiken, Conrad Kopley 30.127
Alabama Caputi 29.18, 19
Albania Gillespie 25.104
Alberti, Juan Bautista Novillo-Corvalán 23.48
Alberti, Leon Battista Ke 29.64, 65n9, 66, 67, 68, 73
Albertini, Tamara Ke 29.66
Alcibiades Dalgarno 22.4, 7–8; Koulouris 25.3, 50n158, 55–57
Aldgate, Anthony Wisor 21.8n16
Alexander, Horace Foster 22.52
Alighieri, Dante Czarnecki 21.66n17; Golden 23.89; Ryan 30.68, 75, 76, 81
Allan, Tuzyline Jita Bond 23.76n17
Allègre, Marie Favre 30.54, 55n2
Allen, Annette Foster 22.42, 59n33
Allen, Clifford Berkowitz 29.132
Allen, Henry M. Dalgarno 22.3n3
Allen, Judith Leach 28.99; Ryan 30.69n8
Allen, Maud Rutherford 24.154
Allen, Paula Gunn Czarnecki 21.50–53, 55–56, 59, 62, 69
Alley, Henry M. Jenkins (Gwyn) 27.23, 37
Alsen, Eberhard Ke 29.68n12
Alt, Christina Czarnecki 21.52n3; Davison 23.7n15; Jones 22.76n2; Livingstone 26.88n2; Lostoski-Ho 28.50, 51; Novillo-Corvalán 23.50; Ryan 30.69
Altenmüller, Eckart Davison 23.2n3
Althusser, Louis Schwartz 29.99
Amato, Joseph van Straten 30.90n7
Ames, Christopher White 24.122n34
Amidon, Stevens Cheney 24.59n6
Anderson, Gerald D. Wisor 21.29

Andrés-Cuevas, Isabel María Foster 22.41
Andrews, Charles Cheney 24.57n1; Delsandro 25.76; Foster 22.67
Andrews, Kerri van Straten 30.85n1, 86
Annan, Noel Gillespie 25.106
Anne of Denmark (Queen) Lauby 27.49, 50
Anrep, Boris Berkowitz 29.138; Gillespie 29.149–50, 151, 152
Ansermet, Ernest Berkowitz 29.128, 132, 133
Anspaugh, Kelly Lauby 27.59
Antarctica Gillespie 25.104
Antell, Judith A. Czarnecki 21.63
Apollodorus of Athens Koulouris 25.50n158
Appardurai, Arjun Chua 30.34
Apuleius, Lucius Rutherford 24.155–56
Aquinas, Thomas Lauby 27.52
Arana, Julio César Novillo-Corvalán 23.54–55
Argentina Novillo-Corvalán 23.passim; Shin 23.131
Aristodemus Koulouris 25.3, 50, 57
Aristophanes Koulouris 25.8, 14, 50n158, 52–53, 57, 69
Aristotle Bunting 30.18; Gilman 29.34; Jenkins (Gwyn) 27.27, 35; Kotler 24.38; Schwartz 29.100, 101; White 24.passim
Armenia Gillespie 25.104
Armstrong, Charles Ke 29.79n17
Armstrong, Philip Williams 26.117
Arnold, Matthew Dalgarno 22.1, 3–4, 14; Gilman 29.46n4; Schwartz 29.96
Arrington, Phillip Ke 29.65n10
Arts Council Gallery (London) Chua 30.31
Asch, Sholem Pająk 24.18
Ashmolean Museum (Oxford) Chua 30.31
Asia Novillo-Corvalán 23.42
Astell, Mary Wisor 21.20
Athens, Greece Bunting 30.26; Dalgarno 22.5, 8; Gillespie 25.104, 123; Golden 23.100–102; Koulouris 25.passim; Reed 29.162
Atkin, Jonathan Berkowitz 29.127n6
Attridge, Derek Williams 26.110
Aubrey, John McVicker 28.83n24
Auden, W. H. de Gay 30.99; Gallego Larrarte 30.111, 113, 115; Kopley 30.127
Auerbach, Erich Koulouris 25.7; White 24.113, 117n30
Augustus Koulouris 25.19n37
Austen, Jane Chua 30.37, 38; Golden 23.93–94; Jenkins (Gwyn) 27.43; Leach 28.102n7; Shin 23.131
Austen-Leigh, J. E. Leach 28.102n7
Australia Gillespie 25.125; Graeber 24.170n4, 171; Pająk 24.23
Austria Gillespie 25.102; Graeber 24.175; Pająk 24.22
Avebury McVicker 28.76, 82, 83, 87
Avery, Todd Davison 29.144
Bacall, Lauren Marcus 24.5
Bach, Johann Sebastian Davison 23.17; Jenkins (Gwyn) 27.34, 40
Bachelard, Gaston Ryan 30.69, 72, 81
Bacon, George Washington Gillespie 25.122n43
Baden-Powell, Agnes Wisor 21.12n20
Baden-Powell, Olave Wisor 21.12n20
Baden-Powell, Sir Robert Kotler 24.51; Wisor 21.2, 8–14, 37
Baedeker, Karl Gillespie 25.100–01, 123; Golden 23.96–97, 99–103
Bagenal, Barbara White 24.103n5
Bahun, Sanja Foster 22.59n33, 60n38; Van Wert 29.109, 112, 117, 119
Bailey, Benjamin Koulouris 25.2n5
Bailey, N. Golden 23.97n22
Baker, Abigail McVicker 28.72n8
Baker, Andrew Berkowitz 29.133
Baker, Houston Caputi 29.6n2
Baker, J. N. L. Gillespie 25.104
Bakhtin, Mikhail Cheney 24.57; McVicker 28.80n18; Sullam 30.118
Bal, Mieke White 24.109n17
Baldwin, Nick Adair/Martin 24.82n8, 85
Baldwin, Stanley Jones 22.83; Kotler 24.51; Wisor 21.2, 15n26, 16, 20–26
The Balkans Gillespie 25.102
Balthus Berkowitz 29.128

Balzac, Honoré Gilman 29.31n13
Banet-Weiser, Sarah Berkowitz 29.135n13
Banfield, Ann Bond 23.67; Jenkins (Amber) 27.5; Layne 21.84, 93, 98–99; Sullam 30.121n4
Bankes, William John Rutherford 24.141–42, 156, 159
Banks, Gemma McVicker 28.82n23
Banks, Joanne Trautmann Bond 23.74; Phillips 26.9
Banner, Louis Humm 29.158
Bantock, G. H. Davison 29.146, 147
Barber, Martyn McVicker 28.82
Baring, Rowland Thomas Wisor 21.8
Barnes, George Fischer 28.26n3
Barnes, John Wisor 21.21–22
Barnes, Julian Williams 26.115
Barnes, Leonard Gillespie 25.102
Barnlund, Dean C. Berkowitz 29.131, 137
Barr, Jr., Alfred H. Berkowitz 29.128–29n8
Barr, Margaret Berkowitz 29.128–29n8
Barr, Tina Rutherford 24.142n4
Barrett, Eileen Bond 23.76n17; Bunting 30.12, 16; Czarnecki 21.51n2; Layne 21.89; McVicker 28.71n7, 75n11; Van Wert 29.120
Barrett, Michèle Gillespie 25.104n16; Jones 22.86; Kotler 24.48; Novillo-Corvalán 23.33–34, 58; Wisor 21.1
Barrows, Adam White 24.113n23
Barthes, Roland Favre 30.59n11; Fischer 28.28, 29–30, 35, 41; Foster 22.66; Jenkins (Gwyn) 27.42; Wisor 21.3
Bartholomew, J.G. Gillespie 25.102–03, 120, 125
Barzun, Jacques Davison 23.3n5
Bassnet, Susan Novillo-Corvalán 23.40
Batchelor, John Novillo-Corvalán 23.36
Bates, Sir Percy Adair/Martin 24.92
Bath Chua 30.31
Batkin, Norton Ke 29.66
Baucom, Ian Caputi 29.5n2
Baudelaire, Charles Bunting 30.18
Bayreuth, Germany Davison 23.4, 26–27; Foster 22.64n44
Bazin, Nancy Favre 30.58
Beard, Mary Jenkins (Gwyn) 27.26
Beasley, Rebecca Fouirnaies 22.38
Beattie, Thomas White 24.127n38
Beaumont, Francis Leach 28.102
Beauvoir, Simone de Delsandro 25.75n4
Beckett, Samuel Cheney 24.70; Shin 23.129
Beddington, Jack Adair/Martin 24.92–93
Bedford Place White 24.116
Beer, Gillian Davison 23.1n1, 7, 24; Davison 29.144; Fischer 28.27; Foster 22.65n45; Gillespie 25.118; Lostoski-Ho 28.50n6; McVicker 28.69n2, 89–90; Shin 23.111n7, 123n22, 124
Beerbohm, Marie Berkowitz 29.128
Beethoven, Ludwig van Davison 23.9, 19; Foster 22.56–57
Belgium Delsandro 25.82n11
Bellamy, Edward Cheney 24.64
Bell, Anne Olivier Koulouris 25.2, 4, 13n16–17
Bell, Clive Adair/Martin 24.79, 91; Berkowitz 29.passim; Chua 30.37, 43; Dalgarno 22.8; Davison 23.6–7, 9, 24–25; Davison 29.passim; Gillespie 29.passim; Humm 29.passim; Hussey 29.passim; Jenkins (Amber) 27.5; Ke 29.57n1, 63, 65n9; Layne 21.83–85, 87–89, 91–98, 100–102; McVicker 28.77; Reed 29.passim; Schwartz 29.96; White 24.101n1, 108n15; Wisor 21.37
Bell, Julian Adair/Martin 24.79, 83, 95; Berkowitz 29.126n4; Chua 30.35; de Gay 30.105; Foster 22.50; Gallego Larrarte 30.111, 112, 115; Gilman 29.53n23; Kopley 30.127; Layne 21.101; Sullam 30.123
Bell, Julian (Q's son) Williams 26.105
Bell, Keith Adair/Martin 24.75n1
Bell, Quentin Adair/Martin 24.80–83; Berkowitz 29.126n4; Dalgarno 22.8; Davison 23.26; Delsandro 25.76; Favre 30.55, 57, 58, 61, 62; Jenkins (Gwyn) 27.35–36, 38; Koulouris 25.2, 13n15; Layne 21.89, 94, 101; Lostoski-Ho 28.63n27; Rutherford

24.141, 152; Shin 23.136; Williams 26.105; Wisor 21.3n7
Bell, Stephen Novillo-Corvalán 23.43n4
Bell, Vanessa Adair/Martin 24.passim; Berkowitz 29.135n11; Davison 23.24–25; Foster 22.44; Fouirnaies 22.25, 36; Gillespie 25.107; Gillespie 29.151, 153; Humm 29.156; Jenkins (Amber) 27.passim; Jenkins (Gwyn) 27.38; Layne 21.passim; Lostoski-Ho 28.63; Pająk 24.30n10; Rutherford 24.141; Ryan 30.80
Bellemin-Noël, Jean Phillips 26.3
Benjamin, Walter Bunting 30.18; Foster 22.41n3, 65; Schwartz 29.101; Wisor 21.1, 4
Bennett, Arnold Cheney 24.61n9; Fischer 28.32, 35; Gallego Larrarte 30.112; Gilman 29.33; Ke 29.59; White 24.107n12
Bennett, Jane Lostoski-Ho 28.64n29
Benson, G. Vere Rutherford 24.141
Benson, Hugh H. Dalgarno 22.5n5
Benson, John Adair/Martin 24.76
Benstock, Shari Camarasana et al. 24.2
Berenson, Bernard Berkowitz 29.127
Berger Jr., Harry Dalgarno 22.1, 4
Berkowitz, Elizabeth Hussey 29.168
Berlant, Lauren Clarke 28.6, 9, 10, 17
Berlin, Germany Gillespie 25.104
Berman, Jessica Chua 30.34; Kotler 24.42, 51; Pająk 24.13, 31–32; White 24.104n6, 110n19, 118, 124n35, 126; Wisor 21.3n8
Berrens, Karla van Straten 30.93
Bersani, Leo Clarke 28.9n6
Bertarelli, L.V. Gillespie 25.101
Besant, Walter Cheney 24.61n10
Best, Stephen Fischer 28.26n4
Bexhill, Sussex Jones 22.81n6
Beylin, Karolina Pająk 24.23–24
Beylin, Marek Pająk 24.23n9
Beylin, Regina Pająk 24.23n9
Big Ben Bond 23.71n12; White 24.113n23
Biron, Chartres Pająk 24.16–17, 25, 28
Bishop, Edward L. Bunting 30.5, 11, 24; Fischer 28.27n5, 30; Gillespie 25.116n33; Ke 29.72n16; Phillips 26.9
Black, Chris Fischer 28.25n1
Black, Naomi Favre 30.60, 61; Wisor 21.2n5, 3n6–7, 4n10
Blake, William Gillespie 29.152; McVicker 28.79
Blakemore, Diane White 24.109n17
Blandford, G. Fielding Czarnecki 21.64n14
Bloch, Ernst Cheney 24.61n8; Livingstone 26.93, 94, 95, 98, 99
Blom-Cooper, Louis Wisor 21.28
Blo' Norton Gillespie 25.104n16
Bloom, Harold Delsandro 25.85; Van Wert 29.107
Blotner, Joseph L. Rutherford 24.142n4, 158
Blumberg, Angie McVicker 28.82n23
Blyth, Ian Graeber 24.175n9
Bobonich, Christopher Dalgarno 22.10
Bodkin, Sir Archibald Pająk 24.28
Boehmer, Elleke Williams 26.114
Bogart, Humphrey Marcus 24.5
Bognor Gillespie 25.107
Boileau, Nicolas Gilman 29.34
Bombay, India Golden 23.83
Bonaparte, Napoleon Koulouris 25.67
Bond, Maurice F. Wisor 21.15, 17
Bond Street Adair/Martin 24.77, 87; Bond 23.63, 66, 70; Gillespie 25.116, 125; Marcus 24.7; White 24.114
Bond, Trevor J. Gillespie 25.129; Golden 23.104
Bone, Robert Caputi 29.17n14
Bongiorno, Andrew White 24.105n7
Bonikowski, Wyatt Czarnecki 21.57–58, 72–73
Boswell, James Gilman 29.54n24
Botticelli, Sandro Jenkins (Gwyn) 27.41
Bourdieu, Pierre Berkowitz 29.129–30, 132, 137; Schwartz 29.100–01
Bourne, Francis Wisor 21.14
Bourriaud, Nicolas Sullam 30.117n1
Bowden, Sue Jones 22.91n9
Bowen, E. E. Jenkins (Gwyn) 27.28, 37
Bowen, Elizabeth White 24.101, 108, 112, 114

Bowlby, Rachel Dalgarno 22.8; Favre 30.56; Fischer 28.38n16; Gillespie 25.107n24; Golden 23.88n14; Schwartz 29.102; Van Wert 29.117, 118; White 24.107n13
Boy-Żeleński, Tadeusz Pająk 24.17–19, 23n9, 31n11
Bradshaw, David Adair/Martin 24.83; Bunting 30.8; Novillo-Corvalán 23.38; Schwartz 29.89n3; White 24.114, 115n27
Brancusi, Constantin Berkowitz 29.128
Braund, Susanna H. Koulouris 25.6n10
Braybrooke, Neville van Straten 30.89
Brazil Novillo-Corvalán 23.33–34, 44, 54–55
Breasted, James Henry Rutherford 24.154
Breckin, Tom de Gay 30.101n2
Bretagne, France Gillespie 25.99
Bridgeman, Teresa White 24.116n29
Briganti, Chiara White 24.113n22
Briggs, Julia de Gay 30.99n1, 103; Kopley 30.125; Lauby 27.53; White 24.113n23, 114n26, 126n37; Wisor 21.3, 32
Briscoe, Arthur Rutherford 24.140
British Library Chua 30.31; Marcus 24.6
British Museum Bunting 30.18, 20; Golden 23.91; Ke 29.76–77, 81; McVicker 28.72n8, 74, 79, 80; Schwartz 29.89, 93, 94–95, 97, 103
Brittain, Vera McVicker 28.86n28
Britton, Dennis Lauby 27.61
Britzolakis, Christina Cheney 24.61n10
Brockington, Grace Reed 29.164
Brontë, Charlotte Kotler 24.40
Brontë, Patrick Kotler 24.44, 52
Brooke, Rupert Czarnecki 21.70n19
Brooks, Peter Van Wert 29.109n4
Brosnan, Leila Fischer 28.25n2
Brothers, Barbara Camarasana et al. 24.2
Brown, Bill Golden 23.83n1; Schwartz 29.102
Brown, Horatio Gillespie 25.100
Brown, Oliver Berkowitz 29.127n5
Brown, Stephanie Favre 30.61
Browne, Henry Schwartz 29.87, 88, 90, 91
Browne, Sir Thomas McVicker 28.79, 84n25, 85–86, 89
Browne, William Lauby 27.59, 60, 61
Browning, Elizabeth Barrett Williams 26.115, 117
Bryher Humm 29.159
Buchan, John Novillo-Corvalán 23.38
Buck, Pearl Pająk 24.18
Bucknill, John Charles Czarnecki 21.64n14
Budge, E.A. Rutherford 24.passim
Bulson, Eric Gillespie 25.100n6, 111, 116; Golden 23.100n29
Bulwer-Lytton, Antony Wisor 21.26n43
Burchardt, Jeremy Jones 22.81, 91n8
Burdekin, Katherine Cheney 24.61
Burden, Robert McVicker 28.86n28
Burke, Edmund Davison 23.17
Burl, Aubrey McVicker 28.77n16, 82, 83
Burma (now Myanmar) Schwartz 29.94
Burton, Diane Wisor 21.3n7
Busse, Rachel M. Van Wert 29.117
Bussy, Janie Davison 29.141, 146
Butler, Judith Caputi 29.21, 22; Clarke 28.9n6; Fouirnaies 22.36; Humm 29.158; Kotler 24.50
Butts, Mary Wisor 21.20
Buxton, Charles Roden Foster 22.51
Byerly, Alison Ke 29.60n7
Byron, George Gordon Bunting 30.13; Gilman 29.53n23; Golden 23.94; Lauby 27.52; Rutherford 24.142; Ryan 30.71; Shin 23.131; Van Wert 29.113
Bywaters, Freddy Wisor 21.26
Bywater, Jr., William G. Gillespie 29.151n4
Cambridge Bunting 30.5, 13; Chua 30.35; Golden 23.83; Jenkins (Gwyn) 27.37, 42; Kopley 30.125; Schwartz 29.94, 97
Cambridge University Davison 23.3, 24–25; Gillespie 25.104; Golden 23.83, 89n15, 94, 98; Koulouris 25.25n63; Novillo-Corvalán 23.39, 41; Rutherford 24.158; Wisor 21.21, 23–24

Cameron, Julia Margaret Adair/Martin 24.87n12; Fouirnaies 22.32, 36
Camus, Albert Berkowitz 29.128; Shin 23.129
Canal, Giovanni Antonio (Canaletto) Wisor 21.39
Caputi Daileader, Celia R. Caputi 29.15n12, 23
Caracciolo, Marco Lostoski-Ho 28.49n5
Carby, Hazel V. Caputi 29.6n3, 15
Cardoso, Eliana A. Novillo-Corvalán 23.44
Carey, John Fouirnaies 22.22n1
The Caribbean Novillo-Corvalán 23.55
Carlyle, Jane Welsh Clarke 28.20–21
Carlyle, Thomas Golden 23.93–94; Schwartz 29.98
Carnarvon, (Lord) George McVicker 28.81; Rutherford 24.154
Carnegie Mellon University Gilman 29.30n9
Carpenter, Edward Wisor 21.17n29
Carr, Helen Novillo-Corvalán 23.54
Carrington, Dora Adair/Martin 24.82; Layne 21.92; McVicker 28.86
Carroll, Lewis Golden 23.99n28
Carter, Howard McVicker 28.81–82; Rutherford 24.143, 146–47, 149, 154
Caruth, Cathy van Straten 30.94
Carver, Katelynn Foster 22.56n30
Casanova, Pascale Chua 30.33
Casas, Bartolomé de las Novillo-Corvalán 23.53
Case, Janet Adair/Martin 24.79; Dalgarno 22.3, 6, 15n15; Golden 23.83n4, 85, 87, 94–95; Jenkins (Gwyn) 27.passim; Sullam 30.121–22
Casement, Roger Novillo-Corvalán 23.52, 54–56
Cassigneul, Adèle Koulouris 25.11
Cassis, France Adair/Martin 24.80–83, 85, 90, 92; Layne 21.99
Catallus Goldman 30.108n1; Kopley 30.126
Cather, Willa Czarnecki 21.52n4
Caughie, Pamela L. Dalgarno 22.15; de Gay 30.99n1; Favre 30.61; Fischer 28.28n9; Jenkins (Amber) 27.5n3; Shin 23.134n26; van Straten 30.86n3
Cavell, Edith Delsandro 25.82n11
Cavitch, Max Shin 23.112n9
Caws, Mary Ann Adair/Martin 24.80n6, 82, 85; Berkowitz 29.126n3
Cebes Dalgarno 22.9–10, 12–13
Cecil, Lady Robert (Nellie) Chua 30.43; Wisor 21.5
Cervantes, Miguel de Gilman 29.54n54
Cézanne, Paul Gillespie 29.151n4; Jenkins (Amber) 27.17; Layne 21.93, 98
Ceylon (now Sri Lanka) Gillespie 25.98; Marcus 24.8
Chakrabarty, Dipesh Chua 30.34; Lostoski-Ho 28.52, 53n11
Chamberlain, Neville Wisor 21.16
Champollion, Jean-François Rutherford 24.141
Chan, Evelyn Tsz Yan Livingstone 26.96
Chancery Lane White 24.115
Channel Islands Lauby 27.58
Chapman, George Davison 29.145
Chapman, Wayne K. Gillespie 25.104n16
Chappell, Mike Wisor 21.38
Charleston Adair/Martin 24.77–79, 81–82, 84–85, 89, 92–94
Chaucer, Geoffrey Foster 22.59; Gilman 29.49n13; Shin 23.134
Chavkin, Allen Czarnecki 21.65n16
Chekhov, Anton Bunting 30.15; Fischer 28.34; Ke 29.80, 81; White 24.102n3
Cheney, Matthew Camarasana et al. 24.4
Chesler, Phyllis Favre 30.58
Chicago Caputi 29.16; Gilman 29.30
Child, Harold Fischer 28.35
Childs, John Wisor 21.35
Childs, Peter Novillo-Corvalán 23.38
Chile Novillo-Corvalán 23.34, 43
China Schwartz 29.101
Chromius of Aetna Shin 23.115
Chuan Guangming Chua 30.46
Chubb, Sir Cecil McVicker 28.82
Chudoba, Ewa Pająk 24.15
Chun, Maureen Fischer 28.27n6
Churchill, Winston Wisor 21.22n37
Cicero Jenkins (Gwyn) 27.30
Claire, René Humm 29.159

Clark, Cumberland Gillespie 25.102
Clark, Kenneth Davison 29.145
Clarke, Stuart N. Clarke 28.7n2; Fischer 28.25n2, 26n3; Reed 29.163n1; Wisor 21.1n2–3, 2, 6n14, 26, 32, 39n57
Claydon, Tim Adair/Martin 24.75
Clegg, Maree Bunting 30.20n4
Clements, Susan Jenkins (Gwyn) 27.33
Clewell, Tammy McVicker 28.71n5; Van Wert 29.117
Clifford-Barney, Natalie Pająk 24.23n9
Clifton College Golden 23.83, 94, 98
Coates, Kimberly Engdahl Dalgarno 22.9n10; Wisor 21.3n8
Cocteau, Jean Berkowitz 29.128
Cohen, Debra Rae Williams 26.114n7
Cole, Sarah Bunting 30.15–16; Delsandro 25.76; Foster 22.62n42
Colefax, Sybil Adair/Martin 24.85
Coleridge, Samuel Taylor Cheney 24.67; de Gay 30.105; Gilman 29.34, 46n4, 53n23; Lauby 27.50
Colet, Louise Sullam 30.122
Colette Humm 29.158
Colla, Elliott McVicker 28.71n7, 79, 81n20, 82n23
Collier, Patrick Gilman 29.47n8
Collins, Judith Gillespie 29.151n4
Coloneus Jenkins (Gwyn) 27.29
Columbus, Christopher Novillo-Corvalán 23.40, 41n3
Comfort, Carol Czarnecki 21.52
Connor, Steven Davison 23.9; Ryan 30.78n20
Conrad, Joseph Fischer 28.34; Gillespie 25.105, 106n22, 118, 121n40; Layne 21.78; Novillo-Corvalán 23.37–39, 50, 52
Constantinople (now Istanbul) Fouirnaies 22.29, 35; Gillespie 25.104; Gillespie 29.151; Golden 23.84; Graeber 24.176, 179–80
Cook, Blanche Wiesen Clarke 28.14n10
Cook, David A. Shin 23.118
Cook, John Harrison McVicker 28.69n1
Cooley, Martha Layne 21.78n1
Cooper, Duff Wisor 21.22n36
Copenhagen, Denmark Caputi 29.16
Cordery, Lindsey Gillespie 25.120n39
Cornish, Vaughan Jones 22.82–83
Cornwall Gillespie 25.108, 123; McVicker 28.76, 80, 86–88; Rutherford 24.137
Cortés, Hernán Novillo-Corvalán 23.40
Corton, Christine L. Ryan 30.77n19
Cosgrove, Denis Gillespie 25.111
Costa Rica Novillo-Corvalán 23.34
Costello, Katherine A. Pająk 24.12
Cotton, Charles Leach 28.99
Courage, Fiona Koulouris 25.2n6, 11
Courington, Chella Czarnecki 21.51
Courtald, Samuel Adair/Martin 24.85
Covent Garden Davison 23.4; Golden 23.passim
Coverley, Merlin van Straten 30.86
Covington, Elizabeth White 24.113n22
Cowper, William Chua 30.38; Van Wert 29.113
Cox, Ka Czarnecki 21.70n19
Cowper, William Adair/Martin 24.82; Davison 23.9
Craig, Sir Maurice Czarnecki 21.65
Crenshaw, Kimberlé Caputi 29.6n4; Delsandro 25.86n18
Crete, Greece Dalgarno 22.14; McVicker 28.72n8
Crook, David Paul Davison 23.15n23
Crook, Steve Chua 30.32
Cromwell, Oliver Wisor 21.38
Crosse, Gordon Wisor 21.15, 17
Crossland, Rachel Livingstone 26.88n2
Crossley, Robert Livingstone 26.92
Crossman, Robert Dalgarno 22.13
Cuba Novillo-Corvalán 23.34
Cuddy-Keane, Melba Czarnecki 21.52n3; Dalgarno 22.1n1, 15n14; Delsandro 25.93; Favre 30.60; Foster 22.59n35, 60n37, 63, 66; Golden 23.83n4; Jenkins (Gwyn) 27.34; McVicker 28.85n27; van Straten 30.85n1, 86, 90n8, 91, 92, 93; White 24.104n6, 111n20
Cumae, Italy Koulouris 25.16
Cunard, Nancy Berkowitz 29.128; Camarasana et al. 24.1; Humm 29.159

Cunningham, Anne Caputi 29.15n13, 21
Cunningham, Michael Favre 30.53; Layne 21.78–80, 86–87, 102
Cunningham, Valentine Gallego Larrarte 30.113
Cunnington, Maud McVicker 28.83
Curl, James Stevens Rutherford 24.154
Curthoys, Mark Golden 23.99n28
Curtis, Vanessa Clarke 28.8
Curzon, Mary Fouirnaies 22.23–24, 26, 36
Czarnecki, Kristin Czarnecki 21.50n1, 52n3; Davison 23.7n15, 13n21; Williams 26.106
Dąbrowska, Maria Pająk 24.23n9
Dakers, Caroline Jenkins (Amber) 27.13n15
Dalgarno, Emily Bunting 30.18; Dalgarno 22.8n9; Golden 23.86, 98n24, 103n33; Jenkins (Gwyn) 27.27; Ke 29.64–65n9; McVicker 28.71n5, 76n14; Schwartz 29.88, 91; Wisor 21.3n7, n9, 5
Daly, Mary Delsandro 25.87–88
Daly, Nicholas Adair/Martin 24.75
Damrosch, David Chua 30.33
Dandelion, Ben Pink Foster 22.46, 47n15
Daniels, Anthony Wisor 21.11, 14
Darwin, Charles Davison 23.passim; Ryan 30.73, 76
Darwin, Emma Davison 23.1
Darwin, Francis Davison 23.1, 25
Darwin, Gwen Davison 23.25
Daugherty, Beth Rigel Chua 30.41–42; de Gay 30.101; Favre 30.57, 61, 63; Gillespie 25.113n32; Gilman 29.31–32n14, 32, 36, 47n7, 48n12, 51n16–19, 52n21, 53n22, 54n25–26; Golden 23.83n3; Jenkins (Gwyn) 27.24; Koulouris 25.11; Sullam 30.119n3
Davidson, Michael Williams 26.111
Davidson, Randall Wisor 21.14
Davidson, R.E. Adair/Martin 24.88–89
Davies, Alistair Koulouris 25.11
Davies, Dominic Novillo-Corvalán 23.42
Davies, Emily Wisor 21.24
Davis, Heather Lostoski-Ho 28.53n10
Davis, Lloyd Wisor 21.3n6, 4n10
Davis, Miles Chua 30.34
Davis, Thadious M. Caputi 29.19n15, 21
Davis, Thomas Delsandro 25.passim
Davison, Claire Hussey 29.167
Day-Lewis, Cecil de Gay 30.99; Gallego Larrarte 30.111, 115; Kopley 30.127
Debussy, Claude Davison 23.22n32
DeChellis Hill, Carol Layne 21.78n1
Defoe, Daniel Sullam 30.119–20
de Gay, Jane de Gay 30.99n1; Foster 22.42n4; Pająk 24.31; Ryan 30.71n12, 75
Dekker, Thomas Leach 28.102
DeKoven, Marianne Caputi 29.6n3, 9n8, 13; Fischer 28.37, 40n19
De la Mare, Walter Fischer 28.35
Delany, Paul Czarnecki 21.70n19
de Lauretis, Theresa Bond 23.76n17
Delgardo-García, Cristina White 24.124n36, 127n38
Delorey, Denise Czarnecki 21.52n3
Deloria Jr., Vine Czarnecki 21.59n9
Delsandro, Erica Gene Delsandro 25.77n7; Gillespie 25.118
DeMeester, Karen Czarnecki 21.54, 57, 63, 66, 71n20
Demosthenes Jenkins (Gwyn) 27.29
Denmark Caputi 29.17, 18
De Quincey, Thomas Dalgarno 22.11
Derain, André Berkowitz 29.128
Derrida, Jacques Dalgarno 22.1; McVicker 28.80n19; Phillips 26.10; Williams 26.108n5, 112
Derry, Julian Davison 23.1
Descartes, René Ke 29.65; Williams 26.116
DeSalvo, Louise Caputi 29.12–13; Davison 23.5; Fischer 28.39n18, 41; Koulouris 25.7n12; Layne 21.88–89
Detloff, Madelyn Clarke 28.6n1, 13n9; Favre 30.63; Foster 22.66; McVicker 28.71n5; Pająk 24.12
Diaghilev, Sergei Berkowitz 29.128, 129; Rutherford 24.154
Díaz-Alejandro, Carlos F. Novillo-Corvalán 23.46–47
DiBattista, Maria Shin 23.111n7, 122n21,

124, 136
Dick, Susan Bond 23.65; Jenkins (Amber) 27.9n8, 11; McVicker 28.87; Shin 23.125n23, 131n24
Dickens, Charles Gillespie 25.119; Golden 23.92, 100n29; Pająk 24.23
Dickey, Colin Wisor 21.3n6–7
Dickinson, Emily Goldman 30.108n1; Kopley 30.126, 127
Dickinson, G. Lowes Dalgarno 22.13–14
Dickinson, Lowes Cato Jenkins (Gwyn) 27.38
Dickinson, Oswald Clarke 28.6
Dickinson, Renée Lostoski-Ho 28.48n2
Dickinson, Violet Chua 30.42; Clarke 28.passim; Gillespie 25.104, 116; Jenkins (Gwyn) 27.27, 32, 37; Koulouris 25.10n14, 25n63
Diderot, Denis Gilman 29.34
DiGaetani, John Louis Davison 23.19n28
Dillard, Annie Shin 23.128
Diment, Gayla Bond 23.65n4
Dimock, Wai Chee Lostoski-Ho 28.53–54n11
Dimyon, Clare Pająk 24.15
Diotima of Mantinea Dalgarno 22.6–8, 12; Koulouris 25.53–55
Dirschauer, Marlene Ryan 30.81n27
Disraeli, Benjamin Wisor 21.22
Doan, Laura L. Pająk 24.21
Dobson, Eleanor McVicker 28.82n23
Docherty, Thomas Bond 23.65n5
Donald, James Humm 29.159n11
Donaldson, Elizabeth Favre 30.59, 63
Donne, John Gillespie 25.127n49; Golden 23.89; Ke 29.81
Doolittle, Hilda (H. D.) Humm 29.159; McVicker 28.71
Douglas, Erin Jenkins (Gwyn) 27.33
Douie, Vera Wisor 21.24n39
Dowland, John Layne 21.87n3
Dowling, Linda Dalgarno 22.9
Doyle, Arthur Conan Novillo-Corvalán 23.38
Doyle, Laura Caputi 29.5n2, 6, 8, 9, 10
Drake, Sir Francis Gillespie 25.105n20
Driscoll, Catherine Adair/Martin 24.77
Driscoll, Leonard McVicker 28.70n2
Drucker, Johanna Berkowitz 29.126
Dryden, John Gilman 29.34, 46n4
Dryden, Linda Novillo-Corvalán 23.38
Dubino, Jeanne Adair/Martin 24.87; Golden 23.83n4, 100; Graeber 24.167
DuBois, W. E. B. Caputi 29.22
Duckworth, George Koulouris 25.6; Layne 21.81; McVicker 28.76n14, 91
Duckworth, Gerald Golden 23.84
Duckworth, Stella Clarke 28.6, 7; Jenkins (Gwyn) 27.25; Koulouris 25.5; McVicker 28.76n14; Shin 23.123n22
Dudziński, Bolesław Pająk 24.30–31
Duff-Gordon, Lady Lucie Rutherford 24.156–57
Duffy, Edna Adair/Martin 24.75
Duffy, Julia Wisor 21.3n6, 4n10
Du Gard, Roger Martin Davison 29.142n4
Du Gay, Roger Martin Pająk 24.18
Du Maurier, Daphne Pająk 24.20
Duncan, Katharine Sinclair Wisor 21.29
Dunlap, Ellen Marcus 24.5, 7
Dunlap, Sarah van Straten 30.91n9, 93n12
Dunn, Carolyn Czarnecki 21.52
Dunn, Jane Adair/Martin 24.77, 95; Jenkins (Amber) 27.13n16; Layne 21.82, 88, 90
DuPlessis, Rachel Blau Czarnecki 21.52n3; Fischer 28.38
Dusinberre, Juliet Foster 22.45n11; Leach 28.99, 101
Duthuit, Georges Berkowitz 29.128; Davison 29.143
Dymond, Justine Czarnecki 21.50n1
Eagleton, Terry Humm 29.160
Earheart, Amelia Gillespie 25.118
Earle, Peter Novillo-Corvalán 23.49–50
Earp, Thomas Wade Berkowitz 29.128
Easedale, Joan Adeney Kopley 30.128
Eastbourne, Sussex Jones 22.81n6
Ecuador Novillo-Corvalán 23.34
Edelman, Lee Lauby 27.59; Van Wert 29.110, 118, 119–20
Edmondson, Annalee White 24.110n19
Edney, Matthew H. Gillespie 25.117, 127
Egypt Marcus 24.7; McVicker 28.71, 81;

Rutherford 24.passim; Schwartz 29.94; Wisor 21.37
Eiland, Howard Wisor 21.4
Einstein, Albert Fouirnaies 22.21; Lostoski-Ho 28.53
Eisenstein, Sergei Humm 29.159
Elam, Caroline Ke 29.65n9
Eliot, T. S. Berkowitz 29.128; Bunting 30.6; Chua 30.37; de Gay 30.99; Fischer 28.26, 32n11; Foster 22.41n1; Humm 29.156; Ke 29.68–69; Kopley 30.128; Kotler 24.40; Lauby 27.48; Layne 21.78; McVicker 28.71, 86n28; Reed 29.164; White 24.101n1, 103, 108n15; Williams 26.108n6
Ellis, Steve Foster 22.63n43; Livingstone 26.90
Emerson, Ralph Waldo Ke 29.61n8, 66, 69, 78; Pająk 24.30
Empson, William Gallego Larrarte 30.111
English, Elizabeth Pająk 24.12
Enloe, Cynthia Wisor 21.11
Erdrich, Louise Czarnecki 21.50n1
Erman, Adolf Rutherford 24.157
Eryximachus Koulouris 25.50n158, 51–52, 56
Estaunié, Edouard Hussey 29.168
Estrada, Ezequiel Martínez Novillo-Corvalán 23.49
Esty, Jed Bunting 30.12; Delsandro 25.76; Gillespie 25.120n38, 121n41; Jones 22.76n2; Lauby 27.47–48; Novillo-Corvalán 23.39
Euripedes Golden 23.95; Koulouris 25.8, 42–50, 67n238, 69–70
Evans, Arthur McVicker 28.72n8
Evans, Billy McVicker 28.85
Evans, Elizabeth Delsandro 25.76n5
Evans, Walker Berkowitz 29.128n8
Ewing, K.D. Wisor 21.29n45, 30
Faderman, Lillian Clarke 28.7, 10
Fagan, Brian Rutherford 24.141
Falcoff, Mark Novillo-Corvalán 23.49
Falcetta, Jennie-Rebecca Bond 23.64n3
Fallaize, E. N. Ryan 30.74n16
Fand, Roxanne Ryan 30.72n13
Farjeon, Herbert Davison 29.143n6
Faucher, Kane X. Berkowitz 29.135
Fawcett Women's Library Marcus 24.5–7
Feigel, Lara Cheney 24.65n12
Feldman, Matthew Chua 30.46
Felman, Shoshana Favre 30.59n10
Felski, Rita White 24.106n6
Ferber, Edna Marcus 24.9
Ferguson, Frances Sullam 30.121n4
Fernald, Anne E. Bond 23.65n4; Bunting 30.13; Cheney 24.55; Czarnecki 21.51n2, 66n17; Golden 23.83n1, 86–87, 88n14; McVicker 28.85n27
Ferrer, Daniel Fischer 28.27n5
Fielding, Henry Bunting 30.17, 18; Ke 29.71, 80
Finch, Annie Kopley 30.125
Fish, Stanley Humm 29.157
Fisher, H.A.L. Wisor 21.6n15
Fitzroy Street, London Adair/Martin 24.92, 95
Flanders Fields Bunting 30.5
Flaubert, Gustave Kopley 30.128; Sullam 30.118n2, 122; Williams 26.114–15
Fleet Street Bond 23.63; White 24.115
Flesher, Erika Fouirnaies 22.22
Fletcher, John Leach 28.102
Fletcher, Rachel Ke 29.67
Flint, Kate Bunting 30.15; Fischer 28.27n7; Jenkins (Amber) 27.7n4; White 24.104n6, 111n21
Florence, Italy Berkowitz 29.127
Foka, Amalia Berkowitz 29.136–37
Fornoff, Carolyn Lostoski-Ho 28.54
Forster, E. M. Davison 29.146; Fischer 28.32n11; Gallego Larrarte 30.112, 113; Gillespie 25.101n11, 111; Golden 23.83n4, 100; Ke 29.63; Kopley 30.128; Lauby 27.48; Marcus 24.7; McVicker 28.90n29; Novillo-Corvalán 23.34; Pająk 24.20; Reed 29.163; Rutherford 24.137, 158–59; Shin 23.114; Schwartz 29.95; Sullam 30.119, 120
Foster, J. Ashley Foster 22.44n7, n9, 51n22; Livingstone 26.90
Fowler, Alistair Sullam 30.118
Fowler, Regina Dalgarno 22.1n1

Fowler, Robert Koulouris 25.20n38
Ford, Ford Madox Novillo-Corvalán 23.50; Rutherford 24.154; Sullam 30.119
Foucault, Michel Clarke 28.14, 19, 21–22; Lauby 27.47, 59; McVicker 28.72–74, 76n14, 79–80, 92
Fouirnaies, Christine Graeber 24.176
Fox, Alice Graeber 24.168, 175n9
Fox, George Foster 22.47n14, 48n16, 54n29
France Adair/Martin 24.77, 80n6; Gillespie 25.101, 103; Golden 23.100; Graeber 24.175; Reed 29.163; Wisor 21.33
Franco, Jeré Bishop Czarnecki 21.53n5, 60
Frank, Joseph Bond 23.64n2; White 24.113
Frattarola, Angela van Straten 30.86n3
Frazer, James Davison 23.4, 11; Rutherford 24.155, 157; Ryan 30.74, 76
Frede, Michael Dalgarno 22.15–16
Frederick, Bonnie Gillespie 25.107, 118
Freedman, Ariela Czarnecki 21.62n11, 66
Freedman, Carl Livingstone 26.94
Freeman, Gillian Layne 21.85–87, 90
Freire, Paolo Cheney 24.58n4
French, Jennifer L. Novillo-Corvalán 23.42
Freud, Sigmund Camarasana et al. 24.2; Caputi 29.9n8; Kotler 24.43n3; Layne 21.78; McVicker 28.71; Rutherford 24.135, 144–45; Ryan 30.72, 74; Van Wert 29.107, 108, 109, 111, 112, 116
Friedberg, Anne Humm 29.159n11
Friedman, Susan Stanford Camarasana et al. 24.2; Caputi 29.6n3, 15n13; Cheney 24.58; Chua 30.33–34; Gillespie 25.111, 115; Lostoski-Ho 28.55n16
Friez, Othon Berkowitz 29.128
Frobisher, Sir Martin Gillespie 25.105n20
Frost, J. William Foster 22.44n6, 46, 47n13, 48
Froude, James Anthony Graeber 24. 167–68
Froula, Christine Adair/Martin 24.77; Bunting 30.5; Caputi 29.6n3, 9n8; Czarnecki 21.54n7, 64, 66, 71, 73; Davison 23.5n11; Delsandro 25.76n5; Foster 22.41n1, 58n31; Kotler 24.46; Novillo-Corvalán 23.43; Shin 23.111n7; White 24.124n36
Fry, Margery Gillespie 29.152; Golden 23.102
Fry, Paul H. Shin 23.110n4
Fry, Roger Adair/Martin 24.80, 82, 85, 94; Berkowitz 29.127n5, 129n8; Chua 30.38, 39, 40; Foster 22.50; Fouirnaies 22.31; Gillespie 29.149, 151, 152, 153; Golden 23.102; Jenkins (Amber) 27.5, 6, 7, 10, 12–13, 17; Ke 29.63, 65n9; Kopley 30.127; Layne 21.82–85, 88, 90–98, 100–102; Reed 29.163, 164; Rutherford 24.135, 141, 149n5, 152; Schwartz 29.96
Frye, Marilyn Delsandro 25.88
Fulton, Lorie Watkins Czarnecki 21.51n2
Fuss, Diana Shin 23.112n9
Fussell, Paul Kopley 30.125–26
Gabler, Hans Walter Jenkins (Amber) 27.5n3, 8n6; Phillips 26.10
Gaipa, Mark Rutherford 24.135
Galef, David Williams 26.111
Gallego Larrarte, Bàrbara Kopley 30.125, 127
Gallop, Jane Fischer 28.27
Galsworthy, John Caputi 29.7; Cheney 24.61n9; Dalgarno 22.8; Fischer 28.32, 35, 36; Ke 29.59; Novillo-Corvalán 23.50; Pająk 24.18
Gandy, Matthew Davison 23.8
Gao Yuanyuan Chua 30.45
Gardner, Edmund G. Gillespie 25.100–01
Garnett, Angelica Adair/Martin 24.82, 91, 94; Fouirnaies 22.25, 34, 36; Layne 21.82, 90, 98; Williams 26.105
Garnett, David Adair/Martin 24.82; Foster 22.50; Humm 29.156; Livingstone 26.96, 97, 98, 100, 102
Garnett, Edward Novillo-Corvalán 23.50
Garrard, Greg Lostoski-Ho 28.53
Garrity, Jane Gillespie 25.120n37, 127; Lostoski-Ho 28.48n2; McVicker 28.88, 89
Garvey, Johanna White 24.102n4

Gaskell, Elizabeth Chua 30.37, 38
Gasset, José Ortega y Novillo-Corvalán 23.43
Gauguin, Paul Reed 29.162
Gay, Ross Shin 23.114n13
Gearty, C.A. Wisor 21.29n45, 30
Genette, Gérard White 24.109n17, 115n28, 116n29
George, Lloyd Berkowitz 29.132
Georgievics, Georg von Golden 23.96n21
Geppert, Alexander C.T. Golden 23.99
Germany Adair/Martin 24.77, 95; Davison 29.144; Gillespie 25.103; Graeber 24.170n4; Novillo-Corvalán 23.45, 47–48; Wisor 21.33
Gerzina, Gretchen Caputi 29.22n18
Gheeraerts, Marcus (the Younger) Fouirnaies 22.23, 25–26
Gheerbrant, Alain Novillo-Corvalán 23.53
Gibbon, Edward Davison 23.15–16, 18; Fischer 28.30, 31; Gillespie 25.105–06, 120, 123; Schwartz 29.101
Gibbons, Jennifer Camarasana et al. 24.2
Gibbons, June Camarasana et al. 24.2
Giddens, Anthony Clarke 28.9n6
Gide, Andre Davison 29.142n4
Gilbert, Sandra Caputi 29.21; Czarnecki 21.53, 70; Favre 30.58; Fouirnaies 22.24; Kotler 24.36; Layne 21.102; Pająk 24.12n5
Gilbert, W.S. Davison 23.16, 19
Giles, Peter Davison 23.4, 6, 10
Gillespie, Diane Adair/Martin 24.78, 91; Davison 23.3n8; Foster 22.51n26; Fouirnaies 22.21; Gillespie 25.97, 100n5, n8, 119, 127n49; Gillespie 29.149n1; Golden 23.83n3, 88; Hussey 29.167; Jenkins (Amber) 27.5, 10, 14; Layne 21.81–85, 90, 93, 96, 100, 102; Wisor 21.3
Gillis, John Wisor 21.12n22
Gilroy, Paul Caputi 29.5n2; Graeber 24.166, 168, 174
Gilmour, Sir John Wisor 21.29
Gilstrap, Lee Czarnecki 21.61–62
Giotto Layne 21.86
Giovanelli, Alessandro White 24.104n6
Girton College Bunting 30.17; Wisor 21.24
Gisges-Zwierzchowska, Ewa Pająk 24.18, 20
Gladstone, William Wisor 21.22
Glasgow, Scotland Gillespie 25.99
Glendinning, Victoria Adair/Martin 24.80, 82–84; Fouirnaies 22.33, 36; Golden 23.102; Humm 29.156n3
Godley, A.D. Rutherford 24.155
Goelet, Ogden Rutherford 24.136, 156
Goethe Chua 30.33
Golden, Amanda Bunting 30.11; Gillespie 25.100n7, 123; Golden 23.83, 84n7, 87n10, 89, 95; Jenkins (Gwyn) 27.37; Ke 29.67n11
Goldhill, Simon Koulouris 25.11, 71n245
Goldman, Jane Adair/Martin 24.75; Bunting 30.9; Davison 23.3n7; Favre 30.60; Foster 22.41n3, 44–45, 54–55; Golden 23.91n16; Goldman 30.108n1; Jenkins (Amber) 27.5, 8, 9, 13, 16; Ke 29.72n15; Kopley 30.125, 126; Layne 21.80, 84, 96–98, 100; Rutherford 24.158, 160; Ryan 30.69n8, 78, 79n21; Shin 23.111, 112n8
Goldman, Mark White 24.104n6
Gomulicki, Juliusz Pająk 24.23n9
Gooch, G.P. Foster 22.51
Goodheart, A.L. Wisor 21.29n45–46
Goodman, Robin Truth Caputi 29.21n16
Goodyear, Charles Novillo-Corvalán 23.53
Gordon, Lydnall Favre 30.64
Gordon Square Adair/Martin 24.77; Koulouris 25.5, 8, 25n63
Gottlieb, Laura Moss Cheney 24.59n6, 62
Graber, Darin Gillespie 25.126
Graff, Agnieszka Pająk 24.26
Graham, R.B. Cunninghame Novillo-Corvalán 23.50
Graham, John Golden 23.96n21
Graham, J. W. Foster 22.51; Lostoski-Ho 28.57–59; Ryan 30.71, 73, 75
Grant, Duncan Adair/Martin 24.79, 80n6, 81–82, 85, 90–93, 95; Foster 22.41n3; Fouirnaies 22.25; Gillespie 29.151; Jenkins (Amber) 27.13; Layne 21.88–89, 95, 101; Rutherford 24.141

Grant, Lady Sybil Adair/Martin 24.86
Graves, Robert Berkowitz 29.128; Rutherford 24.137
Gray, Harold St. George McVicker 28.82
Gray, Thomas Shin 23.116n15
Greeb, Leonard (Lenare) Fouirnaies 22.25, 32
Greece Adair/Martin 24.80n6; Bunting 30.5, 15, 18, 19; Gillespie 25.100–01; Golden 23.passim; Graeber 24.177; Ke 29.67, 77; Koulouris 25.passim; McVicker 28.71, 72n8, 76, 86; Rutherford 24.152; Schwartz 29.101
Green, Christopher Ke 29.65n9
Green, Peter Rutherford 24.159; Koulouris 25.6n9, 16n28, 17n30
Greenaway, Kate Gilman 29.30
Greenblatt, Stephen Novillo-Corvalán 23.41
Greene, Robert Leach 28.102
Gregory, Rosalyn Cheney 24.61n10
Grenfell, Francis Wisor 21.26n43
Grewel, Inderpal Caputi 29.5n2
Grey, Thomas S. Davison 23.3, 27n40
Gribble, David Dalgarno 22.7n8
Griggs, Arthur Kingsland Gillespie 25.102
Griswold, Charles Dalgarno 22.1
Grodzinsky, Ewa Ryan 30.68n2
Groom, Winston Berkowitz 29.128n7
Groover, Kristina Bond 23.65–66, 68n7; Foster 22.42n4; Van Wert 29.114
Gross, Robert Caputi 29.5n2
Grote, George Dalgarno 22.5n5, 10
Gruber, Ruth Favre 30.61
Gualtieri, Elena Koulouris 25.11; Wisor 21.3n6, 4
Guatemala Novillo-Corvalán 23.34
Gubar, Marah Williams 26.108
Gubar, Susan Caputi 29.21; Czarnecki 21.53, 70; Favre 30.58; Kotler 24.36
Guildford Gillespie 25.99
Guillaume, Paul Berkowitz 29.128
Gunew, Sneja Camarasana et al. 24.2
Gunselman, Cheryl Gillespie 25.129
Hackett, Robin Lauby 27.61
Hadow, W.H. Davison 23.4n9
Haefele, Lisa Schwartz 29.88n1
Haffey, Kate Caputi 29.10n9
Hagen, Benjamin D. Caputi 29.21n16; Cheney 24.58n4; Chua 30.41n4; Favre 30.55n2; Kopley 30.125; Leach 28.104; Lostoski-Ho 28.64; McVicker 28.69n1, 85–86n27; Ryan 30.82; White 24.114n25
Haggard, Henry Rider McVicker 28.70n2; Novillo-Corvalán 23.38
Hakluyt, Richard Gillespie 25.105; Graeber 24.166–68, 170, 172, 175n9, 176n10
Halberstam, Jack Caputi 29.15n13; Pająk 24.12, 29
Hall, Radclyffe Marcus 24.9; Pająk 24.passim; Wisor 21.6n14
Hall, Stuart Wisor 21.5
Haller, Evelyn McVicker 28.71n7, 75n11, 82n22; Rutherford 24.137–40, 151, 155, 158–59
Halliday, Sam Davison 23.8, 11, 19n28
Halperin, David M. Dalgarno 22.8
Hammill, Faye Golden 23.84n5
Hampton Court Palace Wisor 21.39
Hancock, Frank Jones 22.80–81
Hancock, Nuala Adair/Martin 24.78
Hankins, Leslie Kathleen Gillespie 25.123n44; Gilman 29.36; Humm 29.157, 158–59; Pająk 24.28
Hanks, Tom Berkowitz 29.128n7
Haraway, Donna Lostoski-Ho 28.53n10
Hardenburg, Walter E. Novillo-Corvalán 23.52–53
Hardy, Thomas Fischer 28.34; McVicker 28.70n2
Hare, Augustus J.C. Gillespie 25.100
Harker, Ben Livingstone 26.89–90
Harley, J.B. Gillespie 25.108, 128
Harmansah, Ömür Lostoski-Ho 28.54
Harpham, Geoffrey Galt Shin 23.124
Harris, Alexandra Jones 22.76n2
Harris, Anne Ryan 30.68n5
Harris, Susan Bunting 30.10
Harrison, Jane Ellen Adair/Martin 24.86n10; Dalgarno 22.3; Davison

23.4, 6, 10–11, 25; Delsandro 25.85, 91; Golden 23.83n4, 100n30; Jenkins (Gwyn) 27.23, 25, 26, 39; McVicker 28.72, 75n12, 79, 84n25
Harrison, Robert Pogue van Straten 30.90–91
Harrod, Roy Gillespie 29.150; Humm 29.160
Harry Ransom Center Camarasana et al. 24.1–2; Marcus 24.passim
Hart, George Rutherford 24.140, 142, 148
Hartley, Jenny Wisor 21.3n7
Harvey, David Lostoski-Ho 28.49n4, 54n12
Harvey, Kathryn Foster 22.51n24
Harvey, T. E. Berkowitz 29.132
Harwood, Brian Wisor 21.33–34, 37n56, 38–39
Haste, Cate Czarnecki 21.68
Hastings, Adrian Wisor 21.15n26, 16–17
Hattaway, Judith Schwartz 29.102
Haule, James Cheney 24.64; Gillespie 25.122n42; Phillips 26.2
Hawkes, Ellen Gillespie 25.116
Hawkins, Sir John Gillespie 25.105n20
Hawley, William McVicker 28.84n24
Hawthorne, Nathaniel Gilman 29.53n23
Hayman, Richard McVicker 28.84
Headlam, Walter Golden 23.85n8; Rutherford 24.141
Heath, Malcolm White 24.105n8–9
Heath-Stubbs, John Shin 23.110n4, 113, 115
The Hebrides Gillespie 25.99–100, 104, 108; Rutherford 24.137
Heffernan, James White 24.102n4
Hegglund, Jon Gillespie 25.100n6, 110, 118–19
Heilbrun, Carolyn Delsandro 25.75, 92
Heine, Elizabeth Davison 23.5n11
Heininge, Kathy Foster 22.43–44
Helal, Kathleen Kotler 24.41
Helwege, Ann Novillo-Corvalán 23.44
Helt, Brenda Clarke 28.6n1, 20
Hemingway, Ernest White 24.108
Henderson, Cathy Marcus 24.9
Henderson, John Golden 23.100
Henderson, Sandra Lauby 27.51
Henig, Suzanne Williams 26.110
Henke, Suzette Czarnecki 21.57; Van Wert 29.113–14; White 24.102n4, 106n10, 107n12
Henrietta Maria of France (Queen) Lauby 27.50
Henry, Holly Gillespie 25.105, 128; Livingstone 26.88n2, 89; Lostoski-Ho 28.50n6; McVicker 28.77, 85n26, 89, 90n29
Henry, Zoë Chua 30.46n6
Hepburn, Allan Delsandro 25.77
Herman, David White 24.109n17, 110n18, 116n29; Williams 26.115
Herman, William Rutherford 24.158
Herodotus Jenkins (Gwyn) 27.31; Rutherford 24.155
Herrick, Robert Gilman 29.50n14, 53n23
Herrmann, Anne Adair/Martin 24.80
Herschel, J. Ryan 30.79n22
Hertslet, Edward Gillespie 25.102
Herzog, Kristin Czarnecki 21.63, 69
Heshong, Lisa Ryan 30.68n4
Heuston, R.F.V. Wisor 21.28
Hewart, Gordon Kotler 24.51; Wisor 21.2, 26–31
Hewitt, John Adair/Martin 24.92–93
Higdon, David White 24.102n3
Higonnet, Margaret R. Gillespie 25.112
Hill, Edwin Chua 30.34
Hill, Katherine C. de Gay 30.101n2; Kopley 30.125, 126
Hill, Lorraine Gilman 29.31n13
Hinnov, Emily Fischer 28.27n6; Foster 22.59n33, 60n36, n40; Lostoski-Ho 28.49n3, 50; Wisor 21.3n7
Hirsh, Elizabeth Fouirnaies 22.22
Hitchmough, Wendy Hussey 29.168–69
Hite, Molly Graeber 24.166; White 24.104n6, 109, 127n38
Hitler, Adolf Chua 30.40; Czarnecki 21.58; Davison 29.144; Gillespie 25.110
Hobbes, Thomas Schwartz 29.101
Hobbs, William Cooper Wisor 21.28
Hoberman, Ruth Schwartz 29.88, 97–98

Hobsbawm, Eric Novillo-Corvalán 23.43
Hobson, J.A. Novillo-Corvalán 23.41–42, 56–57
Hodgkin, Thomas Foster 22.47n13
Hodgkins, Hope Williams 26.108n6
Hoff, Molly Dalgarno 22.1n1; White 24.102n4
Hoffmann, Charles Phillips 26.2
Högberg, Elsa Clarke 28.9n6, 13n9, 21n13; Favre 30.53n1; Lostoski-Ho 28.49n3, 50
Holden, Len Adair/Martin 24.75
Holinshed, Raphael Lauby 27.58n7
Hollander, Rachel Bunting 30.5; Van Wert 29.117
Holleyman, M.G. Koulouris 25.7n12
Hollis, Catherine W. Gillespie 25.107; Gilman 29.31
Holloway Prison Delsandro 25.83; Marcus 24.7
Holroyd, Michael Adair/Martin 24.77, 82; Humm 29.156n4; Marcus 24.8
Holtby, Winifred Bunting 30.11
Homer Bunting 30.19; Dalgarno 22.6, 16; Jenkins (Gwyn) 27.31; Koulouris 25.passim; McVicker 28.79; Rutherford 24.154; White 24.117n30, 118n33, 124n36
Honey, Maureen Caputi 29.6n2
hooks, bell Kotler 24.40, 44
Hooper, Frances Gilman 29.29, 30, 31
Hooper-Greenhill, Eilean Schwartz 29.90, 91
Hope-Allen, Mary Davison 29.143n6
Hope-Wallace, Philip Davison 29.143n6
Horace Dalgarno 22.1n1; Jenkins (Gwyn) 27.30; Shin 23.113, 120n20
Houghton Library Fouirnaies 22.25
Howard, Elizabeth Catherine (Lady Carnarvon) Koulouris 25.6
Howatson, M.C. Dalgarno 22.7n7
Hoyland, John S. Foster 22.49–50
Hubertus, Prince of Löwenstein-Wertheim-Freudenberg Wisor 21.9
Hudson, W. H. Chua 30.35; Novillo-Corvalán 23.38, 49–51
Hughes, Langston Caputi 29.5n1
Humble, Karen Koulouris 25.11
Humboldt, Alexander von Novillo-Corvalán 23.38, 42
Humm, Maggie Adair/Martin 24.93; Fouirnaies 22.21–22; Humm 29.157n7, 159; Hussey 29.168; Kotler 24.49, 51; Layne 21.85; Sullam 30.117n1; Wisor 21.2n5, 3n6
Hungary Gillespie 25.102
Hungerford, Edward Bond 23.65; Gilman 29.28n3
Hunt, Peter Williams 26.108
Hurston, Zora Neale Czarnecki 21.50–1
Hussey, Mark Adair/Martin 24.93; Berkowitz 29.passim; Bunting 30.7; Chua 30.43n5; Czarnecki 21.52; Davison 23.11, 22n32; Davison 29.passim; Delsandro 25.82n11; Foster 22.42, 50n20, 59n35, 66; Gallego Larrarte 30.112; Gillespie 29.passim; Golden 23.84n5; Humm 29.passim; Hussey 29.169; Jenkins (Gwyn) 27.23; Jones 22.76, 80–81, 82n7, 86; Ke 29.59n5, 63, 65n9; Koulouris 25.11; Layne 21.98; McVicker 28.69–70n2, 87, 89; Reed 29.passim; Shin 23.109n1
Hutchinson, George Caputi 29.6n2, 8n7
Hutchinson, Mary Humm 29.157; Layne 21.84
Hutchinson, St. John Wisor 21.30n48
Hutton, James Lostoski-Ho 28.52
Huxley, Aldous Berkowitz 29.128; Cheney 24.62; Foster 22.44; Williams 26.108n6
Huxley, Julian Livingstone 26.93
Huxley, T.H. Davison 23.3n8
Hyde Park Wisor 21.10
Hyde Park Gate Golden 23.94
Hyde, Virginia Gillespie 25.107
Hylson-Smith, Kenneth Wisor 21.17
Hynes, Samuel Wisor 21.12n22
Ibsen, Henrik Marcus 24.5
India Gillespie 25.127; Graeber 24.170n4, 180n14; McVicker 28.81; Novillo-Corvalán 23.41n3; Ryan 30.73; Schwartz 29.94, 101; Wisor 21.37

Inglis, Elizabeth Koulouris 25.11, 13n17
Ingram, Angela Marcus 24.9
Ingram, Penelope Rutherford 24.135
Innes, Kathleen Foster 22.51–52, 62
Inskip, Thomas Walker Hobart Wisor 21.26n40
Irby, Leonard Howard Loyd Golden 23.95
Ireland McVicker 28.81
Irigaray, Luce Clarke 28.9n6
Isaacs, Sir Rufus Wisor 21.14
Isherwood, Christopher Delsandro 25.77; Gallego Larrarte 30.111
Isles of Scilly Golden 23.89
Islington, London Shin 23.132
Italy Adair/Martin 24.77, 80n6; Bunting 30.5; Gillespie 25.101n11, 102; Graeber 24.178–79
Ivins, William M. Ke 29.65
Iwaszkiewicz, Jarosław Pająk 24.22, 23n9
Jackson, H.J. Golden 23.84n5
Jackson, Kevin Humm 29.157n6
Jackson, Robert Wisor 21.26, 28–29, 30n48
Jacob, Max Berkowitz 29.128
Jacobs, Naomi M. van Straten 30.90
Jaeger, Muriel Livingstone 26.96, 97, 98, 100, 101, 102
Jahn, Manfred White 24.109n17, 115n28
Jaillant, Lise Chua 30.34; Golden 23.84
James, David Jones 22.76n2
James, Emily Golden 23.88, 104; Van Wert 29.117
James, Henry Adair/Martin 24.85; Layne 21.78n1, 81–82
Jameson, Fredric Cheney 24.61n8, 63; Livingstone 26.88, 93, 94, 99; Novillo-Corvalán 23.58
Jameson, Storm Cheney 24.61
Jamieson, Andrew Golden 23.96n21
Janta, Aleksander Pająk 24.20
Japan Novillo-Corvalán 23.41
Jarzombek, Mark Ke 29.65
Javadizadeh, Kamren Clarke 28.14n10
Jeal, Tim Wisor 21.10, 12n22, 14
Jebb, Richard Claverhouse Golden 23.103n33; Koulouris 25.8, 14n25, 62n219, 68
Jehlen, Myra Williams 26.114
Jenkins, Ian Schwartz 29.96
Jenkins, William White 24.102n4
Jennings, Michael W. Wisor 21.4
Jewsbury, Geraldine Clarke 28.20–21
Jex-Blake, Thomas Kotler 24.44, 52
Joannou, Maroula Jones 22.76n2
John Herron Art Museum (Indianapolis) Chua 30.31
Johnson, George M. Layne 21.78
Johnson, Jamie Williams 26.115
Johnson, Samuel Davison 23.19; Gilman 29.28, 29, 34, 35, 46n4, 49n12, 53n23, 54n24
Johnston, Georgia Bond 23.71–72, 80
Johnston, John Wisor 21.8n16
Jones, Clara Chua 30.41; Delsandro 25.76; Favre 30.61n13; Gillespie 25.108; Jones 22.77n3
Jones, Gloria White 24.109n17
Jones, Inigo Lauby 27.49, 50
Jones, Mervyn White 24.102n3
Jones, Prudence Rutherford 24.155, 157
Jones, Rufus Foster 22.47n15, 48n17, 49, 54n29
Jones, Tom Wisor 21.25
Jonson, Ben Fouirnaies 22.28; Lauby 27.49, 50
Jouve, Pierre Jean Reed 29.163, 164
Jowett, Benjamin Dalgarno 22.3–4, 6; Koulouris 25.50n160
Jowitt, Claire Graeber 24.165–66
Joyce, James Berkowitz 29.128; Cheney 24.61n9; Chua 30.43; Fischer 28.32, 34; Gillespie 25.116; Humm 29.156, 157; Kopley 30.126, 127; Livingstone 26.94; McVicker 28.71; Novillo-Corvalán 23.38–39; Pająk 24.20; Schwartz 29.93n6; White 24.101–02, 106n6, 113
Joynson-Hicks, William Pająk 24.28; Wisor 21.22n37
Jrade, Cathy Novillo-Corvalán 23.49
Juhasz, Suzanne Jenkins (Amber) 27.17
Juvenal Koulouris 25.passim
Kahane, Claire Fischer 28.27n6, 37–38
Kane, Julie Foster 22.42

Kaplan, Caren Caputi 29.5n2
Kaplan, Cora Layne 21.81
Kapp, Yvonne (Cloud) Berkowitz 29.134–35n10
Karl, Alissa Novillo-Corvalán 23.36, 41, 57
Karshan, Thomas Leach 28.99n1
Katz, Tamar Cheney 24.59n5
Kay, Lindsay Lauby 27.61
Kazan, Francesca Ke 29.58n3
Ke, Lingxiang Bunting 30.8
Keats, John Davison 29.145; Koulouris 25.2; McVicker 28.79; Shin 23.122–23
Keillor, Alexander McVicker 28.83
Keith-Roach, Edward Gillespie 25.102
Kelley, Joyce E. Davison 23.4n10, 5, 9, 19n28
Keller, Evelyn Fox Livingstone 26.93
Kelly, Alice Bunting 30.19–20
Kendall, H. G. O. McVicker 28.83
Kendall-Morrick, Karalyn Williams 26.117
Kennard, Jean E. Caputi 29.22n18
Kennedy, David Shin 23.111n7
Kennedy, Thomas Foster 22.50n18
Kenninghall Gillespie 25.105
Kent Gillespie 25.108n26
Kenya Gillespie 25.117n35
Kenyon, Sir Frederic Schwartz 29.88, 90, 91, 96
Kenyon Jones, Christine Dalgarno 22.9; Gilman 29.47n8; Golden 23.98; Jenkins (Gwyn) 27.24, 25, 36, 43; Koulouris 25.5n8
Kermode, Frank Fischer 28.27n5
Kern, Stephen Lostoski-Ho 28.54n12; White 24.107, 113n23, 114n25
Keynes, John Maynard Adair/Martin 24.83–86, 91, 94–95; Berkowitz 29.132; Davison 29.146; Gillespie 29.150; Humm 29.156, 160; Jones 22.82; Wisor 21.20
Kidd, Ronald Wisor 21.28, 29n44–46, 30
Kincaid, Jamaica Cheney 24.67
King Charles I Gillespie 25.121; Graeber 24.176; Wisor 21.33, 38–39
King Charles II Wisor 21.33–34
King's College London Dalgarno 22.9; Davison 23.1; Jenkins (Gwyn) 27.passim; Gilman 29.47n8; Golden 23.96; Koulouris 25.5n8; Marcus 24.8
King Edward VII Cheney 24.58; Koulouris 25.4
King Edward VIII Wisor 21.10, 12n21, 14, 16–17, 22n36, 32, 39
King George V Wisor 21.14–15, 16n27, 32
King George VI Wisor 21.15–17, 32
King Henry VIII Lauby 27.58n7; Wisor 21.39
King James I Graeber 24.174, 175n9
King, James Chua 30.39, 41n4
King, Julia Gillespie 25.97, 100n9, 102n13, 105n20–21, 106n22, 128n51, 129; Gilman 29.48n10, 50n14; Sullam 30.122n5
King Leopold II Novillo-Corvalán 23.54
King William III Graeber 24.178; Wisor 21.39
Kingsley, Charles Schwartz 29.90
Kingsley, Mary Kotler 24.43
Kingston, England Williams 26.111
Kipling, Rudyard Fischer 28.36; Novillo-Corvalán 23.38
Kirby, William C. Chua 30.34
Kirkpatrick, B. J. Wisor 21.1n2–3
Kirkpatrick, Robin Ryan 30.76n18
Kirstein, Lincoln Berkowitz 29.128n8
Kirstein, Mina Berkowitz 29.128n8
Kisling, Moïse Berkowitz 29.128
Kister, Hanna Pająk 24.18, 20, 22–23
Kister, Marian Pająk 24.20
Kitchener, Horatio Herbert Koulouris 25.67; Wisor 21.14
Kitliński, Tomek Pająk 24.32
Klein, Melanie Clarke 28.13
Kleinbauer, W. Eugene Ke 29.65n9
Knole Fouirnaies 22.23, 30–34, 36
Knowles, Nancy Cheney 24.57n1; Foster 22.58, 66; Wisor 21.2n5
Knox-Shaw, Peter Shin 23.111n7
Kohlmann, Benjamin Cheney 24.61n10
Kofman, Sarah Dalgarno 22.12–13
Kolocotroni, Vassiliki Ke 29.67n11
Konkol, Margaret Golden 23.104

Kopley, Emily de Gay 30.passim; Fischer 28.43n21; Gallego Larrarte 30.passim; Goldman 30.107–08; Sullam 30.passim; White 24.102
Koppen, Randi S. Jenkins (Amber) 27.16; Wisor 21.3n7
Kore-Schröder, Leena Jones 22.76, 81
Kossak, Zofia Pająk 24.18
Kostkowska, Justyna Jenkins (Amber) 27.19; Layne 21.85, 100; Lostoski-Ho 28.49n3, 57n19
Kotler, Margot Camarasana et al. 24.3–4
Koulouris, Theodore Dalgarno 22.1n1; Gilman 29.32, 36; Ke 29.67n11; Jenkins (Gwyn) 27.25, 26; Koulouris 25.5n8, 7n12; McVicker 28.71n5, 76n14, 80n19; Van Wert 29.117
Krasińska, Ewa Pająk 24.26
Kristeva, Julia Clarke 28.9n6; Czarnecki 21.62; Favre 30.53; Fischer 28.27, 28, 31
Krouse, Tonya Bond 23.76n17; Czarnecki 21.57
Krzywicka, Irena Camarasana et al. 24.3; Pająk 24.passim
Krzywicki, Jerzy Pająk 24.31n11
Krzywicki, Piotr Pająk 24.31n11
Kuehn, Julia Fischer 28.38; Novillo-Corvalán 23.36, 39
Kukil, Karen Gilman 29.29–30. 31, 36
Kuncewiczowa, Maria Pająk 24.18
Labouchère, Henry Novillo-Corvalán 23.52
Lacan, Jacques Van Wert 29.107, 108n2, 109, 110, 113n8, 114, 116, 119
Lackey, Michael Layne 21.78–79, 85
Lacourarie, Chantal Ke 29.58n1
Lagerlöf, Selma Gilman 29.30
Lamarck, Jean-Baptiste Davison 23.5n12
Lamb, Charles Kopley 30.125
Lambert, Elizabeth Davison 23.3n8, 7n15, 12–13
Lamos, Colleen Golden 23.88n14
Landowska, Wanda Pająk 24.23n9
Lane, Edward William Rutherford 24.156–57
Lanier, Douglas Lauby 27.61
Lang, William Cosmo Gordon Kotler 24.51; Wisor 21.2, 14–18
Lanone, Catherine van Straten 30.85
Laplanche, Jean Van Wert 29.108n2
Larabee, Mark D. Golden 23.99n28, 100
Larkin, Philip Shin 23.116n18
Larson, Nella Caputi 29.passim
Larsson, Lisbeth Bunting 30.20; Gillespie 25.111n29, 113, 124; van Straten 30.85n1, 87n4
Lascelles, Henry Fouirnaies 22.26–27
László, Philip de Fouirnaies 22.32
Latham, Monica Favre 30.54; Layne 21.78, 80, 83
Latham, Sean Adair/Martin 24.89, 95; Fouirnaies 22.22; Shin 23.111n7
Latin America Novillo-Corvalán 23.passim
Lau, Meghan Lauby 27.48
Laurence, Patricia Chua 30.32–33, 34, 37; Fischer 28.27n7, 42–43n20; Foster 22.58n31; Gillespie 25.104n16
Law, Andrew Bonar Wisor 21.22
Lawrence, D. H. de Gay 30.99; Fischer 28.32n11; Gilman 29.31n13; McVicker 28.71, 77; Pająk 24.20
Lawrence, Karen Bunting 30.10, 12
Lazenby, Donna J. Foster 22.44n10
Leach, Sally Marcus 24.7, 10
Lear, Jonathan Van Wert 29.109
Leaska, Mitchell Czarnecki 21.57; Delsandro 25.76n5, 83; Favre 30.56; Jenkins (Gwyn) 27.24; Phillips 26.1; Rutherford 24.159; Shin 23.109; Wisor 21.40
Lee, Hermione Adair/Martin 24.80; Cheney 24.69n13; Chua 30.40, 41n4; Clarke 28.6; Dalgarno 22.9; Delsandro 25.84; Favre 30.56; Foster 22.44; Gallego Larrarte 30.112; Gilman 29.46n4; Golden 23.83; Jenkins (Gwyn) 27.38; Jones 22.91n9; Ke 29.58n3; Layne 21.79, 82, 87–89, 91; Leach 28.101, 103; Pająk 24.27; Rutherford 24.155, 156n8, 158–59; Shin 23.111n6, 120, 128–29; White 24.102; Wisor 21.1n3, 22n37
Lee, Paula Young Novillo-Corvalán 23.51

Leese, Peter Czarnecki 21.56, 57n8, 64
Lefebvre, Henri Bond 23.64n2; van Straten 30.91, 92
Le Guin, Ursula K. Favre 30.54; Livingstone 26.90, 91
Lehmann, John de Gay 30.99, 100; Gallego Larrarte 30.111, 113; Kopley 30.126, 127
Lei, Jun Chua 30.35
Leighton Park School Jenkins (Amber) 27.7
Lely, Sir Peter Fouirnaies 22.33
Lemke, Sieglinde Caputi 29.6n2
Lenin, Vladimir Novillo-Corvalán 23.41–42, 48
Leonardi, Susan J. Fischer 28.27n5
Lepsius, Karl Richard Rutherford 24.156
Leszkowicz, Paweł Pająk 24.32
Levander, Märta Sund Ryan 30.68n2
Levenback, Karen Delsandro 25.76n5; McVicker 28.71n5
Levitas, Ruth Livingstone 26.98
Levitt, Helen Berkowitz 29.129n8
Levy, Hyman Livingstone 26.100n8
Lewes Gillespie 25.108n26, 109
Lewis, Alison Foster 22.44
Lewis, Andrea Novillo-Corvalán 23.36, 57
Lewis, Colin M. Novillo-Corvalán 23.43
Lewis, Ernest Wisor 21.29n44
Lewis, Pericles Shin 23.111, 117n18, 118n19, 127
Lewis, Wyndham Berkowitz 29.127, 133, 134; Gillespie 25.108; Shin 23.128–29; White 24.102n4
Li, Congshuo Chua 30.34n3
Lianeri, Alexandra Dalgarno 22.5
Liddell, Henry George Golden 23.94, 96, 99, 103
Light, Alison Delsandro 25.86; Fouirnaies 22.22n1; Humm 29.158; Jones 22.81
Lilienfeld, Jane Clarke 28.14; Foster 22.50n19; Ryan 30.69n8
Lilly, Amy M. Wisor 21.4n10
Lim Wan Hui Eva Chua 30.34n3
Lin Xiaoxia Chua 30.45
Lindbergh, Anne Morrow Gillespie 25.118
Lindenberger, Herbert S. Davison 23.6, 18, 19n28
Lindsay, Vachel Humm 29.158
Linett, Maren Delsandro 25.73, 76n5; Williams 26.111, 112
Lipking, Joanna Shin 23.136
Lipking, Lawrence Shin 23.136
Lipson, E. Gillespie 25.102
Little, Judy Bunting 30.10; Van Wert 29.114n10
Liu Ailin Chua 30.37
Liu Xiaoqing Chua 30.35
Lloyd George, David Wisor 21.14, 22, 28
Lock, Rose Koulouris 25.11
Locker-Lampson, Oliver Davison 29.144–45
Lockhart, J.G. Wisor 21.16–18
Lodge, David Layne 21.78
Loeb, Janice Berkowitz 29.128, 129n8
Long Barn Adair/Martin 24.86; Fouirnaies 22.25, 34
Lonnquist, Barbara McVicker 28.76–77n15
Loos, France Wisor 21.37
Lopokova, Lydia Adair/Martin 24.83–84, 94–95; Berkowitz 29.132, 133; Humm 29.156, 157
Lorde, Audre Delsandro 25.passim; Kotler 24.40n1, 44
Los Angeles, USA Czarnecki 21.65
Lostoski-Ho, Leanna Ryan 30.70n11
Louvre Gillespie 29.151
Love, Heather Clarke 28.19
Love, Jean Bond 23.67–68
Low, Lisa Kotler 24.40
Lowe, Gill Adair/Martin 24.75n1; Gillespie 25.116n33
Lowell, James Russell McVicker 28.82n22
Lowerson, John Jones 22.81n6
Lubbock, Percy Kopley 30.128; Sullam 30.119, 120–21
Lucian of Samosata Livingstone 26.90
Luke, Sir Harry Gillespie 25.102
Lurz, John Golden 23.84, 92n18, 94, 98, 102n32
Lyman, Peter Kotler 24.39
Lynas, Mark Ryan 30.68n5
Lyon, Janet Williams 26.111

Lyons, Brenda Dalgarno 22.1n1
Lysias Jenkins (Gwyn) 27.31
Macaulay, Rose Wisor 21.6n14, 26
Macaulay, Thomas Babington Schwartz 29.100, 101
MacCarthy, Desmond Davison 29.144; Reed 29.163, 164
MacColl, James E. Wisor 21.6–7
MacDonald, Ramsay Jones 22.82, 86, 95n14; Wisor 21.12n21–22, 13–14, 22
Mace, Arthur McVicker 28.81
Macintosh, Charles Novillo-Corvalán 23.53
MacKay, Marina Delsandro 25.76; Foster 22.58; Shin 23.129, 136
Mackerell, Judith Adair/Martin 24.84
MacKenzie, John M. Wisor 21.8
Maclagen, Eric Davison 29.145
MacNeice, Louis de Gay 30.99; Gallego Larrarte 30.111; Kopley 30.127
Macpherson, Ken Humm 29.159
Maddison, Carol Shin 23.110n4, 114
Madrid, Spain Gillespie 25.104
Mafeking (now Mahikeng), South Africa Wisor 21.10–12
Magee, Bryan Davison 23.2n4
Maggio, Paula Foster 22.58n31
Mahaffey, Vicki White 24.104n6, 111–12, 117n30
M'ahesa, Sent Rutherford 24.154
Maidenhead Gillespie 25.99
Maika, Patricia Rutherford 24.153, 158
Maitland, Frederic W. de Gay 30.101, 102
Mallarmé, Stéphane Davison 23.22n32; Fischer 28.41
Malle, Louis Chua 30.34
Man Ray Humm 29.157, 159
Manchester Gillespie 25.104
Mangan, James Anthony Bunting 30.14
Mangold, Hilde Livingstone 26.93
Manley Hopkins, Gerard Shin 23.113, 120
Mann, Thomas Pająk 24.18
Mann, Tom Wisor 21.29
Mannheim, Karl Livingstone 26.93, 99
Mansfield, Katherine Berkowitz 29.126, 127n5; Kopley 30.127
Manson, Janet M. Gillespie 25.104n16
Marbot, Marcellin Bond 23.73
Marchand, Jean Berkowitz 29.128
Marchi, Dudley M. Leach 28.99, 104
Marcus, Jane Camarasana et al. 24.passim; Cheney 24.passim; Dalgarno 22.11n13; Davison 23.5; Delsandro 25.75–76, 84n15, 85; Favre 30.58, 59, 60, 62; Foster 22.41, 43, 44n10, 53n28, 64n44; Fouirnaies 22.22n1; Gillespie 25.105, 108, 112–13, 126n46, 128; Golden 23.83n4; Jenkins (Gwyn) 27.27; Kotler 24.passim; Lostoski-Ho 28.48, 49–50; McVicker 28.71n7, 72n8; Novillo-Corvalán 23.36; Pająk 24.passim; Phillips 26.8n6; Van Wert 29.117, 118; Wisor 21.1, 3n7, 4n10–11, 5, 7
Marcus, Laura Cheney 24.65n12; Dalgarno 22.16; Favre 30.57, 61; Fouirnaies 22.38; Humm 29.159; Koulouris 25.11; McVicker 28.71n7, 82n22; White 24.113
Marcus, Sharon Clarke 28.11; Fischer 28.26n4
Marder, Herbert Delsandro 25.84n15
Marett, Robert Ranulph Ryan 30.74n16
Marina, Doña Novillo-Corvalán 23.40
Mark, Marion Marcus 24.10
Markham, Beryl Gillespie 25.117–18
Marler, Regina Layne 21.80
Marlowe, Christopher Bunting 30.17, 18; Ke 29.77; Schwartz 29.88, 93, 94, 100
Marseilles, France Adair/Martin 24.81
Marsh, Moira Caputi 29.22n18
Marshall, Paule Czarnecki 21.51
Marshik, Celia Novillo-Corvalán 23.38; Pająk 24.17; Wisor 21.6
Martin, Alison E. Chua 30.34
Martin, Ann Adair/Martin 24.76n2, 80n7; Gillespie 25.99n4; Williams 26.109, 110
Martin, Linda Bunting 30.10; Van Wert 29.114n10
Martin, Lindsay Chua 30.42
Martini, Arturo Shin 23.113n11
Marx, Karl Novillo-Corvalán 23.49
Mary, Princess Royal Fouirnaies 22.26–27

Maspero, Gaston Rutherford 24.154, 157
Massey, Doreen Gillespie 25.112
Massine, Léonide Berkowitz 29.128
Massumi, Brian Kotler 24.37
Matheson, Hilda Davison 29.143, 144
Matisse, Henri Berkowitz 29.128; Davison 23.22n32; Reed 29.162
Matless, David Gillespie 25.107, 124; Jones 22.83, 91n10, 93n12
Matson, Patricia Czarnecki 21.52n3
Mattison, Laci Ryan 30.74, 75, 82
Maudsley, Henry Czarnecki 21.64n14
Maurice, J.F. Wisor 21.11
Mayfair Bond 23.63
Mayne, John Dawson Gillespie 25.102n12
Mayor, Joseph Bickersteth Golden 23.98; Jenkins (Gwyn) 27.28
Maze, J. R. Fischer 28.37n15
Mbembe, Achille van Straten 30.85n2; 88
McAfee, Helen Kopley 30.128
McCabe, Mary Dalgarno 22.12
McCardie, Henry Wisor 21.37, 143
McCrae, John Bunting 30.7
McDermott, Bridget Rutherford 24.137, 143, 146
McDowell, Deborah E. Caputi 29.16, 17n14, 19n15, 21n17
McDowell, Linda Bunting 30.18
McFarlane, Alexander C. Czarnecki 21.63–64
McGavran Jr., James Holt Shin 23.116n16
McGiff, Shilo Ryan 30.82
McGowan, Todd Van Wert 29.109, 110, 111, 112, 113, 114, 115, 117, 119
McGregor, Wayne Livingstone 26.91
McHale, Brian White 24.116n29
McIntire, Gabrielle Bond 23.77
McKay, Claude Caputi 29.5n1
McKibbin, Ross Jones 22.85
McLachlan, Torin Chua 30.46n6
McLaurin, Allen Jenkins (Amber) 27.5; Layne 21.84; Reed 29.163
McManus, Patricia Fouirnaies 22.22
McMillan, Laurie Czarnecki 21.51n2
McNees, Eleanor Cheney 24.69n13; Gillespie 25.129; Gilman 29.46n4; Phillips 26.1n1
McNeillie, Andrew Dalgarno 22.1n1; Gilman 29.28n3, 53n23
McNicholl, Stella Jenkins (Amber) 27.5n2
McPhee, John Lostoski-Ho 28.52
McPherson, Karen S. Czarnecki 21.57, 63
McVicker, Jeannette Czarnecki 21.51n2
Mediterranean McVicker 28.76
Meisel, Perry Jenkins (Gwyn) 27.27, 28, 33, 34
Melcer, Wanda Pająk 24.30
Melville, Herman Gillespie 25.116, 119
Menand, Louis Van Wert 29.109n4
Mendelssohn, Fanny Marcus 24.8
Mendes, Peter Lauby 27.49
Mendlesohn, Farah Foster 22.44n6, 46, 47n13
Meng, Deyan Chua 30.34n3
Mepham, John McVicker 28.71n5
Meredith, George Foster 22.54
Mew, Charlotte Kopley 30.128
Meyer, Jessica Czarnecki 21.68
Mexico Novillo-Corvalán 23.34
Micir, Melanie Clarke 28.6n1, 19n11
Middeke, Martin Layne 21.79
Middlemas, Keith Wisor 21.21–22
Miletic-Vejzovic, Laila Gillespie 25.97; Gilman 29.48n10, 50n14; Sullam 30.122n5
Mill, John Stuart Dalgarno 22.5
Miller, J. Hillis White 24.110n19, 122n34, 124n36, 127
Miller, Marlowe A. Lauby 27.48n3
Miller, Nancy K. Delsandro 25.74–75, 85, 92; Favre 30.59n11; Kotler 24.36
Miller, Simon Jones 22.77–78
Millett, Kate Kotler 24.36
Mills, Billy McVicker 28.84n25
Mills, Jean Dalgarno 22.3; Delsandro 25.85–86, 91; Foster 22.58n31; Golden 23.83n4, 100n30; Jenkins (Gwyn) 27.23, 26, 27, 39; McVicker 28.71n7, 72n8, 75n11; Wisor 21.3n7
Miłosz, Czesław Pająk 24.15
Milton, John Davison 23.18, 22–25; de Gay 30.101, 102, 103; Fischer 28.41; Gilman 29.48n10; Kopley 30.125; Lauby 27.49, 52, 55–56, 59, 60, 61;

Ryan 30.68
Mitchell, Angus Novillo-Corvalán 23.54
Minow-Pinkney, Makiko Adair/Martin 24.75, 78; Bond 23.65n4, 78; Van Wert 29.113
Miracky, James White 24.113n23, 114n25
Mirrlees, Hope Gallego Larrarte 30.112
Miss Clay Jenkins (Gwyn) 27.27, 31
Miss Lucas Jenkins (Gwyn) 27.27, 31
Mitchell, David Williams 26.112
Moffat, Wendy Golden 23.83n4
Mohanty, Chandra Talpade Caputi 29.5n2
Moi, Toril Czarnecki 21.52n3
Molière Ke 29.81
Monaco, Beatrice Lostoski-Ho 28.56n17
Monk, Ray Humm 29.160
Monk's House Adair/Martin 24.77–78, 89; Gillespie 25.108, 110, 116n34; Jones 22.81, 93n11; Ryan 30.67n1
Monmonier, Mark Gillespie 25.105, 110, 127
Mons, Belgium Wisor 21.37
Montaigne, Michel de Dalgarno 22.3; Fouirnaies 22.26; Gilman 29.53n24; Jenkins (Gwyn) 27.42; Leach 28.passim; Sullam 30.123
Montaldo, Graciela Novillo-Corvalán 23.46
More, Thomas Livingstone 26.93, 94
Moody, Alys Chua 30.37
Moore, Brian White 24.102n3
Moore, G. E. Dalgarno 22.1n1; Rutherford 24.135
Moore, George Chua 30.38
Moore, Jason W. Lostoski-Ho 28.53n10
Moore, Madeline Fouirnaies 22.25
Moore, Marianne Humm 29.159
Moretti, Franco Chua 30.33; White 24.102n3
Morgan, Claire Layne 21.80, 86–87
Morgan, Clare McVicker 28.86n28, 90n30
Morgenstern, Barry Bunting 30.10
Morgenthal, Silvia McVicker 28.86n28
Morice, Francis David Golden 23.98; Jenkins (Gwyn) 27.28
Morley College Chua 30.41–42
Morrell, Lady Ottoline Berkowitz 29.128; Humm 29.156n1; Jones 22.82n7; Wisor 21.14, 39
Morris, F. O. Bunting 30.13
Morris, Jan Adair/Martin 24.80
Morris, Pam Ryan 30.73
Morris, Terence Wisor 21.28
Morris, William Bond 23.73; Cheney 24.64
Morrison, Toni Czarnecki 21.51
Morse, Elizabeth J. Livingstone 26.98n7
Morska, Izabela Pająk 24.26
Morton, Timothy Lostoski-Ho 28.53
Moscow, Russia Gillespie 25.102
Moshenska, Gabriel McVicker 28.71n6
Mosley, Sir Oswald Wisor 21.30n48
Mosse, George Bunting 30.19, 20
Moulton-Barrett, Edward Barrett Kotler 24.43–44, 52
Mourning Dove Czarnecki 21.50n1
Moylan, Tom Livingstone 26.91
Muir, Edwin Kopley 30.128; Sullam 30.119, 120, 121
Mullan, John Clarke 28.14, 15
Mullin, Katherine Novillo-Corvalán 23.38
Muñoz, José Esteban Lauby 27.60n8
Murray, A.T. Koulouris 25.27n70, 28n75
Murray, David Czarnecki 21.59n9
Museum of Modern Art Berkowitz 29.128–29n8
Mussolini, Benito Delsandro 25.80–81; Wisor 21.12
Nagel, Rebecca Ke 29.67n11
Nagy-Seres, Imola Bunting 30.20; Ke 29.58n3, 67n11
Nalbantian, Suzanne Bond 23.65n4, 67
Nash, Jennifer C. Caputi 29.6n4
Nash, John Jones 22.83–84; Schwartz 29.102; van Straten 30.89
Nash, Paul Adair/Martin 24.93
National Gallery (London) Berkowitz 29.138; Davison 29.145; Gillespie 29.149
Negrello, Giulia Novillo-Corvalán 23.34
Nestle, Joan Pająk 24.15
Netherhampton House Gillespie 25.104
Netherlands Adair/Martin 24.80n6; Gillespie 25.103; Graeber 24.175n9; Wisor 21.33

Neumann, Angelo Davison 23.3n5
Neverow, Vara Bunting 30.11, 17; Czarnecki 21.52n3; Davison 23.13n21; Golden 23.83n4, 95, 99n27; Ke 29.57n1, 58n3, 67n11; Kotler 24.43n3; McVicker 28.71n7, 75n11, 80n19; Van Wert 29.120n12; Wisor 21.3n7
Nevill, Dorothy Fouirnaies 22.34
Nevison, C. R. W. Berkowitz 29.133n10
Newhaven Gillespie 25.108n26
New England, USA Graeber 24.173
Newman, Hilary White 24.102n4
New Mexico, USA Czarnecki 21.54–55
New York, USA Gillespie 25.104, 117n35; Golden 23.83
Newnham College Wisor 21.21, 23n38, 24
Newton, Eric Davison 29.146
Newton, K.M. White 24.102n3, 128n39
Ngai, Sianne Kotler 24.37
Nicolai, Philip Cheney 24.64
Nicolson, Benedict Fouirnaies 22.31
Nicolson, Harold Adair/Martin 24.86n11; Fouirnaies 22.23, 25, 36–37; Humm 29.157; Kopley 30.127; Layne 21.79
Nicolson, Nigel Chua 30.32, 35–36; Fouirnaies 22.25; Gilman 29.31n12; Rutherford 24.144
Nicolson, Steve Wisor 21.8
Nietzsche, Friedrich Dalgarno 22.1; Davison 23.4; de Gay 30.99; Gallego Larrarte 30.112; Layne 21.86; White 24.128n39
Nightingale, Andrea Dalgarno 22.4
Nightingale, Florence Rutherford 24.156
Nixon, Rob Lostoski-Ho 28.54n14
Noel-Baker, Philip Foster 22.51n26
Norfolk, England McVicker 28.79
North, Michael Humm 29.157; McVicker 28.81
Nouzeilles, Gabriela Novillo-Corvalán 23.46
Nova Scotia, Canada Gillespie 25.117n35
Novillo-Corvalán, Patricia Gillespie 25.120n39
Nowaczyński, Adolf Pająk 24.18, 30
Nuie, Cornelius Fouirnaies 22.23, 28, 37
Nunez, Sigrid Layne 21.80, 86
Nussbaum, Martha C. Dalgarno 22.4n4, 5–7; Fischer 28.28n9; Kotler 24.37
Nycz, Ryszard Pająk 24.22
Ocampo, Victoria Novillo-Corvalán 23.34–35
O'Connell, Sean Adair/Martin 24.93
O'Conor, Roderic Hussey 29.168
O'Higgins, Paul Wisor 21.7
Olczak-Ronikier, Joanna Pająk 24.23n9
Oldfield, Sybil de Gay 30.102
Oliver, Kelly Williams 26.107–08
Ollard, S.L. Wisor 21.15, 17
Olson, Liesl White 24.124n36
Ortega, Mariana Delsandro 25.88
Ortiz, Raúl Scalabrini Novillo-Corvalán 23.49
Østergaard, Edvin Davison 23.3n5, 26
Ouse (river) Williams 26.106
Outka, Elizabeth Adair/Martin 24.88
Ovid Lauby 27.53
Owen, Wilfrid Wisor 21.9, 27n43
Owens, Louis Czarnecki 21.59–60, 68–70, 72
Oxford University Gillespie 25.104; Golden 23.86; Jenkins (Gwyn) 27.38; Wisor 21.23
Oxner, Alex Shin 23.111n7
Ozick, Cynthia Layne 21.78n1
Paetsasadee, Korrakod McVicker 28.70n2, 90n29
Pająk, Paulina Camarasana et al. 24.3
Palestine Gillespie 25.102; Wisor 21.37
Pall Mall, London Wisor 21.38
Palmerston, Lord Schwartz 29.89–90
Panicacci, Jean-Louis Davison 29.141n2
Pankhurst, Christabel Marcus 24.6–7
Pankhurt, Emmeline Camarasana et al. 24.1; Delsandro 25.83; Marcus 24.5–7
Pankhurst, Richard Marsden Marcus 24.5
Pankhurst, Sylvia Marcus 24.6–7
Pański, Jerzy Pająk 24.23
Pantazzi, Michael Rutherford 24.154
Pape, Fred Adair/Martin 24.79
Parini, Jay Layne 21.79
Paris, France Gillespie 25.102, 104, 123; Humm 29.157; Hussey 29.168; Reed

29.162
Parnell, Charles Stewart Cheney 24.58
Parker, Louis Napoleon Lauby 27.47–48, 49, 58
Parker, S. Emily Foster 22.59n32
Parkes, Adam Gilman 29.45n2
Parrinder, Patrick Livingstone 26.91n5
Parrot, Fiona Novillo-Corvalán 23.34
Partridge, Ralph Adair/Martin 24.82
Passchendaele, Belgium Wisor 21.37
Paston, John Gilman 29.49n13
Pater, Clara Golden 23.95, 98; Jenkins (Gwyn) 27.passim
Pater, Hester (Tottie) Jenkins (Gwyn) 27.26, 33
Pater, Walter Foster 22.44, 53n27; Jenkins (Gwyn) 27.26, 27, 35, 41; Leach 28.104; Rutherford 24.156, 158
Patmore, Coventry Favre 30.56
Patton, Ventria K. Caputi 29.6n2
Paul, Lissa Williams 26.108
Pausanias Koulouris 25.50n158, 51–52
Pawlowski, Merry Delsandro 25.76n5; Fouirnaies 22.22; Wisor 21.3n6, 24n39, 32
Payne, Emma M. Bunting 30.9, 20
Peach, Linden McVicker 28.80; White 24.107n13
Peacock, John Czarnecki 21.59
Peacock, Thomas Love Gilman 29.31n13
Pearson, Nels Gillespie 25.113, 127n48
Pease, Allison Caputi 29.6n3, 15n13
Peat, F. David Czarnecki 21.59n9
Pederson, Elisabeth Skou Reed 29.163n2, 165
Peele, George Leach 28.102
Pelling, Henry Jones 22.95n14
Penner, Erin Kay Shin 23.111n7; van Straten 30.87n4, 90n8
Pennick, Nigel Rutherford 24.155, 157
Pentonville, London Shin 23.131–32
Periyan, Natasha Cheney 24.58n4
Perry, Gill Jenkins (Amber) 27.16
Perry, R. B. Gillespie 25.105n19
Persia (now Iran) Adair/Martin 24.86n11; Rutherford 24.152; Schwartz 29.94, 101
Peterson, Sandra Dalgarno 22.10n12
Pethick-Lawrence, Emmeline Wisor 21.5
Petre, Jonathan Wisor 21.19
Petrie, William Flinders McVicker 28.70n3
Phaedrus Koulouris 25.50n158, 51, 72
Phelan, Jim White 24.104n6
Philippines Czarnecki 21.55
Phillips, Adam Clarke 28.9n6; Van Wert 29.110, 116
Phillips, Joshua Ryan 30.69n8, 79
Phillips, Kathy Gillespie 25.113; Graeber 24.166, 171, 179; Novillo-Corvalán 23.36–37; Wisor 21.13n23
Piazza, Jo Berkowitz 29.136n14
Picabia, Francis Berkowitz 29.128
Picasso, Olga Humm 29.157
Picasso, Pablo Berkowitz 29.128, 129; Foster 22.44; Reed 29.162
Piccadilly Circus Adair/Martin 24.87; Cheney 24.71; White 24.114
Piddinghoe Gillespie 25.109–10
Piłsudski, Józef Pająk 24.18
Pindar Golden 23.88, 93; Shin 23.passim
Pinho, Davi Favre 30.53n1
Pinkney, Tony Adair/Martin 24.76n3
Pintér, Károly Livingstone 26.93
Pitt, William (the Elder) Wisor 21.22
Pitt, William (the Younger) Wisor 21.22
Plath, Sylvia Layne 21.86
Plato Bond 23.73; Bunting 30.18; Dalgarno 22.passim; de Gay 30.102; Golden 23.95, 102; Jenkins (Gwyn) 27.27, 30, 35; Ke 29.64, 66, 67, 68, 75, 79n17, 81; Koulouris 25.3, 5–6, 8, 13–14, 50–57, 72; Schwartz 29.88, 95, 97, 100, 101; White 24.102n3, 105
Plomber, William Gallego Larrarte 30.111
Plutarch Rutherford 24.155
Poland Pająk 24.passim
Politis, Vasilis Dalgarno 22.2, 5
Pollard, Francis Foster 22.52, 61–62, 67
Polo, Marco Gillespie 25.106
Polykleitos Ke 29.64, 66, 67, 68
Poole, Roger Czarnecki 21.61
Pope, Alexander Koulouris 25.58
Portugal Caputi 29.9; Novillo-Corvalán

23.40, 53
Potocki de Montalk, Geoffrey Wisor 21.6n14, 26, 28
Potter, Simon J. Davison 29.142
Pound, Ezra de Gay 30.99
Poussin, Nicolas Gillespie 29.151n4
Pratt, Mary Louise Novillo-Corvalán 23.37, 42
Praxiteles Schwartz 29.88
Pridmore-Brown, Michele Livingstone 26.89n4
Priestley, J. B. Sullam 30.119
Primrose Hill, London Shin 23.131
Prince George, Duke of Cambridge Wisor 21.10
Prins, Yopie Golden 23.83n4, 85, 87; Jenkins (Gwyn) 27.23, 24, 37
Prinsep, Henry Thoby Gillespie 25.127
Proctor, Tammy M. Wisor 21.13
Prosser, Jay Pająk 24.12, 21
Protagoras Dalgarno 22.4–6
Protogenes Koulouris 25.17
Proust, Michel Dalgarno 22.8, 11; Favre 30.54; Humm 29.157; Lauby 27.50
Prussia Pająk 24.22
Ptolemy Rutherford 24.137
Puchner, Martin White 24.102n3
Putzel, Steven Novillo-Corvalán 23.36; White 24.102–03
Pynchon, Thomas Gillespie 25.116
Pyne, Stephen J. Ryan 30.68, 69, 70n10, 73, 77, 81
Pytlak, Magdalena Pająk 24.18
Qian Zhaoming Chua 30.34
Queen Elizabeth I Fouirnaies 22.29; Graeber 24.172–74; Lauby 27.56–57; Shin 23.134
Queen Elizabeth II Wisor 21.16n27
Queen Mary Wisor 21.16n27
Queen Victoria Davison 23.4n9; Graeber 24.181; Koulouris 25.2, 4; Wisor 21.16n27, 38
Quennet, Fabienne C. Czarnecki 21.50n1
Quigley, Megan Fischer 28.28, 39n17; Golden 23.91n17
Radin, Grace Delsandro 25.76n5, 80, 82; Phillips 26.2
Radó, Sandor Gillespie 25.103
Rae, Patricia McVicker 28.71n5, 86n28, 90n30
Raitt, Suzanne Fouirnaies 22.21
Raleigh, Sir Walter Gillespie 25.105n20; Graeber 24.165, 167; Novillo-Corvalán 23.39
Ramazani, Jahan Bunting 30.111, 112; Shin 23.112n9–10
Ramsay, Warren Fischer 28.27
Rancière, Jacques Favre 30.54
Randall, Bryony White 24.113n22
Raphael, Linda Bond 23.73n16
Rasula, Jed Davison 23.4n10, 26; Gallego Larrarte 30.113n3
Ratcliffe, S.K. Foster 22.51
Read, Herbert Sullam 30.119
Reading Prison Pająk 24.27
Reed, Christopher Davison 29.145; Gillespie 29.151n4; Hussey 29.167, 169; Jenkins (Amber) 27.5n1, 6, 15; White 24.107n13, 108n15
Reed, Conor Tomas Wisor 21.3n7
Reeves, Nicholas Rutherford 24.146
Reeve-Tucker, Alice Livingstone 26.89
Regent's Park Adair/Martin 24.80; Czarnecki 21.61, 63
Reid, Alastair Jones 22.95n14
Reid, Panthea Jenkins (Amber) 27.8
Reynier, Christine Ke 29.75
Reynolds, Sir Joshua Schwartz 29.101, 102
Rhodes, Cecil Davison 23.15n23
Rice, David Czarnecki 21.60, 67
Rich, Adrienne Delsandro 25.passim; Kotler 24.41, 44
Richards, Juno Chua 30.46n6
Richardson, Brian White 24.106n7, 114n26
Richardson, Dorothy Humm 29.159
Richardson, Samuel Gilman 29.31n13
Richmond McVicker 28.82
Richmond, Marsha L. Davison 23.3
Richter, Harvena Cheney 24.59n5; Kopley 30.126; White 24.102n4
Ricœur, Paul Lostoski-Ho 28.49
Rieder, John Livingstone 26.90
Riggs, Christina McVicker 28.82

Riley, Matthew Davison 23.4n9
Ritchie, Alick P.F. Wisor 21.2n4
Ritchie, Lady Anne Thackeray Williams 26.108–09
Rives, Rochelle Kotler 24.40
Rivers, Augustus Pitt McVicker 28.70n3
Rizzuto, Nicole Lostoski-Ho 28.49, 50n7
Roberts, Michael Gallego Larrarte 30.111
Robertson, James C. Wisor 21.8n16
Robeson, Paul Foster 22.44
Robins, Elizabeth Camarasana et al. 24.1; Kotler 24.35; Marcus 24.5–7
Robinson, Annabel Davison 23.25
Roca, Julio Argentino Novillo-Corvalán 23.46, 49
Rocchi, Fernando Novillo-Corvalán 23.43
Roche, Hannah Pająk 24.12
Rodmell Gillespie 25.108–10; Jones 22.76, 79–80; Williams 26.111, 112, 116
Rodríguez, Laura Lojo Novillo-Corvalán 23.34
Roe, Sue Bunting 30.11, 19; Dalgarno 22.9; Ke 29.72n16
Roemer, Kenneth M. Cheney 24.61n10
Rogers, Benjamin Bickley Koulouris 25.14n26, 70
Rogers, Gayle Foster 22.50n20; Novillo-Corvalán 23.35
Rohman, Carrie Czarnecki 21.52n3; Lostoski-Ho 28.49n3, n5; Williams 26.106, 113–14
Romains, Jules Hussey 29.169; Reed 29.163–65
Rome, Italy Gillespie 25.104, 123; Koulouris 25.passim; Reed 29.162; Schwartz 29.92, 101
Romney, George Fouirnaies 22.31
Roof, Judith Bond 23.76n17
Rosati, Alessandra van Straten 30.94n13
Rose, Gillian Gillespie 25.112
Rose, Jacqueline Van Wert 29.118
Rose, Marika Van Wert 29.111, 119
Rose, Phyllis Cheney 24.70
Rose, Sam Berkowitz 29.127n5
Rosenbaum, S.P. Adair/Martin 24.76; Gillespie 25.116n33; White 24.102
Rosenberg, Léonce Berkowitz 29.128
Rosenberg, Paul Berkowitz 29.128
Rosenfeld, Natania Delsandro 25.89n20
Rosenthal, Lecia Van Wert 29.117
Rosenthal, Michael Wisor 21.10–11, 12n22, 13–14
Rosetti, Christina Foster 22.41n1
Rosner, Victoria Gillespie 25.116n34; Jones 22.93n11
Ross, Ellen Wisor 21.11
Ross, Janet (Duff Gordon) Berkowitz 29.127
Ross, Stephen J. Chua 30.37; Jenkins (Amber) 27.6
Rossetti, Christina Caputi 29.9n8
Roston, Murray Ke 29.65
Rothenstein, William Berkowitz 29.127n5
Rothman, Roger Shin 23.113
Rowe, M.W. Dalgarno 22.3
Rowse, A.L. Rutherford 24.141
Royal Albert Hall Marcus 24.6
Rubenstein, Roberta Rutherford 24.135
Rubinstein, Arthur Humm 29.157
Ruck, Berta Gillespie 25.118
Rummel, Andrea Bond 23.64n2
Ruoff, A. LaVonne Brown Czarnecki 21.53n5
Ruotolo, Lucio White 24.118n32
Ruppaner, Savina Golden 23.104
Ruskin, John Schwartz 29.89, 90, 96
Russell, Bertrand Berkowitz 29.132; Pająk 24.17, 20
Russell Square White 24.116
Russia Davison 29.144; Gillespie 25.103; Graeber 24.175; Pająk 24.22
Rutherford, Brett McVicker 28.71n7, 82n22
Rutherford, Ernest Livingstone 26.101
Ryan, Derek Davison 23.6, 7n15, 13n21, 16; Foster 22.41n3, 43n5, 44; Jenkins (Amber) 27.6; Lostoski-Ho 28.48–49, 64n28; McVicker 28.76–77n15; Novillo-Corvalán 23.51n6; Phillips 26.2n3; Ryan 30.70n11; Williams 26.107
Rylands, George Sullam 30.119
Saariluoma, Liisa Cheney 24.58, 59n6
Sábato, Hilda Novillo-Corvalán 23.43

Sacks, Oliver Davison 23.2n3
Sackville, Edward Fouirnaies 22.23, 28–29, 37
Sackville, Lionel Fouirnaies 22.24, 26, 28
Sackville, Richard Fouirnaies 22.23, 28–29, 37
Sackville, Thomas Fouirnaies 22.23, 26–27
Sackville-West, Robert Fouirnaies 22.38
Sackville-West, Victoria Adair/Martin 24.86n11
Sackville-West, Vita Adair/Martin 24.80, 86–88; Caputi 29.23; Chua 30.32, 35, 39–40; Clarke 28.17; Dalgarno 22.9; Delsandro 25.84; Fouirnaies 22.passim; Gillespie 25.110, 116; Gillespie 29.153; Gilman 29.31n12; Humm 29.157; Jenkins (Gwyn) 27.23, 32–33; Jones 22.80–81; Ke 29.75; Kopley 30.127; Layne 21.86; McVicker 28.84; Rutherford 24.135, 138, 151–53; Shin 23.128; Sullam 30.118, 122
Saguaro, Shelley Ke 29.58n2
Said, Edward Novillo-Corvalán 23.37, 46
Saint-Amour, Paul K. Chua 30.46n6; Delsandro 25.76; Lostoski-Ho 28.54–55
Saint-Saëns, Camille Davison 23.12n20
Sainte-Beuve, C. A. Gilman 29.34
Salaman, Malcolm C. Rutherford 24.140n2
Salisbury McVicker 28.77
Salmon, André Berkowitz 29.128
Saloman, Randi Dalgarno 22.15n14; Gilman 29.49n13; Golden 23.86n9, 104
Salter, Sir Arthur Foster 22.51
Samarkand, Uzbekistan Gillespie 25.102
Sand, George Cheney 24.67
Sandberg, Eric Ke 29.57n1, 72n16, 78
Sands, Ethel Adair/Martin 24.79, 84; Gillespie 29.152
Sappho Davison 23.18; Layne 21.89; Pająk 24.13; Shin 23.118–20
Sarker, Sonita Graeber 24.166
Sarmiento, Domingo Faustino Novillo-Corvalán 23.43
Sartre, Jean-Paul Foster 22.61–62; Shin 23.129
Sassoon, Siegfried Berkowitz 29.128; McVicker 28.86n28
Satie, Erik Berkowitz 29.128
Savage, George Czarnecki 21.64n14, 65
Savage, Roger Lauby 27.48
Savoie, Tracy Gillespie 25.126n46
Sawyer, Charles J. Gilman 29.54n24
Sayers, Alfred Wisor 21.5
Sayers, Dorothy L. Livingstone 26.98n7
Scarborough Gillespie 25.104
Scarry, Elaine Shin 23.114
Schaffer, Talia Fouirnaies 22.22, 28, 36
Scheman, Naomi Kotler 24.38
Schiff, James White 24.113n22
Schlack, Beverly Ann Fischer 28.41
Schlegel, August Wilhelm Ke 29.68
Schliemann, Heinrich McVicker 28.79
Schotter, Jesse McVicker 28.71n7, 81, 82n22
Schrimper, Michael R. Ke 29.71n14
Schumann, Clara Marcus 24.8
Schwartz, John Pedro Schwartz 29.90n5, 91n6
Scotland Graeber 24.172; McVicker 28.87
Scott, Bonnie Kime Bond 23.65n4; Czarnecki 21.52n3; Fischer 28.27n6; Hussey 29.168; Jenkins (Amber) 27.20; Jones 22.76n2; Ke 29.58n2; Lostoski-Ho 28.49n3, 50n7; van Straten 30.87, 88, 89, 90n7, 91; White 24.102n4
Scott, Laurence White 24.127n38
Scott, Robert Golden 23.94, 96, 99, 103
Scott, Sir Walter Chua 30.38
Scourfield, David Gilman 29.54n25
Scriabin, Alexander Davison 23.22n32
Seaford Gillespie 25.108n26
Sedgwick, Eve Kosofksy Clarke 28.13, 14, 14–15
Sedley, David Dalgarno 22.6, 15
Sedon, Kate Czarnecki 21.72
Sellers, Susan Layne 21.passim
Semonides of Amorgos Koulouris 25.6n10
Seshagiri, Urmila Caputi 29.22n18; Rutherford 24.135
Seton, Elphinstone Gillespie 25.106n23

Seurat, Georges Humm 29.157
Seward, A.C. Davison 23.6, 11
Sewell, Anna Williams 26.109
Shackleton, David Lauby 27.51, 53
Shakespeare, William Bunting 30.17, 18; Caputi 29.15; Czarnecki 21.54; de Gay 30.102; Delsandro 25.84; Favre 30.54; Foster 22.56–57; Gillespie 25.105n20; Gilman 29.34, 47n6, 52n20, 53n23; Golden 23.89; Ke 29.65, 67, 70; Koulouris 25.60; Lauby 27.50, 52; McVicker 28.90; Pająk 24.26, 28; Ryan 30.75; Shin 23.110, 122n21; Schwartz 29.100, 101; White 24.118, 122
Shafer, Robert Shin 23.110n4–5, 117, 124
Sharon-Zisser, Shirly Fischer 28.27n7
Sharpe, Emily Robins Wisor 21.3n7
Shaw, George Bernard Pająk 24.17; Reed 29.165; Rutherford 24.154
Shearman, Monty Berkowitz 29.128
Sheepshanks, Mary Chua 30.41, 42
Sheffield, C.C. Dalgarno 22.7n7
Shellard, Dominic Wisor 21.8
Shelley, Mary Gillespie 29.151; Ryan 30.70n10, 81n26; Schwartz 29.95
Shelley, Percy Bysshe Bond 23.73; Dalgarno 22.8; Davison 23.17; de Gay 30.105; McVicker 28.79; Rutherford 24.148; Ryan 30.70n10; Shin 23.116, 123
Sherry, Vincent Delsandro 25.76; Fischer 28.27n5, 30, 31
Shiach, Morag Wisor 21.1n3
Shih Shumei Chua 30.38
Shipley, A.E. Davison 23.24
Shirkani, Kim Fischer 28.35n13
Shone, Richard Adair/Martin 24.87n12, 91–92
Showalter, Elaine Camarasana et al. 24.2; Czarnecki 21.61, 62n12, 63–64, 66; Favre 30.57; Kotler 24.36, 40
Shuhua, Ling Chua 30.passim
Shuster, G.N. Shin 23.110–11
Sickert, Walter Layne 21.91
Sidney, Philip Leach 28.102
Siebers, Tobin Williams 26.111
Sigurdson, Ola Van Wert 29.115–16
Silko, Leslie Marmon Czarnecki 21.passim
Silver, Brenda Dalgarno 22.7n6, 15; Favre 30.55, 59, 60; Foster 22.44n8, 57; Gillespie 25.116; Golden 23.103n33; Kotler 24.36–37, 39, 41; Koulouris 25.6, 9n13, 14n22, n25–26, 72n247; Layne 21.91; McVicker 28.85n26; Shin 23.134n27
Sim, Lorraine Adair/Martin 24.75; Dalgarno 22.9; Foster 22.42n4, 45
Simmias Dalgarno 22.9, 10n12, 12–13
Simon, Lady Shena Wisor 21.12n21
Simonides Dalgarno 22.14
Simpson, J.C. Davison 23.24
Simpson, Kathryn Fischer 28.42; Gillespie 25.118; Jenkins (Amber) 27.6; Jenkins (Gwyn) 27.33
Simson, Henrietta McVicker 28.86n28
Sirén, Osvald Ke 29.65n9, 66, 67
Sitwell, Sir Osbert Berkowitz 29.138
Skidelsky, Robert Adair/Martin 24.85
Skye (Isle of) Foster 22.41n3; Gillespie 25.99–100, 104; Rutherford 24.137, 150
Śmieja, Wojciech Pająk 24.18, 22
Smith, Amy C. Foster 22.41; McVicker 28.71n7, 72n8, 75
Smith, Craig Williams 26.117
Smith, Jean Andrews Marcus 24.9–10
Smith, Kate Van Wert 29.116n11
Smith, Lindsay Koulouris 25.11
Smith, Philip H. Gillespie 25.122n42
Smith College Gilman 29.28n4, 29, 32, 37
Smith-Rosenberg, Carroll Clarke 28.7, 10
Smocovitis, Vassiliki Betty Davison 23.1n2, 6–7, 16–17
Smollett, Tobias Gilman 29.54n24
Smyth, Ethel Adair/Martin 24.86; Camarasana et al. 24.1; Chua 30.40; Clarke 28.19–20; Davison 23.4; Delsandro 25.82–85; Foster 22.41n1; Gillespie 25.99; Gillespie 29.152; Gilman 29.49n13; Kotler 24.43; Leach 28.100n4; Lostoski-Ho 28.59; Marcus 24.6–8; Ryan 30.67n1; Shin 23.120

Smythe, Karen Shin 23.111n7
Snaith, Anna Cheney 24.69n13; Chua 30.41n4; Dalgarno 22.9, 15; Delsandro 25.76, 84; Fouirnaies 22.22n1; Gillespie 25.107n24, 110; Gilman 29.47n8; Golden 23.98; Graeber 24.167, 169, 171; Jenkins (Gwyn) 27.24, 25, 36, 43; Jones 22.86; Koulouris 25.5n8; Novillo-Corvalán 23.34, 57–58; Pająk 24.31; Phillips 26.2, 8n6; Williams 26.114; Wisor 21.5
Snowden, Margery Adair/Martin 24.80
Snyder, Carey Novillo-Corvalán 23.36
Snyder, R. Claire Delsandro 25.86n18
Snyder, Sharon Williams 26.112
Socrates Dalgarno 22.passim; Koulouris 25.3, 50, 53–57, 72
Soest, Gerard Fouirnaies 22.23
Solnit, Rebecca van Straten 30.85, 93
Son, Youngjoo Livingstone 26.89; van Straten 30.90, 91, 92
Sontag, Susan Kotler 24.49; White 24.106n6
Sophocles Davison 23.17, 20; Delsandro 25.80; Golden 23.95, 98, 103; Jenkins (Gwyn) 27.27, 29, 30; Koulouris 25.5, 8, 14, 60–67, 69; Schwartz 29.100, 101
Sorley, Charles Hamilton Rutherford 24.137
South Africa Wisor 21.37
South America Caputi 29.13; Gillespie 25.120; Novillo-Corvalán 23.passim
Southworth, Helen Foster 22.50n20; Golden 23.84n5
Spain Adair/Martin 24.76, 80n6, 95; Gallego Larrarte 30.115; Gillespie 25.101; Graeber 24.175; Kotler 24.42, 48, 51; Novillo-Corvalán 23.40, 42, 49
Spalding, Frances Adair/Martin 24.81, 90, 92–94; Foster 22.44, 53n27; Gillespie 29.151n3; Jenkins (Amber) 27.7, 14; Layne 21.82, 97, 102
Sparks, Elisa Kay Gillespie 25.111n29, 124n45; Golden 23.83n3; Jones 22.76; van Straten 30.87n4, 90n8, 91n9, 92n11
Spelman, Elizabeth V. Kotler 24.38–39, 43, 45
Spemann, Hans Livingstone 26.93
Spencer, Herbert Davison 23.2
Spender, Stephen Delsandro 25.73; de Gay 30.99; Gallego Larrarte 30.111, 112, 115; Gilman 29.49n13; Kopley 30.127
Spenser, Edmund Golden 23.92; Lauby 27.47, 51–52, 53, 55, 60, 61
Spilsby (Yorkshire) Williams 26.105
Spinoza, Baruch Golden 23.92, 94
Spiro, Mia Lauby 27.48–49
Spiropoulou, Angeliki Ke 29.67n11; Koulouris 25.1, 11
Spivak, Gayatri Chakravorty Camarasana et al. 24.2; Cheney 24.55–56, 60, 67, 69; Chua 30.34
Springhall, John Wisor 21.12n21–22, 13
Squier, Susan M. Gillespie 25.111; Koulouris 25.7n12
Squire, John Collings Chua 30.42
St. Albans, England Gillespie 25.99
Stalla, Heidi McVicker 28.71n7, 78n17, 82n22; Rutherford 24.141, 148, 159
Stam, Robert Davison 23.7n14
Stanfield, Michael Novillo-Corvalán 23.52–53
Stanhope, James Wisor 21.12n21
Stanley, Liz Layne 21.79
Stansky, Peter Caputi 29.22n18; Gallego Larrarte 30.115
Stape, J.H. Gillespie 25.110; Fouirnaies 22.23–24
Stapledon, Olaf Foster 22.50; Livingstone 26.89, 92, 100
Stasi, Paul Graeber 24.165–68, 172, 177n11, 182
Statkiewicz, Max Dalgarno 22.1
Staveley, Alice Kotler 24.51; Wisor 21.1–3, 6, 31
Stawar, Andrzej Pająk 24.23
St. Denis, Ruth Rutherford 24.154
Stead, Lisa Golden 23.87
Stec, Loretta Cheney 24.61
Steel, David Graeber 24.178

Steele, Elizabeth Williams 26.109
Steere, Douglas V. Foster 22.46, 48n16
Stein, Gertrude Adair/Martin 24.80; Czarnecki 21.50n1; Fischer 28.41; Humm 29.159; Kopley 30.126, 127; Shin 23.131; Williams 26.108n6
Stephen, Adrian Adair/Martin 24.82; Gillespie 25.105–06
Stephen, Caroline Emilia Foster 22.passim
Stephen, J. K. Kopley 30.126
Stephen, Judith Wisor 21.5
Stephen, Julia Dalgarno 22.9; Gillespie 25.108; Golden 23.94n19; Jenkins (Amber) 27.13; Jenkins (Gwyn) 27.25; Layne 21.94–95, 97–98; Williams 26.108–09, 110
Stephen, Karin Costelloe Adair/Martin 24.82; Foster 22.44n8
Stephen, Leslie Davison 23.3; de Gay 30.104; Fischer 28.27n7; Foster 22.41n1, 44, 53n27; Gillespie 25.106, 113n32; Golden 23.94, 102; Humm 29.158; Jenkins (Gwyn) 27.36; Ke 29.69; Koulouris 25.5, 7n12; Layne 21.97; Rutherford 24.141; Schwartz 29.98; Sullam 30.119
Stephen, Thoby Caputi 29.14–15; Clarke 28.7; Davison 23.3n8; Golden 23.passim; Jenkins (Gwyn) 27.42n15; Koulouris 25.7n12, 9, 25n63, 72n247; Marcus 24.8; McVicker 28.76n14, 80; Shin 23.111n6, 123n22
Stephens, John S. Foster 22.51
Sterne, Laurence Fischer 28.34; Foster 22.54
Stevanato, Savina Bond 23.64n3
Stevenson, Christina Bond 23.77
Stevenson, Randall Shin 23.111n7
Stewart, Garrett de Gay 30.100; Fischer 28.27
Stewart, Jack Jenkins (Amber) 27.5n1
Stewart, Susan Shin 23.136
St. Ives, Cornwall Layne 21.96–97; McVicker 28.71, 76n14, 87
St. James's Palace Wisor 21.39
St. James's Park Bond 23.63, 69n9; White 24.114
St. John, Christopher Delsandro 25.83
St Leonards, Sussex Jones 22.81n6
St. Margaret's Church White 24.113n23
Still, John Ryan 30.74
Stobaeus Koulouris 25.6n10
Stoeltje, Beverly Marcus 24.9–10
Stoler, Laura Ann van Straten 30.89
Stonehenge McVicker 28.76, 77, 84n24, 88, 89
Stopes, Marie Wisor 21.26
St. Paul Wisor 21.20
St. Paul's Cathedral Bond 23.63; Wisor 21.17
The Strand Bond 23.63; Gillespie 25.122, 125
Strachey, James Golden 23.93
Strachey, Lytton Adair/Martin 24.79–80, 82; Berkowitz 29.125; Fischer 28.32n11; Gallego Larrarte 30.112, 114; Gillespie 29.149, 150, 151, 152; Humm 29.156, 158; Marcus 24.7–8; McVicker 28.86; Pająk 24.20; Rutherford 24.141; White 24.107
Strachey, Nino Humm 29.157, 158
Strachey, Pernel Wisor 21.24
Strachey, Philippa (Pippa) Delsandro 25.83n12
Strachey, Ray Wisor 21.5
Stravinsky, Igor Berkowitz 29.128
Stray, Christopher Golden 23.99
Street, Harry Wisor 21.6
Sudan Wisor 21.37
The Suez Canal Rutherford 24.154n6
Suh, Judy Cheney 24.59n6; Delsandro 25.76n5
Suleri, Sara Chua 30.34
Sullam, Sara Kopley 30.128; Sullam 30.118n2; White 24.102
Sullivan, Anne Ryan 30.68n4
Sullivan, Arthur Davison 23.16, 19
Summers, Anne Wisor 21.12n22
Sussex Adair/Martin 24.78, 84, 87n12, 90, 94–95; Hussey 29.167; Jones 22.75–76, 79–82; Sullam 30.119
Sutcliffe, Peter Golden 23.99
Sutton, Emma Davison 23.4n10, 5, 19n28, 23n33; Fischer 28.31

Suvin, Darko Livingstone 26.87, 91, 96n6, 98, 99, 101
Swan, Edith Czarnecki 21.72
Swanson, Diana Layne 21.89; Czarnecki 21.52n3
Swanson, Roy Arthur Livingstone 26.90
Swift, Jonathan Dalgarno 22.13
Swinburne, Charles Algernon Shin 23.118–19
Switzerland Gillespie 25.106
Sydney-Turner, Saxon Adair/Martin 24.79; Davison 23.27; Ke 29.60; McVicker 28.77; Ryan 30.67n1
Syria Gillespie 25.122
Symons, Arthur Sullam 30.117–18
Szenwald, Lucjan Pająk 24.23–24
Tagg, John Fouirnaies 22.32
Taggard, Genevieve Kopley 30.127
Talland House McVicker 28.76n14
Tallents, Sir Stephen Wisor 21.7–8
Tally Jr., Robert T. Gillespie 25.111–12, 116
Tambling, Jeremy Bond 23.76n17
Tansley Rutherford 24.140
Tate Britain Gillespie 29.152; Pająk 24.27
Tavis, Molly Abel White 24.104n6, 111n21
Tavistock Square Adair/Martin 24.77, 82, 95; Gilman 29.33; McVicker 28.82; Ryan 30.73–74
Taylor, Catherine Layne 21.87
Taylor, Chloë Fischer 28.27n6
Taylor, Melanie A. Pająk 24.12
Taylor, Paul Beekman Czarnecki 21.66
Taylor, Philip M. Wisor 21.7
Taylor, Rod C. Cheney 24.58n4, 71n14; Dalgarno 22.15n14
Taylor, Sunaura Williams 26.107
Tazudeen, Rasheed Fischer 28.27n5
Teed, A.S.H. Adair/Martin 24.81, 85
Telscombe, Sussex Gillespie 25.109–10
Tennyson, Alfred, Lord de Gay 30. 103, 104
Teukolsky, Rachel Berkowitz 29.127
Tew, Philip Jones 22.76n2
Thacker, Andrew Adair/Martin 24.75, 93; Bond 23.64; Gillespie 25.105n20, 113, 117
Thackeray, William Makepeace Fischer 28.34; Gillespie 25.119; Rutherford 24.156
Theocritus Golden 23.102
Thomas, Alun Wisor 21.29
Thomas, Julian McVicker 28.70n3, 71, 72, 75
Thomas, Robert William Novillo-Corvalán 23.53
Thompson, Edith Wisor 21.26
Thompson, Hilary Fischer 28.27n7
Thompson, W.W. Koulouris 25.72n247
Thoms, David Adair/Martin 24.75
Thornton, Amara McVicker 28.72n8
Thornton, Tim Lauby 27.58n7
Thrower, Norman J.W. Gillespie 25.127n47
Thucydides Jenkins (Gwyn) 27.27, 30
Tibullus Rutherford 24.154
Tickner, Lisa Jenkins (Amber) 27.6, 13n17, 19, 20; Layne 21.84, 101
Tobin, Richard Ke 29.66, 67
Todd, Jude Czarnecki 21.55, 66
Todd, Ric Pająk 24.15
Todd, Zoe Lostoski-Ho 28.53n10
Tolstoy, Leo Gilman 29.31n13
Tomasik, Krzysztof Pająk 24.15, 18, 26
Tonks, Nichola McVicker 28.70–71n4, 82n23
Tonning, Erik Chua 30.46
Torgovnick, Marianna Layne 21.84
Toulmin, Stephen Leach 28.103
Townley, Charles Bunting 30.20n4
Townsend, Chris Kopley 30.126
Townsend, Kenneth William Czarnecki 21.58, 60–62
Toth, Leah van Straten 30.86
Transue, Pamela Cheney 24.70
Trautmann Banks, Joanne Chua 30.32; Fouirnaies 22.25; Gilman 29.31
Trefusis, Violet Fouirnaies 22.36
Trevelyan, George McVicker 28.84–85
Trevelyan, R. C. Golden 23.85
Trinity College Bunting 30.14; Kopley 30.125
Trivedi, Harish Novillo-Corvalán 23.40
Trollope, Anthony Gilman 29.31n13

Tromanhauser, Vicki McVicker 28.70n2, 91n30
Trombley, Stephen Favre 30.56
Trotter, David Adair/Martin 24.76, 77n4
Tschacksch, Nadine Pająk 24.12
Tseng, Jui-hua Foster 22.42, 44, 53n27
Tucker, David Chua 30.46
Tung, Charles M. Livingstone 26.89
Tura, Cosimo Davison 29.145
Turchi, Peter Gillespie 25.111
Turkey Adair/Martin 24.80n6; Gillespie 29.151; Graeber 24.175–78; Schwartz 29.94
Tussaud, Marie Wisor 21.10
Tutankhamun McVicker 28.81, 87; Rutherford 24.143, 146, 149, 151, 154
Tuwim, Julian Pająk 24.18
Twain, Mark Berkowitz 29.127
Tziovas, Dimitris Golden 23.100
Uglow, Nathan Golden 23.100n30
Uhlmann, Anthony Jenkins (Amber) 27.5n1, 17; Layne 21.91n4
Umphelby, Fanny Jenkins (Gwyn) 27.41
Undset, Sigrid Pająk 24.18
Unger, Kristina Davison 23.27n40
Uniłowski, Zbigniew Pająk 24.22
United States Kopley 30.128; Sullam 30.119
University College, Dublin Schwartz 29.87
University of Pennsylvania McVicker 28.79
Usick, Patricia Rutherford 24.141–42
Vance, Norman Koulouris 25.11
Van Der Kolk, Bessel Czarnecki 21.63–64
Vandyk, Carl Fouirnaies 22.27
Van Gogh, Vincent Reed 29.162
Vanita, Ruth Dalgarno 22.1
Van Hulle, Dirk Golden 23.85–86, 87n12
Van Wert, Kathryn Czarnecki 21.57; Van Wert 29.113n9
Varga, Adriana Davison 23.4n10
Varon, Daniel Jordan Lostoski-Ho 28.49n4, 50n7, 56
Vaughan, Madge Chua 30.41, 42
Venice, Italy Gillespie 25.100, 104; Gillespie 29.151; Golden 23.84; Rutherford 24.141
Verdi, Giuseppe Rutherford 24.154
Verity, Anthony Shin 23.116n15
Verrall, A.W. Golden 23.85; Koulouris 25.3, 14n22, 42, 44n140, 45n147, 46n148–49, 47n150–51, 48n153
Vickery, John B. Shin 23.111
Vicinus, Martha Clarke 28.10n7, 19n12
Victoria Street White 24.115
Victoria University Humm 29.156n2
Vildrac, Charles Berkowitz 29.128; Reed 29.163
Vince, Gaia Ryan 30.69
Virgil Jenkins (Gwyn) 27.29, 39, 40, 41; Koulouris 25.1, 9, 11, 13–14, 27, 58–59
Virginia, USA Graeber 24.173
Vlasopolos, Anca Gillespie 25.121
Voss, Paul Golden 23.87
Wade, E.C.S. Wisor 21.29n45, 30–31
Wade, Eileen Wisor 21.11
Wade, Francesca McVicker 28.69
Waddell, Nathan Livingstone 26.89
Wagner, Johanna M. Caputi 29.16, 18–19
Wagner, Richard Davison 23.2–4, 6, 8, 11n18, 18n27, 19n28, 20, 26–27
Wakefield, Sir Charles Wisor 21.6n14
Wales Gillespie 25.99
Walker, Alice Camarasana et al. 24.2; Czarnecki 21.51
Walker, Ian Adair/Martin 24.94
Walkowitz, Rebecca Lostoski-Ho 28.54n13; van Straten 30.88n5, 91
Wall, Kathleen Bunting 30.9; Van Wert 29.118
Walpole, Horace Chua 30.38
Walpole, Hugh Sullam 30.119
Walsh, Kelly Van Wert 29.117
Walsh, Rebecca Bond 23.64n2
Walter, Christina Kotler 24.40
Wańkowicza, Zofia Pająk 24.20
Wańkowicz, Krystyna Pająk 24.20
Wańkowicz, Melchior Pająk 24.18, 20, 22
Warner, Marina Wisor 21.3n7
Warner, Michael Clarke 28.9n6
Warner, Sylvia Townsend Camarasana et al. 24.2–3; Rutherford 24.153
Warr, George Jenkins (Gwyn) 27.passim;

Koulouris 25.5
Warren, Allen Wisor 21.10–12, 14
Washington State University Gillespie 25.passim; Golden 23.87; McVicker 28.83
Wasilewska, Wanda Pająk 24.18, 22
Waterlow, Sydney Reed 29.163
Watkins, Alfred McVicker 28.84–85
Watkins, Susan Cotts Berkowitz 29.132, 137
Watson, Frederic Gillespie 25.102, 113–14, 116, 120
Watson, J.N.P. Wisor 21.33–35, 37
Waugh, Evelyn Novillo-Corvalán 23.38
Ważyk, Adam Pająk 24.23
Weber, Gary Novillo-Corvalán 23.52
Webster, John Lauby 27.52, 53
Weinberg, Bernard White 24.105n7
Weinstein, Arnold Bond 23.65
Welland, Sasha Su-Ling Chua 30.37
Wellesley, Arthur Golden 23.92; Rutherford 24.142
Wellesley, Dorothy Adair/Martin 24.86
Wells, Christopher James Bunting 30.12; 120n12
Wells, H. G. Cheney 24.61n9, 63–64; Fischer 28.32, 35; Gallego Larrarte 30.112; Gillespie 25.128n51; Ke 29.59; Livingstone 26.87, 89, 90, 96n6, 99, 100; McVicker 28.90; Pająk 24.17
Wells, Robert Koulouris 25.59n198
Wells, W. T. Wisor 21.6–7
Wellwyn, England Clarke 28.7
Weninger, Robert White 24.102n4
Werner, Marta Golden 23.87
Westminster White 24.116
Westminster Abbey Bond 23.63; Cheney 24.66; Wisor 21.17
West, Rebecca Davison 29.144–45; Rutherford 24.154
Westling, Louise Lostoski-Ho 28.56; McVicker 28.90n29
Wetherell, Charles Berkowitz 29.132, 133, 137
Wheare, Jane Cheney 24.57n2
Whitaker, Joseph Gillespie 25.115
White, Andrea Novillo-Corvalán 23.37
White, Siân White 24.102n4
Whitehall Bond 23.63; White 24.116; Wisor 21.31, 33, 37–40
Whitehead, Alfred Foster 22.56n30
Whitehead, Kate Berkowitz 29.133–34n10, 135
Whitlock, Gillian Pająk 24.12n5
Whitman, Walt Cheney 24.67; Davison 23.18–19; Kopley 30.128; Shin 23.114
Whittier-Ferguson, John Delsandro 25.73, 80; Fischer 28.28n8; Shin 23.134, 136
Whitworth, Michael H. Livingstone 26.88n2, 101; Novillo-Corvalán 23.58; Reed 29.163
Wilde, Niels Ryan 30.68
Wilde, Oscar Pająk 24.27
Wiechert, Nora van Straten 30.86, 88
Wielgoławska, Alicja Pająk 24.23n9
Wilford, John Noble Gillespie 25.111
Wilkinson, Alan Wisor 21.15–17
Williams, D. G. T. Wisor 21.29
Williams, Erika Renée Caputi 29.7n5
Williams, Raymond Berkowitz 29.127; Reed 29.165
Williams, Sandra Wentworth Van Wert 29.112
Williams-Ellis, Clough Jones 22.82, 84–85
Williamson, Philip Wisor 21.20n33, 21, 25
Wilson, Mary Delsandro 25.86; Van Wert 29.120
Wiltshire, England McVicker 28.76, 77, 82
Winckelmann, Johann Joachim Rutherford 24.154n6
Windsor, England Gillespie 25.104
Winkiel, Laura Lostoski-Ho 28.48
Winquist, Martin Adair/Martin 24.88n14
Winslow, Lyttleton Czarnecki 21.64n14
Winterhalter, Teresa Wisor 21.4n10
Wirth-Nesher, Hana White 24.124n35
Wise, Sarah Bond 23.64n1
Wisor, Rebecca Fouirnaies 22.22; Kotler 24.51; Wisor 21.4n10, 5n13, 15n25, 41n59
Withington, Robert Lauby 27.48
Wittgenstein, Ludwig Williams 26.108
Wolf, Naomi Delsandro 25.75n4

Wolfe, Cary Williams 26.107
Wolfe, Jesse Clarke 28.21n13; Czarnecki 21.62; White 24.124n36
Wollaeger, Mark Caputi 29.11, 13–14, 17; Davison 23.23n34; Fischer 28.31n10; Novillo-Corvalán 23.34n2, 35–36
Woodall, Joanna Fouirnaies 22.29n4
Wood, Alice Delsandro 25.76; Foster 22.58, 59n34, 65–66; Fouirnaies 22.22n1; Humm 29.157n5; Phillips 26.2, 8n6; Wisor 21.26n41
Wood, Edward Wisor 21.16
Woolf, Leonard Adair/Martin 24.77, 79–80, 82–85, 88n13, 89, 91; Cheney 24.61; Chua 30.35; Clarke 28.21; Delsandro 25.89; Favre 30.56n5; Foster 22.43–44, 50–51, 59n35, 66; 97–98; Gallego Larrarte 30.114; Gillespie 25.passim; Gilman 29.30, 32; Golden 23.83, 94, 98n25, 100, 102n31; Graeber 24.167, 171; Humm 29.156; Jones 22.82, 86, 91n10; Koulouris 25.2, 13n18; Layne 21.85–90, 92; Lostoski-Ho 28.58; Marcus 24.8; McVicker 28.77, 83; Novillo-Corvalán 23.33–34, 36, 41–42, 44, 53, 56, 58; Pająk 24.30; Reed 29.163; Shin 23.136; Sullam 30.119; Williams 26.106n3, 110, 114; Wisor 21.6, 28
Woolf, Marie Gillespie 25.102n12; Pająk 24.30
Woolf, Sidney Gillespie 25.100n9
Woolley, Charles Leonard McVicker 28.79
Wordsworth, Charles Golden 23.99n28
Wordsworth, William McVicker 28.790
Worth, Aaron Livingstone 26.100
Wright, Elizabeth Adair/Martin 24.87n12; Graeber 24.167; Jenkins (Amber) 27.5n3; Layne 21.81
Wright, Sarah Bird Adair/Martin 24.80n6, 82, 85; Berkowitz 29.126n3
Wright, Winthrop Novillo-Corvalán 23.43
Wroth, Lady Mary Lauby 27.50
Wurtz, James F. Gillespie 25.127n48
Wussow, Helen Adair/Martin 24.75n1; Wisor 21.3n6
Wyatt, Jean Fischer 28.27n6
Wycherley, William Bunting 30.14
Wynne-Davies, Marion Lauby 27.50
Xenophon Dalgarno 22.3
Xie, Yaqing Chua 30.34n3
Xu Wei Chua 30.37
Yeats, W. B. McVicker 28.71
Yoder Jr., Edwin M. Layne 21.78n1
Yoshino, Ayoko Lauby 27.47–48
Young, Kevin Caputi 29.22n18
Ypres, Belgium Wisor 21.37
Z., Y. Gillespie 25.102
Zajączkowski, J.P. Pająk 24.22–23, 25
Zajko, Vanda Koulouris 25.20n38
Zalasiewicz, Jan Lostoski-Ho 28.52n9
Zandvoorde, Belgium Wisor 21.37
Zawada, Andrzej Pająk 24.22, 25
Zawiszewska, Agata Pająk 24.26, 28
Zbyszewska, Paulina Pająk 24.17
Zeiger, Melissa F. Bunting 30.111
Zervos, Christian Berkowitz 29.128n8
Zhang, Dora Fischer 28.33
Zhou Zhuoren Chua 30.36
Zieger, Susan Lauby 27.59
Zink, Suzana van Straten 30.85n1, 87n4
Ziółkowska-Boehm, Aleksandra Pająk 24.20
Žižek, Slavoj Van Wert 29.110n5, 111
Zlatkin, Rachel Czarnecki 21.54
Żmichowska, Narcyza Pająk 24.17
Zola, Émile Cheney 24.58
Zonana, Joyce Shin 23.119
Zupančič, Alenka Van Wert 29.111
Zwerdling, Alex Bond 23.72n15; Bunting 30.7; Cheney 24.59n6, 65; Delsandro 25.76; Foster 22.60n39, 61n41; Fouirnaies 22.22n1; Gillespie 25.112; Shin 23.111n7; Van Wert 29.114

Part 2: Source References

Complied by Oliver Case and Benjamin D. Hagen

2A: Works by Literary Figures and Artists

Aeschylus. *Septem contra Thebas*. Jenkins (Gwyn) 27.31
Alberti, Leon Battista. *On Painting*. Ke 29.64–65, 66
Anne of Denmark (Queen), Ben Jonson, and Inigo Jones. *The Masque of Queens*. Lauby 27.49
Anrep, Boris. *The Awakening of the Muses*. Berkowitz 29.138; Gillespie 29.149–50, 152
Aristophanes. *The Frogs*. Koulouris 25.3, 14, 69–71
Arnold, Matthew. *Complete Prose Works of Matthew Arnold*. Dalgarno 22.3
Arnold. *Essays in Criticism*. Schwartz 29.96
Auden, W. H. *The Orators*. Gallego Larrarte 30.113
Auden and Cecil Day Lewis. Preface. *Oxford Poetry 1927*. Gallego Larrarte 30.111
Barnes, Julian. *Flaubert's Parrot*. Williams 26.115
Baudelaire, Charles. "The Painter of Modern Life." Bunting 30.18
Bell, Clive. *Art*. Berkowitz 29.125, 126, 130; Gillespie 29.151; Layne 21.94, 95, 97, 98, 101, 102; Reed 29.162
Bell. "Cinema Aesthetics: A Critic of the Arts Assesses the Movies." Humm 29.158
Bell. *Civilisation*. Chua 30.43
Bell. "The Creed of an Aesthete." Reed 29.164
Bell. Letter to Vanessa Bell. Berkowitz 29.135
Bell. *Old Friends*. Gillespie 29.149, 151
Bell. *On British Freedom*. Reed 29.165
Bell. *Peace at Once*. Berkowitz 29.125, 132
Bell. *Pot-Boilers*. Reed 29.162
Bell. *Selected Letters of Clive Bell: Art, Love and War in Bloomsbury*. Hussey 29.169
Bell, Julian. Letter to Ling Shuhua. Chua 30.35
Bell. "The Proletariat and Poetry: An Open Letter to C. Day Lewis." Gallego Larrarte 30.115
Bell. "What I Like in Art—I. Tura's *Madonna Enthroned*." Davison 29.145
Bell, ed. *We Did Not Fight: 1914–18 Experiences of War Resisters*. Foster 22.50
Bell, Vanessa. *Abstract Composition* (1914) [painting]. Jenkins (Amber) 27.12
Bell. *Abstract Painting* (1914) [painting]. Jenkins (Amber) 27.12
Bell. "Alfriston." Adair & Martin 24.93
Bell. *The Bathers* (1911) [painting]. Jenkins (Amber) 27.20.
Bell. *The Beach, Studland* (c. 1911) [painting]. Jenkins (Amber) 27.20
Bell. *Figure on the Beach, Studland* (c. 1910–11) [painting]. Jenkins (Amber) 27.20
Bell. "Lecture Given at Leighton Park School." Jenkins (Amber) 27.7; Layne 21.80, 81, 99
Bell. Letter to VW. Lostoski-Ho 28.63n27
Bell. "Life at Hyde Park Gate After 1897." Layne 21.80, 81
Bell. "Notes on Virginia's Childhood." Layne 21.80
Bell. *The Nude* (c. 1922) [painting]. Humm 29.156
Bell. *Selected Letters of Vanessa Bell*. Adair & Martin 24.79, 80, 81, 82, 83, 85, 94; Jenkins (Amber) 27.7–8, 9
Bell. *Studland Beach* (c. 1912) [painting]. Jenkins (Amber) 27.6, 18–20
Bennett, Arnold. *Old Wives' Tale*. Fischer 28.35
Blake, William. *Jerusalem: The Emanation of the Great Albion*. McVicker 28.79
Blast. Berkowitz 29.127
Brontë, Emily. *Wuthering Heights*. Sullam 30.121
Browne, Sir Thomas. *Hydriotaphia, or Urne-Burialle, or A Brief Discourse of*

the Sepulchrall Urnes Lately Found in Norfolk. McVicker 28.79, 85–86
Browne, William. *Circe and Ulysses: The Inner Temple Masque*. Lauby 27.59, 60
Catallus. Tibullus. Pervigilium Veneris. Goldman 30.108
Chekhov, Anton. Letter to Ivan Orlov. Ke 29.80–81n18
Chinese and British (exhibition, 2022–23). Chua 30.31, 32
A Chinese Painter's Choice: Some Paintings from the 14th to the 20th Century from the Collection of Ling Su-hua (exhibition, 1967). Chua 30.31
Chinese Paintings by Ling Su-Hua (exhibition, 1949). Chua 30.31
Cicero. *De Officiis*. Jenkins (Gwyn) 27.30
Conrad, Joseph. *Heart of Darkness*. Gillespie 25.105, 118, 121n40–41; Novillo-Corvalán 23.52
Conrad. *The Congo Diary*. Novillo-Corvalán 23.52
Conrad. *The Collected Letters of Joseph Conrad: 1923–1924*. Novillo-Corvalán 23.37
Conrad. *The Works of Joseph Conrad*. Gillespie 25.106n22
Cooley, Martha. *The Archivist*. Layne 21.78n1
Cunningham, Michael. *The Hours*. Favre 30.53; Layne 21.78, 79, 80, 86, 102
Dante Alighieri. *Commedia*. Ryan 30.81
Dante. *Inferno*. Ryan 30.68, 75, 75
Dante. *Purgatorio*. Ryan 30.81
Defoe, Daniel. *Moll Flanders*. Kopley 30.128; Sullam 30.120
Defoe. *Robinson Crusoe*. Sullam 30.120
Demosthenes. *Meidias and Androtion*. Jenkins (Gwyn) 27.29
Dickinson, Emily. "The reticent volcano keeps." Goldman 30.107–08
Dickinson. "A still—Volcano—Life—." Goldman 30.107–08
Dickinson, Lowes Cato. *Clara Pater* (1860) [painting]. Jenkins (Gwyn) 27.38n14
Dumas, Alexandre. *The Three Musketeers*. Sullam 30.121
Earhart, Amelia. *The Last Flight*. Gillespie 25.118
Eisenstein, Sergei. *Writings, 1922–1934*. Humm 29.159
Eliot, T. S. "Burnt Norton." Fischer 28.26
Eliot. *The Letters*, vol. 1. Bunting 30.6
Eliot. *Old Possum's Book of Practical Cats*. Williams 26.108n6
Eliot. *The Rock*. Lauby 27.48n1
Eliot. "Tradition and the Individual Talent." Chua 30.37; Ke 29.68–69; Reed 29.164
Eliot. *The Waste Land*. Humm 29.156
Emerson, Ralph W. "The American Scholar." Ke 29.61n8, 66, 69, 78
Emerson. *Essays and Lectures*. Pająk 24.31
Euripides. *Ion*. Koulouris 25.3, 8, 14, 42–50
Fielding, Henry. *The History of Tom Jones, a Foundling*. Bunting 30.17, 18; Ke 29.71
Flaubert, Gustave. *The Letters of Gustave Flaubert*. Sullam 30.122
Flaubert. *Three Tales*. Williams 26.114
Flaubert. "Un coeur simple" (A Simple Heart). Williams 26.114–15
Ford, Ford Madox. *Mightier than the Sword: Memories and Criticisms*. Novillo-Corvalán 23.50
Ford. *Parade's End*. Rutherford 24.154
Forster, E. M. *Abinger Pageant*. Lauby 27.48n1
Forster. *Alexandria: A History and a Guide*. Rutherford 24.158n12
Forster. *Aspects of the Novel*. Kopley 30.128; Sullam 30.120
Forster. *Commonplace Book*. Sullam 30.120
Forster. *England's Pleasant Land*. Lauby 27.48n1; McVicker 28.90n29
Forster. *Howards End*. Schwartz 29.95
Forster. *Pharos and Pharillon*. Rutherford 24.137, 158, 159
Forster. *The Rede Lecture*. Gallego Larrarte 30.113
Forster. *A Room with a View*. Gillespie 25.101n11
Freeman, Gillian. *But* Nobody *Lives in*

Bloomsbury Layne 21.85, 86, 88, 90
Froude, James Anthony. *English Seamen in the Sixteenth Century*. Graber 24.167, 168
Fry, Roger. *Cézanne: A Study of His Development*. Jenkins (Amber) 27.12
Fry. "The Friends' Work for War Victims in France." Foster 22.50
Fry. *Vision and Design*. Jenkins (Amber) 27.6, 6–7, 10, 12–13, 17; Layne 21.84; Rutherford 24.149–50n5
Fry, trans. *Men of Europe* (selected poems from Pierre Jean Jouve's *Vous* êtes *hommes*). Reed 29.163–64
Galsworthy, John. "The First and Last." Caputi 29.7n5
Galsworthy. *Fraternity*. Fischer 28.35
Garnett, David. *Lady into Fox*. Humm 29.156; Livingstone 26.96, 97, 98, 100, 102
Gaskell, Elizabeth. *Life of Charlotte Brontë*. Chua 30.32
Gide, André and Roger Martin du Gard. *Correspondance: 1935–1951*. Davison 29.142n4
Goldman, Jane. *Catullus 64*. Goldman 30.108
Grant, Duncan. Letter to VW. Jenkins (Amber) 27.13
Grant. "St. Ives, Huntingdon." Adair & Martin 24.93
Graves, Robert. *Fairies and Fusiliers*. Rutherford 24.137
Green, Peter, trans. *The Sixteen Satires* (Juvenal). Koulouris 25.6n9, 16n28, 17n30
Groom, Winston. *Forrest Gump* (novel). Berkowitz 29.128n7
Hakluyt, Richard. *Divers Voyages Touching the Discoverie of America*. Graber 24.167
Hakluyt. *The Principal Navigations, Voyages, Traffiques & Discoveries of the English Nation*. Graber 24.167, 168
Hakluyt. *Voyages of Hawkins, Frobisher, and Drake: Select Narratives from the Principal Navigations of Hakluyt*. Gillespie 25.105n20
Hall, Radclyffe, and Havelock Ellis. *The Well of Loneliness*. Pająk 24.11, 13, 24, 24n9, 26
Hall, Radclyffe, and Irena Krzywicka. Źródło samotności. Pająk 24.11, 11n1, 13, 16, 18, 20, 21, 22, 23, 24, 25, 26, 28, 29, 30
Hawthorne, Nathaniel. *The House of the Seven Gables*. Gilman 29.53n23
Herodotus. *The Histories*. Jenkins (Gwyn) 27.31
Herrick, Robert. "The Apron of Flowers"; "An Epitaph upon a Virgin"; "His Grange, or private wealth"; "Upon Prew His Maid"; "To the Virgins, to Make Much of Time" (poems). Gilman 29.50n14
Herrick. *The Hesperides and Noble Numbers*. Gilman 29.50n14
Hill, Carol de Chellis. *Henry James's Midnight Song*. Layne 21.78n1
Holroyd, Michael. *Lytton Strachey: The Years of Achievement, 1910–1932*. Humm 29.156n4
Homer, *The Iliad*. Dalgarno 22.6; Jenkins (Gwyn) 27.31; Koulouris 25.29n85
Homer. *Odyssey*. Bunting 30.19; Koulouris 25.3, 4, 5n7, 6, 7–8, 9, 13–14, 20–41, 59n198; Rutherford 24.154
Hopkins, Gerard Manley. "Pied Beauty." Shin 23.120
Horace. *Odes*. Jenkins (Gwyn) 27.30
Hughes, Langston. Letter to Claude McKay. Caputi 29.5n1
Huxley, Aldous. *The Crows of Pearlblossom*. Williams 26.108n6
Indigo Girls. "Virginia Woolf." Delsandro 25.86, 86n17
Isherwood, Christopher. *The Berlin Stories*. Delsandro 25.77n8
Jaeger, Muriel. *The Man with Six Senses*. Livingstone 26.96, 97, 98, 100, 101, 102
James, Henry. *The Ambassadors*. Sullam 30.121

James. *Selected Letters.* Layne 21.82
Jebb, R. C., trans. *Ajax* (Sophocles). Koulouris 25.8, 62n219, 68
Johnson, Samuel. *Life of Gray.* Gilman 29.34
Jonson, Ben and Inigo Jones. *The Masque of Blackness.* Lauby 27.50
Joyce, James. *Finnegans Wake.* Schwartz 29.93n6
Joyce. *A Portrait of the Artist as a Young Man.* Livingstone 26.94
Joyce. *Ulysses.* Chua 30.43; Fischer 28.34; Humm 29.156; Kopley 30.127; Sullam 30.121
Juvenal. *Satires.* Koulouris 25.1n1, 3, 5, 6, 13, 16–19
Keats, John. *The Complete Works of John Keats.* Koulouris 25.2n5
Keats. Letter to Benjamin Bailey. Koulouris 25.2n5
Keats. "Ode on a Grecian Urn." McVicker 28.79
Lamb, Charles. "Oxford at the Vacation." Kopley 30.125
Laocoön and His Sons (sculpture). Bunting 30.20
Larsen, Nella. *Passing.* Caputi 29.5
Larsen. *Quicksand.* Caputi 29.passim
Le Guin, Ursula K. Comment on *F.* Livingstone 26.90
Leonard Woolf Papers, LW to Ramsay MacDonald 3 January 1930. Jones 22.82
Lewis, Wyndham. "Interlude in Bloomsbury." Berkowitz 29.133–34
Lewis. Letters to Rothenstein and Brown. Berkowitz 29.127n5
Lewis. "Standing By …: One Thing and Another." Berkowitz 29.133n10
Lindbergh, Anne Marrow. *North to the Orient.* Gillespie 25.118
Ling Shuhua. *Ancient Melodies.* Chua 30.31, 32, 33, 35, 45, 46
Ling. Letters. Chua 30.35, 36, 37, 38, 43–44
Ling Suhua: A Chinese Painter and her Friends (exhibition, 1983). Chua 30.31
Livy. *The History of Rome.* Jenkins (Gwyn) 27.29
Lorde, Audre. "Age, Race, Class, and Sex: Women Redefining Difference." Delsandro 25.86, 89–90
Lorde. "An Interview: Audre Lorde and Adrienne Rich." Delsandro 25.87, 90
Lorde. "Letter to Mary Daly." Delsandro 25.87–88
Lorde. "The Master's Tools Will Never Dismantle the Master's House." Delsandro 25.90, 91
Lorde. *Sister Outsider.* Delsandro 25.87, 88
Lucian of Samosata. *True Story.* Livingstone 26.90
Lysias. *On the Murder of Eratosthenes* and *Against Agoratus.* Jenkins (Gwyn) 27.31
MacCarthy, Desmond. Dedication [Romains, *The Death of a Nobody*]. Reed 29.164
Malle, Louis. *Ascenseur pour l'échafaud* (film). Chua 30.34
Markham, Beryl. *Westward with the Night* (memoir). Gillespie 25.117, 118
McCrae, John. Bunting 30.7
Milton, John. *Comus.* De Gay 30.103; Fischer 28.41; Lauby 27.49, 55–56, 59, 60
Milton. *Comus: A Masque.* 1634. *As it is now acted at the Theatres Royal, Altered from Milton.* Davison 23.25n37
Milton. *Lycidas.* Kopley 30.125, 126
Milton. *The Masque of Comus, with the Original Music by Henry Lawes.* Davison 23.22
Milton. "Nativity Ode." De Gay 30.101–02
Milton. *Paradise Lost.* Gilman 29.48n10; Ryan 30.68
Milton. *Prose Works of John Milton.* Gilman 29.48n10
Mirrlees, Hope. *Paris.* Gallego Larrarte 30.112
Molière. *The Misanthrope.* Ke 29.81
Montaigne, Michel de. *The Complete Works.* Leach 28.passim

Montaigne. *The Essays of Michel de Montaigne*. Gilman 29.53n24; Sullam 30.123
Montaigne. "On educating children." Jenkins (Gwyn) 27.42
Montaigne. "On Three Kinds of Association." Leach 28.100–01
More, Thomas. *Utopia*. Livingstone 26.94
Morgan, Claire. *A Book for All and None*. Layne 21.80, 86, 87
Nash, Paul. "Kimmeridge Folly, Dorset." Adair & Martin 24.93, 94n17
Newton, Eric. *The Artist in the Witness Box* (radio series). Davison 29.146
Nicolson, Harold. *Harold Nicolson: Diaries and Letters 1930-39*. Fouirnaies 22.23, 25
Nightingale, Florence. *A Journey on the Nile, 1849–1850*. Rutherford 24.156n11
Nunez, Sigrid. *Mitz: The Marmoset of Bloomsbury.* Layne 21.80, 86
Ovid. *Metamorphoses*. Lauby 27.53
Parker, Louis Napoleon. *The Masque of War and Peace*. Lauby 27.48
Parker. *A Pageant for Fair Women*. Lauby 27.48
Parker. *A Pageant of Freedom*. Lauby 27.48
Pater, Walter. *Appreciations*. Jenkins (Gwyn) 27.35, 41
Pater. *Marius the Epicurean*. Rutherford 24.156
Pindar. *The Complete Odes*. Shin 23.115, 116n15, 117, 117n17, 120n20
Plath, Sylvia. *The Journals of Sylvia Plath: Transcribed from the Original Manuscripts at Smith College*. Layne 21.86
Plato. *Ion*. Jenkins (Gwyn) 27.30
Plato. *Meno and Phaedo*. Dalgarno 22.10n11
Plato. *Phaedrus*. Bunting 30.18; De Gay 30.102; Ke 29.67–68; Koulouris 25.3, 14, 72, 81; Schwartz 29.88, 95, 100
Plato. *Symposium*. Dalgarno 22.1n1, 2, 4, 6–8; Ke 29. 79n17; Koulouris 25.3, 5, 8, 14, 50–58
Pope, Alexander. *The Rape of the Lock*. Koulouris 25.58n196
Raleigh, Walter. *English Voyages of the Sixteenth Century*. Graber 24.167
Ritchie, Lady Anne Thackeray. *Bluebeard's Keys and Other Stories*. Williams 26.109
Roberts, Michael, ed. *New Country* (anthology). Gallego Larrarte 30.111
Roberts, ed. *New Signatures* (anthology). Gallego Larrarte 30.111
Rogers, Benjamin Bickley, trans. *Frogs* (Aristophanes). Koulouris 25.70n241, n243–44
Romains, Jules. *The Death of a Nobody* [*Mort de quelqu'un*]. Reed 29.163
Romains. *La vie unanime*. Reed 29.163
Rossetti, Christina. "Goblin Market." Caputi 29.9n8
Sackville-West, Vita. *Knole*. Fouirnaies 22.33
Sackville-West. *Knole and the Sackvilles*. Fouirnaies 22.23, 26, 27, 28, 31, 37
Sackville-West. *The Land*. McVicker 28.84
Sackville-West. *The Letters of Vita Sackville-West to VW*. Rutherford 24.138, 151–52
Sackville-West. "Pater's Sister: The Pin and the Thunderstorm." Jenkins (Gwyn) 27.23–24
Sellers, Susan. *Vanessa and Virginia*. Layne 21.passim
Sewell, Anna. *Black Beauty*. Williams 26.109
Shakespeare, William. *Hamlet*. De Gay 30.102; Ke 29.74
Shakespeare. *Othello*. Caputi 29.15
Shakespeare. *Tempest*. Ke 29.70
Shaw, George Bernarnd. *Caesar and Cleopatra*. Rutherford 24.154
Shelley, Mary. *Frankenstein; or, The Modern Prometheus*. Gillespie 29.151; Ryan 30.70n10, 81n26
Shelley. "The Mortal Immortal." Schwartz 29.95
Shelley, Percy Bysshe. "Mont Blanc." De Gay 30.105

Shelley. "Ozymandias." McVicker 28.79; Rutherford 24.148
Shelley. *Prometheus Unbound*. Ryan 30.70n10
Sidney, Philip. "A Defence of Poesy." Leach 28.102
Silko, Leslie Marmon. *Ceremony*. Czarnecki 21.50, 53, 55, 59, 63, 66, 69, 72
Smyth, Ethel. "The March of Women." Delsandro 25.83
Solo Exhibition: Ling Shuhua (exhibition, 1984). Chua 30.31
Sophocles. *Ajax*. Koulouris 25.8–9, 14, 60–68
Sophocles. *Antigone*. Delsandro 25.80; Jenkins (Gwyn) 27.30; Phillips 26.6
Sophocles. *Oedipus Coloneus*. Jenkins (Gwyn) 27.29
Sorely, Charles Hamilton. *Marlborough and Other Poems*. Rutherford 24.137n1
Spender, Stephen. *The Destructive Element: A Study of Modern Writers and Beliefs*. Gallego Larrarte 30.112
Spender. *Vienna*. Gallego Larrarte 30.112
Spenser, Edmund. *The Faerie Queen*. Lauby 27.51–52
Stapledon, Olaf. *Star Maker*. Livingstone 26.89, 92, 100
Stein, Gertrude. *Tender Buttons*. Kopley 30.127
Stein. *The World is Round*. Williams 26.108n6
Stephen, Julia. *Julia Duckworth Stephen: Stories for Children, Essays for Adults*. Williams 26.109, 110
Sterne, Laurence. *The Life and Opinions of Tristram Shandy, Gentleman*. Sullam 30.121
Stevenson, Robert Louis. *Treasure Island*. Sullam 30.121
Strachey, Lytton. *Books and Characters: French and English*. Humm 29.156
Strachey. *Eminent Victorians*. Humm 29.158
Strachey, Nino. *Young Bloomsbury*. Humm 29.158
Swinburne, Charles Algernon. *Poems and Ballads & Atlanta in Calydon*. Shin 23.118
Swinburne. "Sapphics." Shin 23.119
Tennyson, Alfred, Lord. "The Charge of the Light Brigade." De Gay 30.103
Tennyson. *In Memoriam A. H. H.* De Gay 30.103
Thucydides. *History of the Peloponnesian War*. Jenkins (Gwyn) 27.30
Verdi, Giuseppe. *Aida*. Rutherford 24.154
Verrall, A. W., trans. *Ion* (Euripedes). Koulouris 25.42, 44n140, 45, 46n148–49, 47n150–51, 48n153
Virgil. *Aeneid*. Jenkins (Gwyn) 27.29; Koulouris 25.27n71
Virgil. *Georgics*. Koulouris 25.1n1, 3, 9, 14, 27n71, 58–59
Wagner, Richard. *Richard Wagner's Prose Works*. Davison 23.21, 21n31, 26, 27n40
Warner, Sylvia Townsend. *The True Heart*. Rutherford 24.153
Webster, John. *The Duchess of Malfi*. Lauby 27.52, 53
Webster. *White Devil*. Lauby 27.52
Wells, H. G. *Ann Veronica*. Fischer 28.35
Wells. *The First Men in the Moon*. Livingstone 26.87
Wells. *The Invisible Man*. Livingstone 26.89
Wells. *The Outline of History*. Gillespie 25.128n51; McVicker 28.90
Wells. Preface to *Scientific Romances*. Livingstone 26.96n6, 99
Wells. *The Shape of Things to Come*. Livingstone 26.99
Wells. *A Short History of the World*. Gillespie 25.128n51
West, Rebecca. *The Return of the Soldier*. Rutherford 24.154
West, Clive Bell, and Commander Locker-Lampson. "Living Dangerously." *The Listener*. Davison 29.144–45
Whitman, Walt. *The Complete Poems*. Shin 23.114
Woolf, Leonard. *Downhill All the Way: An Autobiography of the Years 1919–1939.* Adair & Gillespie 25.108; Humm 29.156n3; Lostoski-Ho 28.58;

Martin 24.80n6, 83, 88n13; Novillo-Corvalán 23.53; Wisor 21.28
Woolf. *Empire and Commerce in Africa: A Study in Economic Imperialism.* Graber 24.171; Novillo-Corvalán 23.33, 34, 35, 41, 42, 44, 56; Williams 26.114
Woolf. *The Framework of a Lasting Peace.* Cheney 24.61
Woolf. *Growing: An Autobiography of the Years 1904–1911.* Layne 21.90
Woolf. *The Journey Not the Arrival Matters: An Autobiography of the Years 1939–1969.* Gillespie 25.108, 110
Woolf. "Les Copains" [review of Romains]. Reed 29.163
Woolf. Letter to Ling Shuhua. Chua 30.35
Woolf. "Poetry and Prose" (school essay). Sullam 30.119
Woolf. *The Wise Virgins.* Layne 21.85, 86, 88
Wordsworth, William. *The Prelude.* McVicker 28.79
Wroth, Lady Mary. *The Countess of Montgomery's Urania.* Lauby 27.50
Yoder, Edwin M. Jr. *Lions at Lamb House.* Layne 21.78n1

2B: Scholarship and Miscellaneous Texts

Abbott, Wilbur Cortez. *The Expansion of Europe: A History of the Foundations of the Modern World.* Gillespie 25.102
Abe, Juri. "Fighting a White Man's War: Participation and Representation of the Native American During WWII." Czarnecki 21.58
Abercrombie, Patrick. *Town and Country Planning.* Jones 22.83, 84
Abrams, M.H., and Geoffrey Galt Harpham. "Ode." Shin 23.124
Ackerman, Robert. "Jane Ellen Harrison: The Early Work." McVicker 28.72n8
Adams, Rachel. "Tradition." In *A New Vocabulary for Global Modernism.* Chua 30.34
Ahmed, Sara. "Becoming Unsympathetic." Kotler 24.50
Ahmed. "Introduction: Feel Your Way." Kotler 24.38
Ahmed. "Feminist Killjoys (And Other Willful Subjects)." Kotler 24.40
Ahmed. *Living a Feminist Life.* Favre 30.64
Ahmed. *The Promise of Happiness.* Kotler 24.37, 44
Ahmed. *Queer Phenomenology.* Livingstone 26.98; van Straten 30.88
Ahmed. *Strange Encounters: Embodied Others in Postcoloniality.* Caputi 29.5n2
Aiken, Conrad. "American Literature and American Critics" [Review of Van Doren, ed. *A Short History of American Literature*]. Kopley 30.127
Alberdi, Juan Bautista. *Bases y puntos de partida para la organización política de la República Argentina.* Novillo-Corvalán 23.48
Albertini, Tamara. "Renaissance Italian Aesthetics." *Encyclopedia of Aesthetics* (Kelly, ed.). Ke 29.66
Aldgate, Anthony and James C. Robertson. *Censorship in Theatre and Cinema.* Wisor 21.8n16
Alexander, Horace G. *Justice Among Nations.* Foster 22.52
Allen, Paula Gunn. *The Sacred Hoop: Recovering the Feminine in American Indian Traditions.* Czarnecki 21.50, 51, 52, 53, 55, 56, 59, 62, 69
Alsen, Eberhard. *Romantic Postmodernism in American Fiction.* Ke 29.68n12
Altenmüller, Eckart, Stanley Finger and François Bolter. *Music, Neurology and Neuroscience: Evolution, The Musical Brain, Medical Conditions and Therapies.* Davison 23.2n3
Althusser, Louis. *Lenin and Philosophy, and Other Essays.* Schwartz 29.99
Amato, Joseph. *On Foot: A History of Walking.* van Straten 30.90n7
Anderson, Gerald D. *Fascists, Communists, and the National Government: Civil Liberties in Great Britain, 1931–1937.*

Wisor 21.28, 29, 29n44
Antell, Judith A. "Momaday, Welch, and Silko: Expressing the Feminine Principle Through Male Alienation." Czarnecki 21.63
Aquinas, Thomas. *Summa Theologiae*. Lauby 27.52
"Archive Journeys: Bloomsbury: Roger Fry." Tate Online Layne 21.88
Armstrong, Philip. *What Animals Mean in the Fiction of Modernity*. Williams 26.117
An Atlas of the War: 15 Maps with Explanatory Text. Gillespie 25.104
Attridge, Derek. *The Singularity of Literature*. Williams 26.110
Aubrey, John. *Brief Lives, and Other Select Writings*. McVicker 28.83–84n24
Auerbach, Erich. *Mimesis: The Representation of Reality in Western Literature*. Koulouris 25.7
Austen-Leigh, J. E. *A Memoir of Jane Austen and Other Family Recollections*. Leach 28.102n7
Avery, Todd. "The Trumpets of Autocracies and the Still, Small Voices of Civilisation: Levinas and Radio in a Time of Crisis." *Levinas and Twentieth-Century Literature* (Wehr, ed.). Davison 29.144
Bachelard, Gaston. *The Psychoanalysis of Fire*. Ryan 30.69, 81
Baden-Powell, Sir Robert. *The Young Knights of the Empire*. Wisor 21.14
Baedeker, Karl. *Northern France, from Belgium and the English Channel to the Loire, Excluding Paris and its Environs: Handbook for Travellers*. Gillespie 25.100; Golden 23.96, 97
Baedeker. *Greece: Handbook for Travellers*. Golden 23.99, 100, 101, 102n31
Baker, Abigail. "Myths of the Odyssey in the British Museum (and Beyond): Jane Ellen Harrison's Museum Talks and Their Audience." McVicker 28.72n8, 79
Baker, Andrew M. et. al. "Investigating Word-of-Mouth Conversations About Brands Influence Purchase and Retransmission Intentions." Berkowitz 29.133
Baker, Jr., Houston A. *Modernism and the Harlem Renaissance*. Caputi 29.6n2
Bakhtin, Mikhail. *Epic and the Novel*. Sullam 30.118
Baldwin, Nick. *A–Z of Cars of the 1920s*. Adair & Martin 24.82n8, 85
Baldwin, Stanley. "Freedom and Discipline." Wisor 21.23
Baldwin. "Our Freedom Is Our Own." Wisor 21.26
Baldwin. *This Torch of Freedom: Speeches and Addresses*. Wisor 21.22n35
Baldwin. "Unto Whomsoever Much Is Given." Wisor 21.25
Banner, Louis. "Biography as History." *The American Historical Review*. Humm 29.158
Banet-Weiser, Sarah. "Gender, Social Media, and the Labor of Authenticity." Berkowitz 29.135n13
Bantock, G. H. "The Private Heaven of the Twenties." *The Listener*. Davison 29.146
Barber, Martyn. "'Let sleeping scarabs alone': When Egypt Came to Stonehenge." McVicker 28.82
Barnes, Leonard. *The New Boer War*. Gillespie 25.102
Barnlund, Dean C. "A Transactional Model of Communication." *Language Behavior* (Akin et. al., eds.). Berkowitz 29.131, 137
"Barnlund's Transactional Model of Communication." *Businesstopia* (online). Berkowitz 29.131
Barr, Jr., Alfred H. "A Modern Art Questionaire." *Defining Modern Art* (Sanderly and Newman, eds.). Berkowitz 29.129n8
Barthes, Roland. *Camera Lucido: Reflections on Photography.* Wisor 21.3
Barthes. "The Death of the Author." Favre

30.59n11
Barthes. "Listening." Fischer 28.29–30
Barthes. "The Rustle of Language." Fischer 28.29, 35
Barthes. *S/Z*. Foster 22.66
Bartholomew, J. G. *Citizen's Atlas of the World: Containing 156 Pages of Maps and Plans, with Index, a Gazetteer, and Geographical Statistics*. Gillespie 25.102, 103, 124, 125
Barzun, Jacques. *Darwin, Marx, Wagner: Critique of a Heritage*. Davison 23.3n5
Bassnett, Susan and Harish Trivedi. "Introduction: Of Colonies, Cannibals, and Vernaculars." Novillo-Corvalán 23.40
Batkin, Norton. "Formalism in Analytic Aesthetics." *Encyclopedia of Aesthetics* (Kelly, ed.). Ke 29.66
Baucom, Ian. *Specters of the Atlantic: Finance Capital, Slavery, and the Philosophy of History*. Caputi 29.5n2
Bayreuther Blätter: Deutsche Zeiteschrift im Geiste Richard Wagner. Davison 23.26, 7n40
Beauvoir, Simone de. *The Second Sex*. Delsandro 25.75n4
Beer, Gillian. *Darwin's Plots: Evolutionary Narrative in Darwin, George Eliot and Nineteenth-Century Fiction.* Davison 23.7, 24
Beer. "The Backbone Shiver: Darwin and the Arts." Davison 23.1n1
Bell, Clive. "A Foot-note." *Marcel Proust: an English Tribute*. Dalgarno 22.8
Bell, Stephen. "Aimé Bonpland and Merinomania in Southern South America." Novillo-Corvalán 23.43n4
Bellemin-Noël, Jean. *Le Texte et L'avant-Texte*. Phillips 26.3
Benjamin, Walter. *The Arcades Project*. Bunting 30.18; Schwartz 29.101
Benjamin. "Theses on the Philosophy of History." Wisor 21.1, 4
Bennett, Jane. *Vibrant Matter: A Political Ecology of Things*. Lostoski-Ho 28.64n29
Benson, G. Vere. "Bankes, William John." *DNB*. Rutherford 24.141
Benson, Hugh. "The Dissolution of the Problem of the Elenchus." Dalgarno 22.5n5
Benson, John. *The Rise of Consumer Society in Britain, 1880–1980*. Adair & Martin 24.76
Berger, Harry Jr. "Levels of Discourse in Plato's Dialogues." Dalgarno 22.1, 4
Berlant, Lauren. *The Female Complaint: The Unfinished Business of Sentimentality in American Culture*. Clarke 28.9n6
Berlant. "Intimacy: A Special Issue." Clarke 28.9, 17
Berlant and Michael Warner. "Sex in Public." Clarke 28.9n6
Berman, Jessica. *Modernist Commitments: Ethics, Politics, and Transnational Modernism*. Chua 30.34; Wisor 21.3n8; Pająk 24.13
Berman."Trans Reading and Comparative Modernism." Pająk 24.31, 32
Berrens, Karla. "An Emotional Cartography of Resonance." van Straten 30.93
Bersani, Leo and Adam Phillips. *Intimacies*. Clarke 28.9n6
Bertarelli, L. V. *Northern Italy, from the Alps to Rome (Rome Excepted)*. Gillespie 25.101–02
Bertarelli. *Southern Italy, Including Rome, Sicily, and Sardinia*.. Gillespie 25.102
Best, Stephen and Sharon Marcus. "Surface Reading: An Introduction." Fischer 28.26n4
Beylin, Marek. Personal interview. Pająk 24.23–24n9
Blom-Cooper, Louis and Terence Morris. *With Malice Aforethought: A Study of the Crime and Punishment for Homicide*. Wisor 21.28
Bloom, Harold. "Freud: Frontier Concepts, Jewishness, and Interpretation." *Trauma: Explorations of Memory* (Caruth, ed.). Van Wert 29.107

Blumberg, Angie. "Victorian Literature and Archaeology: Contemporary Excavations." McVicker 28.82n23
Bobonich, Christopher. *Plato's Utopia Recast: His Later Ethics and Politics*. Dalgarno 22.10
Bone, Robert. *The Negro Novel in America*. Caputi 29.17n14
The Book of the Dead: Facsimile of the Papyrus of Ani in the British Museum. Rutherford 24.156n9
Bourdieu, Pierre. *Distinction: A Social Critique of the Judgment of Taste*. Schwartz 29.100
Bourdieu. *Forms of Capital: General Sociology*. Berkowitz 29.129–30, 132, 137
Bourriaud, Nicolas. *Relational Aesthetic*. Sullam 30.117n1
Bowen, E. E. "On Teaching By Means of Grammar." Jenkins (Gwyn) 27.28, 37
Braund, Susanna H. "Juvenal—Misogynist or Misogamist?" Koulouris 25.6n10
Braybrooke, Nevile. *London Green: The Story of Kensington Gardens, Hyde Park, Green Park & St. James's Park*. van Straten 30.89
Breasted, James Henry. *Ancient Records of Egypt: Historical Documents from the Earliest Times to the Persian Conquest*. Rutherford 24.154n7
British Broadcasting Company. "Stonehenge: Last owner's letter found inside book." McVicker 28.82
Brooks, Peter. "The Death Drive at 100." Van Wert 29.109n4
Brown, Horatio. *Venice: An Historical Sketch of the Republic*. Gillespie 25.100
Browne, Henry. *Our Renaissance: Essays on the Reform and Revival of Classical Studies*. Schwartz 29.87, 88, 90, 91, 94
Budge, E. A., trans. *The Book of the Dead; The Papyrus of Ani in the British Museum*. Rutherford 24.138, 143, 145, 146, 150, 156
Budge. *Egyptian Magic*. Rutherford 24.142, 146, 148
Budge. *Legends of the Egyptian Gods: Hieroglyphic Texts and Translations*. Rutherford 24.155
Budge. *The Mummy*. Rutherford 24.142, 148
Budge. *Osiris and the Egyptian Resurrection*. Rutherford 24.135–36, 140, 146, 150
Bulson, Eric. *Novels, Maps, Modernity: The Spatial Imagination, 1850–2000*. Gillespie 25.100n6, 116; Golden 23.100n29
Burden, Robert. "Introduction: Englishness and Spatial Practices." McVicker 28.86n28
Butler, Judith. *Bodies That Matter: On the Discursive Limits of "Sex."* Caputi 29.21, 22
Butler. *Frames of War: When is Life Grievable?* Kotler 24.50
Butler. *Gender Trouble: Feminism and the Subversion of Identity*. Humm 29.158
Burchardt, Jeremy. *Paradise Lost: Rural Idyll and Social Change Since 1800*. Jones 22.81
Burl, Aubrey. *A Guide to the Stone Circles of Britain, Ireland and Brittany*. McVicker 28.77n16, 82, 83
Buxton, Charles Roden. *The Race Problem in Africa*. Foster 22.51
Byerly, Alison. *Realism, Representation, and the Arts in Nineteenth-Century Literature*. Ke 29.60n7
Bywater, William G. *Clive Bell's Eye*. Gillespie 29.151n4
Carby, Hazel V. *Reconstructing Womanhood: The Emergence of the Afro-American Woman Novelist*. Caputi 29.6n3, 15
Cardoso, Eliana A. and Ann Helwege. *Latin America's Economy: Diversity, Trends and Conflicts*. Novillo-Corvalán 23.44
Carey, John. *The Intellectuals and the Masses: Pride and Prejudice among the Literary Intelligentsia, 1880–1939*.

Fouirnaies 22.22n1
Carlyle, Thomas. *The French Revolution: A History*. Golden 23.94
Carlyle. *Hero-Worship*. Schwartz 29.98
Carlyle. *Sartor Resartus*. Schwartz 29.98
Carpenter, Edward. *Cantuar: The Archbishops in Their Office.* Wisor 21.17n29
Carr, Helen. "Roger Casement in the Amazon, The Congo, and Ireland." Novillo-Corvalán 23.54
Carter, Howard. *The Tomb of Tutankhamen: Discovered by the Late Earl of Carnarvon and Howard Carter* (Vol. II). Rutherford 24.149
Carter. *The Tomb of Tut-Ankh-Amen: Discovered by the Late Earl of Carnarvon and Howard Carter* (Vol. III). Rutherford 24.146, 147
Caruth, Cathy. "The Wound and the Voice." *Unclaimed Experience*. van Straten 30.94
Casanova, Pascale. *The World Republic of Letters*. Chua 30.33
Casement, Roger. *The Amazon Journal of Roger Casement*. Novillo-Corvalán 23.54, 55,
Chappell, Mike. *The Guards Division 1914–45.* Wisor 21.38
Cavitch, Max. *The American Elegy: The Poetry of Mourning from the Puritans to Whitman* Shin 23.112n9
Chakrabarty, Dipesh. "Anthropocene Time." Lostoski-Ho 28.53n10
Chakrabarty. "The Climate of History: Four Theses." Lostoski-Ho 28.52
Chavkin, Allen. Introduction. *Leslie Marmon Silko's Ceremony: A Casebook* (Chavkin, ed.). Czarnecki 21.65n16
Child, Harold. "Ann Veronica." *TLS*. Fischer 28.35
Child. "Fraternity." *TLS*. Fischer 28.35
Childs, John. *Army of Charles II.* Wisor 21.35
Childs, Peter. *Modernism and the Post-Colonial: Literature and Empire 1885–1930.* Novillo-Corvalán 23.38
Clark, Cumberland. *Britain Overseas: The Story of the Foundation and Development of the British Empire from 1497–1921*. Gillespie 25.102
Clegg, Maree. *Eighteenth-Century Restoration of Ancient Sculptures: Questions of Authenticity in the Collection of Charles Townley*. Bunting 30.20n4
Cloud, Yvonne. "Bohemia—Old and New: The Cave-Dwellers of Bloomsbury." Berkowitz 29.134n10
Cockerell, Douglas. *Bookbinding and the Care of Books: A Textbook for Bookbinders and Librarians*. Golden 23.96n20
Cole, Sarah. *At the Violet Hour: Modernism and Violence in England and Ireland.* Delsandro 25.76; Foster 22.62n42
Connor, Steven. "Rustications: Animals in the Urban Mix." Davison 23.9
"Convocation of Canterbury, Loyal Tributes, Archbishop and 'A Very Dear Friend.'"" *The Times.* 23 Jan. 1936: 6 Wisor 21.16n27
Cook, David A. "The Content and Meaning of Swinburne's 'Anactoria.'" Shin 23.118
Cooper, Duff. *Old Men Forget.* Wisor 21.22n36
Cornish, Vaughan. *The Scenery of England: A Study of Harmonious Grouping in Town and Country*. Jones 22.83
Corton, Christine L. *London Fog: The Biography*. Ryan 30.77n19
Cosgrove, Denis. "Introduction: Mapping Meaning." Gillespie 25.111
Coverley, Merlin. "Guy Debord and the Situationist International." *Psychogeography*. van Straten 30.86
Crenshaw, Kimberlé. "Demarginalizing the Intersection of Race and Sex: A Black Feminist Critique of Anti-discrimination Doctrine Feminist Theory and Antiracist Politics." Caputi 29.6n4; Delsandro 25.86

Crook, David Paul. *Darwin's Coat-Tails: Essays on Social Darwinism*. Davison 23.15n23
Crossley, Robert. "Olaf Stapledon and the Idea of Science Fiction." Livingstone 26.92
Crossman, Robert. *Plato Today*. Dalgarno 22.13
Cunningham, Valentine. *British Writers of the Thirties*. Gallego Larrarte 30.113
Curl, James Stevens. *Egyptomania: The Egyptian Revival, A Recurring Theme in the History of Taste*. Rutherford 24.154
Curthoys, Mark. "The Press and the University." Golden 23.99n28
Dakers, Caroline. *The Holland Park Circle: Artists and Victorian Society*. Jenkins (Amber) 27.13n15
Daly, Nicholas. *Literature, Technology, and Modernity, 1860-2000*. Adair & Martin 24.75
Damrosch, David. *What Is World Literature?* Chua 30.33
Dandelion, Pink. *An Introduction to Quakerism*. Foster 22.47n15
Daniels, Anthony. "The Man Who Made Scouting." Wisor 21.11, n18, n19, 14
Darwin, Charles. *On the Origin of Species and The Voyage of the Beagle*. Davison 23.7, 8, 8n16, 9, 10, 13, 20
Darwin. *The Descent of Man, and Selection in Relation to Sex*. Davison 23.1, 2, 11n18, 14, 15, 16, 17, 18; Ryan 30.73
Darwin. *The Expression of the Emotions in Man and Animals*. Davison 23.16, 19
Darwin. *The Voyage of the Beagle*. Ryan 30.73–74
Darwin, Francis, editor. *The Life and Letters of Charles Darwin*. Davison 23.1, 1n1
"Darwin and Lord Kelvin and Music." Davison 23.1n1
Davidson, R. E. "A New Lanchester Car." Adair & Martin 24.88, 89, 89n15
Davies, Dominic. "Critiquing Global Capital and Colonial (in)justice: Structural Violence in Leonard Woolf's *The Village in the Jungle* (1913) and *Economic Imperialism* (1920)." Novillo-Corvalán 23.42
Davis, Heather and Zoe Todd. "On the Importance of a Date, or, Decolonizing the Anthropocene." Lostoski-Ho 28.53n10
Davis, Thadious M. *Nella Larsen: Novelist of the Harlem Renaissance*. Caputi 29.19n15, 21
Delany, Paul. '"The Death of a Beautiful Man': Rupert Brooke in Memory and Imagination." Czarnecki 21.70n19
De la Mare, Walter. "An Old Wives' Tale." *TLS*. Fischer 28.35
de Lauretis, Teresa. *The Practice of Love: Lesbian Sexuality and Perverse Desire* Bond 23.76n17
Derrida, Jacques. *The Animal That Therefore I Am*. Williams 26.108n5, 112
Derrida. "Plato's Pharmacy." Dalgarno 22.1n2
Derrida. *Specters of Marx*. Phillips 26.10
Derry, Julian. "Bravo Emma! Music in the Life and Work of Charles Darwin." Davison 23.1, 1n2
Descartes, René. "Discourse on the Method." Williams 26.116n8
Díaz Alejandro, Carlos F. *Essays on the Economic History of the Argentine Republic*. Novillo-Corvalán 23.46
Dickinson, G. Lowes. *After Two Thousand Years: A Dialogue Between Plato and A Modern Young Man*. Dalgarno 22.13
Dickinson. *Plato and His Dialogues* Dalgarno 22.14
Dictionary of National Bibliography. Livingstone 26.98n7
DiGaetani, John Louis. *Richard Wagner and the Modern British Novel* Davison 23.20n28
Dillard, Annie. *Pilgrim at Tinker Creek* Shin 23.128
Dimock, Wai Chee. *Through Other Continents: American Literature Across Deep Time*. Lostoski-Ho

28.53–54n11
Doan, Laura L, and Jay Prosser. *Palatable Poison: Critical Perspectives on the Well of Loneliness* Pająk 24.11, 21
Dobson, Eleanor and Gemma Banks. Introduction: "Strata: Geology, Archaeology, and Psychology in Victorian and Edwardian Literature." McVicker 28.82n23
Dobson and Nichola Tonks. "Introduction: Ancient Egypt in Nineteenth-Century Culture." McVicker 28.82n23
Dobson and Tonks, editors. *Ancient Egypt in the Modern Imagination: Art, Literature and Culture*. McVicker 28.82n23
Docherty, Thomas. *Reading (Absent) Character: Towards a Theory of Characterization in Fiction* Bond 23.65n5
Donald, James, Anne Friedberg, and Laura Marcus, eds. *Close Up: CInema and Modernism*. Humm 29.159n11
Donaldson, Elizabeth. "The Corpus of the Madwoman: Toward a Feminist Disability Studies Theory of Embodiment and Mental Illness.' Favre 30.59, 63
Dowling, Linda. *Hellenism and Homosexuality in Victorian Oxford.* Dalgarno 22.9
Doyle, Laura. *Freedom's Empire: Race and the Rise of the Novel in Atlantic Modernity, 1640–1940*. Caputi 29.5n2
Driscoll, Catherine. *Modernist Cultural Studies*. Adair & Martin 24.77
Drucker, Johanna. *Theorizing Modernism: Visual Art and the Critical Tradition.* Berkowitz 29.126
Dryden, Linda. *Joseph Conrad and H. G. Wells: The Fin-de-Siècle Literary Scene.* Novillo-Corvalán 23.38
Dudziński, Bolesław. "Z nowych książek." Pająk 24.30, 31
Duff-Gordon, Lucie (Austin), Lady. *Letters from Egypt, 1863–65*. Rutherford 24.157
Duffy, Enda. *The Speed Handbook: Velocity, Pleasure, Modernism*. Adair & Martin 24.75
Dunn, Carolyn, and Carol Comfort. *Through the Eye of the Deer: An Anthology of Native American Women Writers*. Czarnecki 21.52
DuPlessis, Rachel Blau. *Writing Beyond the Ending: Narrative Strategies of Twentieth-Century Women Writers.* Czarnecki 21.52n3; Fischer 28.38
Dymond, Justine. "Modemism(s) Inside Out: History, Space, and Modern American Subjectivity in *Cogewea, the Half-Blood."* Czarnecki 21.50n1
Eagleton, Terry. "Theri Final Bows." *TLS*. Humm 29.160
Earle, Peter G. *The Works of Ezequiel Martínez Estrada*. Novillo-Corvalán 23.49
Edelman, Lee. *No Future: Queer Theory and the Death Drive*. Lauby 27.59; Van Wert 29.110, 118, 119–20
Edney, Matthew H. *Mapping an Empire: The Geographical Construction of British India, 1765–1843*. Gillespie 25.117, 127
Eiland, Howard and Michael W. Jennings, eds. *Walter Benjamin: Selected Writings, Vol. 4: 1938-1940.* Wisor 21.4, n12
Elam, Caroline. *Roger Fry and Italian Art*. Ke 29.65n9
English, Elizabeth. *Lesbian Modernism: Censorship, Sexuality and Genre Fiction* Pająk 24.12, 24
English Heritage. "Prehistoric Monuments" (website). McVicker 28.83
Enloe, Cynthia. *Bananas, Beaches & Bases: Making Feminist Sense of International Politics.* Wisor 21.11, n19
Erman, Adolf. *Life in Ancient Egypt*. Rutherford 24.157
Ewing, K. D. and C. A. Gearty. *The Struggle for Civil Liberties: Political Freedom and the Rule of Law in Britain, 1914-*

1945. Wisor 21.29n45, 30, n48
Faderman, Lillian. *Surpassing the Love of Men: Romantic Friendship and Love Between Women from the Renaissance to the Present*. Clarke 28.7, 10
Fagan, Brian. *The Rape of the Nile: Tomb Robbers, Tourists, and Archaeologists in Egypt*. Rutherford 24.141
Falcoff, Mark. "Raúl Scalabrini Ortiz: The Making of an Argentine Nationalist." Novillo-Corvalán 23.49
Fallaize, E. N. "Prehistory" [Review of Frazer, *Myths*]. Ryan 30.74n16
Farjeon, Herbert. "Concerning Julius Caesar." *Radio TImes*. Davison 29.143n6
Faucher, Kane X. "Online Social Capital as Capital." *Social Capital Online*. Berkowitz 29.135
Feldman, Matthew et. al. *Historicizing Modernists: Approaches to 'Archivalism.'* Chua 30.46
Felman, Shoshana. "Women and Madness: The Critical Phallacy." Favre 30.59n10
Ferguson, Frances. "Jane Austen, Emma, and the Impact of Form." Sullam 30.121n4
Finch, Annie. "Poetics: A Taxonomy." *The Body of Poetry*. Kopley 30.125
Fish, Stanley. "Just published: minutiae without meaning." Humm 29.157–58n10
Fletcher, Rachel. "Golden Proportions in a Great House: Palladio's Villa Emo." *Architecture and Mathematics* (Williams and Ostwald, eds.). Ke 29.67
Foka, Amalia. "Constructing an Artworld Influencer Network by Mining Social Media." *Leonardo*. Berkowitz 29.136–37
Fornoff, Carolyn et. al. "Coda." *Timescales: Thinking across Ecological Temporalities*. Lostoski-Ho 28.54
Foster, J. Ashley, in collaboration with students of the "Peace Testimonies in Literature & Art" Spring 2015 Writing Seminar. *Testimonies in Art & Action: Igniting Pacifism in the Face of Total War Exhibition Catalogue*. Foster 22.44n9
Foucault, Michel. "Different Spaces." McVicker 28.73, 74, 79–80, 92
Foucault. "Friendship as a Way of Life." Clarke 28.19, 21–22
Foucault. *The History of Sexuality, Volume 1: An Introduction*. Lauby 27.47, 59
Foucault. *Madness and Civilization: A History of Insanity in the Age of Reason*. Clarke 28.14
Foucault. *The Order of Things: An Archaeology of the Human Sciences*. McVicker 28.73, 74
Fox, George. *An Autobiography*. Foster 22.54n29
Franco, Jere' Bishop. *Crossing the Pond: The Native American Effort in World War II*. Czarnecki 21.53n5, 60
Frank, Joseph. "Spatial Form in Modern Literature: An Essay in Three Parts." Bond 23.64n2
Frazer, James George. *Adonis, Attis, Osiris: Studies in the History of Oriental Religion*. Rutherford 24.155, 157
Frazer. *The Golden Bough*. Ryan 30.74
Frazer. *Myths of the Origin of Fire*. Ryan 30.74
Frede, Michael. "Plato's Arguments and the Dialogue Form." Dalgarno 22.15
Frederick, Bonnie and Virginia Hyde. Introduction. *Women and the Journey: The Female Travel Experience* (Frederick and McLeod, eds.). Gillespie 25.107, 118
Freedman, Carl. "Science Fiction and Utopia: A Historico-Philosophical Overview." Livingstone 26.94
French, Jennifer L. Nature, *Neo-Colonialism and the Spanish American Regional Writers* Novillo-Corvalán 23.42
Freud, Sigmund. "The Acquisition and Control of Fire." Ryan 30.72
Freud. *Beyond the Pleasure Principle*. Van

Wert 29.108, 110
Freud. *Civilization and Its Discontents*. Van Wert 29.108n3, 109
Freud. *Project for Scientific Psychology*. Van Wert 29.108n2
Freud. *Totem and Taboo*. Ryan 30.74
Frost, J. William. "Modernist and Liberal Quakers, 1887-2010." Foster 22.44n6, 46, 47n13, 48
Fry, Paul H. *The Poet's Calling in the English Ode* Shin 23.110n4
Fuss, Diana. *Dying Modern: A Meditation on Elegy* Shin 23.112n9
Fussell, Paul. *Poetic Meter & Poetic Form*. Kopley 30.125–26
Gallop, Jane. *Feminist and Psychoanalysis: The Daughter's Seduction*. Fischer 28.27
Gandy, Matthew. "Acoustic Terrains: An Introduction." *The Acoustic City* (Gandy and Nilsen, eds.). Davison 23.8
Gardner, Edmund G. *The Story of Florence*. Gillespie 25.100, 101
Garnett, Angelica. *Deceived With Kindness: A Bloomsbury Childhood*. Adair & Martin 24.82; Layne 21.82
Gay, Ross. *A Catalog of Unabashed Gratitude*. Shin 23.114n13
Georgievics, Georg von. *A Text-Book of Dye Chemistry (The Chemistry of Dye-Stuffs)*. Golden 23.96n21
Gibbon, Edward. *Decline and Fall of the Roman Empire*. Fischer 28.30, 31; Gillespie 25.105, 106, 120
Giddens, Anthony. *The Transformation of Intimacy: Sexuality, Love, and Eroticism in Modern Societies*. Clarke 28.9n6
Gilbert, Sandra. "Dead Poet's Society." Layne 21.102
Gilbert, Sandra and Susan Gubar. Introduction [Larsen, *Quicksand*; *Norton Anthology of Literature by Women*]. Caputi 29.21
Gilbert and Gubar. *No Mans Land: The Place of the Woman Writer in the Twentieth Century* Czarnecki 21.53, 53n6, 70
Gilberg and Gubar. *Still Mad: American Women Writers and the Feminist Imagination*. Favre 30.58n8
Gillis, John. *Youth and History: Tradition and Change in European Age Relations*. Wisor 21.12n22
Gilroy, Paul. *The Black Atlantic: Modernity and Double Consciousness*. Caputi 29.5n2; Graber 24.166, 168
Gisges-Zwierzchowska, Ewa. *Rój 1924-1945: próba monografii* Pająk 24.18, 20
Glendinning, Victoria. *Leonard Woolf: A Biography*. Adair & Martin 24.82, 83, 85; Golden 23.102, 102n31; Humm 29.156n3;
Glendinning. *Vita: The Life of V. Sackville-West*. Adair & Martin 24.80, 86n11; Fouirnaies 22.33, 36
Godley, A. D. Introduction. *Herodotus* (Books I and II). Rutherford 24.155
Goelet, Ogden. Introduction [*The Egyptian Book of the Dead: The Book of Going Forth by Day*, Faulkner and Goelet, trans.]. Rutherford 24.136, 156
Gomulicki, Juliusz Wiktor. *Aleje czarów* Pająk 24.24n9
Goodheart, A. L. "*Thomas v. Sawkins:* A Constitutional Innovation." *Cambridge Law Journal*. Wisor 21.29n45, n46
Graham, John. *The Compositor's Text-Book, or, Instructions in the Elements of the Art of Printing* Golden 23.96n21
Graham, John W. *Britain and America*. Foster 22.51
Green, Christopher. "Expanding the Canon: Roger Fry's Evaluations of the 'Civilized' and the 'Savage.'" *Art Made Modern* (Green, ed.). Ke 29.65n9
Green, Peter. *Alexander to Actium: The Historical Evolution of the Hellenistic Age*. Rutherford 24.159
Greenblatt, Stephen. *Marvellous*

Possessions: The Wonder of the New World Novillo-Corvalán 23.41
Gregory, Rosalyn, and Benjamin Kohlmann, editors. *Utopian Spaces of Modernism: British Literature and Culture, 1885-1945* Cheney 24.62
Grewal, Inderpal and Caren Kaplan. *An Introduction to Women's Studies: Gender in a Transnational World.* Caputi 29.5n2
Grey, Thomas S. *Wagner's Musical Prose – Texts and Contexts*. Davison 23.3, 3n5, 27n40,
Gribble, David. *Alcibiades and Athens: A Study in Literary Presentation* Dalgarno 22.7n8
Griggs, Arthur Kingsland. *Paris for Everyman: Her Present, her Past, and her Environs*. Gillespie 25.102
Griswold, Charles L., ed. *Platonic Writings/ Platonic Readings* Dalgarno 22.1
Grodzinsky, Ewa and Märta Sund Levander. *Understanding Fever and Body Temperature: A Cross-disciplinary Approach to Clinical Practice*. Ryan 30.68n2
Gross, Robert. "The Transnational Turn: Rediscovering American Studies in a Wider World." Caputi 29.5n2
Grote, George. *Plato and the Other Companions of Sokrates*. Dalgarno 22.5n5, 10
Gubar, Marah. "On Not Defining Children's Literature." Williams 26.108
Hadow, W. H. *The Oxford History of Music*, Vol. 5 Davison 23.4n9
Halberstam, Jack. *"Transgender Butch: Butch/FtM Border Wars and the Masculine Continuum."* Pająk 24.12, 29
Halliday, Sam. *Sonic Modernity. Representing Sound in Literature, Culture and the Arts*. Davison 23.8, 11n18, 20n28
Halperin, David. *One Hundred Years of Homosexuality and other Essays on Greek Love* Dalgarno 22.8
Hammill, Faye and Mark Hussey. *Modernism's Print Cultures.* Golden 23.84n6
Haraway, Donna J. *Staying with the Trouble: Making Kin in the Chthulucene.* Lostoski-Ho 28.53n10
Hardenburg, W. E. "The Devil's Paradise: A British-owned Congo." Novillo-Corvalán 23.53
Hardenburg. *The Putumayo: The Devil's Paradise: Travels in the Peruvian Amazon Region and an Account of the Atrocities Committed Upon the Indians Therein.* Novillo-Corvalán 23.53
Hare, Augustus J. C. *Venice*. Gillespie 25.100
Harley, J. B. "Deconstructing the Map." Gillespie 25.128
Harmansah, Ömür. "Deep Time and Landscape History: How Can Historical Particularity Be Translated?" Lostoski-Ho 28.54
Harris, Anne. Pyromena: Fire's Doing." *Elemental Ecocriticism* (Cohen and Duckert, eds.). Ryan 30.68n5
Harrison, Robert Pogue. *Gardens: An Essay on the Human Condition.* van Straten 30.90–91
Hart, George. *A Dictionary of Egyptian Gods and Goddesses*. Rutherford 24.142, 148
Harvey, David. *The Condition of Postmodernity: An Enquiry into the Origins of Cultural Change*. Lostoski-Ho 28.49n4, 54n12
Harvey, Kathryn. "'Driven by War into Politics!': A Feminist Biography of Kathleen Innes." Foster 22.51
Harwood, Brian. *Chivalry and Command: 500 Years of Horse Guards.* Wisor 21.33, 34, 37n56, 38, 39
Haste, Cate. *Rules of Desire: Sex in Britain: World War I to the Present.* Czarnecki 21.68
Hastings, Adrian. *A History of English Christianity 1920-1985.* Wisor

21.15n26, 16, n27, 17
Hayman, Richard. *Riddles in Stone: Myths, Archaeology and the Ancient Britons*. McVicker 28.84
Hazlitt, William. *The Complete Works of William Hazlitt*. Schwartz 29.90
Heath-Stubbs, John. *The Ode*. Shin 23.110n4, 113, 115
Hegglund, Jon. "Introduction: The Modernist Novel as Metageography." *World Views: Metageographies of Modernist Fiction*. Gillespie 25.119
Hegglund. "*Ulysses* and the Rhetoric of Cartography." Gillespie 25.110, 118
Heilbrun, Carolyn. *The Last Gift of Time: Life Beyond Sixty*. Delsandro 25.75, 92
Henderson, John. *"Oxford Reds": Classic Commentaries on Latin Classics* Golden 23.100
Henry, Zoë, Juno Richards, and Paul K. Saint-Amour. "Transracial Circuits, Transnational Modernism" (conference seminar). Chua 30.46n6
Hepburn, Allan. Review of Davis, *The Extinct Scene*. Delsandro 25.77
Herrmann, Anne. *Queering the Moderns: Poses/Portraits/Performances*. Adair & Martin 24.80
Hertslet, Edward. *Map of Africa by Treaty: With Numerous Maps*. Gillespie 25.102
Herzog, Kristin. "Thinking Woman and Feeling Man: Gender in Silko's *Ceremony*." Czarnecki 21.63, 69
Heshchong, Lisa. *Thermal Delight in Architecture*. Ryan 30.68n4
Heuston, R. F. V. *Lives of the Lord Chancellors 1885-1940*. Wisor 21.28
Hewitt, John. "The Nature and Art of Shell Advertising in the Early 1930s." Adair & Martin 24.92, 93
Higonnet, Margaret R. "New Cartographies, an Introduction." *Reconfigured*. Gillespie 25.112
Higonnet and Joan Templeton, eds. *Reconfigured Spheres: Feminist Explorations of Literary Space*. Gillespie 25.112
Hill, Edwin. "*Noir* Film's Soundtracks: Jazz, Black Transnationalism, and Postcolonial Genres of Criminality." Chua 30.34
Hinnov, Emily. *Encountering Choran Community: Literary Modernism, Visual Culture, and Political Aesthetics in the Interwar Years*. Wisor 21.3n7
Hinnov, Emily M., Laurel Harris, and Lauren M. Rosenblum. Introduction. *Communal Modernisms: Teaching Twentieth-Century Literature and Culture in the Twenty-First-Century Classroom*. Foster 22.60n36
Historical Dictionary of the Friends (Quakers). Foster 22.49
Hoberman, Ruth. *Museum Trouble: Edwardian Fiction and the Emergence of Modernism*. Schwartz 29.88
Hoberman. "Women in the British Museum Reading Room during the Late-Nineteenth and Early-Twentieth Centuries: From Quasi- to Counterpublic." *Feminist Studies*. Schwartz 29.98
Hobsbawm, Eric. *Industry and Empire: From 1750 to the Present Day* Novillo-Corvalán 23.43
Hobson, J. A. *The Psychology of Jingoism* Novillo-Corvalán 23.41, 42
Hodgkin, Thomas. "Caroline Stephen and the Society of Friends." Foster 22.47n14
Holinshed, Raphael. *Chronicles: England, Scotland, and Ireland*. Lauby 27.58n7
Holroyd, Michael. *Lytton Strachey: The New Biography* Adair & Martin 24.82
Holroyd. *On Wheels: Five Easy Pieces* Adair & Martin 24.77
Hooper-Greenhill, Eilean. *Museums and the Interpretation of Visual Culture*. Schwartz 29.91
Hooper-Greenhill. "The Re-birth of the Museum." *Papers Delivered to*

the Nordic Museums Leadership Programme. Schwartz 29.90
Hope-Allen, Mary. "Producer's Memorandum." BBC Written Archive Centre. Davison 29.143n6
Hope-Wallace, Philip. "Critic on the Hearth." *Listener*. Davison 29.143n6
Hoyland, John S. *The Light of Christ*. Foster 22.49, 50
Hsai Chih-tsing. "Ling Shuhua." Chua 30.36
Hudson, William Henry. *Far Away and Long Ago: A Childhood in Argentina.* Chua 30.35; Novillo-Corvalán 23.49, 50
Hunt, Peter. *Criticism, Theory, and Children's Literature*. Williams 26.108
"The 13th Hussars." http://www.pinetreeweb.com/bp-hussars.htm. Wisor 21.37
Hutchinson, George. *The Harlem Renaissance in Black and White*. Caputi 29.6n2
Hutchinson. *In Search of Nella Larsen: A Biography of the Color Line*. Caputi 29.8n7
Huxley, Julian. "The Stream of Life—Development" (radio). Livingstone 26.93
Hylson-Smith, Kenneth. *High Churchmanship in the Church of England* Wisor 21.17
Hynes, Samuel. *The Edwardian Turn of Mind.* Wisor 21.12n22
Innes, Kathleen E. *Defense of the Weak.* Foster 22.52
Innes, *The Story of the League of Nations: Told for Young People*. Foster 22.51
Irby, Leonard Howard Lloyd. *British Birds: Key List* Golden 23.95
Ivins, William M. *Art and Geometry: A Study in Space Intuitions*. Ke 29.65
Jackson, H. J. *Marginalia: Readers Writing in Books* Golden 23.84n5
Jackson, Kevin. *Constellation of Genius 1922: Modernism Year One*. Humm 29.167n6
Jackson, Robert. *The Chief The Biography of Gordon Hewart, Lord Chief Justice of England, 1922-1940.* Wisor 21.26, 28, 29, n44, n47, 30n48
Jacobs, Naomi M. "Consuming Beauty: The Urban Garden as Ambiguous Utopia." van Straten 30.90
Jaillant, Lise. *Modernism, Middlebrow and the Literary Canon: The Modern Library Series, 1917-1955.* Golden 23.84
Jaillant and Alison E. Martin. "Introduction: Global Modernism." Chua 30.34
Jameson, Fredric. *Archaeologies of the Future: The Desire Called Utopia and Other Science Fictions* Cheney 24.61n8, 63; Livingstone 26.88, 94
Jamieson, Andrew. *A Text-Book of Applied Mechanics and Mechanical Engineering* Golden 23.96n21
Jarzombek, Mark. "Alberti, Leon Battista." *Encyclopedia of Aesthetics* (Kelly, ed.). Ke 29.65
Jeal, Tim. *The Boy-Man: The Life of Lord Baden-Powell.* Wisor 21.10, 12n22, 14
Jehlen, Myra. "Félicité and the Holy Parrot." Williams 26.114
Jenkins, Ian. *Archaeologists and Aesthetes*. Schwartz 29.96
Johnson, George M. *Dynamic Psychology in Modern British Fiction* Layne 21.78
Johnston, John. *The Lord Chamberlains Blue Pencil.* Wisor 21.8n16
Jones, Rufus. *Rufus Jones Speaks to Our Time*. Foster 22.47n15, 48n17, 49
Jones, Prudence and Nigel Pennick. *A History of Pagan Europe*. Rutherford 24.155, 157
Jowett, Benjamin. Trans. *The Dialogues of Plato Translated into English.* Dalgarno 22.3, 4
Jowitt, Claire. *The Culture of Piracy, 1580–1630: Literature and Seaborne Crime*. Graber 24.165, 166
Jrade, Cathy L. *Modernismo, Modernity and the Development of Spanish American Literature.* Novillo-Corvalán 23.49

Kaplan, Cora. *Victoriana: Histories, Fictions, Criticism* Layne 21.81
Karl, Alissa G. *Modernism and the Marketplace: Literary Culture and Consumer Capitalism in Rhys, Woolf, Stein, and Nella Larsen* Novillo-Corvalán 23.36, 41, 57
Keller, Evelyn Fox. *Refiguring Life: Metaphors of Twentieth-Century Biology*. Livingstone 26.93
Kennard, Jean E. "Power and Sexual Ambiguity: The Dreadnought Hoax, *VO*, *MD*, and *O*." Caputi 29.22n18
Kennedy, David. *Elegy* Shin 23.111n7
Kennedy, Thomas C. *British Quakerism 1860-1920: The Transformation of a Religious Community.* Foster 22.50n18
Kenyon, Frederic. "Museums and National Life." Schwartz 29.88, 90, 94, 96
Kenyon. Preface [Browne, *Essays on the Reform and Revival of Classical Studies*]. Schwartz 29.91
Kern, Stephen. *The Culture of Time and Space, 1880–1918*. Lostoski-Ho 28.54n12
Kidd, Ronald. *British Liberty in Danger: An Introduction to the Study of Civil Rights.* Wisor 21.28-29, n44, n45, n46, 30, n48
Kirkpatrick, Robert. Introduction [Dante, *Inferno*]. Ryan 30.76n18
Kister, Hanna. *Pegazy na Kredytowej.* Pająk 24.18, 20, 22, 23, 24
Kitliński, Tomek, and Paweł Leszkowicz. "Miłość odmieńcow, myśl, gość-inność i inne uczucia. Afektywność fotografii Roberta Mapplethorpea i Nan Goldin?" Pająk 24.32
Kleinbauer, W. Eugene. *Modern Perspectives in Western Art History: An Anthology of Twentieth-Century Writings on the Visual Arts*. Ke 29.65n9
Kofman, Sarah. "Beyond Aporia?" *Post-Structuralist Classics*. Dalgarno 22.12, 13
Kristeva, Julia. *Revolution in Poetic Language*. Fischer 28.27
Krouse, Tonya. *The Opposite of Desire: Sex and Pleasure in the Modernist Novel* Bond 23.76n17
Krzywicka, Irena, and Agata Tuszyńska. *Wyznania Gorszycielki*. Pająk 24.13
Lacan, Jacques. *The Ethics of Psychoanalysis, 1959–1960: The Seminar of Jacques Lacan*. Van Wert 29.110n5
Lacan. *The Seminar of Jacques Lacan, Book II: The Ego in Freud's Theory and in the Technique of Psychoanalysis, 1954–1955*. Van Wert 29.108n2
Lacan. *The Seminar of Jacques Lacan, Book XI: The Four Fundamental Concepts of Psychoanalysis, 1963–1964*. Van Wert 29.110
Lackey, Michael. *Truthful Fictions: Conversations with American Biographical Novelists.* Layne 21.78, 79, 85
Lane, Edward William. *An Account of the Manners and Customs of the Modern Egyptians*. Rutherford 24.157–58
Laplanche, Jean. *Life and Death in Psychoanalysis*. Van Wert 29.108n2
Larabee, Mark D. *Front Lines of Modernism: Remapping The Great War*. Golden 23.99n28, 100
Latham, Sean. "*Am I a Snob?*" *Modernism and the Novel*. Fouirnaies 22.22
Lau, Meghan. "Performing History: The War-Time Pageants of Louis Napoleon Parker." Lauby 27.48
Lear, Jonathan. *Happiness, Death, and the Remainder of Life*. Van Wert 29.109
Leese, Peter. *Shell Shock: Traumatic Neurosis and the British Soldiers of the First World War.* Czarnecki 21.56, 57n8, 64, 65
Lefebvre, Henri. *The Production of Space*. van Straten 30.91, 92
Lei, Jun. "Capitalizing China: Writing Autography into World Literature." Chua 30.35

"L'Emploi de la Radiophonie dans l'Intérêt de la Paix." Davison 29.143n7
Lemke, Sieglinde. *Primitivist Modernism: Black Culture and the Origins of Transatlantic Modernism*. Caputi 29.6n2
Lenin, Vladimir. *Imperialism: The Highest Stage of Capitalism* Novillo-Corvalán 23.41
"'Lest We Run Too Far,' Aims of Scout and Guide Movements.'" *The Times* 30 Sep. 1937: 34 Wisor 21.11, 12n20
Levenback, Karen L. *VW and the Great War*. McVicker 28.71n5
Levitas, Ruth. *The Concept of Utopia*. Livingstone 26.98
Levy, Hyman. "The Web is Spun" (radio). Livingstone 26.100n8
Lewis, Colin M. *British Railways in Argentina* 1857 Novillo-Corvalán 23.36, 43, 57
Lewis, Pericles. *Religious Experience and the Modernist Novel* Shin 23.111, 117n18, 118n19, 127
Lianeri, Alexandra. "Effacing Socratic Irony: Philosophy and techne in John Stuart Mill's Translation of the Protagoras." Dalgarno 22.5
Liddell, Henry George. *An Intermediate Greek-English Lexicon Founded upon the Seventh Edition of Liddell and Scott's Greek-English Lexicon* Golden 23.94
Liddell and Robert Scott, comp. *A Greek-English Lexicon* Golden 23.96, 99, 99n28
Lindenberger, Herbert S. *Opera, The Extravagant Art*. Davison 23.6, 18, 20n29
Lindsay, Vachel. *The Art of the Moving Picture*. Humm 29.158
Lipson, E. *Europe in the Nineteenth Century: An Outline History Containing Eight Portraits and Four Maps*. Gillespie 25.102
Listy Roy Publisher w Nowym Yorku do Aleksandra Janty i inne materiały Pająk 24.21
Liu Xiaoqing. "The Danger of Foreignization: Ling Shuhua's *Ancient Melodies*." Chua 30.35
Lockhart, J. G. *Cosmo Gordon Lang*. Wisor 21.16, 17, n29, 18
Lodge, David. *The Year of Henry James: The Story of a Novel* Layne 21.78
"Lord Hewart: Tributes at the Law Courts." *Times* 7 May 1943: 8. Wisor 21.26n40
"Londonist" (website). Gillespie 25.104
Love, Heather. *Feeling Backward: Loss and the Politics of Queer History*. Clarke 28.19
Lowerson, John. "Battles for the Countryside." Jones 22.81n6
Lubbock, Percy. *The Craft of Fiction*. Sullam 30.120–21
Luke, Sir Harry and Edward Keith-Roach, eds. *The Handbook of Palestine and Trans-Jordan*. Gillespie 25.102
Lurz, John. *The Death of the Book: Modernist Novels and the Time of Reading*. Golden 23.84, 85, 92n18, 94, 98, 102n32
Lynas, Mark. *The God Species: Saving the Planet in the Age of Humans*. Ryan 30.68n5
MacColl, James E. and W. T. Wells, "The Incitement to Disaffection Bill, 1934." Wisor 21.6, 7
MacDonald, Robert H. *Sons of the Empire: The Frontier and the Boy Scout Movement, 1890-1918*. Wisor 21.12n22, 13, 14
MacKay, Marina. "Going Nowhere in Modernist London." Shin 23.129
MacKay. *Modernism and World War II* Shin 23.136
MacKenzie, John M. *Propaganda and Empire: The Manipulation of British Popular Opinion 1880-1960*. Wisor 21.8
Mackerell, Judith. *Bloomsbury Ballerina: Lydia Lopokova, Imperial Dancer and Mrs John Maynard Keynes* Adair & Martin 24.84

Maddisson, Carol. *Apollo and the Nine: A History of the Ode* Shin 23.110n4, 114
Magee, Bryan. *The Tristan Chord: Wagner and Philosophy* Davison 23.2n4
Maitland, Frederic W. *The Life and Letters of Leslie Stephen.* De Gay 30.101, 102
Mangan, James Anthony. *Athleticism in the Victorian and Edwardian Public School: The Emergence and Consolidation of an Educational Ideology*. Bunting 30.14
Marbot, Jean-Baptiste-Antoine-Marcelin, Baron de. *The Memoirs of Baron de Marbot, Late Lieutenant-General in the French Army* Bond 23.73, 73n16
Marcus, Laura. *The Tenth Muse: Writing about Cinema in the Modernist Period.* Cheney 24.65n12; Humm 29.159
Marcus, Sharon. *Between Women: Friendship, Desire, and Marriage in Victorian England.* Clarke 28.11
Marett, Robert Ranulph. "The Origin of Fire" [Review of Frazer, *Myths*]. Ryan 30.74n16
Marshik, Celia. *British Modernism and Censorship.* Wisor 21.6; Novillo-Corvalán 23.38
Marshik. "History's 'Abrupt Revenges': Censoring War's Perversions in *The Well of Loneliness* and *Sleeveless Errand.*" Pająk 24.17
Martínez Estrada, Ezequiel. *Radiografía de la Pampa.* Novillo-Corvalán 23.49
Martini, Arturo, "Sculpture Dead Language." Shin 23.113n11
Maspero, Gaston. *History of Egypt, Syria, Babylonia, and Assyria*. Rutherford 24.157
Massey, Doreen. *Space, Place, and Gender*. Gillespie 25.112
Matheson, Hilda. "Broadcasting." *Week-End Review*. Davison 29.144n8
Matheson. *Broadcasting*. Davison 29.144n8
Matless, David. *Landscape and Englishness*. Jones 22.83
Matless. "The Uses of Cartographic Literacy: Mapping, Survey and Citizenship in Twentieth-Century Britain." Gillespie 25.107, 124
Mayne, John Dawson. *Mayne's Hindu Law*. Gillespie 25.102n12
Mayor, Joseph Bickersteth. *Greek for Beginners*. Jenkins (Gwyn) 27.28
Mbembe, Achille. "Introduction: Time on the Move." *On the Postcolony*. van Straten 30.85n2, 88
McCabe, Mary. "Irony in the Soul: Should Plato's Socrates be Sincere?" Dalgarno 22.12
McDermott, Bridget. *Decoding Egyptian Hieroglyphics: How to Read the Secret Language of the Pharaohs.* Rutherford 24.137, 142–43, 146
McDowell, Deborah. Introduction [Larsen, *Quicksand and Passing*]. Caputi 29.16, 17n14, 19n15, 21n17
McDowell, Linda. *Gender, Identity, and Place: Understanding Feminist Geographies*. Bunting 30.18
Mcfarlane, Alexander C., and Bessel A. van Der Kolk. "Trauma and its Challenge to Society." Czarnecki 21.63, 64, 64n15
McGowan, Todd. *Enjoying What We Don't Have: The Political Project of Psychoanalysis*. Van Wert 29.109, 110, 111, 113, 114, 115, 117, 119
McKibbin, Ross. *Classes and Cultures: England, 1918–1951*. Jones 22.85
McLachlan, Torin. "Migration-Innovation-Labour." (Conference presentation.) Chua 30.46n6
McMillan, Laurie. "Telling a Critical Story: Alice Walker's 'In Search of Our Mothers' Gardens.'" Czarnecki 21.51n2
McPhee, John. *Basin and Range*. Lostoski-Ho 28.52
McPherson, Karen S. *Incriminations: Guilty Women/Telling Stories.* Czarnecki 21.57, 63
Meisel, Perry. *The Absent Father*. Jenkins (Gwyn) 27.27–28, 33, 34

Melcer, Wanda. "Dwie powieści kobiece." Pająk 24.30
Menand, Louis. "Why Freud Survives." Van Wert 29.109n4
Mendes, Peter. "Arcades & Comus." Lauby 27.49
Mendlesohn, Farah. *Quaker Relief Work in the Spanish Civil War*. Foster 22.44n6, 46, 47n13
Merriam-Webster. dress, v. Graber 24.175n8
Middeke, Martin. Introduction. *Biofictions: The Rewriting of Romantic Lives in Contemporary Fiction and Drama*. Layne 21.79
Middlemas, Keith and John Barnes, *Baldwin: A Biography*. Wisor 21.21, 22
Miller, Nancy K. "Changing the Subject: Authorship, Writing, and the Reader." Favre 30.59n11
Miller. "A Feminist Friendship Archive." Delsandro 25.74–75, 92
Miller. "Getting Personal: Autobiography as Cultural Criticism." Kotler 24.36
Miller, Simon. "Urban Dreams and Rural Reality: Land and Landscape in English Culture, 1920-1945." Jones 22.77
Mills, Billy. "*The Old Straight Track* by Alfred Watkins: walking through the past." *The Guardian*. McVicker 28.84n25
Mitchell, Angus. "The Diaries Controversy." Novillo-Corvalán 23.54
Mitchell, David and Sharon Snyder. *Narrative Prosthesis: Disability and the Dependencies of Discourse*. Williams 26.112
Moffat, Wendy. *A Great Unrecorded History: A New Life of E. M. Forster* Golden 23.84n4
Mohanty, Chandra Talpade. *Feminist without Borders: Decolonizing Theory, Practicing Solidarity*. Caputi 29.5n2
Moi, Toril. *Sexual/Textual Politics: Feminist Literary Theory*. Czarnecki 21.52n3
Monk, Ray. "Biography as an Exemplar of Philosophical Understanding." *Poetics*. Humm 29.160
Monmonier, Mark. *How to Lie with Maps*. Gillespie 25.104–05, 110, 127
Moody, Alys and Stephen J. Ross. *Global Modernists on Modernism*. Chua 30.37
Moore, Jason. "The Capitalocene, Part I: On the Nature and Origins of Our Ecological Crisis." Lostoski-Ho 28.53n10
Moran, Leslie J. *The Homosexual(ity) of Law*. Pająk 24.27
Moretti, Franco. "Conjectures on World Literature." Chua 30.33
Morice, Francis David. *Stories in Attic Greek: Forming a Greek Reading Book*. Golden 23.98; Jenkins (Gwyn) 27.28
Morris, F. O. *A History of British Butterflies*. Bunting 30.13
Morse, Elizabeth J. "Jaeger, Muriel." Livingstone 26.98n7
Morse, H. K. Elizabethan *Pageantry: A Pictorial Survey of Costume and its Commentators from c. 1560-1620: Special Spring Number of The Studio*. Fouirnaies 22.26
Moshenska, Gabriel. "The Archaeological Gaze." McVicker 28.71n6
Morton, Timothy. *Hyperobjects: Philosophy and Ecology after the End of the World*. Lostoski-Ho 28.53
Mosse, George L. *The Image of Man: The Creation of Modern Masculinity*. Bunting 30.19, 20
Moylan, Tom. *Scraps of the Untainted Sky: Science Fiction, Utopia, Dystopia*. Livingstone 26.91
Muir, Edwin. *The Structure of the Novel*. Kopley 30.128; Sullam 30.119, 120
Mullan, John. *Sentiment and Sociability: The Language of Feeling in the Eighteenth Century*. Clarke 28.14, 15
Mullin, Katherine. *James Joyce, Sexuality and Social Purity*. Novillo-Corvalán 23.38

Muñoz, José Esteban. *Cruising Utopia: The Then and There of Queer Futurity*. Lauby 27.60n8
Murray, David. "Sovereignty and the Struggle for Representation in American Indian Nonfiction." Czarnecki 21.59n9
Nalbantian, Suzanne. *Memory in Literature: From Rousseau to Neuroscience* Bond 23.65n4, 67
Nash, Jennifer C. *Black Feminism Reimagined: After Intersectionality*. Caputi 29.6n4
Nature. "The Fogs of London" (23 Dec. 1880). Ryan 30.77n19
Neumann, Angelo. *Personal Recollections of Wagner.* Davison 23.3n5
Nevison, C. R. W. "Wild Parties in Three Countries." Berkowitz 29.133n10
Ngai, Sianne. Introduction. *Ugly Feelings*. Kotler 24.37
Nicolson, Nigel. Letter to Ling Shuhua. Chua 30.36
Nietzsche, Friedrich. *The Joyful Wisdom [Gay Science]*. De Gay 30.99
Nietzsche. "Richard Wagner in Bayreuth." Davison 23.4
Nightingale, Andrea. "Plato on Aporia and Self-knowledge." Dalgarno 22.4
Nixon, Rob. *Slow VIolence and the Environmentalism of the Poor*. Lostoski-Ho 28.54n14
North, Michael. *Reading 1922: A Return to the Scene of the Modern*. Humm 29.157; McVicker 28.81
Nouzeilles, Gabriela and Montaldo, Graciela. "Frontiers." Novillo-Corvalán 23.46
Nowaczyński, Adolf. "Safona z Y.P.S.U." Pająk 24.18, 30
Nussbaum, Martha. *The Fragility of Goodness*. Dalgarno 22.4n4, 5, 6, 7, 7n8
Nycz, Ryszard. "Literatura polska w cieniu cenzury: wykład." Pająk 24.22
"Occasional Notes." Davison 23.1n1
O'Connell, Sean. *The Car in British Society: Class, Gender and Motoring 1896-1939*. Adair & Martin 24.93
O'Higgins, Paul. *Censorship in Britain.* Wisor 21.7
Okopień, Jan. "Towarzystwo Wydawnicze "Rój"." Pająk 24.18
Olczak-Ronikier, Joanna. *In the Garden of Memory: A Memoir* Pająk 24.23-24n9
Oliver, Kelly. "Service Dogs: Between Animal Studies and Disability Studies." Williams 26.107–08
Ollard, S. L., Gordon Crosse, and Maurice F. Bond, eds. *A Dictionary of English Church History.* Wisor 21.15, 17
Ortega y Gasset, José. *Obras completes* Novillo-Corvalán 23.43
Østergaard, Edvin. "Darwin and Wagner: Evolution and Aesthetic Appreciation." Davison 23.3n5, 26
Outka, Elizabeth. *Consuming Traditions: Modernity, Modernism, and the Commodified Authentic*. Adair & Martin 24.88
Owens, Louis. '"The Very Essence of Our Lives': Leslie Silko's Webs of Identity." Czarnecki 21.60, 68, 69, 70, 72
Oxford English Dictionary. Livingstone 26.93
OED. Collins, n2. Clarke 28.7n5
OED. dress, v. Graber 24.175n8
OED. duffle. Graber 24.173
OED. grating, n2. Gilman 29.54n26
OED. heatwave. Ryan 30.79n22
OED. paduasoy. Graber 24.179
Ozick, Cynthia, "Dictation." *Dictation: A Quartet.* Layne 21.78n1
Panicacci, Jean-Louis. "Le temps des Pénuries (1939–1949) dans les Alpes-Maritimes." *Cahiers de la Méditerranée*. Davison 29.141n2
Pantazzi, Michael. "Tutankhamen and Art Deco." *Egyptomania* (Muir, ed.). Rutherford 24.154
Parini, Jay. *Some Necessary Angels* Layne 21.69
Parker, S. Emily. *From the Devotional Diary*

of a Relief Worker in Spain. Foster 22.59
Parrinder, Patrick. "Revisiting Suvin's Poetics of Science Fiction." Livingstone 26.91n5
Patton, Ventria K. and Maureen Honey, eds. *Double-take: A Revisionist Anthology of the Harlem Renaissance*. Caputi 29.6n2
Paul, Lissa. "Enigma Variations: What Feminist Theory Knows about Children's Literature." Williams 26.108
Payne, Emma M. *Casting the Parthenon Sculptures from the Eighteenth Century to the Digital Age*. Bunting 30.9n2, 20
Peacock, John. "Unwriting Empire by Writing Oral Tradition: Leslie Marmon Silko's *Ceremony.*" Czarnecki 21.59
Peat, F. David. *Blackfoot Physics*. Czarnecki 21.59n9
Perry, Gill. *Women Artists and Parisian Avant-Garde*. Jenkins (Amber) 27.16
Perry, R. B. and C. R. Perkins. *World Mapping Today*. Gillespie 25.105n19
Peterson, Sandra. *Socrates and Philosophy in the Dialogues of Plato*. Dalgarno 22.10n12
Petre, Jonathan. *By Sex Divided: The Church of England and Women Priests.* Wisor 21.19, 19n31
Phillips, Adam. *On Flirtation: Psychoanalytic Essays on the Uncommitted Life*. Van Wert 29.110
Phillips. *The Beast in the Nursery: On Curiosity and Other Appetites*. Van Wert 29.116
Piazza, Jo, narrator. *Under the Influence* (podcast series). Berkowitz 29.136n14
Pinkney, Tony. Introduction. *The Politics of Modernism* (Williams). Adair & Martin 24.76n3
Pintér, Károly. *The Anatomy of Utopia: Narration, Estrangement and Ambiguity in More, Wells, Huxley and Clarke*. Livingstone 26.93
Politis, Vasilis. "Aporia and Searching in the Early Plato." Dalgarno 22.2, 5
Pollard, Francis E. *War and Human Values*. Foster 22.52, 62, 67
Polo, Marco. *The Travels of Marco Polo the Venetian*. Gillespie 25.106
Potter, Simon J. *Wireless Internationalism & Distant Learning*. Davison 29.142
Pratt, Mary Louise. Imperial Eyes: *Travel Writing and Transculturation* Novillo-Corvalán 23.37, 42
Proctor, Tammy M. '"A Separate Path': Scouting and Guiding in Interwar South Africa." Wisor 21.11, 13
Pyne, Stephen J. *Fire: A Brief History*. Ryan 30.68, 81
Pyne. *The Pyrocene*. Ryan 30.68–69; 70n10, 73, 77
Pytlak, Magdalena. "Polish Women Translators outside the Canon. On a Forgotten Translation of Dostoyevsky's *The Devils*." Pająk 24.18
Quennet, Fabienne C. *Where "Indians" Fear to Tread?: A Postmodern Reading of Louise Erdrich s North Dakota Quartet.* Czarnecki 21.50n1
Quigley, Megan. *Modernist Fiction and Vagueness: Philosophy, Form, and Language.* Golden 23.91-92n17
Rádo, Sandor. *The Atlas of To-Day and To-Morrow*. Gillespie 25.103–04
Ramazani, Jahan. *Poetry of Mourning: The Modern Elegy from Hardy to Heaney* Bunting 30.11, 12; Shin 23.112n9, n10
Raphael, Linda S. *Narrative Skepticism: Moral Agency and Representations of Consciousness in Fiction* Bond 23.73n16
Rasula, Jed. "Endless Melody." Davison 23.5n10, 26
Rasula. "Make It New." Gallego Larrarte 30.113n3
Ratcliffe, S. K. *The Roots of Violence*. Foster 22.51
Read, Herbert. *Phases of English Poetry*.

Sullam 30.119
Reed, Conor Tomas. "'Q. And babies? A. And babies': On Pacifism, Visual Trauma, and the Body Heap." Wisor 21.3n7
Reeve-Tucker, Alice and Nathan Waddell, eds. *Utopianism, Modernism, and Literature in the Twentieth Century*. Livingstone 26.89
Reeves, Nicholas. *The Complete Tutankhamun: The King, The Tomb, The Royal Treasure*. Rutherford 24.146
Rice, David A. "Witchery, Indigenous Resistance, and Urban Space in Leslie Mannon Silko's *Ceremony.*" Czarnecki 21.60, 67
Rich, Adrienne. "Toward a More Feminist Criticism." Delsandro 25.93
Rich. "What Does a Woman Need to Know?" Delsandro 25.91
Rich. "When We Dead Awaken: Writing as Re-Vision." Delsandro 25.92; Kotler 24.41, 44
Richmond, Marsha L. "The 1909 Darwin Celebration. Reexamining Evolution in the Light of Mendel, Mutation and Meosis." Davison 23.3
Rieder, John. "Fiction, 1895–1926." Livingstone 26.90
Riggs, Christina. "Tutankhamun Goes to the Fair." *Photographing Tutankhamun* (blog). McVicker 28.82
Riley, Matthew, editor. *British Music and Modernism* Davison 23.4n9
Rocchi, Fernando. *Chimneys in the Desert: Industrialization in Argentina during the Export Boom Years* Novillo-Corvalán 23.43
Roemer, Kenneth M. "Paradise Transformed: Varieties of Nineteenth Century Utopias." Cheney 24.61n10
Rogers, Gayle. *Modernism and the New Spain.* Foster 22.50n20; Novillo-Corvalán 23.35
Rose, Gillian. *Feminism and Geography*. Gillespie 25.112
Rose, Jacqueline. "To Die One's Own Death." Van Wert 29.118
Rose, Marika. *A Theology of Failure: Žižek* Against Christian Innocence. Van Wert 29.111, 119
Rose, Sam. *Art and Form: From Roger Fry to Global Modernism*. Berkowitz 29.127n5
Rosenthal, Michael. *The Character Factory: Baden-Powell and the Origins of the Boy Scout Movement.* Wisor 21.10, 11, 12n22, 13, 14
Ross, Ellen. *Love and Toil: Motherhood in Outcast London.* Wisor 21.11, 11n19
Roston, Murray. *Renaissance Perspectives in Literature and the Visual Arts*. Ke 29.65
Rothman, Roger. "On Beauty," Shin 23.113
Rowe, M. W. "Arnold, Plato, Socrates." Dalgarno 22.3
Rowse, A. L. *Homosexuals in History: A Study of Ambivalence in Society, Literature and Arts*. Rutherford 24.141
Rummel, Andrea. "People in the Crowd: British Modernism, the Metropolis, and the Flâneur." Bond 23.64n2
Ruoff, A. Lavonne Brown. "Introduction to American Indian Literatures." Czarnecki 21.53n5
Ruskin, John. *The Works of John Ruskin* (Cook and Wedderburn, eds.). Schwartz 29.89, 96
Ruskin and Henry W. Acland. *The Oxford Museum*. Schwartz 29.89
Ryland, Dadie. *Words and Poetry*. Sullam 30.119
Rytlowa, Jadwiga. "Rodzina Wołków." Pająk 24.24n9
Sacks, Oliver. *Musicophilia* Davison 23.2n3
Said, Edward. "Yeats and Decolonization." Novillo-Corvalán 23.37
Said. *Culture and Imperialism* Novillo-Corvalán 23.46
Salaman, Malcolm C. Introduction [*Arthur Briscoe*]. Rutherford 24.141n2
Salter, Sir Arthur. *Economic Policies and*

Peace. Foster 22.51
Savage, Roger. *Masques, Mayings and Music-Dramas: Vaughan Williams and the Early Twentieth-Century Stage*. Lauby 27.48
Scalabrini Ortiz, Raúl. *Historia de los ferrocarriles argentinos.* Novillo-Corvalán 23.49
Scheman, Naomi. "Anger and the Politics of Naming." Kotler 24.38
Schlegel, August Wilhelm. *A Course of Lectures on Dramatic Art and Literature*. Ke 29.68n12
Schlegel. *Lectures on Literature and Art*. Ke 29.68n12
Schwartz, John Pedro. "'In greater support of his word': Monument and Museum Discourse in *Finnegans Wake*." Schwartz 29.93n6
Schwartz. "Object Lessons: Teaching Multiliteracies through the Museum." *College English*. Schwartz 29.90n5
Sedgwick, Eve Kosofsky. "Jane Austen and the Masturbating Girl." Clarke 28.14, 15
Sedgwick. *Touching Feeling: Affect, Pedagogy, Performativity*. Clarke 28.13
Sedley, David. *The Midwife of Platonism: Text and Subtext in Plato's* Theaetetus Dalgarno 22.6, 15
Seward, A. C., editor. *Darwin and Modern Science: Essays in Commemoration of the Centenary of the Birth of Charles Darwin and of the Fiftieth Anniversary of the Publication of* The Origin of Species Davison 23.6, 11, 11n19
Shafer, Robert. *The English Ode to 1660: An Essay in Literary History* Shin 23.110n4, n5, 117, 124
Shellard, Dominic and Steve Nicolson, with Miriam Handley. *The Lord Chamberlain Regrets...: A History of British Theatre Censorship.* Wisor 21.8
Shih Shumei. *The Lure of the Modern: Writing Modernism in Semicolonial China, 1917–1937*. Chua 30.38
Shipley, A. E. and Simpson, J. C., editors. *The Darwin Centenary: The Portraits, Prints and Writings of Charles Robert Darwin Exhibited at Christ's College, Cambridge in 1909* Davison 23.24, 24n36
Shone, Richard. *The Art of Bloomsbury: Roger Fry, Vanessa Bell and Duncan Grant*. Adair & Martin 24.87n12, 91
Shone. *Bloomsbury Portraits: Vanessa Bell, Duncan Grant, and Their Circle* Adair & Martin 24.92
Showalter, Elaine. *The Female Malady: Women, Madness, and English Culture, 1830-1980.* Czarnecki 21.61, 62n12, 63, 64, 64n14, 66
Shuster, G.N. *The English Ode from Milton to Keats* Shin 23.110
Siebers, Tobin. *Disability Theory*. Williams 26.111
Sigurdson, Ola. [On Incarnation.] Van Wert 29.115–16
Silver, Brenda. "Are You a Quaker?" Foster 22.44n8
Simson, Henrietta. "Heterotopia and Perspective: Toward a DIfference Perspective of Landscape." McVicker 28.86n28
Sirén, Osvald. *Essentials in Art*. Ke 29.65n9, 66, 67
Skidelsky, Robert. *John Maynard Keynes Adair & Martin 24.85*
Small Houses and Bungalows Suitable for the Peak District. Jones 22.83
Śmieja, Wojciech. "Boy i homoseksualizm. Literatura, prawo i ten przerażający homoerota we własnej osobie." Pająk 24.18
Śmieja. "'Topografia pożądania' - konstruowanie przestrzeni wokół homoseksualnych bohaterów polskiej prozy międzywojennej (Iwaszkiewicz, Choromański, Gombrowicz, Breza)." Pająk 24.22
Smith-Rosenberg, Carroll. "The Female

World of Love and Ritual." Clarke 28.7, 10
Smocovitis, Vassiliki Betty. "Darwin and his Theory in Song and Musical Production." Davison 23.1n2, 6, 7, 16n25, 16-17
Solnit, Rebecca. *Wanderlust: A HIstory of Walking*. van Straten 30.85, 93
Sontag, Susan. *Regarding the Pain of Others* Kotler 24.49
Snyder, R. Claire. "What is Third Wave Feminism? A New Directions Essay." Delsandro 25.86n18
Spalding, Frances. *Vanessa Bell*. Adair & Martin 24.81, 85, 90, 90n16, 92, 93, 94, 95; Jenkins (Amber) 27.14; Layne 21.82, 97, 102
Spalding. *Roger Fry: Art and Life*. Gillespie 29.151n3
Spelman, Elizabeth V. "Anger and Insubordination." Kotler 24.38, 39, 43, 44, 45
Spivak, Gayatri Chakravorty. *An Aesthetic Education in the Era of Globalization*. Cheney 24.55, 56, 60, 60n7, 67, 69
Spivak. *Readings* Cheney 24.60
Springhall, John. "Baden-Powell and the Scout Movement Before 1920: Citizen Training or Soldiers of the Future?" Wisor 21.12n21
Springhall. "The Boy Scouts, Class and Militarism in Relation to British Youth Movements, 1908-1930." Wisor 21.12n22
Springhall. *Youth, Empire and Society: British Youth Movements, 1883-1940.* Wisor 21.13
Squire, John Collings. *Tricks of the Trade*. Chua 30.42
"St. James's Park." *Britain Express* (online). van Straten 30.89
St. John, Christopher. *Ethel Smyth: A Biography*. Delsandro 25.83
Stam, Robert. *Reflexivity in Film and Literature, From Don Quixote to Jean-Luc Godard* Davison 23.7n14
Stanley, Liz. *The Auto/Biographical I: The Theory and Practice of Feminist Auto/Biography.* Layne 21.79
Stansky, Peter and William Abrahams. *Journey to the Frontier: Two Roads to the Spanish Civil War*. Gallego Larrarte 30.115
Statkiewicz, Max. *Rhapsody of Philosophy: Dialogues with Plato in Contemporary Thought*. Dalgarno 22.2
Stead, Lisa. Introduction. *The Boundaries of the Literary Archive: Reclamation and Representation*. Golden 23.87
Steel, David. *The Art of Sail-Making…* Graber 24.178
Steele, Elizabeth. "Stories for Children." Williams 26.109
Steere, Douglas V. Introduction. *Quaker Spirituality*. Foster 22.46, 46n12, 48n16, 64
Stephen, Caroline Emelia. *Quaker Strongholds*. Foster 22.44, 47, 47n14, 55, 63
Stephen. *Light Arising: Thoughts on the Central Radiance*. Foster 22.44, 44n10, 47, 47n15, 48, 54, 56
Stephen. *The Vision of Faith and Other Essays*. Foster 22.47, 48-9
Stephen, Leslie. "Emerson." *Studies of a Biographer*. Ke 29.69
Stephen. *Studies of a Biographer*. Humm 29.158
Stephens, John S. *Danger Zones of Europe: A Study of National Minorities.* Foster 22.51
Stray, Christopher. "Educational Publishing." Golden 23.99, 99n28
Street, Harry. *Freedom, the Individual, and the Law.* Wisor 21.6
Still, John. "The Childhood of Thought" [Review of Frazer, *Myths*.] Ryan 30.74
Stoler, Laura Ann. "Imperial Debris and Ruination." *Duress*. van Straten 30.89
Suleri, Sara. *The Rhetoric of English India*. Chua 30.34
Sullivan, Anne. "Animating Flames:

Recovering Fire-Gazing as a Moving-Image Technology." Ryan 30.68n4
Summers, Anne. "Militarism in Britain before the Great War." Wisor 21.12n22
Sutcliffe, Peter. *The Oxford University Press: An Informal History*. Golden 23.99
Suvin, Darko. *Metamorphoses of Science Fiction*. Livingstone 26.87, 91, 96n6, 98, 99, 101
Swan, Edith. "Laguna Symbolic Geography and Silko's *Ceremony.*" Czarnecki 21.72
Swanson, Roy Arthur. "The True, the False, and the Truly False: Lucian's Philosophical Science Fiction." Livingstone 26.90
Symons, Arthur. *Figures of Several Centuries*. Sullam 30.117–18
Tagg, John. *The Burden of Representation*. Fouirnaies 22.32
Taggard, Genevieve. *The Life and Mind of Emily Dickinson*. Kopley 30.127
Tallents, Sir Stephen. *The Projection of England* Wisor 21.8
Tally, Jr., Robert T. Introduction. *Literary Cartographies*. Gillespie 25.112
Tally, Jr., *Spatiality*. Gillespie 25.111, 112, 116
Tally, Jr., ed. *Literary Cartographies: Spatiality, Representation, and Narrative*. Gillespie 25.112
Tarczałowicz, Jacek. *Lucjan Szenwald: życie i twórczość* Pająk 24.24
Taylor, Catherine. "Catherine Taylor's first novel choice - reviews." Layne 21.87
Taylor, Paul Beekman. "Silko's Reappropriation of Secrecy." Czarnecki 21.66
Taylor, Philip M. *The Projection of Britain: British Overseas Publicity and Propaganda, 1919-1939.* Wisor 21.7
Taylor, Sunaura. *Beasts of Burden: Animal and Disability Liberation*. Williams 26.107
Teukolsky, Rachel. *The Literate Eye: Victorian Art Writing and the Prose of Modern Aesthetics*. Berkowitz 29.127
Thacker, Andrew. *Moving Through Modernity: Space and Geography in Modernism*. Bond 23.64; Adair & Martin 24.75, 93
Thomas, Julian. *Archaeology and Modernity*. McVicker 28.70n3, 71, 72, 75
Thoms, David, Len Holden, and Tim Claydon. Introduction. *The Motor Car and Popular Culture in the 20th Century* Adair & Martin 24.75
Thornton, Amara. "The Allure of Archaeology: Agnes Conway and Jane Harrison at Newnham College, 1903–1907." McVicker 28.72n8
Thornton, Tim. Introduction. *The Channel Islands, 1370–1640: Between England and Normandy*. Lauby 27.58n7
Thrower, Norman J. W. *Maps and Man: An Examination of Cartography in Relation to Culture and Civilization.* Gillespie 25.127n47
Tickner, Lisa. *Modern Life and Modern Subjects: British Art in the Early Twentieth Century*. Jenkins (Amber) 27.6, 13n17, 19, 20
Tickner. "Vanessa Bell: Studland Beach, Domesticity, and 'Significant Form.'" Layne 21.84, 101
Times. "Authors and the Law of Libel, Plea for Reform" (13 March 1936). Wisor 21.26n42
Times. "From a Correspondent" (8 July 1911). Ryan 30.80
Times. "Hot Weather and Milk" (11 July 1911). Ryan 30.80
Times. "Effects of the Heat" (22 July 1911). Ryan 30.80
Times. "Heroes Unhorsed" (6 Jan 1936). Wisor 21.32
Times. "The Hottest Day for Thirty Years" (24 July 1911). Ryan 30.80
Times. "Crops and Live Stock" (24 July 1911). Ryan 30.80n24
Times. "Horses' Sufferings from the Heat"

(2 August 1911). Ryan 30.80
Times. "Drought and Thunderstorms" (14 August 1911). Ryan 30.80
Times. "The Great Heat" (14 August 1911). Ryan 30.80n23
Times. "Drought and Sanitation" (14 August 1911). Ryan 30.80n23
Times. "The Heat and Infant Mortality" (17 August 1911). Ryan 30.80n23
Times. "From a Correspondent: The Avebury Circles" (14 Aug 1922). McVicker 28.83
Tobin, Richard. "The Canon of Polykleitos." *American Journal of Archaeology*. Ke 29.66–67
Todd, Jude. "Knotted Bellies and Fragile Webs: Untangling and Re-Spinning in Tayo's Healing Journey." Czarnecki 21.55, 66
Tomasik, Krzysztof. *Homobiografie* Pająk 24.15, 18, 26
Tonks, Nichola. "Obituaries and Obelisks: Egyptianizing Funerary Architecture and the Cemetery as a Heterotopic Space." McVicker 28.70–71n4
Townsend, Kenneth William. *World War II and the American Indian.* Czarnecki 21.58, 60, 60n10, 61-62
Trevelyan, George *M. A Shortened History of England.* McVicker 28.84–85
Trotter, David. "Modernism's Material Futures: Glass, and Several Kinds of Plastic." Adair & Martin 24.77n4
Trotter. "Techno-Primitivism: Á Propos of *Lady Chatterley's Lover*." Adair & Martin 24.76
Turchi, Peter. *Maps of the Imagination: The Writer as Cartographer*. Gillespie 25.111
Umphelby, Fanny. *The Child's Guide to Knowledge*. Jenkins (Gwyn) 27.41
Usick, Patricia. *Adventures in Egypt and Nubia: The Travels of William John Bankes (1786–1855).* Rutherford 24.141, 141
Van Hulle, Dirk. *Modern Manuscripts: The Extended Mind and Creative Undoing from Darwin to Beckett and Beyond* Golden 23.85, 86, 87n12
Verrall, A. W. Introduction. *Ion*. Koulouris 25.3, 14n22
Vicinus, Martha. *Intimate Friends: Women Who Loved Women, 1778–1928.* Clarke 28.10n7, 19n12
Vince, Gaia. *Transcendence: How Humans Evolved through Fire, Language, Beauty and Time*. Ryan 30.69
Vlasopolos, Anca. "Staking Claims for No Territory: The Sea as Woman's Space." *Reconfigured Spheres* (Higonnet and Templeton). Gillespie 25.121
Wade, E. C. S. "Police Powers and Public Meetings." Wisor 21.29n45, 30, 31
Wade, Eileen K. *The Piper of Pax: The Life Story of Sir Robert Baden-Powell.* Wisor 21.11
Wagner, Johanna M. "(Be)Longing in 'Quicksand': Framing Kinship and Desire More Queerly." Caputi 29.16, 18–19
Walker, Ian. *So exotic, so homemade: Surrealism, Englishness, and documentary photography*. Adair & Martin 24.94, 94n17
Walkowitz, Rebecca. "What is the Scale of the Literary Object?" Lostoski-Ho 28.54n13
Walsh, Rebecca. *The Geopoetics of Modernism* Bond 23.64n2
Wang Yiyan. "Fiction in Modern China: Modernity through Storytelling." Chua 30.36
Wańkowicz, Melchior. "Wspomnienia wydawcy." Pająk 24.18, 22-23
Wańkowicz. *Tędy i owędy* Pająk 24.18
Warner, Marina. "Report to the Memoir Club: Scenes from a Colonial Childhood." Wisor 21.3n7
Warren, Allen. "Sir Robert Baden-Powell, the Scout Movement and Citizen." Wisor 21.10, 10n17, 11, 12, 12n20
Warren. "Powell, Robert Stephenson Smyth Baden." Wisor 21.12n22

"Wateler Peace Prize for Lord Baden-Powell." *The Times* 9 Jul. 1937: 15. Wisor 21.14
Watkins, Alfred. *Ancient British Trackways.* McVicker 28.84
Watkins. *The Ley Hunger's Manual.* McVicker 28.84
Watkins. *The Old Straight Track.* McVicker 28.84
Watkins, Susan Cotts. "Social Networks and Social Science History." *Social Science History*. Berkowitz 29.132, 137
Watson, Frederic et. al. *A New & Complete Geographical Dictionary: Containing a Full and Accurate Description of the Several Parts of the Known World as Divided into Continents, Islands, Oceans, Seas, Rivers, Lakes, Etc.* Gillespie 25.102, 113, 114, 120, 121
Watson, J. N. P. *Through Fifteen Reigns: A Complete History of the Household Cavalry.* Wisor 21.33, 34, 35
Weber, Gary. "Henry Labouchere, 'Truth' and the New Journalism of Late Victorian Britain." Novillo-Corvalán 23.52
Welland, Sasha Su-Ling. *A Thousand Miles of Dreams: The Journeys of Two Chinese Sisters*. Chua 30.37
Wetherell, Charles. "Historical Social Network Analysis." *International Review of Social History*. Berkowitz 29.132, 137
White, Andrea. "Conrad and Imperialism." Novillo-Corvalán 23.37
Whitehead, Kate. "Broadcasting Bloomsbury." *The Year of English Studies*. Berkowitz 29.133–34n10, 135
Wielgoławska, Alicja. *Dziennikarze. Byli wśród nas. Są z nami*. Pająk 24.24n9
Wilde, Niels. "Anthropocene Horcruxes: Toward a Theory of Distributed Identities." Ryan 30.68
Wilford, John Noble. *The Mapmakers*. Gillespie 25.111
Wilkinson, Alan. *Oxford Dictionary of National Biography.* Wisor 21.15, 16, 16n27, 17
Williams, D. G. T. "Preventive Action and Public Order: The Principle of *Thomas* v. *Sawkins*." Wisor 21.29, 29n45
Williams, Erika Renée. "A Lie of Omission: Plagiarism in Nella Larsen's *Quicksand*." Caputi 29.7n5
Williams-Ellis, Clough. *England and the Octopus*. Jones 22.84, 85
Williamson, Philip. "Baldwin's Reputation: Politics and History, 1937-1967." Wisor 21.20, 20n33
Williamson. *Stanley Baldwin: Conservative Leadership and National Values.* Wisor 21.21, 22n35, 25
Winckelmann, Johann Joachim. *History of Ancient Art*. Rutherford 24.154n6
Wise, Sarah. *The Blackest Streets: The Life and Death of a Victorian Slum* Bond 23.64n1
Withington, Robert. *English Pageantry: An Historical Outline, vol 2.* Lauby 27.48
Wolf, Naomi. *The Beauty Myth*. Delsandro 25.75n4
Wolfe, Cary. *What is Posthumanism?* Williams 26.107
"Women at Cambridge, New Buildings for Girton." *The Times* 31 Oct. 1930: 10. Wisor 21.24
Woodall, Joanna. *Portraiture: Facing the Subject*. Fouirnaies 22.29n4
"Wooley's Excavations." *Ur-Online: The British Museum and Penn Museum* (website). McVicker 28.79
Worth, Aaron. "The Imperial Transmissions: H. G. Wells, 1897–1901." Livingstone 26.100
Wright, Winthrop R. *British-Owned Railways in Argentina: Their Effect on Economic Nationalism* Novillo-Corvalán 23.43
Wynne-Davies, Marion. "The Queen's Masque: Renaissance Women and the Seventeenth-Century Court Masque."

Lauby 27.50
Vickery, John B. *The Prose Elegy: An Exploration of Modern American and British Fiction* Shin 23.111, 111n7
Zalasiewicz, Jan et. al. "Petrifying Earth Process: The Stratigraphic Imprint of Key Earth System Parameters in the Anthropocene." Lostoski-Ho 28.52n9
Zawada, Andrzej. *Dwudziestolecie literackie* Pająk 24.22, 25
Zawiszewska, Agata. Życie świadome Pająk 24.17, 26, 27, 29
Zeiger, Melissa F. *Beyond Consolation: Death, Sexuality, and the Changing Shapes of Elegy*. Bunting 30.11
Qian, Zhaoming. *Modernism and Orientalism*. Chua 30.34
Z., Y. *From Moscow to Samarkand.* Gillespie 25.102
Ziółkowska-Boehm, Aleksandra. *Na tropach Wańkowicza po latach* Pająk 24.20
Žižek, Slavoj. *Less Than Nothing: Hegel and the Shadow of Dialectical Materialism*. Van Wert 29.110n5–6, 111
Zlatkin, Rachel. "The Flesh of Citizenship: Red Flowers Grew." Czarnecki 21.54
Zonana, Joyce. "*Swinburne's Sappho: The Muse as Sister-Goddess*." Shin 23.119
Zupančič, Alenka. "Ontology and the Death Drive: Lacan and Deleuze." Van Wert 29.111–12

2C: Woolf/Woolf-Adjacent Scholarship (VW = Virginia Woolf)

Abel, Elizabeth. *VW and the Fictions of Psychoanalysis*. Rutherford 24.135
Adams, David. *Colonial Odysseys: Empire and Epic in the Modernist Novel.* McVicker 28.81n20, 87
Adair, Robin and Ann Martin. "A Driving Bloomsbury: VW, Vanessa Bell, and the Meaning of the Motor-Car." Gillespie 25.99n4
Adkins, Peter. "Bloomsbury and Nature." Jenkins (Amber) 27.14n18
Adkins. *The Modernist Anthropocene*. Ryan 30.69
Adkins, ed. *VW and the Anthropocene*. Ryan 30.69
Allan, Tuzyline Jita. "The Death of Sex and the Soul in *MD* and Nella Larsen's *Passing*." Bond 23.76n17
Allègre, Marie. *VW Beyond Psychoanalysis.* Favre 30.54
Allen, Annette. "VW's Spirituality: 'We are the words; we are the music.'" Foster 22.42, 55n33
Allen, Judith. "Feminist Politics: 'Repetition' and 'Burning' in *TG* (Making It New)." Ryan 30.69n8
Allen. *VW and the Politics of Language*. Leach 28.99
Alley, Henry M. "A Rediscovered Eulogy: VW's 'Miss Janet Case: Classical Scholar and Teacher.'" Dalgarno 22.3n3; Jenkins (Gwyn) 27.23, 37
Alt, Christina. "VW and the Anticipations of the Anthropocene." Ryan 30.69
Alt. *VW and the Study of Nature.* Czarnecki 21.52n3; 23.7n15; Livingstone 26.88n2; Lostoski-Ho 28.50–51; Novillo-Corvalán 23.50
Amidon, Stevens. "*TY*: Mapping a Genre." Cheney 24.59n6
Andrews, Charles. "'beauty, simplicity, and peace': Faithful Pacifism, Activist Writing & *TY*." Foster 22.67; Cheney 24.57n1
Andrews. *Writing Against War: Literature, Activism, and the British Peace Movement.* Delsandro 25.76
Andrews, Kerri. "VW." *Wanderers: A History of Women Walking*. van Straten 30.85n1, 86
Anspaugh, Kelly. "Circe Resartus: *TTL* and William Browne of Tavistock's *Circe and Ulysses* Masque." Lauby 27.59
Apuleius. *The Golden Ass of Apuleius*. Rutherford 24.155
Armstrong, Phillip. "Why Phaedrus? Plato in VW's Novel *JR*." *Nordic Journal of English Studies*. Ke 29.79n17

Arrington, Phillip. "A Most Copious Digression: An Erasmian Analysis of the Rhetoric of VW's Comments on Letters in *JR*." Ke 29.65n10

Atkin, Jonathan. *A War of Individuals: Bloomsbury Attitudes to the Great War*. Berkowitz 29.127n6

Bahun, Sanja. *Modernism & Melancholia: Writing as Countermourning*. Foster 22.5n33, 60n38; Van Wert 29.112, 117, 119

Bahun. "Woolf and Psychoanalytic Theory." *VW in Context* (Randall and Goldman, eds.). Van Wert 29.109

Banfield, Ann. *The Phantom Table: W, Fry, Russell, and the Epistemology of Modernism*. Jenkins (Amber) 27.5; Layne 21.84, 93, 98, 99

Banfield. *Unspeakable Sentences: Narration and Representation in the Language of Fiction*. Sullam 30.121n4

Banks, Joanne Trautmann. "The Editor as Ethicist." Phillips 26.9

Banks. "Through a Glass, Longingly." Bond 23.74

Barr, Tina. "Divine Politics: VW's Journey toward Eleusis in *TTL*." *boundary 2*. Rutherford 24.142n4

Barrett, Eileen. "Indecency: *JR*, Modernist Homosexuality, and the Culture of War." Bunting 30.12, 16; Van Wert 29.120

Barrett. Introduction. *VW Lesbian Readings* Layne 21.89

Barrett. "Matriarchal Myth on a Patriarchal Stage: VW's *BTA*." McVicker 28.71n7, 75n11

Barrett. "Septimus and Shadrack: Woolf and Morrison Envision the Madness of War." Czarnecki 21.51n2

Barrett. "Unmasking Lesbian Passion: The Inverted World of *MD*." Bond 23.76n17

Barrett, Michèle. "VW's Research for Empire and Commerce in Africa (Leonard Woolf, 1920)." Gillespie 25.104n16; Novillo-Corvalán 23.33, 58

Batchelor, John. *VW: The Major Novels*. Novillo-Corvalán 23.36

Bazin, Nancy. *VW and the Androgynous Vision*. Favre 30.58

Bell, Anne Olivier. Introduction. *D1*. Koulouris 25.4

Bell, Quentin. Afterword to *The Widow and the Parrot*. Williams 26.105

Bell. "*AROO* and *TG*." *VW and Fascism: Resisting the Dictators' Seduction*. Wisor 21.3n7

Bell. *Bloomsbury Recalled*. Adair & Martin 24.82; Layne 21.94

Bell. *VW: A Biography*. Adair & Martin 24.80; Davison 23.26; Delsandro 25.76; Favre 30.55; Jenkins (Gwyn) 27.35–36, 38; Layne 21.89; Lostoski-Ho 28.63n27; Rutherford 24.141; Shin 23.136

Beer, Gillian. *Arguing with the Past: Essays in Narrative from W to Sidney*. McVicker 28.89–90

Beer. "Hume, Stephen, and Elegy in *TTL*." Shin 23.111n7, 123n22, 124

Beer. "The Island and the Aeroplane: The Case of VW." Gillespie 25.118

Beer. "Physics, Sound, and Substance: Later W." Fischer 28.27

Beer. *VW: The Common Ground*. Lostoski-Ho 28.50n6

Beer. "'Wireless': Popular Physics, Radio and Modernism." *Cultural Babbage* (Spufford and Uglow, eds.). Davison 29.144

Berman, Jessica. "Intimate and Global: Ethical Domains from Woolf to Rhys." Kotler 24.42, 51

Bishop, Edward L. "The Alfa and the *Avant-Texte*: Transcribing VW's Manuscripts." Phillips 26.9

Bishop. "Getting a Hold on Haddock: VW's Inks." Gillespie 25.116n33

Bishop. Introduction [*JR: The Holograph*]. Ke 29.72n16

Bishop. "The Shaping of *JR*: Woolf's Manuscript Revisions." Bunting 30.11

Bishop. "Toward the Far Side of Language:

VW's *VO.*" Fischer 28.27n5, 30–31
Bishop, ed. *JR: The Holograph Drafts.* Bunting 30.5, 24
Black, Naomi. Introduction. *TG.* By VW. Wisor 21.3n7, 4n10
Black. "'Not a Novel, They Said': Editing VW's *TG.*" *Editing Women.* Wisor 21.2n5, 3n6
Black. *VW as Feminist.* Favre 30.60, 61
Blotner, Joseph L. "Mythic Patterns in *TTL.*" *PMLA.* Rutherford 24.142n4, 158
Blyth, Ian. "*O* and the Tudor Voyages." *Locating Woolf: The Politics of Space and Place* (Snaith and Whitworth, eds.). Graber 24.175n9
Bowlby, Rachel. "Jacob's Type." *VW: Feminist Destinations.* Van Wert 29.117–18
Bowlby. *VW: Feminist Destinations.* Dalgarno 22.8; Favre 30.56; 38n16; Schwartz 29.102
Bowlby. "Walking, Women and Writing." Gillespie 25.107n24
Bonikowski, Wyatt. *Shell Shock and the Modernist Imagination: The Death Drive in Post-World War I British Fiction.* Czarnecki 21.57, 58, 73
Bradshaw, David. "'Tut, Tut': Censorship, Propriety and Obscenity in *VO.*" Novillo-Corvalán 23.38
Bradshaw. "'Vanished, Like Leaves': The Military, Elegy and Italy in *MD.*" Bunting 30.8
Bradshaw, ed. *Carlyle's House and Other Sketches* [VW]. Schwartz 29.89n3
Breckin, Tom. "Hours in a Library: VW and Leslie Stephen." De Gay 30.101n2
Briggs, Julia. "'Almost Ashamed of England Being so English': Woolf and Ideas of Englishness." Lauby 27.53
Briggs. "Between the Texts: VW's Acts of Revision." Kopley 30.125
Briggs. *VW: An Inner Life.* De Gay 30.99n1, 103; Wisor 21.3, 3n7, 32
Brockington, Grace. *Above the Battlefield: Modernism and the Peace Movement in Britain, 1900–1918.* Reed 29.164
Brosnan, Leila. "'Words Fail Me': VW and the Wireless." Fischer 28.25n2
Brown, Bill. "The Secret Life of Things (VW and the Matter of Modernism)." Golden 23.83n1; Schwartz 29.102
Brown, Stephanie. Favre 30.61
Burton, Diane. *An Aesthetic of Witness: The Interaction of Photographs and Nonfiction Prose in George Orwell's* The Road to Wigan Pier, *James Agee and Walker Evans's* Let Us Now Praise Famous Men, *and VW's* TG. Wisor 21.3n7
Caputi Daileader, Celia R. "Othello's Sister: Racial Hermaphroditism and Appropriation in VW's *O.*" Caputi 29.15n12, 23
Caracciolo, Marco. "Cosmic Time and the Rhythm of Narrative." Lostoski-Ho 28.49n5
Carver, Katelynn. "Behind the Cotton Wool: Process Philosophy in the Works of VW." Foster 22.56n30
Caughie, Pamela. "Feminist Woolf." Favre 30.61
Caughie. *VW and Postmodernism: Literature in Quest & Question of Itself.* Dalgarno 22.15; Fischer 28.28n9; Shin 23.134n26
Caughie. "VW: Radio, Gramophone, Broadcasting." van Straten 30.86n3
Caughie et. al., eds. *W Online.* De Gay 30.99n1; Jenkins (Amber) 27.5n3
Caws, Mary Ann and Sarah Bird Wright. *Bloomsbury and France: Art and Friends.* Adair & Martin 24.80n6, 82, 85; Berkowitz 29.126n3
Chan, Evelyn Tsz Yan. *VW and the Professions.* Livingstone 26.96
Chapman, Wayne K. "Collaborative Reviewing by Leonard and VW." Gillespie 25.104n16
Chapman and Janet M. Manson. "Carte and Tierce: Leonard, VW, and War for Peace." Gillespie 25.104n16
Chesler, Phyllis. *Women and Madness.* Favre 30.58

Chun, Maureen. "Between Sensation and Sign: The Secret Language of *TW*." Fischer 28.27n6
Clarke, Stuart N. "The Lord Chief Justice and the Woolfs." Wisor 21.26, 32
Clarke. "The Horse with a Green Tail." Wisor 21.39n57
Clarke. "VW's Broadcasts and Her Recorded Voice." Fischer 28.26n3
Clements, Susan. "The Point of 'Slater's Pins': Misrecognition and the Narrative Closet." Jenkins (Gwyn) 27.33
Clewell, Tammy. "Consolation Refused: VW, The Great War, and Modernist Mourning." McVicker 28.71n5; Van Wert 29.117
Coates, Kimberly Engdahl. "Phantoms, Fancy (and) Symptoms: VW and the Art of Being Ill." Dalgarno 22.9n10
Coates. "Photographing Violence: *TG* and Contemporary Feminist Responses to Images of War." Wisor 21.3n8
Cole, Sarah. *At the Violet Hour: Modernism and Violence in England and Ireland.* Bunting 30.15–16
Colla, Elliott. *Conflicted Antiquities: Egyptology, Egyptomania, Egyptian Modernity*. McVicker 28.71n7, 79, 81, 82n23
Collier, Patrick. *Modernism on Fleet Street*. Gilman 29.47n8
Collins, Judith. *The Omega Workshops*. Gillespie 29.151n4
Connor, Steven. "VW, the Baby, and the Bathwater" (online). Ryan 30.78n20
Cook, Blanche Wiesen. "'Women Alone Stir My Imagination': Lesbianism and the Cultural Tradition." Clarke 28.14n10
Cordery, Lindsey. "VW and South America: Border-Reading." Gillespie 25.120n39
Courington, Chella. "Virginia Woolf and Alice Walker: Family as Metaphor in the Personal Essay." Czarnecki 21.51
Crossland, Rachel. *Modernist Physics*. Livingstone 26.88n2
Cuddy-Keane, Melba. "'Collateral Truths': Global and International Discourse in VW, T. S. Eliot, and Sir Thomas Browne." McVicker 28.85n27
Cuddy-Keane. Introduction and Notes (*BTA*). Foster 22.59n35, 60, 63, 66
Cuddy-Keane. "Mind-wandering and Mindfulness: A Cognitive Approach to *MD* and *TTL*." van Straten 30.85n1, 91, 92, 93
Cuddy-Keane. "Modernist Soundscapes and the Intelligent Ear: An Approach to Narrative Through Auditory Perception." van Straten 30.86n3
Cuddy-Keane. "Movement, Space, and Embodied Cognition in *TTL*." van Straten 30.86
Cuddy-Keane. "The Rhetoric of Feminist Conversation: Virginia Woolf and the Trope of the Twist." Czarnecki 21.52n3
Cuddy-Keane. *VW, The Intellectual and the Public Sphere*. Dalgarno 22.1n1, 15n14; Delsandro 25.93; Favre 30.60; Golden 23.84n4; Jenkins (Gwyn) 27.34
Cunningham, Anne. "Negative Feminism and Anti-Development in VW's *VO*." Caputi 29.6n3, 15n13
Cunningham, Michael. Introduction [*VO*]. Caputi 29.21
Curtis, Vanessa. *VW's Women*. Clarke 28.8
Czarnecki, Kristin. "Two-Spirits and Gender Variance in VW's *O* and Louise Erdrich's *The Last Report on the Miracles at Little No Horse*." Czarnecki 21.50n1
Czarnecki. "VW, Authorship, and Legacy: Unravelling Nurse Lugton's Curtain." Williams 26.106
Czarnecki, and Vara Neverow, eds. *Woolf and Animals*. VW Miscellany. Czarnecki 21.52n3; Davison 23.7n15, 13n21
Czarnecki and Carrie Rohman, eds. *Virginia Woolf and the Natural World: Selected Papers from the Twentieth Annual International Conference on Virginia*

Woolf. Czarnecki 21.52n3
Dalgarno, Emily. *VW and the Migrations of Language*. Dalgarno 22.8n9; Golden 23.86, 98n24; McVicker 28.71n5, 76n14
Dalgarno. *VW and the Visible World.* Bunting 30.18; Jenkins (Gwyn) 27.27; Ke 29.64–65n9; Schwartz 29.88, 91; Wisor 21.3n9, 5
Daugherty, Beth Rigel. "Chronological List of Essays by VW Published Only in U.S. (lifetime and posthumous publication noted)." *VW Miscellany.* Sullam 30.119n3
Daugherty. "Feminist Approaches." Favre 30.57, 61, 63; Gilman 29.31–32n14
Daugherty. "Learning VW: Of Leslie, Libraries, and Letters." Gillespie 25.113n32
Daugherty. "A Library of Her Own: Virginia Stephen's Books." Golden 23.83n3
Daugherty. "Mary Sheepshanks, V Stephen, and Morley College: Learning to Teach, Learning to Write." Chua 30.41–42
Daugherty. "Teaching W/W Teaching." Jenkins (Gwyn) 27.24
Daugherty. *VW's Apprenticeship: Becoming an Essayist.* Chua 30.41; De Gay 30.101
Davidson, Michael. *Invalid Modernism: Disability and the Missing Body of the Aesthetic*. Williams 26.111
Davis, Thomas. *The Extinct Scene*. Delsandro 25.76, 77, 77–78n9, 78, 79, 82, 89, 91, 93
Davis. "The Historical Novel and History's End: VW's *TY.*" Delsandro 25.75, 76, 77, 78, 79, 82, 89, 91, 93
De Gay, Jane. *VW's Novels and the Literary Past*. De Gay 30.99n1; Pająk 24.31; Ryan 30.71n12, 75
De Gay. "Challenging the Family Script: Woolf, the Stephen Family, and Victorian Evangelical Theology." Foster 22.42n3
DeKoven, Marianne. *Rich and Strange: Gender, History, Modernism*. Caputi 29.6n3; 9n8, 13; Fischer 28.37, 40n19
Delorey, Denise. "Parsing the Female Sentence: The Paradox of Containment in Virginia Woolf's Narratives." Czarnecki 21.52n3
Delsandro, Erica Gene. "Flights of Imagination: Aerial Views, Narrative Perspectives, and Global Perceptions." Gillespie 25.118
Delsandro. "Modernism and Memorials: VW and Christopher Isherwood." Delsandro 25.77n7
DeMeester, Karen. "Trauma and Recovery in Virginia Woolf's *MD.*" Czarnecki 21.54, 57, 63, 66, 71n20
DeSalvo, Louise. Introduction [*MEL*]. Caputi 29.12–13
DeSalvo. "Sorting, Sequencing, and Dating the Drafts of VW's *VO.*" Davison 23.5n11
DeSalvo. *VW: The Impact of Childhood Sexual Abuse on her Life and Work.* Layne 21.88
DeSalvo. *VW's First Voyage: A Novel in the Making*. Fischer 28.41
Detloff, Madelyn. "Gender Please, Without the Gender Police: Rethinking Pain in Archetypal Narratives of Butch, Transgender, and FtM Masculinity." Pająk 24.12, 12n7
Detloff. *The Persistence of Modernism: Loss and Mourning in the Twentieth Century*. McVicker 28.71n5
Detloff. *The Value of Virginia Woolf.* Clarke 28.13n9
Detloff. "W and Crip Theory." Favre 30.63
Detloff. "W and Lesbian Culture: Queering Woolf Queering." Clarke 28.6n1
Detloff and Brenda Helt. "Queering Woolf—An Introduction." Clarke 28.6n1
DiBattista, Maria. "VW's Winter's Tale." Shin 23.111n7, 122n21, 124
Dick, Susan. Introduction. *TTL*. Jenkins (Amber) 27.9n8, 11
Dick. "The Tunnelling Process: Some

Aspects of VW's Use of Memory and the Past." Bond 23.65; McVicker 28.87
Dickey, Colin. "VW and Photography." Wisor 21.3n6, n7
Dickinson, Renée. "Exposure and Development: Re-Imagining Narrative and Nation in the Interludes of *TW*." Lostoski-Ho 28.48n2
Diment, Galya. *The Autobiographical Novel of Co-Consciousness: Goncharov, Woolf, and Joyce*. Bond 23.65n4
Dirschauer, Marlene. *Modernist Waterscapes: Water, Imagination and Materiality in the Works of VW*. Ryan 30.68n2, 81n27
Douglas, Erin. "Queering Flowers, Queering Pleasures in 'Slater's Pins Have No Points.'" Jenkins (Gwyn) 27.33
Doyle, Laura. "Transnational History at Our Backs: A Long View of Larsen, W, and Queer Racial Subjectivity in Atlantic Modernism." Caputi 29.6, 8, 9, 10
Driscoll, Leonard. *The Archaeological Encounter in British Fiction, 1880–1940*. McVicker 28.70n2
Dubino, Jeanne. "Engendering Voyages in VW's Fiction." *Voyages Out, Voyages Home* (De Gay and Dell, eds.). Graber 24.167
Dubino. "From 'Greece 1906' to '[A Dialogue upon Mount Pentelicus]': From Diary Entry to Traveler's Tale." Golden 23.83n4, 100
Dubino. Introduction. *VW and the Literary Marketplace*. Adair & Martin 24.87
Duffy, Julia and Lloyd Davis. "Demythologizing Facts and Photographs in *TG*." Wisor 21.3n6, 4n10
Dunlap, Sara. "'One Must be Scientific': Natural History and Ecology in *MD*." *Interdisciplinary/Multidisciplinary W* (Martin and Holland, eds.). van Straten 30.91n9, 93n12
Dunn, Jane. *VW and Vanessa Bell: A Very Close Conspiracy*. Adair & Martin 24.77, 95; Jenkins (Amber) 27.13n16; Layne 21.82, 88, 90
Dusinberre, Juliet. *VW's Renaissance: Woman Reader or Common Reader?* Foster 22.45n11; Leach 28.99
Edmondson, Annalee. "Narrativizing Characters in *MD*." Bond 23.71
Ellis, Steve. *British Writers and Approaches of World War II*. Livingstone 26.90
Ellis. "VW and the Theatre of War." Foster 22.63n43
Esty, Jed. *A Shrinking Island: Modernism and National Culture in England*. Delsandro 25.76; Lauby 27.47–48
Esty. *Unseasonable Youth: Modernism, Colonialism, and the Fictions of Development*. Bunting 30.12; Gillespie 25.120n38, 121n41
Esty. "VW's Colony and the Adolescence of Modernist Fiction." Novillo-Corvalán 23.39
Falcetta, Jennie-Rebecca. "Geometries of Space and Time: The Cubist London of MD." Bond 23.64n3
Fand, Roxanne J. *The Dialogic Self: Reconstructing Subjectivity in W, Lessing, and Atwood*. Ryan 30.72n13
Fernald, Anne E. "A Room, A Child, A Mind of One's Own: VW, Alice Walker, and Feminist Personal Criticism." Czarnecki 21.51n2
Fernald. *VW: Feminism and the Reader* Bond 23.65n4; Bunting 30.13; Cheney 24.55; Golden 23.83n1, 83n4, 86, 88n14; McVicker 28.85n27
Ferrer, Daniel. *VW and the Madness of Language*. Fischer 28.27n5
Flesher, Erika. "Picturing the Truth in Fiction: Re-visionary Biography and the Illustrative Portraits for *O*." Fouirnaies 22.22
Flint, Kate. "Reading Uncommonly: VW and the Practice of Reading." Jenkins (Amber) 27.7n4
Flint. "Revising *JR*: VW, Women, and Language." Bunting 30.15; Fischer

28.27n7
Forster, E. M. "The Novels of VW." Gillespie 25.111; Novillo-Corvalán 23.34; Shin 23.114
Foster, J. Ashley. "Recovering Pacifisms Past: Modernist Networks, the Society of Friends, and the Peace Movement of the Spanish Civil War." Foster 22.44n7, 51, 51n22
Foster. "Writing in the 'White Light of Truth': History, Ethics, and Community in VW's *BTA*." Livingstone 26.90
Fouirnaies, Christine. "Was VW a Snob? The Case of Aristocratic Portraits in *O*." Graber 24.176
Fowler, Regina. "Moments and Metamorphoses: VW's Greece." Dalgarno 22.1n1
Fox, Alice. *VW and the Literature of the English Renaissance*. Graber 24.167, 168, 175n9, 176n10
Frattarola, Angela. "Developing an Ear for the Modernist Novel: VW, Dorothy Richardson, and James Joyce." van Straten 30.86n3
Freedman, Ariela. *Death, Men, and Modernism: Trauma and Narrative in British Fiction from Hardy to Woolf.* Czarnecki 21.62n11, 66
Friedman, Susan Stanford. *Mappings: Feminism and the Cultural Geographies of Encounter*. Chua 30.33–34; Gillespie 25.111
Friedman. *Planetary Modernisms.* Lostoski-Ho 28.55n16
Friedman. "Spatialization, Narrative Theory, and VW's *VO*." *Ambiguous Discourse* (Mezei, ed.). Caputi 29.6n3, 15n13
Friedman. "VW's Pedagogical Scenes of Reading: *VO*, *CR1*, and Her 'Common Readers" Cheney 24.58, 58n3
Friedman. "Wartime Cosmopolitanism: Cosmofeminisms in VW's *TG* and Majane Satrapi's *Persepolis*." Gillespie 25.115
Froula, Christine. "*MD*'s Postwar Elegy: Women, War, and the Art of Mourning." Shin 23.111n7
Froula. "On French and British Freedoms: Early Bloomsbury and the Brothels of Modernism." Adair & Martin 24.77
Froula. "Out of the Chrysalis: Female Initiation and Female Authority in VW's *VO*." Caputi 29.6n3, 9n8; Davison 23.5n11
Froula. "St. Virginia's Epistle to an English Gentleman: Sex, Violence, and the Public Sphere in *TG*." Kotler 24.46
Froula. *Virginia Woolf and the Bloomsbury Avant-Garde: War, Civilization, Modernity.* Czarnecki 21.54n7, 64, 66, 71, 73; Foster 22.41n1, 58n31; Novillo-Corvalán 23.43
Fulton, Lorie Watkins. "'A direction of one's own': Alienation in *MD* and *Sula*." Czarnecki 21.51n2
Gabler, Hans. "A Tale of Two Texts: Or, How One Might Edit VW's *TTL*." Jenkins (Amber) 27.5n3, 8n6; Phillips 26.10
Gaipa, Mark. "An Agnostic's Daughter's Apology: Materialism, Spiritualism, and Ancestry in W's *TTL*." *Journal of Modern Literature*. Rutherford 24.135
Gao Yuanyuan. "An Analysis of Ling Shuhua's Linguistic Qualities in *Ancient Melodies*." Chua 30.45
Garrard, Greg. "Worlds Without Us: Some Types of Disanthropy." Lostoski-Ho 28.53
Garrity, Jane. "Global Objects in *TW*." Gillespie 25.120n37; Lostoski-Ho 28.48n2
Garrity. *Step-Daughters of England: British Women Modernists and the National Imaginary*. McVicker 28.88–89
Gerzina, Gretchen. "Bushmen and Blackface: Bloomsbury and Race." Caputi 29.22n18
Gerzina. "VW, Performing Race." Caputi 29.22n18
Gilbert, Sandra M. A Note on the Illustrations. *O*. Fouirnaies 22.24

Gilbert and Susan Gubar. *The Madwoman in the Attic: The Woman Writer and the Nineteenth-Century Literary Imagination*. Favre 30.58
Gillespie, Diane. "'Her Kodak Pointed at His Head': VW and Photography." Fouirnaies 22.21, 22; Wisor 21.3, 3n6
Gillespie. Introduction. *The Library of Leonard and VW*. Davison 23.3n8; Koulouris 25.97; Gillespie 25.97, 100n5, n8; Golden 23.83n3, 88
Gillespie. Introduction (VW, *RF*). Gillespie 29.149n1
Gillespie. *The Sisters' Arts: The Writing and Painting of VW and Vanessa Bell*. Adair & Martin 24.78, 91; Jenkins (Amber) 27.5, 10, 14; Layne 21.81, 82, 83, 84, 85, 90, 93, 96, 100, 102
Gillespie. "The Texture of the Text: Editing *RF*." Gillespie 29.149n1
Gillespie. "Through Woolf's 'I's: Donne and *TW*." Gillespie 25.127n49
Gillespie. "VW and the Curious Case of Berta Ruck." Gillespie 25.118–19
Gillespie. "'Woolfs in Sheep's Clothing: The Hogarth Press and 'Religion.'" Foster 22.52n26
Golden, Amanda. "'A Brief Note in the Margin:' VW and Annotating." Golden 23.84n7, 87n10
Golden. "Textbook Greek: Thoby Stephen in *JR*." Bunting 30.11; Gillespie 25.100n7, 123; Jenkins (Gwyn) 27.37; Ke 29.67n11
Golden. "VW's Marginalia Manuscript." Golden 23.83, 83n2
Goldman, Jane. "Burning Feminism: VW's Laboratory of Intimacy." Ryan 30.69n8, 78, 79n21
Goldman. *The Cambridge Introduction to VW*. Bunting 30.9; Ke 29.72n15
Goldman. *The Feminist Aesthetics of VW: Modernism, Post-Impressionism and the Politics of the Visual*. Adair & Martin 24.75; Foster 22.45; Jenkins (Amber) 27.5, 13, 16; Layne 21.84, 92, 96, 97, 98, 100
Goldman. "From *MD* to *TW*: New elegy and lyric experimentalism." Shin 23.111, 111n7, 112n8
Goldman, *Modernism, 1910-1945: Image to Apocalypse*. Foster 22.54, 55
Goldman. "Modernist Studies." Favre 30.60
Goldman. "*TTL*'s Use of Language and Form." Jenkins (Amber) 27.8, 9; Rutherford 24.158, 160
Goldman. "Two Postcards from Skye: VW in the Hebrides." Foster 22.42n3
Goldman. "VW: Prophet of 'Pure Loss.'" Golden 23.91n16
Goldman and E. H. Wright. "The Cambridge W." Jenkins (Amber) 27.5n3
Gooch, G.P. *Politics and Morals*. Foster 22.51
Goodman, Robin Truth. "Woolf and Women's Work." *Literature and the Development of Feminist Thought* (Goodman, ed.). Caputi 29.21n16
Gordon, Lyndall. "Too much Suicide." Favre 30.64
Gottlieb, Laura Moss. "*TY*: A Feminist Novel." Cheney 24.59n6, 62
Graham, J. W. Introduction. *TW: The Two Holographs*. Lostoski-Ho 28.57–60
Graham, ed. and transcriber. *TW: The Two Holographs*. Ryan 30.71, 73, 75
Groover, Kristina. "Enacting the Sacred in *MD*." Foster 22.42n4
Gualtieri, Elena. "*TG* and the Photograph: The Art of Propaganda." Wisor 21.3n6, 4
Graber, Darin. "*H. M. S. Orlando*: The Metamorphosing, Imperial Vessel." Gillespie 25.126
Groover, Kristina K. "'The Conditions of Our Love': Seeking and Desiring in *JR*." *South Atlantic Review*. Van Wert 29.114
Groover. "Taking the Door off the Hinges: Liminal Space in VW's *MD*." Bond 23.65, 66
Gruber, Ruth. *VW: The Will to Create as a Woman*. Favre 30.61
Haefele, Lisa. "Violent Conversions,

Rhetorical Weapons: *MD* and the Influence of a Nationalist Literary History." *VW and Her Influences* (Davis and McVicker, eds.). Schwartz 29.88n1

Haffey, Kate. "Exquisite Moments and the Temporality of the Kiss in *MD* and *The Hours*." Caputi 29.10n9

Hagen, Benjamin D. "Feeling Shadows: VW's Sensuous Pedagogy." Cheney 24.58n4; Lostoski-Ho 28.64

Hagen. *The Sensuous Pedagogies of VW and D. H. Lawrence*. Chua 30.41n4

Hagen. "Sir Thomas Browne and the Reading of Remains in *O*." McVicker 28.85–86n27

Hagen. "Woolfian Love in Aggregate: Posthuman—Queer—Feminist." Caputi 29.21n16

Haller, Evelyn. "Alexandria as Envisioned by VW and E. M. Forster." Rutherford 24.158, 159

Haller. "The Anti-Madonna in the Work and Thought of VW." Rutherford 24.137, 138, 139–40, 158

Haller. "Isis Unveiled: VW's Use of Egyptian Myth." McVicker 28.71n7, 75n11, 82n22; Rutherford 24.155, 158

Hancock, Nuala. *Charleston and Monk's House: The Intimate House Museums of VW and Vanessa Bell*. Adair & Martin 24.78

Hankins, Leslie Kathleen. "'Across the Screen of My Brain': VW's 'The Cinema' and Film Forums of the Twenties." Humm 29.157n9, 158–59

Hankins. "*O*: 'A Precipice Marked V' Between 'A Miracle of Discretion' and 'Lovemaking Unbelievable: Indiscretions Incredible.'" Pająk 24.28

Hankins. "VW and Film." Gilman 29.36

Hankins. "VW's 'The Cinema': Sneak Previews of the Holograph Pre-texts Through Post-Publication Revisions." Humm 29.157n9, 159

Harker, Ben. "'On Different Levels Ourselves Went Forward': Pageantry, Class Politics and Narrative Form in VW's Late Writing." Livingstone 26.89–90

Harris, Susan C. "The Ethics of Indecency: Censorship, Sexuality, and the Voice of the Academy in the Narration of *JR*." Bunting 30.10

Harrod, Rod. *The Life of John Maynard Keynes*. Gillespie 29.150; Humm 29.160

Hartley, Jenny. "Clothes and Uniform in the Theatre of Fascism: Clemence Dane and VW." Wisor 21.3n7

Hattaway, Judith. "VW's *JR*: History and Memory." Schwartz 29.102

Haule, James. "Reading Dante, Misreading Woolf: New Evidence of VW's Revision of *TY*." Cheney 24.64; Phillips 26.2

Haule and Philip H. Smith. *Concordances to the Novels of VW*. Vlasopolos, Anca. "Staking Claims for No Territory: The Sea as Woman's Space." Gillespie 25.122n42

Hawkes, Eileen, ed. "Friendships Gallery" (VW). Gillespie 25.116

Heine, Elizabeth. "The Earlier Voyage Out: VW's First Novel." Davison 23.5n11

Heine. "VW's Revisions of *VO*." Davison 23.5n11

Heininge, Kathy. "VW: Quaker Pacifist?" Foster 22.43-4

Heininge. "The Search for God: VW and Caroline Emelia Stephen." Foster 22.43-4

Helal, Kathleen M. "Anger, Anxiety, Abstraction: VW's 'Submerged Truth.'" Kotler 24.41

Helt, Brenda. "Passionate Debates on 'Odious Subjects': Bisexuality and Woolf's Opposition to Theories of Androgyny and Sexual Identity." Clarke 28.20

Helt and Madlyn Detloff, eds. *Queer Bloomsbury*. Clarke 28.6n1

Henig, Suzanne. Introduction. "A Cockney's Farming Experiences." Williams

26.110
Henke, Suzette A. "Virginia Woolf's Septimus Smith: An Analysis of 'Paraphrenia' and the Schizophrenic Use of Language." Czarnecki 21.57
Henke. "*TW* as Ontological Trauma Narrative: The Anxiety of a Death (Un)Foreseen." *VW and Trauma: Embodied Texts* (Eberly and Henke, eds.). Van Wert 29.113–14
Henry, Holly. "From Edwin Hubble's Telescope to VW's 'Searchlight.'" Gillespie 25.127–28
Henry. "Science and Technology." McVicker 28.77, 85n26, 89, 90n29
Henry. *VW and the Discourse of Science: The Aesthetics of Astronomy.* Livingstone 26.88n2, 89; Lostoski-Ho 28.50n6
Herman, David. "Modernist Life Writing and Nonhuman Lives: Ecologies of Experience in VW's *F.*" Williams 26.115
Herman, William. "VW and the Classics: Every Englishman's Prerogative Transmuted into Fictional Art." *VW: Centennial Essays* (Ginsberg and Gottlieb, eds.). Rutherford 24.158
Hill, Katherine C. "VW and Leslie Stephen: History and the Literary Revolution." De Gay 30.101n2
Hill, Lorraine. "More about Library Holdings of Woolf Materials." Gilman 29.31n13
Hinnov, Emily M. "'Each is part of the whole: we act different parts; but are the same': From Fragment to Choran Community in the Late Work of VW." Foster 22.59n33, 60n40
Hinnov. "Shufflings of Kristeva: The Choran Moment in VW." Fischer 28.27n6
Hinnov. "'To Give the Moment Whole': The Nature of Time and Cosmic (Comm) Unity in VW's *TW.*" Lostoski-Ho 28.49n3, 50
Hirsh, Elizabeth. "VW and Portraiture." Fouirnaies 22.22
Hitchmough, Wendy. *The Bloomsbury Look.* Reed 29.169
Hite, Molly. "The Public Woman and the Modernist Turn: VW's *VO* and Elizabeth Robins's *My Little Sister.*" Graber 24.166–67
Hodgkins, Hope. "High Modernism for the Lowest: Children's Books by Woolf, Joyce, and Greene." Williams 26.108n6
Hoff, Molly. "A Feast of Words in *MD.*" Dalgarno 22.1n1
Hoffmann, Charles. "VW's Manuscript Revisions of TY." Phillips 26.2
Högberg, Elsa. *VW and the Ethics of Intimacy.* Clarke 28.9n6, 13n9, 21n13; Favre 30.53n1
Högberg. "VW's Object-Oriented Ecology." Lostoski-Ho 28.49n3, 50
Hollander, Rachel. "Novel Ethics: Alterity and Form in *JR.*" Van Wert 29.117
Hollis, Catherine W. "Editor's Introduction: The Common Book Collector." *VW Miscellany*. Gilman 29.31
Holtby, Winifred. *VW: A Critical Memoir.* Bunting 30.11
Humm, Maggie. "Bloomsbury and the Arts." Sullam 30.117n1
Humm. "Cinema and Photography." Wisor 21.3n6
Humm. "Memory, Photography, and Modernism: The 'dead bodies and ruined houses' of VW's *TG.*" Kotler 24.49, 51
Humm. *Modernist Women and Visual Cultures: VW, Vanessa Bell, Photography and Cinema.* Adair & Martin 24.93; Humm 29.157n7, 159; Layne 21.85; Wisor 21.2n5, 3n6
Humm. "VW and Visual Culture." *The Cambridge Companion to VW*. 2nd ed (Sellers, ed.). Wisor 21.2n5, 3n6; Fouirnaies 22.22
Hungerford, Edward A. "'My Tunnelling Process': The Method of *MD.*" Bond 23.65

Hussey, Mark. "Case Study: Clive Bell and the Legacies of Significant Form." *The Handbook to the Bloomsbury Group* (Ryan and Ross, eds.). Reed 29.162, 164

Hussey. *Clive Bell and the Making of Modernism*. Berkowitz 29.passim; Davison 29.passim; Gillespie 29.passim; Humm 29.passim; Hussey 29.passim; Ke 29.59n5, 63, 65n9; Reed 29.passim

Hussey. "The Fall of a Flower." Jenkins (Gwyn) 27.23–24

Hussey. Introduction. *BTA*. Foster 22.50n20, 59n35, 66; Shin 23.109n1

Hussey. Introduction. *TTL*. McVicker 28.87

Hussey. "'I'd Make it Penal': The Rural Preservation Movement in VW's *BTA*." Adair & Martin 24.93; Jones 22.76, 80, 81, 82n7

Hussey. *The Singing of the Real World: The Philosophy of VW*. McVicker 28.69–70n2, 89

Hussey. *VW A to Z: A Comprehensive Reference for Students, Teachers and Common Readers to Her Life, Work and Critical Reception.* Delsandro 25.82n11; Layne 21.98

Hussey. "'W. H. Day Spander' Had a Sister: Joan Adeney Easdale." *Leonard and VW, the Hogarth Press, and the Networks of Modernism* (Southworth, ed.). Gallego Larrarte 30.112

Hussey. "Woolf: After Lives." Foster 22.42

Hussey, ed. *VW and War: Fiction, Reality, and Myth*. Bunting 30.7

Hussey, ed. "Living in a War Zone: An Introduction to VW as a War Novelist." Czarnecki 21.52, 52n4

Ingram, Penelope. "'One Drifts Apart': *TTL* as Art of Response." *Philosophy and Literature*. Rutherford 24.135

James, Emily. "VW and the Child Poet." Golden 23.88

James and Rachel M. Busse. "The Forms of War: Pocket Diaries and Post Cards in *JR*." *Journal of Modern Literature*. Van Wert 29.117

Javadizadeh, Kamran. "How VW Kept Her Brother Alive in Letters." Clarke 28.14n10

Johnson, Jamie. "VW's Flush: Decentering Human Subjectivity through the Nonhuman Animal Character." Williams 26.115

Johnston, Georgia. "Politics of Retrospective Space in VW's Memoir 'A Sketch of the Past.'" Bond 23.71, 71n14, 72

Jones, Clara. *VW: Ambivalent Activist*. Chua 30.41; Delsandro 25.76; Favre 30.61n13

Jones. "VW and 'The Villa Jones.'" Gillespie 25.108

Jones. "VW's 1931 'Cook Sketch.'" Jones 22.77, 77n3

Juhasz, Suzanne. *A Desire for Women: Relational Psychoanalysis, Writing and Relationships between Women.* Jenkins (Amber) 27.17

Kahane, Claire. *Passions of the Voice: Hysteria, Narrative, and the Figure of the Speaking Woman, 1850–1915.* Fischer 28.27n6, 37–38

Kane, Julie. "Varieties of Mystical Experience in the Writings of VW." Foster 22.42

Karshan, Thomas. "What is an Essay? Thirteen Essays from VW." Leach 28.99n1

Katz, Tamar. "Pausing, Waiting, Repeating: Urban Temporality in *MD* and *TY*." Cheney 24.59n5

Kazan, Francesca. "Description and the Pictorial in *JR*." *ELH*. Ke 29.58n3

Ke, Lingxiang. "'The Real Flower; Part Earth; Part Flower': VW's Statuesque Form in *JR*." Bunting 30.8

Kelley, Joyce E. "VW and Music." Davison 23.5, 5n10, 9, 20n28

Kelly, Alice. *Commemorative Modernisms: Women Writers, Death and the First World War*. Bunting 30.19–20

Kendall-Morrick, Karalyn. "Mongrel Fiction: Canine Bildung and the

Feminist Critique of Anthropocentrism in VW's *F.*" Williams 26.117
Kenyon Jones, Christine and Anna Snaith. "'Tilting at Universities': Woolf at King's College London." Dalgarno 22.9; Gilman 29.47n8; Golden 23.98; Jenkins (Gwyn) 27.24, 25, 36, 43; Koulouris 25.5n8
Kermode, Frank. Introduction. *BTA*. Fischer 28.27n5
King, James. *VW*. Chua 30.39, 41n4
King, Julia and Laila Miletic-Vejzovic, editors. *The Library of Leonard and VW: A Short-Title Catalog*. Gillespie 25.97, 100, 101n11, 102n13, 105n20–21; Gilman 29.48n10, 50n14; Golden 23.83n3; Sullam 30.122n5
Kirkpatrick, B. J. and Stuart N. Clarke. *A Bibliography of VW*. Wisor 21.1n2, n3
Knowles, Nancy. "A Community of Women Looking at Men: The Photographs in VW's *TG*." Wisor 21.2n4
Knowles. "Active Pacifism in a World at War: The Legacy of VW's Pacifist Theory on Narrative Structure." Foster 22.58, 66
Knox-Shaw, Peter. "*TTL:* The Novel as Elegy." Shin 23.111n7
Kolocotroni, Vassiliki. "Strange Cries and Ancient Songs: Woolf's Greek and the Politics of Intelligibility." *VW in Context* (Randall and Goldman, eds.). Ke 29.67n11
Kopley, Emiily. *VW and Poetry*. De Gay 30.passim; Fischer 28.43n21; Gallego Larrarte 30.passim; Goldman 30.107–08; Kopley 30.passim; Sullam 30. passim
Koppen, Randi S. "Embodied Form: Art and Life in VW's *TTL*." Jenkins (Amber) 27.16
Koppen. *VW, Fashion and Literary Modernity.* Wisor 21.3n7
Kore-Schröder, Leena. "'Reflections in a Motor Car': VW's Phenomenological Relations of Time and Space." Jones 22.76, 81, 81n6
Kostkowska, Justyna. *Ecocriticism and Women Writers: Environmentalist Poetics of VW, Jeanette Winterson, and Ali Smith*. Lostoski-Ho 28.49n3
Kostkowska. "*Studland Beach* and *JR:* Vanessa Bell's and VW's Experiments in Portrait Making 1910–1933." Jenkins (Amber) 27.19; Layne 21.85, 100
Kostkowska. *VW's Experiment in Genre and Politics, 1926–1931: Visioning and Versioning* TW. Lostoski-Ho 28.57n19
Koulouris, Theodore. *Hellenism and Loss in the Work of VW*. Dalgarno 22.1n1; Jenkins (Gwyn) 27.25–26; Koulouris 25.5n8; McVicker 28.71n5, 76n14, 80n19
Koulouris. "Jacques Derrida in VW: Death, Loss and Mourning in *JR*." McVicker 28.71n5, 80n19; Van Wert 29.117
Koulouris. "VW's 'Greek Notebook' (VS Greek and Latin Studies): An Annotated Transcription." Gilman 29.32, 36n17; Ke 29.67n11
Kraskowska, Ewa. "On the Circulation of Feminist Discourse via Translation (VW, S. de Beauvoir, J. Butler)." Pająk 24.26
Kristeva, Julia. "About Chinese Women." Favre 30.53
Krouse, Tonya. "Sexual Deviancy in *MD:* The Case of Septimus Smith." Czarnecki 21.57
Kuehn, Julia. *A Female Poetics of Empire: From Eliot to Woolf.* Novillo-Corvalán 23.36, 39
Kuehn. "*VO* as Voyage In: Exotic Realism, Romance and Modernism." Fischer 28.38
Kukil, Karen V. "The Frances Hooper Collection of VW Books and Manuscripts." Gilman 29.29–30, 31
Lacourarie, Chantal. "Painting and Writing: A Symbiotic Relation in VW's Works." Ke 29.58n1
Lambert, Elizabeth L. "'And Darwin Says They Are Nearer The

Cow': Evolutionary Discourse in *Melymbrosia* and *VO*." Davison 23.3n8, 7n15, 12, 13
Lamos, Colleen. "VW's Greek Lessons." Golden 23.88n14
Lanone, Catherine. "The Non-Linear Dynamics of VW's London: From Elation to Street Haunting." van Straten 30.85
Larsson Lisbeth. "A Brief Moment in Bloomsbury—*JR*." Bunting 30.20
Larsson. *Walking VW's London: An Investigation in Literary Geography*. Gillespie 25.111n29, 113, 124; van Straten 30.85n1, 87n4
Latham, Monica. "Serv[ing] Under Two Masters: VW's Afterlives in Contemporary Biofictions." Layne 21.78, 80, 83
Latham. *VW's Afterlives*. Favre 30.54
Latham, Sean. *"Am I a Snob?": Modernism and the Novel*. Adair & Martin 24.89, 95
Latham, S. "Elegy for the Snob: VW and the Victorians." Shin 23.111n7
Laurence, Patricia. "The Facts and Fugue of War: From *TG* to *BTA*." Foster 22.58n31
Laurence. *Lily Briscoe's Chinese Eyes: Bloomsbury, Modernism, and China*. Chua 30.32–33, 37, 44
Laurence. *The Reading of Silence: VW in the English Tradition*. Fischer 28.27n7, 42–43n20
Laurence. "A Writing Couple: Shared Ideology in VW's *TG* and Leonard Woolf's *Quack, Quack!*" Gillespie 25.104n16
Lawrence, Karen. "Gender and Narrative Voice in *JR* and *A Portrait of the Artist as a Young Man*." Bunting 30.10, 12
Lazenby, Donna J. *A Mystical Philosophy: Transcendence and Immanence in the Works of VW and Iris Murdoch*. Foster 22.44n10
Le Guin, Ursula K. "TGAN Again." Favre 30.54
Leaska, Mitchell. *Granite and Rainbow: The Hidden Life of VW*. Rutherford 24.159
Leaska. Introduction. *PA*. Favre 30.56
Leaska. *The Novels of Virginia Woolf From Beginning to End*. Czarnecki 21.57
Leaska, ed. *The Pargiters*. Delsandro 25.76n5, 83
Leaska, ed. *Pointz Hall: The Earlier and Later Typescripts of* BA. Wisor 21.40
Lee, Hermione. "Biomythographers: Rewriting the Lives of VW." Layne 21.79
Lee. "'Crimes of Criticism': VW and Literary Journalism." Gilman 29.46n4
Lee. *The Novels of VW*. Ke 29.58n3
Lee. "*TTL*: Completed Forms." *VW's* TTL (Bloom, ed.). Rutherford 24.158–59
Lee. *VW*. Adair & Martin 24.80; Chua 30.40, 41n4; Clarke 28.6; Davison 23.24; Delsandro 25.84; Favre 30.56; Foster 22.44; Gallego Larrarte 30.112; Golden 23.83; Jenkins (Gwyn) 27.24, 38; Layne 21.87, 88, 89, 91; Leach 28.101, 103; Pająk 24.27; Rutherford 24.153, 154, 155, 156; Shin 23.120, 128, 129; Wisor 21.22, 23n37
Lehmann, John. "VW." *The Open Night*. Kopley 30.126
Lewis, Alison. "Caroline Emelia Stephen (1834-1909) and VW (1882-1941): A Quaker Influence on Modern English Literature." Foster 22.44
Lewis, Andrea. "The Visual Politics of Empire and Gender in VW's *VO*." Novillo-Corvalán 23.36, 43, 57
Li, Congshuo. "Degenderizing Modernity in Ling Shuhua's Boudoir School Writing: With a Comparison to VW." Chua 30.34n3
The Library of Leonard and VW (online catalogue). Washington State University. McVicker 28.83n24
Light, Alison. *Mrs. W and the Servants*. Humm 29.158
Lilienfeld, Jane. "'The Gift of a China

Inkpot': Violet Dickinson, VW, Elizabeth Gaskellk, Charlotte Brontë, and the Love of Women in Writing." Clarke 28.14
Lilienfeld. "W: War and Peace." Ryan 30.69n8
Lin Xiaoxia. "Shijie Wenxue Shiyuzhong de Wenhua Fanyi Yanjiu—Jianlun *Guyun* de Fanyi Chuangzuo." Chua 30.45
Linett, Maren. "The Jew in the Bath: Imperiled Imagination in W's *TY*." Delsandro 25.73
Lim Wan Hui Eva. "Private and Common Ground: The Work of Ling Shuhua and VW in the Late 1930s." Chua 30.34n3
Lilly, Amy M. "*TG,* Two Exhibits: Woolf's Politics of Display." Wisor 21.4n10
Light, Alison. *Mrs. Woolf and the Servants*. Fouirnaies 22.22n1
Linett, Maren. *Bodies of Modernism: Physical Disability in Transatlantic Modernist Literature*. Williams 26.111, 112
Little, Judy. "*JR* as Comedy: Woolf's Parodic Bildungsroman." *New Feminist Essays on VW* (Marcus, ed.). Van Wert 29.115n10
Lojo Rodríguez, Laura María. "'A gaping mouth, but no words': VW Enters the Land of Butterflies" Novillo-Corvalán 23.34
Lonnquist, Barbara. "Homeless in Nature: Solitary trampings and Shared Errantry in Cornwall, 1905." McVicker 28.76–77n15
Lostoski-Ho, Leanna. "'Against time and sea': The Deep Temporality of the Interludes in *TW*." Ryan 30.70n11
Low, Lisa. "Refusing to Hit Back: VW and the Impersonality Question." Kotler 24.40
Lowe, Gill. "'Penning and Pinning': VIta, V, and *O*." Gillespie 25.116n33
Lyon, Janet. "On the Asylum Road with W and Mew." Williams 26.111
Lyons, Brenda. "VW and Plato: The Platonic Background of *JR*." Dalgarno 22.1n1
MacKay, Marina. *Modernism and World War II*. Delsandro 25.76
MacKay. "VW and the pastoral patria." Foster 22.58
Maggio, Paula. "Taking Up Her Pen for World Peace: VW, Feminist Pacifist. Or Not?" Foster 22.58n31
Maika, Patricia. *VW's* BTA *and Jane Harrison's Con/spiracy*. Rutherford 24.153, 158
Marchi, Dudley M. *Montaigne Among the Moderns*. Leach 28.99, 104
Marcus, Jane. "Alibis and Legends: The Ethics of Elsewhereness, Gender, and Estrangement." Camarasana, *et al* 24.2, 3
Marcus. "Afterword: Some Notes on Radical Teaching." Pająk 24.31
Marcus. *Art and Anger: Reading Like A Woman*. Cheney 24.55, 60, 72; Favre 30.59; Kotler 24.35, 36, 39, 41, 42, 44, 46, 47, 48, 49
Marcus. "Britannia Rules *The Waves*." Gillespie 25.126n46; Novillo-Corvalán 23.36
Marcus. *Hearts of Darkness: White Women Write Race* Cheney 24.56; Lostoski-Ho 28.48, 49–50; Pająk 24.11n2
Marcus. Introduction. *TG*. Wisor 21.1, 3n7, 4n10, n11.
Marcus. "Introduction: Changing the Subject." Favre 30.58n9
Marcus. "Middlebrow Feminism." Pająk 24.13
Marcus. "'No More Horses': VW on Art and Propaganda." Foster 22.53n28; Fouirnaies 22.22n1; Wisor 21.5
Marcus. "The Niece of a Nun: VW, Caroline Stephen, and the Cloistered Imagination." Foster 22.41, 42n3, 43
Marcus. "Pathographies: The VW Soap Operas." Favre 30.59n12
Marcus. "Quentin's Bogey." Favre 30.59, 60, 62
Marcus. "Registering Objections:

Grounding Feminist Alibis." Gillespie 25.105, 112–13, 127, 128
Marcus, "Some Sources for *BA*." Foster 22.64n44
Marcus. "Storming the Toolshed." Pająk 24.13
Marcus. "Taking the Bull by the Udders: Sexual Difference in VW—A Conspiracy Theory." Gillespie 25.108
Marcus. "Thinking Back through Our Mothers." Delsandro 25.84n15, 85; Favre 30.58; Foster 22.41–42n3; Wisor 21.7
Marcus. "To the Women's Review of Books (letter)." Pająk 24.13
Marcus. *VW*. Van Wert 29.117, 118
Marcus. *VW and the Languages of Patriarchy*. Cheney 24.56, 59n5, 59n6, 62, 64n11; Dalgarno 22.11n13; Jenkins (Gwyn) 27.27; McVicker 28.71n7, 72n8; Pająk 24.15, 16, 27, 28; Phillips 26.8n6
Marcus, Laura. *Dreams of Modernity*. McVicker 28.82n22
Marcus. "'Hieroglyphics in Motion': Repressing Ancient Egypt and the Middle East in Film Theory and Criticism of the Silent Period." McVicker 28.71n7, 82n22
Marcus. "Woolf's Feminism and Feminism's Woolf." Dalgarno 22.16; Favre 30.57, 61
Marder, Herbert. *The Measure of Life: VW's Last Years*. Delsandro 25.84n15
Marsh, Moira. "Bunga Bunga on the Dreadnought: Hoax, Race, and W." Caputi 29.22n18
Martin, Ann. "Modernist Transformations: VW, Cinderella, and the Legacy of Lady Ritchie." Williams 26.109, 110
Martin, Linda. "Elegy and the Unknowable Mind in *JR*." Bunting 30.10; Van Wert 29.114n10
Martin. "Sky Haunting: The British Motor-Car Industry and the World Wars." Adair & Martin 24.76n2
Martin. "'Unity-Dispersity': VW and the Contradictory Motif of the Motor-Car." Adair & Martin 24.80n7
Martin, Lindsay. "VW at Morley College." Chua 30.42
Matson, Patricia. "The Terror and the Ecstasy: The Textual Politics of Virginia Woolf's *MD*." Czarnecki 21.52n3
Mattison, Laci. "VW's Ethical Subjectivity: Deleuze and Guattari's Worlding and Bernard's 'Becoming-Savage.'" Ryan 30.74, 75
Maze, J. R. "VW: Ideas of Marriage and Death in *VO*." Fischer 28.37n15
McGregor, Wayne. "Why VW?" Livingstone 26.91
McGregor. *WoolfWorks*. Livingstone 26.91
McIntire, Gabrielle. *Modernism, Memory, and Desire: T.S. Eliot and VW* Bond 23.77
McLaurin, Allen. *VW: The Echoes Enslaved*. Layne 21.84; Jenkins (Amber) 27.5
McLaurin. "VW and Unanimism." *Journal of Modern Literature*. Reed 29.163
McManus, Patricia. "The 'Offensiveness' of VW: From a Moral to a Political Reading." Fouirnaies 22.22
McNees, Eleanor. "The 1914 'Expurgated Chunk': The Great War in and out of *The Years*." Phillips 26.1n1
McNees. "Woolf as Reviewer-Critic." Gilman 29.46n4
McNeillie, Andrew. "Bloomsbury." Dalgarno 22.1n1
McNeillie. Introduction. "Byron & Mr Briggs" (*E*3). Gilman 29.28n3
McNicholl, Stella, ed. *TTL*. Jenkins (Amber) 27.5n2
Meng, Deyan. "Ling Shuhua and VW: Female Communion, Resistance, and Individuality." Chua 30.34n3
Mepham, John. "Mourning and Modernism." McVicker 28.71n5
Meyer, Jessica. "'Not Septimus Now': Wives of Disabled Veterans and Cultural Memory of the First World War in Britain." Czarnecki 21.68

Micir, Melanie. *The Passion Projects: Modernist Women, Intimate Archives, Unfinished Lives*. Clarke 28.19n11
Micir. "Queer Woolf." Clarke 28.6n1
Miller, Marlowe A. "Unveiling 'the Dialectic of Culture and Barbarism' in British Pageantry: VW's *BTA*." Lauby 27.48n3
Mills, Jean. "*TG:* The Movie?" Wisor 21.3n7
Mills. *VW, Jane Ellen Harrison, and the Spirit of Modernist Classicism*. Dalgarno 22.3, 3n3; Delsandro 25.85–86, 91; Foster 22.58n31; Golden 23.84n4, 100n30; Jenkins (Gwyn) 27.23, 26–27, 39; McVicker 28.71n7, 72n8, 75n11
Minow-Pinkney, Makiko. *VW & the Problem of the Subject.* Bond 23.65n4, 78; Van Wert 29.113
Minow-Pinkney. "VW and the Age of Motor Cars." Adair & Martin 24.75, 78
Monaco, Beatrice. *Machinic Modernism: The Deleuzian Literary Machines of Woolf, Lawrence and Joyce*. Lostoski-Ho 28.56n17
Moore, Madeline. *The Short Season Between Two Silences*. Fouirnaies 22.25
Morgan, Clare. "Vanishing Horizons: VW and the Neo-Romantic Landscape in *BTA*." McVicker 28.86n28, 91n30
Morgenstern, Barry. "The Self-Conscious Narrator in *JR*." Bunting 30.10
Morris, Jan. *Travels with VW*. Adair & Martin 24.80, 80n6
Morris, Pam. *Jane Austen, VW and Worldly Realism*. Ryan 30.73
Nagel, Rebecca. "VW on Reading Greek." *The Classical World*. Ke 29.67n11
Nagy-Seres, Imola. "Malleable Sculptures in VW's *JR* and Early Travel Diaries." *Journal of Modern Literature*. Bunting 30.20; Ke 29.58n3, 67n11
Nash, John. "Exhibiting the Example: VW's Shoes." Schwartz 29.102
Neverow, Vara. "Contrasting Urban and Rural Transgressive Sexualities in *JR*." *VW and the City* (Evans and Cornish, eds.). Van Wert 29.120n12
Neverow. "Desiring Statues and Ambiguous Sexualities in VW's *JR* and Early Travel Diaries." *Interdisciplinary/ Multidisciplinary Woolf* (Martin and Holland, eds.). Ke 29.58n3, 67n11
Neverow. "Documenting Fascism in *TG* and *The Handmaids Tale:* An Examination of Woolf's Textual Notes and Scrap Books and Atwood's 'Historical Notes.'" Wisor 21.3n7
Neverow, Vara S. "Freudian Seduction and the Fallacies of Dictatorship." Kotler 24.43n3; Wisor 21.3n7
Neverow. Introduction. *JR*. Golden 23.84n4, 95, 99; Ke 29.57n1; McVicker 28.80n19
Neverow. "The Return of the Great Goddess: Immortal Virginity, Sexual Autonomy, and Lesbian Possibility in *JR*." McVicker 28.71n7, 75n11
Neverow. "The Woolf, the Horse, and the Fox: Recurrent Motifs in *JR* and *O*." Bunting 30.17
Neverow. "Woolf's Editorial Self-Censorship and Risk-Taking in *JR*." Bunting 30.11
Negrello, Giulia. "Wild Nature, Afternoon Teas and Butterflies: VW, Victoria Ocampo and the South-American Dream." Novillo-Corvalán 23.34
Nicolson, Nigel. *VW*. Rutherford 24.144
Nicolson and Joanne Trautmann, eds. *L6*. Chua 30.32
Novillo-Corvalán, Patricia. "Empire and Commerce in Latin America: Historicizing W's *VO*." Gillespie 25.120n39
Nussbaum, Martha C. "The Window: Knowledge of Other Minds in VW." Fischer 28.27n9
Oldfield, Sybil. *The Child of Two Atheists: VW's Humanism*. De Gay 30.102
Oxner, Alex. "Characterizing Absence: VW's New Elegy in *JR*." Shin

23.111n7
Paetsasadee, Korrakod. *VW and the Sciences of Prehistory: A Reading of Five Major Novels*. McVicker 28.70n2, 90n29
Parkes, Adam. *A Sense of Shock: The Impact of Impressionism on Modern British and Irish Writing*. Gilman 29.45n2
Parrott, Fiona G. "Friendship, Letters and Butterflies: Victoria Ocampo and VW" Novillo-Corvalán 23.34
Pawlowski, Merry. "VW's Veil: The Feminist Intellectual and the Organization of Public Space." Fouirnaies 22.22; Wisor 21.32, 32n50
Pawlowski. "'Seule la culture desinteressee': VW, Gender, and Culture in Time of War." Wisor 21.3n6
Pawlowski. "The VW and Vera Douie Letters: Woolf's Connections to the Women's Service Library." Wisor 21.24n39
Peach, Linden. *VW*. McVicker 28.80
Pearson, Nels. "Woolf's Spatial Aesthetics and Postcolonial Critique." *A Companion to VW*. Gillespie 25.113, 127n48
Pease, Allison. *Modernism, Feminism and the Culture of Boredom*. Caputi 29.6n3, 15n13
Pedersen, Elisabeth Skou. "'One Thing Melts into Another': Unanimism, Affect, and Imagery in VW's *The Waves*." *Structures of Feeling* (Sharma and Tygstrup, eds.). Reed 29.163n2, 165
Penner, Erin Kay. "Crowding Clarissa's Garden." *VW and the Natural World* (Czarnecki and Rohman, eds.). van Straten 30.87n4, 90n8
Penner. "The Order of a Smashed Window-Pane: Novel Elegy in Woolf's *TW*." Shin 23.111n7
Periyan, Natasha. "'Altering the Structure of Society': An Institutional Focus on VW and Working-Class Education in the 1930s." Cheney 24.58n4
Phillips, Josh. "Thoughts on Peace in a Wine Cellar: On Transcribing the 1917 Dinner Party in the Holograph *Y*." Ryan 30.69n8, 79
Phillips, Kathy J. *VW against Empire*. Gillespie 25.113; Graber 24.166, 171, 179; Novillo-Corvalán 23.36, 37; Wisor 21.13
Pinho, Davi. "From Julia Kristeva to Paulo Mendes Campos: Impossible Conversations with VW." Favre 30.53n1
Poole, Roger. "'We all put up with you V': Irreceivable Wisdom about War." Czarnecki 21.61
Pridmore-Brown, Michele. "1939–40: Of VW, Gramophones, and Fascism." Livingstone 26.89n4
Prins, Yopie. "OTOTOTOI: VW and the 'Naked Cry' of Cassandra." Golden 23.85, 85n8, 87
Prins. *Ladies' Greek*. Jenkins (Gwyn) 27.23, 24, 37
Prins, "The Sexual Politics of Translating *Prometheus Bound*." Golden 23.85, 88n13
Putzel, Steven. "VW and British 'Orientalism.'" Novillo-Corvalán 23.36
Quigley, Megan. *Modernist Fiction and Vagueness: Philosophy, Form, and Language*. Fischer 28.39n17
Quigley. "Reading VW Logically: Resolute Approaches to *VO* and Wittegenstein's *Tractatus*." Fischer 28.28n9
Radin, Grace. "'Two Enormous Chunks': Episodes Excluded during the Final Revisions of TY." Phillips 26.2n2
Radin. *VW's* TY: *The Evolution of a Novel*. Delsandro 25.76n5, 82; Phillips 26.2
Rae, Patricia. "Proleptic Elegy and the End of Arcadianism in 1930s Britain." McVicker 28.71n5, 86n28, 91n30
Raitt, Suzanne. *Vita and Virginia: The Work and Friendship of Vita Sackville-West and VW*. Fouirnaies 22.21

Ramsay, Warren. "The Claims of Language: VW as Symbolist." Fischer 28.27
Reed, Christopher. "Bloomsbury Bashing: Homophobia and the Politics of Criticism in the Eighties." *Genders*. Berkowitz 29.127
Reed. *Bloomsbury Rooms: Modernism, Subculture, Domesticity*. Berkowitz 29.127; Davison 29.145; Gillespie 29.151n4
Reed. "Through Formalism: Feminism and VW's Relation to Bloomsbury Aesthetics." Jenkins (Amber) 27.5n1, 6, 15
Reid, Panthea. *Art and Affection: A Life of VW*. Jenkins (Amber) 27.8
Reynier, Christine. *VW's Ethics of the Short Story*. Ke 29.75
Richter, Harvena. "The Hidden Poetry of VW." *VW Miscellany*. Kopley 30.126
Ricoeur, Paul. *Time and Narrative, Volume 2*. Lostoski-Ho 28.49
Rizzuto, Nicole. "Maritime Modernism: The Aqueous Form of VW's *TW*." Lostoski-Ho 28.49, 50n7
Roe, Sue. "The Impact of Post-Impressionism." *Cambridge Companion to VW* (Roe and Sellers, eds.). Ke 29.72n16
Roe. Introduction [*JR*]. Bunting 30.11, 19
Roe. *Writing and Gender: VW's Writing Practice*. Dalgarno 22.9
Rohman, Carrie. *Choreographies of the Living: Bioaesthetics in Literature, Art, and Performance*. Williams 26.106, 113–14
Rohman. "'We Make Life': Vibration, Aesthetics and the Inhuman in *TW*." Lostoski-Ho 28.49n3, n5
Roof, Judith. *A Lure of Knowledge: Lesbian Sexuality and Theory* Bond 23.77n18
Roof. "The Match in the Crocus: Representations of Lesbian Sexuality." Bond 23.76n17
Rosati, Alessandra. "Wounded Cities, Fragmented Selves: Walking, Melancholia and the Interwar Novel. W's *MD* and Bontempelli's *La vita operosa*." van Straten 30.94n13
Rose, Phyllis. *Woman of Letters: A Life of VW* Cheney 24.70
Rosenbaum, S.P. Foreword. *The Bloomsbury Group*. Adair & Martin 24.76
Rosenfeld, Natania. *Outsiders Together: V and Leonard W*. Delsandro 25.89n19
Rosenthal, Lecia. *Mourning Modernism: Literature, Catastrophe, and the Politics of Consolation*. Van Wert 29.117
Rosner, Victoria. "VW and Monk's House." Gillespie 25.116n34
Rubenstein, Roberta. "'I meant nothing by The Lighthouse': VW's Poetics of Negation." *Journal of Modern Literature*. Rutherford 24.135
Rutherford, Brett. "VW's Egyptomania: Echoes of *The Book of the Dead* in *TTL*." McVicker 28.71n7, 82n22
Ryan, Derek. "Following Snakes and Moths: Modernist Ethics and Posthumanism." Williams 26.107
Ryan. "From Spaniel Club to Animalous Society: VW's *F*." Davison 23. 7n15, 13n21, 16
Ryan. "'Nature who has played so many tricks upon us': Digging Granite and Chasing Rainbows with VW." McVicker 28.76–77n15
Ryan. "Posthumanist Interludes: Ecology and Ethology in *TW*." Lostoski-Ho 28.48–49; Ryan 30.70n11
Ryan. *VW and the Materiality of Theory: Sex, Animal, Life*. Foster 22.42n3, 43n5, 45; Davison 23.6, 7n15, 13n21; Lostoski-Ho 28.49n3, 64n28; Phillips 26.2n3
Ryan and Stephen Ross. Introduction. *The Handbook to the Bloomsbury Group*. Jenkins (Amber) 27.6
Saariluoma, Liisa. "VW's *TY*: Identity and Time in an Anti- Family Novel." Cheney 24.58, 59n6
Saguaro, Shelley. "'Something that would stand for the conception':

The Inseminating world in the Last Writings of VW." *Green Letters*. Ke 29.58n2
Saint-Amour, Paul. "Deep Time's Hauntings: Modernism and Alternative Chronology." Lostoski-Ho 28.54–55
Saint-Amour. *Tense Future: Modernism, Total War, Encyclopedic Form*. Delsandro 25.76
Saloman, Randi. *VW's Essayism*. Dalgarno 22.5n14; Gilman 29.49n13; Golden 23.86n8
Sandberg, Eric. *VW: Experiments in Character*. Ke 29.57n1; 72n16, 78
Sarker, Sonita. "Woolf and Theories of Postcolonialism." *VW in Context* (Randall and Goldman, eds.). Graber 24.166
Savoie, Tracy. "Caged Tiger: Louis as Colonial Subject in VW's *TW*." Gillespie 25.126n46
Schaffer, Talia. "Posing *O*." Fouirnaies 22.22, 28, 36
Schlack, Beverly Ann. *Continuing Presence: VW's Use of Literary Allusion*. Fischer 28.41
Schrimper, Michael R. "'the young gentlemen taking in the room next door': Privileged Spaces in *JR*." Ke 29.71n14
Scott, Bonnie Kime. "Ecocritical Woolf." Lostoski-Ho 28.49n3, 50n7
Scott. "Ecofeminism, Holism, and the Search for Natural Order in W." *VW and the Natural World* (Czarnecki and Rohman, eds.). Ke 29.58n2
Scott. *In the Hollow of the Wave: Virginia Woolf and Modernist Uses of Nature*. Czarnecki 21.52n3; Lostoski-Ho 28.49n3, 50n7; van Straten 30.87, 88, 89, 91
Scott. Introduction. *MD*. Bond 23.65n4
Scott. "VW's Personal Landscapes." Jenkins (Amber) 27.20
Scott. "A Modernist Walk in the Park with VW." *Modernism in the Green* (Daniel and Konkol, eds.). van Straten 30.87n4, 88n5, 90n7, 91
Scott. "'The Word Split Its Husk': W's Double Vision of Modernist Language." Fischer 28.27n6
Schotter, Jesse. *Hieroglyphic Modernisms: Writing and New Media in the Twentieth Century*. McVicker 28.71n7, 81, 82n22
Sedon, Kate. "Moments of Aging: Revising Mother Nature in Virginia Woolf's *MD*." Czarnecki 21.72
Sellers. *The Cambridge Companion to VW*. Layne 21.80
Sellers, Susan, and Elizabeth Wright. "Painting in Prose: Performing the Artist in Susan Sellers's *Vanessa and Virginia*." Layne 21.81
Seshagiri, Urmila. "Orienting VW: Race, Aesthetics, and Politics in *TTL*." *MFS*. Rutherford 24.135
Seshagiri. *Race and the Modernist Imagination*. Caputi 29.22n18
Shackleton, David. "The Pageant of Mutabilitie: VW's *BTA* and *The Faerie Queene*." Lauby 27.51–52
Sharon-Zisser, Shirley. "'Some Little Language Such as Lovers Use': VW's Elemental Erotics of Simile." Fischer 28.27n7
Sharpe, Emily Robins. "Pacifying Bloomsbury: VW, Julian Bell, and the Spanish Civil War." Wisor 21.3n7
Sherry, Vincent. *The Great War and the Language of Modernism*. Delsandro 25.76; Fischer 28.27n5, 30
Shirkani, Kim. "Small Language and Big Men in VW." Fischer 28.35n13
Showalter, Elaine. *The Female Malady: Women, Madness, and English Culture*. Favre 30.57
Showalter. Introduction. *MD*. Favre 30.57n7
Showalter. *A Literature of Their Own*. Favre 30.57
Showalter. "VW and the Flight Into Androgyny." Favre 30.57; Kotler 24.36, 40

Silver, Brenda. "'Anon' and 'The Reader': VW's Last Essays." Foster 22.57; Layne 21.91
Silver. "The Authority of Anger: *TG* as Case Study." Dalgarno 22.15; Kotler 24.36, 39, 41
Silver. *VW Icon*. Favre 30.55, 59, 60
Silver ed. *VW's Reading Notebooks*. Dalgarno 22.7n6; Gillespie 25.116; Koulouris 25.6, 9n13, 14n22, n25–26
Sim, Lorraine. *VW: The Patterns of Ordinary Experience*. Adair & Martin 24.75; Dalgarno 22.9, 9n10; Foster 22.42n4, 45
Simpson, Kathryn. "Bloomsbury and Class." Jenkins (Amber) 27.6
Simpson. "Economies and Desire: Gifts and the Market in 'Moments of Being: "Slater's Pins Have No Points."'" Jenkins (Gwyn) 27.33
Simpson. "'Queer Fish': W's Writing of Desire Between Women in *VO* and *MD*." Fischer 28.42
Simpson. "To 'Write About Mrs Lindbergh': W, Flight, and Anne Morrow Lindbergh's *North to the Orient*." Gillespie 25.118
Smith, Amy C. "Bad Religion: The Irrational in *MD*." McVicker 28.75n12
Smith. "Loving Maidens and Patriarchal Mothers: Revisions of the *Homeric Hymn to Demeter* and *Cymbeline* in *MD*." McVicker 28.75n12
Smith. *VW's Mythic Method*. McVicker 28.71n7, 72n8, 75
Smith. "Woolf's Paratactic Method" (presentation). McVicker 28.75n12
Smith and Isabel Ma Andrés Cuevas. "To the Readers: VW and Spirituality." Foster 22.41
Smith and Andrés Cuevas. "Woolf and Spirituality." *VW Miscellany* (special issue). McVicker 28.75n12
Smith, Craig. "Across the Widest Gulf: Nonhuman Subjectivity in VW's *F*." Williams 26.117
Smith, Kate. Introduction [VW, *F*]. Van Wert 29.116n11
Smythe, Karen. "VW's Elegiac Enterprise." Shin 23.111n7
Snaith, Anna. Introduction. *TY*. Phillips 26.2, 8n6
Snaith. "Leonard and VW: Writing against Empire." *Journal of Commonwealth Literature*. Graber 24.167, 171; Novillo-Corvalán 23.57
Snaith. "Race, Empire, and Ireland." Graber 24.169, 171
Snaith. *VW: Public and Private Negotiations*. Delsandro 25.76, 84; Fouirnaies 22.22n1; Gillespie 25.107n24, 110; Pająk 24.31
Snaith. "Wide Circles: The *TG* Letters." Dalgarno 22.15; Wisor 21.5
Snaith. "Woolf and Education." Chua 30.41n4
Snaith and Elleke Boehmer. "Leonard and VW: Writing against Empire." Williams 26.114
Snaith and Michael H. Whitworth. "Introduction: Approaches to Space and Place in W." Novillo-Corvalán 23.58
Snyder, Carey. "W's Ethnographic Modernism: Self-Nativizing in *VO* and Beyond." Novillo-Corvalán 23.36
Son, Youngjoo. *Here and Now: The Politics of Social Space in D. H. Lawrence and VW*. Livingstone 26.89; van Straten 30.90, 91, 92
Southworth, Helen. Introduction. *Leonard & VW, The Hogarth Press, and the Networks of Modernism*. Foster 22.50n20; Golden 23.84n6
Spalding, Frances. *VW: Art, Life and Vision*. Foster 22.44, 53n27
Sparks, Elisa Kay. "'Everything tended to set itself in a garden': VW's Literary and Quotidian Flowers, A Bar-Graphical Approach." *VW and the Natural World* (Czarnecki and Rohman, eds.). van Straten 30.91n9
Sparks. "Leonard and Virginia's London Library: Mapping London's Tides,

Streams and Statues." Gillespie 25.124n45; Golden 23.83n3
Sparks. "Metropolis Unbound: VW's Heterotopian Utopian Impulse." *W and the City* (Evans and Cornish, eds.). van Straten 30.91n9, 92n11
Sparks. "Sunflower Suture: Disseminating the Garden in *TY*." *Interdisciplinary/Multidisciplinary W* (Martin and Holland, eds.). van Straten 30.91n9
Sparks. *A VW Herbarium*. van Straten 30.91n9
Sparks. "'Whose Woods These Are': VW and the Primeval Forest of the Mind." *VW: Writing the World*. van Straten 30.87n4
Sparks. "Woolf on the Downs." Jones 22.76
The Sphere. "A Literary Letter: Books from the Hogarth Press" (7 June 1924). Gilman 29.54n24
Spiro, Mia. "Between Public and Private Acts: W's Anti-Fascist Strategies." Lauby 27.48–49
Spiropoulou, Angeliki. "'On Not Knowing Greek': VW's Spatial Critique of Authority." Ke 29.67n11; Koulouris 25.1n1
Squire, Susan M. and Louise A. DeSalvo. "VW's 'The Journal of Mistress Joan Martyn.'" Koulouris 25.7n12
Stalla, Heidi. "The Play of Fact and Fiction in V Stephen's 'The Journal of Mistress Joan Martyn.'" McVicker 28.78n17
Stalla. "William Bankes: Echoes of Egypt in VW's *TTL*." McVicker 28.71n7, 82n22; Rutherford 24.141, 148, 159
Stansky, Peter. *On or About December 1910: Early Bloomsbury and Its Intimate World*. Caputi 29.22n18
Stape, John H. "'The Man at Worthing' and the Author of 'The Most Insipid Verse She had Ever Read': Two Allusions in *O*." Fouirnaies 22.23
Stape, Notes to *O*. Fouirnaies 22.24
Stape, ed. *VW: Interviews and Recollections*. Gillespie 25.110
Stasi, Paul. *Modernism, Imperialism, and the Historical Sense*. Graber 24.165–66, 167–68, 177
Staveley, Alice. "Name That Face." Wisor 21.1, 3, 6, 31; Kotler 24.51
Stec, Loretta. "Dystopian Modernism vs Utopian Feminism: Burdekin, Woolf, and West Respond to the Rise of Fascism." Cheney 24.61
Stevanato, Savina. *Visuality and Spatiality in VW's Fiction* Bond 23.64n3
Stevenson, Christina. "'Here was One Room, There was Another': The Room, Authorship, and Feminine Desire in *A Room of One's Own* and *MD*" Bond 23.77
Stevenson, Randall, and Jane Goldman. "'But what? Elegy?': Modernist Reading and the Death of Mrs. Ramsay." Shin 23.111n7
Stewart, Garrett. "Catching the Stylistic D/rift: Sound Defects in W's *TW*." De Gay 30.100; Fischer 28.27
Stewart, Jack. "A 'need for distance and blue': Space, Color and Creativity in *TTL*." Jenkins (Amber) 27.5n1
Suh, Judy. "The Comedy of Outsiders in VW's *TY*." Cheney 24.59n6
Sullam, Sara. "Figures of Contradiction: VW's Rhetoric of Genres." *Contradictory Woolf* (Bolaki and Ryan, eds.). Sullam 30.118n2
Sutton, Emma. "'Within a Space of Tears': Music, Writing, and the Modern in VW's *VO*." Davison 23.5n10
Sutton. "'Putting words onto the back of music': Woolf, 'Street Music' and *VO*." Davison 23.23n33; Fischer 28.31
Sutton, "Fiction as Musical Critique: VW, *VO* and the Case of Wagner." Davison 23.5n10
Sutton, *VW and Classical Music* Davison 23.5, 20n28
Swanson, Diana L. "Lesbian Approaches." *Palgrave Advances in VW Studies* (Snaith, ed.). Layne 21.89
Swanson, Diana, ed. *VW Miscellany* 81.

Czarnecki 21.52n3
Tambling, Jeremy. "Repression in MD's London." Bond 23.76n17
Taylor, Chloë. "Kristevan Themes in VW's *TW*." Fischer 28.27n6
Taylor, Rod C. "Narrow Gates and Restricted Paths: The Critical Pedagogy of VW." Dalgarno 22.15n14; Cheney 24.58n4, 71n14
Tazudeen, Rasheed. "'Discordant Syllabling': The Language of the Living World in VW's *BTA*." Fischer 28.27n5
Thacker, Andrew. "Woolf and Geography." Gillespie 25.105n20, 113, 117
Thompson, Hilary. "VW and Michèle Montrelay's Unconscious Signifier." Fischer 28.27n7
Torgovnick, Marianna. *The Visual Arts, Pictorialism, and the Novel: James, Lawrence, and Woolf.* Layne 21.84
Toth, Leah. "Re-Listening to VW: Sound Transduction and Private Listening in *MD*." van Straten 30.86
Toulmin, Stephen. *Return to Reason*. Leach 28.103
Townsend, Chris. "Meter and Modernist Prose Verse Fragments in W's *TY*." Kopley 30.126
Transue, Pamela J. *Virginia Woolf and the Politics of Style* Cheney 24.70
Trautmann Banks, Joanne. "The Editor as Ethicist." *VW: Interpreting the Modernist Text* (Haule and Stape, eds.). Gilman 29.31
Tromanhauser, Vicki. "VW's London and the Archaeology of Character." McVicker 28.70n2, 91n30
Trombley, Stephen. *All That Summer She Was Mad: VW: Female Victim of Male Medicine*. Favre 30.56
Tseng, Jui-hua. "Walter Pater, the Stephens and VW's Mysticism." Foster 22.42, 44, 53n27
Tung, Charles M. "Baddest Modernism." Livingstone 26.89
Twitchell, Beverly H. *Cézanne and Formalism in Bloomsbury*. Gillespie 29.151
Uhlmann, Anthony. "VW and Bloomsbury Aesthetics." Jenkins (Amber) 27.5n1, 17; Layne 21.91n4
Van Wert, Kathryn. "The Early Life of Septimus Smith." *Journal of Modern Literature*. Czarnecki 21.57; Van Wert 29.113n9
Vanita, Ruth. "Plato, Wilde, and Woolf: The Poetics of Homoerotic 'intercourse' in *AROO*." Dalgarno 22.1n1
Varga, Adriana, editor. *VW and Music* Davison 23.5n10
Varon, Daniel Jordan. "'The Drop Fell'—Time-Space Compression in *TW*." Lostoski-Ho 28.49n4, 50n7, 56n17
Wade, Francesca. *Portrait of VW by Jeanette Winterson with Charlotte Casiraghi and Keira Knightley*. McVicker 28.69
Wall, Kathleen. "Significant Form in *JR*: Ekphrasis and the Elegy." Bunting 30.9; Van Wert 29.118
Walkowitz, Rebecca. "Woolf's Evasion." *Cosmopolitan Style*. van Straten 30.88n5, 91
Walsh, Kelly. "The Unbearable Openness of Death: Elegies of Rilke and W." Van Wert 29.117
Weinstein, Arnold. *Recovering Your Story: Proust, Joyce, Woolf, Faulkner, Morrison*. Bond 23.65n4
Wells, Christopher James. "Doubt, Havelock Ellis, and Bisexuality in *JR*." Bunting 30.12; Van Wert 29.120n12
Westling, Louise. "VW and the Flesh of the World." Lostoski-Ho 28.56; McVicker 28.90n29
Wheare, Jane. *Virginia Woolf: Dramatic Novelist* Cheney 24.57n2
Whittier-Ferguson, John. "The Burden of Drafts: Woolf's Revisions of *BA*." Shin 23.134, 134n27, 136
Whittier-Ferguson. "Repetition, Remembering, Repetition: VW's Late Fiction and the Return of War."

Delsandro 25.73, 80; Fischer 28.28n8
Whitworth, Michael. *Einstein's Wake*. Livingstone 26.88n2, 101
Whitworth. *VW*. Reed 29.163
Wiechert, Nora. "'No Sense of Proportion': Urban Green Space and Mental Health in *MD*." van Straten 30.86, 88, 93n12
Williams, Raymond. "The Bloomsbury Fraction." Berkowitz 29.127
Williams. "The Significance of 'Bloomsbury' as a Social and Cultural Group." Berkowitz 29.127; Reed 29.165
Wilson, Mary. "'Chasms in the Continuity of our Ways': Queering Domesticity in *JR* and *TTL*." Van Wert 29.120
Winkiel, Laura. "A Queer Ecology of the Sea: Reading VW's *TW*." Lostoski-Ho 28.48
Winterhalter, Teresa. "'What Else Can I Do But Write?': Discursive Disruption and the Ethics of Style in VW's *TG*." Wisor 21.4n10
Wisor, Rebecca. "About Face: The *TG* Photographs in Cultural Context." Kotler 24.51
Wisor. "*My Country is the Whole World*": TG *and the Culture of Pacifist Dissent* (Dissertation.) Wisor 21.4n10, 5n13
Wisor. "Versioning VW: Notes toward a Post-eclectic Edition of *TG*." Wisor 21.41n59
Wolfe, Jesse. *Bloomsbury, Modernism, and the Reinvention of Intimacy*. Clarke 28.21n13
Wolfe. "The Sane Woman in the Attic: Sexuality and Self-Authorship in *MD*." Czarnecki 21.62
Wollaeger, Mark A. "Woolf, Postcards, and the Elision of Race: Colonizing Women in *VO*." Caputi 29.13–14; Davison 23.23n34
Wollaeger. "The Woolfs in the Jungle: Intertextuality, Sexuality, and the Emergence of Female Modernism in *VO, The Village in the Jungle,* and *Heart of Darkness*." Caputi 29.11, 17; Fischer 28.31n10; Novillo-Corvalán 23.34n2, 35, 36
Wood, Alice. *Modernism and Modernity in British Women's Magazines*. Humm 29.157n5
Wood. *VW 's Late Cultural Criticism.* Wisor 21.26n41; Foster 22.58, 59n34, 65, 66; Fouirnaies 22.22n1; Phillips 26.2, 8n6
"Woolf in the World: A Pen and a Press of Her Own" (Smith College exhibition; website). Gilman 29.30n7, 31
Wright, E. H. "The 'girl-novel': *Chance* and W's *VO*." *The Conradian*. Graber 24.167
Wright, Elizabeth. "Bloomsbury at Play." Adair & Martin 24.87n12
Wurtz, James F. "'I have had my vision': Empire and the Aesthetic in W's *TTL*." Gillespie 25.127n48
Wyatt, Jean. "Avoiding Self-Definition: In Defense of Women's Right to Merge (Julie Kristeva and *MD*)." Fischer 28.27n6
Xie, Yaqing. "'A Genteel Form of Suicide': Julian Bell's Chinese Journey." Chua 30.34n3
Xu Wei and Liu Ailin. "A Comparison of Feminism between the Works of Ling Shuhua and VW." Chua 30.37
Yoshino, Ayako. "*BTA* and Louis Napoleon Parker—the Creator of the Modern English Pageant." Lauby 27.47–48
Young, Kevin. "The Time VW Wore Blackface." Caputi 29.22n18
Zhang, Dora. "Naming the Indescribable: W, Russell, James, and the Limits of Description." Fischer 28.33
Zieger, Susan. "Dickens's Queer Children." Lauby 27.59
Zink, Suzana. *VW's Rooms and the Spaces of Modernity*. van Straten 30.85n1, 87n4
Zwerdling, Alex. "*JR:* Woolf's Satiric Elegy." *ELH*. Bunting 30.7; Shin 23.111n7; Van Wert 29.114
Zwerdling. *VW and the Real World*. Bond

23.72n15; Cheney 24.59n6, 65; Delsandro 25.76; Foster 22.60, 61n4; Fouirnaies 22.22n1; Gillespie 25.112

Part 3: Topics
Compiled by Jenny Ann Cubin and Benjamin D. Hagen

ableism
Woolf's critique of in "The Widow and the Parrot," Williams 26.passim

absence
in *TG*, Wisor 21.41

academy, the
and inequality, Delsandro 25.87

actor-network theory Reed 29.165

advertising
Shell-Mex campaign, Adair and Martin 24.92–94

aevum
concept of in *BTA*, Lauby 27.52–53

Alexandria
and *TTL*, Rutherford 24.137
See also influences, myth

androgyny
in *AROO*, Gillespie 25.116; Lauby 27.50; Pająk 24.28–29
in *MD*, Czarnecki 21.63
See also impersonality

Angel in the House Golden 23.94n19

anger Favre 30.58–59; Kotler 24.passim
See also emotion, feminism, impersonality

animal/s
and human relations in "The Widow and the Parrot," Williams 26.passim
and human relations in *VO*, Davison 23.passim
and modernism, Williams 26.114–15, 118
and music, Davison 23.16–17, 25
as nicknames, Clarke 28.10
bird imagery in *BTA*, Lauby 27.53
bird imagery in *TW*, Lostoski-Ho 28.50–51
cows in *BTA*, Foster 22.42–43
in children's literature, Williams 26.109, 112
in Woolf's writing, Livingstone 26.87, 89, 91
insects in "Kew Gardens," Ke 29.62–63
metaphor of, Clarke 28.14
Shag, Williams 26.113
snail in "Kew Gardens," Ke 29.63–64
See also bioethics, imagery, metaphor, music, sound

annotation
Woolf's practice of, Golden 23.83–85, 88; Jenkins 27.37
Woolf's "VS Greek and Latin Studies" notebook, Koulouris 25.passim
See also, transcription, translation writing

Anthropocene
and *TW*, Lostoski-Ho 28.passim
concept of, Lostoski-Ho 28.52–54
effects of combustion on environment, Ryan 30.69
See also climate change, fire, history, time

antisemitism
and Leonard's career, Marcus 24.8

aporia Dalgarno 22.passim

archaeology McVicker 28.70–71, 75
and biography, Hussey 29.167
artifacts, McVicker 28.81
Egyptology, McVicker 28.81–82
Woolf as literary archaeologist, McVicker 28.passim
See also history/historiography, land/ landscape

archive
confirmation of *TG* photographs, Kotler 24.51
Harry Ransom Center, Marcus 24.passim
JR notebook, Bunting 30.5
Mortimer Rare Book Collection (Smith College), Gilman 29.passim
Woolf's correspondence with Ling Shushua, Chau 30.passim
Woolf's letters to Violet Dickinson, Clarke 28.passim
Woolf's maps, Gillespie 25.passim

art
aesthetics of, Jenkins 27.34–36, 41–42
and decadence, Fouirnaies 22.29
and domesticity, Adair and Martin 24.90–91
and egotism, Delsandro 25.83–85
and feminism in *TTL*, Jenkins 27.passim
and social action, Foster 22.53–67
and women, Jenkins 27.34–35; Lauby 27.58–60
and women in *TTL*, Jenkins 27.passim
and unity, Rutherford 24.149
architecture, Ke 29.64–69
artistic form, Ke 29.passim
Jacob as artist in *JR*, Bunting 30.9–12
Keatsian "negative capability," Shin 23.122
neo-individualism, Reed 29.64–65
one-centric perspective, Ke 29.66–74
politics of, Adair and Martin 24.87
role of art/artist, Jenkins 27.7, 13; Jenkins 27.41–42; Layne 21.93–95; Shin 23.122; White 24.101n2
silence in *JR*, Ke 29.75–76
snapshot aesthetic in *O*, Fouirnaies 22.33
statuesque form in "Kew Gardens," Ke 29.61–64
statuesque form in *JR*, Bunting 30.15–16, 19–24; Ke 29.64–82
the visual arts in *TTL*, Jenkins 27.passim
unanimism, Reed 29.163–64
Vanessa Bell's aesthetics of, Jenkins 27.7–9, 13–14, 17. 20
See also formalism, music, painting, photograph/photography, post-impressionism

atlas
See books, geography

autoeroticism
Woolf and writing, Clarke 28.14–18, 21

autoethnography Koulouris 25.1–5; Phillps 26.9–10

automobile
and war, Adair and Martin 24.95
modernism and the motor-car, Adair and Martin 24.passim
road maps, Gillespie 25.99
See also advertising, consumerism, literary aesthetics, travel

avant-texte
Woolf's drafts of the 1917 chapter of *TY*, Phillips 26.passim
See also writing

beauty
politics of, Shin 23.113–14

Bildungsroman Livingstone 26.88
in *VO*, Novillo-Corvalán 23.39

bioethics Williams 26.107
in "The Widow and the Parrot," Williams, 26.passim
See also animals, the Anthropocene, disability, nature, nonhuman

biofiction Layne 21.78–80
Susan Sellers's *Vanessa and Virginia,* Layne 21.passim

biography and life-writing
and biofiction, Layne 21.passim
aristocratic backgrounds in *O*, Fouirnaies 22.31
biographical tropes in Woolf and Hussey's *Clive Bell*, Gillespie 29.passim
facts, Gillespie 29.153–54
in *TG*, Kotler 24.42–43
mosaic trope, Gillespie 29.150–52

Woolf's, Clarke 28.6–7, 21; Favre 30.56; McVicker 28.76–78
Woolf's autobiographical practices, Bond 23.71–72

Bloomsbury Group
aesthetics of, Jenkins 27.5–6, 8, 10, 17
and class, Adair and Martin 24.83–86, 88–89
and Clive Bell, Berkowitz 29.passim; Davison 29.passim;
and the motor-car, Adair and Martin 24.passim
anti-Bloomsbury sentiment, Davison 29.146–47
See also literary aesthetics, modernism

body
in "On Being Ill," Dalgarno 22.9–13
in Plato, Dalgarno 22.9–13
politics of in *O*, Graber 24.passim
See also walking

books
academic textbooks, Golden 23.83–85, 96–97, 99
atlas, Gillespie 25.102–04, 124–26
dust jacket, Fouirnaies 22.23
geographical dictionaries, Gillespie 25.102
guide books, Gillespie 25.97, 100; Golden 23.99–101
in *JR*, Golden 23.passim
See also genre, libraries, translation

Boy Scouts, the Wisor 21.10–14
See also masculinity, patriarchy

capital
impact capital, Berkowitz 29.30–33, 136–38
social capital, Berkowitz 29.129–30

capitalism
capitalist imperialism and Latin America in *VO*, Novillo-Corvalán 23.passim
See also economics

cartography
and colonialism, Gillespie 25.112–13, 115–16, 128
and patriarchy, Gillespie 25.112–13, 115–16
and sociocultural change, Gillespie 25.102–03
and war, Gillespie 25.110
and women, Gillespie 25.118
map as document of cultural change, Gillespie 25.104
road maps, Gillespie 25.99
Woolf's literary, Gillespie 25.108, 111–13, 115–24, 127–29
Woolf's maps, Gillespie 25.passim
See also imperialism, nationalism, transport, travel, walking

cemetery
as heterotopia, McVicker 28.73–74
See also death, ghosts, grief, hauntology,

censorship
and cinema, Wisor 21.8
of *The Well of Loneliness*, Pająk 24.passim
Radclyffe Hall trial, Pająk 24.16, 27
Woolf's self-censorship, Kotler 24.41; Pająk 24.27–29

characterization
and cartography in Woolf's fiction, Gillespie 25.98, 116–19, 122–24, 127–28
and scenic memory in *MD*, Bond 23.passim
Egyptian myth and *TTL*, Rutherford 24.passim
in "A Sketch of the Past," Ke 29.59–60
in *JR*, Golden 23.91–93; Ke 29.64–82
in "Kew Gardens," Ke 29.61–64
in *MD*, White 24.passim
Woolf's "tunnelling process," Bond 23.65
Woolf's "tunnelling process" in *MD*, Bond 23.66
See also identity, subjectivity

chorus
in *VO*, Davison 23.19–22, 28
See also community, music

cinema
and pacifism, Wisor 21.8
Clive Bell's views on, Humm 29.passim
Woolf's essay, Humm 29.159

class
and driving, Adair and Martin 24.78, 83–84
and the Bloomsbury Group, Adair and Martin 24.83–86, 88–89
and the English countryside, Jones 22.passim
and writing, Delsandro 25.86
aristocracy, Fouirnaies 22.passim
critique of in *O*, Fouirnaies 22.passim; Graber 24.passim
difference in *JR*, Ke 29.79–80
gender as, Fouirnaies 22.34–37
snobbery, Fouirnaies 22.21, 38; Marcus 24.7
Woolf's self-criticism, Jones 22.79
See also education, politics, society

climate change, Lostoski-Ho 28.54
See also the Anthropocene

clothing
See fashion

colonialism
and cartography, Gillespie 25.112–13, 115–16, 128
and gender, Novillo-Corvalán 23.40, 54, 57
and Latin American in *VO*, Novillo-Corvalán 23.passim
and vessels in *VO*, Graber 24.166–67
role of vessels, Gillespie 25.125–26; Graber 24.166, 169, 170
See also imperialism, nationalism/patriotism, ships

color
and feminism in *TTL*, Jenkins 27.13–17

common reader Gilman 29.passim; Layne 21.85
See also reading

community
and fire, Ryan 30.68, 73
and utopia/utopianism, Cheney 24.65–72; Livingstone 26.94–96
and women in *TY*, Delsandro 25.passim
and Woolf's writing, McVicker 28.71
communal modernism, Pająk 24.31
social networks, Berkowitz 29.passim
See also chorus, feminism, fire, interconnection, subjectivity, utopia/utopianism

consumerism
and motor-cars, Adair and Martin 24.75–78, 87–89
See also advertising, automobile, capitalism, economics

countryside Jones 22.passim

creativity
Woolf's conception of, Leach 28.101–02
See also art, women, writing

criticism
and women, Fischer 28.36

culture
and geographical dictionaries, Gillespie 25.102
cartography and sociocultural change, Gillespie 25.102–04
cultural heritage and Woolf's writing, McVicker 28.passim
"Egyptomania," Rutherford 24.154, 156
print culture, Golden 23.84–85
Woolf and Egyptomania, Rutherford 24.passim
See also archaeology, art, history/historiography, literary history/tradition, society, women

death Shin 23.123n22
and elegy in *TTL*, Shin 23.124
burial practices, McVicker 28.70–71, 79
elegy, Shin 23.111–12; Van Wert 29.117–18
The Egyptian Book of the Dead, Rutherford

24.136–37, 150
in *JR*, Ke 29.70–71
in *VO*, Caputi 29.10, 14–15
morbidity in *O*/at Knole, Fouirnaies 22.30
The Egyptian Book of the Dead and *TTL*, Rutherford 24.passim
See also cemetery, ghosts, hauntology, monuments, mourning, suicide

disability
and modernism, Williams 26.111–12
and the academy, Delsandro 25.87
in "The Widow and the Parrot," Williams 26.passim
in *TY*, Delsandro 25.79–80, 86
Woolf's representation of, Williams 26.111–12
See also ableism, animals, bioethics,

domesticity
and art, Adair and Martin 24.90–91
in *VO*, Shin 23.115–16
See also Angel in the House

drama
and the Socratic dialogue, Dalgarno 22.4
Aristotle's poetics of, White 24.105–06
poetics of in *MD*, White 24.passim
See also genre, literary aesthetic, pageant

driving
and British identity, Adair and Martin 24.92–95
and class, Adair and Martin 24.78, 83–84
and gender, Adair and Martin 24.77–78, 82, 89
and land/landscape, Adair and Martin 24.88, 93–94
See also automobile, cartography, consumerism, modernism, transport, travel

ecocriticism
and *TW,* Lostoski-Ho 28.49–50
weather in *TY*, Ryan 30.79–81
See also animals, the Anthropocene, fire, nature, nonhuman

economics
and gender, Wisor 21.23–25
capitalist imperialism and Latin American in *VO*, Novillo-Corvalán 23.passim
colonialism and English vessels, Graber 24.170
Leonard's "economic imperialism," Novillo-Corvalán 23.41–42
See also advertising, capitalism, consumerism, imperialism

education
and gender, Bunting 30.12–18; Golden 23.87, 89, 97–98
and women, Caputi 29.passim; Gillespie 25.115; Jenkins 27.43; Wisor 21.23–25
in *JR*, Bunting 30.12–18; Ke 29.77–82
in Nella Larsen's *Quicksand* and *VO*, Caputi 29.passim
Woolf at Morley College, Chua 30.40–42
Woolf's, Dalgarno 22.1, 9; Gillespie 25.100, 105; Jenkins 27.passim; Koulouris 25.5–6
Woolf's "VS Greek and Latin Studies" notebook, Koulouris 25.passim
writing as unteachable, Chua 30.40–44
See also feminism, influences, masculinity, museum, pedagogy, reading, writing

egotism
and art, Delsandro 25.83–85
Woolf's, Clarke 28.passim

ekphrasis Layne 21.83–84, 94, 100

emotion
and music, Davison 23.17–18
happiness, Kotler 24.44–45, 52–53
See also anger

epistolary
Woolf's and Ling Shushu's letters, Chua 30.passim

Woolf's and Violet Dickinson's letters, Clarke 28.passim

eroticism
Woolf's letters to Violet Dickinson, Clarke 28.passim

ethics
call for feminist ethics, Favre 30.62–63
of empathy, Clarke 28.13–15
Quaker thought and ethics in *BTA*, Foster 22.58–67
See also ableism, the Anthropocene, bioethics, disability, interconnection, nonhuman, pageant

exceptional moment
Woolf's moments of being, Livingstone 26.87–88; Lostoski-Ho 28.63–64
See also reality, representation

exercise
and gender, Gillespie 25.106

exoticism
Woolf and Latin America, Novillo-Corvalán 23.34–36
See also imperialism

exploration Gillespie 25.105–07
and women, Gillespie 25.118
See also cartography, influences, travel

fact
and biofiction, Layne 21.passim
See also reality, representation

failure
of intimacy, Clarke 28.17–21
of quest for unity in *TY*, Cheney 24.65
of Woolf's "mentorship" of Ling Shuhua, Chua 30.passim

fascism
and Woolf's study of Plato, Dalgarno 22.13–16
nationalism and fascism in *BTA*, Lauby 27.passim
Quakers as anti-fascists, Foster 22.passim
Woolf's opposition to, Livingstone 26.89–90; Wisor 21.5–6
Woolf's opposition to in *BTA*, Lauby 27.50
See also anger, antisemitism, economics, imperialism, pacifism, race, war

fashion
in *JR*, Schwartz 29.91–92
politics of in *O,* Fouirnaies 22.35–36; Graber 24.169–74, 177–82

femininity
and empathy, Clarke 28.14–15
and the Girl Guides, Wisor 21.12
See also empathy, feminism, gender, women

feminism
and ancient philosophy, Dalgarno 22.passim
and color in *TTL*, Jenkins 27.13–17
and geography, Gillespie 25.112–13
and heteronormativity, Delsandro 25.87–88
and intersectionality, Caputi 29.6, 20; Delsandro 25.86
and matriarchy in Ancient Egypt, Rutherford 24.157
and Michel de Montaigne, Leach 28.99
and pedagogy, Delsandro 25.74–75, 88, 90–93
and race, Delsandro 25.87–88
and resistance in *BTA*, Lauby 27.passim
and the Goddess Isis, Rutherford 24.157
and the masque, Lauby 27.49–50
and Vanessa Bell, Jenkins 27.13
female speakers in *JR*, Bunting 30.24–27
feminist politics in *TY*, Delsandro 25.passim
Jane Marcus's legacy, Camarasana et. al. 24.1–4
killjoy, Kotler 24.37, 45
suffrage, Camarasana et. al. 24.1; Marcus 24.5–6
transnational, Caputi 29.5–6
Woolf's, Czarnecki 21.52; Novillo-Corvalán

23.35, 37; Phillips 26.7–8; Shin 23.111, 116–17; White 24.107; Wisor 21.19–20, 23
See also Angel in the House, anger, animals, femininity, friendship, gender, heteronormativity, hysteria, influences, intersectionality, intimacy, lesbian desire/relation/identity, literary history/tradition, love, marriage, matriarchy, patriarchy, philology, queer, reception, sisterhood, subjectivity, walking, women

fiction
and modernism, Layne 21.84
science fiction and Woolf, Livingstone 26.passim
See also biofiction, genre, language, literary aesthetics,

fire Ryan 30.passim

flâneur/flâneuse
See walking, women

food
and imperialism in *VO*, Novillo-Corvalán 23.43–47, 51

formalism
and Roger Fry, Jenkins 27.6–7, 12–13
and *TTL*, Jenkins 27.passim
pedagogical form in *TY*, Cheney 24.passim
responses to innovations of *JR*, Bunting 30.6
significant form, Layne 21.83–84, 92–98, 101
See also art, literary aesthetics, painting

friendship
female, Jenkins 27.25, 32–33
romantic, Clarke 28.5–7, 20
Woolf and Violet Dickinson, Clarke 28.passim
Woolf's view of, Clarke 28.20–21
See also intimacy, queer, romance, sisterhood

gender
and ancient philosophy, Dalgarno 22.2, 8
and colonialism, Novillo-Corvalán 23.40, 54, 57
and driving, Adair and Martin 24.77–78, 82, 89
and education, Bunting 30.12–16; Golden 23.87, 89, 97–98
and exercise, Gillespie 25.106
and geography, Gillespie 25.112–13
and imperialism in *O*, Graber 24.passim
and *MD*, Czarnecki 21.50, 63, 66, 68, 70–71
and music, Davison 23.18–19, 25
and nationalism, Wisor 21.27
and otherness, Graber 24.166
and the ode, Shin 23.115–16, 119
and travel, Graber 24.167
and walking, Gillespie 25.106–07
and war, Czarnecki 21.53
and writing, Koulouris 25.6–7
and/as class, Fouirnaies 22.34–37
critique of in *O*, Graber 24.passim
cross-dressing, Fouirnaies 22.36
female friendship in *TY*, Delsandro 25.83
in Native American culture, Czarnecki 21.51–53, 66, 69–70
in *VO*, Shin 23.115–17
politics in *TY*, Delsandro 25.passim
transgender reading of *O*, Pająk 24.12–13
See also androgyny, femininity, feminism, heteronormativity, masculinity, matriarchy, patriarchy, women

General Strike, 1926 Wisor 21.22–23

genre
academic textbooks, Golden 23.83–84, 96–99
Bildungsroman, Livingstone 26.88
Bildungsroman in *VO*, Novillo-Corvalán 23.39
biofiction, Layne 21.passim
children's literature, Williams 26.108–10, 115–17
dialogue, Dalgarno 22.passim
drama and *MD*, White 24.passim

elegy, Shin 23.111–12
elegy and *JR*, Bunting 30.10–12
elegy and *TTL*, Shin 23.124–28
essay, Leach 28.99
family saga, Livingstone 26.88
guide books, Gillespie 25.97; Golden 23.99–100
imperial adventure fiction, Novillo-Corvalán 23.38–39
JR as abbreviated *Künstlerroman*, Bunting 30.5
marriage plot, Caputi 29.15, 20–21
masque, Lauby 27.49–50
polemic, Livingstone 26.88
science fiction, Livingstone 26.87, 89–91
the ode, Shin 23.110, 112–13
the relational nature of, Sullam 30.passim
TY as historical novel, Delsandro 25.73, 80–82
travel writing in *VO*, Novillo-Corvalán 23.39
Woolf and science fiction, Livingstone 26.passim
Woolf's study of, White 24.102–03
Woolf's "The Decay of Essay Writing," Leach 28.passim
See also epistolary, literary aesthetics, parody, poetry, tragedy

geography
and feminism, Gillespie 25.112–13
and gender, Gillespie 25.112
and spatial theory, Gillespie 25.98, 111–13
atlas, Gillespie 25.102–04, 124–26
geographical dictionaries, Gillespie 25.102
urban space in *MD*, Bond 23.passim
See also cartography, geopolitics

geopolitics
Latin America and *VO,* Novillo-Corvalán 23.passim

ghosts
in *TTL*, Rutherford 24.139
in "The Widow and the Parrot," Williams 26.114–15
See also death, ghosts, hauntology, psychoanalysis

Girl Guides, the Wisor 21.10–12
See also imperialism, women

grief
postwar, McVicker 28.71
See also mourning

handwriting
Leonard's, Gillespie 25.109
Woolf's, Gilman 29.31–32; Koulouris 25.3–4, 10; Phillips 26.4–5, 8

hauntology
and reading, Phillips 26.10–11
See also cemetery, death, ghosts, heterotopia, psychoanalysis

health
of soldiers, Wisor 21.11

heritage
cultural heritage and Woolf's writing, McVicker 28.passim

heteronormativity
and feminism, Delsandro 25.87–88
critique of in *Quicksand*, Caputi 29.21
in *TY*, Delsandro 25.79–80
Woolf's critique of in *O*, Graber 24.172
Woolf's resistance to, Jenkins 27.33–35
See also feminism, gender, marriage

heterotopia
Foucault's theory of, McVicker 28.72–74
Woolf's heterotopic aesthetic, McVicker 28.passim
See also, cemetery, libraries, mourning, museum, utopia/utopianism

history/historiography
"ancient song" in *MD*, Lostoski-Ho 28.55
and geographical dictionary, Gillespie 25.102

Egyptian, Rutherford 24.155–57
fire and ancestral past, Ryan 30.73–75
human, Lostoski-Ho 28.52
prehistory and Woolf's writing, McVicker 28.passim
transpersonal, Delsandro 25.86
women's, Marcus 24.passim
Woolf's historical practices, McVicker 28.passim; Novillo-Corvalán 23.passim; Phillips 26.7
See also archaeology, colonialism, land/landscape, museum

Hogarth Press Golden 23.98n25
and pacifism, Wisor 21.6–7
and Quakers, Foster 22.44

hysteria Clarke 28.14

identity
and imperialism in *VO*, Livingstone 26.91–92
and science fiction in Woolf's late writing, Livingstone 26.passim
Woolf's as writer, Livingstone 26.88
See also nationalism/patriotism, subjectivity

illness
and language, Fischer 28.41–42
in Plato, Dalgarno 22.9–13
in *Quicksand*, Caputi 29.20
in *VO*, Caputi 29.14; Fischer 28.41–42
Woolf's aesthetic strategy of, Livingstone 26.92–94
See also psychoanalysis/psychology

imagery
cartological in Woolf's fiction, Gillespie 25.98, 111–12, 117–24, 127
in *TW*, Livingstone 26.100–02; Lostoski-Ho 28.50, 61–63
pictorial strategy in *O*, Fouirnaies 22.passim
water and suicide, Layne 21.89–90
water in *VO*, Davison 23.23–24, 27–28
See also animals, metaphor

immunity Cheney 24.69–70

imperialism
and cartography, Gillespie 25.102–04, 124–29
and gender in *O*, Graber 24.passim
and identity in *VO*, Livingstone 26.91–92
and Latin American in *VO*, Novillo-Corvalán 23.passim
and masculinity, Wisor 21.9–10–12
and nationalism, Novillo-Corvalán 23.56–57; Wisor 21.25–26
and patriarchy in *VO*, Delsandro 25.89; Novillo-Corvalán 23.38–39
and radio, Wisor 21.25
and religion, Wisor 21.14–15
and science, Livingstone 26.100
and ships, Gillespie 25.124
and the Boy Scouts, Wisor 21.10–14
and the Girl Guides, Wisor 21.10–12
and the other/Other, Williams 26.113–14
and the rubber trade, Novillo-Corvalán 23.51–56, 58
and *TW*, Lostoski-Ho 28.49–50
critique of in *O*, Graber 24.passim
critique of in *VO*, Caputi 29.11
in *TG*, McVicker, 28.74
Leonard's "economic imperialism," Novillo-Corvalán 23.41–42
Woolf's critique of, Novillo-Corvalán 23.37–38; Williams 26.113–14; Wisor 21.5–7, 14–15
Woolf's critique of in *VO*, Novillo-Corvalán 23.passim
Woolf's research for Leonard's work on economic imperialism, Novillo-Corvalán 23.33–34, 44–45, 47–49
See also colonialism, nationalism/patriotism, race, research

impersonality Kotler 24.passim; Layne 21.93–96, 98

influences
academic textbooks, Golden 23.83–85, 98–99

Aristotle, White 24.101–03
Aristotle's mimetic theory and *MD*, White 24.passim
Vanessa Bell, Adair and Martin 24.78–79, 82, 87n12; Jenkins 27.5, 7, 9, 10, 13, 17–20; Layne 21.passim
Clive Bell as "influence," Berkowitz 29.133–36
Sir Thomas Browne, McVicker 28.85–86
William Browne, Lauby 27.59
Janet Case, Golden 23.87, 95; Jenkins 27.23–27, 36, 38, 40; Phillips 26.6–7
classical Greek texts, Golden 23.passim
Charles Darwin, Davison 23.passim
Violet Dickinson, Clarke 28.passim
Amelia Earhart, Gillespie 25.118
Egyptian myth, McVicker 28.71, 75; Rutherford 24.passim
Sigmund Freud, Rutherford 24.144–45
Edward Gibbon, Gillespie 25.105
Greek myth, McVicker 28.71–72, 75
Richard Hakluyt, Gillespie 25.105; Graber 24.167–68, 170
Jane Ellen Harrison, Jenkins 27.23–27, 39; McVicker 28.72
Homer, Koulouris 25.6–78
William Henry Hudson, Novillo-Corvalán 23.49–50
James Joyce, White 24.101–02
John Milton, Davison 23.22–25
Michel de Montaigne, Dalgarno 22.3
Michel de Montaigne and *AROO*, Leach 28.passim
Victoria Ocampo, Novillo-Corvalán 23.34–35
Clara Pater, Golden 23.95; Jenkins 27.passim
Pindar, Shin 23.113, 115, 123
Plato, Dalgarno 22.passim
Plato's *Symposium*, Dalgarno 22.6–7; Koulouris 25.8
Sappho, Shin 23.118–20
science, Livingstone 26.88, 93; Lostoski-Ho 28.50
Shag, Williams 26.113
Ethel Smyth, Delsandro 25.82–85
Edmund Spenser, Lauby 27.passim
Julia Stephen, Williams 26.109–10
Alfred, Lord Tennyson, Caputi 29.12; De Gay 30.103–04
Thoby Stephen's library, Golden 23.89, 93–95
travel, Golden 23.88
Richard Wagner, Davison 23.2–5, 19, 21, 26–27

interconnection Foster 22.45, 49, 51, 56–57, 59, 64–65

intermediality
and Woolf's writing, Davison 23.passim

interruptions
in *TY*, Delsandro 25.73

intersectionality
and feminism, Delsandro 25.86
and Woolfian scholarship, Czarnecki 21.50–51; Delsandro 25.passim
See also ableism, disability, literary aesthetics

intimacy
failure of, Clarke 28.17–21
of snapshot aesthetic in *O*, Fouirnaies 22.33
public/private, Clarke 28.10–11
queer politics of, Clarke 28.passim
Woolf and Violet Dickinson, Clarke 28.9–10
See also friendship, lesbian desire/relation/identity, love

land/landscape
and archaeology, McVicker 28.70
and driving, Adair and Martin 24.88, 93–94
and geographical dictionaries, Gillespie 25.102
as soundscape, Davison 23.7–9
Latin American and *VO*, Novillo-Corvalán 23.34–37
Neolithic British landscapes in Woolf's narratives, McVicker 28.passim
patriarchal ownership of, Gillespie 25.112–

13, 115–16
See also the Anthropocene, imagery, metaphor, nature, nonhuman

language
and illness, Fischer 28.41–42
functional language in "Modern Novels," Fischer 28.passim
functional language in *VO*, Fischer 28.passim
Kristeva's theory of, Fischer 28.27
sound of, Fischer 28.27–30, 35–36, 41
Woolf's conception of, Fischer 28.26–29, 33–37
See also philology

law, the
and *TG*, Wisor, 21.26–31

lesbian desire/relation/identity
and love, Shin 23.118–19
in *BTA*, Lauby 27.59–60
in *MD*, Bond 23.70–71, 73–79
in "Slater's Pins Have No Points," Jenkins 27.33–35
in Radclyffe Hall and Woolf, Pająk 24.passim
in *TY*, Delsandro 25.79–80
Woolf and Violet Dickinson, Clarke 28.passim
Woolf's, Delsandro 25.89; Layne 21.89
See also friendship, intimacy, matriarchy, queer, women

libraries
as heterotopia, McVicker 28.74
Harry Ransom Center, Marcus 24.passim
in *JR*, Golden 23.91–94, 103
Thoby Stephen's library, Golden 23.89, 93–94
Woolf's, Golden 23.87, 100–01, 103
See also annotation, book, education, influences, reading, translation, writing

listening
and language, Fischer 28.27–30, 42
Charles Darwin's "transposition," Davison 23.8, 10
in *VO,* Davison 23.9–11, 21; Fischer 28.30–31
naturalist as listener, Davison 23.7–10
Roland Barthes concept of, Fischer 28.28–30, 35–37, 41
See also language, music, sound, soundscape

literary aesthetics
and painting, Adair and Martin 24.93; Layne 21.82–85, 87, 91–92, 100–01
and painting in *TTL*, Jenkins 27.passim; Layne 21.95–99
and the motor-car, Adair and Martin 24.passim
and the visual arts in *TTL*, Jenkins 27.passim
biofiction, Layne 21.passim
in *JR*, Golden 23.86
music and *VO,* Davison 23.passim
ontology of literature, Foster 22.43, 53–58
Woolf and children's literature, Williams 26.108–10, 115–18
Woolf and maps, Gillespie 25.passim
Woolf and Native American literature, Czarnecki 21.passim
Woolf and science fiction, Livingstone 26.passim
Woolf's, Bond 23.64–69; Davison 23.1; Fischer 28.passim; Golden 23.83–85; Koulouris 25.3–8; Layne 21.passim; Lostoski-Ho 28.passim; Rutherford 24.152–53, 159–60; Shin 23.111–12; White 24.101–03
Woolf's heterotopic aesthetic, McVicker 28.passim
Woolf's mythic method, McVicker 28.75
Woolf's odes, Shin 23.passim
See also art, bioethics, biofiction, culture, drama, epistolary, formalism, genre, illness, imagery, intermediality, listening, literary history/tradition, masque, metaphor, mimesis, music, narrative, poetics, poetry, repetition,

sound, soundscape, space, time, tragedy, writing

literary history/tradition
cross-cultural and global modernism, Chua 30.33–34, 46
late modernism, Delsandro 25.76–77
Shakespeare's sister, Jenkins 27.11; Jenkins 27.23, 43
See also biofiction, genre, literary aesthetics, poetry, writing

London
Woolf's maps of, Gillespie 25.98–99

love
and lesbian desire, Shin 23.118–19
in *JR*, Ke 29.81–82
Woolf's odes, Shin 23.passim
See also failure, friendship, intimacy, lesbian desire/relation/identity, queer

maps
See cartography

marriage
in *MD,* Bond 23.74–78
in *TTL*, Rutherford 24.139
in *VO*, Davison 23.17–22, 24–25; Fischer 28.31n10, 37–40, 42
See also feminism, heteronormativity, research, women

masculinity
and imperialism, Wisor 21.9–10–11
and military dress, Wisor 21.9–10
and sexual aggression, Caputi 29.9–10, 17–18
and the Boy Scouts, Wisor 21.11
martial masculinity in *JR*, Bunting 30.7, 12–14, 19–24
See also education, feminism, patriarchy

masque
and feminism, Lauby 27.49–50
pageant as in *BTA*, Lauby 27.passim

masturbation
phobia of, Clarke 28.14
See also autoeroticism

matriarchy
and Kristeva's semiotic language, Fischer 28.27
and myth in *TTL*, Rutherford 24.135, 144, 151
and Native American culture, Czarnecki 21.52–53, 66, 69–70
in Ancient Egypt, Rutherford 24.157
Woolf's view of, Czarnecki 21.50, 52–53
See also community, feminism, influences, mother/motherhood, patriarchy, women

memory
scenic memory in *MD*, Bond 23.passim

mental health
Woolf's, Layne 21.90
See also grief, mourning, suicide, trauma

metaphor
and ships in *O*, Graber 24.passim
animals, Clarke 28.14
cartographical in Woolf's fiction, Gillespie 25.111–12, 117–24, 127–28
caves, Bond 23.66n6
in "Slater's Pins Have No Points," Jenkins 27.33
in *TW*, Livingstone 26.100–02
metaphorical pyrotechnics, Ryan 30.70–76
ships in Woolf's writing, Graber 24.169–71
See also animals, imagery, literary aesthetics

mimesis White 24.105
Woolf's revision of Aristotelian mimesis in *MD*, White 24.passim
See also drama, influences, poetry

mirror Foster 22.62

misogyny

and E.M. Forster, Rutherford 24.159
See also patriarchy

modernism
and animals, Williams 26.114–15, 118
and disability, Williams 26.111–12
and elegy, Shin 23.112
and fiction, Layne 21.84
and music, Davison 23.2–4
and painting, Adair and Martin 24.91–92
and the motor-car, Adair and Martin 24.passim
late modernism, Delsandro 25.76–77
modernist networks, Berkowitz 29.passim; Pająk 24.13
modernist publishers, Pająk 24.18–22
practices of writing, Golden 23.85–86
See also literary aesthetics, literary history/historiography, painting, postmodernism

monuments
and mourning, McVicker 28.75

mother/motherhood
pronatalism, Wisor 21.11n19–12n20
See also Angel in the House, marriage

mourning
and heterotopias in Woolf's writing, McVicker 28.passim
and monuments, McVicker 28,75
practices of, McVicker 28.71n5
See also death, ritual

museum
and *JR*, Schwartz 29.passim
as heterotopia, McVicker 28.74
See also education

music
"ancient song" in *MD*, Lostoski-Ho 28.55
and animals, Davison 23.16–17, 25
and Charles Darwin, Davison 23.passim
and emotion, Davison 23.17–18
and gender, Davison 23.18–19, 25
and modernism, Davison 23.2–4
and nature, Davison 23.passim
and nonhuman life, Davison 23.1, 6–7
and *VO,* Davison 23.passim
and Woolf's writing, Davison 23.3–5
birdsong in *TW*, Lostoski-Ho 28.51
gramophone in *BTA*, 63
in "Slater's Pins Have No Points," Jenkins 27.34–35, 39–40
royal musician, Wisor 21.32–35
See also art, emotion, listening, opera, sound, soundscape

myth
and science, McVicker 28.75
Antigone, Phillips 26.6–7
Egyptian in *TTL*, Rutherford 24.passim
Greek mythology in Woolf's "VS Greek and Latin Studies" notebook, Koulouris 25.passim
Isis, Rutherford 24.155–57
matriarchal in *TTL*, Rutherford 24.135, 144, 151
Woolf's mythic method, McVicker 28.75
See also influences

narrative
and biofiction, Layne 21.79
method, Williams 26.110, 112; Jenkins 27.40; Koulouris 25.6–7
method in *F*, Williams 26.115
method in *JR*, Golden 23.85–86
method in *MD*, Bond 23.68–70; White 24.passim
method in "Slater's Pins Have No Points," Jenkins 27.33–34, 38–39
method in *TTL*, Rutherford 24.148–49, 159–60
See also formalism, literary aesthetics

nationalism/patriotism
and cartography in Woolf's fiction, Gillespie 25.120–21
and Englishness in Woolf's writing, McVicker 28.passim
and gender, Wisor 21.27
and imperialism, Novillo-Corvalán 23.56–57; Wisor 21.25–26

and religion, Wisor 21.15–18
and the Boy Scouts, Wisor 21.10–14
and the Girl Guides, Wisor 21.10–12
British identity and driving, Adair and Martin 24.92–95
English identity and fascism in *BTA*, Lauby 27.passim
English identity and vessels, Graber 24.165–68, 177
in *TG*, Wisor 21.passim
See also colonialism, imperialism, land/landscape, race, women

nature
and music, Davison 23.passim
imagery in *TW*, Lostoski-Ho 28.50, 61, 63
listening to, Davison 23.7–9
See also animals, the Anthropocene, ecocriticism, land/landscape, nonhuman, the other/Other, representation

nonhuman
and human relations in "The Widow and the Parrot," Williams 26.passim
and human relations in *VO*, Davison 23.passim
and music, Davison 23.1
and music in *VO,* Davison 23.6–7, 11
in *TW*, Livingstone 26.100–02; Lostoski-Ho 28.passim
in Woolf's writing, Livingstone 26.87, 89, 91
life in *MD*, Lostoski-Ho 28.55
See also animal, the Anthropocene, imagery, land/landscape, metaphor, nature

nostalgia
and Englishness, McVicker 28.86–87
in *BTA*, Lauby 27.54–55
See also nationalism/patriotism

objects Schwartz 29.101–03
See also museum

ode
See poetry

opera Davison 23.26–27
and *VO,* Davison 23.17–21, 23
See also music

other/Other
and gender, Graber 24.166
and the other/Other, Williams 26.113–14
and race, Delsandro 25.88–90
human and nonhuman relations in "The Widow and the Parrot," Williams 26.passim
in *BTA*, Lauby 27.53, 58–59
in Woolf's writing, Livingstone 26.87, 89–91
See also animals, exoticism, feminism, gender, intersectionality, nature, patriarchy, race

pacifism
and censorship, Wisor 21.8
and cinema, Wisor 21.8
and fire scenes in Woolf, Ryan 30.77–79
and Quakerism, Foster 22.passim
and the Hogarth Press, Wisor 21.6–7
and Woolf's interest in masculine behavior, Gallego Larrarte 30.115
Clive Bell's, Berkowitz 29.125; Davison 29.145
in *BTA*, Foster 22.58–67
in *JR*, Bunting 30.25–27
Woolf's, Wisor 21.5–8
Woolf's in *TG*, Wisor 21.9
See also fascism, interconnection

pageant
and ethics, Foster 22.58–67
audience in *BTA*, Foster 22.60–67
history of, Lauby 27.48–49
pageantry and imperialism, Wisor 21.9–10
politics of in *BTA*, Gillespie 25.119; Lauby 27.passim; Livingstone 26.95
royal in *TG*, Wisor 21.31–35
See also drama, nationalism/patriotism

painting
and literary aesthetics, Adair and Martin 24.93; Layne 21.82–85, 87, 91–92, 100–01
and literary aesthetics in *TTL*, Jenkins 27.passim; Layne 21.95–99
and modernism, Adair and Martin 24.91–92
Bell's *Interior with the Artist's Daughter*, Adair and Martin 24.91
in *O*, Fouirnaies 22.passim
See also art, formalism, influences

parataxis Cheney 24.67–72

parody
and travel writing in *VO*, Novillo-Corvalán 23.39

patriarchy
and cartography, Gillespie 25.112–13, 115–16, 128
and imperialism in *VO*, Delsandro 25.89; Novillo-Corvalán 23.37–39
and Kristeva's symbolic language, Fischer 28.27
and philology, Jenkins 27.38
and politics, Wisor 21.22
and society in *TG*, McVicker 28.74; Wisor 21.passim
and the academy, Delsandro 25.87
and women, Delsandro 25.75
ownership of land, Gillespie 25.112–13, 115–16
patriarchal images in *TG*, Wisor 21.passim
Woolf's critique of, Novillo-Corvalán 23.37–39; Phillips 26.7–8
Woolf's critique of in *BTA*, Foster 22.65; Lauby 27.passim
Woolf's critique of in *MD*, Bond 23.70–79; Czarnecki 21.72–73
Woolf's critique of in *TY*, Delsandro 25.79–80
See also education, feminism, gender, masculinity, matriarchy, misogyny, society, violence, women

pedagogy
and dialogue, Dalgarno 22.15
and feminism, Delsandro 25.74–75, 88, 90–93
and reading, Cheney 24.passim
Clara Pater's role in Woolf's education, Jenkins 27.passim
discovery, Camarasana et. al. 24.2
in Plato's *Protagoras*, Dalgarno 22.4
Woolf's "mentorship" of Ling Shuhua, Chua 30.passim
See also class, education, influences, philology, women, writing

philology Jenkins 27.28, 36–38
and the patriarchy, Jenkins 27.38
Woolf's view of, Jenkins 27.24–25, 38, 42–43
See also education, influences, pedagogy, women, writing

philosophy
and bodies, Dalgarno 22.9–13, 15
and contradiction, Dalgarno 22.8
and definitions, Dalgarno 22.6, 14
and doubt, Dalgarno 22.6, 12
and personal experience, Dalgarno 22.2
and politics, Dalgarno 22.8, 13–16
and social interaction, Dalgarno 22.1
and solitude, Dalgarno 22.10
and the question, Dalgarno 22.3
virtue and knowledge, Dalgarno 22.4, 6, 10
See also anger

photograph/photography Layne 21.85
and *TG*, Kotler 24.48–53; Wisor 21.passim
Hall's documentary photographs, Wisor 21.5
in *O*, Fouirnaies 22.passim
snapshot aesthetic in *O*, Fouirnaies 22.33

poetics
of loss in Woolf's "VS Greek and Latin Studies" notebook, Koulouris 25.9–10
of tragedy in *MD*, White 24.passim

poetry de Gay 30.passim; Gallego Larrarte

30.passim; Goldman 30.passim; Kopley 30.passim; Sullam 30.passim
and form, Sullam 30.passim
and gender difference, Gallego Larrarte 30.111–12
and generational difference, Gallego Larrarte 30.113
and genre, Sullam 30.passim
and prose, Goldman 30.107–08; Kopley 126–27
and queer feeling, Goldman 30.107–08
and the Socratic dialogue, Dalgarno 22.4
antiquity, Goldman 30.108
aurality, de Gay 30.101–02
definition, Kopley 30.125
elegy, de Gay 30.100–05; Shin 23.111–12, 124–28
Pindar's odes and *TTL*, Shin 23.123–24
Pindar's odes and *VO*, Shin 23.115–17
the ode, Shin 23.110, 112–13
Woolf's odes, Shin 23.passim
See also art, formalism, genre, impersonality, influences, literary aesthetics, poetics, tragedy, witness

police Schwartz 29.99–100

politics
and publishing, Pająk 24.passim
and the patriarchy, Wisor 21.22
and society, Wisor 21.21–22, 27–31
and war, Wisor 21.22
of art, Adair and Martin 24.87
of beauty, Shin 23.113–14
of fashion in *O*, Fouirnaies 22.35–37; Graber 24.169–74, 177–82
of Quakerism, Foster 22.passim
of reading, White 24.103–04, 107–09
of rural preservation, Jones 22.passim
of sexuality in *O*, Graber 24.172–75, 177, 181
of the body in *O*, Graber 24.passim
public/private, Wisor 21.22, 39
queer politics of intimacy, Clarke 28.passim
See also bioethics, ethics, feminism, geopolitics, imperialsim, nationalism, pageant, patriarchy, patriotism, society, women

post-impressionism Layne 21.84, 93, 96
in *TTL*, Jenkins 27.10, 14, 16–17
See also art

postmodernism
and biofiction, Layne 21.78

postwar
and gendered politics in England, Czarnecki 21.68
grief, McVicker 28.71
postwar life in *MD*, Czarnecki 21.64–68, 70
See also economics, politics, trauma, war

power
Woolf's resistance to in *BTA*, Lauby 27.passim

prehistory
See history

pronatalism Wisor 21.11n19
Woolf's critique of, Wisor 21.12

psychoanalysis/psychology
death drive, Van Wert 29.passim
desire v. drive, Van Wert 29.111–12
effects of urban parks on Septimus in *MD*, van Straten 30.93–94
Freud's Oedipus complex and *TTL*, Rutherford 24.144–45
Freud's uncanny, Camarasana et. al. 24.2; McVicker 28.71
Klein's "depressive position," Clarke 28.13
Woolf's "madness," Favre 30.passim
See also illness, influences, language

public/private
and driving, Adair and Martin 24.89–90
and intimacy, Clarke 28.9–10
and politics, Wisor 21.22, 39
life in *MD*, White 24.119–21, 123–27
selfhood in *MD*, Bond 23.71
space, McVicker 28.91–92

war and memorials, London 16.passim

queer
homosexuality in ancient texts, Dalgarno 22.2, 8
politics of intimacy, Clarke 28.passim
queer feeling, Goldman 30.107–08
queer subtext in *Quicksand*, Caputi 29.16
theory and utopias, Livingstone 26.98–100
theory of friendship, Clarke 28.19–20
theory of futurity, Van Wert 29.119–20
See also failure, friendship, lesbian desire/relation/identity, romance

race
and feminism, Delsandro 25.87–88
and inequality, Delsandro 25.87–88
Black modernity, Caputi 29.5–6
primitivism in *VO* and Larsen's *Quicksand*, Caputi 29.13–14, 16–18
racial difference in *VO*, Caputi 29.13–14
See also colonialism, exoticism, imperialism, racism, the other/Other

racism
and the other/Otherness, Delsandro 25.88–90
and Woolf in *VO*, Novillo-Corvalán 23.35–36
See also colonialism, exoticism, imperialism, race, the other/Other

radio
and Clive Bell, Davison 29.passim
and imperialism, Wisor 21.25

reading
and criticism, Gilman 29.passim
and hauntology, Phillips 26.10–11
and pedagogy, Cheney 24.passim
interaction with a text, Dalgarno 22.6
politics of, White 24.103–04, 107–08
surface reading, Fischer 28.26
the reader and *MD*, White 24.103–04, 109–10, 112, 114, 119, 128
transpersonal feminism and *TY*, Delsandro 25.passim
Woolf and classical Greek texts, Dalgarno 22.passim; Golden 23.passim
Woolf's practice of, Jenkins 27.37, 40–42
Woolf's readers, Fischer 28.34–35; Leach 28.103
Woolf's "VS Greek and Latin Studies" notebook, Dalgarno 22.6–7; Koulouris 25.passim
See also annotation, common reader, education, influences, language, libraries, pedagogy, research, transcription, translation, writing

reality
representation of, Fischer 28.31–32, 34; Golden 23.85–86; Livingstone 26.87–88; White 24.106–10
representation of in *MD*, White 24.111–13, 116, 128
See also exceptional moment

reception
feminist reception of Woolf/Woolf's feminism, Favre 30.passim
of *The Well of Loneliness*, Pająk 24.passim
of Woolf and Radclyffe Hall in Poland, Pająk 24.passim

religion
and imperialism, Wisor 21.14–15
and nationalism, Wisor 21.15–18
and skepticism, Caputi 29.11
and women, Wisor 21.18–20
church scenes in *VO* and *Quicksand*, Caputi 29.
in *TG,* Wisor 21.17, 19
Quakerism, Foster 22.passim
Woolf's critique of, Wisor 21.15
See also aevum, spirituality

repetition
in *VO*, Fischer 28.38–39

representation
of nature in *TW*, Lostoski-Ho 28.50–51
of reality, Fischer 28.31–32, 34; Golden 23.85–86; White 24.106–10

of reality in *MD*, White 24.111–13, 116, 128

research
Woolf's research for Leonard's work on economic imperialism, Novillo-Corvalán 23.33–34, 44–45, 47–49
Woolf's "VS Greek and Latin Studies" notebook, Koulouris 25.passim
See also literary aesthetics, reading, writing

romance
romantic friendship, Clarke 28.5–7, 20
Woolf's and Violet Dickinson's romantic friendship, Clarke 28.passim
See also friendship, intimacy, lesbian desire/relation/identity, love, queer, sisterhood

royalty
in *TG*, Wisor 21.31–35
royal musician, Wisor 21.32–35

science
and imperialism, Livingstone 26.100
and myth, McVicker 28.75
and Woolf's writing, Livingstone 26.88, 93, 97
archaeology, McVicker 28.70–71
See also technology

sexuality
comparison between Woolf and Vanessa Bell, Layne 21.85–89
politics of in *O*, Graber 24.172–75, 177, 181
virginity in *VO* and *Quicksand*, Caputi 29.19–20
Woolf's, Delsandro 25.89
See also friendship, intimacy, lesbian desire/relation/identity, love, queer

Shakespeare's sister
See literary history/tradition

shell shock
See war

ships
and imperialism, Gillespie 25.124–26
and metaphor in *O*, Graber 24.passim
and metaphor in Woolf's writing, Graber 24.169, 171
vessels and English identity, Graber 24.165–69, 177
See also capitalism, colonialism, commerce, imperialism

significant form
See formalism

sisterhood
Woolf and Bell, Layne 21.passim
See also feminism, friendship, influences, lesbian desire/relation/identity, love, romance

smoking
cigarette cards in *TG*, Wisor 21.2

society
and politics, Wisor 21.21–22, 27–31
and the Boy Scouts, Wisor 21.10–11, 13–14
and the Girl Guides, Wisor 21.10–11
and the motor-car, Adair and Martin 24.75–78
and the patriarchy in *TG*, Wisor 21.passim
cartography and sociocultural change, Gillespie 25.102–04
Woolf's critique of social hierarchies, Davison 23.25–26; Gillespie 25.112–13, 115–16, 128; Wisor 21.10
Woolf's critique of social hierarchies in *O*, Graber 24.passim
Woolf's heterotopias, McVicker 28.passim
See also automobile, consumerism, culture, economics, politics

Society of Outsiders Delsandro 25.87; Phillips 26.1, 8; Wisor 21.35
soldiers
health of, Wisor 21.11
Horse Guard Parade, Wisor 21.38–40
Household Cavalry, Wisor 21.32–38, 40
See also health, trauma, war

sound
birdsong in *TW*, Lostoski-Ho 28.51
Charles Darwin's views of, Davison 23.passim
gramophone in *BTA*, Foster 22.63
in *VO,* Davison 23.passim
of language, Fischer 28.27
See also listening, music, opera, soundscape

soundscape
Charles Darwin's "transpositions," Davison 23.8, 10
in *VO*, Davison 23.9–11, 20
landscape as, Davison 23.7–9
See also listening, music, sound

space
and subjectivity, Bond 23.64–66
geography and spatial theory, Gillespie 25.98, 111–13
heterotopias, McVicker 28.73–74
in *AROO*, Leach 28.102–04
in *MD*, White 24.113–17
public/private, McVicker 28.91–92
urban space in *MD*, Bond 23.passim
Woolf's conception of, Bond 23.64–65; Gillespie 25.112–13, 116, 119–20
See also history/historiography, memory, time

spirituality
and literature's mission, Foster 22.53–67
asceticism, Dalgarno 22.11
mysticism/materialism, Foster 22.passim
Quakerism, Foster 22.passim
the soul, Dalgarno 22.9–10; Ke 29.62, 76–77
Woolf's mythic method, McVicker 28.75
See also religion

stream of consciousness
in *JR*, Golden 23.86
Woolf's "tunnelling process," Bond 23.65–66
See also literary aesthetics, poetry, writing

subjectivity
and biofiction, Layne 21.79
and space, Bond 23.64–66
and the motor-car, Adair and Martin 24.75, 82
and trauma, Van Wert 29.109–10, 115
female subjectivity and urban space in *MD*, Bond 23.passim
intersubjectivity in *MD*, White 24.110
See also community, identity

suicide
and water imagery, Layne 21.89–90
in *MD*, White 24.122–25
in Plato, Dalgarno 22.10
Woolf's, Favre 30.passim; Gillespie 25.110; Layne 21.80, 89, 91
See also death, mental health

technology
and the motor-car, Adair and Martin 24.76–77, 95
See also consumerism, economics, science

temporality
See time

time
and heterotopia, McVicker 28.73–74
and *TW*, Lostosko-Ho 28.passim
concept of deep time, Lostoski-Ho 28.52–53
in *MD*, Bond 23.passim; Lostoski-Ho 28.55; White 24.113–17
in *TTL*, Lostoski-Ho 28.55–56
the future, Cheney 24.63–65; Van Wert 29.119–20
Woolf's conception of, Livingstone 26.93–96
Woolf's "tunneling process," Bond 23.65–66
See also history/historiography, space

tradition
See literary history/tradition

tragedy
Aristotle's poetics of, White 24.105

poetics of in *MD*, White 24.passim
See also genre, influences, literary aesthetics, poetry

transcription
transcript of the 1917 Dinner Party scene from holograph of *TY*, Phillips 26.passim
transcript of Woolf's "As to criticism," Gilman 29.45–55
transcript of Woolf's "VS Greek and Latin Studies" notebook, Koulouris 25.13–72
transcript of Woolf's "The Villa Jones," Jones 22.89–95
Woolf's practice, Phillips 26.9–11
See also annotation, archive, literary aesthetics, translation, writing

translation
JR and Woolf's strategies of, Golden 23.passim
Woolf's strategies of, Golden 23.86–87; Jenkins 27.27, 35–37; Koulouris 25.4
Woolf's training in, Dalgarno 22.1, 16
See also annotation, literary aesthetics, transcription, writing

transport
the motor-car, Adair and Martin 24.passim
See also automobile, gender, travel, ships

trauma
and recovery in *MD* and Leslie Marmon Silko's *Ceremony*, Czarnecki 21.passim
and war, Czarnecki 21.50–53, 64–65; Van Wert 29.108–09
in *BTA*, Lauby 27.53–53

travel
and gender, Graber 24.167
English vessels and colonialism, Graber 24.169
guide books and *JR*, Gillespie 25.97, 100; Golden 23.99–100, 102–03
motor-cars, Adair and Martin 24.75–76, 89–90
road maps, Gillespie 25.99
Woolf and England, McVicker 28.79
Woolf and Greece, Golden 23.102; Ke 29.67, 77–78; McVicker 28.78
Woolf and maps, Gillespie 25.100–01
See also automobile, transport, walking

unity
and art, Rutherford 24.149

utopia/utopianism
and science fiction in Woolf's late writing, Livingstone 26.passim
in *TY*, Cheney 24.passim
of urban parks, van Straten 30.passim
theories of, Livingstone 26.93–94, 98–99
See also cemetery, hetrotopias, libraries, museum, queer

violence
in *BTA*, Lauby 27.55–57

voice
recording of Woolf's, Fischer 28.25–26

walking
and gender, Gillespie 25.106–07
and women, Gillespie 25.106–08
in London parks, van Straten 30.passim
spatiotemporal suspension, van Straten 30.87–88, 91
wanderings of mind and body, van Straten 30.86
Woolf and maps, Gillespie 25.97–98, 104–07, 109–10

war
and cartography, Gillespie 25.110
and gender, Czarnecki 21.53
and military dress, Wisor 21.9–10, 36–37
and politics, Wisor 21.22
and the Boy Scouts, Wisor 21.13–14
and the motor-car, Adair and Martin 24.95
and trauma, Czarnecki 21.50–53, 64–65
as background for Woolf/Ling

correspondence, Chua 30.39–40
history without the military, Foster 22.65–67
Horse Guard Parade, Wisor 21.38–40
Household Cavalry, Wisor 21.32–38, 40
in *TY*, Delsandro 25.81–82
JR as anti-war novel, Bunting 30.passim
shell shock in *MD*, Bunting 30.8; Czarnecki 21.50
Woolf's conception of, McVicker 28.80–81; Wisor 21.9–10, 40–41
See also fascism, postwar, soldiers, trauma

women
and art, Jenkins 27.34–35; Lauby 27.58–60
and art in *TTL*, Jenkins 27.passim
and criticism, Fischer 28.36
and education, Gillespie 25.115; Jenkins 27.43; Wisor 21.23–25
and exploration, Gillespie 25.118
and map-making, Gillespie 25.118
and patriarchy, Delsandro 25.75
and religion, Wisor 21.18–20
and walking, Gillespie 25.106–08
and writing, Clarke 28.14; Fischer 28.31; Leach 28.101–04
definition of, Delsandro 25.88
female subjectivity in *MD*, Bond 23.passim
the Girl Guides, Wisor 21.10–12
See also Angel in the House, community, domesticity, feminism, friendship, gender, heteronormativity, intimacy, lesbian desire/identity/relation, literary history/tradition, love, marriage, sisterhood

writing
and autoeroticism, Clarke 28.14–18, 21
and class, Delsandro 25.86
and gender, Koulouris 25.6–7
and women, Clarke 28.14; Fischer 28.31; Leach 28.101–04
culture of, Clarke 28.14
epistolary culture, Clarke 28.11
modernist practices of writing, Golden 23.85–86
Woolf's editing practice, Jenkins 27.8–10; Leach 28.101; Lostoski-Ho 28.56–60
Woolf's stationary, Koulouris 25.3
Woolf's "tunnelling process," Bond 23.65–66
Woolf's drafts of the 1917 chapter of *TY*, Phillips 26.passim
Woolf's "VS Greek and Latin Studies" notebook, Koulouris 25.passim
See also annotation, epistolary, history/tradition, reading, transcription, translation, women

Part 4: Woolf References

Compiled by Benjamin D. Hagen and Skylar Kovacs

Part 4A: The Diaries

"Greek Notebook" Koulouris 25.passim
PA Favre 30.56
11 February 1897 Gillespie 25.107
23 May 1897 Gilman 29.53n23
"Diary. Hyde Park Gate. 1903?" Golden 23.87
"Miss Case" (*PA* 181–84) Jenkins (Gwyn) 27.23, 24, 32, 33, 35, 36, 38
"Netherhampton House, Salisbury. August: 1903" (*PA* 187ff.) Gillespie 25.104, 107
"Stonehenge" (*PA* 198–200) McVicker 28.77
28 March 1905 Gillespie 25.100
"Cornwall 1905" Gillespie 25.104, 108
"Blo' Norton 1906" Gillespie 25.100, 104–05
"Greece, 1906" Gillespie 25.100–02; Golden 23.100; Koulouris 25.33n106
"Street of Tombs" (*PA* 322–23) McVicker 28.78
"Eleusis" (*PA* 324–25) McVicker 28.78
"Appendix E: Experiments and Exercises: Warboys 1899" Koulouris 25.3
9 January 1915 Williams 26.111
22 November 1917 Sullam 30.121
8 September 1918 Livingstone 26.87
18 September 1918 Golden 23.100
23 September 1918 Novillo-Corvalán 23.50

3 November 1918 Golden 23.95
11 October 1919 Golden 23.93
26 January 1920 Ke 29.64
18 May 1920 Davison 23.26n39
25 October 1920 Gilman 29.47n7
29 April 1921 Gilman 29.47n7
23 May 1921 Dalgarno 22.6
3 December 1921 Gilman 29.47n7
26 July 1922 Ke 29.64, 70n13; McVicker 28.80
16 August 1922 Gilman 29.29, 33
28 August 1922 Gilman 29.51n19; White 24.103n5
3 September 1922 Gilman 29.33; White 24.103n5
4 October 1922 White 24.103n5
14 October 1922 Favre 30.57n7
29 October 1922 Golden 23.86
7 November 1922 Humm 29.156
7 January 1923 White 24.103n5
28 January 1923 Dalgarno 22.11
19 February 1923 Fouirnaies 22.21
19 June 1923 Humm 29.157
28 July 1928 Gilman 29.32
6 August 1923 Gilman 29.55n27
17 August 1923 Gilman 29.27, 52n20, 53n24
29 August 1923 Gilman 29.27
30 August 1923 Bond 23.65, 66n6; McVicker 28.87
5 September 1923 Gilman 29.27
11 September 1923 Gilman 29.47n7
15 October 1923 Bond 23.65; White 24.113
16 November 1923 Gillespie 29.152; Gilman 29.27, 32
12 January 1924 Gilman 29.53n24
3 February 1924 Gilman 29.32, 33
5 April 1924 Gilman 29.33, 50n15, 55n27
5 May 1924 Gilman 29.55n27
5 July 1924 Fouirnaies 22.30
15 August 1924 Goldman 30.107–08; Graeber 24.168n3
7 September 1924 White 24.112, 127
15 September 1924 Gillespie 29.152
18 March 1925 Gilman 29.27–28
17 May 1925 Gilman 29.48n9
18 June 1925 Bond 23.67
27 June 1925 de Gay 30.100, 103
7 December 1925 Gilman 29.36; Sullam 30.119
21 December 1925 Layne 21.86
7 May 1926 Schwartz 29.97
9 May 1926 Wisor 21.22
"Rodmell. 1926" [July 1926] Jenkins (Amber) 27.8–9
5 September 1926 Sullam 30.121
23 November 1926 Foster 22.41, 65
21 February 1927 de Gay 30.100
14 March 1927 Sullam 30.122
18 June 1927 de Gay 30.99; Wisor 21.10
4 July 1927 Davison 29.142
11 July 1927 Adair/Martin 24.82, 84
10 August 1927 Adair/Martin 24.80
4 September 1927 de Gay 30.104; Hussey 29.167
5 September 1927 Adair/Martin 24.81
18 February 1928 Jenkins (Amber) 27.9n7
17 April 1928 Adair/Martin 24.83
21 April 1928 Adair/Martin 24.86n10
7 November 1928 Bunting 30.26n5; de Gay 30.99, 100
28 November 1928 Fischer 28.26, 27n7
4 January 1929 Foster 22.41, 45
28 May 1929 Lostoski-Ho 28.51
31 May 1929 Adair/Martin 24.86
5 August 1929 Lostoski-Ho 28.47n1
21 August 1929 Adair/Martin 24.86
11 October 1929 Davison 23.6
16 September 1929 Lostoski-Ho 28.51
5 November 1929 Lostoski-Ho 28.47
8 December 1929 Gillespie 25.105; Graeber 24.168n3
28 December 1929 Adair/Martin 24.84
26 January 1930 Lostoski-Ho 28.47n1
16 February 1930 Fischer 28.42
11 March 1930 Lostoski-Ho 28.47n1
28 March 1930 Gillespie 29.152
9 April 1930 Ke 29.58n4
20 August 1930 Ryan 30.75
24 September 1930 Ryan 30.75
2 December 1930 Lostoski-Ho 28.47n1
12 December 1930 Lostoski-Ho 28.59n23
30 December 1930 Ryan 30.67, 76
10 January 1931 Gallego Larrarte 30.113

20 January 1931 Delsandro 25.83n12
4 February 1931 Delsandro 25.84
9 March 1931 Delsandro 25.84
13 May 1931 Lostoski-Ho 28.58n20
30 May 1931 Lostoski-Ho 28.59n22
23 June 1931 Lostoski-Ho 28.58n20, 61
7 July 1931 Lostoski-Ho 28.57n18
17 July 1931 Lostoski-Ho 28.47n1, 58n20
19 July 1931 Jones 22.75
7 August 1931 Jones 22.75
15 August 1931 Jones 22.79
14 October 1931 Jones 22.77; Lostoski-Ho 28.47
16 November 1931 Gilman 29.49n12
25 December 1931 Gallego Larrarte 30.114
11 February 1932 Cheney 24.63
16 February 1932 Cheney 24.59; Wisor 21.5
22 April 1932 Golden 23.102
8 May 1932 Golden 23.102; McVicker 28.86–87
10 May 1932 Golden 23.102n31
3 July 1932 Gilman 29.48n9
6 July 1932 Gilman 29.48n9
14 July 1932 Cheney 24.70
17 August 1932 Gilman 29.48n9
13 October 1932 Gilman 29.48n9
2 November 1932 de Gay 30.99, 100
21 July 1933 Golden 23.103
29 October 1934 Golden 23.103n33
15 November 1934 Cheney 24.67
20 February 1935 Cheney 24.62
29 August 1935 Gillespie 25.118
1 April 1936 Wisor 21.24n39
10 December 1936 Wisor 21.39–40
6 August 1937 Chua 30.40
22 March 1938 Chua 30.39
26 April 1938 Chua 30.40
29 April 1938 Chua 30.40
3 May 1938 Gillespie 29.153
3 June 1938 Delsandro 25.93n23; Phillips 26.3
16 June 1938 Schwartz 29.92
17 August 1938 Gillespie 25.110; Gillespie 29.153
22 September 1938 Gillespie 29.153
6 October 1938 Gillespie 29.154
13 October 1938 Gillespie 29.154
28 February 1939 de Gay 30.105
6 September 1939 Shin 23.136
24 September 1939 Gillespie 25.110
7 October 1939 Gillespie 29.153
29 November 1939 Gillespie 29.154
16 December 1939 Gillespie 29.154
26 January 1940 Gillespie 29.154
9 February 1940 Gillespie 29.154
11 February 1940 Gillespie 25.110
30 May 1940 Gillespie 25.110
31 May 1940 Gillespie 25.110
22 June 1940 Gilman 29.49n12
25 July 1940 Gillespie 29.154
10 August 1940 de Gay 30.105
13 September 1940 Gillespie 25.110
17 September 1940 Gillespie 25.110
29 September 1940 Gillespie 25.110

Part 4B: The Essays and Other Nonfiction

"22 Hyde Park Gate" Layne 21.80
"Abbeys and Cathedrals" McVicker 28.74–75
"Am I a Snob?" Adair/Martin 24.84–85; Fouirnaies 22.21–23
"American Fiction" Kopley 30.127
"The American Scholar" Ke 29.61n8, 66, 74
"Anon" Davison 23.11; Foster 22.53, 57–58; Lauby 27.51; Layne 21.91; McVicker 28.85n26; Shin 23.134n27; White 24.103
AROO. Bunting 30.17; Caputi 29.5, 7, 22; Chua 30.39; Clarke 28.12, 20; Czarnecki 21.51n2; Dalgarno 22.1n1, 13; de Gay 30.99, 100; Delsandro 25.83n12, 84, 89; Favre 30.55, 57, 58, 60, 63; Fischer 28.31n10, 36; Foster 22.51, 53–56; Fouirnaies 22.21, 31; Gallego Larrarte 30.112; Gillespie 25.98, 113, 116; Golden 23.89; Jenkins (Amber) 27.11, 13; Jenkins (Gwyn) 27.43; Kopley 30.125; Kotler 24.36, 40–41, 43; Kopley 30.127; Koulouris 25.17n31; Lauby 27.50; Leach 28.passim; Marcus 24.6; McVicker 28.74, 79; Novillo-Corvalán 23.36; Pająk 24.11, 13,

26–28, 31; Schwartz 29.89, 97, 99; Sullam 30.118, 119; White 24.108n15; Wisor 21.1, 4
"The Art of Biography" Gillespie 29.154, 160
"The Art of Fiction" Sullam 30.120
"As to modern criticism" Gilman 29.passim
"The Art of Biography" Layne 21.79
"Aunt Maria" Clarke 28.6
"Aurora Leigh" Kopley 30.128
"Byron & Mr Briggs" Gilman 29.28, 29, 34, 45n1, n2, n3, 46n4, n5, 47n6, 48n10, 48–49n12, 50n14, 51n19, 52n20, 53n23
"Cambridge" Schwartz 29.89n3
"Character in Fiction" Cheney 24.61; Fischer 28.32, 33; Ke 29.60–61, 65
"The Cheapening of Motor-Cars" Adair/Martin 24.93–94
"The Cinema" Humm 29.157, 158, 159; Wisor 21.4
"The Common Reader" Gilman 29.28n2, 29, 34, 35, 46n3, 47n8, 49n13, 53n23; Leach 28.103
CR1. Fouirnaies 22.31; Gilman 29.27, 28–29, 31n13, 32, 34–36, 48n9, 49n12, n13, 51n19, 55n27; McVicker 28.74, 86
CR2. Gilman 29.48n9, 49n12
"Craftsmanship" Chua 30.42; Dalgarno 22.14–16; Fischer 28.25–27, 28, 29, 32
"The Decay of Essay Writing" Kotler 24.39–40; Leach 28.99
"The Docks of London" Gillespie 25.125; Graeber 24.169, 170n4, 171, 174, 175n8
"Donne After Three Centuries" Gillespie 25.127n49; Ke 29.81
"Dr. Bentley" Gilman 29.33
"The Dramatic in Life and Art" White 24.102
"The Elizabethan Lumber Room" Graeber 24.168, 170; Leach 28.102
"English Prose" Kopley 30.127; Sullam 30.117
"Evening Over Sussex: Reflections in a Motor Car" Adair/Martin 24.80
"Flying Over London" Adair/Martin 24.86; Gillespie 25.118
"Friendships Gallery" Clarke 28.7, 13–14, 15
"Geraldine and Jane" Clarke 28.20–21
Granite and Rainbow Layne 21.84
"The Historian and 'The Gibbon'" Gillespie 25.105n21
"Hours in a Library" De Gay 30.99
"How It Strikes a Contemporary" Gilman 29.46n4, n5
"How Should One Read a Book?' Jenkins (Gwyn) 27.41; Kopley 30.128; Sullam 30.117, 119
"The Humane Art" Clarke 28.11
"Impassioned Prose" Sullam 30.118, 121
"Impressions at Bayreuth" Davison 23.4, 9–10
"Impressions of Sir Leslie Stephen" Kopley 30.126
Introduction to *Life as We Have Known It* Favre 30.61n13; Jones 22.86
Introduction to *MD* van Wert 29.111n7
"Joseph Conrad" Gillespie 25.106n22
"Journeys in Spain" Gillespie 25.101
"Julia Margaret Cameron" Fouirnaies 22.32
"Lady Dorothy Nevill" Fouirnaies 22.34
"The Leaning Tower" Gallego Larrarte 30.111, 112, 114, 115; Gillespie 25.110; Kopley 30.127–28; Lauby 27.60n9
"A Letter to a Young Poet" Cheney 24.71n15; Chua 30.42; Gallego Larrarte 30.111, 113–14; Jones 22.75n1, 77, 80; Ke 29.68; Kopley 30.128
"Life and the Novelist" Ryan 30.72n12
"Literary Geography" Gillespie 25.119; Golden 23.100n29
London Scene Phillips 26.2
"Lord Jim" Gillespie 25.106n22
"The Love of Reading" Cheney 24.56
"Middlebrow" Chua 30.42–43; Jones 22.75, 86, 93n12
MOB. Fischer 28.27n7, 36; Foster 22.41, 45–46, 67; Gillespie 25.116, 128–29;

Koulouris 25.6, 9n14; Shin 23.128
"The Modern Essay" Kotler 24.40
"Modern Fiction" Fischer 28.27, 33–35; Foster 22.41, 53–56; Gillespie 25.112; Gilman 29.45n2, 49n12; Novillo-Corvalán 23.50; White 24.106–08, 113, 117
"Modern Novels" Fischer 28.27, 28, 31, 32, 33–35, 39
"Modern Novels (Joyce)" White 24.101
"Montaigne" Leach 28.100
"The Movies and Reality" Gillespie 29.159
"Mr. Bennett and Mrs. Brown" Fischer 28.32; Shin 23.121; White 24.106, 107n12, n14, 111
"Mr. Conrad's Crisis" Gillespie 25.106n22
"Mr. Conrad's 'Youth'" Gillespie 25.106n22
"Mr. Hudson's Childhood" Novillo-Corvalán 23.50
"Mr. Symons's Essays" Sullam 30.117–18
"The New Biography" Gillespie 25.98; Humm 29.160; Layne 21.79
"Notes on an Elizabethan Play" Leach 28.102
"The Novels of Defoe" Sullam 30.120
"Old Bloomsbury" Layne 21.80
"On a Faithful Friend" Williams 26.113
"On Being Ill" Dalgarno 22.2, 9–13; de Gay 30.102–03; Fischer 28.42, 43; Goldman 30.107–08; Livingstone 26.88n3, 92–93, 94, 97, 99, 102; Williams 26.112
"On Not Knowing French" Fischer 28.29
"On Not Knowing Greek" Bunting 30.16; Dalgarno 22.2–9; Gilman 29.33; Golden 23.91n17, 103; Jenkins (Gwyn) 27.25, 41; Ke 29.67; Kotler 24.40; Koulouris 25.1, 20n38; White 24.108, 124n36
"On Re-Reading Novels" Sullam 30.122n5; Williams 26.114
"The Opera" Davison 23.4, 27n41
"Oxford Street Tide" Gillespie 25.125; Graeber 24.169
"Parodies" Chua 30.42
"The Pastons and Chaucer" Gilman 29.45–46
"The Perfect Language" Fischer 28.29; Jenkins (Gwyn) 27.36
"Phases of Fiction" Kopley 30.128; Leach 28.103; Sullam 30.117, 119
"Pictures" Layne 21.91–92
"Poetry, Fiction and the Future" Davison 29.142; Kopley 30.128; Shin 23.112, 129; Sullam 30.117, 118, 119, 122; White 24.103
"Portrait of a Londoner" Graeber 24.180
"Professions for Women" Delsandro 25.83; Favre 30.57; Fischer 28.27–28; Golden 23.94n19; Phillips 26.2
"The Reader" Shin 23.134n27
"To Spain" Gillespie 25.101
"Reading" McVicker 28.86
"Reading at Random" Gilman 29.49n12; McVicker 28.91n30
"Reminiscences" Layne 21.80–81
"Report on Teaching at Morley College" Chua 30.41
"Reviewing" Adair/Martin 24.87
"The Rights of Youth" Cheney 24.61n9
RF Gillespie 29.150, 153, 154; Hussey 29.167; Jenkins (Amber) 27.6; Ke 29.65n9; Layne 21.92
"Sir Thomas Browne" McVicker 28.85
"A Sketch of the Past" Bond 23.64–65, 67, 74; Cheney 24.58n4; Czarnecki 21.51; Fischer 28.35n14; Foster 22.53, 56–57; Fouirnaies 22.31; Gallego Larrarte 30.113; Gillespie 25.116, 128–29; Gillespie 29.154n5; Golden 23.86, 88–89, 93–94, 103; Goldman 30.107–08; Jenkins (Gwyn) 27.27–28; Ke 29.58, 59–60, 73, 79; Layne 21.80–81, 98; Lostoski-Ho 28.64; McVicker 28.76n14, 77, 91
"Speech to the London and National Society for Women's Service" Jenkins (Gwyn) 27.35n12
"Street Haunting" Williams 26.111
"The Sun and the Fish" McVicker 28.89
"This is the House of Commons" Wisor 21.20
"Thoughts on Peace in an Air Raid" Foster 22.45, 66; Gillespie 25.116; McVicker

28.85n27, 86; Wisor 21.10
TG. Bond 23.71n13; Bunting 30.16–17, 25; Caputi 29.7, 8, 14, 22, 23; Cheney 24.56–57, 58n4, 61–62, 66–67; Clarke 28.9, 12; Dalgarno 22.2, 14–15; Davison 29.145; de Gay 30.104; Delsandro 25.76, 83, 87, 89–90, 93; Foster 22.41, 43–44, 51–52, 58, 66; Fouirnaies 22.21, 31, 35, 37; Gallego Larrarte 30.115; Gillespie 25.98, 113, 115–16, 118, 124, 128; Gillespie 29.154; Hussey 29.169; Jenkins (Gwyn) 27.36, 41; Jones 22.86; Kotler 24.passim; Lauby 27.47, 50, 53, 57–60; McVicker 28.74, 87; Pająk 24.26; Phillips 26.passim; Ryan 30.69n8, 78; Shin 23.116; Wisor 21.passim
"Thunder at Wembley" Gillespie 25.128; McVicker 28.82; Novillo-Corvalán 23.46, 57
"Venice" Golden 23.84
"The Villa Jones" Jones 22.passim
"Walter Sickert: A Conversation" Layne 21.91–92
"William Hazlitt" Cheney 24.67
"Women and Fiction" Jenkins (Gwyn) 27.35n12; White 24.108n15
"Women Must Weep" Wisor 21.1n2

Part 4C: The Letters

No. 9, 24 Oct [1897], To Thoby Stephen. Golden 23.98
No. 19, 17 Sept [1898], To Emma Vaughan. Jenkins (Gwyn) 27.39
No. 25, 13 June 1899, To Emma Vaughan. Dalgarno 22.15n15; Jenkins (Gwyn) 27.38
No. 31, [17? June 1900], To Emma Vaughan. Jenkins (Gwyn) 27.32, 41; Koulouris 25.5
No. 32, 6 Aug [1900], To Emma and Margaret Vaughan. Jenkins (Gwyn) 27.32
No. 34, 23 Oct [1900], To Emma Vaughan. Jenkins (Gwyn) 27.32, 33
No. 36, [July 1901], To Thoby Stephen. Koulouris 25.5
No. 50, [Sept 1902], To Violet Dickinson. Clarke 28.10
No. 51, [Sept 1902?], To Violet Dickinson. Clark 28.10
No. 54, [Oct/Nov 1902], To Violet Dickinson. Clark 28.11
No. 55, [Oct/Nov 1902], To Violet Dickinson. Clark 28.11
No. 57, [Oct/Nov 1902], To Violet Dickinson. Clark 28.9
No. 62, [27? Dec 1902], To Violet Dickinson. Clark 28.10
No. 66, [25? Jan 1903], To Thoby Stephen. Jenkins (Gwyn) 27.42, 42n15; Leach 28.99–100
No. 72, [1903?], To Violet Dickinson. Clark 28.10
No. 74, [March 1903], To Violet Dickinson. Clark 28.8
No. 75, [early April 1903], To Violet Dickinson. Clark 28.8
No. 78, 28 April [1903], To Violet Dickinson. Clark 28.10
No. 79, 30 April [1903], To Violet Dickinson. Clark 28.10
No. 80, [4 May? 1903], To Violet Dickinson. Clarke 28.7, 11, 16, 21
No. 83, [4 June? 1903], To Violet Dickinson. Clark 28.14
No. 85, [June 1903], To Violet Dickinson. Clark 28.10
No. 88, [30 June? 1903], To Violet Dickinson. Clarke 28.15, 16
No. 89, [June/July 1903], To Violet Dickinson. Clark 28.14
No. 91, [7? July 1903], To Violet Dickinson. Goldman 30.107–08
No. 92, [22 July 1903], To Violet Dickinson. Clark 28.8, 10
No. 97, [Aug 1903], To Violet Dickinson. Clark 28.10
No. 98, 30 Aug [1903], To Violet Dickinson. Clarke 28.16
No. 100, 2 Sept [1903], To Emma Vaughan. Jenkins (Gwyn) 27.32, 41
No. 101, [19? Sept 1903], To Violet

Dickinson. Clark 28.8, 12
No. 105, 2 Oct [1903], To Violet Dickinson. Clark 28.9
No. 107, [11? Oct 1903], To Violet Dickinson. Clarke 28.18
No. 109, [Oct/Nov 1903], To Violet Dickinson. Clark 28.11
No. 113, [Autumn 1903], To Violet Dickinson. Clarke 28.16
No. 152, [25 Jan 1904], To Violet Dickinson. Clark 28.8
No. 171, [March 1904], To Violet Dickinson. Clark 28.12
No. 205, [30 Dec 1904], To Violet Dickinson. Clarke 28.16
No. 208, [early Jan 1905], To Madge Vaughan. Chua 30.41
No. 218, 23 Feb [1905], To Emma Vaughan. Jenkins (Gwyn) 27.41
No. 221, [11? March 1905], To Violet Dickinson. Clark 28.12
No. 227, [May 1905], To Violet Dickinson. Clarke 28.12, 17
No. 236, [July 1905], To Lady Robert Cecil. Chua 30.43
No. 248, 27 Aug [1905], To Violet Dickinson. Clark 28.9
No. 250, 1 Oct [1905], To Violet Dickinson. Koulouris 25n63
No. 251, 9 Nov [1905], To Violet Dickinson. Chua 30.42
No. 254, [3 Dec 1905], To Violet Dickinson. Clark 28.12
No. 266, [16 April 1906], To Violet Dickinson. Clarke 28.16–17
No. 282, [4 Aug 1906], To Violet Dickinson. Gillespie 25.104
No. 296, [15 Nov 1906], To Violet Dickinson. Clark 28.15
No. 310, [29 Nov 1906], To Violet Dickinson. Clark 28.5–6
No. 348, [17 Feb 1907], To Violet Dickinson. Clark 28.12
No. 369, [7 July 1907], To Violet Dickinson. Clarke 28.17
No. 380, [25 August 1907], To Violet Dickinson. Clarke 28.12, 16
No. 381, [1 Sept 1907], To Violet Dickinson. Clarke 28.18
No. 383, [22 Sept 1907], To Violet Dickinson. Clarke 28.17
No. 428, [7 Aug 1908], To Vanessa Bell. Layne 21.80
No. 438, 19 Aug 1908, To Clive Bell. Davison 23.6–7
No. 454, 1 Nov [1908], To Madge Vaughan. Gillespie 25.101n11
No. 471, [7? Feb 1909], To Clive Bell. Davison 23.28
No. 502, [12 Aug 1909], To Vanessa Bell. Davison 23.4
No. 534, [4 Sept 1910], To Clive Bell. McVicker 28.77
No. 574, [21 July 1911], To Vanessa Bell. Ryan 30.80
No. 933, 17 May 1918, To Harriet Weaver. Chua 30.43
No. 1112, [5 Jan 1920], To Janet Case. Novillo-Corvalán 23.42
No. 1172, [28] March 1921, To Saxon Sydney-Turner. McVicker 28.77
No. 1267, 6 Aug [1922], To Ottoline Morrell. Wisor 21.14–15
No. 1287, [21 Sept 1922], To Barbara Bagenal. White 24.103n5
No. 1311, 1 Nov 1922, To Lady Ottoline Morrell. Humm 29.156n1
No. 1337, 25 Dec 1922, To Gerald Brenan. Bunting 30.17
No. 1433, 1 Dec 1923, To Gerald Brenan. Gilman 29.32
No. 1441, [end of Jan 1924], To Ethel Sands. Gillespie 29.152
No. 1500, 2 Oct [1924], To Molly MacCarthy. Rutherford 24.144
No. 1573, [1 Sept 1925], To Vita Sackville-West. Ke 29.75
No. 1576, [3 Sept 1925], To Vanessa Bell. Jenkins (Amber) 27.9n7
No. 1583, 16 Sept 1925, To Roger Fry. Dalgarno 22.9
No. 1585, [18 Sept 1925], To Janet Case. Sullam 30.122
No. 1624, 16 March 1926, To Vita

Sackville-West. Sullam 30.122
No. 1656, [19? July 1926], To Vita Sackville-West. Sullam 30.118
No. 1718, 18 Feb 1927, To Vita Sackville-West. Rutherford 24.152
No. 1725, 5 March 1927, To Vanessa Bell. Layne 21.103
No. 1750, 8 May 1927, To Vanessa Bell. Layne 21.99
No. 1762, 25 May 1927, To Vanessa Bell. Jenkins (Amber) 27.13; Layne 21.96
No. 1764, 27 May 1927, To Roger Fry. Jenkins (Amber) 27.7; Layne 21.97; Rutherford 24.152–53
No. 1781, [8? July 1927], To Vita Sackville-West. Jenkins (Gwyn) 27.32
No. 1789, 23 July [1927], To Vanessa Bell. Adair/Martin 24.79
No. 1793, 1 Aug 1927, To Ethel Sands. Adair/Martin 24.81
No. 1800, 21 Aug [1927], To Saxon Sydney-Turner. Ke 29.60
No. 1806, 2 Sept [1927], To Ethel Sands. Adair/Martin 24.84
No. 1815, 29 Sept [1927], To Vanessa Bell. Adair/Martin 24.81
No. 1820, 9 Oct [1927], To Vita Sackville-West. Fouirnaies 22.21
No. 1821, 13 Oct [14 1927], To Vita Sackville-West. Fouirnaies 22.23
No. 1829, [11 Nov 1927], To Vita Sackville-West. Fouirnaies 22.25
No. 1834, [19 Nov? 1927], To Clive Bell. Chua 30.43
No. 1852, 29 Jan [1928], To Vanessa Bell. Adair/Martin 24.81
No. 1864, 21 Feb [1928], To Vanessa Bell. Adair/Martin 24.82
No. 1865, [26 Feb 1928], To Julian Bell. Adair/Martin 24.81, 83
No. 1870, 12 March 1928, To Vita Sackville-West. Adair/Martin 24.81
No. 1875, 25 March [1928], To Vanessa Bell. Adair/Martin 24.83n9
No. 1876, 31 March 1928, To Vita Sackville-West. Adair/Martin 24.80
No. 1877, 5 April 1928, To Quentin Bell. Adair/Martin 24.83
No. 1883, [17 April 1928], To Vita Sackville-West. Fouirnaies 22.25
No. 1886, [27 April 1928], To Vita Sackville-West. Fouirnaies 22.25
No. 1894, 12 May [1928], To Vanessa Bell. Adair/Martin 24.82; Layne 21.91
No, 1916, 22 Aug 1928, To Ethel Sands. Adair/Martin 24.84
No. 1919, [2 Sept 1928], To Vanessa Bell. Pająk 24.30
No. 2003, 17 Feb 1929, To Quentin Bell. Adair/Martin 24.85
No. 2020, 24 April 1929, To Vanessa Bell. Adair/Martin 24.85
No, 2026, 5 May 1929, To Vanessa Bell. Adair/Martin 24.81
No. 2028, 11 May 1929, To Quentin Bell. Adair/Martin 24.85
No. 2118, 30 Dec 1929, To Vanessa Bell. Adair/Martin 24.84
No. 2218, 15 Aug 1930, To Ethel Smyth. Clarke 28.20
No. 2224, 28 Aug [1930], To Ethel Smyth. Lostoski-Ho 28.59
No. 2292, Christmas day 1930, To Ethel Smyth. Ryan 30.67n1
No. 2297, 30 Dec 1930, To Sydney Saxon-Turner. Ryan 30.67n1
No. 2300, 1 Jan 1931, To Vita Sackville-West. Delsandro 25.84
No. 2360, 24 April [1931], To Vita Sackville-West. Leach 28.100n4
No. 2558, 19 March 1932, To Harmon H. Gladstone. Rutherford 24.144
No. 2647, [21 Oct 1932], To Ethel Smyth. Adair/Martin 24.89
No. 2699, [27 Jan 1933], To Ethel Smyth. Adair/Martin 24.86
No. 2703, 14 Feb [1933], To Vanessa Bell. Adair/Martin 24.87
No. 2746, 8 June 1933, To Ethel Smyth. Kotler 24.43
No. 2783, 22 Aug [1922], To Ethel Smyth. Gillespie 25.100
No. 2850, 24 Jan [1934], To Quentin Bell. Dalgarno 22.8

No. 2879, 20 April [1934], To R.C. Trevelyan. Dalgarno 22.14
No. 2887, 4 May [3 1934], To Vanessa Bell. Layne 21.81
No. 2910, 10 July [1934], To Stephen Spender. Gilman 29.49n13
No. 2955, [27 Nov 1934], To Victoria Ocampo. Novillo-Corvalán 23.35
No. 2977, 22 Jan 1935, To Victoria Ocampo. Novillo-Corvalán 23.35
No. 3140, [6 June 1936], To Ethel Smyth. Gillespie 29.153
No. 3197, 6 Dec [1936], To Violet Dickinson. Clarke 28.21
No. 3212, [20 Jan 1937], To Ethel Smyth. Gillespie 29.153
No. 3230, 7 April [1937], To Stephen Spender. Delsandro 25.73
No. 3294, [17 Aug 1937], To Vanessa Bell. Layne 21.81
No. 3307, 18 Sept [1937], To Margaret Llewelyn Davies. Gillespie 29.153
No. 3377, 5 April 1938, To Ling Shuhua. Chua 30.37, 39, 40, 43, 44
No. 3379, 9 April 1938, To Ling Shuhua. Chua 30.35
No. 3383, 3 May [1938], To Ling Shuhua. Chua 30.39–40; Favre 30.56; Gillespie 29.153
No. 3425, 27 July 1938, To Ling Shuhua. Chua 30.39, 43, 44
No. 3428, [7] Aug 1938, To Ethel Smyth. Gillespie 29.153
No. 3435, 29 Aug [1938], To Ethel Smyth. Gillespie 29.153
No. 3442, 11 Sept 1938, To R. C. Trevelyan. Gillespie 29.153
No. 3454, 8 Oct [1938], To Vanessa Bell. Gillespie 29.153; Layne 21.92
No. 3457, 15 Oct 1938, To Ling Shuhua. Chua 30.39, 45
No. 3460, 24 Oct 1938, To Vanessa Bell. Ke 29.60
No. 3505, 14 April [1939], To Ethel Smyth. Gillespie 29.153
No. 3506, 17 April 1939, To Ling Shuhua. Chua 30.44
No. 3536, 16 July 1939, To Ling Shuhua. Chua 30.37, 39, 44
No. 3571, 3 Dec [1939], To Vita Sackville-West. Gillespie 29.153
No. 3582, 1 Feb 1940, To Ethel Smyth. Gillespie 29.154
No. 3583, [4 Feb 1940], To Vanessa Bell. Layne 21.91
No. 3612, 9 June 1940, To Ethel Smyth. Gilman 29.50n14
No. 3615 9 July [1940], To Ethel Smyth. Chua 30.40
No. 3633, [24 Aug 1940], To Benedict Nicolson. Fouirnaies 22.31
No. 3678, 12 Jan 1941, To Ethel Smyth. Jones 22.76
No. 3680, 19 Jan [1941], To Vita Sackville-West. Gillespie 25.116

Part 4D: The Novels (and Play)

BTA. Cheney 24.65; Chua 30.40; Czarnecki 21.52n3; Davison 23.11; de Gay 30.99, 100, 105; Delsandro 25.76; Fischer 28.28n8; Gillespie 25.119, 128; Gillespie 29.154; Chua 30.39; Humm 29.165; Jones 22.76, 93n13; Lauby 27.passim; Livingstone 26.89, 94–96, 102; Lostoski-Ho 28.54–55; McVicker 28.69n2, 86, 89–91, 92; Rutherford 24.158; Shin 23.109, 122, 128–29, 131, 132n25, 134–35; Schwartz 29.93n7, 99n8; Wisor 21.39–40
F. Humm 29.158; Layne 21.82; Livingstone 26.88n3, 89, 90; Phillips 26.9; van Wert 29.116n11; Williams 26.113, 115, 117
"The Hours" Czarnecki 21.57; White 24.101
JR. Bunting 30.passim; Cheney 24.61n10, 65, 67; Dalgarno 22.1n1; de Gay 30.102; Foster 22.passim; Gillespie 25.100n7, 122–23, 125; Gilman 29.52n20; Golden 23.passim; Graeber 24.168; Humm 29.156, 157; Hussey 29.167; Jenkins (Gwyn) 27.39–40, 42; Ke 29.passim; Layne 21.85;

McVicker 28.69, 80, 87, 92: Schwartz 29.passim; Shin 23.111, 122; Sullam 30.121; van Wert 29.107, 108, 109, 110–11, 112–20
JR Holograph. Bunting 30.5, 24
MD. Adair/Martin 24.77–78, 85, 87; Bond 23.passim; Bunting 30.8; Caputi 29.10; Cheney 24.61n10; Clarke 28.20; Czarnecki 21.passim; Dalgarno 22.1n1; Davison 29.142; Favre 30.57n7; Gillespie 25.104, 116, 123–24; Gilman 29.28, 29, 45n2, 52n20; Golden 23.84; Goldman 30.107–08; Jenkins (Amber) 27.9; Layne 21.80; Livingstone 26.88n3; Lostoski-Ho 28.54, 55; McVicker 28.70n2, 87; Ryan 30.69n8; Schwartz 29.93–94, 98, 99; Shin 23.111–12, 127, 132; Sullam 30.121; van Straten 30.passim; van Wert 29.108, 109, 111, 112, 113; White 24.passim
MEL. Caputi 29.11, 12–13, 14; Davison 23.5, 24n35, 27; Fischer 28.39–40; Novillo-Corvalán 23.35, 47
ND. Caputi 29.21; Gillespie 25.107, 111, 117, 120–22, 124–25; Jenkins (Gwyn) 27.34; Ryan 30.70n10; Schwartz 29.103n9; Shin 23.120–21; Williams 26.109
O. Adair/Martin 24.75, 85; Caputi 29.23; Clarke 28.7; Czarnecki 21.50n1; Fouirnaies 22.passim; Gillespie 25.107–08, 118–19, 126; Gillespie 29.150; Golden 23.98n23; Graeber 24.passim; Humm 29.158; Layne 21.79; Livingstone 26.90, 91; Lostoski-Ho 28.55n15; McVicker 28.85n27; Pająk 24.28; Schwartz 29.99; Shin 23.114n13, 128; Sullam 30.118, 122; Williams 26.109; Wisor 21.31n49, 37
The Pargiters. Cheney 24.63, 67; Chua 30.39; de Gay 30.99; Delsandro 25.83; Gallego Larrarte 30.114; Golden 23.103; Jenkins (Gwyn) 27.23, 24, 43–44; Phillips 26.1–2; Shin 23.128
Pointz Hall. Shin 23.109–110, 129, 133–35
RF. Jenkins (Amber) 27.6
TTL. Adair/Martin 24.85, 93; Bunting 30.11n3; Dalgarno 22.1n1, 6; de Gay 30.99n1, 100, 103–04; Favre 30.57; Gillespie 25.107–08, 122, 128; Jenkins (Amber) 27.passim; Jones 22.75; Ke 29.72; Kopley 30.126; Lauby 27.59; Layne 21.85, 95–99, 102; Lostoski-Ho 28.53, 55–56, 58; McVicker 28.87–88; Rutherford 24.passim; Ryan 30.69n8; Shin 23.111, 114–15, 117, 123–28, 131; Sullam 30.121; White 24.113n24
TTL: Holograph ms. *Woolf Online*. Jenkins (Amber) 27.passim; Rutherford 24.138–39, 140–41, 142, 153
TTL: The Original Holograph Draft. Rutherford 24.153
TW. Adair/Martin 24.93; Bunting 30.26n5; Cheney 24.56; Czarnecki 21.73n21; de Gay 30.99; Fischer 28.26–27, 28, 43; Gillespie 25.113, 124–28; Gillespie 29.152, 153; Ke 29.58n4, 82; Kopley 30.125; Koulouris 25.8; Layne 21.99–100; Livingstone 26.100–02; Lostoski-Ho 28.passim; McVicker 28.88–89; Reed 29.163, 165; Ryan 30.passim; Shin 23.111; Sullam 30.118, 122
TW: The Two Holograph Drafts. Lostoski-Ho 28.57–60, 61n26
TY. Camarasana et al. 24.4; Cheney 24.passim; Czarnecki 21.52n3; Delsandro 25.passim; Fischer 28.28n8; Foster 22.67; Gillespie 25.118, 120, 124; Gillespie 29.154; Golden 23.86, 103; Jenkins (Gwyn) 27.27; Jones 22.75–76; Livingstone 26.89, 94–95; Phillips 26.passim; Rutherford 24.159; Ryan 30.passim; Shin 23.128
VO. Caputi 29.passim; Cheney 24.67; Davison 23.4n10, 5–28; de Gay 30.101–02, 103; Fischer 28.passim; Gillespie 25.106n22, 120–21, 124; Gilman 29.52n20; Graeber 24.166–71, 177n11, 179; Lauby 27.56; Layne

21.100; Livingstone 26.88n3, 91; Lostoski-Ho 28.54; McVicker 28.87; Novillo-Corvalán 23.passim; Reed 29.163; Shin 23.112, 114–21, 123
VO Earlier Typescript (Berg). Fischer 28.39–40

Part 4Ea: The Poem

"Ode Written Partly in Prose on Seeing the Name of Cutbush Above a Butcher's Shop in Pentonville." Novillo-Corvalán 23.51; Shin 23.111, 116, 128–35

Part 4Eb: The Short Fiction

"A Cockney Farming Experience" Williams 26.109
"[A Dialogue Upon Mount Pentelicus]" Golden 23.100, 102
"The Experiences of a Pater-familias" Williams 26.109
"The Journal of Mistress Joan Martyn" Gillespie 25.104n18; Koulouris 25.7–8; McVicker 28.76, 78
"Kew Gardens" Adair/Martin 24.93; Ke 29.58, 61–64, 65, 69, 73, 79; Layne 21.92; Livingstone 26.88n3; van Straten 30.86
"Lappin and Lapinova" Livingstone 26.87, 88n3, 97
"The Mark on the Wall" Golden 23.87; Jenkins (Gwyn) 27.26; Schwartz 29.93
"Moments of Being: Slater's Pins Have No Points" Jenkins (Gwyn) 27.23, 24, 25, 27, 32, 33–35, 37, 38–39, 40
"Mrs Dalloway in Bond Street" Gillespie 25.116; Schwartz 29.99
"Nurse Lugton's Curtain" Williams 26.106, 110, 117
"The Patron and the Crocus" Gilman 29.30, 31n13
""Scenes from the Life of a British Naval Officer" Gillespie 25.126; Wisor 21.13n23
"The Searchlight" Gillespie 25.105; Gilman 29.30
"Solid Objects" Schwartz 29.89n3
"Street Haunting: A London Adventure" Jones 22.75; Shin 23.122, 124, 129, 132; van Straten 30.1
"An Unwritten Novel" Shin 23.109, 119–24, 129, 132, 135
"The Widow and the Parrot" Williams 26.passim

Part 5: Bibliography of Articles, Reviews, and Other Materials in Volumes 21–30 (2015–2024)

Articles, Comments, and Introductions

*(entries marked with a * comprise the vol. 24 section "Essays in honor of Jane Marcus)*

Adair, Robin, and Ann Martin. "A Driving Bloomsbury: Virginia Woolf, Vanessa Bell, and the Meaning of the Motor-Car." *Woolf Studies Annual*, vol. 24, 2018, pp. 75–100.
Bond, Candis E. "Remapping Female Subjectivity in *Mrs. Dalloway*: Scenic Memory and Woolf's 'Bye-Street' Aesthetic." *Woolf Studies Annual*, vol. 23, 2017, pp. 63–82.
Bunting, Galen. "'Brought Up in An Illusion': *Jacob's Room* as Modernist Anti-War Novel." *Woolf Studies Annual*, vol. 30, 2024, pp. 5–29.
*Camarasana, Linda, J. Ashley Foster, Robin Hackett, Clara Jones, and Jean Mills. "Jane Marcus in the Archives: Politics and Pleasures." *Woolf Studies Annual*, vol. 24, 2018, pp. 1–4.
Caputi, Celia R. "Belated Epiphanies: Intersectionality and Education in Virginia Woolf's *The Voyage Out* and Nella Larsen's *Quicksand*." *Woolf Studies Annual*, vol. 29, 2023, pp. 5–26.
*Cheney, Matthew. "The Reader Awakes: Pedagogical Form and Utopian

Impulse in *The Years*." *Woolf Studies Annual*, vol. 24, 2018, pp. 55–74.

Chua, Han Au. "We Misunderstood Them: The Correspondence between Virginia Woolf and Ling Shuhua." *Woolf Studies Annual*, vol. 30, 2024, pp. 31–52.

Clarke, Matthew. "My Poor Intimate: Virginia Woolf and Violet Dickinson." *Woolf Studies Annual*, vol. 28, 2022, pp. 5–24.

Czarnecki, Kristin. "Melted Flesh and Tangled Threads: War Trauma and Modes of Healing in Virginia Woolf's *Mrs. Dalloway* and Leslie Marmon Silko's *Ceremony*." *Woolf Studies Annual*, vol. 21, 2015, pp. 50–77.

Dalgarno, Emily. "Virginia Woolf Reinvents the Socratic Dialogue." *Woolf Studies Annual*, vol. 22, 2016, pp. 1–20.

Davison, Claire. "Hearing the World 'in Full Orchestra': Voyaging Out with Woolf, Darwin, and Music." *Woolf Studies Annual*, vol. 23, 2017, pp. 1–32.

Delsandro, Erica Gene. "No More Missed Connections: A Lesson in Transpersonal Feminism with Virginia Woolf, Audre Lorde, and Adrienne Rich." *Woolf Studies Annual*, vol. 25, 2019, pp. 73–96.

Favre, Valérie. "(Un)Framing the Mad Woman in the River? The Questions of Virginia Woolf's 'Madness' and Suicide in Her Feminist Reception." *Woolf Studies Annual*, vol. 30, 2024, pp. 53–66.

Fischer, Niklas Cyril. "Slipping in the Inaudible: Making Sense of Deictic Words in The Voyage Out." *Woolf Studies Annual*, vol. 28, 2022, pp. 25–46.

Foster, J. Ashley. "Writing in the 'White Light of Truth': History, Ethics, and Community in Virginia Woolf's *Between the Acts*." *Woolf Studies Annual*, vol. 22, 2016, pp. 41–74.

Fouirnaies, Christine. "Was Virginia Woolf a Snob? The Case of Aristocratic Portraits in Orlando." *Woolf Studies Annual*, vol. 22, 2016, pp. 21–40.

Gillespie, Diane F. "Maps of Her Own: Virginia Woolf In and Beyond the Archives." *Woolf Studies Annual*, vol. 25, 2019, pp. 97–136.

Gilman, Danielle N. Introduction. "Virginia Woolf's 'As to Criticism': An Annotated Transcription." *Woolf Studies Annual*, vol. 29, 2023, pp. 27–38.

Golden, Amanda. "Textbook Greek: Thoby Stephen in Jacob's Room." *Woolf Studies Annual*, vol. 23, 2017, pp. 83–108.

Graber, Darin. "H. M. S. Orlando: The Metamorphosing, Imperial Vessel." *Woolf Studies Annual*, vol. 24, 2018, pp. 165–84.

Jenkins, Amber. "Drafting Mrs. Ramsay and Lily Briscoe: Visual Aesthetics and the Manuscript of Virginia Woolf's *To the Lighthouse*." *Woolf Studies Annual*, vol. 27, 2021, pp. 5–22.

Jenkins, Gwyn. "Pater's Pins Stuck: Virginia Woolf and Clara Pater at King's College Ladies' Department." *Woolf Studies Annual*, vol. 27, 2021, pp. 23–46.

Jones, Clara. "Virginia Woolf and 'The Villa Jones' (1931)." *Woolf Studies Annual*, vol. 22, 2016, pp. 75–88.

Ke, Lingxiang. "'The Real Flower; Part Earth; Part Flower': Virginia Woolf's Statuesque Form in Jacob's Room." *Woolf Studies Annual*, vol. 29, 2023, pp. 57–86.

*Kotler, Margot. "After Anger: Negative Affect and Feminist Politics in Virginia Woolf's *Three Guineas*." *Woolf Studies Annual*, vol. 24, 2018, pp. 35–54.

Koulouris, Theodore. "Virginia Woolf's 'Greek Notebook' (VS Greek and Latin Studies): An Annotated Transcription." *Woolf Studies Annual*,

vol. 25, 2019, pp. 1–72.
Lauby, Daniel G. "Fascism, Resistance, Failure: Woolf's Adaptations of Masques in Between the Acts." *Woolf Studies Annual*, vol. 27, 2021, pp. 47–62.
Layne, Bethany. "The 'Supreme Portrait Artist' and the 'Mistress of the Phrase': Contesting Oppositional Portrayals of Woolf and Bell, Life and Art, in Susan Sellers's 'Vanessa and Virginia.'" *Woolf Studies Annual*, vol. 21, 2015, pp. 78–106.
Leach, Stephen. "A Back Shop All Our Own: Montaigne as a Possible Source for A Room of One's Own." *Woolf Studies Annual*, vol. 28, 2022, pp. 99–106.
Livingstone, Catriona. "'Unacted Part[s]': Subjunctive Science-Fictional Identities in Virginia Woolf's Later Work." *Woolf Studies Annual*, vol. 26, 2020, pp. 87–104.
Lostoski-Ho, Leanna. "'Against Time and Sea': The Deep Temporality of the Interludes in *The Waves*." *Woolf Studies Annual*, vol. 28, 2022, pp. 47–68.
*Marcus, Jane. "Flirting with the HRC." *Woolf Studies Annual*, vol. 24, 2018, pp. 5–10.
McVicker, Jeanette. "Archaeological Woolf: Prehistory, Heterotopias, and Envisioning the Future." *Woolf Studies Annual*, vol. 28, 2022, pp. 69–98.
Novillo-Corvalán, Patricia. "Empire and Commerce in Latin America: Historicizing Woolf's *The Voyage Out*." *Woolf Studies Annual*, vol. 23, 2017, pp. 33–62.
*Pająk, Paulina. "'Echo Texts': Woolf, Krzywicka, and *The Well of Loneliness*." *Woolf Studies Annual*, vol. 24, 2018, pp. 11–34.
Phillips, Josh. "Thoughts on Peace in a Wine Cellar: On Transcribing the 1917 Dinner Party in the Holograph *Years*." *Woolf Studies Annual*, vol. 26, 2020, pp. 1–12.
Rutherford, Brett. "Virginia Woolf's Egyptomania: Echoes of *The Book of the Dead* in *To The Lighthouse*." *Woolf Studies Annual*, vol. 24, 2018, pp. 135–64.
Ryan, Derek. "Virginia Woolf and the Pyrocene: Fire Ecologies in *The Waves* and *The Years*." *Woolf Studies Annual*, vol. 30, 2024, pp. 67–84.
Schwartz, John Pedro. "Not So 'Solid Objects': Monuments and Character in *Jacob's Room*." *Woolf Studies Annual*, vol. 29, 2023, pp. 87–106.
Shin, Jacqueline. "It's You I Adore: On the Odes of Virginia Woolf." *Woolf Studies Annual*, vol. 23, 2017, pp. 109–40.
Van Straten, Lisa. "A Walk in the Park through the Past, Present and Future: Entangled Temporalities in *Mrs. Dalloway*'s Urban Parks." *Woolf Studies Annual*, vol. 30, 2024, pp. 85–97.
Van Wert, Kathryn. "'Driven by An Unseizable Force': Virginia Woolf and the Invention of the Death Drive." *Woolf Studies Annual*, vol. 29, 2023, pp. 107–24.
White, Siân. "The Dramatic Modern Novel: Mimesis and The Poetics of Tragedy in *Mrs. Dalloway*." *Woolf Studies Annual*, vol. 24, 2018, pp. 101–34.
Williams, Sebastian. "Woolf's Bioethics: Animals and Dependency in 'The Widow and the Parrot.'" *Woolf Studies Annual*, vol. 26, 2020, pp. 105–20.
Wisor, Rebecca. "About Face: The 'Three Guineas' Photographs in Cultural Context." *Woolf Studies Annual*, vol. 21, 2015, pp. 1–49.

Forums

Mark Hussey's Clive Bell and the Making of Modernism *(2021)*

Berkowitz, Elizabeth. "On the Significance of Clive Bell: 'Impact Capital' and the Life of an Idea." *Woolf Studies Annual*, vol. 29, 2023, pp. 125–40.

Davison, Claire. "Alternative Currents? Listening in to Mark Hussey's Clive Bell and the Making of Modernism." *Woolf Studies Annual*, vol. 29, 2023, pp. 141–48.

Gillespie, Diane F. "Biographical Tropes: The Making of Modernist Biographies." *Woolf Studies Annual*, vol. 29, 2023, pp. 149–55.

Humm, Maggie. "1922, Cinema, Biography, and Clive Bell." *Woolf Studies Annual*, vol. 29, 2023, pp. 156–61.

Hussey, Mark. "Keeping My Distance: Response to Readers." *Woolf Studies Annual*, vol. 29, 2023, pp. 167–70.

Reed, Christopher. "Art Words." *Woolf Studies Annual*, vol. 29, 2023, pp. 162–66.

On Emily Kopley's Virginia Woolf and Poetry *(2021)*

De Gay, Jane. "'[T]he voices of the poets, answering each other': Virginia Woolf's Elegiac Imagination." *Woolf Studies Annual*, vol. 30, 2024, pp. 99–106.

Goldman, Jane. "That Queer Feeling in the Hot Grass: *Virginia Woolf and Poetry*." *Woolf Studies Annual*, vol. 30, 2024, pp. 107–09.

Gallego Larrarte, Bárbara. "Prompting Woolf: The Rise of the Thirties Generation." *Woolf Studies Annual*, vol. 30, 2024, pp. 111–16.

Kopley, Emily. "Print Does Not Settle it: Response to Readers." *Woolf Studies Annual*, vol. 30, 2024, pp. 125–29.

Sullam, Sara. "A Relational View of Literary Genres: Virginia Woolf and Poetry." *Woolf Studies Annual*, vol. 30, 2024, pp. 117–24.

Archival Materials, Corrections, Notes, and Reference Materials

Alcrim, Mitchell, Case, Oliver, Jenny Ann Cubin, Niklas Cyril, Benjamin D. Hagen, Skylar Kovacs, Maria Trejling, and Pamela Weidman. "Index of *Woolf Studies Annual* Volumes 1–10 (1995–2004)." *Woolf Studies Annual*, vol. 28, 2022, pp. 129–300.

Alcrim, Mitchell, Case, Oliver, Jenny Ann Cubin, Niklas Cyril, Benjamin D. Hagen, Skylar Kovacs, and Pamela Weidman. "Index of *Woolf Studies Annual* Volumes 11–15 (2005–2009)." *Woolf Studies Annual*, vol. 29, 2023, pp. 193–265.

Bolchi, Elisa. "International Notes." *Woolf Studies Annual*, vol. 23, 2017, pp. 203–04.

Case, Oliver, Jenny Ann Cubin, Benjamin D. Hagen, Skylar Kovacs, and Pamela Weidman. "Index of *Woolf Studies Annual* Volumes 16–20 (2010–2014)." *Woolf Studies Annual*, vol. 30, 2024, pp. 153–249.

Hagen, Benjamin D. Editor's Note. *Woolf Studies Annual*, vol. 28, 2022, p. 3–4

———. Editor's Note. *Woolf Studies Annual*, vol. 29, 2023, p. 3–4.

———. Editor's Note. *Woolf Studies Annual*, vol. 30, 2024, p. 3.

Hussey, Mark. "Editor's Note." *Woolf Studies Annual*, vol. 27, 2021, pp. 3–4.

Gilman, Danielle. Transcription of Virginia Woolf's Draft: "As to criticism." *Woolf Studies Annual*, vol. 30, 2024, pp. 39–55.

Jones, Clara. Transcription: "The Villa Jones." *Woolf Studies Annual*, vol. 22, 2016, pp. 89–95.

Koulouris, Theodore. "Virginia Woolf's 'Greek Notebook' (VS Greek and Latin Studies): An Annotated Transcription." *Woolf Studies Annual*, vol. 25, 2019, pp. 1–72.

Phillips, Josh. "Thoughts on Peace in a Wine Cellar: A Transcription of the

1917 Dinner Party in the Holograph *Years*." *Woolf Studies Annual*, vol. 26, 2020, pp. 13–86.

Reviews

Allen, Carolyn, and Monica Latham. Review of *A Poetics of Postmodernism and Neomodernism: Rewriting* Mrs. Dalloway by Monica Latham. *Woolf Studies Annual*, vol. 22, 2016, pp. 140–44.
Banerjee, Ria. Review of *Threshold Modernism: New Public Women and the Literary Spaces of Imperial London* by Elizabeth Evans; *Virginia Woolf's Rooms and the Spaces of Modernity* by Suzana Zink. *Woolf Studies Annual*, vol. 26, 2020, pp. 164–67.
Barkway, Stephen. Review of *Virginia Woolf's Garden: The Story of the Garden at Monk's House* by Caroline Zoob. *Woolf Studies Annual*, vol. 21, 2015, pp. 181–84.
Battershill, Claire. Review of *Modernism, Middlebrow and the Literary Canon* by Lisa Jaillant. *Woolf Studies Annual*, vol. 21, 2015, pp. 160–63.
Berman, Jessica. Review of *On Beauty and Being: Hans-Georg Gadamer's and Virginia Woolf's Hermeneutics of the Beautiful* by Małgorzata Bielecka-Hołda. *Woolf Studies Annual*, vol. 28, 2022, pp. 301–03.
Botwick, Aaron. Review of *Shakespeare in Bloomsbury* by Majorie Garber. *Woolf Studies Annual*, vol. 30, 2024, pp. 251–53.
Bright, Jennifer Burns. Review of *The Bloomsbury Cookbook: Recipes for Life, Love and Art* by Jans Ondaatje Rolls. *Woolf Studies Annual*, vol. 21, 2015, pp. 184–87.
Caleb, Amanda. Review of *Virginia Woolf and Nineteenth-Century Women Writers: Victorian Legacies and Literary Afterlives* by Anne Reus. *Woolf Studies Annual*, vol. 30, 2024, pp. 253–56.
Carluccio, Cristina. Review of *Trans-Woolf: Thinking Across Borders* edited by Claire Davison and Anne-Marie Smith-Di Biasio. *Woolf Studies Annual*, vol. 25, 2019, pp. 175–78.
Caws, Mary Ann. Review of *Cross-Channel Modernisms* edited by Claire Davison, Derek Ryan, and Jane Goldman. *Woolf Studies Annual*, vol. 27, 2021, pp. 93–95.
Chapman, Wayne K. Review of *Leonard Woolf: Bloomsbury Socialist* by Fred Leventhal and Peter Stansky. *Woolf Studies Annual*, vol. 26, 2020, pp. 161–63.
Clarke, Darren. Review of *Bloomsbury Stud: The Life of Stephen 'Tommy' Tomlin* by Michael Bloch and Susan Fox. *Woolf Studies Annual*, vol. 27, 2021, pp. 112–14.
Collier, Patrick. Review of *Virginia Woolf and the Professions* by Evelyn Tsz Yan Chan. *Woolf Studies Annual*, vol. 23, 2017, pp. 186–90.
Cornish, Sarah E. Review of *The Cambridge Companion to Modernist Culture* edited by Celia Marshik; *The Cambridge Companion to The Bloomsbury Group* edited by Victoria Rosner. *Woolf Studies Annual*, vol. 22, 2016, pp. 144–47.
———. Review of *Modernism, Fashion, and Interwar Women Writers* by Vike Martina Plock. *Woolf Studies Annual*, vol. 24, 2018, pp. 215–17.
Czarnecki, Kristin. Review of *Rooms: Women, Writing, Woolf* by Sina Queyras. *Woolf Studies Annual*, vol. 29, 2023, pp. 267–69.
———. Review of *Virginia Woolf Writing the World: Selected Papers from the Twenty-Fourth Annual International Conference on Virginia Woolf* edited by Pamela L. Caughie and Diana L.

Swanson. *Woolf Studies Annual*, vol. 24, 2018, pp. 236–40.

Daugherty, Beth Rigel. Review of *Becoming Virginia Woolf: Her Early Diaries & the Diaries She Read* by Barbara Lounsberry. *Woolf Studies Annual*, vol. 21, 2015, pp. 193–96.

Davies, Madeleine. Review of *Virginia Woolf & Heritage: Selected Papers from the Twenty-Sixth Annual Conference on Virginia Woolf* edited by Jane de Gay, Tom Breckin, and Anne Reus. *Woolf Studies Annual*, vol. 24, 2018, pp. 242–46.

———. Review of *Virginia Woolf's Portraits of Russian Writers: Creating the Literary Other* by Darya Protopopova. *Woolf Studies Annual*, vol. 26, 2020, pp. 167–70.

De Gay, Jane. Review of *The Cambridge Companion to* To the Lighthouse edited by Allison Pease. *Woolf Studies Annual*, vol. 22, 2016, pp. 148–51.

———. Review of *Orlando: A Biography* edited by Suzanne Raitt and Ian Blyth. *Woolf Studies Annual*, vol. 25, 2019, pp. 159–61.

Delsandro, Erica. Review of *Tense Future: Modernism, Total War, Encyclopedic Form* by Paul K. Saint-Amour; *Writing Against War: Literature, Activism, and the British Peace Movement* by Charles Andrews. *Woolf Studies Annual*, vol. 24, 2018, pp. 207–11.

Detloff, Madelyn. Review of *The Sensuous Pedagogies of Virginia Woolf and D. H. Lawrence* by Benjamin D. Hagen. *Woolf Studies Annual*, vol. 27, 2021, pp. 85–87.

Dickson, Jay. Review of *Behind the Mask: The Life of Vita Sackville-West* by Matthew Denn. *Woolf Studies Annual*, vol. 21, 2015, pp. 200–03.

Doyle, Laura. Review of *A Companion to Virginia Woolf* edited by Jessica Berman. *Woolf Studies Annual*, vol. 23, 2017, pp. 179–82.

Dubino, Jeanne. Review of *Recycling Virginia Woolf in Contemporary Art and Literature* edited by Monica Latham, Caroline Marie, Anne-Laure Rigeade. *Woolf Studies Annual*, vol. 29, 2023, pp. 269–72.

Edmondson, Annalee. Review of *Feminist Narrative Ethics: Tacit Persuasion in Modernist Form* by Katherine Saunders Nash. *Woolf Studies Annual*, vol. 21, 2015, pp. 174–77.

Elkin, Lauren, et al. Review of *Contemporary Woolf/Woolf Contemporaine* edited by Claire Davison-Pegon and Anne-Marie Smith Di- Biasio. *Woolf Studies Annual*, vol. 22, 2016, pp. 125–28.

Favre, Valérie. Review of *The Edinburgh Companion to Virginia Woolf and Contemporary Global Literature* edited by Dubine et. al. *Woolf Studies Annual*, vol. 29, 2023, pp. 272–75.

Fernald, Anne E. Review of *Virginia Woolf's Mythic Method* by Amy C. Smith. *Woolf Studies Annual*, vol. 30, 2024, pp. 256–59.

Foster, J. Ashley. Review of *Virginia Woolf, Europe, and Peace: Transnational Circulations, Volume 1* edited by Ariane Mildenberg and Patricia Novillo-Corvalán; *Virginia Woolf, Europe, and Peace: Aesthetics and Theory, Volume 2*, edited by Peter Adkins and Derek Ryan. *Woolf Studies Annual*, vol. 28, 2022, pp. 304–10.

Fox, Meghan C. Review of *Virginia Woolf: Ambivalent Activist* by Clara Jones. *Woolf Studies Annual*, vol. 23, 2017, pp. 175–78.

Gerzina, Gretchen Holbrook, et al. Review of *Vanessa and Her Sister* by Priya Parmar; *Adeline* by Norah Vincent; *Virginia Woolf in Manhattan* by Maggie Gee. *Woolf Studies Annual*, vol. 22, 2016, pp. 120–25.

Golden, Amanda, and Dirk Van Hulle.

Review of *Modern Manuscripts: The Extended Mind and Creative Undoing from Darwin to Beckett and Beyond* by Dirk Van Hulle. *Woolf Studies Annual*, vol. 22, 2016, pp. 131–34.

Goldman, Jane. Review of *Queer Bloomsbury* edited by Brenda Helt and Madelyn Detloff. *Woolf Studies Annual*, vol. 23, 2017, pp. 161–71.

Goldman, Jonathan, et al. Review of *Modernism and Autobiography* edited by Maria DiBattista and Emily O. Wittman. *Woolf Studies Annual*, vol. 22, 2016, pp. 138–40.

Greaves, Margaret. Review of *Modernist Physics: Waves, Particles, and Relativities in the Writings of Virginia Woolf and D.H. Lawrence* by Rachel Crossland. *Woolf Studies Annual*, vol. 25, 2019, pp. 169–71.

Griesinger, Emily. Review of *Religion Around Virginia Woolf* by Stephanie Paulsell. *Woolf Studies Annual*, vol. 26, 2020, pp. 158–60.

Hagen, Benjamin D. Review of *The Value of Virginia Woolf* by Madelyn Detloff. *Woolf Studies Annual*, vol. 23, 2017, pp. 171–74.

Hammill, Faye. Review of *Modernism and Modernity in British Women's Magazines* by Alice Wood. *Woolf Studies Annual*, vol. 27, 2021, pp. 101–03.

Hankins, Gabriel. Review of *Scholarly Adventures in the Digital Humanities: Making the Modernist Archives Publishing Project* by Claire Battershill et. al. *Woolf Studies Annual*, vol. 24, 2018, pp. 231–33.

Hankins, Gabriel. Review of *Jacob's Room* edited by Stuart N. Clarke. *Woolf Studies Annual*, vol. 29, 2023, pp. 275–78.

Hobson, Suzanne. Review of *Virginia Woolf and Christian Culture* by Jane de Gay. *Woolf Studies Annual*, vol. 25, 2019, pp. 172–74.

Holland, Kathryn. Review of *Virginia Woolf and Her Female Contemporaries: Selected Papers from the Twenty-Fifth Annual International Conference on Virginia Woolf* edited by Julie Vandivere and Megan Hicks. *Woolf Studies Annual*, vol. 24, 2018, pp. 240–42.

Humm, Maggie. Review of *Virginia Woolf: Art, Life and Vision* by Frances Spalding. *Woolf Studies Annual*, vol. 21, 2015, pp. 156–59.

Hunter, Dianne M. Review of *Literary Aesthetics of Trauma: Virginia Woolf and Jeanette Winterson* by Reina Van der Wiel. *Woolf Studies Annual*, vol. 21, 2015, pp. 188–90.

Hussey, Mark. Review of *The Bloomsbury Group Memoir Club* by S. P. Rosenbaum, edited by James M. Haule. *Woolf Studies Annual*, vol. 21, 2015, pp. 151–55.

———. Review of *The Oxford Handbook of Virginia Woolf* edited by Anne E. Fernald. *Woolf Studies Annual*, vol. 28, 2022, pp. 310–13.

———. Review of *Square Haunting: Five Writers in London Between the Wars* by Francesca Wade; *Virginia Woolf and the Women Who Shaped Her World* by Gillian Gill. *Woolf Studies Annual*, vol. 27, 2021, pp. 95–101.

———. Review of *Virginia Woolf's Afterlives: The Author as Character in Contemporary Fiction and Drama* by Monica Latham. *Woolf Studies Annual*, vol. 29, 2023, pp. 279–81.

Jaillant, Lise. Review of *Modernist Lives: Biography and Autobiography at Leonard and Virginia Woolf's Hogarth Press* by Claire Battershill; *Virginia Woolf and the World of Books* edited by Nicola Wilson and Claire Battershill. *Woolf Studies Annual*, vol. 26, 2020, pp. 146–49.

James, Emily. Review of *At the Mercy of Their Clothes: Modernism, the*

Middlebrow, and British Garment Culture by Celia Marshik. *Woolf Studies Annual*, vol. 24, 2018, pp. 212–14.

———. Review of *The Work of Revision* by Hannah Sullivan. *Woolf Studies Annual*, vol. 21, 2015, pp. 163–66.

Johnson, Erica L. Review of *Modernism and the Rhythms of Sympathy: Vernon Lee, Virginia Woolf, and D. H. Lawrence* by Kirsty Martin. *Woolf Studies Annual*, vol. 21, 2015, pp. 171–74.

Kimber, Gerri. Review of *Commemorative Modernisms: Women Writers, Death and the First World War* by Alice Kelly. *Woolf Studies Annual*, vol. 27, 2021, pp. 106–09.

Kohlmann, Benjamin. Review of *Edward Upward: Art and Life* by Peter Stansky. *Woolf Studies Annual*, vol. 23, 2017, pp. 199–202.

Konkol, Margaret."Review of *The Sky of Our Manufacture: The London Fog in British Fiction from Dickens to Woolf* by Jesse Oak Taylor. *Woolf Studies Annual*, vol. 24, 2018, pp. 234–36.

Laing, Kathryn. Review of *Fresca: A Life in the Making. A Biographer's Quest for a Forgotten Bloomsbury Polymath* by Helen Southworth. *Woolf Studies Annual*, vol. 24, 2018, pp. 225–28.

Levine-Keating, Helane. Review of *Translation as Collaboration: Virginia Woolf, Katherine Mansfield and S. S. Koteliansky* by Claire Davison. *Woolf Studies Annual*, vol. 21, 2015, pp. 134–36.

Love, Heather A. Review of *Virginia Woolf, Science, Radio, and Identity* by Catriona Livingstone. *Woolf Studies Annual*, vol. 29, 2023, pp. 281–84.

Marshik, Celia. Review of *Modernism à La Mode: Fashion and the Ends of Literature* by Elizabeth M. Sheehan. *Woolf Studies Annual*, vol. 26, 2020, pp. 150–52.

Martin, Ann. Review of *Woolf: A Guide for the Perplexed* by Kathryn Simpson. *Woolf Studies Annual*, vol. 23, 2017, pp. 183–86.

Mills, Jean. Review of *Interdisciplinary/ Multidisciplinary Woolf: Selected Papers from the Twenty-Second Annual International Conference on Virginia Woolf* edited by Ann Martin and Kathryn Holland; *Virginia Woolf and the Common(Wealth) Reader: Selected Papers from the Twenty-Third Annual International Conference on Virginia Woolf* edited by Helen Wussow and Mary Ann Gillies. *Woolf Studies Annual*, vol. 22, 2016, pp. 151–56.

Neverow, Vara. Review of *Clive Bell and the Making of Modernism: A Biography* by Mark Hussey. *Woolf Studies Annual*, vol. 28, 2022, pp. 314–18.

Ophir, Ella. Review of *Virginia Woolf and Poetry* by Emily Kopley. *Woolf Studies Annual*, vol. 28, 2022, pp. 318–21.

Outka, Elizabeth. Review of *Night and Day* by Michael Whitworth. *Woolf Studies Annual*, vol. 26, 2020, pp. 143–45.

Paul, Catherine. Review *Crafting Feminism from Literary Modernism to the Multimedia Present* by Amy E. Elkins. *Woolf Studies Annual*, vol. 30, 2024, pp. 260–62.

Pouliot, Amber. Review of *Homes and Haunts: Touring Writers' Shrines and Countries* by Alison Booth. *Woolf Studies Annual*, vol. 25, 2019, pp. 190–93.

Protopopova, Darya. Review of *The Common Reader* (1st and 2nd Series in One Volume) translated and edited with notes by Natalya Reinhold; *Night and Day* by translated and edited with notes by Natalya Reinhold. *Woolf Studies Annual*, vol. 21, 2015, pp. 127–33.

Ranger, Holly. Review of *Ladies' Greek:*

Victorian Translations of Tragedy by Yopie Prins. *Woolf Studies Annual*, vol. 27, 2021, pp. 109–12.
Reus, Anne. Review of *Behind the Times: Virginia Woolf in Late-Victorian Contexts* by Mary Jean Corbett. *Woolf Studies Annual*, vol. 28, 2022, pp. 321–24.
Rosen, Jeff. Review of *Virginia Woolf's Influential Forebears: Julia Margaret Cameron, Anny Thackeray Ritchie and Julia Prinsep Stephen* by Marion Dell. *Woolf Studies Annual*, vol. 25, 2019, pp. 183–86.
Ryan, Derek. Review of *Sentencing Orlando: Virginia Woolf and the Morphology of the Modernist Sentence* edited by Elsa Högberg and Amy Bromley. *Woolf Studies Annual*, vol. 25, 2019, pp. 178–81.
Saloman, Randi. Review of *Virginia Woolf: Experiments in Character* by Eric Sandberg. *Woolf Studies Annual*, vol. 21, 2015, pp. 196–99.
Schorr, C. S. W. Review of *Virginia Woolf, Jane Ellen Harrison, and the Spirit of Modernist Classicism* by Jean Mills. *Woolf Studies Annual*, vol. 21, 2015, pp. 177–81.
Scott, Bonnie Kime. Review of *Women Making Modernism* edited by Erica Gene Delsandra. *Woolf Studies Annual*, vol. 27, 2021, pp. 87–90.
Sellers, Annalee. Review of *Woolf's Ambiguities: Tonal Modernism, Narrative Strategy, Feminist Precursors* by Molly Hite. *Woolf Studies Annual*, vol. 25, 2019, pp. 165–68.
Shannon, Drew Patrick. Review of *Virginia Woolf: Critical and Primary Sources, Volume 1: 1975–1984* edited by Vara Neverow; *Virginia Woolf: Critical and Primary Sources, Volume 2: 1985–1994*, edited by Jeanne Dubino; *Virginia Woolf: Critical and Primary Sources, Volume 3: 1995–2004*, edited by Kathryn Simpson; *Virginia Woolf: Critical and Primary Sources, Volume 4: 2005–2014*, edited by Gill Lowe. *Woolf Studies Annual*, vol. 28, 2022, pp. 324–27.
———. Review of *Virginia Woolf: The War Without, the War Within: Her Final Diaries & the Diaries She Read* by Barbara Lounsberry. *Woolf Studies Annual*, vol. 25, 2019, pp. 193–96.
———. Review of *Virginia Woolf's Apprenticeship: Becoming an Essayist* by Beth Rigel Daugherty. *Woolf Studies Annual*, vol. 29, 2023, pp. 284–87.
———. Review of *Virginia Woolf's Modernist Path: Her Middle Diaries & the Diaries She Read* by Barbara Lounsberry. *Woolf Studies Annual*, vol. 24, 2018, pp. 228–31.
Sim, Lorraine. Review of *A Mystical Philosophy: Transcendence and Immanence in the Works of Virginia Woolf and Iris Murdoch* by Donna J. Lazenby. *Woolf Studies Annual*, vol. 21, 2015, pp. 190–93.
Smith, Amy C. Review of *Modernist Waterscapes: Water, Imagination and Materiality in the Works of Virginia Woolf* by Marlene Dirschauer. *Woolf Studies Annual*, vol. 30, 2024, pp. 263–67.
———. Review of *Virginia Woolf and the Ethics of Intimacy* by Elsa Högberg. *Woolf Studies Annual*, vol. 29, 2023, pp. 287–89.
Smith, Angela. Review of *Natural Connections: Virginia Woolf and Katherine Mansfield* by Bonnie Kime Scott; *"Eternally in Yr Debt": The Personal and Professional Relationship Between Virginia Woolf & Elizabeth Robins* by Hilary Newman; *Saxon Sydney-Turner: The Ghost of Bloomsbury* by Todd Avery; *Virginia Woolf as Memoirist: 'I Am Made and Remade Continually'* by

Alice Lowe; *Mistress of the Brush and Madonna of Bloomsbury, The Art and Life of Vanessa Bell: A Biographical Sketch and Comprehensive Annotated Bibliography of Writings on Vanessa Bell* by Suellen Cox; *Septimus Smith: Modernist and War Poet: A Closer Reading* by Vara S. Neverow. *Woolf Studies Annual*, vol. 23, 2017, pp. 191–95.

Sorensen, Jennifer. Review of *Cheap Modernism: Expanding Markets, Publishers' Series, and the Avant-Garde* by Lise Jaillant. *Woolf Studies Annual*, vol. 24, 2018, pp. 218–21.

Sorum, Eve. Review of *Character and Mourning: Woolf, Faulkner, and the Novel Elegy of the First World War* by Erin Penner. *Woolf Studies Annual*, vol. 27, 2021, pp. 90–92.

Sparks, Elisa Kay. Review of *Critical Insights: Virginia Woolf and 20th-Century Women Writers*, by Kathyrn Stelmach Artuso. *Woolf Studies Annual*, vol. 22, 2016, pp. 157–60.

———. Review of *The Handbook to the Bloomsbury Group* edited by Derek Ryan and Stephen Ross. *Woolf Studies Annual*, vol. 25, 2019, pp. 162–65.

———. Review of *Walking Virginia Woolf's London: An Investigation in Literary Geography* by Lisbeth Larsson. *Woolf Studies Annual*, vol. 25, 2019, pp. 181–83.

Sriratana, Verita. Review of *Virginia Woolf and the Problem of the Subject: Feminine Writing in the Major Novels*; *Virginia Woolf and December 1910: Studies in Rhetoric and Context* by Makiko Minow-Pinkney. *Woolf Studies Annual*, vol. 21, 2015, pp. 166–71.

Stalter-Pace, Sunny. Review of *Moving Modernisms: Motion, Technology, and Modernity* edited by David Bradshaw, Laura Marcus, and Rebecca Roach. *Woolf Studies Annual*, vol. 23, 2017, pp. 196–98.

Stansky, Peter. Review of *The Politics of 1930s British Literature: Education, Class, Gender* by Natasha Periyan. *Woolf Studies Annual*, vol. 26, 2020, pp. 152–54.

———. Review of *Selected Letters of Clive Bell: Art, Love and War in Bloomsbury* edited by Mark Hussey. *Woolf Studies Annual*, vol. 30, 2024, pp. 265–67.

Sutton, Emma. Review of *Virginia Woolf: Music, Sound, Language* by Elicia Clements. *Woolf Studies Annual*, vol. 26, 2020, pp. 155–57.

Swanson, Diana L. Review of *Ecocriticism and the Idea of Culture: Biology and the Bildungsroman* by Helena Feder; *Ecocriticism and Women Writers: Environmentalist Poetics of Virginia Woolf, Jeanette Winterson, and Ali Smith* by Justyna Kostkowska. *Woolf Studies Annual*, vol. 21, 2015, pp. 146–51.

Terry, Sarah. Review of *Virginia Woolf and Music* by Elicia Clements. *Woolf Studies Annual*, vol. 21, 2015, pp. 137–42.

Tromanhauser, Vicki. Review of *Dissensuous Modernism: Women Writers, the Senses, and Technology* by Allyson C. Demaagd. *Woolf Studies Annual*, vol. 29, 2023, pp. 289–92.

Utell, Janine. Review of *Virginia Woolf: Twenty-First-Century Approaches* edited by Jeanne Dubino, Gill Lowe, Vara Neverow, and Kathryn Simpson. *Woolf Studies Annual*, vol. 22, 2016, pp. 128–31.

Vechinski, Matthew James. Review of *Roomscape: Women Writers in the British Museum from George Eliot to Virginia Woolf* by Susan David Bernstein. *Woolf Studies Annual*, vol. 22, 2016, pp. 135–38.

Walsh, Kelly S. Review of *Modernism and Melancholia: Writing as*

Countermourning by Sanja Bahun. *Woolf Studies Annual*, vol. 21, 2015, pp. 142–46.
———. Review of *Virginia Woolf and Being-in-the-World: A Heideggerian Study* by Emma Simone. *Woolf Studies Annual*, vol. 25, 2019, pp. 186–89.
Winkiel, Laura. Review of *Modernism at the Beach: Queer Ecologies and the Coastal Commons* by Hannah Freed-Thall. *Woolf Studies Annual*, vol. 30, 2024, pp. 267–70.
Wolfe, Jesse. Review of *Bloomsbury, Beasts, and British Modernism* by Derek Ryan. *Woolf Studies Annual*, vol. 30, 2024, pp. 270–73.
———. Review of *Literary Couples and 20th-Century Life Writing: Narrative and Intimacy* by Janine Utell. *Woolf Studies Annual*, vol. 27, 2021, pp. 103–06.
Young, John K. Review of Virginia Woolf's *Mrs. Dalloway* edited by Anne E. Fernald. *Woolf Studies Annual*, vol. 22, 2016, pp. 117–19.
Zox-Weaver, Annalisa. Review of *Ordinary Matters: Modernist Women's Literature and Photography* by Lorraine Sim. *Woolf Studies Annual*, vol. 24, 2018, pp. 221–25.
Zumhagen-Yekplé, Karen. Review of *Modernist Fiction and Vagueness: Philosophy, Form, and Language* by Megan Quigley. *Woolf Studies Annual*, vol. 22, 2016, pp. 160–64.

Reviews

The Artist Helen Coombe (1864–1937): The Tragedy of Roger Fry's Wife. Martin Ferguson Smith (London: Hogarth Arts, Ltd., 2023). pp. 338.

The forced incarceration inflicted upon the postpartum, psychosis-suffering, unnamed protagonist in Charlotte Perkins Gilman's "The Yellow Wall Paper" (1890) and the general paradox of mental health "care" for nineteenth- and twentieth-century women are inescapable, contemporaneous references that loom over Martin Ferguson Smith's *The Artist Helen Coombe (1864–1937): The Tragedy of Roger Fry's Wife*. Helen was an artist of great, unrealized promise as well as the wife of Bloomsbury art critic Roger Elliot Fry. Due to what physicians now believe to have been schizophrenia, Helen was committed to an asylum in 1910 where she remained until her death in 1937, never again to see her and Roger's two children. Yet, while patriarchal control softly coded as "treatment" is essential to understand aspects of Helen Fry's biography, there is a critical difference that prevents making too direct of an analogy between Gilman's semi-fictional "The Yellow Wall Paper" and the tragedy of Helen Coombe Fry.

Gilman's short story connects her protagonist's suffering directly to multiple perpetrators of injustice. There is blame to go around. In the case of Helen Coombe Fry, however, such "blame" is not so clear-cut, no matter how much one might want—as Smith sometimes appears to—to assign a villain to explain the depths of heart-wrenching tragedy that defined much of Helen's life. The story of Helen Fry is instead a tale of a talented, charismatic woman with the devastating misfortune to become a casualty of an oppressive era in women's mental health treatment, who lived within and among a community of professionals and loved ones who ultimately caused harm in the service of trying to help and provide compassionate support.

The Artist Helen Coombe is an overdue showcase for Helen, a woman long functioning merely as a plot device to preface the Bloomsbury group's flourishing, but about whom scholars, until now, have known precious little. As Bloomsbury art critic Roger Elliot Fry's institutionalized wife, Helen embodied a clearly demarcated "before" to Roger Fry's "after" as the propellant of the younger circle around Virginia Woolf, Vanessa Bell, Clive Bell, Duncan Grant, and all their creative peers into aesthetic modernism. Helen was admitted to her final place of residence, the Quaker mental asylum known as The Retreat, York, on November 7, 1910; coincidentally, one day later, Roger's groundbreaking exhibition *Manet and the Post-Impressionists*—one credited with altering the course of English painting as well as modern art historiography—opened on November 8, 1910.[1] In the annals of Bloomsbury, the break point of Helen's consignment in tandem with the opening

[1] *Manet and the Post-Impressionists,* today known as the "First Post-Impressionist Exhibition," was referred to variously by Bloomsbury and Bloomsbury-adjacent members as an "art-quake," and the impetus for an overall change or shift in human character, reeling from the inspirational shock of French late-nineteenth century art (Cork).

of *Manet and the Post-Impressionists* supercharged Roger's story—and that of canonical Bloomsbury.

Yet Helen Coombe Fry was far more than a narrative obstacle to be overcome, disappearing into the ether as soon as she was committed. As quoted in Smith, "Goldie" (Goldsworthy Lowes Dickinson), Roger's far-more-than-close friend, referred to Helen as "[t]hat brilliant beautiful woman"; art historian Tancred Borenius called her "one of the truly great 'might-have-beens' of English art" with a mind of "singular distinction"; and Bernard Berenson, Roger's future mentor, preferred Helen over Roger, calling Helen the "superior person" of the pair in an 1868 letter to his sister (1, 62, 188). In Smith's recounting, Helen, rather than Roger, was publicly perceived to be the "catch" of the two in terms of wit, talent, and pleasurable company.

Starting at age seventeen, Helen received thirteen to fourteen years of rigorous, professional art education in both England and Paris, winning prizes for her work. Unusually, she supported herself financially such that she could afford her own studio at thirty-one, likely through work as a well-regarded portraitist (19–29, 52). Helen was a known and respected member of the Arts and Crafts collective around architect Arthur Heygate Mackmurdo (31–32). Helen was friends with Oscar Wilde, served as matchmaker for critic Will Rothenstein, and was friendly with William Morris and his family (48, 62). It was likely within the Mackmurdo circle that Helen began her exploration of stained glass, a medium for which she would later receive several commissions, through the influence of Selwyn Image.[2] Helen's *Green Harpsichord* (1896), in addition to the surviving examples of her stained glass, are perhaps her most well-known extant works.

With the inclusion of so many full examples of Helen's correspondence, Smith returns Helen's voice to the public record and, simultaneously, takes pains to correct the work of previous, well-regarded Bloomsbury scholars. With a diligence and precision that at times feels more personal than productive, Smith is careful to point out where scholars of Bloomsbury fell short in their research, or where they mischaracterized Helen in the service of furthering alternative theses (11, 43, 47, 57). While breaking up the storytelling, such moments of correction do underscore the myriad, glaring, missed scholarly opportunities to *notice* Helen Coombe Fry, with the consequence of Helen's previously unexamined life the shameful outcome.

Smith identifies the genealogy of Helen's mental illness in her paternal lineage and notes the preponderance of "serious mental instability" among Helen's brothers and sisters, resulting in several suicides and institutionalizations (14–17). Helen's psychiatric struggles began early in her marriage and only increased in frequency and severity (185). She tried to jump from a window, threatened her loved ones, became irrationally belligerent and hateful towards Roger, and chewed on glass (191, 192, 266). She had long bouts of schizophrenic madness—mania

[2] It should also be noted that while Roger's "aesthetic ideals" have traditionally explained his draw to Mackmurdo, with Smith's new details, it was undoubtedly the superior connection between his spouse and the Mackmurdo circle that inspired such an interest (Reed 36).

coupled with delusions, sadness, and periods where her temperament was deemed a physical risk to her children and nursing team (271). She was institutionalized at various asylums; she was subjected to the nineteenth-century American physician Silas Weir Mitchell's infamous "rest cure" (x–xvi, 270). In between these bouts, Helen had moments of productivity, joy, and calm—working on her commissions for stained glass, enjoying her children, visiting art exhibitions, going on holiday with Roger—albeit moments that decreased in number as the years progressed. In 1907, it became too much: Helen's brother Howard formally registered her under the 1845 Lunacy Act, a petition for her legal classification as a "person of unsound mind," thereafter requiring the approval of a physician to return to many aspects of everyday life (vi, 271). Helen's registration under the Lunacy Act was the death knell, signaling the beginning of the end of her personal and creative autonomy.

As her schizophrenic periods waxed and waned and Helen's personality shifted and changed as did the disease, Roger was increasingly advised to remove Helen from regular domestic life, leading to her final institutionalization at The Reach, York, in 1910. Finally, whether through the progression of her condition or the self-protection of a defeated soul, Helen became, in her patient records from The Retreat, York, "deeply demented" albeit with "wonderful flashes of memory" (The Retreat, York, June 30, 1926). Helen died at The Retreat at the age of 73.

Arguably one of the greatest cruelties inflicted upon an already-afflicted Helen was neither her misfortune to be born in an era of pre-pharmacological mental health treatment nor the uncontrollable biological destiny of her genetic predisposition to mental illness. It was not even, as Smith argues repeatedly (and, as I will note, perhaps unfairly), the lack of support for her art while under the oversight of Roger Fry. It was not even the two pages of chronology that *succeed* the November 1910 date of her admittance to The Retreat. (From November 1910 until Helen's 1937 death, the years that record and encompass the entirety of the Bloomsbury heyday *all* pass by without her engagement, perhaps even her knowledge, or her deserved participation).

The ultimate cruelty was instead that Helen Coombe Fry was essentially erased from the record of Bloomsbury. Between the lines of Bloomsbury travels, acclaim, and drama, Helen in the asylum screamed to return home and occasionally was able to return to art-making. To the extent possible, given her mental state, Helen fought back against her imprisonment at The Retreat. Helen wrote to the powerful Sir Edward Fry, Roger's father, begging him to help her "rejoin her family" (289). Roger continued to pay for her upkeep at The Retreat (upon his death, Helen asked Roger's sister who would now pay for her care [The Retreat, York, October 9, 1934]). Roger corresponded regularly with Helen's attending physicians and received updates in return—from occasional watercolors, to back-and-forth letters talking about the impact of color on the mentally disabled. Roger visited Helen in 1911, 1912, 1913, and they mutually wrote letters to one another until 1919 (Smith 53–54). During this time, Roger was also mounting the *Second Post-Impressionist Exhibition,* the Omega Workshop, dealing with the onset of various affairs, the post-War era—all of this while still maintaining a connection to Helen as part of his engagements. Helen's cries, requests, care, and financial burden thus remain in the narrative, uncomfortably concurrent with the more joyful, well-known Bloomsbury moments.

And Helen found a way to be *in* the Bloomsbury story in other ways. Roger tended to slip Helen's work into his exhibitions—both before and after her committal. In his first solo exhibition in 1903, Roger included a watercolor of Helen's (judged to be the best of the show); during a 1917 Omega exhibition on copies, Roger included four works by Helen—they were received with acclaim (3, 38). Similarly, one should look at Fry's longstanding interest in children's art as a connection to Helen.[3] This passionate side interest of Roger's is like an answer to a question about madness and the art instinct—a quest, however subconscious, to see what remained of his beloved, brilliant wife. Though relegated to the ghostly edge of Bloomsbury, Helen Fry never actually left the plot. Smith's meticulously researched text constitutes an implied as well as a direct, barbed critique of over a century of scholarly oversight.[4]

In bringing Helen's story to the fore, Smith also necessarily reintroduces Roger Fry. The vision of Roger as the empathetic, professorial elder statesman of Bloomsbury becomes tarnished through recall of his early years with Helen. Roger, in these early years, appears as the weaker of the two in terms of social group affection and power within the art world. A stained-glass commissioner for Helen and Roger noted, for instance, that while she adored Helen's work, Roger's was merely "growing on her" (213). It is not a stretch to see in Roger's seemingly lighthearted poems—a loving (?) Christmas poem to Helen that notes her "Frank unashamed pride," "Aping humility", "An anger ready as your wit," and comments that she will not "submit" (183–84)—his own insecurities rising to the surface with an aim to diminish her. The Roger in Smith's telling is selfish and self-absorbed. Shortly after his marriage to Helen, Roger disappeared for long, intimate excursions with his friend and former (or current?) lover Goldie Dickinson—reassuring Goldie that nothing really had to change now that he was married (123, 135, 136, 174). While in America working for the Metropolitan Museum of Art, Roger neglected

[3] Winifred Gill in a letter to Duncan Grant from April 18, 1967, notes Roger's "enthusiastic delight" in "Miss Marion Richardson's revolutionary methods of 'teaching' drawing to school children," which primarily consisted in letting their natural, untutored intuition create (Gill).

[4] The network of care necessary to sustain not only Helen as a mentally ill person, but also Roger, as a successful creative force in the world emerges as an additional "hidden-in-plain-sight" character in Smith's text. Over the course of hundreds of pages, for instance, Roger's multiple unmarried sisters are called in to service (willingly or at the behest of Sir Edward Fry) in support of Roger, Helen, and the children with a frequency that became a norm following Helen's institutionalization–Roger's sisters ultimately running all aspects of his household and domestic life so that he had the freedom to travel, create, and live without burden. With Helen now released from historiographic purgatory, one may also wish that these equal prime movers in Bloomsbury—the sisters of Roger Fry—should also be given their due, their worlds examined and rendered valuable to scholarship.

to send home sufficient money for Helen and the kids; she resorted to begging him and angrily demanding he rectify this error (255).

However, there is much—including my summary above—that is conjecture. For all we know, Roger's offensive and mean-spirited Christmas poem to Helen was neither written nor perceived as such between the two. Equally, the particular intimacy of his relationship with Goldie Dickinson: we do not know what arrangements or understandings may have been made between Roger and Helen regarding Goldie.

It is this risk of conjecture that plagues Smith's analysis of Roger. Smith, for instance, chides Roger for traveling following one of Helen's episodes, concluding that the "most plausible explanation is that the pursuit of pictures and fame remained his first priority" (253). Smith may be correct, and examples do appropriately raise questions about Roger's priorities and his appreciation of Helen's needs.[5] However, Smith editorializes correspondences, assuming value systems aligned with contemporary views about labor, marriage, and work. Did Helen submit to Roger's demands under duress, because of his own patronizing, patriarchal values and a financial dependence on him, or was she a product of the gender expectations of the time, and, as a woman who married at thirty-two, a series of expectations she embarked upon with eyes wide open?[6] There is much that is tremendously tragic about Helen's life—but it is possible that evidence doesn't point to *this* particular tragedy as fully accurate, or accounted for in the record.[7]

Yet the most troublesome supposition in *The Artist Helen Coombe*, one that threatens to compromise the importance of Smith's diligent scholarship on Helen, is the thesis regarding Roger's impact on Helen's mental illness. While acknowledging Helen's significant genetic lineage for psychiatric disorders, Smith qualifies this conclusion by noting that at "the same time, it will be contended that Roger's character and behavior are likely to have triggered or at least aggravated some of her breakdowns," and Smith speculates whether "the story of Helen's mental illness would have been significantly different if she had stayed single or married a man" unlike Roger (1, 5). Smith's evidence is, in part, that "in every episode of her mental illness she turned against him" (1). During one of her episodes in 1909, Helen called Roger a "cheat," which Smith states was "probably because she reckoned he was cheating her of her life as a wife and mother" (5). In response to her vitriol against Roger, Smith responds that "she had much justification for resenting the

[5] Indeed, Vanessa Bell, writing in her 1934 "Memories of Roger Fry" with a brief mention of her first and only meeting with Helen, cites Helen complaining that "she had no time for work" (Bell).

[6] Helen's fate as a female artist after marriage and children is not so dissimilar from that of her peers, if the stories in Virginia Woolf's great-niece Virginia Nicholson's still-illuminating text, *Among the Bohemians*, are any indication (Nicholson).

[7] Smith is not the first to take Roger Fry down a peg in historical narrative, as holes in his celebrated persona have been present all along, most notably with the testimony of his children, Pamela and Julian.

way she had sacrificed a large measure of her independence and a promising career to marry a man who put his own interests and career first" (267, 277).

By linking the extremity of Helen's condition to Roger's selfishness, Smith unintentionally removes focus from Helen's lived humanity by inaccurately assigning rational causation to what was, in all likelihood, the common symptomatology of Helen's severe mental illness. Was the depth of Helen's schizophrenic rage exacerbated by or caused by Roger's inability to make space for her needs in their relationship, or were the content of those rages simply the expected and not uncommon byproduct of a terrible mental illness—where deluded lashing out at loved ones is typical, even if hurtful?[8] Such attempts to privilege the former narrative at the expense of the more probable latter unnecessarily superimpose a potentially false, stereotypical story of female professional and personal subjugation onto Helen and Roger at the expense of Helen's actual recounted experience of life and trauma. As historian Elaine Showalter notes about the nineteenth-century mental illness catchall "hysteria" in *The Female Malady: Women, Madness and English Culture, 1830–1980* (1987), while it is "certainly possible to see hysteria within the specific historical framework of the nineteenth century as an unconscious form of feminist protest … Such claims … come dangerously close to romanticizing and endorsing madness as a desirable form of rebellion rather than … the desperate communication of the powerless …" (Showalter 5).

Helen Coombe Fry, whether through the oppressions of her spouse, realities of her own time, and/or ignorance of her caregivers, was not well-served by the world in which she had the fortune (or misfortune?) to inhabit. Her cries echo through the lines of her letters, maintaining their potency and raising the specter of shame when juxtaposed to the exuberance of the Bloomsbury life Roger was leading simultaneously with her suffering. *The Artist Helen Coombe* is at once a restoration of personhood to a talented, forgotten artist, and at the same time a warning. Helen, like many others in the background before and after, was dramatically, visibly *there* all along; it is incumbent upon researchers to have the wisdom and desire to pay attention.

—Elizabeth Berkowitz,
Independent Scholar & Executive Director,
The American Trust for the British Library

[8] The recent *DSM-5TR* description of schizophrenic symptomatology notes the commonality of "dysphoric mood", bouts of irrational anger while under a delusion, etc., all as caused by mental illness rather than necessarily grounded in reality (American Psychiatric Association 101–108). Psychiatrist Peter Dally describes, in the context of manic depression: "In a sense, every manic depressive breakdown reflects battle with a close companion, suppressed anger, fear of rejection, resentment, struggling against love" (Dally 99). Though not referring to schizophrenia, the patterning of lashing out at those closest while in the grip of a mental health episode remains.

Works Cited

American Psychiatric Association. *Diagnostic and Statistical Manual of Psychiatric Disorders, Fifth Edition, Text Revision.* American Psychiatric Association, 2022.

Bell, Vanessa. "Memories of Roger Fry (1934)." TGA20096/1/8-9. Charleston Trust, Correspondence and Other Papers Relating to Roger Fry, Vanessa Bell, Clive Bell, Duncan Grant, and Others. Tate Archive, London.

Cork, Richard. "From 'Art-Quake' to 'Pure Visual Music': Roger Fry and Modern British Art, 1910–1916." *Art Made Modern: Roger Fry's Vision of Art,* edited by Christopher Green, Merrell Holberton, 1999, pp. 57–72.

Dally, Peter. *The Marriage of Heaven and Hell: Manic Depression and the Life of Virginia Woolf.* St. Martin's, 1999.

Gill, Winifred. Letter to Duncan Grant. April 18, 1967. TAM24M 10/12. Winifred Gill Collection.Tate Archive, London.

Nicholson, Virginia. *Among the Bohemians: Experiments in Living 1909–1939.* Viking, 2002.

Reed, Christopher. *Bloomsbury Rooms: Modernism, Subculture, and Domesticity.* Yale University Press, 2004.

The Retreat, York. Case Book 24, Helen Coombe Fry. Digitized File from the Borthwick Institute for Archives, University of York, York. Accessed October 2015.

Showalter, Elaine. *The Female Malady: Women, Madness and English Culture, 1830-1980.* Virago, 1987.

Woolf, Virginia. *Roger Fry: A Biography*. Harcourt, Brace and Company, 1940.

In and Out of Bloomsbury:
Biographical Essays on Twentieth-Century Writers and Artists.
Martin Ferguson Smith (Manchester: Manchester University Press, 2021).
x + 316pp.

There is something to be said for the mouse that roars rather than the lion that squeaks. Not everything in art or literature needs to be momentous or earth-shattering; sometimes, small discoveries simply make scholarship incrementally—but noticeably—better. This belief is the import of Martin Ferguson Smith's compilation *In and Out of Bloomsbury: Biographical Essays on Twentieth-Century Writers and Artists.*

Martin Ferguson Smith is a renowned classicist who has long diligently and meticulously pursued a research interest in the work and lives of the Bloomsbury group. As Smith states in his preface, the essays reproduced in *In and Out of Bloomsbury* were written in his seventies, created with the "same priority" he "had and ha[s] as a classicist": to "make known new material rather than recycle old" and to "extend our knowledge" through "presentation of previously unpublished" material (ix).[1] *In and Out of Bloomsbury* is Smith's anthology of these writings on nineteenth- and twentieth-century British authors and creatives. The texts are predominantly connected to the Bloomsbury group, but they also discuss J. R. R. Tolkien's teacher Richard Williams Reynolds, popular mystery author Dorothy L. Sayers, and painter Tristram Hillier. Smith makes these divergences from the purely Bloomsbury-themed essays with "no apology," arguing that his subject-matter "variety" adds to the overall understanding of "the cultural scene in the first half of the twentieth century" (4). The title *In and Out of Bloomsbury* is intended to mark topical continuity *and* discontinuity.

The essays each adopt an archaeological exhaustiveness. Smith's chapters explore in depth scholarly errors or archival discoveries, critique preceding researchers, and transcribe the archival source(s) mentioned. In chapter 8, on popular mystery author Dorothy L. Sayers's teenage contribution to a local historical pageant, Smith notes this was a "forgotten contribution" of Sayers, and he locates the photograph documenting her participation at the Marion E. Wade Center at Illinois' Wheaton College (200–01). In other essays, such as chapter 6, "Virginia Woolf and 'the hermaphrodite,'" Smith reproduces primary sources in full, and in chapter 4, documenting "Virginia Woolf's second visit to Greece," he includes an in-depth, down-to-the-hour itinerary of the Woolfs', Roger Fry, and his sister Margery Fry's travels (e.g., "Tuesday 19 April / At sea. Virginia took her sponge-bag with her to breakfast…") (157, 98).

These choices constitute rich archival nuggets, but they can also make for extremely challenging reading. Each essay is disjointed. Stories stop and start as primary source records are introduced, extended background research intercedes, or when Smith digresses to critique a previous scholar's oversight. In addition, with each chapter built around record correction or discovery rather than a specific thesis, readers experience a plethora of meticulously researched detail, but little sense of the *purpose* of this new information. Though chapter 10 ("The secret love-

[1] Smith's background as a classicist, while ensuring that each research "shard" of data is given its due, does also, perhaps, contribute to a jarring aspect of the essays—notably his visual analysis of works of art. Visual analysis of portraits of Helen Coombe Fry and Vanessa Bell, as well as nude photographs of Vanessa, Clive Bell, and Roger Fry, suffer from a lack of an art historian's eye, which would be better positioned to provide the type of ekphrastic writing needed to bring the images to life. For example: "The expression is enigmatic, but probably to be interpreted as wistful rather than as vacant" with the "red of the fruit and of the lips" conveying the "suggestion that both are ripe and ready—the apple for eating, the lips for kissing." The headscarf "is plainer than the one she is wearing" but "arranged in a not dissimilar fashion, so as to reveal some tufts of hair" (21, 23, 34). One might also wish for an art historian's disciplinary insight—quickly contextualizing the portrait of Vanessa from 1911–1912 with lips parted, offering an apple to the viewer, as a modern Eve temptress in the context of Vanessa and Roger's nascent affair, rather than overreading the image and requiring a reference to the "apple [as] a potent symbol of love and desire" to understand the composition (image reproduced 19, 23).

child of an American Civil War commander") traces in exquisite depth the Arkansas and Confederate lineage of Richard Williams Reynolds, the man who eventually became J.R.R. Tolkien's teacher at King Edward's School in Birmingham, England, it is unclear what such detail, however interesting, adds to scholarship on Tolkien, on Tolkien's writing, or even on the cultural scene in the early twentieth century (238-271). In his chapter on Virginia Woolf's 1932 trip to Greece, Smith notes that the essay's purpose is to "put the record straight or straighter," specifically focusing on the misidentification of a photograph in Hermione Lee's 1996 Virginia Woolf biography (a text Smith describes as "factually unreliable") (95). Lee, and several other subsequent scholars who Smith names, describes the photograph of the Bloomsbury travelers as having been taken at the Acropolis—exhibiting, as Smith puts it, a "breath-taking ignorance of the architecture of one of the most celebrated groups of ancient monuments in the world"; according to Smith, the image clearly shows the Temple of Olympian Zeus in Athens (95, 109–10).[2] Precision should be expected of any scholar, much less a widely published one, but, beyond publicly shaming the previous authors, it remains unstated why, beyond scholarly integrity (no small concern, of course!) it *matters* to our understanding of Virginia's second trip to Greece that she took a photo at the Temple of Olympian Zeus in Athens. Readers now have a more accurate record of the 1932 trip but little guidance to coalesce the factual pieces into a meaningful whole.

This is a pattern that repeats throughout Smith's essays: archival research truly unrivaled, defined by comprehensive searching of previously unthought-of collections and holdings, corrections and descriptions made and supported by every possibly discoverable fact. Yet, the relevance and purpose of each archival discovery, of each correction, remains less apparent, leaving a reader to marvel at both the exhaustiveness of the finds, and equally wonder: what does knowing the specific details of Clive Bell's deflowering in the seductive arms of the nineteenth-century "Mrs. Robinson" Annie Raven-Hill bring to our wider comprehension of the historical actor or of the period overall (82)?

Such an absence of broader significance is less a fault of Smith's than it is, perhaps, a consequence of misleading marketing. Whether through personal choice or the overzealousness of an editorial team committed to the headline that shouts rather than informs, the content value of each essay is overstated as if it were a monumental discovery, missed by all before Smith. What *In and Out of Bloomsbury actually* is is a collection of invaluable breadcrumbs for scholars of the period. *In and Out of Bloomsbury* is not a groundbreaking collection of essays but instead a testament to a classicist's lifework extending beyond his famed translations and scholarship on Lucretius and Diogenes. Smith's writings on Bloomsbury and its widening circles apply a classicist's archaeological precision, necessary to piece together the ancient past, to a far-better-documented, but often incompletely sifted

[2] Record correction continues with an extended section of the chapter in which Smith corrects the "published versions" of Virginia Woolf's letters from this trip based on "copies of the manuscripts" (118).

through, relatively recent era.

Smith's fervent pursuit of details—dismissed archival collections scoured, long-forgotten photographic records decoded, persons looming in the shadows identified—is not only a testament to Smith's skill but also constitutes an essential service for future scholars who can subsequently mine Smith's biographical tales for broader meaning or pore over footnotes and endnotes to find rich, never-before-considered primary sources. These research discoveries don't shape data into a grand thesis but instead exist as a model of good scholarship and a guide to begin a researcher's journey. Though not earth-shattering in its revelations, Smith's *In and Out of Bloomsbury* is a masterclass in pursuing and documenting research, wherever it takes you.

—Elizabeth Berkowitz,
Independent Scholar &
Executive Director, The American Trust for the British Library

Edible Arrangements: Modernism's Queer Forms.
Elizabeth Blake (Cambridge: Cambridge University Press, 2023). x + 225 pp.

I'm going to resist, in this review, all temptations to adorable food jokes, such as pronouncing Elizabeth Blake's monograph "yummy" or "delicious." Indeed, I don't feel such adjectives quite suffice. If one were to describe this project in the simplest of terms, as an examination of queer, or queered, scenes of eating in modernist works, it might at first seem an intriguing intervention into food studies, a contribution to queer studies, but also perhaps something of a niche project. But this description severely understates the significance of *Edible Arrangements.* Blake here brilliantly weds feminist scholarship and queer theory to enlarge on the importance of domestic sites of feeding as loci of pleasure and enculturation, seeing in the queering of such sites and practices by modernist writers the potential for utopic disruption. The exemplary close readings that stud the monograph—intensely surprising and gratifying in their own right—cohere into a revelatory argument that winds up being less about food per se than the possibilities inherent in the representation of consumption for the queering and revivification of genre itself. The book is a fascinating and important contribution to modernist studies, benefiting from the recent recuperation of affect and embodiment as key elements of modernist aesthetic practice.

Beginning with the erotic danger of Prufrock's peach, Blake traces the limning of queer pleasure—an embodied adherence to the moment and the everyday—through the works of a host of modernist writers and a number of established literary modes: satire, obscenity, dinner-party drama, the motif of mother and child. In each case, in the works she reads, the centrality of sensation opens up a new world of disruptive possibility. Satire, for instance, in works by Bruce Nugent, Virginia

Woolf, and Katherine Mansfield, uses counternormative oral pleasures as a model for interrupting the normative trudge to conformity. Similarly, what Blake terms "dinner theatricality" in the stage works of Jane Bowles, Tennessee Williams, and Thornton Wilder—the staged recognition of the theatricality inherent in the dinner party itself—allows for the queer reinvention of the very practice of commensality, as "the question of what one will eat and with whom one will eat it becomes a question of identity, identification, and desire" (120). As in the influential work of Caroline Levine, Blake recognizes the way in which literary form is not unitary, but mutable and capacious, susceptible to dismantling and reimagining with political import.

Blake's brief treatment of Woolf features as part of Chapter One, "Bad Taste: Satire and the Senses"—thus, not by way of the bourgeois triumph of Mrs. Ramsay's boeuf en daube, but in relation to the dinner dichotomies of *A Room of One's Own*. Rather than dwelling on privation, as do most accounts of Woolfian scenes of eating, Blake suggests that we engage Woolf's essays as offering an expansion of the definition of pleasure. Inviting "careful thinking about the normative pressures of systematized taste itself," such essays as "Middlebrow" are best understood, she argues, as satire, "witty reposte[s] in an ongoing conversation" in which Woolf "takes on an exaggerated version of the persona that has been assigned to her" (40). In lampoonishly portraying herself as an enforcer of taste "brandishing a muffin on the point of a tea spoon" (*DM* 183), she is demonstrating by way of this "failure of commensality" (41) less the failures of the middlebrows themselves than of "the very system that assigns the term" (40).

Similarly if more complexly, argues Blake, in Woolf's famous appreciation of the gustatory pleasures offered in the men's college of *A Room of One's Own*, she is once again "inhabiting, for a moment, a particular position … performing for her readers the kind of complacency that rich foods and good wine can produce, enabling the men she is eating with to believe that all is right with the world, when the primary argument of her essay is that precisely the opposite is true" (44). By contrast, it is the mediocre food at the women's college that "evokes social conscience as a form of duty," provoking in the narrator an explosion of leading—and "transformative" (44)—questions. Thus, counter-intuitively, Woolf's essays offer up as a liberatory tack the embrace of "challenging and counter-normative pleasure" including the "disruptive potential of bad food" (39, 46).

Every one of Blake's chapters is stunningly effective, but I must take particular note of two readings. Chapter Two, organized around the idea of obscenity, which Blake carefully defines in purely literary (rather than legal or historical) terms as "writing that allows transgressive or excessive desire to dictate its form" (61), focuses on hunger and its antinormative intensity in the work of James Joyce, Djuna Barnes, and Rabindrinath Tagore. The reading of Barnes's *Nightwood* here is astonishingly good, parsing the notoriously difficult last scene of the book—"obscene and visceral" (80)—through Robin's own "hunger," which, substituting for subjectivity, determines the way the novel rotates around her as absent center, circling the black hole of her desire. I can honestly say that this chapter has transformed my own reading of the novel.

Equally revelatory, though in relation to a much less familiar work, is Blake's approach to Olive Moore's 1930 novel *Spleen*, the centerpiece of Chapter Four, in which she argues that disrupting the expected figure of the mother feeding her child can produce a version of queer futurity (*contra* Lee Edelman) that supplants maternal coercion. In the figure of *Spleen*'s protagonist Ruth—usually seen, in the few existing readings, as rejecting her disabled son by insisting he be fed by others—Blake finds instead a resistance to imposed normativity that allows for her son's difference and newness. She pairs this analysis with a second strong section on *Nightwood* focusing on the way in which Nora fails in her attempt to "mother" Robin through feeding, in which the metaphor of mother and child proves inadequate, casting doubt on the viability of metaphor itself.

If one can locate a flaw in *Edible Arrangements*—and to do so feels almost unfair, given the superb quality of the volume as a whole—it's that this use of *Nightwood* in two different chapters feels like a questionable decision. It muddies the argument about the novel, especially since Blake never completely dovetails her reading in Chapter Four with the earlier explication of Robin's hunger. Each reading works on its own, but in the context of the monograph they feel like less than the sum of their parts—the opposite of the cumulative effect one gets from *Edible Arrangements* as a whole, in which each chapter gloriously supplements and transfigures Blake's larger argument about the genre-transforming potentialities of queer pleasure.

—Debra Rae Cohen,
University of South Carolina

Bring No Clothes: Bloomsbury and the Philosophy of Fashion.
Charlie Porter (London: Particular Books, 2023). 358 pp.

This book originated in a 2023 exhibition curated by the fashion journalist Charlie Porter. "Bring No Clothes: Bloomsbury and Fashion" was the inaugural show at Charleston's new cultural center and exhibition space in Lewes, Sussex, an addition to the well-known house museum located in nearby Firle. As well as photographs and artefacts of those associated with the Bloomsbury Group, the exhibition also incorporated catwalk fashion by Dior, Fendi, Burberry, Comme des Garçons, Erdem, and S. S. Daley.

The association of Bloomsbury with high fashion is nothing new. Scholars such as Jane Garrity, Randi Koppen, Nicola Luckhurst, Celia Marshik, Claire Nicholson, and Elizabeth Sheehan, among others, have written extensively about Virginia Woolf, fashion, clothing, and commodity culture. Woolf's deep ambivalence about dress, as well as her fascination with "frock consciousness," have been explored in many contexts. Brenda Silver's *Virginia Woolf Icon* (1999) remains indispensable for anyone seeking to navigate the differences between the Woolf known to scholars and the image of her (and "Bloomsbury") that circulates in newspapers, magazines, and inexpensive trade books aimed at a general readership. In her chapter "Fashion Stills," Silver cites a July 1996 article in *W* that pointed out how "Bloomsbury has long been a significant player in the fashion world, experiencing a revival about every five years" (188). Quentin Bell, for that matter, published *On Human Finery* in 1947, thanking his sister, Angelica, for allowing him to "make use of her large collection of fashion plates" (10).

There are, then, different demands and expectations for a book by an academic published by a university press (and typically priced far beyond the reach of most readers) and that by a journalist such as Porter, who has written an idiosyncratic and often very personal account of his encounter with what some of those associated with the Bloomsbury Group wore. The book (reissued in paperback in September 2024 with a new Afterword) argues—convincingly—that the clothing worn by Woolf, Forster, Grant, Keynes, Vanessa Bell, and Ottoline Morrell provides an index to their understanding of, and challenge to, the patriarchal and heterosexist strictures bequeathed them by the long history of fashion. The inclusion of Morrell as a "member" (7) of the Bloomsbury Group will surprise many readers of this journal, but, again, Silver provides a useful context. Doing publicity for the film *Tom & Viv*, Miranda Richardson appeared on the *Charlie Rose* show on December 7, 1994. Rose asked her who was in the Group:

> Rose: clearly, Vita Sackville-West was, along with—
> Richardson: And there's Ottoline Morrell, and the Sitwells, and
> Virginia Woolf, Lytton Strachey, yeah, all those people (Silver 181).

Virginia Woolf was photographed for *Vogue* magazine's Hall of Fame wearing, it has long been assumed, a dress that had belonged to her mother. (Nicola Luckhurst notes that another image from the same shoot was given by Woolf to *Atalanta's Garland*, a publication of the Edinburgh University Women's Union, in which the formal pose with which she was depicted in *Vogue* is replaced by one in which she "looks provocatively, even coquettishly at the camera" [4]). Porter argues that the dress in fact probably belonged to Ottoline Morrell, a conclusion he arrives at in part because no photograph of Julia Stephen in such a dress exists. His supposition has been supported by Maggie Humm, whom Porter dubiously cites as representing the "opinion of the [Virginia Woolf] Society" (17). It is an interesting hypothesis, but Porter withholds the more sensational reason for his claim until near the end of his book, in a chapter on Ottoline wherein he argues that Woolf and Morrell had a sexual liaison (300). It's unclear yet whether this notion has gained traction, but it seems to me rather a stretch given what we know about Woolf and Morrell's relationship and opinions of one another.

In his introduction, Porter claims that "for nearly a century, biographers have tiptoed around" the subject of Woolf's queerness, "talking of her love for

Vita Sackville-West and [Violet] Dickinson as jolly japes" (9). Such a claim is at odds with the facts of biographical writing about Woolf but, again, to make such statements without needing to explain them in any detail is a prerogative enjoyed by journalists. There are a number of such throwaway lines throughout the book, and I admit they often distracted me from what are Porter's more useful and interesting insights about the main topic: clothing. In addition to sweeping generalizations, the narrative at times runs off into irrelevancies: we learn that Welbeck Abbey, Ottoline Morrell's childhood home, is not far from Heathrow, that Thorpe Park is on the other side of the M3, where there is a theme park which has Porter's favorite rides, the Saw and Stealth, "the fastest roller coaster in the UK" (272). Okay.

If we read *Bring No Clothes* as a kind of memoir, or even a journal, such flights will appear less obtrusive. And it is, indeed, a deeply personal book. The narrative is interrupted by the sudden death of the author's mother, a loss which leads him to begin making clothes for himself as a form of grieving (97). Compounding this grief, and emphasizing the memoir-like tone of the book, a moving postscript recounts the death of Porter's father as he was nearing the end of writing it. Photographs of the clothing he has made for himself, as well as rag rugs he taught himself to make, blend with the history he has recovered from the archives he plumbed for both the exhibition in Lewes and the book it gave rise to. He describes his book as a series of observations, and these are often very perceptive.

Porter makes the insightful comment that there is a tension between most people's professing to "know nothing" about fashion and the unconscious knowledge they undoubtedly possess about clothes' meaning and codes. The book is constructed as a series of reflections on photographs, reflections often presented in the style of captions: "The simplicity of the outfit in this photograph from 1926: T-shirt length sleeves, the headscarf, the Mary Janes" (96) describes a photograph of Vanessa Bell, for example. The photographs themselves are a treasure-trove of candid and formal scenes from the everyday life of Porter's subjects (although the paper quality on which they have been printed sadly often makes detail difficult to discern), and provide their own kind of archive for readers to explore further. In the excellent chapter on E. M. Forster, Porter states his aim as to disrupt the idea "that only the clothes of someone engaged with fashion are interesting to us" (154). Any man who has noticed how differently he is treated when wearing a suit and tie will understand Forster's point about the suit as a form of disguise (181). Porter acknowledges Forster for helping him "come to terms with my own repressed queer life, as a young man in the second half of the 20th century" (155). For all its questionable assertions, extraneous information, and grandiose claims to articulating "a philosophy," *Bring No Clothes* nevertheless will find a place on the capacious shelves of Bloomsbury lore.

—Mark Hussey,
Independent Scholar

Works Cited

Bell, Quentin. *On Human Finery*. Hogarth, 1947.
Luckhurst, Nicola. *Bloomsbury in Vogue*. Cecil Woolf, 1998.
Silver, Brenda. *Virginia Woolf Icon*. U of Chicago P, 1999.

Virginia Woolf and Capitalism.
Clara Jones, ed. (Edinburgh: Edinburgh University Press, 2024). xiv + 319 pp.

In the opening essay of this collection, Michèle Barrett points out that "Marxist thinking, and the category of 'capitalism' that over time it engendered, went into decline in the aftermath of the collapse of the Soviet Union in 1979 and the ending of the cold war" (32). However, it was around 1979 that an acrimonious argument in the relatively young field of Woolf studies erupted between Quentin Bell and Jane Marcus over the latter's use of the word "marxist" to describe Woolf's politics. Clara Jones rightly argues in the introduction to this volume that this argument's fixation on the definition of "marxist" obscured the "details of Woolf's real-world political action" (7). At the time, an exasperated Marcus wrote that Bell knew perfectly well she did not mean that Woolf was "a card-carrying member of a Communist party" ("Quentin's Bogey" 490). That long-ago contretemps, nevertheless, is a significant chapter in the history of Woolf scholarship, which is itself a significant chapter in the history of feminist literary criticism. Marcus's prescience in describing *Night and Day* (1919) and *The Years* (1937) as "deeply subversive of patriarchal and capitalist British culture," and "The Legacy" as "an allegory of Woolf's primary commitment to the struggle of the working class" (Introduction xvii) is borne out by the contributors Jones has assembled.[1]

[1] A book review is not the place to go into detail about this history, but the following sources, listed chronologically, will be relevant for anyone wishing to see Jones's collection in a longer view. See also the Spring and Fall 1983 volumes (numbers 20 and 21) of the *Virginia Woolf Miscellany*:
Marcus, Jane. "Tintinnabulations." *Marxist Perspectives*, vol. 2, no. 1, Spring 1979, pp. 144–67. Reprinted in *Art & Anger: Reading Like a Woman*, Ohio State UP, 1988, pp. 157–81.
Bell, Quentin. "Bloomsbury and the Vulgar Passions." *Critical Inquiry*, vol. 6, no. 2, Winter 1979, pp. 239–56.
Marcus, Jane. Introduction and "Thinking Back Through Our Mothers." *New Feminist Essays on Virginia Woolf*, U of Nebraska P, 1981, pp. xiii–xx, 1–30.
Bell, Quentin. "A 'Radiant' Friendship." *Critical Inquiry*, vol. 10, no. 4, 1984, pp. 557–66.
Marcus, Jane. "Quentin's Bogey." *Critical Inquiry*, vol. 11, no. 3, 1985, pp. 486–97. Reprinted in *Art & Anger: Reading Like a Woman*, Ohio State UP, 1988, pp. 201–12.
Bell, Quentin. "Reply to Jane Marcus." *Critical Inquiry*, vol. 11, no. 3, 1985, 498–501.
Marcus, Jane. "Storming the Toolshed." *Art & Anger: Reading Like a Woman*, Ohio State UP, 1988, pp. 182–200.
London, Bette. "Guerilla in Petticoats or Sans-Culotte? Virginia Woolf and the Future of Feminist Criticism." *diacritics*, vol. 21, no. 2/3, 1991, pp. 11–29,

Even before the collapse of the Soviet Union, capitalism had moved through several phases that rendered Marx's labor theory of value somewhat anachronistic. Jones notes that Woolf's own lifetime spanned not only two World Wars, but also the 1917 Bolshevik revolution's offer of a wholesale alternative economic model, the crash of 1929, and the continuing colonial exploitation of raw materials that filled capitalists' coffers. And since 1945, technology and globalism have further eroded the usefulness of a traditionally Marxist analysis. *Virginia Woolf and Capitalism* is a volume in the series "Virginia Woolf—Variations," whose editor, Derek Ryan, intends to publish "agenda-setting research" (ix). Jones's contributors have been well-chosen to fulfil this mission, although over the course of their thirteen pieces the term "capitalism" has to become quite elastic as it is enlisted to fit a variety of emphases. Woolf described herself in "A Sketch of the Past" (1939–40) as "a fish in a stream; deflected; held in place," but said she could not describe that stream, which consisted of the "immense forces society brings to play upon each of us" (*MOB* 80). The way the term "capitalism" is used in this volume often calls to mind that "stream"—life itself, perhaps.

Barrett's essay—"'The eagle claws other peoples lands, & goods': Virginia Woolf on the Desire to Dominate"—provides a helpful framework for those that follow it. Questioning whether capitalism is an adequate description of the "social system" that Woolf wished to criticize in *Mrs. Dalloway* (1925), Barrett argues that Woolf is closer to Foucault than to Marx given that the novel "is an exercise in the criticism of power more generally" (36). Revisiting her own research, Barrett reminds us that Woolf "had read and taken notes from all the Consular Reports from Turkey" as she assisted Leonard Woolf with his book *Empire and Commerce in Africa*: Clarissa Dalloway's muddling of Albanians and Armenians could not be farther from the political acumen of her creator (38). Anna Snaith, in the essay following Barrett's, remarks that those notes made by Woolf "are more anti-imperialist, more tending towards the damning quotation," than the book Leonard published (qtd. 52; see Barrett 113). Barrett establishes that Virginia Woolf saw capitalism as underpinned by the "desire for aggression, the desire to dominate and enslave" (40), and Snaith follows this up, in "Empire, Slavery and Capitalism," by pointing out that in both *A Room of One's Own* (1929) and *Three Guineas* (1938) Woolf was focused "consistently on the exploitative economics of imperial extraction alongside more culturally-based forms of conquest and control" (48). As Barrett says, Woolf studies has only recently caught up with its own subject's analyses of how "colonial violence" is a persistent theme in her fiction (40).

Part One of *Virginia Woolf and Capitalism* is titled "Class, Empire, Capital." Its five essays demonstrate both the flexibility of the term "capitalism" as used across the collection and also the nature of the connective tissue linking one essay to another. Unsurprisingly, the issue of class recurs, though with diverse emphases. Woolf's political prescience also emerges from these essays. Despite Snaith's calling out of the "occlusions and silences around race, slavery and empire" in Woolf's major essays, she notes also that they are "deeply radical and creative explorations of capitalist imperialism and its impacts on women's lives" (60). Woolf was drawing attention to the streams of gold and silver flowing from colonial exploitation into the coffers of major universities long before our current moment's investigation of how many venerable institutions are built on an immoral foundation.

Charlotte Taylor Suppé, in "'my comfortable capitalistic head': Virginia Woolf on Consumption, Co-operation and Motherhood," and Natasha Periyan, in "Biometric Feminism: *A Room of One's Own* and the Politics of Intelligence," concentrate on issues of class with particular attention to capitalism's effect on the lives of women. Suppé, in my opinion, restricts the range of her reference perhaps a little too tightly in order to support her view that Woolf was prejudiced against the women of the Co-Operative Guild. A "general reticence about fictionalising the lived realities of working-class women" (78) slides in a footnote into Woolf's "elimination of working-class characters" (88n24). The treatment of class is always a fraught topic in Woolf studies, but perhaps that reticence could be seen as another instance of her prescience from the vantage point of our current situation when writers are "canceled" if they dare to create characters outside of their own lived experience (cf. *American Dirt*!). Woolf's complaint to Margaret Llewelyn Davies about the conventionality of the Guildswomen whose narratives she introduced in the "Introductory Letter" to *Life as We have Known It* (1931) is taken by Suppé as an example of her antipathy to the working class, though a broader analysis might have cast a wider net and tempered this conclusion. (Although it has not survived, Woolf's prompt reply to a letter about *Three Guineas* from an unemployed weaver named Agnes Smith in 1938 suggests how she was always ready to engage thoughtfully with criticisms of her own thinking about class. Smith's own long letter, inaugurating a correspondence that continued until Woolf's death, is one among several examples of how Woolf's writing was received positively, if critically, by those who identified as working class [see Smith].)

Periyan shows that although Woolf leaves unclear just how women are supposed to come by the necessary £500 a year, she makes capital central in *A Room* to the issue of how environmental factors "shape female creativity" (93). The rise of intelligence testing in the twentieth century was part of meritocracy's "biological solution to the capriciousness of inherited capital" (94), and despite Woolf's blind spot about how race contributed to the "scientific understanding" of intelligence, her attention to the importance of material conditions to creativity was a welcome shift away from "Romantic notions of creative genius" (107).

Concluding Part One, Charles Andrews, in "'Merchant of this city': Capitalism and the Liturgies of Peace and War in *Jacob's Room*," describes a "web-like" narrative in that novel which summons in every paragraph the system within which Jacob is enmeshed. Capitalism here, similarly to how Barrett reads *Mrs. Dalloway*, becomes one element in a system comprised of militarism, masculinity, imperialism and what Andrews describes as "cultural liturgies," the "civil religion" in which "the market" now receives the devotion and "enchanted belief" once offered to religion.

Part Two, "Labour and the Marketplace," begins with Rachel Bowlby's witty account of Woolf's adventures in the property market. In midsummer 1919, Woolf either owned or had an interest in nine different properties—an image of Woolf as real estate mogul rather at odds with how she is typically seen. But, as Bowlby notes, houses "are perfect manifestations of the symbolic force of capitalism as invisible organiser and transformer of cultural perceptions" (140). Woolf took pride in being an owner of the Hogarth Press. When the man from the company moving the Woolfs' belongings from Hogarth House to Tavistock Square in 1924 shook Leonard's hand, Woolf commented that his gesture was "because we are real people & own a press" (*D*2 293). Although publishing "has always resisted its association with the capitalist marketplace" (162), Nicola Wilson points out that such disingenuousness was not shared by Virginia Woolf. Wilson is one of a dynamic group of scholars who are rewriting the history of the Hogarth Press within a much more archives-based, nuanced, and historically aware context than that bequeathed by a long-received narrative. In "Publishing and Capitalism at the Hogarth Press," Wilson dispels the myth that the Press was "a triumph of imagination over capitalism," as Phyllis Rose put it in 1978 (103). Not only were the Woolfs clear-eyed about the fact that what had begun on their dining-room table as a hobby quickly grew into a proper business concern, they were committed to "exploring the contemporary crises of capitalism" in what they chose to publish (169). Jane Marcus, again, was prescient when she began her introduction to *New Feminist Essays* in 1981 by quoting Miss Marchmont in *Jacob's Room* (1922): "'Publishers are capitalists—publishers are cowards'" (xiii).

Wilson's attention to the business of writing and publishing is picked up in Bryony Randall's "'It's rather distinguished to be as ordinary as I am'. Woolf's Working Women Writers." The historian Rosamond Merridew (from "The Journal of Mistress Joan Martyn"), Miss Willatt ("Memoirs of a Novelist"), and Miss Allan, in *The Voyage Out* (1915), provide a way to explore "Woolf's evolving feminist critique of the capitalist structures within which the work of writing is inevitably embroiled" (187). Randall's essay reminds us that *cultural* (or social) capital is a significant aspect of this collection's landscape, an aspect particularly salient in the work of a writer: however much she may wish to think only of her art, a writer cannot escape the material conditions in which it is produced.

The point is sharpened in Stanislava Dikova's innovative reading of *Night and Day* as a "problem novel." Often read as anomalous in Woolf's canon, *Night and Day* returns in Dikova's reading to being what Marcus saw decades ago, a politically subversive work. Drawing on Habermas, Dikova argues in "The Literary Public Sphere in Virginia Woolf's *Night and Day*" that the novel stages a conflict between the individual and the "insidious encroachment of state power and market forces on the most intimate aspects of self-relation" (213). Her example is Ralph Denham, who rigidly separates his life between the "hours of work" and those "of dreams" (213). Evelyn Tsz Yan Chan reiterates the example in "Capitalism and Woolf's Beyond-Work" where she reads Denham's lament about the meaninglessness of his work as a solicitor as resonating with contemporary ideas of automation and universal basic income as a release from drudgery: "If we were to live not just as vehicles of labour for capitalism, if the idea of waged work shifted, then what would be our role as humans?" (226) is a question implied by Denham's ennui. In *Three Guineas* (where, incidentally, Woolf championed wages for housework), Woolf spoke of capitalism's production of "cripples in a cave." Chan notes that Woolf was not alone in discussing what would now be termed "postwork," citing her friend John Maynard Keynes's "Economic Possibilities for our Grandchildren" as another example of similar thinking (230). It is depressing, though, to recognize that in so many areas of our lives the same battles are being fought as were raging a hundred years ago.

In 1984, Jane Marcus wrote that she did "not think we have begun to explore [Woolf's] complexities" ("Quentin's Bogey" 494). Although those complexities have certainly been much explored since then, Jones's volume reinforces the sense of Woolf's prescience, of the contemporary power of her writing, and the fact that there is still plenty of room for continued exploration. Brenda Silver's "Virginia Woolf: A Sound Investment" closes Part Two by revisiting talks Silver gave between 2001 and 2003 when the phenomenon of *The Hours* had brought Woolf's name and image before new audiences and readers. Both the novel and its movie version provide "an excellent case study for exploring the intersections of stardom, fandom and capital in the cultural struggles over who 'owns' Virginia Woolf and her texts" (247). This is, as it has in a sense always been, the crux of Woolf studies: who "owns" her name, her image, the interpretation of her works. In 1991, Bette London warned against "the knowing quotation" that risked "making 'Woolf' a code word" for a homogenized feminism (London 27). Silver's penetrating analysis of the cultural and financial power accruing to what she named "Virginia Woolf Icon" takes in both the economics of book publishing, and the vastly expanded media world of the twenty-first century within which that icon circulates.

A coda titled "Critical/Creative Approaches" closes *Virginia Woolf and Capitalism*. Helen Tyson's "Scrapbooking the Present Day: The *Three Guineas* Scrapbooks," and Kabe Wilson's "Work Cut Out" (made by isolating every reference in *Mrs. Dalloway* to a paid occupation, business name, or personal title) both return us to the materiality of Woolf's texts. *Mrs. Dalloway* has often lent itself to map-making, and Wilson concludes this provocative collection with "a demographic map of how British interwar capitalist society" is depicted in the novel (295). In a final example of how Woolf speaks loudly in our present moment, Tyson recounts how her undergraduate students at the University of Sussex use the scrapbooks that Woolf created as the matrix from which *Three Guineas* arose as models for compiling their own present-day versions. Noting that her women students now place physical safety above economic concerns, Tyson has been led by this experience to recognize a thread in the scrapbooks she had hitherto overlooked, about "abortion, childbirth, the maternal death rate, birth control, war and male sadism" (283). As early as 1932, Woolf recorded that she had "collected enough gunpowder to blow up St. Pauls" (*D4* 77). Her "feminist archives," as Tyson describes the scrapbooks (now available on WoolfNotes.com), show us "just how far Woolf went in tracking the extent to which capitalism shaped the most intimate aspects of women's lives" (286). In an America hurtling towards realizing Margaret Atwood's Gilead, that shaping continues.

—Mark Hussey,
Independent Scholar

Works Cited

Barrett, Michèle. "Virginia Woolf's Research for *Empire and Commerce in Africa* (Leonard Woolf, 1920)." *Woolf Studies Annual*, vol. 19, 2013, pp. 83–122.
London, Bette. "Guerilla in Petticoats or Sans-Culotte? Virginia Woolf and the Future of Feminist Criticism." *diacritics*, vol. 21, no. 2/3, 1991, pp. 11–29.
Marcus, Jane. Introduction. *New Feminist Essays on Virginia Woolf*, U of Nebraska P, 1981, pp. xiii–xx.
——. "Quentin's Bogey." *Critical Inquiry*, vol. 11, no. 3, 1985, pp. 486–97.
Smith, M. Agnes. Letter to Virginia Woolf. 7 Nov 1938. Snaith, pp. 98–103.
Snaith, Anna, editor. *Three Guineas* Letters. *Woolf Studies Annual*, vol. 6, 2000, pp. 17–168.

Cybernetic Aesthetics: Modernist Networks of Information and Data.
Heather A. Love (New York City: Cambridge University Press, 2024).
pp. vii–xii + 210.

For Woolf scholars, Heather A. Love's revelatory *Cybernetic Aesthetics: Modernist Networks of Information and Data* should be welcomed as the culmination of an arc of criticism that launched on or about the year 2000, with Pamela Caughie's edited collection *Virginia Woolf in the Age of Mechanical Reproduction.* Subsequent investigations of modernism and technology explored the conceptualization of data, the aesthetics of networks, the rhetoric of innovation, the rise of the information age, and the cognitive and communal ontologies of radio and other media—all of which are neatly enfolded within *Cybernetic Aesthetics*. For modernist scholars more generally, Love's book offers a fresh model for investigating and articulating the mutual interdependence of literary aesthetics and STEM frameworks, as well as a long overdue masterclass in the history of information theory in the twentieth century. Such an impactful treatment of technology and modernism is the paradoxical consequence of Love's focus on cybernetics, the transdisciplinary field of inquiry that developed in the twentieth century to study feedback systems (looped causal mechanisms whereby the endpoint of one process becomes the beginning of another). The circular processes examined by cyberneticists include social, biological, ecological, cognitive, and communicative systems, though in the popular imagination they are associated most with technological systems that process information. These latter systems happen to be the ones theorized during the first wave of cybernetics, making modernist literature a supremely appropriate cultural territory for reflecting critically upon the machine learning feedback mechanisms that are of immediate concern for Love's twenty-first-century readers.

Science and Technology Studies scholars—or any scholar who relishes concrete and specific historical grounding—will be relieved that Love does not use "cybernetics" loosely or figuratively. Love thoroughly understands its constitution as a field and respects its foundational concepts even though she "reconceives cybernetics historiography by locating a cultural pre-history ... in modernist literature's formal experiments" (9). When the conclusion summarizes the book as having "explored literary feedback loops, modernist information systems, and self-reflexive communication pedagogy" (145), the claim does not ring hollow, as it is infused by accounts of key thinkers Ross Ashby, Gregory Bateson, Mary Catherine Bateson, Margaret Mead, Claude Shannon, Silvan Tomkins, and Norbert Wiener. While Love clearly concurs with the field's foundational premise that the emergence of cybernetics was one of the twentieth century's most important events (surely one could not withstand the pressures of writing such a book were this not the case), she does not treat cybernetics as an independent domain that unilaterally influences modernism. Rather, Love explores the modernism of cybernetics itself. Though the first wave of cybernetics theory circulated during WWII, Love excavates its buried groundworks in the first half of the century, "shifting the cybernetics timeline back in time by several decades" to demonstrate how modernism and cybernetics inhabited the same "cybernetic fold" generated by "modernity's dizzying informational matrix" (8, 2). If modernism was permeated by the same historical pressures, communicative media, and information processes that are associated with postwar cybernetics, modernism also permeated the information systems that would later produce cybernetics, making it necessary to appreciate "the often-absent aesthetic dimensions of the cybernetics story," so often reduced to a matter of armaments (7). In recovering these dimensions, Love claims more space at the cybernetics table for literary critics, whose presence alongside engineers, scientists, and social scientists has mostly been limited to literature of science scholars.

Kindly razing a primary obstacle that has prevented a broader swathe of literary scholars from concerning themselves with cybernetics, Love explains the field's fundamentals clearly and approachably without sacrificing rigor or sophistication. This is very much a book for literature scholars; they need not know anything about cybernetics in advance. Scholars who suppose that such a topic could not interest them may well find themselves drawn in by Love's understanding of cybernetics as an intermedial phenomenon or by her keen eye for the rich and strange particulars of modernist literature and culture.

Each of the four body chapters links a cybernetics concept with a modernist author: Ezra Pound employs feedback loops to communicate vast amounts of data in

Chapter 1; John Dos Passos textually reconciles Wiener and Shannon's disagreement about the relationship between information and noise in Chapter 2; Virginia Woolf uncovers the unexpected affective and communal potential of black boxes (technological mechanisms insufficiently understood by the public) in Chapter 3; and Gertrude Stein's modeling of cultural self-reflexivity contributes to the formation of the cybernetic social sciences in Chapter 4. The usefulness of Love's cybernetics framework is apparent throughout *Cybernetic Aesthetics*, which presents a series of stunningly new and utterly convincing interpretations. Some of modernism's most intractable texts, its most angular structures and frustrating cruxes—Dos Passos's disorienting "Newsreels," Stein's hypnotic repetitions, Pound's unreckonable *Cantos* and notorious broadcasts, Woolf's crackling gramophone—neatly resolve into cybernetic loops, boxes, and folds. The individual readings are comprehensive in scope, eclectic in evidentiary support, and crystalline in analysis. Love never overreaches in drawing literary and cybernetic parallels or resorts to the flimsier work of arguing by analogy or implication. Certainly, the backward reach toward Sherlock Holmes as a data processor in the Coda might have been better replaced with more sustained contemporary examples of cybernetic aesthetics to solidify the monograph's claim to immediate relevance in the twenty-first century, but Holmes aside, *Cybernetic Aesthetics* is an enormous achievement that creates what has thus far proved elusive: a convincing theory of modernist literature and information completely free of anachronism.

The decision to frame a book about modernism and technology as an argument about information, rather than media, computation, algorithms, or even networks or data per se, bears particularly juicy fruit in Chapter 3, "Black Box Subjectivity: Associative Language, Affect, and Radio Blindness in Virginia Woolf's *The Waves*." Here, Love strikes fresh ground in bypassing the well-studied aural media of *Between the Acts* and the more familiar registers of affect theory that entered Woolf scholarship via Eve Kosofsky Sedgwick, Lauren Berlant, and Sara Ahmed. To contend that Woolf and psychologist/cyberneticist Silvan Tomkins similarly create methods for discerning patterns within apparently random conditions, the chapter deploys the second-order (that is, second wave) cybernetics theory of the black box. The black box serves as a figure for the technological unknown, a common modern situation in which only the inputs and outputs of a given mechanism are known, leaving the rest—how it works, how it is implemented, what materials it contains, what processes it runs—opaque. Focusing on *The Waves* and "A Ramble about Words," a talk broadcasted by the BBC in 1937 (published in *The Listener* with the title "Craftsmanship"), Love argues that Woolf presented language itself as a black box and radio as a channel for new kinds of subjectivity through its "inherent aesthetic possibilities" (75). Love's reading of *The Waves* by way of Tomkins's *Affect Imagery Consciousness* will likely prove a watershed moment in criticism on this notoriously esoteric novel, and the extended analysis of "A Ramble about Words" brilliantly plumbs its political and cultural messages, its aesthetic properties as an oral performance, and its canny mobilization of "radio's distinct transmission aesthetic" (96). Chapter 3's most ambitious claim is that *The Waves* pushed black-box subjectivity further than Tomkins by creating modernist media ecology long before "media ecology" was coined. Positing the broader existence of this ecology across Woolf's canon, moreover, "allows us to understand Woolf's literary production not simply in terms of the formative influence a technology like radio may have had on her aesthetics, but also according to the new feedback loops she adds to technological, cybernetic, and media discourses" (104). With Chapter 3 ending on this note, Love has delivered a strong serve. The ball is now in our court.

—Shawna Ross
Texas A&M University

Notes on Contributors

Ramathi Bandaranayake is a third year PhD student in English and Comparative Literature at Columbia University. She researches early twentieth century comparative British and Russian literature, with a focus on war literature, medical humanities, and the intersections between literary works and the history and philosophy of science. She is also currently a contributing writer for *Synapsis: A Health Humanities Journal.*

Oliver Case is a lecturer in 20th-century literature at Birmingham City University. His PhD, completed in April 2024, was a study of the relationship between Woolf's representations of nonhuman subjects, human extinction, and experiments with narrative temporality in her late novels. His most recent publication is an article for *English: Journal of the English Association* titled "'There was a star riding through clouds one night, and I said to the star, "Consume me"': Post-human extinction in Virginia Woolf's *The Waves*." He also has a forthcoming chapter on *To the Lighthouse* in *Revisiting Modernism: Texts and Contexts* (Lexington Books).

Han Au Chua is a DPhil candidate at the University of Oxford. His doctoral studies are supported by the HASS International PhD Scholarship. Han Au's research is on the works of twentieth-century British writers who wrote about Asia, including Burma (Myanmar), China, Ceylon (Sri Lanka), Hong Kong, India, Malaysia, and Singapore, from the Asian perspective during the modernist period. He is interested in modernist engagement across cultures, the Bloomsbury Group, and digital technologies. He has published in *Leonardo*, *Prose Studies*, *Textual Practice*, *Woolf Studies Annual*, and elsewhere.

Jenny Ann Cubin is a musicologist, researcher, and writer. She holds a PhD from Lancaster University where she developed a method of "listening out" for the musical expression of androgyny through a comparative analysis of Virginia Woolf's novel *The Waves* and Kate Bush's song cycle, *A Sky of Honey*. She is currently consolidating research that examines ecofeminist expressions of female pastoral in Kate Bush's music and is exploring the intersections between Bush, her music and career, and women's creative histories.

Anne E. Fernald is Professor of English and Women's, Gender, and Sexuality Studies at Fordham University. She is the editor of the Cambridge University Press *Mrs. Dalloway* (2014), the *Norton Critical Edition* of *Mrs. Dalloway* (2021), and *the Oxford Handbook to Virginia Woolf* (2021). She has published on Woolf and feminist modernism more generally. She was co-editor of *Modernism/modernity*, 2019–2023. She is currently writing a collective biography of modernist women writers.

Skylar Kovacs is a PhD candidate in English Literature at Queen's University. Her dissertation examines depictions of trauma and resilience in the fiction of Virginia Woolf, Nella Larsen, Emily Holmes Coleman, and Jean Rhys.

Cristina Testa holds a Master Degree in Comparative Languages and Literatures at the University of Perugia (Italy), where she was also an academic tutor. She subsequently obtained a doctorate from the University of Florence with a thesis on Virginia Woolf and ancient Greece, which focuses on the study and philological analysis of unedited manuscripts, among them Woolf's "Agamemnon Notebook." She currently alternates her research activity with professional school teaching.

Submission Guidelines for Woolf Studies Annual

Woolf Studies Annual invites articles on the work and life of Virginia Woolf and her milieu. The *Annual* intends to represent the breadth and eclecticism of critical approaches to Woolf and particularly welcomes new perspectives and contexts of inquiry. Articles discussing relations between Woolf and other writers and artists are also welcome.

Articles are sent for review anonymously to a member of the Editorial Board and at least one other reader. Manuscripts should not be under consideration elsewhere or have been previously published. It is strongly advised that those submitting work to WSA be familiar with the journal's content. Among criteria on which evaluation of submissions depends are

- whether an article demonstrates familiarity with scholarship already published in the field,
- whether the article is written clearly and effectively,
- and whether it makes a genuine contribution to Woolf studies.

Preparation of Copy

1. Articles typically do not exceed 8000 words. This word count is a guide rather than a stipulation, though inquiries about significantly shorter or longer submissions should be sent to the journal editor at woolfstudiesannual@gmail.com.
2. A separate file should include the article's title, author's name, address, phone, and email address. The author's name and any other identifying references should not appear on the manuscript to preserve anonymity for our readers.
3. All submissions must include an abstract of no more than 250 words. Revised abstracts will accompany published articles.
4. Manuscripts should conform to the most recent MLA style (9th edition).
5. Submissions should be sent as MS Word attachments to woolfstudiesannual@gmail.com.
6. Authors of accepted manuscripts are responsible for any necessary permissions fees and for securing any necessary permissions.

All editorial inquiries should be addressed to woolfstudiesannual@gmail.com. Inquiries concerning orders, advertising, reviews, etc. should be addressed to PaceUP@pace.edu.

TULSA STUDIES IN WOMEN'S LITERATURE

SPRING 2025, VOL.44, NO.1

@TSWLJOURNAL // UTULSA.EDU/TSWL // LIKE US ON FACEBOOK

CALL FOR PAPERS

The Burney Journal

A peer-reviewed publication of the Burney Society, *The Burney Journal* is available in print and online (OPEN ACCESS); it is indexed by EBSCO Host and MLA International Bibliography. *The Burney Journal* accepts submissions from 1 June to 1 November, with prospective publication occurring the following June.

The Burney Journal is dedicated to the study of the works of the Burney family, especially Frances Burney d'Arblay, her life, her contemporaries, and her times. This annual, interdisciplinary publication invites submissions on all aspects of the Burneys' lives and careers, in a variety of disciplines including literature, history, art, music, and politics. The aims of the journal center on supporting and advocating for eighteenth-century studies broadly, and particularly author studies, women's studies, and cultural studies.

Manuscripts should be submitted electronically on our website: https://theburneyjournal.library.mcgill.ca/about/submissions.
We accept submissions that vary in length from 5,000 to 7,500 words; for shorter or longer submissions, please contact the editor, Sophie Coulombeau (burney.editor@gmail.com). Submissions must follow MLA guidelines and the journal style sheet.

For further information, please visit the journal website: https://theburneyjournal.library.mcgill.ca.

The thirty-first volume of *Woolf Studies Annual*
was published in Spring 2025
by Pace University Press

Cover and interior layout by Zetta Whiting
The journal was typeset in Times New Roman and Arial
and printed by Lightning Source in La Vergne, Tennessee

Pace University Press

Director: Manuela Soares
Faculty Advisor: Eileen Kreit
Production Consultant: Joseph Caserto

Graduate Assistants: Vidhi Sampat and Zetta Whiting
Student Aide: Kianna Swingle

www.ingramcontent.com/pod-product-compliance
Lightning Source LLC
Chambersburg PA
CBHW060237100726
47907CB00003B/661
9781965246016